I0822949

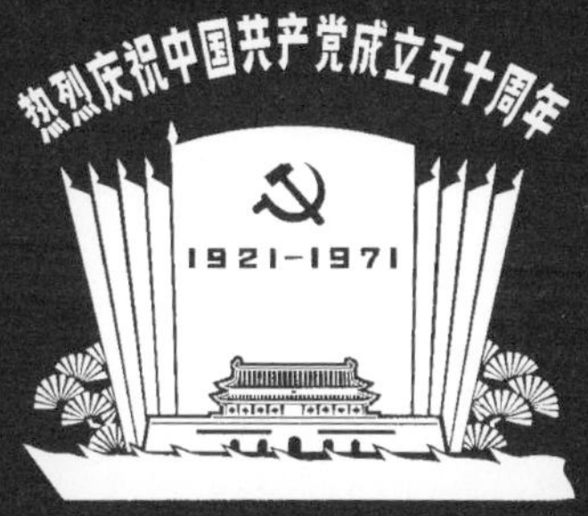

CHINESE
PROPAGANDA POSTERS

TASCHEN

CONTENTS

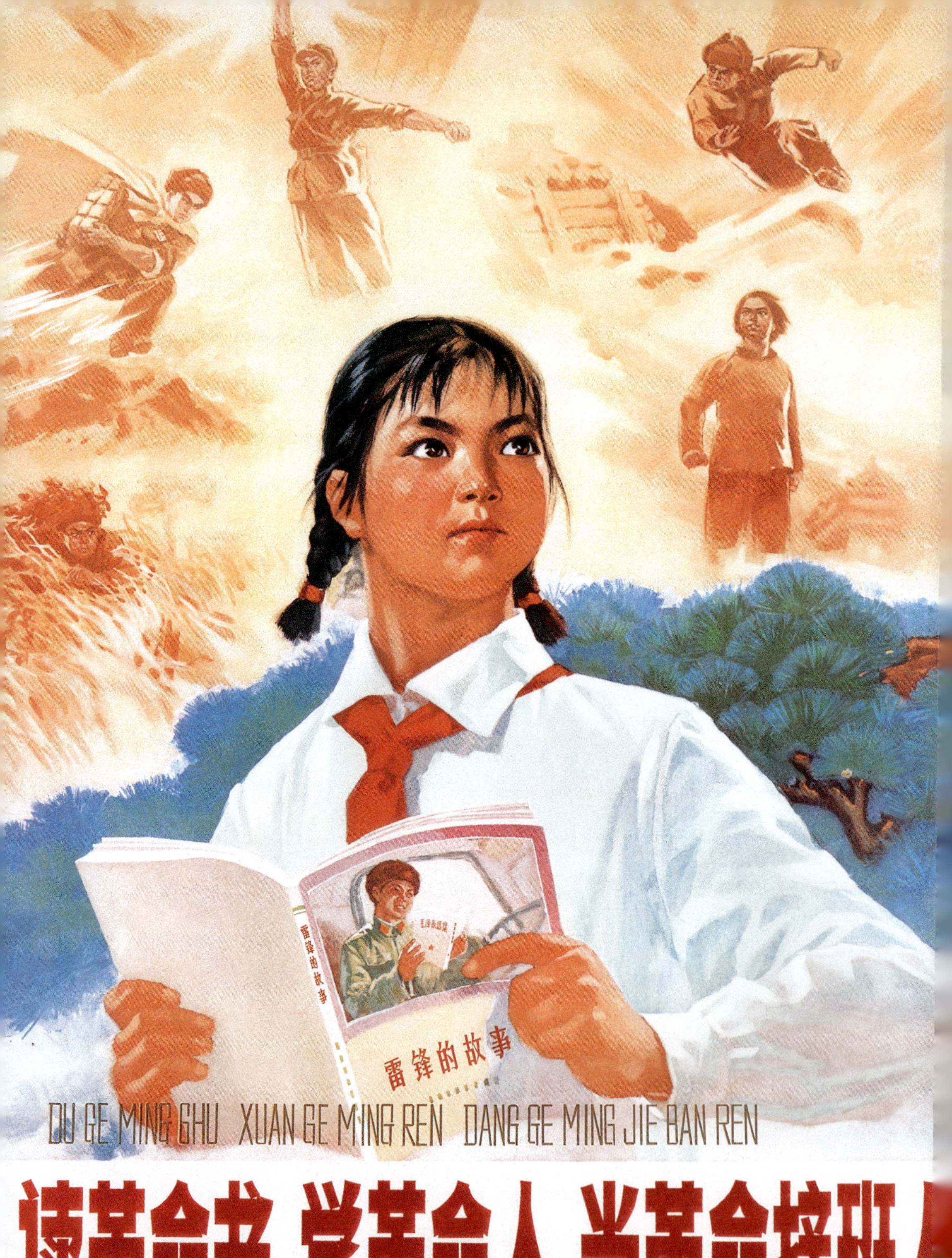

读革命书 学革命人 当革命接班人

THE GIRL IN THE POSTER

I wanted to be the girl in the poster (opposite) when I was growing up. Every day I dressed up like that girl in a white cotton shirt with a red scarf around my neck, and I braided my hair the same way. I liked the fact that she was surrounded by the revolutionary martyrs, whom I was taught to worship since kindergarten. The one on the far right was Liu Hulan, the teenage girl whose head was chopped off by the Nationalists because she wouldn't betray her faith in Communism. The soldier above her was Huang Ji-guang (see page 20), who used his chest to block American machine-gun fire in the Korean War. The one next to him was Dong Cunrui, who used his own body as a post supporting explosives when blowing up an enemy bridge. The soldier on the far left was Cai Yong-xiang, who was run over by a train while rescuing others. The book, which the girl in the poster carries in her hands, is *Stories of Lei Feng*, a soldier/hero/martyr, who was a truck-driver who died protecting others.

My passion for the posters began when I was eight years old. One day I brought home from school a poster of Chairman Mao (see page 11). Although I did not know that the Cultural Revolution had started, my action made me a participant—I removed my mother's "Peace and Happiness" painting with children playing in a lotus pond from the wall, and replaced it with the Mao poster. My mother was not pleased but she tried not to show her disappointment. I remember my thoughts: why wasn't she happy about Mao looking down at us during every meal while others couldn't have enough of Mao?

The posters had a great impact on my life. They taught me to be selfless and to be loyal to Mao and Communism. To be able to feel closer to Mao, I filled my house with posters. I looked at Mao before I closed my eyes at night and again when I woke. When I saved a few pennies, I would go to the bookstores to buy new Mao posters.

The place where I lived in Shanghai became a war zone during the heat of the Cultural Revolution in the late sixties and early seventies. Violence between factions often led to death. Everyone fought in the name of Mao. To be a Maoist was the goal of the time. For ten years I was in charge of the "Blackboard Newspaper" in my school. For the head art, I copied every image from *Samples of illustrations and decorative designs for newspapers and magazines* (see page 22). Week after week, month after month and year after year, I tirelessly drew pictures. I put out extra editions of the blackboard newspaper

Read revolutionary books, learn from revolutionaries and become an heir of the revolution *Book title:* Stories of Lei Feng *Artist:* Mo Shuzi; Jiangsu People's Publishing House, 1974

Revolutionäre Bücher lesen, von Revolutionären lernen und Erbe der Revolution werden *Buchtitel:* Geschichten von Lei Feng *Gemalt von* Mo Shuzi; Volksverlag Jiangsu, 1974

Lisez des livres révolutionnaires, instruisez-vous des actes des révolutionnaires et devenez les héritiers de la révolution *Titre du livre :* Histoires de Lei Feng *Peintre :* Mo Shuzi, Éditions Populaires du Jiangsu, 1974

during the summers and winters when the schools were out. I didn't mind that only a few people would see my work. My hands were swollen from frostbite and I could barely hold the chalk. But I was inspired by the heroes and heroines in the posters, and I believed that hardship would only toughen me and make me strong.

I continued to dream that one day I would be honored to have an opportunity to sacrifice myself for Mao, and become the girl in the poster. I graduated from middle school and was assigned by the government to work in a collective labor farm near the East China Sea. Life there was unbearable and many youths purposely injured themselves, for example, cut off their foot or hand in order to claim disability and be sent home. My strength and courage came from the posters that I grew up with. I believed in heroism and if I had to, I preferred to die like a martyr.

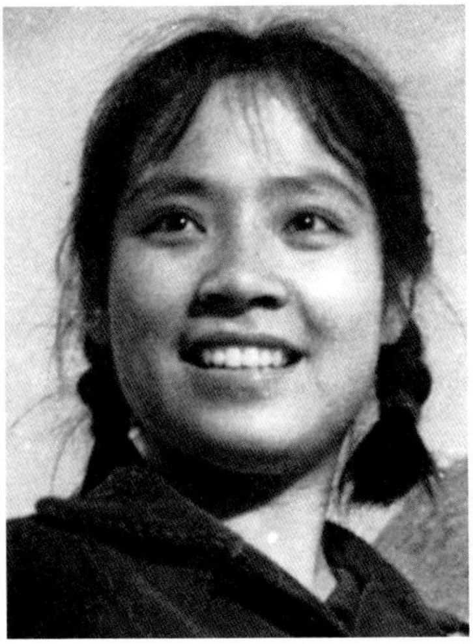

I slaved in the rice and cotton fields for three years until Madame Mao, Jiang Qing, changed my fate. In early 1976, no one knew that Mao was dying and Madame Mao was preparing herself to take over China after him. She was making a propaganda film to show the masses, and she had sent out talent scouts all over the country to look for a "proletarian face" to star in her film. I was chosen when hoeing in the cotton field. I was brought to the Shanghai Film Studio to be trained to act in Madame Mao's film. It was there I encountered the famous poster-painter Mr. Ha Qiongwen from the Shanghai Art Institute *Hun-Yuan*. I was brushing my teeth one morning in a public sink when Mr. Ha approached me. He showed me a piece of paper authorizing him to look for models for his posters. He said that he liked my look and asked if I would model for him. I was flattered but asked if my puffy eyes would be a bother because I had just woken up. He said no. Mr. Ha followed me back to my dorm to choose costumes from my clothes. I was surprised that he picked my green-colored worn-out army jacket which I had brought back with me from the labor camp. I told him that it would only take a moment for me to wash off the muddy dirt on the shoulder. He stopped me and said that the dirt was the effect that he had been looking for.

Anchee Min, 1976

I began posing after Mr. Ha set up the camera. I didn't know how to pose and was just doing what he asked of me, which was to look into the far distance with confidence. I apologized for my sun-beaten skin and hair, and I tried to hide my fungicide-stained fingernails. He said that he liked the fact that I looked like a real peasant. He asked me what I would wear when working in the rice paddy. I replied that I would wear a straw hat, I wouldn't wear shoes, and I would have my sleeves rolled up to the elbows and the pants up to the knees. He told me to do that. I obeyed. I kicked off my shoes and he saw the fungicide-stained toenails. I was embarrassed, but he told me that I shouldn't be. Instead, I should be proud. "I have been painting posters featuring peasants for years," he said, "and I have never realized my mistake. From now on I will paint peasants' toenails in a brown color." A week later, Mr. Ha sent me a print of his favorite shot of me. I looked quite heroic, like the girl in the poster I had admired as a child. Months passed and I didn't hear from him. One day during the Chinese New Year, when I was walking near Shanghai's busiest street, Central Xi-Zang Road and East Yan-an Road, I saw myself in a poster on the front window of the largest bookstore. The woman in the poster had my face, my jacket, but her arms and legs were thicker. She wore a straw hat, her sleeves and pants were rolled up, and all her nails were brown-colored!

I rushed home to share the news with my family, and everyone was excited and proud. I wished that I could have purchased a print of that poster, but it was not for sale. The clerk in the bookstore told me that it was distributed by the government for displaying in public spaces.

Max Gottschalks's collection of Chinese propaganda posters is unique and marvellous. The posters are a representation of a generation's fantasy. They reflect an important era in Chinese history, which has been falsely recorded for the most part.

A picture is worth a thousand words, so let them speak.

Anchee Min

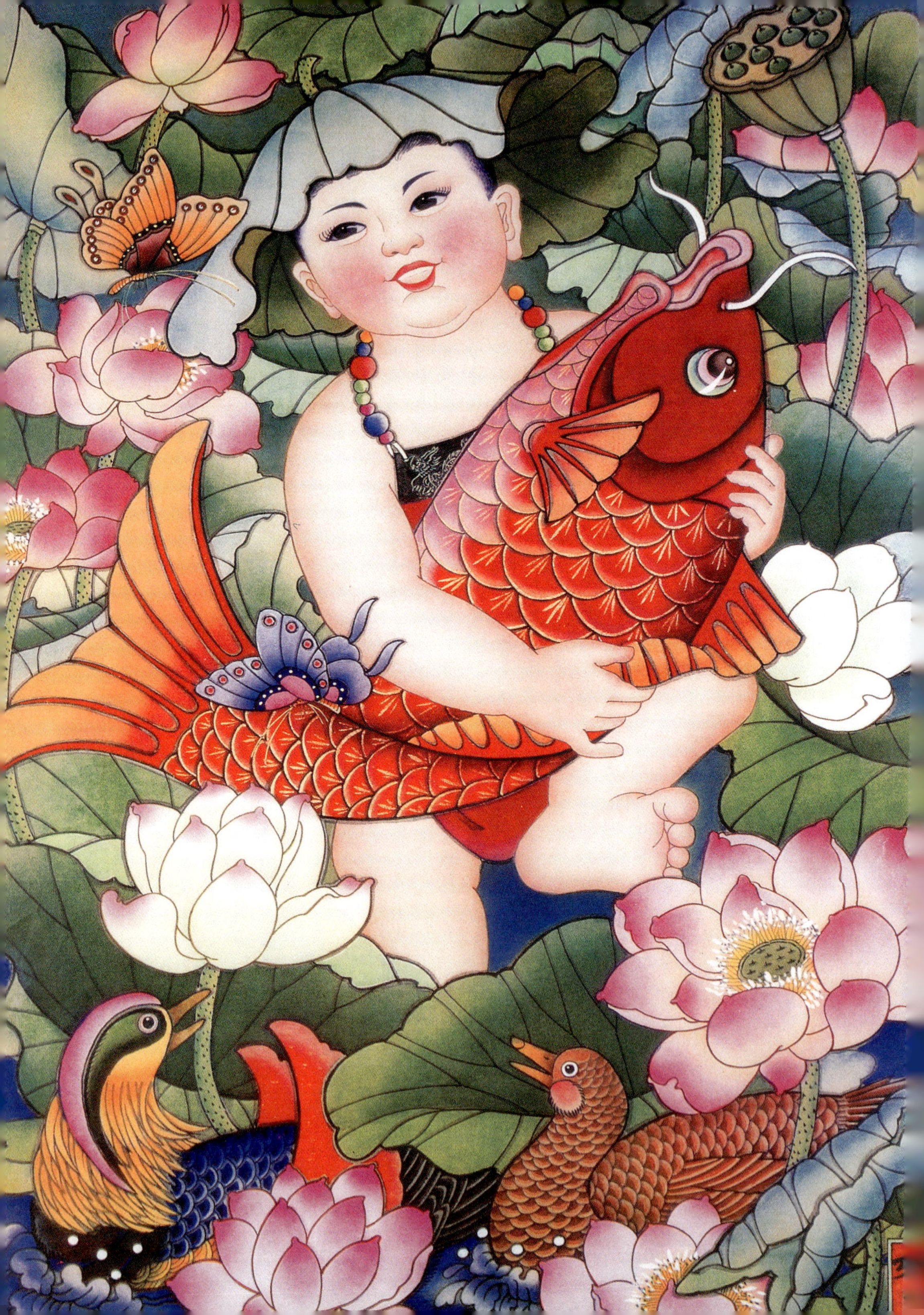

LOOKING AT THE PROPAGANDA POSTERS

Four hundred propaganda posters to look at. After about two minutes I feel kind of numb. I try to be patient and flick through them all again from the beginning. Suddenly 10,000 eternally blooming red flowers float before my eyes—each one exactly the same as the others. Suddenly I discover myself among them; I see my family, my neighbors, millions of people. A whole era comes flooding back. I keep looking at the posters. The person I am today observes the first half of my life. What emotions am I feeling? Apathy? Shame? Disgust? Abhorrence? Or nostalgia? None of the above? Or maybe a mixture of all of them?

Could that be me, that pale-skinned, chubby little chap in the red apron sitting on a lotus leaf holding up a large carp? From earliest memories to an old New Year picture. I sit on my father's shoulder. In my hand I am clutching some candied fruit on a long stick. Past the huge cooking pots of porridge made from wheat flour fried in fat, past the entertainers turning somersaults, we stroll through Beijing's New Year Market. (In those days, the city walls and their towers were still there. So were the Siheyuan, the rectangular courtyard houses.) The pictures of Sun Wukong and Zhao Zilong, which I painted at the age of five, reappear before my eyes. And suddenly, I see myself with the red neckerchief of the Young Pioneers, sitting on a tractor, and hear myself singing a song in praise of the high-voltage power line. I run along behind the heroic-looking comrade worker as he climbs a ladder and builds a rainbow.

The childhood memories gradually blur. Cut to another image. From an old New Year poster to a propaganda poster.

"What do you want to be when you grow up?" a nursery-school teacher asks me. "I would like to be a member of a geological exploration team and search for treasure for the fatherland." I am shy and do not trust myself to say the second half of the sentence out loud.

The picture of myself changes. I see a helmeted artilleryman gazing angrily in the direction of Taiwan.

A neighbor's son shouts at the top of his voice: "I have three arrows that can work miracles. When I shoot the first arrow, our building will turn into a 30-story skyscraper. When I shoot the second, skyscrapers will spring up all over China. When I shoot the third, Communism will be implemented all over the world!"

I am impressed and I admire him, so much so that I want to paint his picture.

Had I really painted him, it would have been my first propaganda poster. Perhaps I might have won first prize in an all-China children's painting competition.

From the day I was born in 1951, I was subjected to a visual education from children's picture books, through school textbooks and books for teenagers, to the huge number of other images and propaganda posters. They all dealt with similar

Playing with the fish, 1981 **Mit dem Fisch spielen**, 1981 **Jouer avec le poisson**, 1981

subjects and were my signposts through life. They made sure we did not make mistakes. They showed rich green meadows across which fat sheep rolled towards us like pearl beads. In 1958 green trees appeared in the same pictures. Children dangled from the branches like pears, armed with catapults and brooms to hunt sparrows. Destroy them! Everyone went on banging the gong until the sparrows fell down dead.

Only once did I just happen to paint a garden with artificial mountains, pavilions, and winter flowers. I was immediately told off by my brother. "That is a garden of the land-owning class!" he said. Then I was only painting what I had done on holiday (watch goldfish). The teacher's comment: "Of absolutely no educational value."

Time to get back to business and turn my attention to propaganda posters. I notice that the hands on the posters grow bigger and bigger. The hands that harvested corn-on-the-cob and carried watermelons now caress rockets. Looming over the enormous hands of the working class are the even more enormous hands of the Great Leader. Thousands upon thousands of waving hands, among them my own, moving vigorously back and forth in the air, imitating Lenin in 1918: "Bolsheviks, comrade sailors, forward!" Commands, slogans, huge hands wiping away sweat, patting the shoulder of a comrade, hurling hand grenades at the heads of the enemy. Hand in hand we formed a large circle and played hide-and-seek when we were small. Hand in hand, we would later defeat imperialism. I do not know who invented propaganda posters. One thing I do know: my life is reflected in them. There was never any doubt about it until a certain event happened.

It was shortly before the beginning of the Cultural Revolution. On the wall next to my bed hung a poster with a quotation from Mao Zedong: "While working the fields during the high season, eat solid food; in the time when there is not much to do, eat half solid and half liquid food, supplemented by potatoes and sweet potatoes." I knew every word but even so I did not understand what it meant. Every day before going to sleep and after getting up, I stared at the poster and reread it. No way could I grasp the meaning. Why was our leader lecturing us about what we should eat? I now think if this quotation had been turned into a visual image, it would have been understandable to anyone. In the vast fields there was nothing to harvest; 20 million peasants were starving because they had nothing to eat. Therefore ... therefore it should not be expressed in pictorial language, only in words.

When I was 16, I was sent to work on the land. For the first time I learnt about how peasants lived. The physical work was very hard. People barely had enough to eat. In that poverty-stricken village I once saw the bedroom of a newly married peasant couple. On the wall was a poster with good luck symbols like the phoenix and the dragon and a scroll bearing the words: "The Mandarin duck and his mate swim in the revolutionary ocean, married couples are comrades." For me it was terribly depressing but at the same time something to be envied. I walked along the muddy track and saw the propaganda

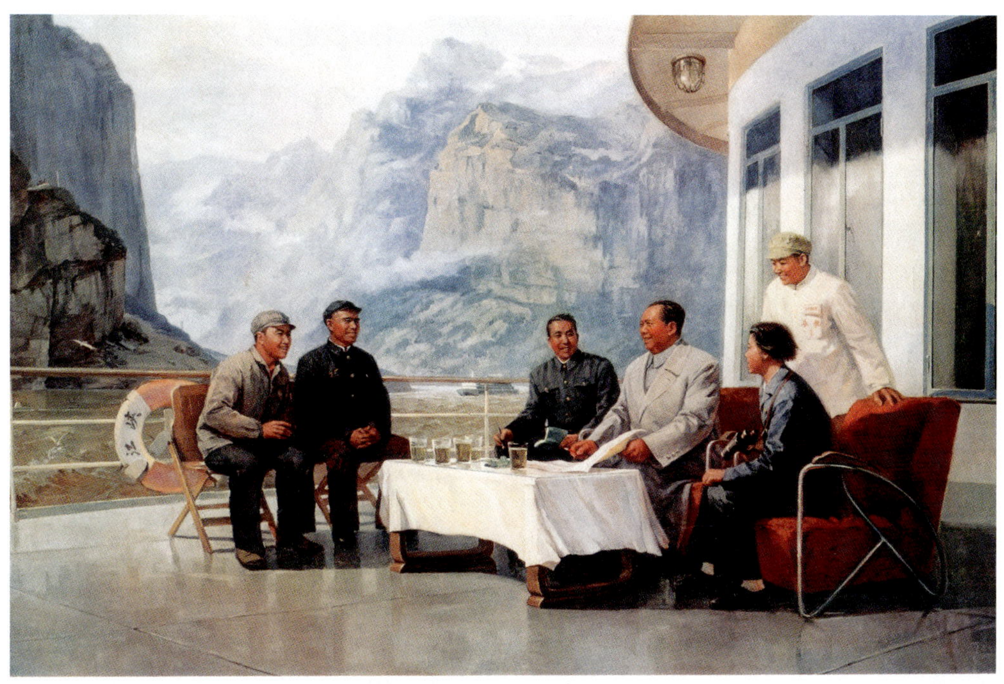

The victorious journey, 1972 **Die siegreiche Fahrt**, 1972 **La traversée de la victoire**, 1972

poster on the clay wall. In it, thick smoke rose from the chimneys, carrying within it the hope that poverty could be overcome by work! How romantic the painted smoke was! Like clouds in paradise. In a village where people and livestock lived together, what comfort was there in looking at a picture of chimneys rising up into the sky? I am sure that if, at that time, I had seen pictures of Jesus or Buddha, they would have been just as meaningless to me, since I knew nothing about them.

I am a city-dweller and that was the way it struck me. How would it have appeared to a country child who had never seen any pictures other than propaganda posters? In the country I came across many very gifted young local artists. All they ever painted were propaganda posters like these. All their love, all their yearnings went into their pictures. Their highest ambition was to become a professional propaganda poster artist.

What might they paint today? Perhaps pretty pictures for advertising posters. Perhaps they have long since returned to traditional Chinese landscape painting. I believe that under the surface of the political propaganda poster there has always been an undercurrent. It is folk art's hidden gene. It has its roots in traditional myths and legends and in the notion of bringing together ancient history, people, and nature. It is the source from which the soul of a nation springs. If we look more closely at the posters we recognize that, despite constraints, many images persistently try to express themselves. Perhaps it is precisely because a few of these weak, even distorted, beams of light shine through in the pictures that I felt a touch of nostalgia. It cannot be said that that era was a complete wasteland.

I am a lucky man. At the age of 20 I got to know Vincent van Gogh and Picasso. Since then no one can force me to relate to a poster. When, under the permanently watchful eye of our leader, I cycled alone past walls covered with posters of big, strong workers, peasants, and soldiers, I saw myself as a figure from a Kafka novel. That is when I began to write and to feel lonely. That was the beginning of my life in exile. Today, political propaganda posters have become expensive antiques. But I will never be a collector. For, the moment I look at them, 10,000 red flowers appear before my eyes. One of them is my father. He is nearly 90 years old. He often falls out of bed, yelling and thrashing about like mad, because in his dreams he is fighting against class enemies and probably still defending Chairman Mao. I believe, at least for the next few decades, several generations of leaders will continue to appear in living rooms and bedrooms, and on the street. They will demand that we feel good, be grateful, and smile, smile like the people in the posters, broadly enough to show all our white teeth, right down to our molars.

My sofa is covered with a throw of brightly colored, traditional Chinese cotton cloth, with a phoenix and peony pattern. I am waiting for the phoenix to come flying out of the distance.

Duo Duo

Playing with cats, 1981
Mit Katzen spielen, 1981
Jouer avec les chats, 1981

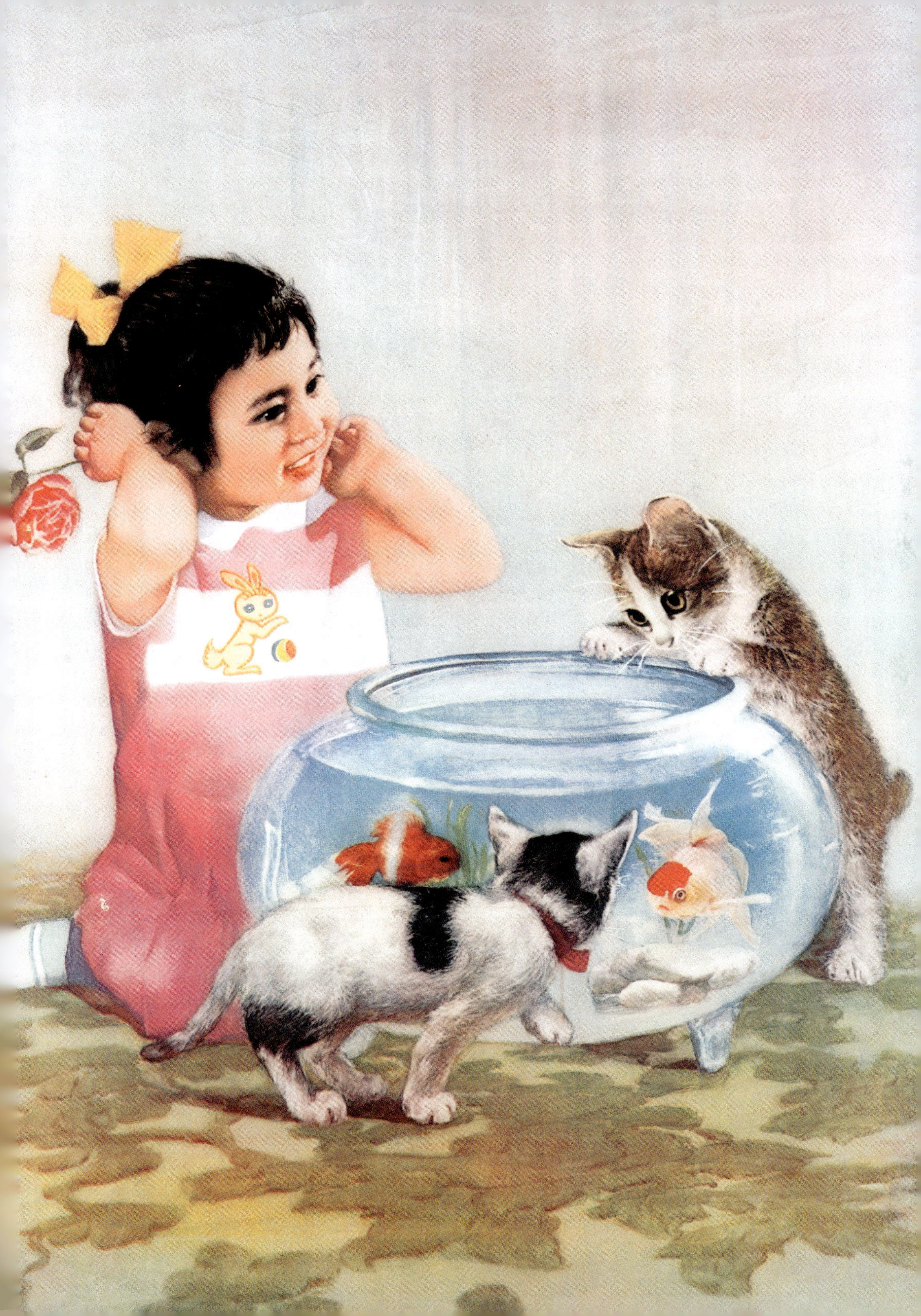

THE RISE AND FALL OF THE CHINESE PROPAGANDA POSTER

The image that used to prevail in the People's Republic of China was defined by the political images that were provided by propaganda art. Through all of its long history, the Chinese political system used the arts to propagate correct behavior and thought. Literature, poetry, painting, stage plays, songs, and other artistic expressions were produced to entertain, but they also were given an important didactic function: they had to educate the people in what was considered right and wrong at any one time. As long as the State provided examples of correct behavior, this automatically would make the people believe what was considered proper to believe.

Once the People's Republic was established in 1949, propaganda art continued to be one of the major means to provide examples of correct behavior. But it also gave a concrete expression to many different policies, and to the many different visions of the future the Chinese Communist Party had over the years. In a country with as many illiterates as China had in the 1940s and 1950s, this method of visualizing abstract ideas and in this way educating the people worked especially well. Propaganda posters, which were cheaply and easily produced, became one of the most favored vehicles for this type of communication. Because they were widely available, they could be seen everywhere. And they were an excellent way to brighten up the otherwise drab places where people lived. In this way they could penetrate every level of social organization and cohabitation, even the lowliest ones: the multicolored posters could be seen adorning walls not only in offices and factories, but in houses and dormitories as well. Most people liked the posters for their composition and visual content, and did not pay too much attention to the slogans printed underneath. This allowed the political message of the posters to be passed on in an almost subconscious manner.

The most talented artists were employed to visualize the political trends of the moment in quite detailed fashion. Many of them had worked on the commercial calendars that had been so popular before the People's Republic was founded. These artists were quickly coopted and incorporated in the various governmental and party organizations that were set up to produce propaganda posters. They were, after all, well versed in design techniques and able to visualize a product in a commercially attractive way. The images they made were often figurative and realistic, almost as if photographs had been directly copied. Their aim was to portray the future in the present, not only showing "life as it really is," but also "life as it ought to be." They were painted in a naïve style, with all forms outlined in black, filled in with bright pinks, reds, yellows, greens, and blues. These works created a kind of "faction," a hybrid of "fact" and "fiction," stressing the positive and papering over anything negative. What defined them as propaganda art were the politically inspired slogans.

These original works of art were reproduced in journals and magazines, and then reprinted as large- or smaller-format posters, and sometimes even turned into postage stamps. The large posters could be seen on the streets, in railway stations, and in other public spaces, while the smaller ones were distributed through the network of the *Xinhua* (New China) bookshops for mass consumption. Given the frequent changes in what was deemed correct, these political posters came to be more carefully studied than newspapers for spotting the subtle changes in tone, ideology, and slogans.

The content of the posters was largely taken up with the topics of politics and economic reconstruction that dominated China after 1949. Hyper-realistic, ageless, larger-than-life peasants, soldiers, workers, and youngsters in dynamic poses peopled the images. They pledged allegiance to the Communist cause, or obedience to Chairman Mao Zedong, or were engaged in the glorious task of rebuilding the nation. As a result, most of the posters served strictly utilitarian, abstract goals: they glorified work and personal sacrifice for the greater well-being. At the same time, they paid scant attention to the personal and private dimension of people's lives, to rest and recreation.

The strong and healthy bodies of the people shown in the posters functioned as metaphors for the strong and healthy productive classes the State wanted to propagate. In the process, the gender distinctions of the subjects were by and large erased over time. The physical differences between males and females practically disappeared–something that was also attempted in real life. Men and women alike had stereotypical, "masculinized" bodies, which almost made them look like Superpersons. Their clothes were baggy and sexless, the only colors available being cadre gray, army green or worker/peasant blue. And their faces, including short-cropped hairdos and chopped-off pigtails, were done according to a limited repertoire of acceptable standard forms.

The years of the great mass movements such as the Great Leap Forward (1958–1960) and the subsequent Cultural Revolution (1966–1976), when millions of people were mobilized into action, saw the climax in poster production. The propaganda poster reached the peak of artistic expression, both in form and content. In particular during the Cultural Revolution, politics increasingly took precedence over any other subject in propaganda posters. Chairman Mao Zedong, as the Great Teacher, the Great Leader, the Great Helmsman, and the Supreme Commander, seemed to have become the only permissible subject of the era. His face was painted usually in red and other warm tones, and in such a way that it appeared smooth and seemed to radiate as the primary source of light in a composition, illuminating the faces of the people that looked towards him. His image was considered more important than the occasion for which the propaganda poster was designed: in a number of cases, identical posters were published in different years but bearing different slogans in order to serve different propaganda causes. There was something in the images featuring Mao

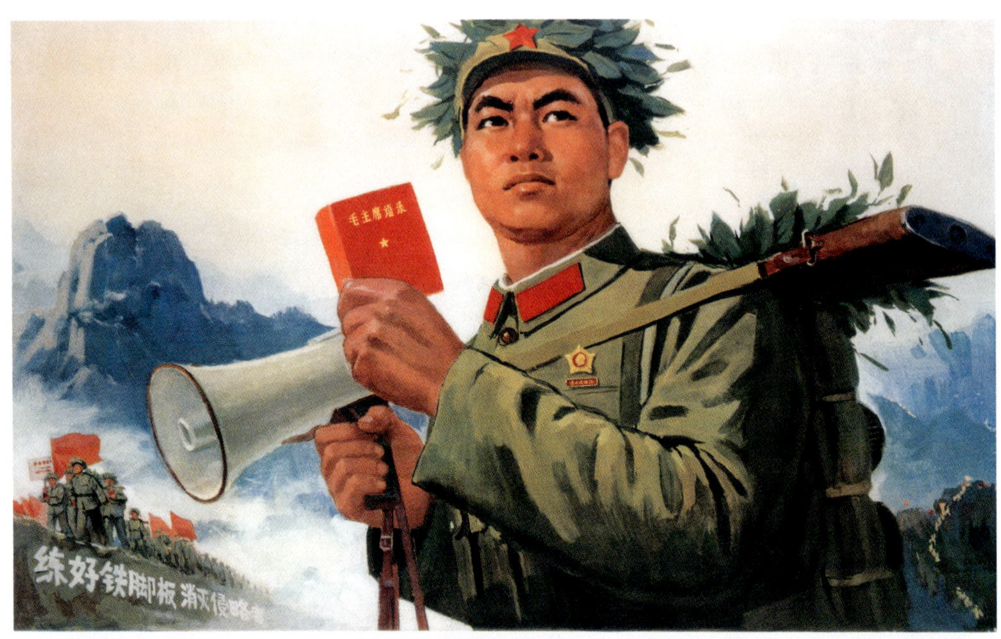

From now on we must be prepared, 1971

Ab jetzt muss man darauf vorbereitet sein, 1971

À partir de maintenant, il faut nous tenir prêts à cette éventualité, 1971

that struck a chord with the people. He somehow remained united with them, whether he inspected fields and factories, shook hands with the peasants and workers, sat down to smoke a cigarette with them; stood on the bow of a ship, dressed in a terry-cloth bathrobe after an invigorating swim in the Yangtse River; or even when he headed a column of representatives of the national minorities, or floated above a sea of red flags.

Mao also became a regular presence in every home, usually in the form of his official portrait. It is estimated that during the Cultural Revolution, some 2.2 billion of these official Mao portraits were printed, which means three for every person in the nation. Not having the Mao portrait on display indicated an apparent unwillingness to go with the revolutionary flow of the moment, or even a counter-revolutionary outlook, and refuted the central role Mao played not only in politics, but in the day-to-day affairs of the people. This formal portrait often occupied the central place in the home. Not only was the man himself made into a divine being; his portrait had to be treated with special care as well, as if it contained the divinity himself. Nothing could be placed above it, and its frame should not have a single blemish.

Mao continued to be an enduring icon over the years, both in China and abroad. Andy Warhol, for example, made paintings on the basis of the official portrait of Mao. But such subversions of the image of the Great Leader did not, somehow, resonate in China. Many people revered him as before and he remained a regular presence in many homes. Even as late as the 1990s, any depictions of Mao that did not conform to the stylistic dictates of *hong, guang, liang* (red, bright, and shining) elicited surprisingly negative responses from the many elderly and even young Chinese I spoke with. The general opinion was that such a representation was simply "not done" for a leader of Mao's stature.

The decline in the popularity of propaganda posters started in the early 1980s. Under Deng Xiaoping, who succeeded Mao Zedong at the helm of the People's Republic, the economic rehabilitation of China became the Party's main consideration, to the exclusion of anything else. Moreover, China opened itself to the West. From now on, the aim was to design and produce posters that created public support for the new, multifaceted policies that made up the reform package. At the same time, political orthodoxy still had to be upheld and the leading role of the Party within society had to be maintained. In the process of doing this, the people had to be made aware that the modernization policies were here to stay, and would not be revoked in the near future. Where Mao's continuous efforts at mobilization in the name of revolutionary movements would have been unthinkable without posters, the second revolution that was engineered by Deng could do well without them. These developments had enormous consequences for propaganda art. Propaganda themes became less heroic and militant, and more impressionistic, while bold colors were replaced with more subdued tones. Likewise, the slogans employed were less strident and militaristic, and more normative in content: the people were no longer called upon to struggle against enemies or nature, but instead were urged to adopt more cultured, hygienic, and educated lifestyles. Abstract images replaced realism; explicit political contents were replaced by an emphasis on economic construction, or even by ordinary commercial advertisements. Design and representational techniques borrowed from Western advertising were frequently employed. Although these changes in style may have made the images less accessible to the more backward sections of the population, they greatly invigorated the overall product.

The themes of the posters that the government continued to publish can best be termed as glimpses of "living the good life in a material world." All this was a far cry from the propaganda of the previous decades. After all, propaganda must always reflect reality, even in a society that has seen such fundamental changes as China has since the 1980s. A number of developments in the content of propaganda art really stand out because they are so far removed from the practices of the past. The improvement in living conditions was reflected in the greater diversity in clothing, both in material, design, cut, and color, that people wear in the posters. Gone were the blue, gray, or black unisex "Mao-suits" that previously had vouched for the people's proletarian outlook. The accoutrements of the revolutionary past were traded in for running shoes, leather jackets, and designer suits for men, while hot pants, spiked heels, and more feminine dresses–including the Shanghai dress, with its high slits–became *de rigueur* for women. Gone were the chopped hairdos and ponytails of bygone posters, making way for fancifully permed or styled hairdos. More and more attention was paid to the details of the new affluence that manifested itself in Chinese society, in particular in the urban areas. The increased openness, the higher level of personal freedom that was allowed, was translated into such visual icons as the jumbo jet, representing the new opportunities for travel, both within the country and abroad. The television set was seen as an embodiment of personal success in the new era. Owned by ever-growing numbers of people, it became a regular presence in many posters.

But most importantly, people were shown enjoying themselves, and actually having fun. An example of this complete turnaround can be found in the genre of the starlet poster. They could be seen everywhere once the publication of cheap, single-sheet calendars featuring photographs of actresses commenced in the 1980s. Most of them initially were devoted to film and entertainment celebrities exclusively from Hong Kong. Later, stars and starlets from Taiwan also came to be included. But a real increase in these posters occurred as the Chinese entertainment industry started generating its own celebrities. Movie actors and actresses and female television personalities no longer strictly appear on calendars: they now have joined forces with advertising agencies to endorse the numerous products on sale in China's contemporary consumer society. Despite these attempts to modernize, propaganda art has lost all contact with the population. The images, slogans, and messages that the Party continues to produce are seen as increasingly irrelevant and fall on unseeing eyes and deaf ears. With popular interest in politics at an all-time low, people no longer care about being ideologically or politically pure. They are more interested in having fun, and therefore in the size of their paychecks and whether they'll still be employed tomorrow. Posters have lost their credibility and appeal, and the numbers produced have declined dramatically. The people consider them to be old-fashioned, even though propaganda posters are now printed on thick, high-quality glossy paper, or even on plastic sheeting. The emergence of artists who no longer needed to work within the arts bureaucracy ushered in the gradual development of an increasingly unregulated art market that was no longer hampered by government control. The establishment of private companies, galleries, and other outlets to act as dealers for these young artists has greatly facilitated the marketing of their works. With a rich choice of truly desirable paintings and posters becoming more widely available than ever before, there is no longer any need to buy the dull political messages. By consciously avoiding political or moralizing subjects in their works, artists provide the people with visual materials that they consider more meaningful or that appeal aesthetically. This is illustrated by the return of traditional auspicious imagery and New Year prints—not only with traditional but with modern contents as well—in both urban and rural domestic interiors.

Not much is left, in short, of a pictorial genre that once was aimed to inspire the Chinese people, to mobilize them and point the way to a future Communist utopia. Politics is dead, and consumerism very much alive. After the turn of the century, four different types of mass art have remained, all consumed by different groups. The urban yuppies desire poster-sized reproductions of Western art. The less well-off buy fairly inexpensive calendar posters, preferably featuring pretty girls. The majority of the Chinese, the peasants, are more and more inspired by traditional images, even though the picture of Mao may have taken the space formerly reserved for deities such as the Kitchen God. There are still some political posters available, but only collectors from China and the West seem to be interested in them. The images that once defined the image of China have disappeared.

Stefan R. Landsberger

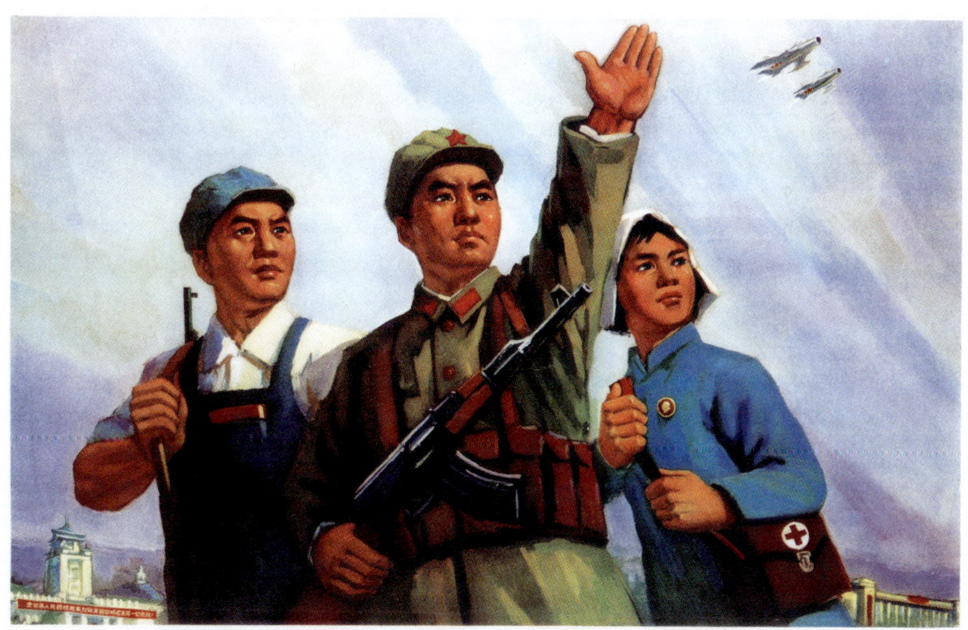

Air-raid protection poster
Designed by the People's Air Raid Protection Committee in the capital, 1970

Plakat des Volksluftschutzes
Entworfen vom Leitungsbüro des Volksluftschutzes der Hauptstadt, 1970

Affiche de la défense antiaérienne populaire
Conception : Siège principal de la défense antiaérienne populaire de la capitale, 1970

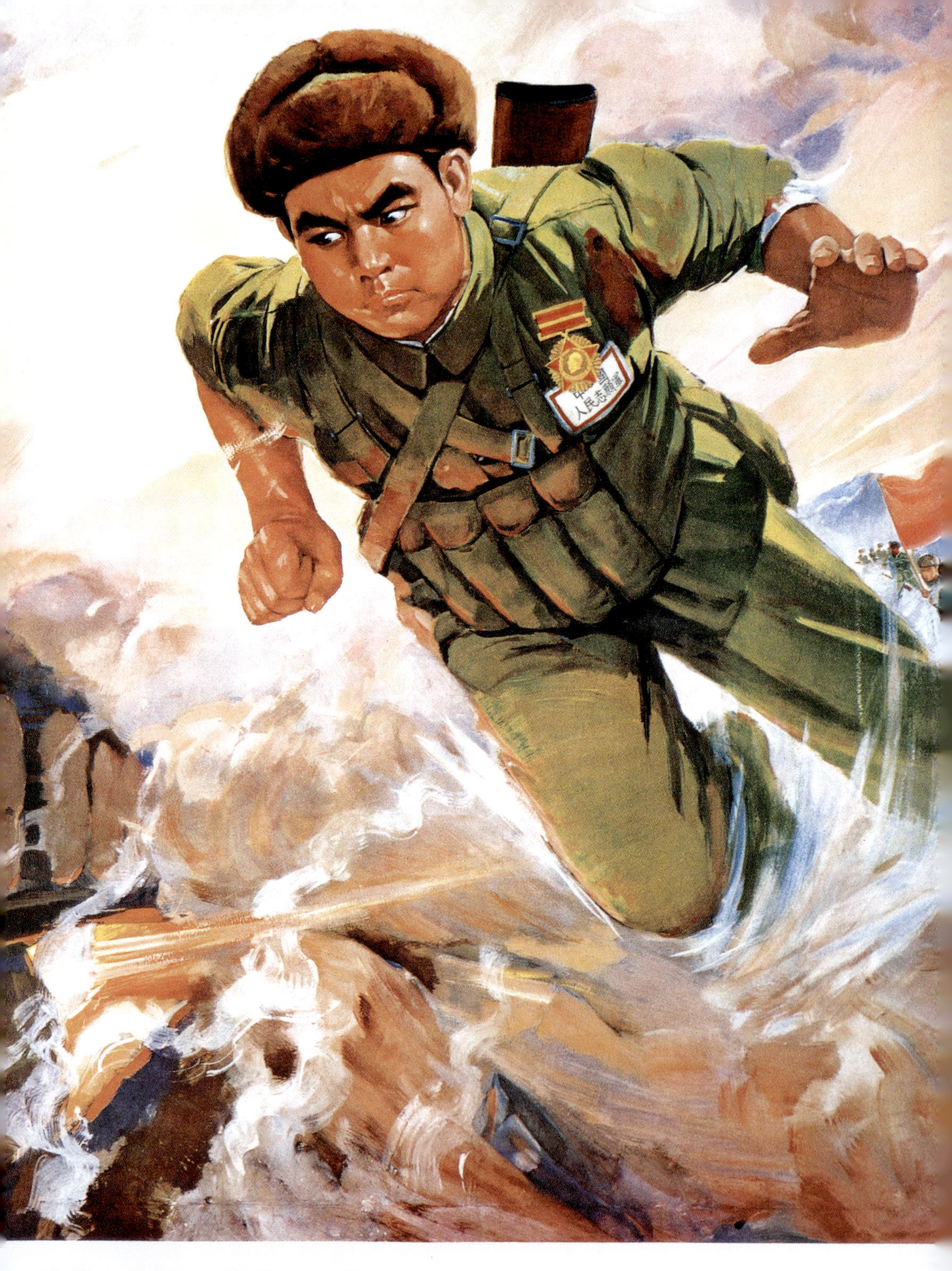

英雄黄继光

DAS MÄDCHEN AUF DEM POSTER

Als Kind wollte ich das Mädchen auf dem Poster (Seite 4) sein. Tag für Tag kleidete ich mich wie dieses Mädchen, trug ein weißes Baumwollhemd, ein rotes Tuch um den Hals und Zöpfe wie sie. Es gefiel mir, dass sie von den Märtyrern der Revolution umgeben war, zu deren Verehrung man mich seit dem Kindergarten angehalten hatte. Ganz rechts war Liu Hulan zu sehen, eine Jugendliche, die von den Nationalisten geköpft worden war, weil sie ihrem Glauben an den Kommunismus nicht abschwören wollte. Der Soldat über ihr war Huang Jiguang (siehe links), der sich im Koreakrieg mit seiner Brust in das Maschinengewehrfeuer der Amerikaner stellte. Der Mann neben ihm war Dong Chunrui, der mit Sprengstoff am eigenen Körper eine feindliche Brücke in die Luft fliegen ließ. Der Soldat ganz links war Cai Yong-xiang, der von einem Zug überfahren wurde, als er anderen das Leben rettete. Das Buch, das das Mädchen auf dem Poster in den Händen hält, *Geschichten von Lei Feng,* handelt von einem Soldaten, der als Lastwagenfahrer ums Leben kam, als er andere schützte.

Meine Leidenschaft für die Plakate wurde geweckt, als ich acht Jahre alt war. Eines Tages brachte ich ein Bild des Vorsitzenden Mao (Seite 11) aus der Schule mit nach Hause. Obwohl ich nicht wusste, dass die Kulturrevolution begonnen hatte, nahm ich durch diese Handlung daran teil – ich nahm das „Frieden und Glück"-Gemälde meiner Mutter mit Kindern, die in einem Lotos-Teich spielen, von der Wand und ersetzte es durch das Mao-Poster. Meiner Mutter gefiel das nicht, doch sie versuchte, ihre Enttäuschung zu verbergen. Ich erinnere mich noch, wie ich damals dachte: Warum freut sie sich nicht, dass Mao bei jeder Mahlzeit auf uns herabblickt, wo doch andere von Mao nie genug bekommen können?

Die Plakate hatten großen Einfluss auf mein Leben. Sie lehrten mich, selbstlos zu sein und Mao und dem Kommunismus treu ergeben. Um mich Mao näher zu fühlen, hängte ich weitere Poster in der Wohnung auf. Vor dem Einschlafen und beim Aufwachen schaute ich auf Mao. Wenn ich etwas Geld gespart hatte, ging ich in die Buchhandlung und kaufte mir neue Mao-Bilder.

Der Ort, an dem ich in Shanghai lebte, wurde im Eifer der Kulturrevolution in den späten sechziger und den frühen siebziger Jahren zum Kriegsgebiet. Die Gewalt zwischen den Splittergruppen hatte oft tödliche Folgen. Jeder kämpfte im Namen Maos. Höchstes Ziel war es in dieser Zeit, Maoist zu sein. Zehn Jahre lang war ich für die Wandzeitung an unserer Schule verantwortlich. Für Illustrationen sorgte ich, indem ich alle Abbildungen aus dem Heftchen *Illustrations- und Dekorationsmuster für Zeitungen*

Huang Jiguang the hero
Artist: Zhou Pengzhuang; Shanghai People's Publishing House, 1973; 0.15 Yuan

Der Held Huang Jiguang
Gemalt von Zhou Pengzhuang; Volksverlag Shanghai, 1973; 0,15 Yuan

Le héros Huang Jiguang
Peintre : Zhou Pengzhuang ; Éditions Populaires de Shanghai, 1973 ; 0,15 yuan

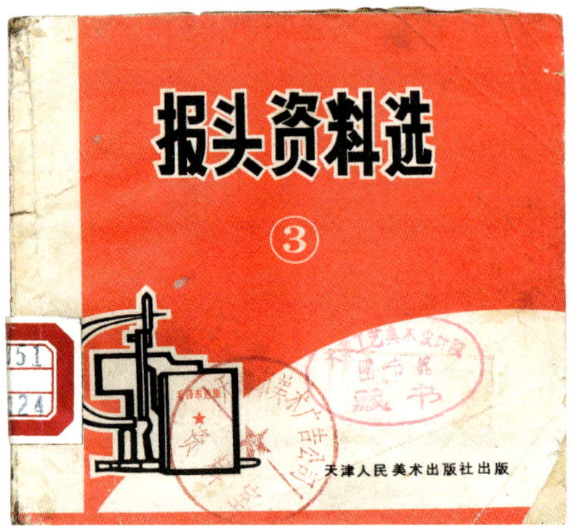

und Zeitschriften (siehe oben) kopierte. Wochen-, monate-, ja jahrelang zeichnete ich unermüdlich Bilder. Während im Sommer und Winter die Schulen geschlossen waren, brachte ich Sonderausgaben der Wandzeitung heraus. Es machte mir nichts aus, dass nur wenige Menschen mein Werk sahen. Frostbeulen ließen meine Hände anschwellen und ich konnte kaum die Kreide halten. Doch die Helden und Heldinnen auf den Plakaten inspirierten mich und ich war der Überzeugung, dass mich Entbehrungen nur abhärteten und stärker machten.

Es war immer noch mein Traum, eines Tages die Ehre zu haben, mich für Mao zu opfern und das Mädchen auf dem Poster zu werden. Ich schloss die Mittelschule ab und wurde von der Regierung dazu bestimmt, in der Nähe des Ostchinesischen Meers in einem Arbeitslager auf dem Land zu arbeiten. Das Leben dort war unerträglich und viele Jugendliche fügten sich absichtlich Verletzungen zu. Sie schlugen sich zum Beispiel den Fuß oder die Hand ab, damit sie als Behinderte nach Hause geschickt wurden. Meine Kraft und Tapferkeit verdanke ich den Plakaten, mit denen ich aufgewachsen war. Ich glaubte an das Heldentum, und wenn es denn sein musste, wollte ich lieber als Märtyrerin sterben. Drei Jahre lang wurde ich in den Reis- und Baumwollfeldern geknechtet, bis sich mein Schicksal durch Madame Mao, Jiang Qing, wendete. Anfang 1976 ahnte niemand, dass Maos Tod bevorstand und dass Madame Mao sich darauf vorbereitete, die Macht in China zu übernehmen. Sie arbeitete an einem Propagandafilm für die Massen. In ihrem Auftrag waren Talentsucher im ganzen Land unterwegs, um „proletarische Gesichter" aufzuspüren, die die Hauptrollen in ihrem Film spielen sollten. Während ich in den Baumwollfeldern schuftete, wurde ich ausgewählt.

Man brachte mich zum Shanghai-Filmstudio, wo ich für den Auftritt in Jiang Qings Film geschult wurde. Dort begegnete ich dem berühmten Plakatmaler Ha Qiongwen vom Shanghaier Kunstinstitut Hua-Yuan. Als ich mir eines Morgens an einer öffentlichen Waschrinne die Zähne putzte, kam Herr Ha näher. Er zeigte mir ein Papier, das ihn dazu berechtigte, Modelle für seine Plakate zu suchen. Er sagte, dass ihm mein Aussehen gefalle, und bat mich, ihm Modell zu sitzen. Ich fühlte mich geschmeichelt, fragte aber, ob meine geschwollenen Augen – ich war gerade aufgestanden – nicht störend seien. Er verneinte.

Herr Ha ging mit mir in den Schlafsaal, um aus meiner Kleidung die passenden Stücke auszusuchen. Ich war erstaunt, dass er meine grüne, abgetragene Armeejacke auswählte, die ich aus dem

Arbeitslager mitgebracht hatte. Ich sagte, es würde nur ein paar Minuten dauern, den Dreck von der Schulter abzuwaschen. Doch er hielt mich zurück und sagte, gerade auf den Schmutz komme es ihm an. Nachdem Herr Ha die Kamera aufgestellt hatte, saß ich ihm Modell. Ich wusste nicht, welche Pose ich einnehmen sollte, und folgte einfach seiner Anweisung, zuversichtlich in die Ferne zu schauen. Ich entschuldigte mich für meine sonnenverbrannte Haut und mein ausgeblichenes Haar und versuchte meine von den Pflanzenschutzmitteln verfärbten Fingernägel zu verstecken. Er meinte, es gefalle ihm, dass ich wie eine echte Bäuerin aussähe. Er fragte, wie ich denn bei meiner Arbeit im Reisfeld gekleidet gewesen sei. Ich antwortete, dass ich normalerweise einen Strohhut aufgehabt, aber keine Schuhe getragen hätte, die Ärmel hätte ich bis zu den Ellenbogen, die Hosenbeine bis zu den Knien hochgekrempelt. Er bat mich, das auch jetzt zu tun. Ich zog meine Schuhe aus und er sah meine von den Pflanzenschutzmitteln verfärbten Fußnägel. Ich war verlegen, doch er meinte, ich sollte lieber stolz darauf sein. „Seit Jahren male ich Bilder von Bauern“, sagte er, „und erst jetzt fällt mir der Fehler auf. Von nun an werde ich die Fußnägel der Bauern braun malen.“

Eine Woche später schickte mir Herr Ha einen Druck seiner Lieblingsaufnahme von mir. Ich sah recht heldenhaft aus, wie das Mädchen auf dem Plakat, das ich als Kind angebetet hatte. Monate gingen ins Land, ohne dass ich etwas von Herrn Ha hörte. Als ich eines Tages während des chinesischen Neujahrsfestes auf der belebtesten Straße von Shanghai, der Mittleren Xi-Zang-Straße und der Östlichen Yan-An-Straße, unterwegs war, entdeckte ich mich auf einem Poster im Schaufenster der größten Buchhandlung. Die Frau auf dem Poster hatte mein Gesicht, sie trug meine Jacke, aber ihre Arme und Beine waren dicker. Sie hatte einen Strohhut auf, ihre Ärmel und Hosenbeine waren hochgekrempelt und ihre Nägel waren alle braun! Ich eilte nach Hause, um die Neuigkeiten meiner Familie mitzuteilen, und alle waren aufgeregt und stolz. Ich hätte zu gern einen Druck dieses Plakats erworben, doch es war unverkäuflich. Der Buchhändler erzählte mir, dass die Regierung es verteile, damit es öffentlich ausgestellt werde.

Max Gottschalks Sammlung chinesischer Propagandaplakate ist einzigartig und beeindruckend. Die Plakate zeigen die Vorstellungswelt einer ganzen Generation und spiegeln einen wichtigen Abschnitt chinesischer Geschichte wider, der oft falsch dargestellt wird.

Ein Bild ist mehr wert als tausend Worte, deshalb lasst die Bilder sprechen!

Anchee Min

BEIM BETRACHTEN DER PROPAGANDAPLAKATE

400 Propagandaplakate ansehen. Nach ungefähr zwei Minuten bin ich wie betäubt. Ich versuche, geduldig zu sein und blättere alles noch einmal von vorn durch. Plötzlich schweben 10 000 rote, auf ewig und immer blühende Blumen an meinen Augen vorbei – eine gleicht der anderen. Plötzlich entdecke ich unter ihnen auch mich, meine Familie, meine Nachbarn, Millionen von Menschen. Eine Epoche kehrt zurück …

Ich betrachte die Plakate weiter. Das heutige Ich betrachtet die erste Hälfte meines Lebens. Welche Gefühle empfinde ich? Stumpfheit? Scham? Ekel? Abscheu? Oder Nostalgie? Nichts von all dem? Oder vielleicht eine Mischung aus allem?

Jener hellhäutige, pummelige, einen großen Karpfen tragende Knabe mit der roten Schürze auf dem Lotosblatt – könnte das nicht ich sein? Raus aus den frühesten Erinnerungen, hinein in ein altes Neujahrsbild: Ich, einen langen Stiel mit kandierten Früchten in der Hand haltend, sitze auf der Schulter meines Vaters. Vorbei an den gigantischen Töpfen mit dem Brei aus in Fett geröstetem Weizenmehl, vorbei an den Purzelbäume schlagenden Varieteekünstlern schlendern wir über den Jahrmarkt Pekings. Damals waren die Stadtmauern mit ihren Türmen noch da, und die viereckigen Wohnhöfe „Siheyuan" auch. Die Bilder von Sun Wukong und Zhao Zilong, die ich mit fünf Jahren gemalt habe, erscheinen wieder vor meinen Augen. Und plötzlich sehe ich mich mit dem roten Halstuch der Jungen Pioniere auf einem Traktor sitzen und höre, wie ich ein Loblied auf die Hochspannungsleitung singe. Ich laufe hinter den heldenhaft aussehenden Onkeln Arbeitern her, die gerade eine Leiter hochsteigen und einen Regenbogen bauen …

Die Erinnerungen aus meiner Kindheit verschwimmen allmählich. Ein anderes Bild taucht auf. Das alte Neujahrsplakat verwandelt sich in ein Propagandaplakat: „Was willst du werden, wenn du groß bist?", fragt mich eine Kindergärtnerin. „Ich möchte Mitglied einer geologischen Forschungsbrigade sein und für das Vaterland nach Schätzen suchen." Aufgrund meiner Schüchternheit traue ich mich nicht, die zweite Hälfte des Satzes auszusprechen.

Mein Bild ist wiederum verwandelt: Ein behelmter Artillerist blickt zornig in Richtung Taiwan. Ein Nachbarsjunge ruft lauthals: „Ich besitze drei Wunderpfeile. Wenn ich den ersten Pfeil abschieße, wird aus unserem Gebäude ein 30-geschossiges Hochhaus. Wenn ich den zweiten abschieße, werden überall in China Hochhäuser entstehen. Wenn ich den dritten abschieße, hat sich der Kommunismus auf der ganzen Welt durchgesetzt!" Ich bin beeindruckt und bewundere ihn, so dass ich ein Bild davon malen möchte. Hätte ich es wirklich gemalt, wäre es mein erstes Propagandaplakat gewesen. Vielleicht hätte ich den ersten Preis für Kindermalerei in China erhalten. Seit meiner Geburt im Jahr 1951 war ich einer visuellen Didaktik ausgeliefert: von Kinder-Bilderbüchern über Schulbücher, Jugendlektüre, bis hin zu den großen Mengen anderer Bilder und Propagandaplakaten. Sie hatten alle ähnliche Themen und waren Wegweiser für mein Leben. Sie sorgten dafür, dass wir keinen Fehler machten, sie zeigten fruchtbares Grasland, auf dem sich fette Schafe wie Perlen vorwärts rollten. 1958 tauchten auf solchen Bildern auch grüne Bäume auf, auf denen Kinder wie Birnen hingen und mit Katapulten und Besen nach Spatzen jagten. Vernichtet sie! Alle schlugen unaufhörlich den Gong, bis die Spatzen tot herunterfielen.

Einmal hatte ich zufällig einen Garten mit künstlichen Bergen, Pavillons und Winterblüten gemalt. Sofort wurde ich von meinem Bruder zurechtgewiesen: „Das ist ein Garten der Gutsbesitzerklasse!“ Dann schilderte ich meine Ferienerlebnisse im Bild: Goldfische beobachten. Kritik des Lehrers: „Absolut keine erzieherische Bedeutung!“

Also zurück zu meinen Vorbildern, den Propagandaplakaten. Ich stellte fest, dass die Hände auf den Plakaten immer größer wurden: Die Hände, die Maiskolben ernteten und Wassermelonen trugen, streichelten nun die Raketen. Über gigantischen Händen der Arbeiterklasse ragte die noch gigantischere Hand des Großen Vorsitzenden hervor. Tausende und Abertausende winkende Hände, darunter auch meine Hand, die sich heftig in der Luft auf und ab bewegte und Lenin im Jahr 1918 imitierte: „Bolschewiken, Genossen Matrosen, vorwärts!“ Befehle, Parolen, eine große Handfläche, Schweiß abwischen, Schulter des Genossen schütteln, Handgranaten auf die Köpfe der Feinde werfen. Hand in Hand einen großen Kreis bilden und Verstecken spielen, als wir klein waren. Später schlugen wir Hand in Hand den Imperialismus zu Boden.

Ich weiß nicht, wer Propagandaplakate erfunden hat. Eins steht für mich fest: Mein Leben spiegelt sich in ihnen wider. Nie hat es Zweifel daran gegeben, bis auf ein Ereignis. Das war kurz vor Beginn der Kulturrevolution. An der Wand neben meinem Bett hing ein Plakat mit einem Zitat von Mao Zedong: „Während der Hauptsaison der Feldarbeit feste Nahrung essen; in der Zeit, in der nicht viel zu tun ist, zur Hälfte Festes, zur Hälfte Flüssiges essen, ergänzt durch Kartoffeln und Süßkartoffeln.“ Jedes Wort kannte ich, trotzdem konnte ich nicht verstehen, was es bedeutete. Jeden Tag, vor dem Einschlafen und nach dem Aufstehen, starrte ich auf dieses Plakat und las es immer wieder. Ich war nicht im Stande, es zu begreifen. Warum lehrt uns unser Führer, wie wir zu essen haben? Heute denke ich, wenn man dieses Zitat in ein Bild umgewandelt hätte, hätte es jeder verstanden: Auf großflächigen Feldern gibt es nichts zu ernten; 20 Millionen Bauern verhungern, weil sie nichts zu essen haben. Deshalb … deshalb durfte es nicht durch Bildsprache zum Ausdruck gebracht werden, sondern nur gesagt werden.

Mit 16 Jahren wurde ich zum Arbeitseinsatz aufs Land geschickt. Zum ersten Mal lernte ich das Leben der Bauern kennen. Die körperliche Arbeit war sehr hart. Man hatte kaum zu essen. In jenem armen Dorf betrat ich einmal eine bäuerliche Brautkammer. An der Wand sah man das Plakat mit Glückssymbolen wie Phönix und Drachen und die Schriftrolle:

„Das Mandarinentenpaar schwimmt im revolutionären Ozean; die Eheleute sind Genossen“. Für mich war es bitterlich trostlos und beneidenswert zugleich. Ich ging einen schlammigen Pfad entlang und sah das Propagandaplakat an der Lehmmauer: Dichter Rauch stieg aus Schornsteinen empor. Darin lag die Hoffnung verborgen: Durch Arbeit kann die Armut bekämpft werden! Wie romantisch der gemalte Rauch war! Wie die Wolken im Paradies. Was für ein Trost sollte es sein, in einem Ort, in dem Menschen und Vieh zusammenlebten, in die Höhe ragende Schornsteine auf einem Bild zu sehen? Ich bin mir sicher, wenn ich damals Bilder von Jesus oder Buddha gesehen hätte, wären sie ebenso bedeutungslos für mich gewesen, weil ich sie nicht kannte.

Ich bin ein Stadtkind und habe es so empfunden. Wie hätte es auf ein Kind vom Land gewirkt, das noch nie im Leben andere Bilder gesehen hatte als Propagandaplakate? Ich war manchen künstlerisch sehr begabten jungen Menschen vom Land begegnet. Sie malten nichts anderes als solche Propagandaplakate. Alle ihre Sehnsüchte und ihre Liebe verarbeiteten sie in ihren Bildern. Ihr höchstes Ideal war, ein professioneller Propagandaplakat-Künstler zu werden.

Was mögen sie wohl heute malen? Vielleicht schöne Bilder für Werbeplakate? Vielleicht sind sie längst zur traditionellen chinesischen Landschaftsmalerei zurückgekehrt? Meines Erachtens hat es unter dem Mantel des politischen Propagandaplakats stets eine Unterströmung gegeben. Das ist das verborgene Gen der Volkskunst. Sie basiert auf den volkstümlichen Mythen und Sagen und der Vorstellung, Geschichte, Menschen und Natur zu vereinen. Sie ist der Ursprung der Seele einer Nation. Wenn man die Plakate genauer betrachtet, kann man erkennen, dass manche Bilder trotz politischer Zwänge hartnäckig versuchten, sich selbst auszudrücken. Vielleicht gerade aufgrund einiger weniger schwacher, ja verzerrter Lichtstrahlen in den Bildern habe ich einen Hauch von Nostalgie empfunden. Man kann nicht behaupten, jene Epoche sei eine reine Ödnis gewesen.

Ich bin ein Glücklicher. Mit 20 Jahren habe ich Vincent van Gogh und Picasso kennengelernt. Seitdem konnte man mich nicht mehr zwingen, eine innere Beziehung zu einem Plakat aufzubauen. Als ich allein mit dem Fahrrad unter den immer wachsamen Blicken unseres Führers an den mit Plakaten von großen und starken Arbeitern, Bauern und Soldaten verhängten Mauern vorbeifuhr, kam ich mir vor wie eine Figur aus Kafkas Romanen. Von da an begann ich zu schreiben und einsam zu sein. Von da an begann mein Leben im Exil.

Heute sind politische Propagandaplakate teure Antiquitäten geworden. Aber ich werde sie nie sammeln. Denn sobald ich sie erblicke, erscheinen 10 000 rote Blumen vor meinen Augen, eine davon ist mein Vater. Er ist fast 90 Jahre alt, fällt oft nachts aus dem Bett, schreit und schlägt wie wild um sich, weil er im Traum gegen Klassenfeinde kämpft und wahrscheinlich auch noch den Großen Vorsitzenden verteidigt. Ich glaube, zumindest in den nächsten Jahrzehnten werden noch mehrere Generationen von Führern in unseren Wohnzimmern, Schlafzimmern und auf der Straße auftauchen und von uns verlangen, uns wohlzufühlen, dankbar zu sein und zu lächeln, so zu lächeln wie die Menschen auf den Plakaten und dabei die weißen Zähne, sogar die Backenzähne zu zeigen …

Mein Sofa ist mit einem traditionellen chinesischen, farbenprächtigen Tuch aus Baumwolle bedeckt, auf dem Phönix und Pfingstrosen abgebildet sind. Ich warte auf den Phönix, der aus der Ferne geflogen kommen wird …

Duo Duo

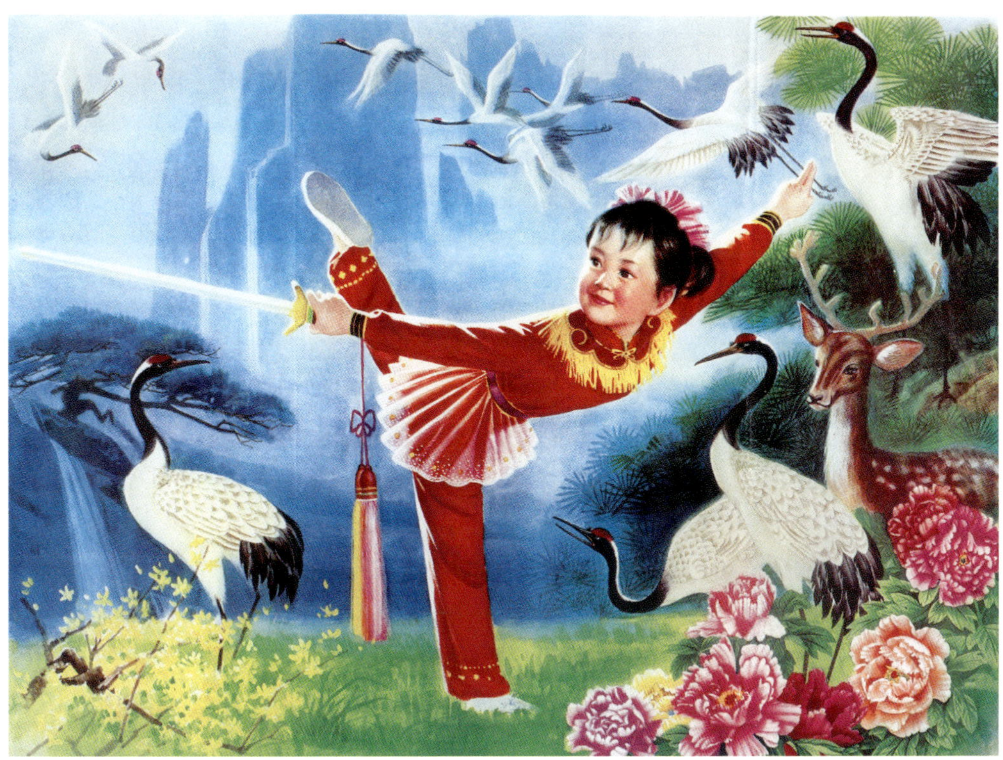

The new generation of traditional martial arts practitioners, 1983

Nachwuchs der traditionellen Kampfkunst, 1983

La relève des arts martiaux traditionnels, 1983

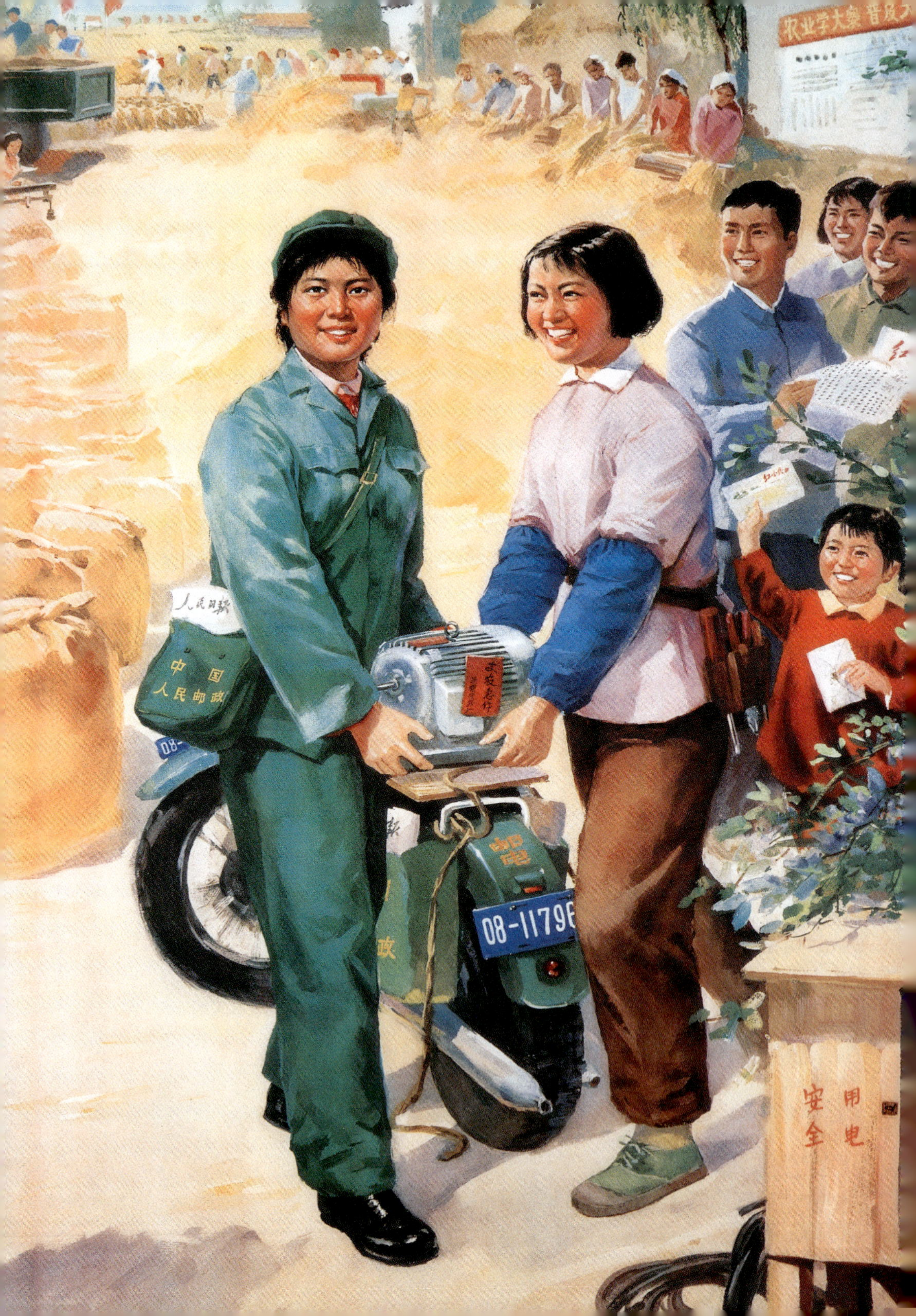

农业学大寨 普及大
人民日报
中国
人民邮政
邮电
08-11796
安全用电

AUFSTIEG UND NIEDERGANG DES CHINESISCHEN PROPAGANDAPLAKATS

Das vorherrschende Bild in der Volksrepublik China wurde durch die politischen Plakate der Propagandakunst definiert. In der langen chinesischen Geschichte wurden stets die Künste benutzt, um korrektes Verhalten und Denken zu propagieren. Prosa und Dichtung, Malerei, Theater, Gesang und alle anderen künstlerischen Ausdrucksformen dienten der Unterhaltung, doch kam ihnen auch eine bedeutende didaktische Aufgabe zu: Sie sollten das Volk darin unterweisen, was zu einer bestimmten Zeit als richtig und falsch betrachtet wurde. Solange der Staat Beispiele für korrektes Verhalten lieferte, würden die Menschen automatisch diejenige Meinung vertreten, die als die richtige angesehen wurde.

Nach der Gründung der Volksrepublik 1949 blieb die Propagandakunst eines der wichtigsten Mittel, um Vorbilder für richtiges Verhalten zu liefern. Darüber hinaus war sie jedoch ein konkreter Ausdruck wechselnder politischer Linien und Zukunftsvisionen, die die Kommunistische Partei Chinas über die Jahre in großer Zahl verfolgte. In einem Land mit einer hohen Analphabetenquote, wie es China in den vierziger und fünfziger Jahren des 20. Jahrhunderts war, funktionierte die Methode, abstrakte Vorstellungen zu visualisieren und auf diese Weise das Volk zu erziehen, besonders gut. In der Herstellung einfache und billige Propagandaplakate entwickelten sich zu den bevorzugten Medien, wenn es um diese Form der Mitteilung ging. Da diese Plakate vielerorts erhältlich waren, sah man sie auch überall. Und sie waren bestens geeignet, die ansonsten grauen und düsteren Orte, an denen die Menschen lebten, freundlicher erscheinen zu lassen. Auf diese Weise konnten die Plakate in alle Ebenen der sozialen Organisation und des Zusammenlebens vordringen, sogar in die untersten: Die Farbplakate schmückten die Wände nicht nur in Büros und Fabriken, sondern auch in Häusern und Wohnheimen. Den meisten Menschen gefielen die Gestaltung und die Motive und den darunter gedruckten Parolen schenkten sie nicht viel Aufmerksamkeit. So konnte die politische Botschaft der Plakate auf nahezu unbewusste Weise weitergegeben werden.

Die begabtesten Künstler wurden eingesetzt, um die aktuellen politischen Trends bis in die Einzelheiten zu visualisieren. Die Bilder, die sie schufen, waren oft figürlich und realistisch, als ob es sich um Kopien von Fotografien handelte. Ihr Ziel war es, in der Gegenwart die Zukunft darzustellen. Sie wollten das Leben nicht nur zeigen, „wie es wirklich ist", sondern auch, „wie es sein sollte". Diese Plakate waren in einem naiven Stil gestaltet: Schwarze Linien bildeten Umrisse, die in strahlendem Rosa, Rot, Gelb, Grün und Blau ausgemalt waren. Diese Werke schufen eine Art „faction" – eine Kreuzung

It makes me happy to contribute something to support agriculture, 1977

Es ist eine Freude, etwas zur Unterstützung der Landwirtschaft beizutragen, 1977

C'est une joie de faire quelque chose pour soutenir l'agriculture, 1977

aus Fakten und Fiktionen –, indem sie das Positive herausstrichen und alles Negative aufpolierten. Zur Propagandakunst wurden sie durch die politischen Parolen.

Diese Originalkunstwerke wurden in Zeitschriften und Magazinen reproduziert und dann als groß- oder kleinformatige Plakate nachgedruckt; manchmal lieferten sie sogar das Motiv für Briefmarken. Die großen Plakate konnte man auf den Straßen, in Bahnhöfen und an anderen öffentlichen Plätzen sehen, während die kleineren Formate über das Vertriebsnetz der Buchhandlungen von *Xinhua* (Neues China) an die Massen gelangten. Da die Vorstellungen von dem, was als korrekt galt, häufig wechselten, wurden diese politischen Plakate bald sorgfältiger studiert als die Zeitungen, um die feinen Veränderungen hinsichtlich der Haltung, der Ideologie und der Parolen aufzuspüren.

Die Inhalte der Plakate wurden in hohem Maße von den Themen der Politik und des wirtschaftlichen Wiederaufbaus bestimmt, die in China nach 1949 vorherrschend waren. Hyperrealistisch gestaltete, alterslose, überlebensgroße Bauern, Soldaten, Arbeiter und Jugendliche in dynamischen Posen bevölkerten die Bilder. Sie gelobten, der kommunistischen Sache treu ergeben zu sein oder dem Vorsitzenden Mao Zedong zu gehorchen oder sie waren mit der ruhmreichen Aufgabe betraut, die Nation wiederherzustellen – mit dem Ergebnis, dass die Plakate streng nützlichen, abstrakten Zielen verpflichtet waren: Sie glorifizierten die Arbeit und das persönliche Opfer für das allgemeine Wohlergehen. Der privaten Dimension des Lebens, der Erholung und Entspannung, widmeten sie nur wenig Aufmerksamkeit.

Die starken und gesunden Körper der Menschen auf den Plakaten standen metaphorisch für die starken und gesunden werktätigen Klassen, die Gegenstand staatlicher Propaganda waren. Im Laufe der Zeit wurden die Geschlechtsmerkmale der dargestellten Figuren weitgehend getilgt. Die körperlichen Unterschiede zwischen Mann und Frau verschwanden praktisch – auch im wirklichen Leben gab es Versuche in diese Richtung. Männer ebenso wie Frauen hatten typisierte, „vermännlichte" Körper, die sie fast wie Übermenschen erscheinen ließen. Ihre Kleidung war sackartig und geschlechtslos, als einzige Farben standen das Grau der Kader, das Grün der Militärs oder das Blau der Arbeiter und Bauern zur Verfügung. Und ihre Gesichter, ihre Kurzhaarfrisuren und kurzen Zöpfe waren in einem begrenzten, standardisierten Formenrepertoire gestaltet.

In den Jahren der großen Massenbewegungen wie des Großen Sprungs nach vorn (1958 bis 1960) und später der Kulturrevolution (1966 bis 1976), als Millionen von Menschen mobilisiert wurden, erreichte der Ausstoß an Plakaten seinen Höhepunkt. Das Propagandaplakat stand formal und inhaltlich auf dem Gipfel des künstlerischen Ausdrucks. Insbesondere während der Kulturrevolution hatten die politischen Themen Vorrang vor allen anderen. Der Vorsitzende Mao Zedong als Großer Lehrer, Großer Führer, Großer Steuermann und Großer Oberkommandierender war in dieser Zeit anscheinend das einzig zulässige Motiv. Sein Gesicht wurde normalerweise in rötlichen und anderen warmen Farbtönen gemalt. Es wirkte glatt und überstrahlte als Hauptlichtquelle die Komposition, indem es die Gesichter der Menschen, die sich ihm zuwandten, erleuchtete. Maos Abbild wurde wichtiger als die Gelegenheit, für die das Propagandaplakat entworfen war: Vielfach wurden identische Plakate zu unterschiedlichen Zeiten mit wechselnden Parolen herausgegeben, um verschiedenen propagandistischen Zwecken zu dienen. Irgendetwas an den Mao-Darstellungen brachte in den Menschen eine Saite zum Klingen. Er blieb in gewisser Weise mit ihnen verbunden, ob er nun Felder oder Fabriken inspizierte, den Bauern und Arbeitern die Hand schüttelte, im Sitzen mit ihnen eine Zigarette rauchte oder nach kräftigendem Schwimmen im Jangzi-Fluss im Frotteebademantel am Bug eines Schiffes stand – und sogar, wenn er eine Kolonne mit Repräsentanten nationaler Minderheiten anführte oder über einem Meer roter Fahnen schwebte.

Bald war das Mao-Bild in jedem Haus ein gewohnter Anblick, meist in Form seines offiziellen Porträts. Schätzungen zufolge wurden im Verlauf der Kulturrevolution etwa 2,2 Milliarden dieser offiziellen Mao-Porträts gedruckt, das heißt: Auf jeden Bürger der Volksrepublik kamen drei Stück. Wenn kein Mao-Bild im Haus zu entdecken war, lieferte dies einen Hinweis darauf, dass man sich offenbar dem revolutionären Strom des Augenblicks entgegenstemmen und nicht zulassen wollte, dass Mao eine zentrale Rolle nicht nur in der Politik, sondern auch im Alltagsleben spielte. Dieses offizielle Porträt nahm häufig den wichtigsten Platz in der Wohnung ein. Nicht nur der Mensch Mao wurde zu einem göttlichen Wesen erhoben, auch sein Porträt musste mit besonderer Sorgfalt behandelt werden, als ob es die Göttlichkeit selbst in sich barg: Es durfte nichts darüber gehängt werden und der Rahmen durfte keinen Kratzer haben.

Mao blieb jahrelang eine dauerhafte Ikone – in China wie auch im Ausland. Andy Warhol zum Beispiel schuf Bilder auf der Grundlage des offiziellen Mao-Porträts. Doch solch subversiver Umgang mit dem Bild des Großen Führers fand in China keinen Widerhall. Viele Menschen verehrten ihn nach wie vor, und er gehörte in Häusern und Wohnungen durchaus zum üblichen Inventar. Bis in die neunziger Jahre riefen Mao-Bilder, die nicht den Stildiktaten von *hong, guang, liang* (rot, hell und leuchtend) entsprachen, erstaunlich negative Reaktionen bei vielen älteren und auch jungen Chinesen hervor, mit denen ich sprach. Nach allgemeiner Auffassung war es einfach unschicklich, einen Führer von Maos Statur auf diese Weise darzustellen.

Ab Anfang der achtziger Jahre verloren Propagandaplakate allmählich an Popularität. Unter Deng Xiaoping, dem Nachfolger Mao Zedongs am Steuer der Volksrepublik, wurde die Gesundung der Wirtschaft zum wichtigsten, ja zum einzigen Anliegen der Partei. Darüber hinaus vollzog China eine Öffnung gegenüber dem Westen. Von nun an bestand das Ziel darin, Propaganda zu entwerfen und zu schaffen, die der neuen, facettenreichen Politik und damit dem Reformprogramm insgesamt öffentliche Unterstützung sicherte. Gleichzeitig musste das orthodoxe politische Denken hochgehalten werden und die führende Rolle der Partei in der Gesellschaft musste gewahrt bleiben. Ebenso war den Menschen ins Bewusstsein zu rücken, dass die Modernisierungspolitik fortgesetzt und in absehbarer Zeit nicht widerrufen würde. Während Maos ständiges Bemühen um Mobilisierung im Namen revolutionärer Bewegungen ohne Plakate nicht denkbar war, konnte die zweite, von Deng in die Wege geleitete Revolution gut ohne sie auskommen.

Diese Entwicklung hatte gewaltige Auswirkungen auf die Propagandakunst. Ihre Themen wurden weniger heroisch und militant, eher impressionistisch, und an die Stelle der strahlenden traten eher gedämpfte Farben. Ebenso wurden weniger schneidige und militaristische Parolen, sondern eher solche normativen Inhalts eingesetzt: Die Menschen wurden nicht mehr zum Kampf gegen Feinde oder gegen die Natur aufgerufen, sondern zu einer kultivierteren, hygienischeren und gebildeteren Lebensweise angehalten. Abstraktes trat an die Stelle der realistischen Darstellung und offenkundig politische Inhalte wurden durch eine Betonung des wirtschaftlichen Aufbaus oder sogar durch gewöhnliche kommerzielle Anzeigen ersetzt. Gestaltungs- und Darstellungstechniken mit Anleihen an die westliche Reklame kamen häufig zur Anwendung. Zwar führten diese stilistischen Veränderungen dazu, dass die Bilder für die eher traditionsverbundenen Teile der Bevölkerung schwerer zugänglich waren, doch belebten sie insgesamt das Medium des Propagandaplakates.

Hinsichtlich der Motive lassen sich die Plakate, die von der Regierung weiterhin veröffentlicht wurden, am besten als flüchtiger Blick „auf ein gutes Leben in einer materialistischen Welt" charakterisieren. All dies erinnert nur von Ferne an die Propaganda früherer Jahrzehnte. Doch Propaganda gibt immer auch die Realität wieder, selbst in einer Gesellschaft, die so fundamentale Veränderungen erlebt hat wie China seit den achtziger Jahren. Beim Inhalt der Propagandakunst gibt es eine Reihe wirklich auffälliger Entwicklungen, die sich von der früher geübten Praxis deutlich absetzen.

Die Verbesserung der Lebensumstände zeigte sich darin, dass die auf den Plakaten dargestellten Personen Kleidung in einer großen Vielfalt von Stoffen, Mustern, Schnitten und Farben trugen. Die blaue, graue oder schwarze Mao-Kluft, die früher bei Mann und Frau für ein proletarisches Aussehen gesorgt hatte, war verschwunden. An die Stelle der Revolutionsausstattung der Vergangenheit traten bei den Männern Turnschuhe, Lederjacken und Designer-Anzüge, während für Frauen Hotpants, Stilettos und femininere Kleider – darunter das hoch geschlitzte Shanghai-Kleid – unerlässlich wurden. Verschwunden waren die Stoppelhaarfrisuren und die Pferdeschwänze früherer Plakate, stattdessen gab es nun modisch dauergewellte oder gestylte Frisuren. Mit viel Aufmerksamkeit und Sorgfalt wandte man sich den Einzelheiten zu, in denen sich der Überfluss in der chinesischen Gesellschaft manifestierte, insbesondere in den Städten. Die zunehmende Offenheit, das höhere Maß an zulässiger persönlicher Freiheit wurden in visuelle Zeichen wie den Jumbojet übersetzt, der neue Reisemöglichkeiten innerhalb des

Landes und ins Ausland symbolisierte. Das Fernsehgerät sollte für persönlichen Erfolg in einem neuen Zeitalter stehen. Da die Menschen in immer größerer Zahl ein solches Gerät besaßen, war es bald auf vielen Plakaten zu finden.

Das Wichtigste aber war, dass Menschen dargestellt wurden, die ihren Vergnügungen nachgingen und offensichtlich Spaß hatten. Ein Beispiel für diese totale Umkehr findet sich im Bereich der Starlet-Poster. Nachdem in den achtziger Jahren die ersten billigen Kalenderblätter mit Fotos von Schauspielerinnen veröffentlicht worden waren, konnte man solche Poster bald überall sehen. Anfangs waren darauf ausschließlich Berühmtheiten aus der Welt des Entertainments und Films abgebildet, die aus Hongkong stammten. Später kamen Stars und Sternchen aus Taiwan hinzu. Einen echten Zuwachs erlebten diese Poster, als die chinesische Unterhaltungsindustrie ihre eigenen Berühmtheiten hervorbrachte. Männliche und weibliche Filmstars und Frauen aus dem TV-Geschäft tauchen heute nicht mehr nur auf Kalenderblättern auf: Sie haben sich inzwischen mit Werbeagenturen verbündet, um den Verkauf zahlreicher Waren, die in der chinesischen Konsumgesellschaft der Gegenwart erhältlich sind, zu fördern.

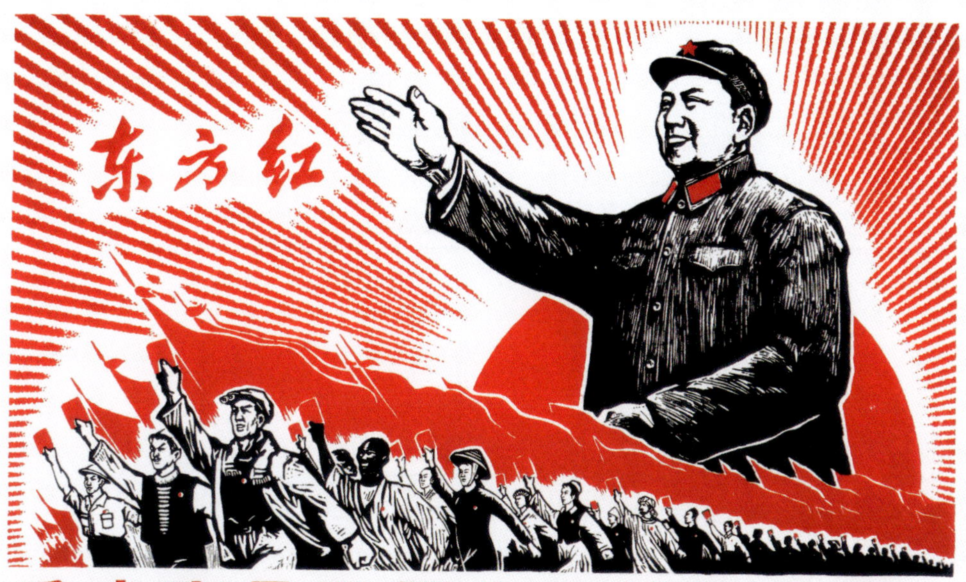

Chairman Mao is the red sun in our hearts, September 1968
In the image: The east is red

Der Vorsitzende Mao ist die rote Sonne in unserem Herzen, September 1968
Im Bild: Der Osten ist rot

Le président Mao est le soleil rouge de notre cœur, Septembre 1968
Dans l'image : L'Est est rouge

Trotz ihrer Modernisierungsversuche hat die Propagandakunst jeden Kontakt mit der Bevölkerung verloren. Die Bilder, Parolen und Botschaften, die von der Partei weiterhin produziert werden, erscheinen zunehmend unbedeutend. Sie stoßen auf blicklose Augen und taube Ohren. Da das Interesse der Leute für Politik auf einem nie erlebten Tiefpunkt angelangt ist, liegt ihnen nichts mehr daran, ideologisch oder politisch „rein" zu sein. Ihr Interesse gilt eher dem eigenen Vergnügen und in diesem Zusammenhang auch der Höhe ihres Gehalts und der Frage, ob sie morgen noch Arbeit haben werden. Propagandaplakate haben ihre Glaubwürdigkeit und ihren Reiz verloren, die Produktionszahlen sind drastisch gesunken. Die Leute halten sie für altmodisch, auch wenn Propagandaplakate heute auf dickes Hochglanzpapier bester Qualität oder sogar auf Plastikfolien gedruckt werden. Als Künstler auftraten, die nicht mehr innerhalb der Kunstbürokratie arbeiten mussten, entwickelte sich ein zunehmend deregulierter, den Beschränkungen der Regierungskontrolle entzogener Kunstmarkt. Es entstanden private Gesellschaften, Galerien und andere Verkaufsstellen für diese jungen Künstler, was ihnen die Vermarktung ihrer Werke sehr erleichterte. Da heute wirklich reizvolle Gemälde und Poster in nie gekannter reicher Auswahl erhältlich sind, besteht keine Nachfrage mehr nach den stumpfsinnigen politischen Botschaften. Indem sie politisch oder moralisierend auftretende Personen absichtlich aus ihren Werken verbannt haben, stellen Künstler visuelles Material zur Verfügung, das den Menschen bedeutungsvoller oder ästhetisch ansprechender erscheint. Dies wird durch die Rückkehr traditioneller Glücksmotive und Neujahrsdrucke – nicht nur traditionellen, sondern auch modernen Inhalts – in die Häuser und Wohnungen im städtischen wie auch im ländlichen Raum belegt.

Kurzum, es ist wenig übrig von einem Bildgenre, das einst mit dem Ziel geschaffen wurde, das chinesische Volk zu begeistern, zu mobilisieren und ihm den Weg in eine zukünftige kommunistische Utopie zu weisen. Die Politik ist tot, die Konsumgesellschaft höchst lebendig. Nach der Wende zum 21. Jahrhundert sind vier Typen von Massenkunst geblieben, die von jeweils unterschiedlichen Gruppen rezipiert werden. Die städtischen Yuppies bevorzugen Reproduktionen westlicher Kunst in Postergröße. Leute mit weniger Geld kaufen preiswerte Kalenderposter, am liebsten mit Darstellungen hübscher Mädchen. Die Bauern, die in China die Mehrheit stellen, begeistern sich zunehmend für traditionelle Bilder, auch wenn das Mao-Bild den Raum besetzt hat, der früher dem Küchengott oder anderen Gottheiten vorbehalten war. Es sind zwar noch einige politische Plakate erhältlich, doch nur Sammler aus China oder aus dem Westen interessieren sich anscheinend dafür. Die Bilder, die einst das China-Bild prägten, sind verschwunden.

Stefan R. Landsberger

Chairman Mao visits high-yielding fields, 1963

Vorsitzender Mao besichtigt Felder mit hohem Ertrag, 1963

Le président Mao visite des champs à fort rendement, 1963

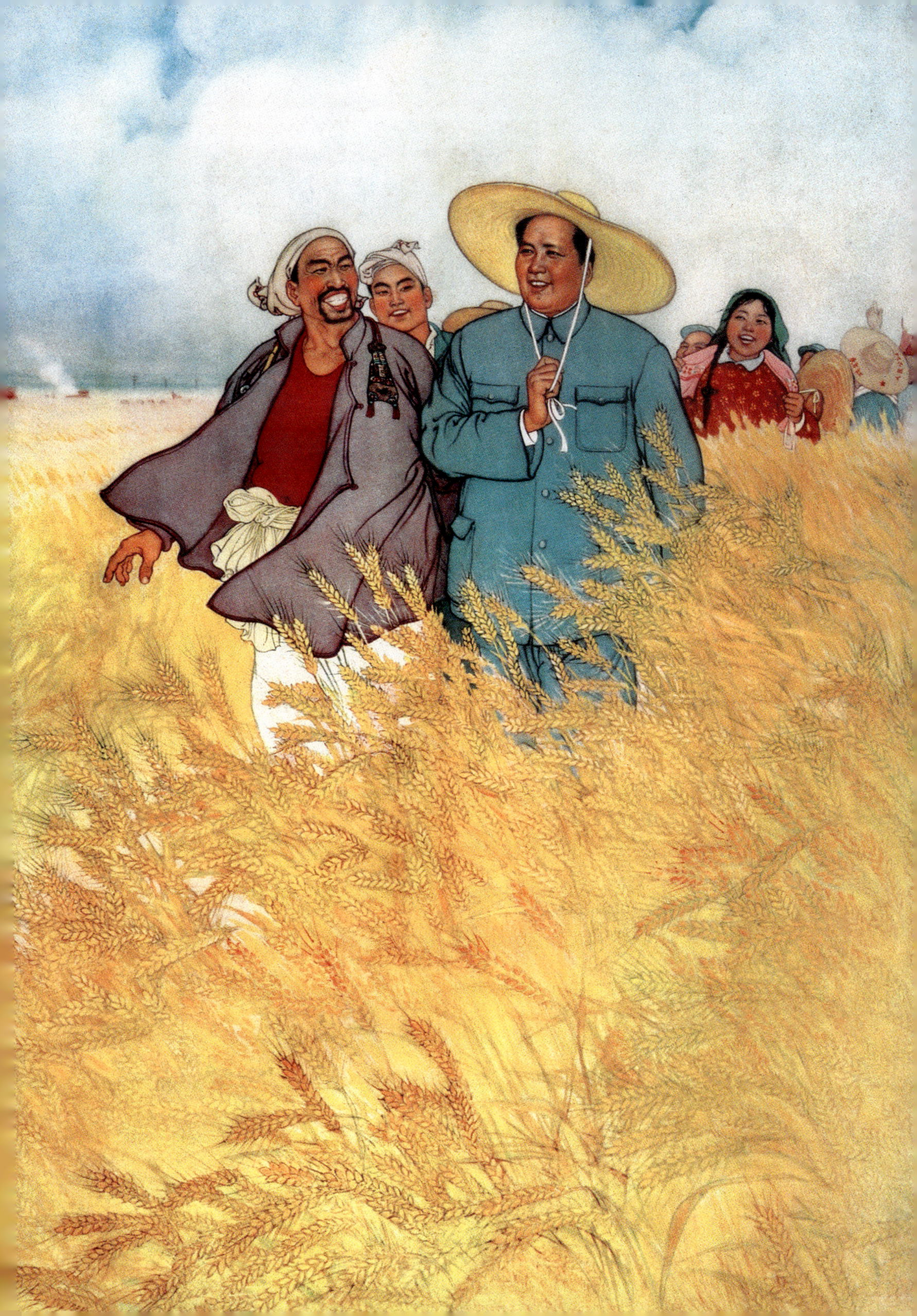

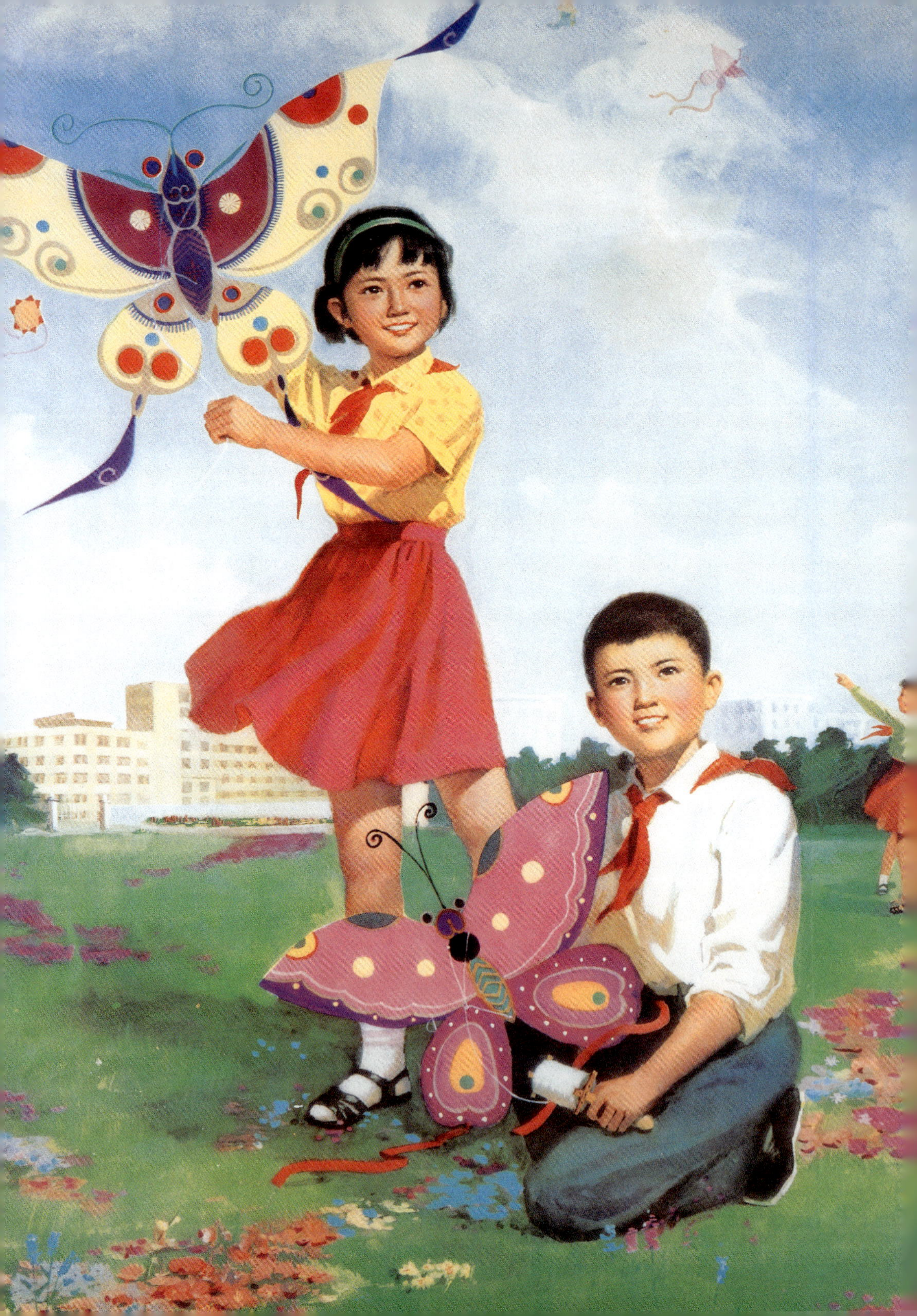

LA FILLE DE L'AFFICHE

Toute mon enfance, j'ai voulu être la fille de l'affiche (page 4). Jour après jour, je m'habillais comme cette fille : robe de coton blanc, petit foulard rouge noué autour du cou et, comme elle, je me faisais des nattes. Le fait qu'elle était entourée des martyrs de la révolution, que j'avais appris à vénérer au jardin d'enfants, me plaisait énormément. Celle qui se trouvait tout à fait à droite était Liu Hu-lan, l'adolescente qui avait été décapitée parce qu'elle refusait d'abjurer sa foi dans le communisme. Le soldat qui la surplombait s'appelait Huang Ji-guang (voir aussi page 20) ; pendant la guerre de Corée, avec sa poitrine, il avait intercepté le tir d'une mitrailleuse américaine. À côté de lui se tenait Dong Chun-rui, qui s'était couvert le corps d'explosifs pour faire sauter un pont ennemi. Tout à fait à gauche, il y avait Cai Yong-xiang, le soldat qui fut écrasé par un train en secourant des camarades. La fille de l'affiche tenait à la main un livre, *L'Histoire de Lei Feng* – soldat, héros et martyr –, qui racontait le destin de ce conducteur de camion, mort en voulant protéger les autres.

C'est à l'âge de huit ans que je me pris de passion pour les affiches. Un jour, je rapportai de l'école un portrait du président Mao Zedong (page 11). Même si j'ignorais à ce moment-là que la Révolution culturelle avait commencé, mon acte faisait de moi une activiste : je retirai du mur le tableau de ma mère, « Paix et Bonheur », qui représentait des enfants jouant dans un étang couvert de lotus, et le remplaçai par le portrait de Mao. Cela ne plut guère à ma mère, mais elle essaya de cacher sa déception. Je me souviens de ce que je pensais alors : comment ne pas être heureux que Mao daigne baisser les yeux pour nous regarder manger, alors que d'autres n'avaient pas leur content de lui ?

Les affiches eurent une profonde influence sur ma vie. Elles m'ont appris à être dévouée et loyale envers Mao et le communisme. Pour me sentir plus proche de lui, je remplissais la maison de ses portraits. Je regardais le Grand Timonier le soir avant de m'endormir et le matin à mon réveil. Quand j'arrivais à économiser quelques sous, je courais les librairies pour m'acheter d'autres affiches de lui. L'endroit où j'habitais à Shanghai devint une zone de combats au plus fort de la Révolution culturelle, fin des années 60, début des années 70. La violence entre factions était telle que beaucoup mouraient. Tout le monde se battait au nom de la pensée de Mao. Être maoïste – tel était alors le but suprême. Pendant dix ans, je fus responsable du journal de l'école, le « Blackboard Newspaper » ; je recopiais chaque dessin paru dans le « Head Art for Propaganda Publishing » (page 22). Je dessinais à longueur de journée, de semaine, d'année. Je publiais des éditions spéciales du journal, même

Whose kite flies higher? 1970

Wessen Drachen fliegt höher? 1970

Qui a un cerf-volant qui vole plus haut ? 1970

pendant la fermeture estivale et hivernale de l'école. Une poignée de personnes seulement voyaient mon travail, mais peu m'importait. Mes mains enflaient sous les gelures et je pouvais à peine tenir un bout de craie. Mais j'étais inspirée par les héros et les héroïnes des affiches, et je croyais que les privations ne feraient que m'endurcir et me rendre forte.

Je continuais de rêver qu'un jour j'aurais l'insigne honneur de pouvoir me sacrifier pour Mao, et de devenir la fille de l'affiche. Ma scolarité primaire achevée, le gouvernement m'envoya travailler dans une ferme collective située non loin de la mer de Chine orientale. La vie y était si dure, si insoutenable que nombre de jeunes se blessaient à dessein, en se coupant un pied ou une main par exemple, pour être déclarés inaptes au travail et être renvoyés chez eux. Quant à moi, je tirais ma force et mon courage des affiches qui avaient enchanté mon enfance. Je croyais dur comme fer à l'héroïsme, et tant qu'à faire, je préférais mourir en martyre.

Je travaillais comme un forçat dans les champs de riz et de coton pendant trois ans, jusqu'au jour où Madame Mao, Jiang Qing, donna un autre cours à mon destin. Début 1976, personne ne savait que Mao agonisait et que son épouse se préparait à prendre le pouvoir après sa disparition. Elle était en train de réaliser un film de propagande pour les masses, et elle avait envoyé partout dans le pays des découvreurs de talents pour dénicher le « visage prolétarien » convenant au premier rôle du film. Je fus choisie un jour que je binais dans un champ de coton. On m'emmena au studio de cinéma de Shanghai pour m'apprendre à jouer dans le film. C'est là que je fis la connaissance du célèbre peintre d'affiches Ha Quiongwan du Hua-Yuan, l'institut des Arts de Shanghai. Un matin que je me brossais les dents au-dessus du lavabo public, monsieur Ha m'aborda. Il me montra un papier officiel l'autorisant à recruter des modèles pour ses affiches. Il me dit qu'il aimait mon allure et me demanda si je voulais poser pour lui. J'étais flattée bien entendu, mais je lui demandai si mes yeux bouffis de sommeil ne le dérangeaient pas. Il me dit que non.

Il me suivit jusqu'à mon dortoir pour y choisir des costumes parmi mes vêtements. Je fus surprise de le voir prendre ma veste verte et déchirée de l'armée, que je portais au camp de travail. Je lui dis d'attendre quelques secondes, le temps d'enlever la boue sur l'épaule. Il m'arrêta net et me dit qu'un peu de saleté était exactement l'effet qu'il recherchait.

La séance de pose commença dès que monsieur Ha eut installé l'appareil photo. Ne sachant pas poser, je me contentai de prendre l'attitude voulue par lui, qui était de regarder droit dans le lointain, avec assurance. Je m'excusai pour ma peau et mes cheveux abîmés par le soleil, et essayai de cacher mes ongles teintés par les fongicides. Il me dit beaucoup apprécier mon authentique allure de paysanne. Il voulut savoir ce que je portais pour travailler dans les rizières. Un chapeau de paille, mais pas de chaussures, lui répondis-je, et puis je roulais mes manches jusqu'aux coudes et les jambes de mon pantalon jusqu'aux genoux. Il me dit de le faire. J'obéis. J'ôtai mes chaussures et vis mes ongles de pied brunis par les fongicides. J'étais très gênée, mais il me dit de ne pas l'être. Au contraire, j'avais, d'après lui, toutes les raisons d'être fière. « Je peins des affiches de paysans depuis des années », dit-il, « et je ne me suis jamais rendu compte de mon erreur. Dorénavant, je peindrai en brun les ongles de pied des paysans. »

Une semaine plus tard, monsieur Ha m'envoya une épreuve de la photo de moi qu'il préférait. J'arborais un air vraiment héroïque, à l'instar de la fille de l'affiche, que j'avais admirée enfant. Les mois passèrent et je n'entendis plus parler de lui. Un jour, pendant le Nouvel An chinois, je marchais non loin de la rue la plus commerçante de Shanghai, Central Xi-Zang Road et East Yan-an Road, quand j'aperçus une affiche dans la vitrine de la plus grande librairie du quartier : la jeune femme représentée avait mon visage, ma veste, mais ses bras et ses jambes étaient nettement plus forts. Elle portait un chapeau de paille, ses manches et les jambes de son pantalon étaient relevées, et ses ongles étaient bruns !

Je rentrai vite à la maison pour annoncer la nouvelle à ma famille. Mes parents étaient tout excités et fiers. J'aurais voulu acheter un exemplaire de l'affiche, mais elle n'était pas en vente. L'employé de la librairie m'expliqua que le gouvernement distribuait les affiches pour qu'elles soient exposées dans les lieux publics.

La collection d'affiches de propagande chinoises que possède Max Gottschalk est unique et merveilleuse. Les affiches représentent le rêve de toute une génération et sont le reflet d'une période capitale de l'histoire de la Chine, qui a été en grande partie mal documentée.

Les images en disent souvent plus que les mots, alors laissons-leur la parole.

Anchee Min

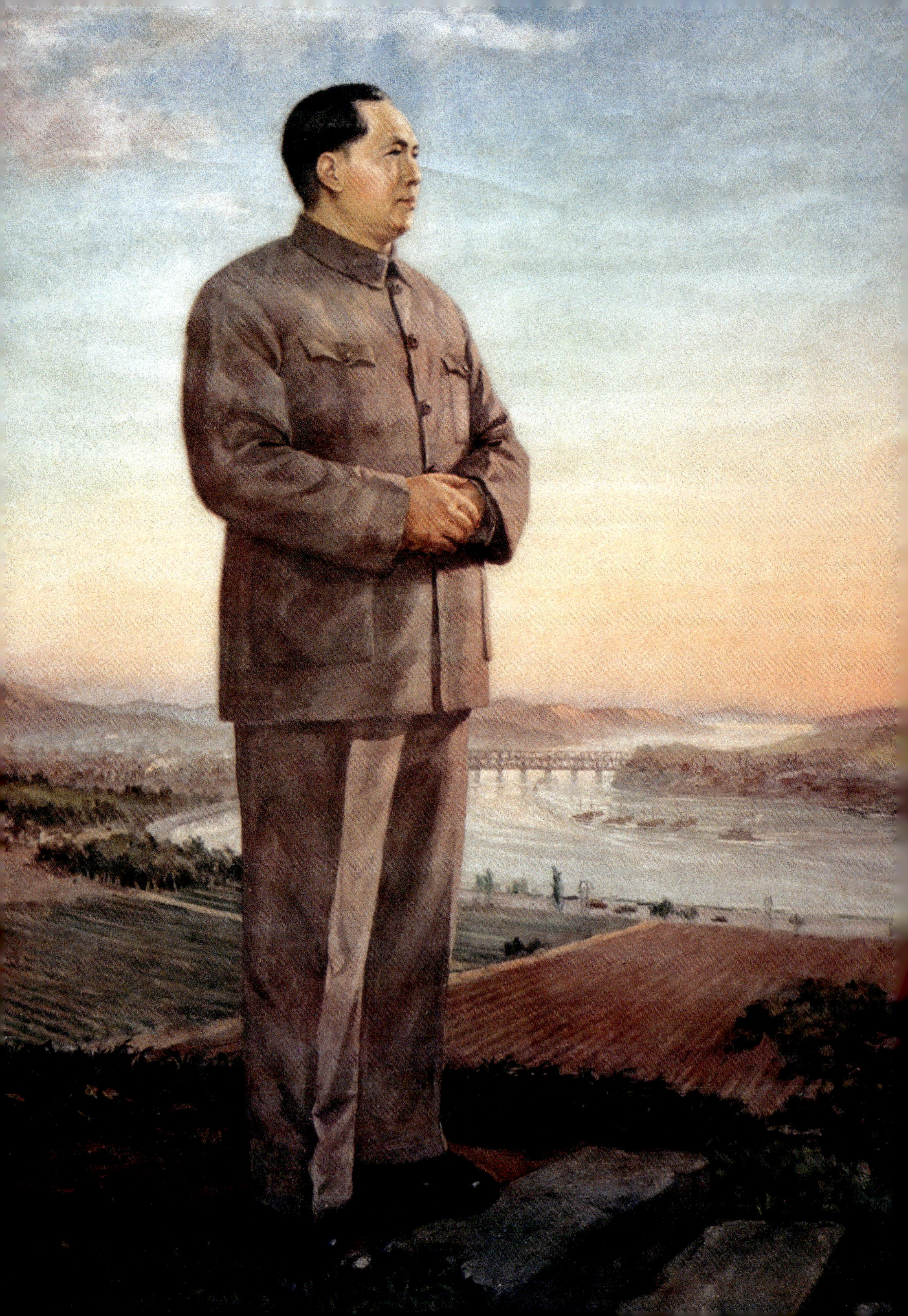

EN REGARDANT LES AFFICHES DE PROPAGANDE

400 affiches de propagande à regarder. Au bout de deux minutes environ, je suis comme engourdi. J'essaie d'être patient et je me remets à feuilleter le tout depuis le début. 10 000 fleurs rouges, figées dans un épanouissement éternel, toutes semblables les unes aux autres, me passent tout à coup devant les yeux. Je me découvre soudain moi aussi au milieu d'elles, moi, ma famille, mes voisins, des millions de gens. Une époque fait retour ...

Je continue de regarder les affiches. Mon moi d'aujourd'hui regarde la première moitié de ma vie. Qu'est-ce que je ressens ? De l'apathie ? De la honte ? Du dégoût ? De l'horreur ? Ou de la nostalgie ? Rien de tout cela ? Ou peut-être un mélange de tous ces sentiments ?

Ce petit garçon replet à la peau claire, assis dans son tablier rouge sur la feuille de lotus, une grosse carpe dans les bras, ce pourrait être moi ? Mais quittons les souvenirs les plus reculés et entrons dans une vieille image de Nouvel An. Une grande brochette de fruits confits à la main, je suis perché sur les épaules de mon père. Passons devant les gigantesques marmites de bouillie à base de farine de blé frite, devant les artistes de variété en train de faire des culbutes, et promenons-nous dans la foire annuelle de Pékin (à cette époque, les murs de la ville étaient encore là avec leurs tours, et les maisons à cour carrées, les « Siheyuan », aussi). Les images de Sun Wukong et de Zhao Zilong que j'ai peintes quand j'avais 5 ans me reviennent en mémoire. Et soudain je me vois assis sur un tracteur, le foulard rouge des Jeunes pionniers autour du cou, et je m'entends chanter un hymne à la gloire de la ligne à haute tension. Je cours derrière les oncles ouvriers qui ressemblent à des héros, et qui sont justement en train de grimper à une échelle pour construire un arc-en-ciel ...

Les souvenirs d'enfance s'estompent peu à peu. Une nouvelle image émerge. La vieille affiche de Nouvel An se métamorphose en affiche de propagande. « Qu'est-ce que tu veux faire quand tu seras grand ? », me demande une jardinière d'enfants. « Je voudrais être membre d'une brigade d'exploration géologique et chercher des trésors pour la patrie. » Je n'ose pas, à cause de ma timidité, prononcer la seconde moitié de la phrase. Mon image elle aussi se voit métamorphosée. Un artilleur casqué regarde avec colère en direction de Taiwan. Un jeune voisin crie à tue-tête : « Je possède trois flèches magiques. Si je décoche la première flèche, notre bâtiment se transformera en un immeuble de trois étages. Si je décoche la deuxième, des immeubles surgiront partout en Chine. Si je décoche la troisième, le communisme sera réalisé dans le monde entier ! » Je suis impressionné et je l'admire, au point que je voudrais faire une peinture de cette histoire. Si je l'avais vraiment faite, ça aurait été ma

The east is red *Artist:* Li Zongjian; People's Art Publishing House, 1953

Der Osten ist rot *Gemalt von* Li Zongjian; Volkskunstverlag, 1953

L'Est est rouge *Peintre :* Li Zongjian ; Éditions Populaires d'Art, 1953

première affiche de propagande. Peut-être que j'aurais reçu le premier prix de peinture d'enfants de Chine.

J'ai été livré dès ma naissance (1951) à une éducation visuelle, des livres d'images pour enfants à la multitude des affiches de propagande et autres, en passant par les ouvrages scolaires et les lectures pour la jeunesse. Toutes ces images avaient les mêmes thèmes et jouaient dans ma vie le rôle de balises. Elles veillaient à ce que nous ne fassions pas de fautes. De riches prairies dans lesquelles se roulaient comme des perles de gras moutons. En 1958, on vit apparaître sur ces mêmes images des arbres verts dans lesquels des enfants, accrochés comme des poires, chassaient les moineaux à l'aide de catapultes et de balais. Détruisez-les ! Tous frappaient le gong sans discontinuer jusqu'à ce que les moineaux tombent morts à terre.

Une fois seulement j'avais peint par hasard un jardin avec des montagnes artificielles, des pavillons et des fleurs d'hiver. Je fus aussitôt rappelé à l'ordre par mon frère : « C'est un jardin de la classe possédante ! » Je peignis dans l'image les expériences de mes vacances, à savoir regarder les poissons rouges. Commentaire de l'instituteur : « Absolument aucune vertu pédagogique ! »

Vint le temps de l'imitation et de l'alignement sur les affiches de propagande. Je constatai que les mains sur les affiches devenaient de plus en plus grosses. Les mains qui récoltaient des épis de maïs et portaient des pastèques caressaient à présent des fusées. Au-dessus de ces mains gigantesques de la classe ouvrière, dont elle se détachait, planait celle, encore plus gigantesque, du Grand président. Des milliers et des milliers de mains que l'on agitait, et parmi elles la mienne imitant, dans un mouvement de haut en bas et de bas en haut, Lénine en 1918 : « Bolcheviks, camarades marins, en avant ! » Ordres, slogans, des mains énormes, épongeant la sueur, secouant l'épaule du camarade, lançant des grenades sur la tête de l'ennemi. Quand nous étions petits, il s'agissait de former un grand cercle en nous donnant la main et de jouer à la cache-cache. Plus tard, toujours en nous donnant la main, nous terrassions l'impérialisme.

Je ne sais pas qui a inventé les affiches de propagande. Une chose pour moi est sûre, c'est que ma vie s'y reflète. Jamais il n'y eut place en moi pour le doute, jusqu'à cet incident. C'était un peu avant le début de la révolution culturelle. À côté de mon lit était accrochée une affiche portant une citation de Mao Zedong : « Pendant la saison des gros travaux des champs, mangez de la nourriture solide ; dans les périodes où il n'y a pas grand chose à faire, mangez pour moitié du solide, pour moitié du liquide, avec un complément de pommes de terre et de patates douces. » Je connaissais chaque mot, et pourtant je n'arrivais pas à comprendre ce que cela voulait dire. Tous les jours, avant de m'endormir et à mon lever, je regardais fixement cette affiche et la relisais inlassablement. Je n'étais pas en mesure de la comprendre. Pourquoi notre dirigeant nous disait-il comment nous devions manger ? Je pense aujourd'hui que, si on traduisait cette citation en image, tout le monde la comprendrait : il n'y a rien à récolter sur ces champs immenses ; 20 millions de paysans meurent de faim parce qu'ils n'ont rien à manger. Voilà pourquoi ... voilà pourquoi cela ne devait pas être exprimé en langage visuel, mais seulement verbal.

À 16 ans, je fus envoyé à la campagne comme main-d'œuvre. Pour la première fois, j'ai appris à connaître la vie des paysans. Le travail physique était très dur. C'est à peine si on avait de quoi manger à notre faim. Un jour, je suis entré dans la chambre nuptiale d'un jeune couple du village. Au mur, on voyait l'affiche du phénix et du dragon, symboles de bonheur, qu'accompagnait ce rouleau de parchemin : « Le couple de mandarins nage dans l'océan révolutionnaire ; les époux sont des camarades. » C'était pour moi affreusement triste et cela me faisait envie en même temps. En suivant l'étroit chemin boueux, je vis, placardée sur le mur de torchis, cette affiche de propagande montrant une épaisse fumée s'élevant de cheminées. Quels espoirs cela ne recouvrait-il pas ! Le travail pouvait combattre la pauvreté ! Comme cette fumée peinte était romantique ! Comme les nuages du paradis. Quel immense réconfort c'était, pour les gens de ce village qui faisaient vie commune avec le bétail, de lever les yeux et de voir se dresser des cheminées sur une image ! Je suis sûr que, si j'avais vu à cette époque des images de Jésus ou de Bouddha, elles n'auraient eu pour moi aucun sens, pour la raison que je ne les connaissais pas.

Je suis quelqu'un de la ville et c'est ainsi que je l'ai ressenti. Qu'en eût-il été d'un enfant de la campagne qui n'aurait encore jamais vu de sa vie d'autres images que les affiches de propagande ? J'avais rencontré beaucoup de jeunes gens de la campagne très doués pour l'art. Ils ne peignaient rien d'autre que ce genre d'affiches de propagande. C'étaient tous leurs désirs et tout leur amour qu'ils transposaient dans leurs images. Leur idéal artistique suprême était de devenir des professionnels de l'affiche de propagande.

Qu'est-ce qu'ils peuvent bien peindre aujourd'hui ? Peut-être des beautés pour des affiches publicitaires ? Peut-être qu'ils sont retournés depuis longtemps à la tradition chinoise de la peinture de paysage ? À mon avis, il y a toujours eu un courant de fond sous l'habillage de l'affiche de propagande politique, à savoir le gène enfoui de l'art populaire. Basé sur les mythes et les légendes populaires et sur l'idéal antique de fusion de l'homme et de la nature, c'est lui qui est à l'origine de l'âme d'une nation. Si l'on regarde plus attentivement ces affiches, on peut se rendre compte que certaines d'entre elles essaient obstinément de s'exprimer en dépit de la muselière politique. C'est peut-être justement à cause de ces quelques rares rayons de lumière, même déformés, que j'ai éprouvé des relents de nostalgie. On ne peut pas dire que cette époque soit un vide.

J'ai de la chance. J'ai découvert à 20 ans Vincent van Gogh et Picasso. Depuis, il n'a plus été possible de me faire peindre une affiche. Quand, seul, je passais en vélo, sous la surveillance permanente des regards de nos dirigeants, devant les affiches d'ouvriers, de paysans et de soldats grands et forts dont étaient placardés nos murs, je me faisais l'effet d'un personnage d'un roman de Kafka. C'est alors que j'ai commencé à écrire et à être solitaire. C'est alors qu'a commencé mon existence en exil.

Aujourd'hui, les affiches de propagande politique sont des antiquités qui se vendent cher. Mais je ne les collectionnerai jamais. Car dès que je les aperçois, 10 000 fleurs rouges apparaissent devant mes yeux, et l'une d'elles est mon père. Il a presque 90 ans, il tombe souvent de son lit la nuit, il crie et donne des coups de poings comme un fou autour de lui parce qu'en rêve, il se bat contre les ennemis de classe et défend encore probablement le Grand président. Je crois que, pendant les prochaines décennies au moins, plusieurs générations de nos dirigeants vont encore surgir dans nos salles de séjour, nos chambres à coucher et dans la rue pour exiger de nous que nous nous sentions bien, que nous soyons reconnaissants et que nous souriions comme les gens sur les affiches, en montrant des dents blanches et même les dents du fond ...

Mon canapé est recouvert d'une cotonnade chinoise traditionnelle aux couleurs somptueuses, sur laquelle sont reproduits le phénix et la pivoíne. J'attends le phénix qui viendra de loin en fendant l'air de ses ailes ...

Duo Duo

The springtime of science has arrived, 1978

Der Frühling der Wissenschaft ist gekommen, 1978

Voici venu le printemps de la science, 1978

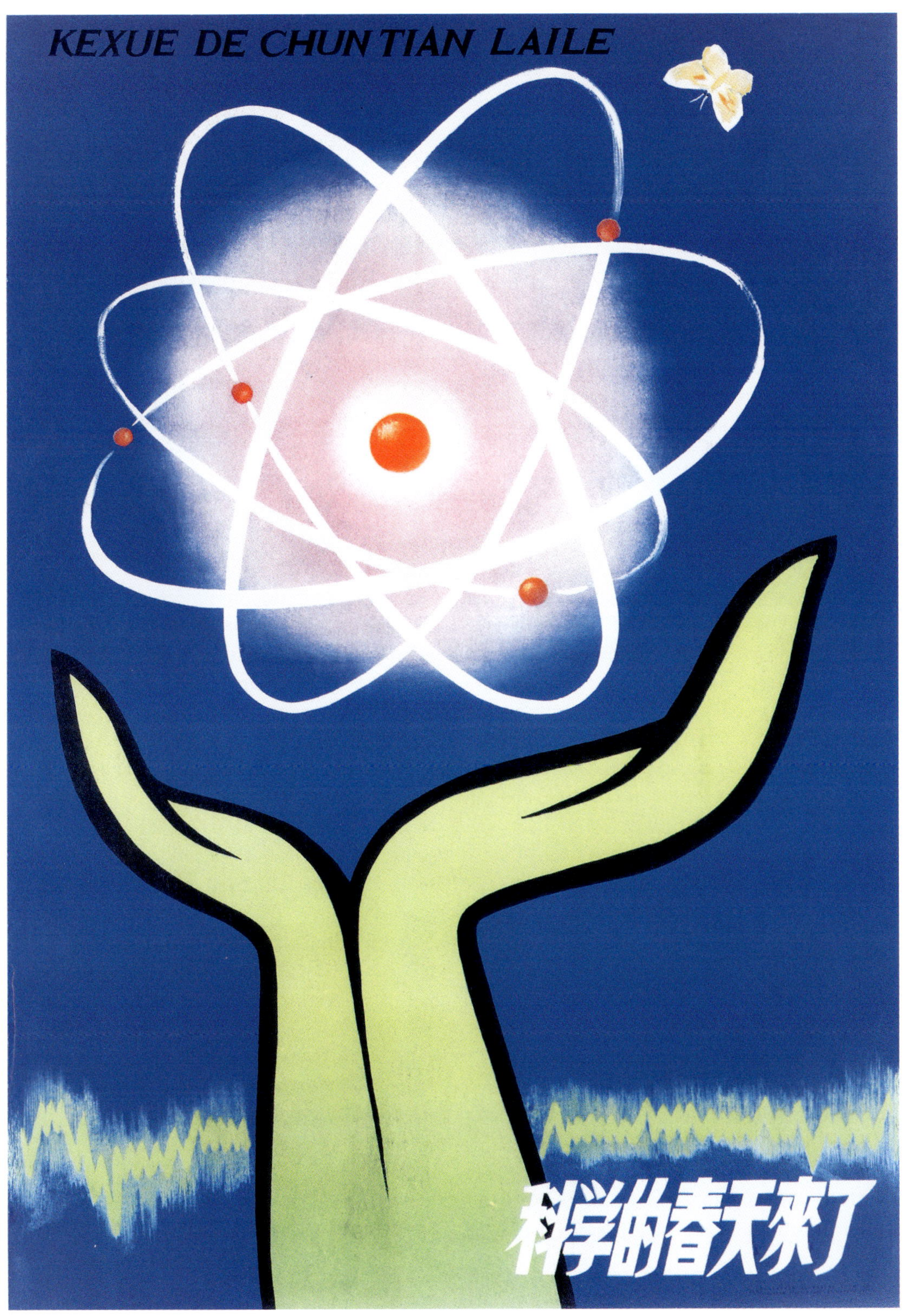
KEXUE DE CHUN TIAN LAILE
科学的春天來了

APOGÉE ET DÉCLIN DE L'AFFICHE DE PROPAGANDE CHINOISE

L'image prévalente en République populaire de Chine était largement définie par les images politiques que livrait l'art de propagande révolutionnaire. Tout le long de son histoire millénaire, le système politique chinois s'est servi des arts pour propager un comportement et une pensée conformes à une idéologie. Si la littérature, la poésie, la peinture, le théâtre, l'opéra, les chansons et d'autres expressions artistiques étaient conçus avant tout pour divertir, ils avaient aussi une fonction didactique capitale : éduquer le peuple dans ce qui était jugé juste ou faux à un moment donné. Tant que l'État montrerait des exemples de ce qu'était une conduite « correcte », les masses populaires seraient automatiquement portées à croire à ce qu'il était juste de croire.

Après l'établissement de la République populaire en 1949, l'art de propagande demeura l'un des moyens majeurs de fournir des exemples édifiants de vertu idéologique ou politique. Mais il donna aussi une forme concrète aux nombreuses politiques et visions différentes du futur que le Parti communiste chinois forgea au cours des ans. Dans un pays comme la Chine, qui comptait dans les années 40 et 50 des millions d'illettrés, cette méthode pour représenter des idées abstraites, et par là éduquer le peuple, fut particulièrement efficace. Les affiches de propagande, qui étaient bon marché et faciles à produire, devinrent l'un des véhicules privilégiés de ce type de communication. Comme elles étaient en vente libre, on pouvait les voir absolument partout. Elles étaient en outre un excellent moyen d'égayer les espaces de vie, fort tristes par ailleurs, de la population. Elles pouvaient ainsi pénétrer l'organisation sociale et la vie communautaire, à tous les niveaux, même les plus modestes : les affiches multicolores ornaient non seulement les murs des bureaux et des usines, mais aussi ceux des maisons et des dortoirs. La plupart des gens les appréciaient pour leur composition et leur contenu optique et ne prêtaient guère attention aux slogans inscrits dans la partie inférieure. Ainsi le message politique passait-il de manière presque subconsciente.

Les artistes les plus talentueux furent employés pour donner aux tendances politiques du moment une forme visuelle précise et minutieuse. Parmi ces artistes, beaucoup avaient travaillé sur les almanachs publicitaires, si prisés avant la fondation de la République populaire. Ils furent rapidement récupérés et intégrés dans les divers organismes que le gouvernement et le Parti avaient créés pour produire des affiches de propagande. Ces artistes étaient après tout très versés dans les techniques de la conception et du dessin, donc capables de représenter de façon attrayante n'importe quel produit. Les images qu'ils façonnaient étaient souvent figuratives et réalistes, comme si elles avaient été des copies fidèles de photographies. Elles avaient pour dessein de représenter le futur dans le présent, en ne montrant pas seulement « la vie comme elle est », mais aussi « comme elle devrait être ». Elles étaient peintes dans un style naïf ; toutes les formes étaient soulignées de noir et saturées de couleurs vives : rose, rouge, jaune, vert et bleu. Ces œuvres créaient une sorte de « faction », un hybride de « fait » et de « fiction », mettant l'accent sur ce qui était positif et faisant l'impasse sur tout ce qui était négatif. Ce qui les définissait comme un art de propagande, c'étaient les slogans d'inspiration politique.

Ces œuvres d'art originales étaient publiées dans les journaux et les magazines, puis imprimées sous forme d'affiches, de grand ou petit format, et quelquefois même sur les timbres-poste. Les grandes affiches étaient exposées dans les rues, les gares et d'autres lieux publics, tandis que les plus petites étaient diffusées par le réseau de librairies *Xinhua* (Nouvelle Chine) pour une consommation de masse. Étant donné que ce que l'on considérait comme « correct » était soumis à de fréquentes fluctuations, ces affiches politiques finirent par être réalisées avec plus de circonspection que les journaux, car elles observaient les subtiles modifications de ton, d'idéologie et de slogan.

Les affiches reprenaient les thèmes de la reconstruction politique et économique, prédominant après 1949. Des jeunes, des paysans et des ouvriers sans âge, démonstratifs et hyperréalistes, figurés dans des poses dynamiques, peuplaient les images. Ils faisaient allégeance à la cause communiste ou obédience au président Mao Zedong, ou s'étaient engagés dans l'œuvre glorieuse de reconstruire la nation. La plupart des affiches avaient donc une finalité abstraite, strictement utilitaire : elles glorifiaient le travail et le sacrifice personnel pour le bien-être général. En même temps, elles se préoccupaient peu de la dimension individuelle et privée de la vie des gens, de leur délassement et de leurs distractions.

Les corps sains et puissants symbolisaient les classes productives, fortes et toniques – une image que l'État voulait propager. Les distinctions génériques entre les personnages s'estompèrent au fil du temps. Les caractères féminins et masculins avaient pratiquement disparu – un gommage qui avait été aussi tenté dans la vie réelle. Femmes et hommes avaient des corps stéréotypés, « masculinisés », leur donnant presque l'apparence de surhommes. Leurs vêtements étaient larges et unisexes ; les seules couleurs disponibles étaient le gris des cadres du parti, le vert de l'armée et le bleu des masses laborieuses – les ouvriers et les paysans. Les visages, aux cheveux coupés court ou nattés, s'inscrivaient dans un répertoire restreint de formes standardisées acceptables.

C'est dans les années de gigantesques mouvements populaires, tels le Grand Bond en avant (1958–1960) et la Révolution culturelle subséquente (1966–1976), qui mobilisèrent des millions de gens, que la production d'affiches atteignit son point culminant. L'affiche propagandiste trouva aussi dans ces grandes périodes son expression artistique la plus achevée, dans le fond comme dans la forme. Le président Mao Zedong, Grand Éducateur, Grand Leader, Grand Timonier et Commandant suprême, semblait être devenu le seul sujet admissible à l'époque. Son visage était peint d'ordinaire en rouge et dans d'autres couleurs chaudes, et ce de telle manière qu'il dégageait de la douceur et semblait rayonner, comme une source de lumière illuminant les visages tournés vers lui. Son image était jugée plus importante que l'occasion qui avait donné lieu à la création de l'affiche : il arrivait que les mêmes affiches fussent publiées plusieurs années, mais avec des slogans différents, afin de servir différentes causes de propagande. Il y avait dans les images de Mao un je ne sais quoi qui trouvait un écho chez les gens. Il était toujours uni à eux, d'une manière ou d'une autre : qu'il inspectât les champs et les usines, serrât la main à des paysans et des ouvriers, qu'il s'assît pour fumer une cigarette avec eux, ou se tînt debout à la proue d'un navire, se montrât dans un peignoir en tissu éponge, après un bain revigorant dans le Yangzijiang, ou même qu'il fût en tête d'une colonne de délégués des minorités nationales ou flottât sur une mer de drapeaux rouges.

Mao trouva place aussi dans chaque foyer, généralement sous forme de portrait officiel. On estime que, durant la Révolution culturelle, quelque 2,2 millions de portraits officiels de Mao furent imprimés, ce qui fait trois par personne. Le fait de n'avoir chez soi aucun portrait de lui était l'indice d'une réticence à suivre le mouvement révolutionnaire du moment, ou, pire, celui d'un esprit contre-révolutionnaire, et d'une réfutation du rôle central joué par Mao, non seulement en politique mais aussi dans la vie courante de chacun. Ce portrait occupait souvent une place de choix dans la maison. La personne de Mao n'était pas la seule à être l'objet d'une véritable vénération, son portrait recevait lui aussi les marques de la plus grande déférence, comme s'il renfermait la divinité elle-même : on ne plaçait rien au-dessus et son cadre devait rester immaculé.

Mao devint une icône, en Chine comme à l'étranger, et devait le demeurer avec le temps. Andy Warhol, par exemple, peignit des tableaux basés sur le portrait officiel de Mao. Mais pareilles subversions de l'image du Grand Timonier n'eurent aucune répercussion en Chine. Comme par le passé, il était exposé à la vénération de beaucoup de gens et restait omniprésent dans nombre de foyers. Encore à la fin des années 90, toute représentation de Mao qui n'était pas conforme aux règles stylistiques de *hong*, *guang*, *liang* (rouge, radieux, brillant) provoquait, à ma grande surprise, des réponses négatives de la part de vieux Chinois, et même de jeunes, avec qui je m'entretenais. L'opinion était unanime : pareille représentation n'était tout simplement pas digne de quelqu'un de la stature de Mao.

La popularité des affiches propagandistes commença à décliner au début des années 80. Sous Deng Xiaoping, qui avait succédé à Mao Zedong en tant que premier personnage politique de la République populaire, le Parti décida d'une nouvelle orientation en donnant la priorité absolue à la modernisation de l'économie. Le processus d'ouverture de la Chine à l'Occident s'amorçait lui aussi. Dès lors, l'objectif était d'élaborer et de produire le support public des nouvelles politiques constituant le vaste programme de réformes. En même temps, il fallait maintenir la barre de l'orthodoxie politique et préserver le rôle dominant du Parti dans la société. Pour ce faire, il était essentiel que la population prenne conscience que la politique de modernisation était définitive et ne serait pas révoquée dans un proche avenir. Alors que les efforts constants de Mao pour mobiliser les masses au nom des mouvements révolutionnaires auraient été impensables sans les affiches, la seconde révolution conduite par Deng était à même de se passer d'elles.

La nouvelle orientation eut d'énormes répercussions sur l'art de propagande. Les thèmes se firent moins héroïques et militants, mais plus impressionnistes ; des tons plus sobres se substituèrent aux couleurs criardes. De même, les slogans perdirent de leur ton véhément et militariste, ils devinrent plus normatifs dans leurs messages : le peuple n'était plus exhorté à combattre les ennemis ou la nature, mais incité à adopter un mode de vie où la culture, l'hygiène et l'instruction tiendraient une plus grande place. Les images abstraites remplacèrent les images hyperréalistes ; l'accent mis sur la construction économique ainsi que l'apparition de la publicité ordinaire détrônèrent le message politique explicite. L'emprunt aux techniques et au design de la pu-blicité occidentale était fréquent. Bien que ces changements de style eussent pu rendre les images moins compréhensibles aux couches sociales plus arriérées, ils redonnèrent une grande vigueur au produit global.

Les thèmes des affiches, que le gouvernement continuait de publier, peuvent au mieux se définir comme des visions fugitives du « bien vivre dans un monde matériel ». On était donc fort loin du slogan propagandiste des décennies précédentes. Mais, après tout, la propagande doit toujours refléter la réalité, même dans une société ayant connu des mutations aussi profondes que celle de la Chine depuis les années 80. Maintes nouveautés dans la teneur de l'art de propagande se démarquaient complètement des pratiques du passé.

L'amélioration des conditions de vie était visible sur les affiches : les protagonistes portaient à présent des vêtements plus variés, tant dans le tissu et le style que dans la coupe et la couleur. Fini le costume « Mao » unisexe de couleur bleue, grise ou noire, qui relevait d'une conception prolétarienne du peuple. Les accoutrements du passé révolutionnaire faisaient place aux chaussures de sport, aux vestes en cuir et aux costumes de couturiers pour les hommes, tandis que s'imposaient les shorts moulants, les talons hauts et les robes plus féminines, dont la robe shanghaienne, haut fendue, pour les femmes. Finis aussi les cheveux courts et les queues de cheval des anciennes affiches ; le temps des coiffures originales, permanentées ou à la dernière mode, était venu.

La richesse, un phénomène nouveau qui touchait à présent la société chinoise, surtout dans les zones urbaines, faisait l'objet d'une attention accrue et minutieuse. L'ouverture croissante sur le monde, les libertés individuelles qui se développaient avec l'assentiment tacite des autorités étaient transposées sur les affiches au moyen de divers symboles, parmi eux l'avion gros-porteur qui représentait, fait nouveau, la possibilité de voyager, dans le pays comme à l'étranger. Le poste de télévision était devenu l'incarnation de la réussite personnelle ; comme il était en passe de conquérir les foyers, il figurait régulièrement sur les affiches.

Mais plus important encore : elles montraient les gens en train de se divertir, ou carrément en train de s'amuser. L'affiche de starlette est un exemple de ce revirement manifeste. Depuis l'apparition dans les années 80 de calendriers bon marché, illustrés de photos d'actrices, elle était présente un peu partout. À l'origine, la plupart étaient consacrées exclusivement à des vedettes du cinéma et du spectacle de Hong Kong. Par la suite s'y ajoutèrent les stars et les starlettes de Taiwan. Mais sitôt que l'industrie du spectacle chinoise se mit à produire ses propres vedettes, le nombre des affiches s'accrut considérablement. Les acteurs et actrices de cinéma ainsi que les vedettes féminines de la télévision n'apparaissent plus seulement sur les almanachs : ils ont rejoint aussi les troupes de choc des agences de publicité, pour vanter les nombreux produits vendus sur le marché de la société de consommation chinoise.

Malgré ces efforts de modernisation, l'art de propagande a fini par perdre tout contact avec la population. Les images, slogans et messages que le Parti continue de diffuser sont perçus comme ayant de moins en moins de rapport avec la réalité et ne trouvent plus d'écho. L'intérêt pour la politique en général étant au plus bas, les gens se moquent bien de faire preuve de vertu idéologique ou politique. S'amuser, voilà ce qui les intéresse vraiment, leurs autres préoccupations étant bien entendu le montant de leur salaire et la préservation de leur emploi. Les affiches ont perdu leur crédibilité et leur charme, et leur fabrication a diminué de façon dramatique. On les juge démodées, bien qu'elle soient à présent imprimées sur du papier luxueux ou du vinyle.

L'émergence d'une jeune génération d'artistes n'ayant plus besoin de travailler dans le cadre bureaucratique a permis le développement progressif d'un marché de l'art échappant de plus en plus à la régulation et au contrôle étatique. Par ailleurs, la création de sociétés privées, de galeries et d'autres points de vente a grandement facilité la commercialisation des œuvres de ces jeunes artistes. Étant donné le grand choix de tableaux et d'affiches réellement attrayants, et le fait qu'ils sont d'ores et déjà en vente libre, plus besoin d'acheter les messages politiques édifiants et lénifiants. Les artistes, qui évitent soigneusement les sujets politiques ou moralisateurs, proposent des œuvres plastiques que les gens jugent plus éloquentes ou attirantes sur le plan esthétique. Le retour en force, dans les intérieurs citadins et ruraux, des traditionnelles « images du Nouvel An », représentant à l'origine divers symboles d'heureux auspices, mais qui se sont enrichies aujourd'hui de motifs plus modernes, est l'illustration de cette évolution.

Ce qui subsiste d'un genre artistique, naguère destiné à inspirer le peuple chinois, à le mobiliser et à lui montrer la voie d'une utopie communiste future, est bien maigre. La politique est morte et enterrée, le consumérisme, lui, est bien vivant. Il reste, à l'aube du nouveau millénaire, quatre types d'art de masse, tous consommés par des groupes différents. Les yuppies des centres urbains aiment les reproductions au format de poster d'œuvres d'art occidentales. Les gens moins aisés achètent des calendriers postérisés plutôt bon marché, enjolivés de préférence de belles filles. La majorité des Chinois – les paysans – sont de plus en plus attirés par les images traditionnelles, bien que le portrait de Mao ait pu occuper la place autrefois réservée aux divinités, tel le dieu du foyer. Il existe encore quelques affiches politiques, mais les collectionneurs chinois et occidentaux semblent être les seuls à leur trouver de l'intérêt. Les images qui ont jadis défini l'image de la Chine ont bel et bien disparu.

Stefan R. Landsberger

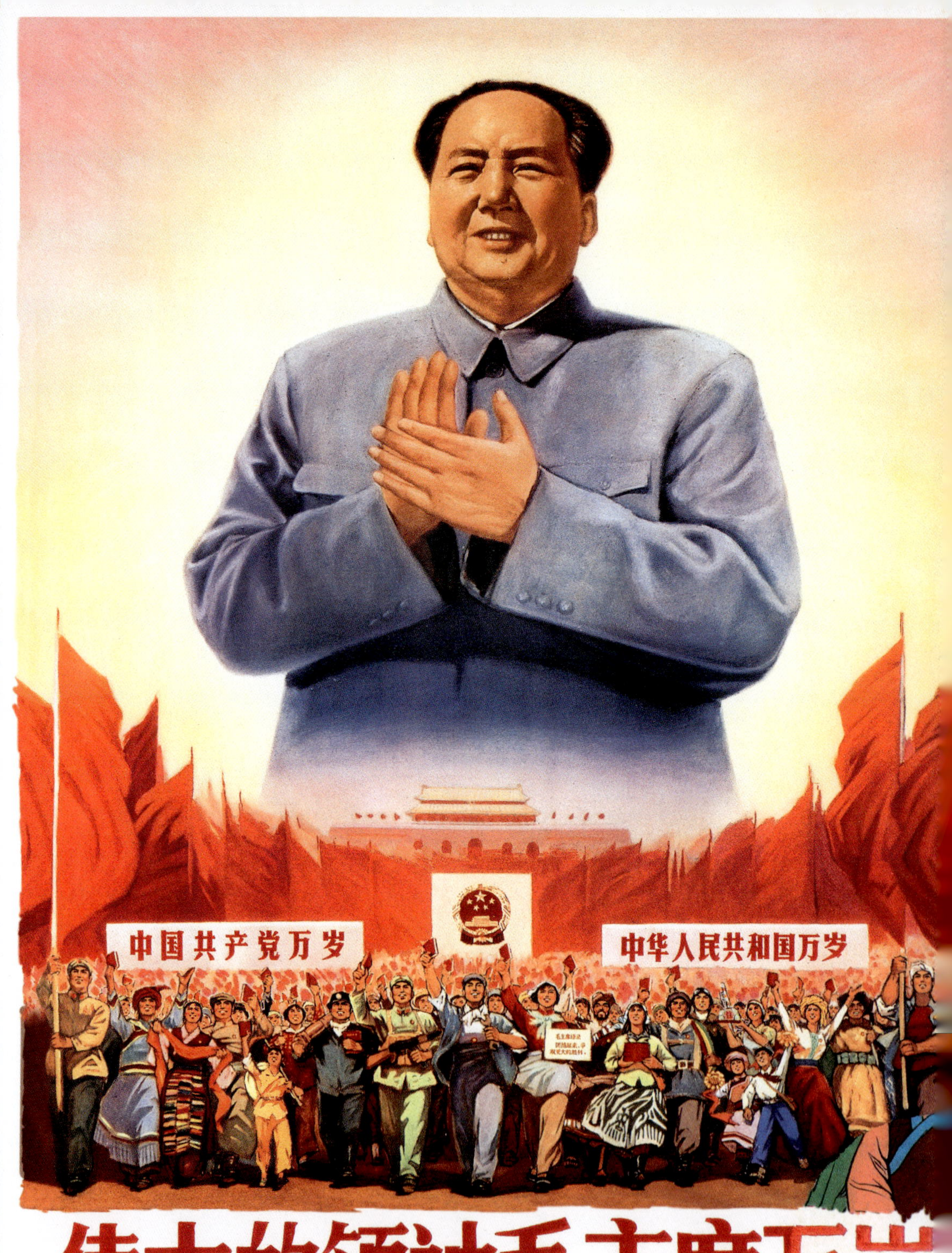
中国共产党万岁
中华人民共和国万岁
伟大的领袖毛主席万岁
热烈欢呼第四届全国人民代表大会的胜利召开

I

THE COMMUNIST PARTY

DIE KOMMUNISTISCHE PARTEI
LE PARTI COMMUNISTE

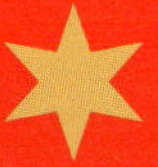

Page 52
Long live our great leader Chairman Mao We cheer the successful opening of the 4th National People's Congress *Banner, left:* Long live the Chinese Communist Party *Banner, right:* Long live the People's Republic of China; 1975

Es lebe der Große Führer, der Vorsitzende Mao Mit begeisterten Ausrufen die erfolgreiche Eröffnung des 4. Nationalen Volkskongresses begrüßen *Transparent links:* Es lebe die Kommunistische Partei Chinas *Transparent rechts:* Es lebe die Volksrepublik China; 1975

Vive le Grand Timonier, le président Mao Saluons par des clameurs d'enthousiasme l'ouverture du 4e Congrès national populaire *Banderole de gauche :* Vive le Parti Communiste Chinois *Banderole de droite :* Vive la République Populaire de Chine; 1975

"What really counts in the world is conscientiousness, and the Communist Party is most particular about being conscientious."

Was wirklich in der Welt Geltung hat, das ist Gewissenhaftigkeit, und Gewissenhaftigkeit ist das, was sich die kommunistische Partei am meisten angelegen sein lässt. ✶ Ce qui compte réellement dans le monde, c'est d'être consciencieux ; et c'est ce à quoi le Parti communiste est le plus attaché.

The most spectacular of landscapes is found on the most dangerous of summits. *Banners from left to right:* Long live Chairman Mao! Long live the CCP! Long live Marxism, Leninism and Mao Zedong's ideas! *Artists:* Pan Jinba and Xia Hua; Shanghai People's Publishing House, 1976; 0.14 Yuan

Die herrlichsten Landschaften sind auf den gefahrvollen Gipfeln zu finden. *Transparente von links nach rechts:* Es lebe der Vorsitzende Mao! Es lebe die KP Chinas! Es lebe Marxismus, Leninismus und Mao Zedongs Ideen! *Gemalt von* Pan Jinba und Xia Hua; Volksverlag Shanghai, 1976; 0,14 Yuan

C'est sur les sommets au milieu des dangers que se trouvent les paysages les plus sublimes. *Banderoles de gauche à droite :* Vive le président Mao ! Vive le Parti communiste chinois ! Vive le marxisme, le léninisme et les idées de Mao Zedong ! *Peintres :* Pan Jinba et Xia Hua ; Éditions Populaires de Shanghai, 1976 ; 0,14 yuan

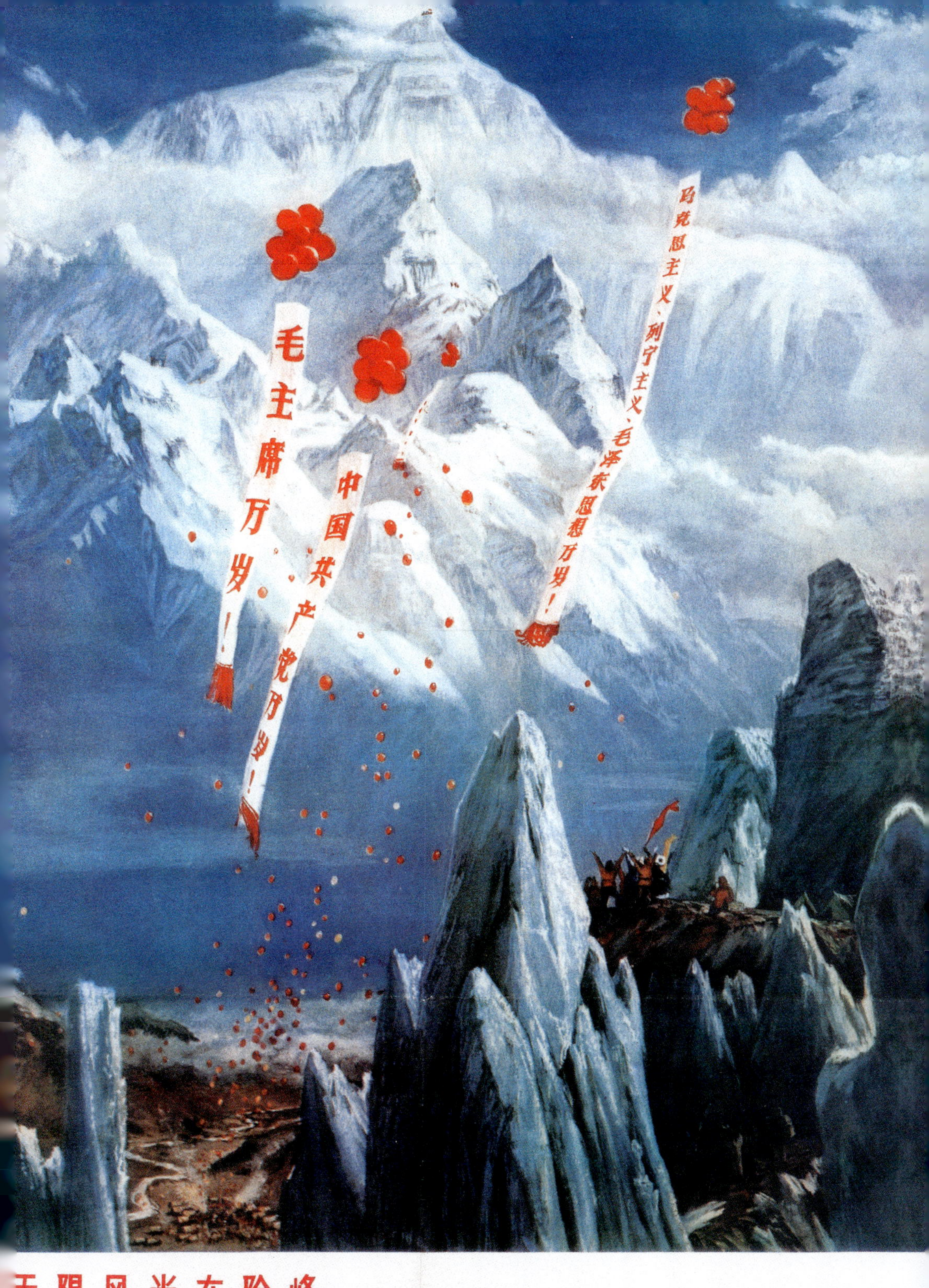

无限风光在险峰

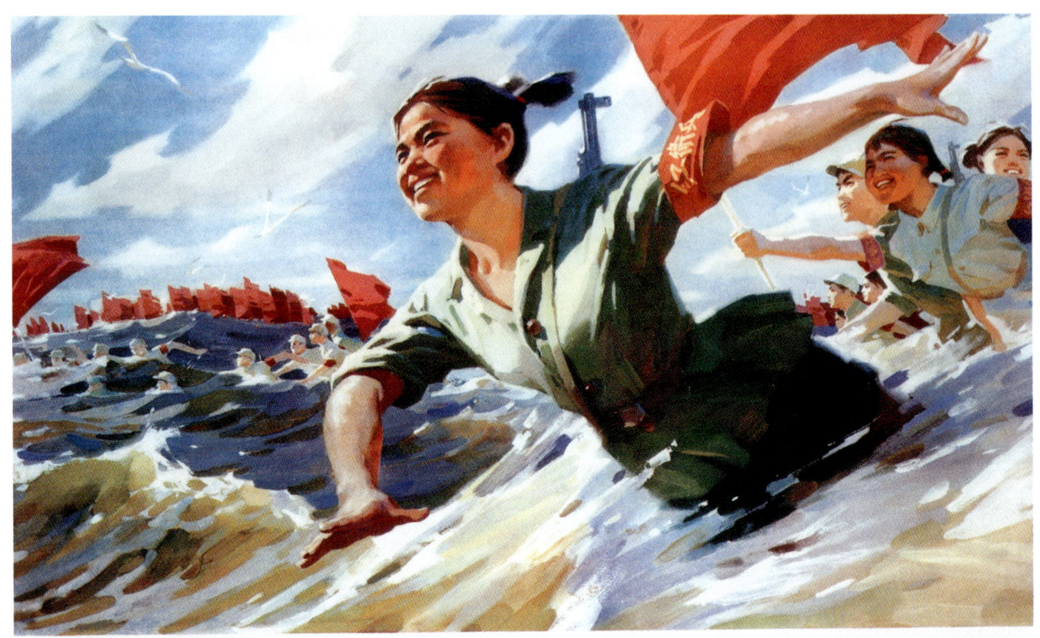

Steeling ourselves against the strength of the wind and storms
On armband: Red Guard
Artists: Ying Xiaohe and Mu Li; The People's Sports Publishing House, 1976 *Print run:* 200,000; 0.11 Yuan

Sich im starken Wind und Sturm stählen *Auf der Armbinde*: Rote Garde *Gemalt von* Ying Xiaohe und Mu Li; Volks-Sportverlag, 1976 *Auflage:* 200 000; 0,11 Yuan

Aguerrissons-nous dans la violence du vent et de la tempête
Sur le brassard : Garde Rouge *Peintres :* Ying Xiaohe et Mu Li ; Éditions Populaires Sportives, 1976 *Tirage :* 200 000 ; 0,11 yuan

Resume the march to victory in the glow of the 11th Party Congress *Artist:* Yang Yongzang; Guangxi People's Publishing House, 1977 *Print run:* 30,000; 0.11 Yuan

Im Glanz des 11. Parteitags den Siegesmarsch fortsetzen *Gemalt von* Yang Yongzang; Volksverlag Guangxi, 1977 *Auflage:* 30 000; 0,11 Yuan

Poursuivez votre marche triomphale dans l'éclat de ce 11e congrès du Parti *Peintre :* Yang Yongzang ; Éditions Populaires de Guangxi, 1977 *Tirage :* 30 000 ; 0,11 yuan

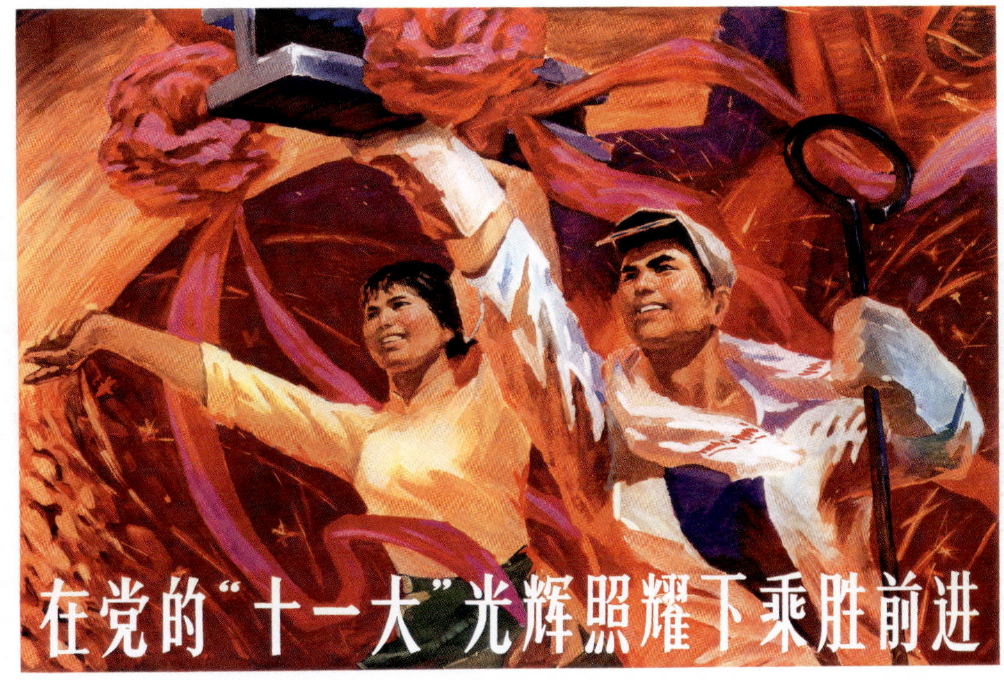

"Policy and tactics are the life of the Party; leading comrades at all levels must give them full attention and must never on any account be negligent."

Politik und Taktik sind das Leben der Partei; die führenden Genossen aller Ebenen müssen der Politik und Taktik höchste Aufmerksamkeit zuwenden, dürfen sie unter keinen Umständen auf die leichte Achsel nehmen. ✶ Politique et tactique sont la vie même du Parti ; les camarades dirigeants à tous les échelons doivent leur accorder la plus grande attention et ne jamais se montrer négligents à cet égard.

The red flag of the Party Poster (No. 2) used for primary school "Ideological Education" lessons *Artist:* Zheng Naobin *Published by:* Shanghai Working Group for the Compilation of Primary and Middle School Teaching Materials

Die rote Parteiflagge Plakat (Nr. 2) für den Unterricht „Ideologische Erziehung" der Grundschule *Gemalt von* Zheng Naobin *Herausgeber:* Arbeitsgruppe für die Zusammenstellung des Unterrichtsmaterials der Grund- und Mittelschulen Shanghai

Le drapeau rouge du Parti Affiche (n°2) destinée aux cours d'« éducation idéologique » de l'école primaire *Peintre :* Zheng Naobin *Éditeur :* Groupe de travail de Shanghai chargé de l'élaboration du matériel d'enseignement destiné aux écoles primaires et secondaires

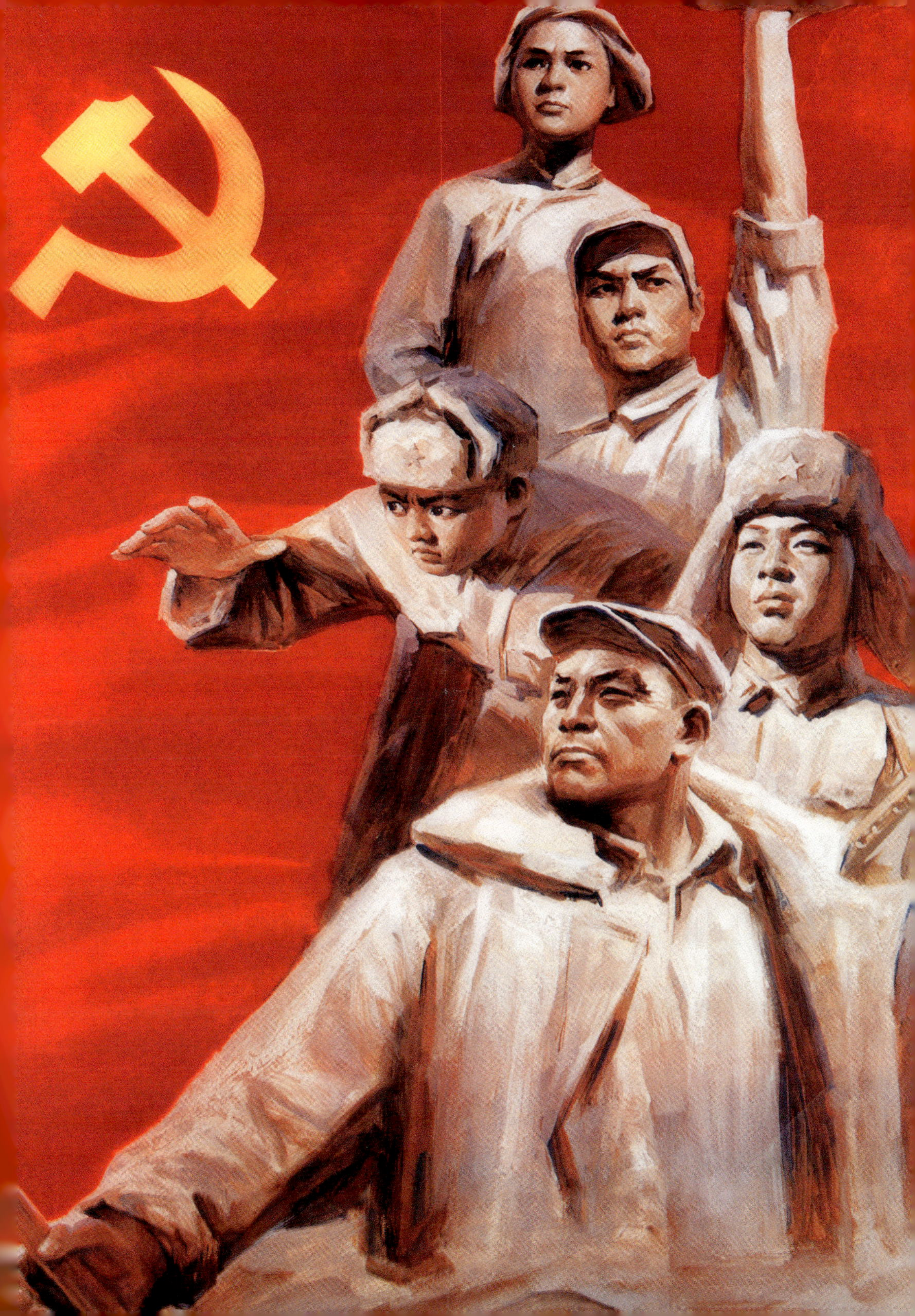

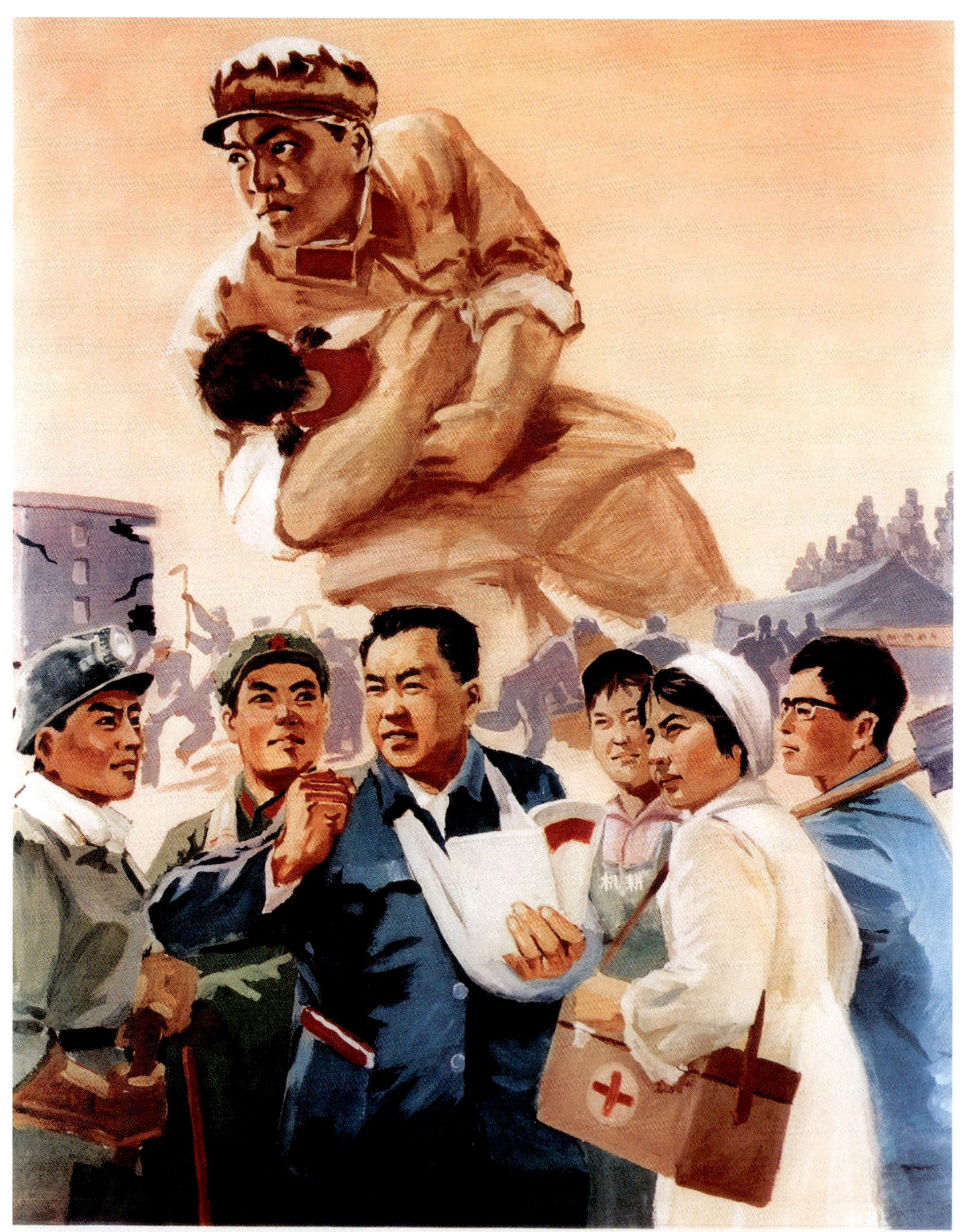

加强党的领导发挥共产党员共青团员模范带头作用

《抗震救灾宣传画》（四）　《抗震救灾宣传画》编绘组绘

Great celebration of the victorious people *Banners, top left:* Carry out to the full the strategic decision to "correctly govern affairs of state by grasping the most important link in the chain." Unite under the leadership of the Central Committee led by Chairman Hua *Artist:* Jin Jifa; Shanghai People's Publishing House, 1977

Großes Fest des triumphierenden Volkes *Transparente links oben:* Die strategische Entscheidung „durch Anpacken des wichtigsten Kettengliedes die Angelegenheiten des Landes gut regeln" in vollem Umfang durchführen. Vereint sein unter der Führung des vom Vorsitzenden Hua geleiteten Zentralkomitees *Gemalt von* Jin Jifa; Volksverlag Shanghai, 1977

Grande fête du triomphe du peuple *Banderoles, en haut à gauche :* Exécutons dans toute son ampleur la décision stratégique selon laquelle « les affaires du pays ne seront bien réglées que si l'on aborde de front le maillon principal. » Soyons unis sous la conduite du comité central et de son dirigeant le président Hua *Peintre :* Jin Jifa ; Éditions Populaires de Shanghai, 1977

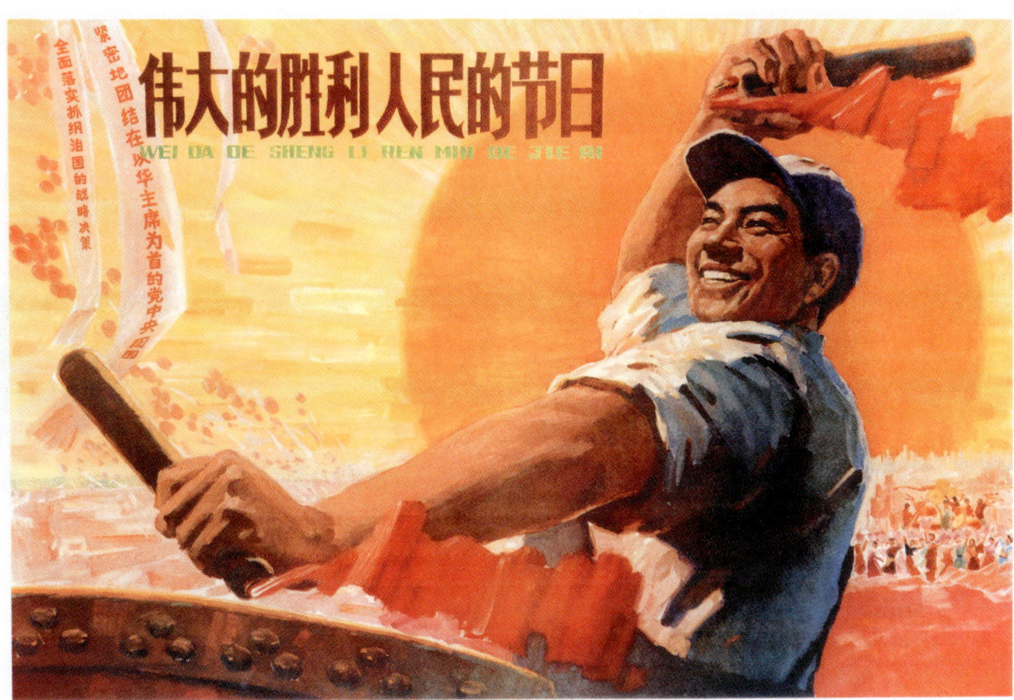

Opposite

Strengthen the Party leadership, fulfill the exemplary function of communists and members of the Communist League of Youth "Propaganda posters for emergency works after an earthquake (4)" *Designed by:* The editorial office of "Propaganda posters for emergency works after an earthquake"; Earthquake Publishing House

Die Parteiführung verstärken, die Vorbildfunktion der Kommunisten und der Mitglieder des Kommunistischen Jugendverbandes wahrnehmen „Propagandaplakate für die Notstandsarbeiten nach einem Erdbeben (4)" *Entwurf:* Redaktion der „Propagandaplakate für die Notstandsarbeiten nach einem Erdbeben"; Erdbeben-Verlag

Renforçons la direction du Parti ; les communistes et les membres des associations de la jeunesse communiste doivent montrer l'exemple « Affiche de propagande pour les travaux d'urgence à entreprendre après un séisme (4) » *Conception :* Rédaction des « Affiches de propagande pour les travaux d'urgence à entreprendre après un séisme » ; Éditions du Séisme

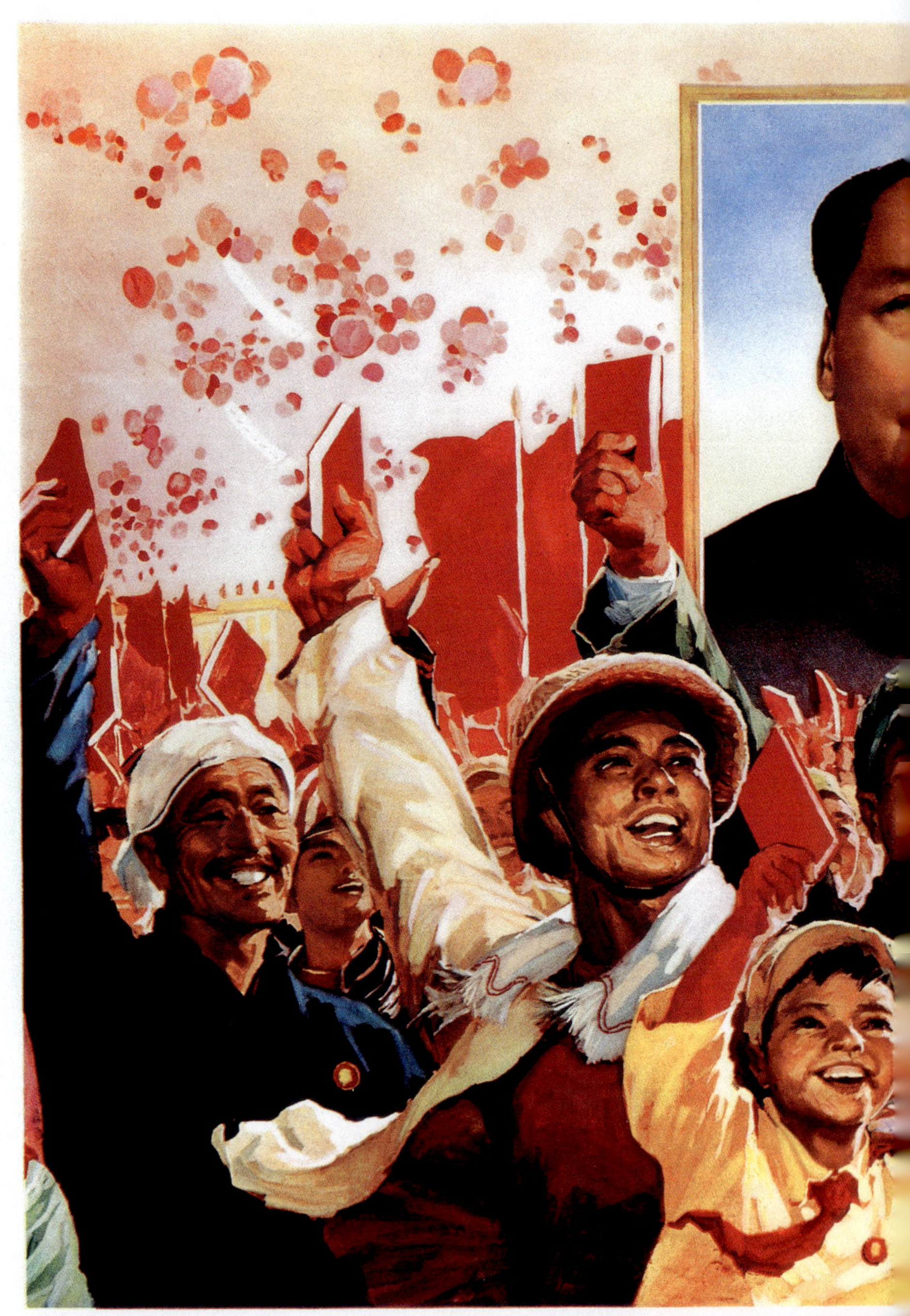
热烈欢呼第四届全国

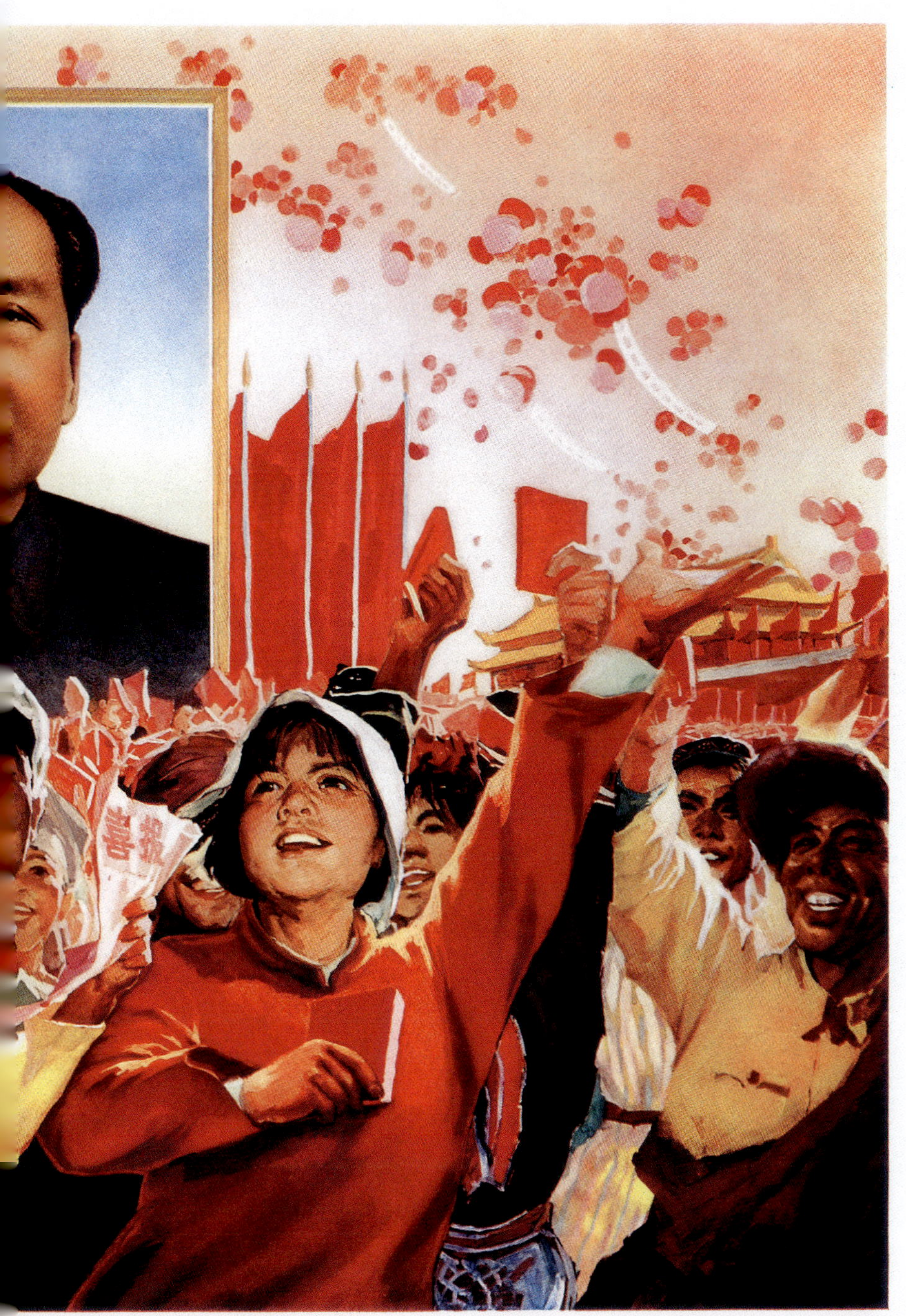

民代表大会胜利召开

Pages 62–63
We cheer the successful opening of the 4th National People's Congress *On the sheet of paper held by the child:* Good news *Designed by:* Shandong Province Exhibition Hall Studio *Published by:* Shandong People's Publishing House, 1971; 0.28 Yuan

Mit begeisterten Ausrufen die erfolgreiche Eröffnung des 4. Nationalen Volkskongresses begrüßen *Auf dem Blatt in der Hand des Kindes:* Freudige Nachricht *Entwurf:* Studio der Ausstellungshalle der Provinz Shandong *Herausgeber:* Volksverlag Shandong, 1971; 0,28 Yuan

Saluons par des clameurs d'enthousiasme l'ouverture du 4e Congrès National populaire *Sur la feuille dans la main de l'enfant :* Bonne nouvelle *Conception :* Studio de la Maison des Expositions de la province du Shandong *Éditeur :* Éditions Populaires de Shandong, 1971 ; 0,28 yuan

"We must have faith in the masses and we must have faith in the Party. These are two cardinal principles."

Wir müssen an die Massen glauben, wir müssen an die Partei glauben: Das sind zwei Grundprinzipien. ✶ Il faut faire confiance aux masses ; il faut faire confiance au Parti : ce sont là deux principes fondamentaux.

Continue the march to victory *Banner:* Under the leadership of the Central Committee led by Chairman Hua, continue the march to victory *Artist:* Wang Yupin, Rongcheng District House of Culture; Shandong People's Publishing House, 1977; 0.11 Yuan

Den Siegesmarsch fortsetzen *Transparent:* Unter Führung des vom Vorsitzenden Hua geleiteten Zentralkomitees den Siegesmarsch fortsetzen. *Gemalt von* Wang Yupin, Kulturhaus des Kreises Rongcheng; Volksverlag Shandong, 1977; 0,11 Yuan

Poursuivons la marche vers la victoire *Banderole :* Poursuivons la marche vers la victoire sous la conduite du comité central que dirige le président Hua. *Peintre :* Wang Yupin, Maison de la Culture du canton de Rongcheng ; Éditions Populaires du Shandong, 1977 ; 0,11 yuan

Pages 66–67
Eagerly looking forward to our arrival. *Bottom left, on life ring:* Shanghai *Artists:* Sun Xikun, Gu Juanhua, and Shen Liangrong of the Shanghai Port Authority; Shanghai People's Publishing House, 1st edn 1973, 4th edn 1974 *Print run:* 1,800,001–2,300,000; 0.14 Yuan

Sehnlichste Erwartungen *Links unten auf dem Rettungsring:* Shanghai. *Gemalt von* Sun Xikun, Gu Juanhua und Shen Liangrong von der Hafenaufsicht Shanghai; Volksverlag Shanghai, 1. Aufl. 1973, 4. Aufl. 1974 *Auflage:* 1 800 001–2 300 000; 0,14 Yuan

De grandes espérances *En bas à gauche sur la bouée de sauvetage :* Shanghai. *Peintres :* Sun Xikun, Gu Juanhua et Shen Liangrong, de l'organe de surveillance du port de Shanghai ; Éditions Populaires de Shanghai, 1ère éd. 1973, 4e éd. 1974 *Tirage :* 1 800 001–2 300 000 ; 0,14 yuan

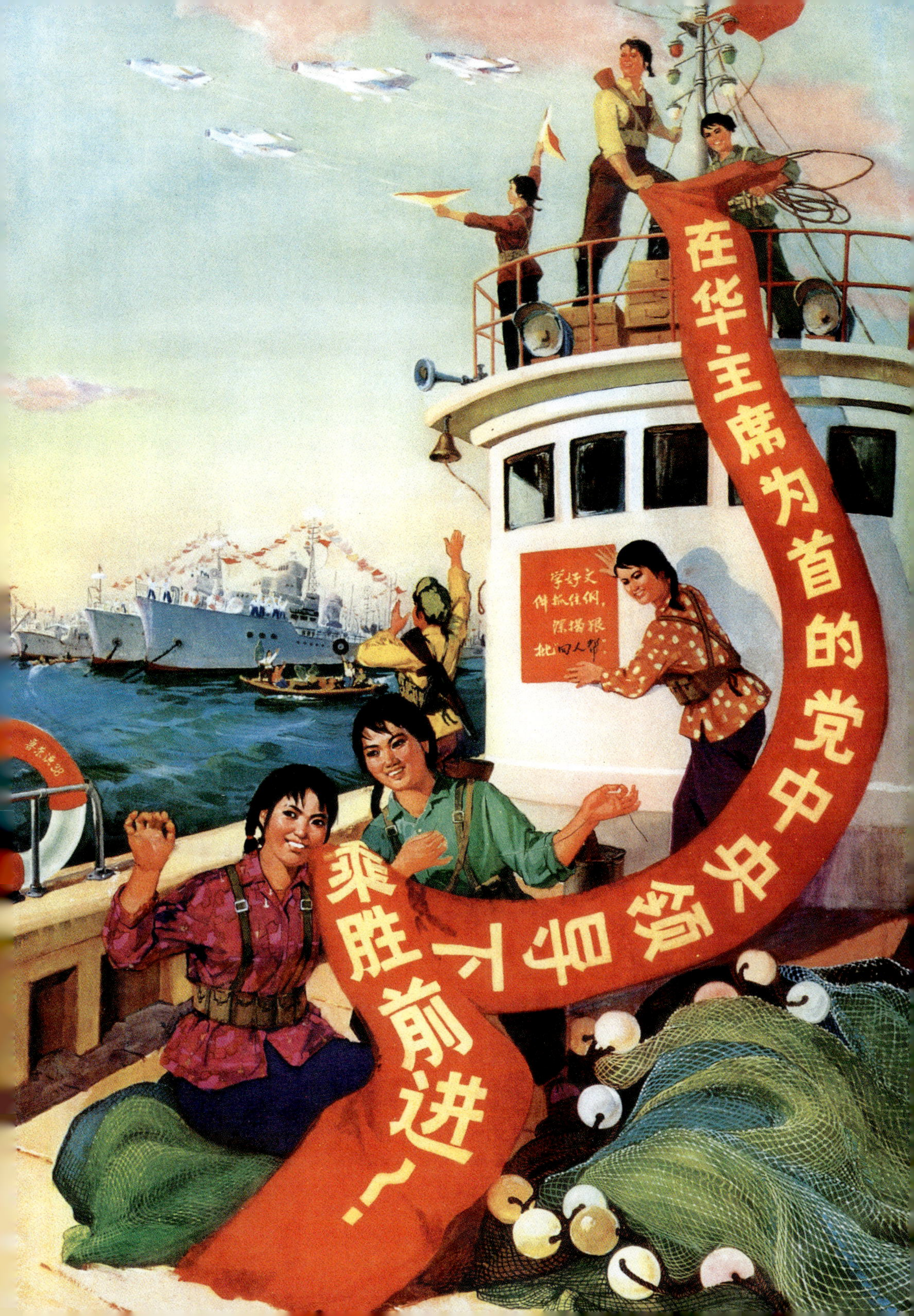
在华主席为首的党中央领导下
乘胜前进！
学好文件抓住纲，
深揭狠批四人帮

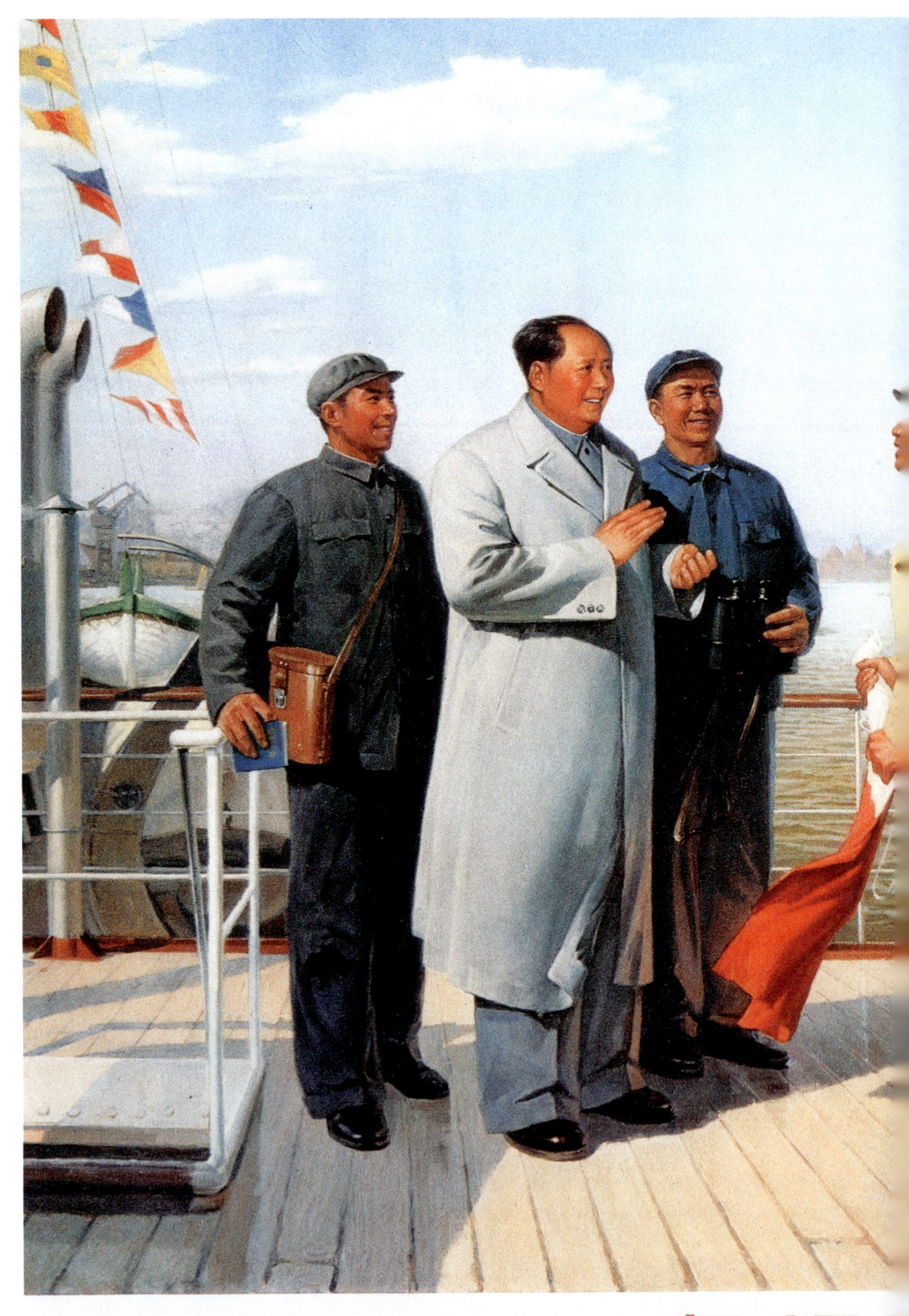

殷切

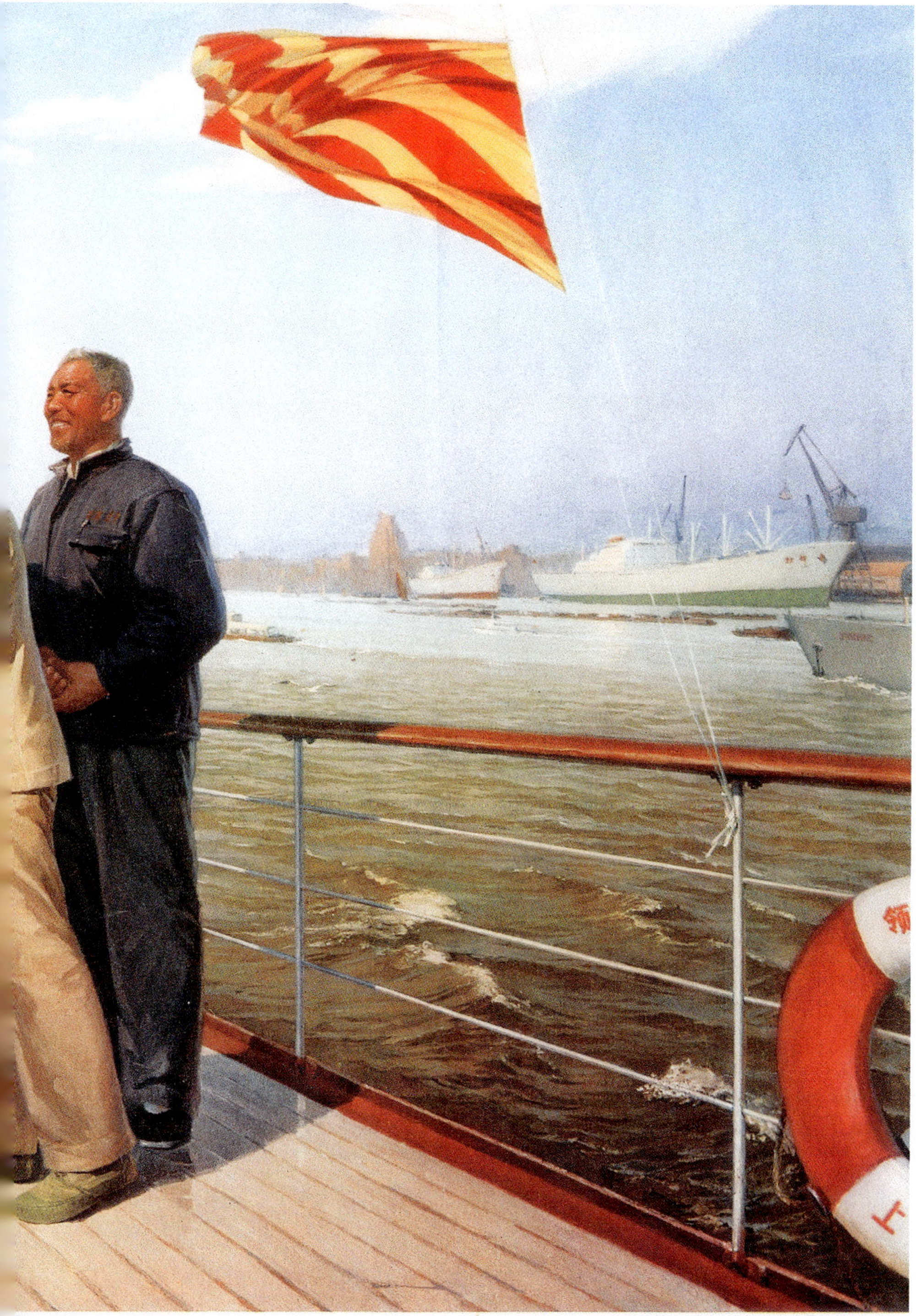

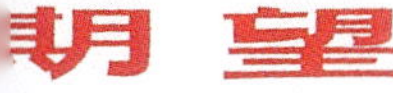

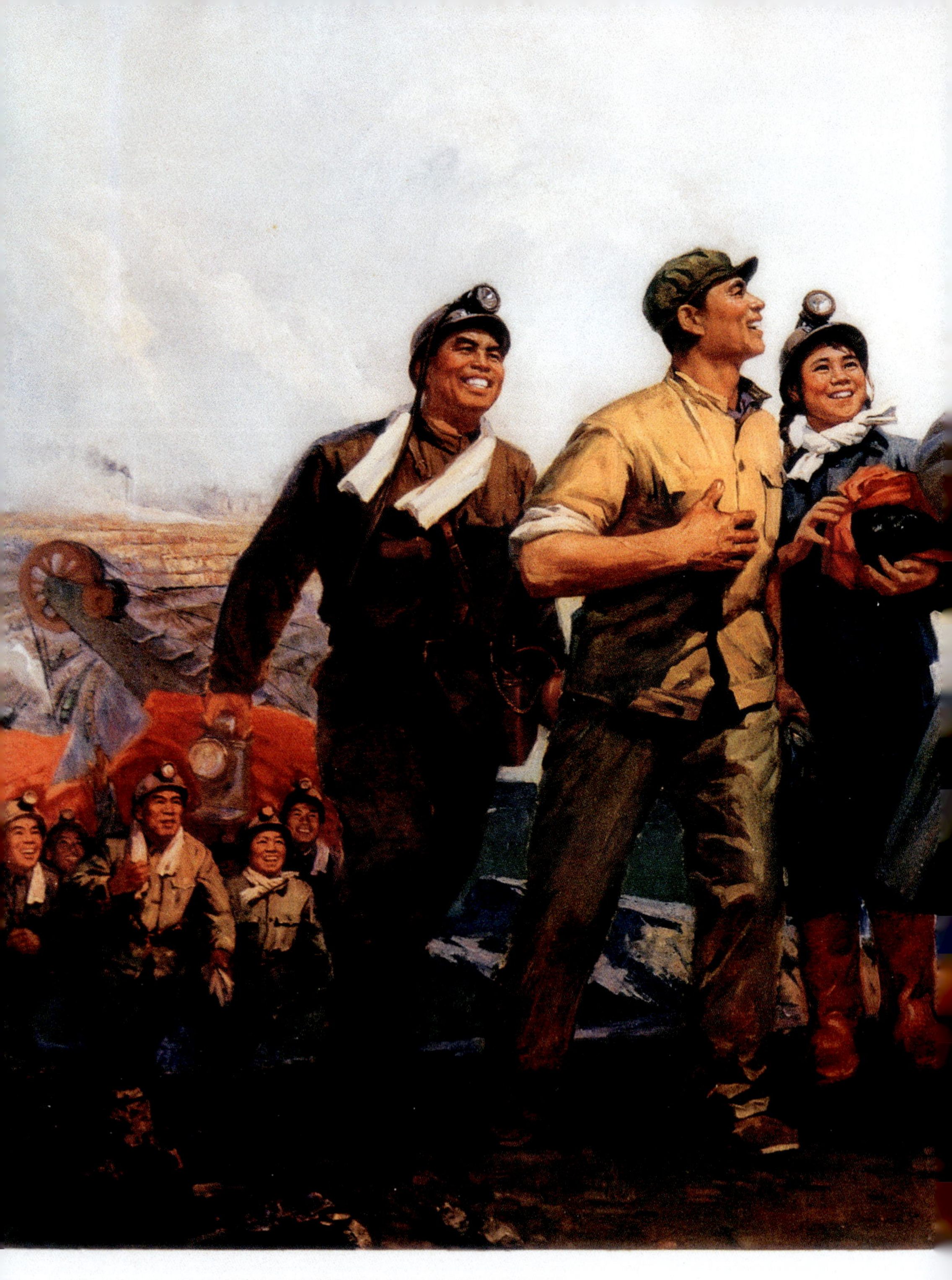

毛主席视察抚顺

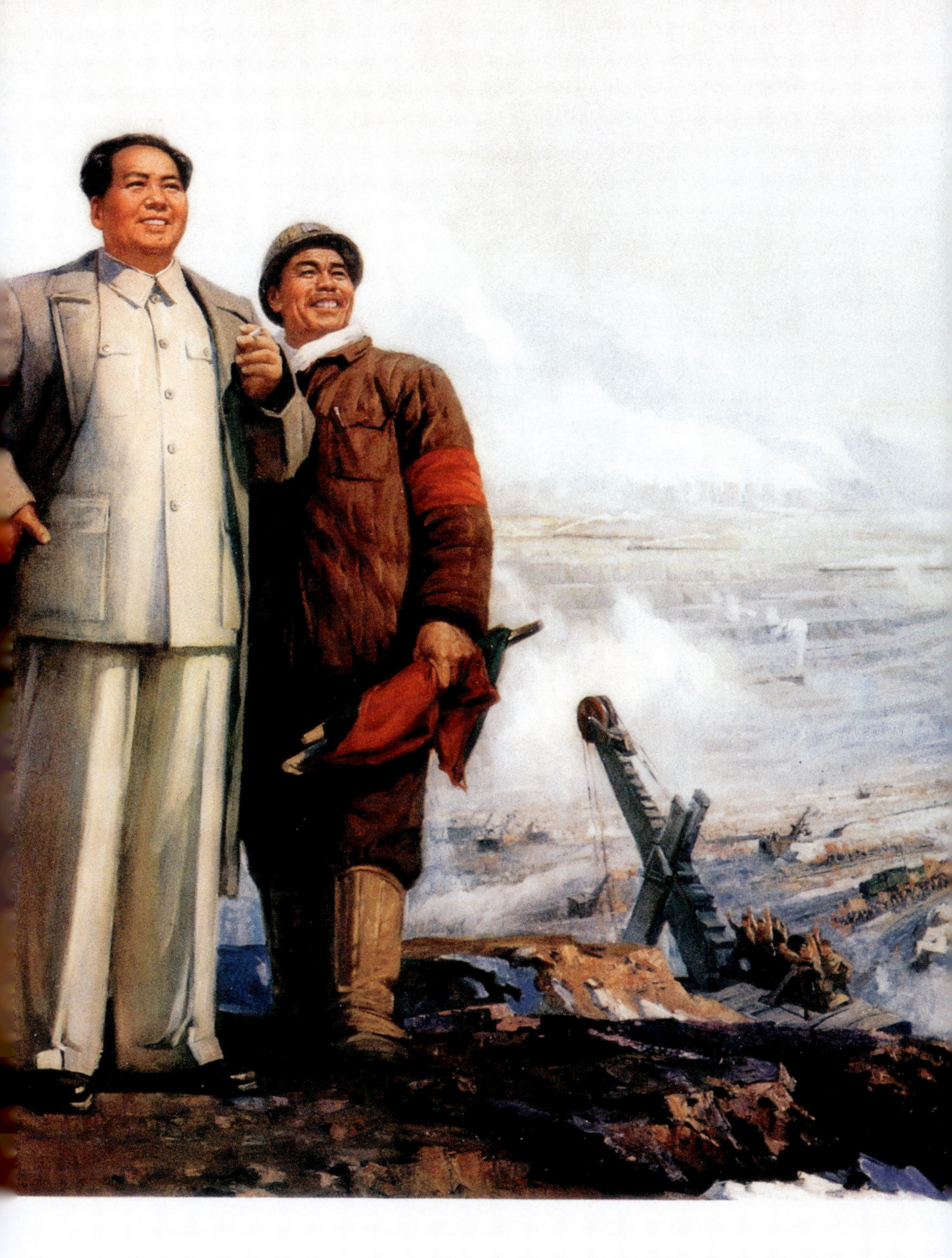

Pages 68–69
Chairman Mao on a tour of inspection in Fushun. *Designed by:* Liaoning Province Propaganda Hall for the Ideas of Mao Zedong; Liaoning People's Publishing House, 1972; 0.12 Yuan

Vorsitzender Mao auf einer Inspektionsreise durch Fushun. *Entwurf:* Propaganda-Halle für Mao Zedong-Ideen der Provinz Liaoning; Volksverlag Liaoning, 1972; 0,12 Yuan

Le président Mao lors d'un voyage d'inspection à Fu-shun. *Conception :* Maison de la propagande des idées de Mao Zedong de la province du Liaoning ; Éditions Populaires du Liaoning ; 1972 ; 0,12 yuan

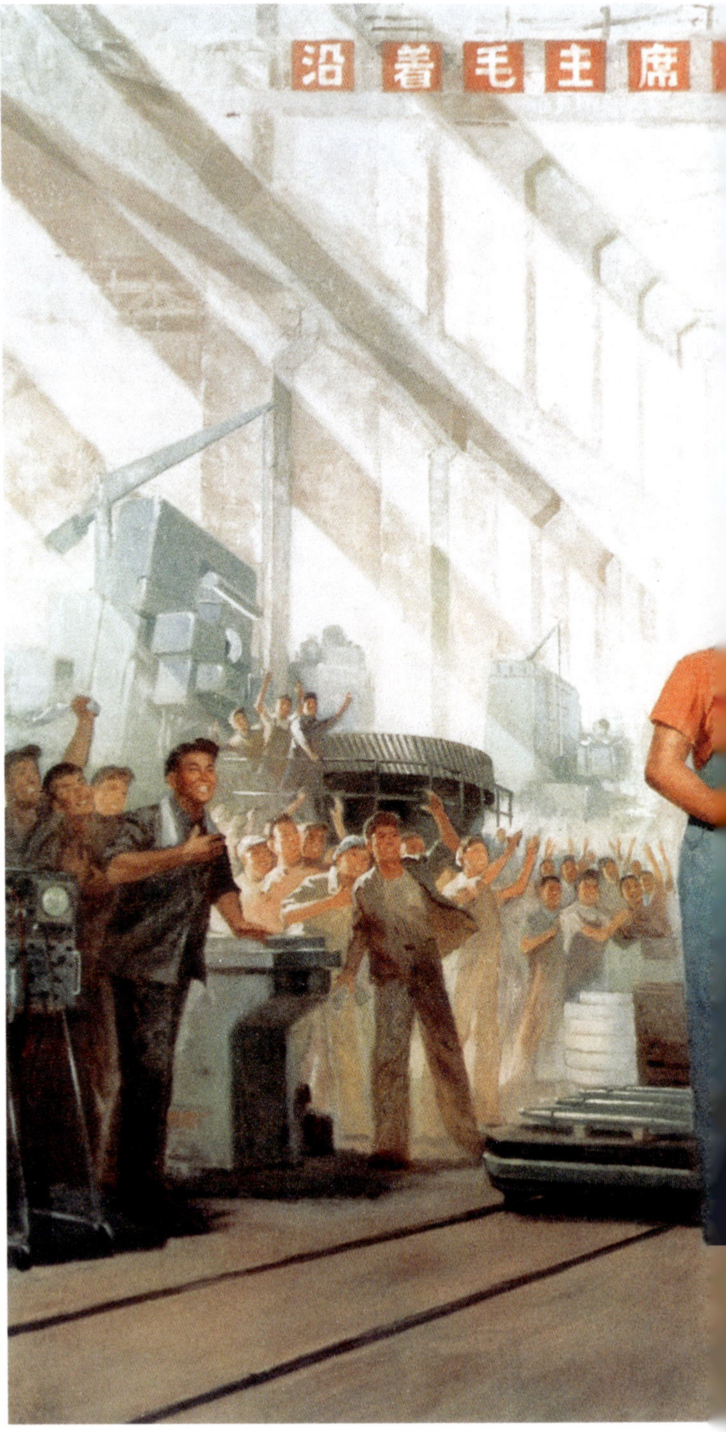

Shining path, glittering future. *Banner, above:* Stride triumphantly forward along the revolutionary path of Chairman Mao *Designed by:* Workers' Art Study Group of the Shanghai Office for Mechanical Engineering and Electronics; Shanghai People's Publishing House, 1975; 0.14 Yuan

Strahlender Weg, Glänzende Zukunft. *Transparent oben:* Auf der revolutionären Linie des Vorsitzenden Mao triumphierend vorwärts schreiten *Entwurf:* Kunst-Arbeitsgruppe der Arbeiter beim Amt für Maschinenbau und Elektronik Shanghai; Volksverlag Shanghai, 1975; 0,14 Yuan

La voie étincelante de l'avenir radieux. *Banderole, en haut :* Avançons triomphalement dans la ligne révolutionnaire du président Mao *Conception :* Groupe de travail artistique des ouvriers du Service de construction mécanique et électronique de Shanghai ; Éditions Populaires de Shanghai, 1975 ; 0,14 yuan

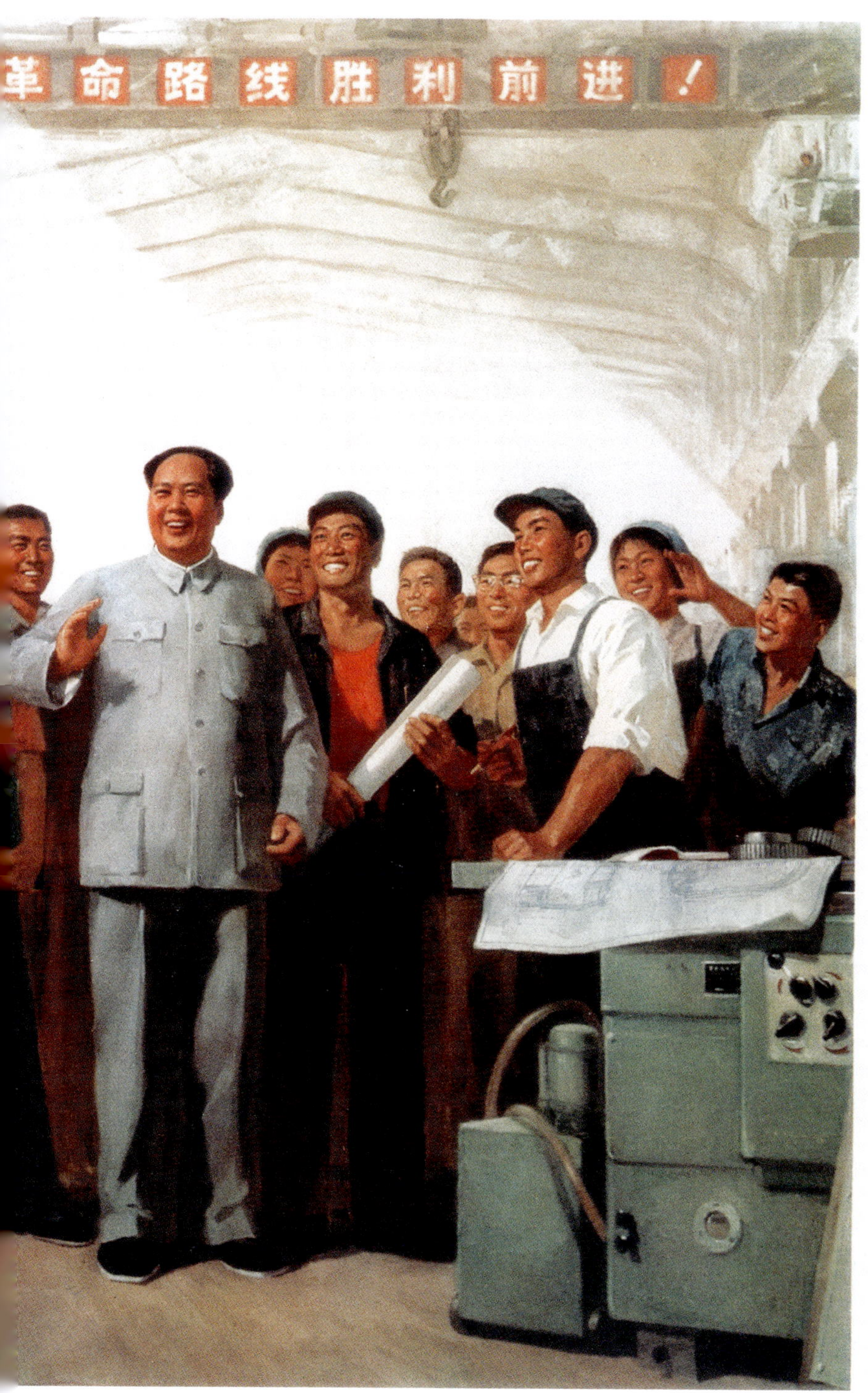

光辉的道路 灿烂的前程

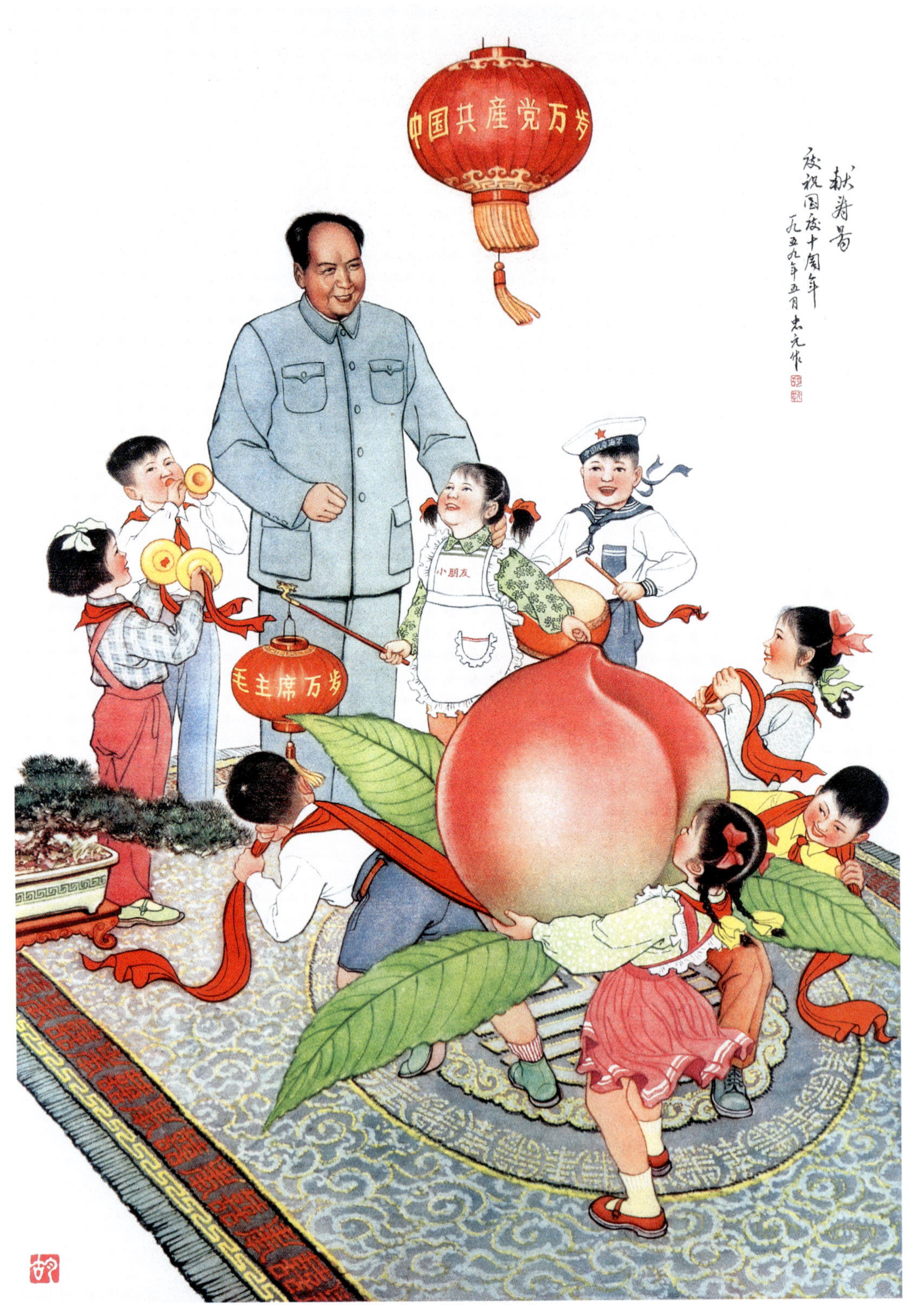
中国共産党万岁
献寿图
庆祝国庆十周年
一九五九年五月 忠元作
小朋友
毛主席万岁

Opposite

Wishing (Chairman Mao) a long life. *Lantern, top:* Long live the Chinese Communist Party *Lantern, below:* Long live Chairman Mao *Top right:* In celebration of the 10th anniversary of the foundation of the People's Republic of China, May 1959, Hu Zhongyuan *Artist:* Hu Zhongyuan; Tianjin Art Publishing House, 1st edn 1958, 2nd edn 1959, 3rd edn 1959; 0.13 Yuan

„(Dem Vorsitzenden Mao) ein langes Leben wünschen. *Laterne oben:* Es lebe die Kommunistische Partei Chinas *Laterne unten:* Es lebe der Vorsitzende Mao *Oben rechts:* Zur Feier des 10. Gründungstages der Volksrepublik China, im Mai 1959, Hu Zhongyuan *Gemalt von* Hu Zhongyuan; Kunstverlag Tianjin, 1. Aufl. 1958, 2. Aufl. 1959, 3. Aufl. 1959; 0,13 Yuan

Longue vie (au président Mao) *Lampion du haut :* Vive le Parti communiste chinois *Lampion du bas :* Vive le président Mao *En haut à droite :* Célébration du 10e anniversaire de la fondation de la République Populaire de Chine, mai 1959, Hu Zhongyuan *Peintre :* Hu Zhongyuan; Éditions d'Art de Tianjin, 1ère éd. 1958, 2e éd. 1959, 3e éd. 1959 ; 0,13 yuan

"With you in charge, my heart is at ease" *Border, right:* To the families of the young people sent to work on the land
Border, left: Tianjin City Revolutionary Committee, 1977

„Hast du die Sache in der Hand, ist mir leicht ums Herz."
Rechter Rand: Den Familien der Jugendlichen gewidmet, die zum Arbeitseinsatz aufs Land gehen
Linker Rand: Revolutionskomitee der Stadt Tianjin, 1977

« Si tu as l'affaire en main, j'ai le cœur léger. » *Marge de droite :* Dédié aux familles des adolescents qui vont travailler à la campagne
Marge de gauche : Comité révolutionnaire de la ville de Tianjin, 1977

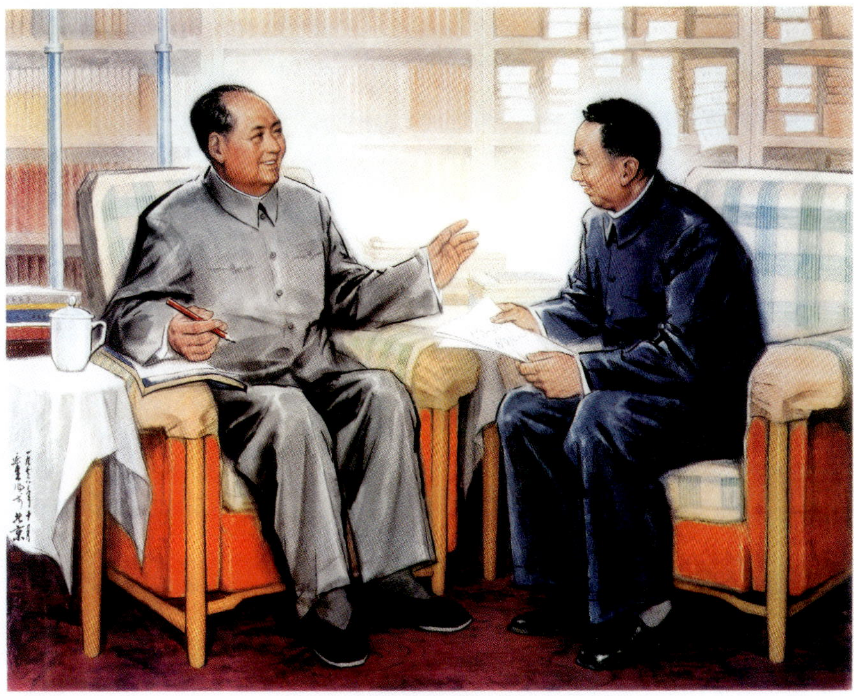

Opposite
A gift for Chairman Mao. *Banner around the peach:* Long live Chairman Mao *Artist:* Gao Ruqian; Ninxia People's Publishing House, 1963
Print run: 100,000; 0.18 Yuan

Ein Geschenk für den Vorsitzenden Mao. *Transparent auf dem Pfirsich*: Es lebe der Vorsitzende Mao *Gemalt von* Gao Ruqian; Volksverlag Ninxia, 1963
Auflage: 100 000; 0,18 Yuan

Un cadeau pour le président Mao. *Banderole sur la pêche :* Vive le président Mao *Peintre :* Gao Ruqian ; Éditions Populaires de Ninxia, 1963
Tirage : 100 000 ; 0,18 yuan

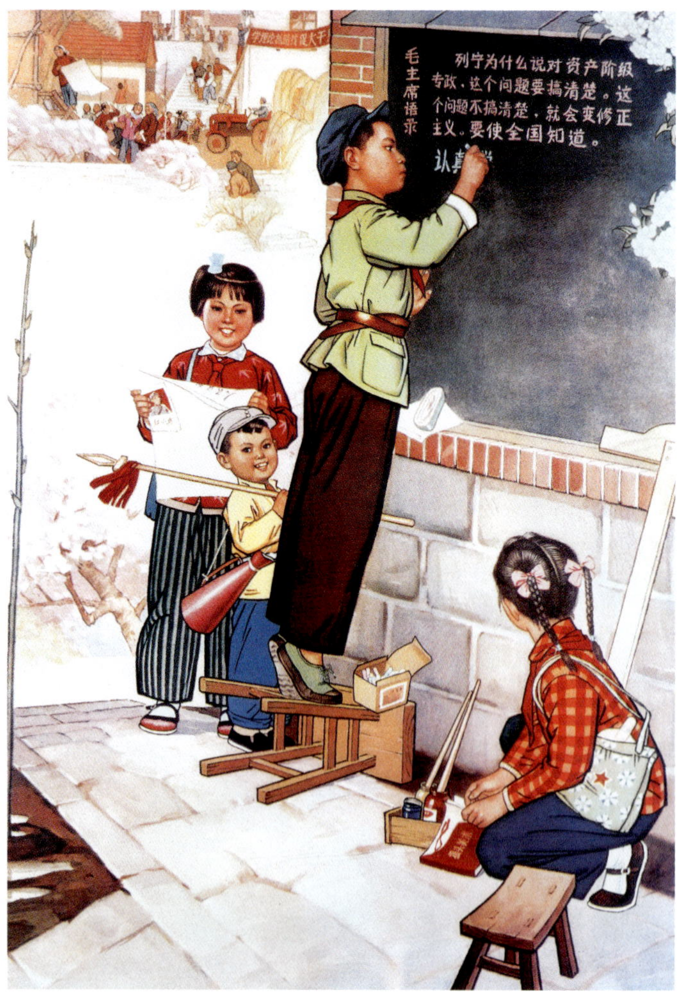

In every street and alley
On the blackboard: "Why does Lenin say we must get to the root of the question of the dictatorship of capitalism? Because it would bring about a transformation of revisionism if we were not to get to the root of this question. The whole country must deal with this issue." Mao Zedong *Artist:* Su Geng; Hebei People's Publishing House, 1976
Print run: 230,000; 0.11 Yuan

In allen Straßen und Gassen
An der Tafel: „Warum sagt Lenin, man müsse der Frage der Diktatur des Kapitalismus auf den Grund gehen? Weil die Umwandlung in den Revisionismus stattfinden würde, wenn man dieser Frage nicht auf den Grund geht. Das ganze Land muss sich damit befassen." Mao Zedong *Gemalt von* Su Geng; Volksverlag Hebei, 1976
Auflage: 230 000; 0,11 Yuan

Dans toutes les rues et ruelles
Au tableau : « Pourquoi Lénine dit-il qu'il faut étudier à fond la question de la dictature du capitalisme ? Parce que, si on n'étudie pas cette question, on risque de tomber dans le révisionnisme. Le pays tout entier doit s'en préoccuper. » Mao Zedong *Peintre :* Su Geng; Éditions Populaires du Hebei, 1976
Tirage : 230 000 ; 0,11 yuan

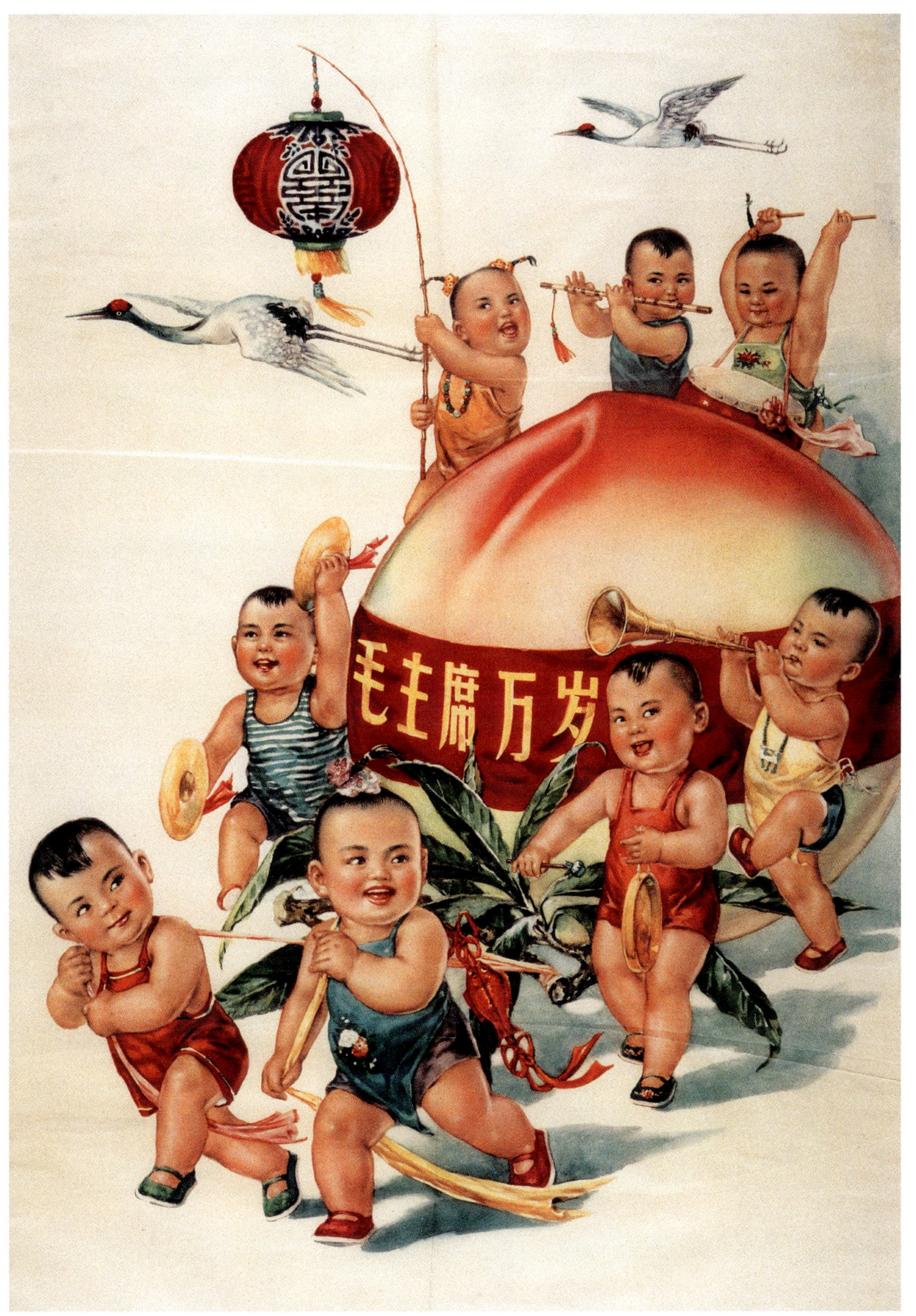
毛主席万岁

Opposite
Chairman Mao visits the blast furnace, 1964

Der Vorsitzende Mao am Hochofen, 1964

Le président Mao au haut-fourneau, 1964

Pages 78–79
The People's Commune is good, 1961

Die Volkskommune ist gut, 1961

La Commune populaire, c'est bien, 1961

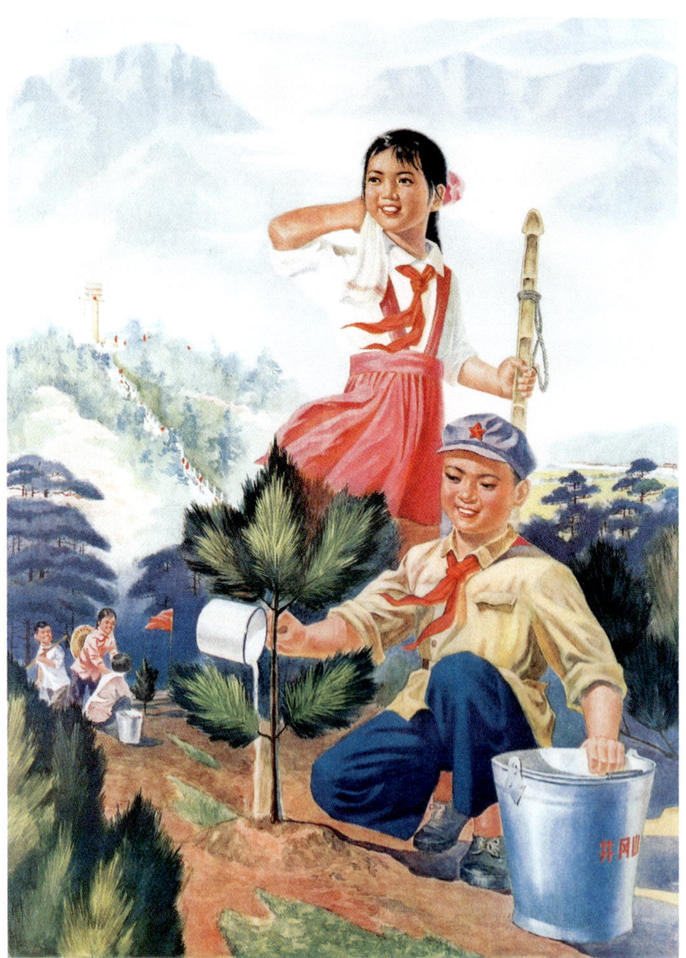

Young tree shoots on Jinggang* Mountain
*Jiangxi Province, where the first CCP base was established, referred to as the "Cradle of the Revolution."

Neue Baumsetzlinge auf dem Berg Jinggang*
*Provinz Jiangxi; der Ort des ersten Stützpunktes der KP China wird als „Wiege der Revolution" bezeichnet.

De nouveaux plants d'arbres sur le mont Jinggang*
*Province du Jiangxi, premier bastion du Parti communiste chinois, qualifiée de « berceau de la révolution ».

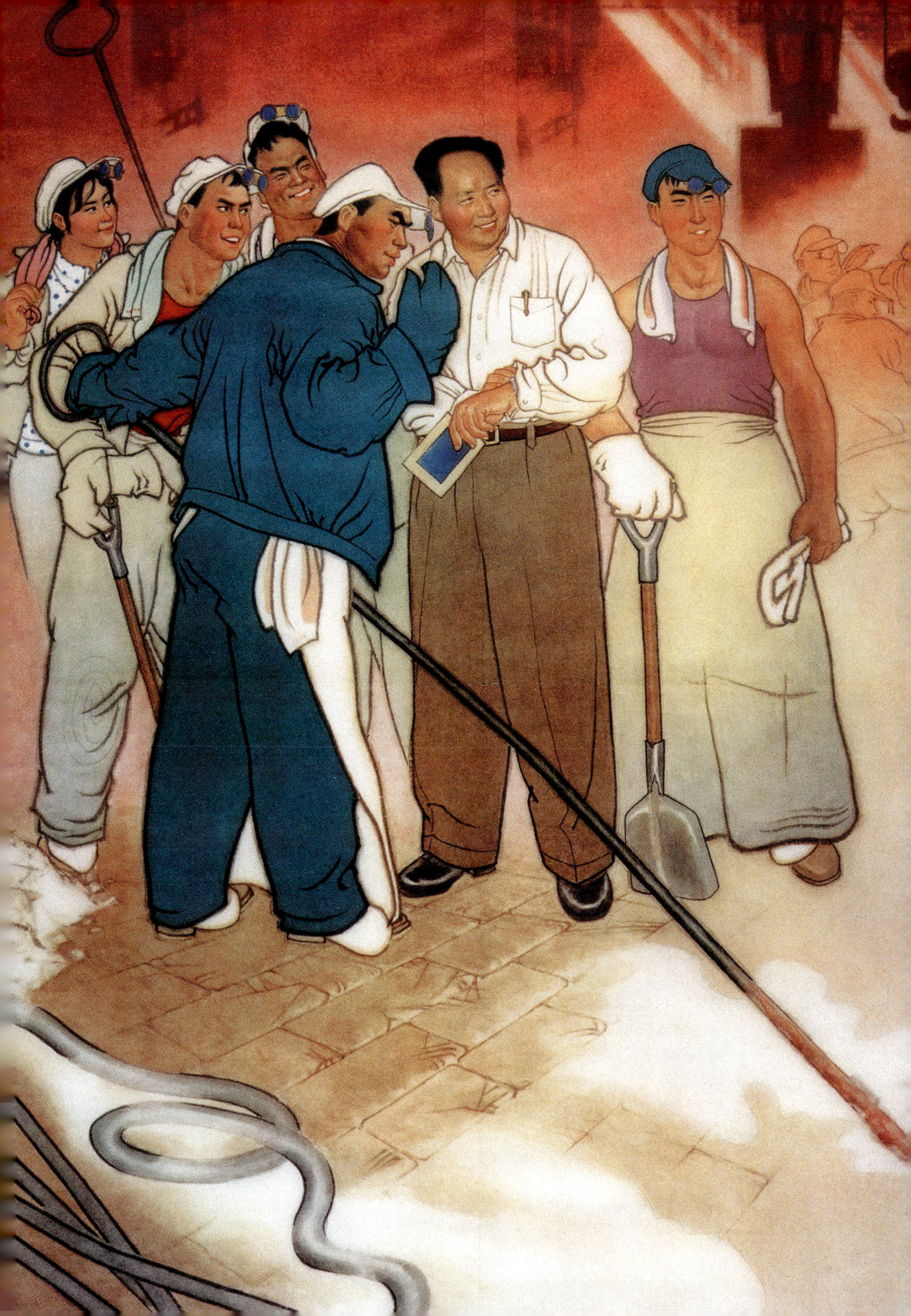

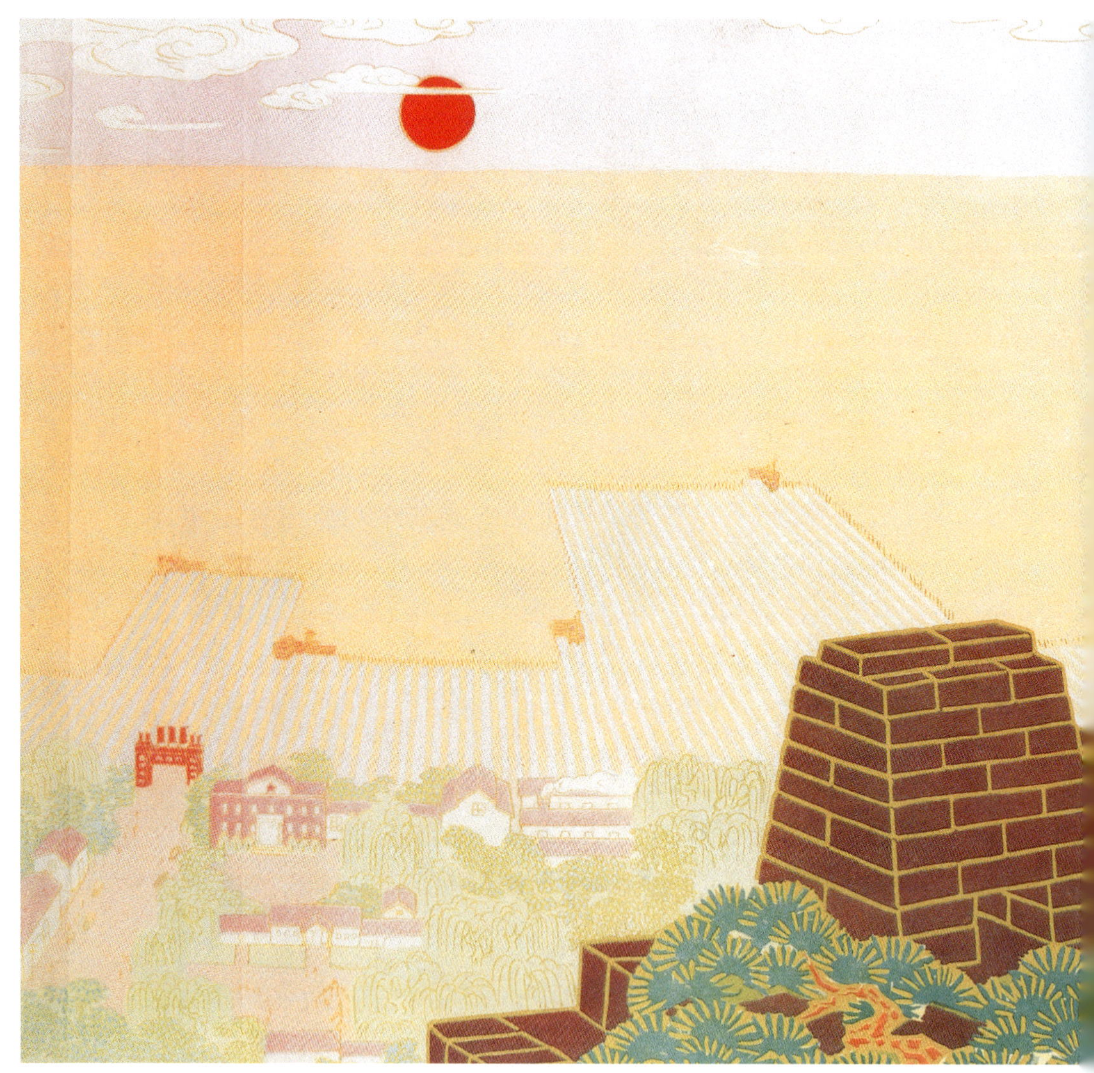

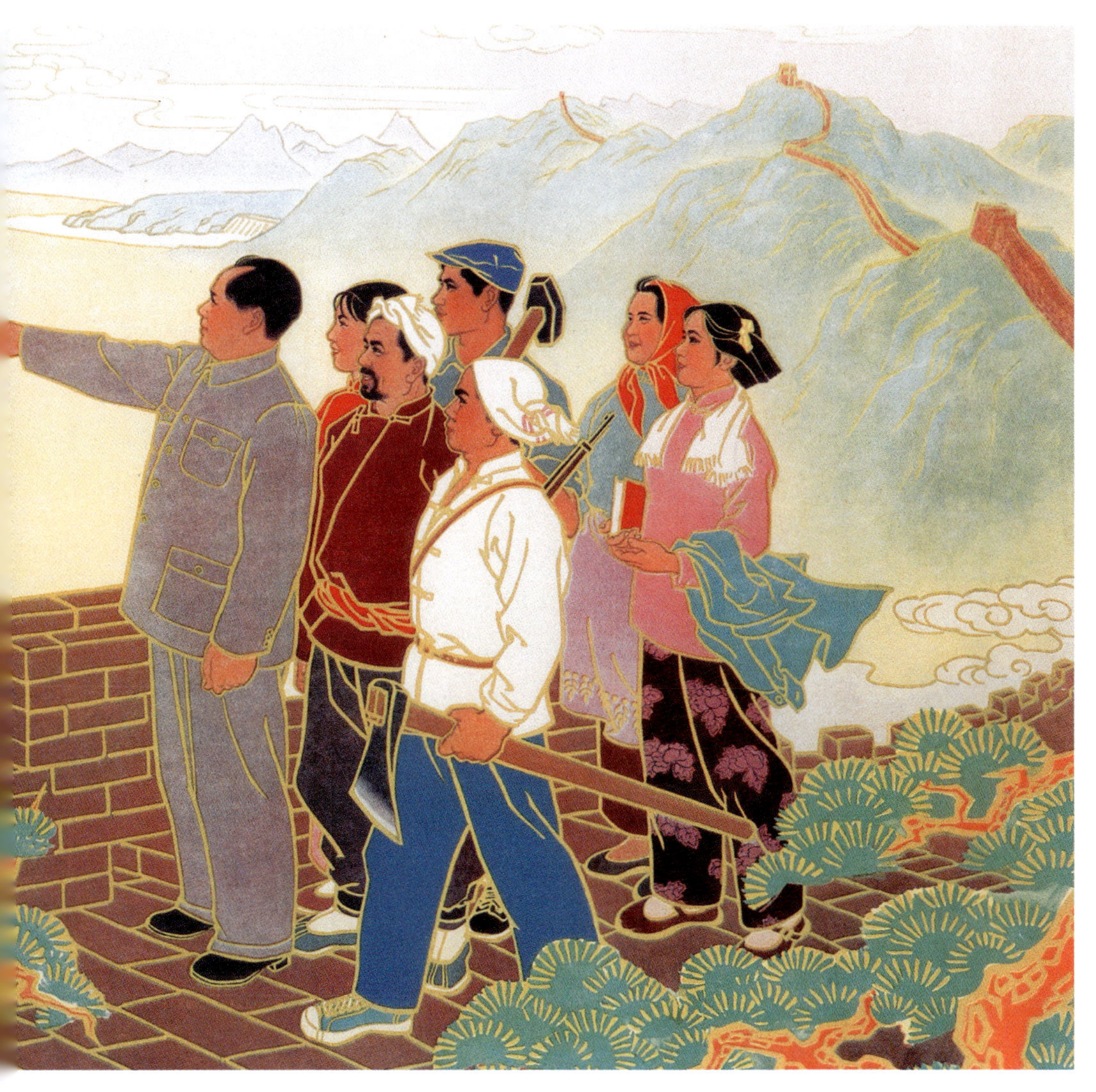

Opposite
Follow the Communist Party and promote China's upturn *Artist:* Zhu Dunjian; Jiangsu People's Publishing House, 1982; 0.18 Yuan

Der Kommunistischen Partei folgen und Chinas Aufschwung fördern *Gemalt von* Zhu Dunjian; Volksverlag Jiangsu, 1982; 0,18 Yuan

Suivons le Parti communiste et favorisons l'essor de la Chine *Peintre :* Zhu Dunjian ; Éditions Populaires du Jiangsu, 1982 ; 0,18 yuan

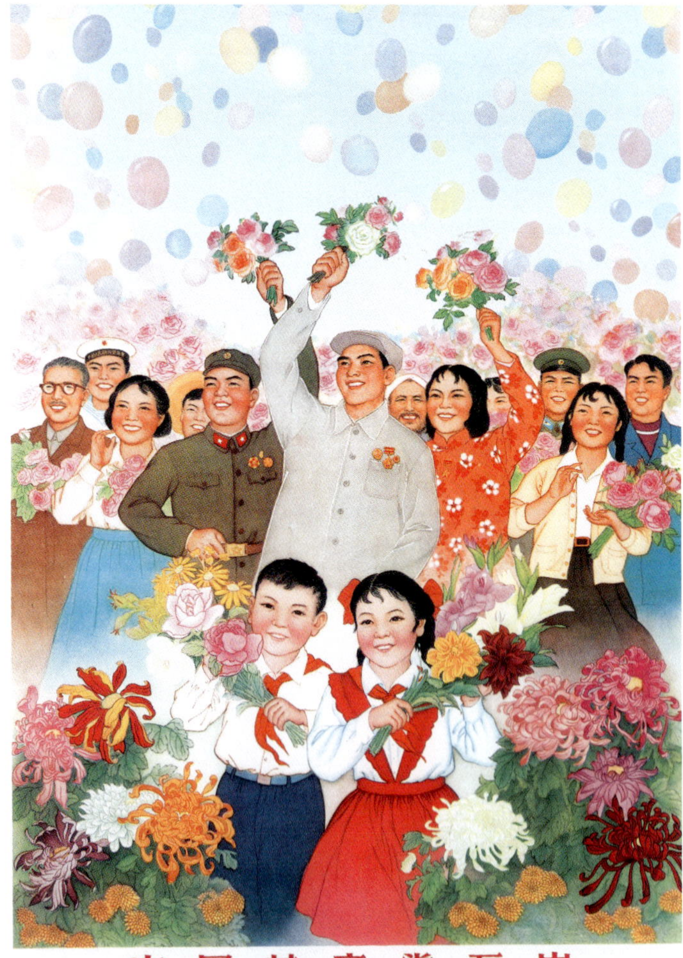

Long live the Chinese Communist Party *Artists:* Zhang Ruji, Sheng Cijun and Tian Yuwen; People's Art Publishing House, 1964 *Print run:* 30,000; 0.15 Yuan

Es lebe die Kommunistische Partei Chinas *Gemalt von* Zhang Ruji, Sheng Cijun und Tian Yuwen; Volkskunstverlag, 1964 *Auflage:* 30 000; 0,15 Yuan

Vive le Parti communiste chinois *Peintres :* Zhang Ruji, Sheng Cijun et Tian Yuwen, Éditions Populaires d'Art, 1964 *Tirage :* 30 000 ; 0,15 yuan

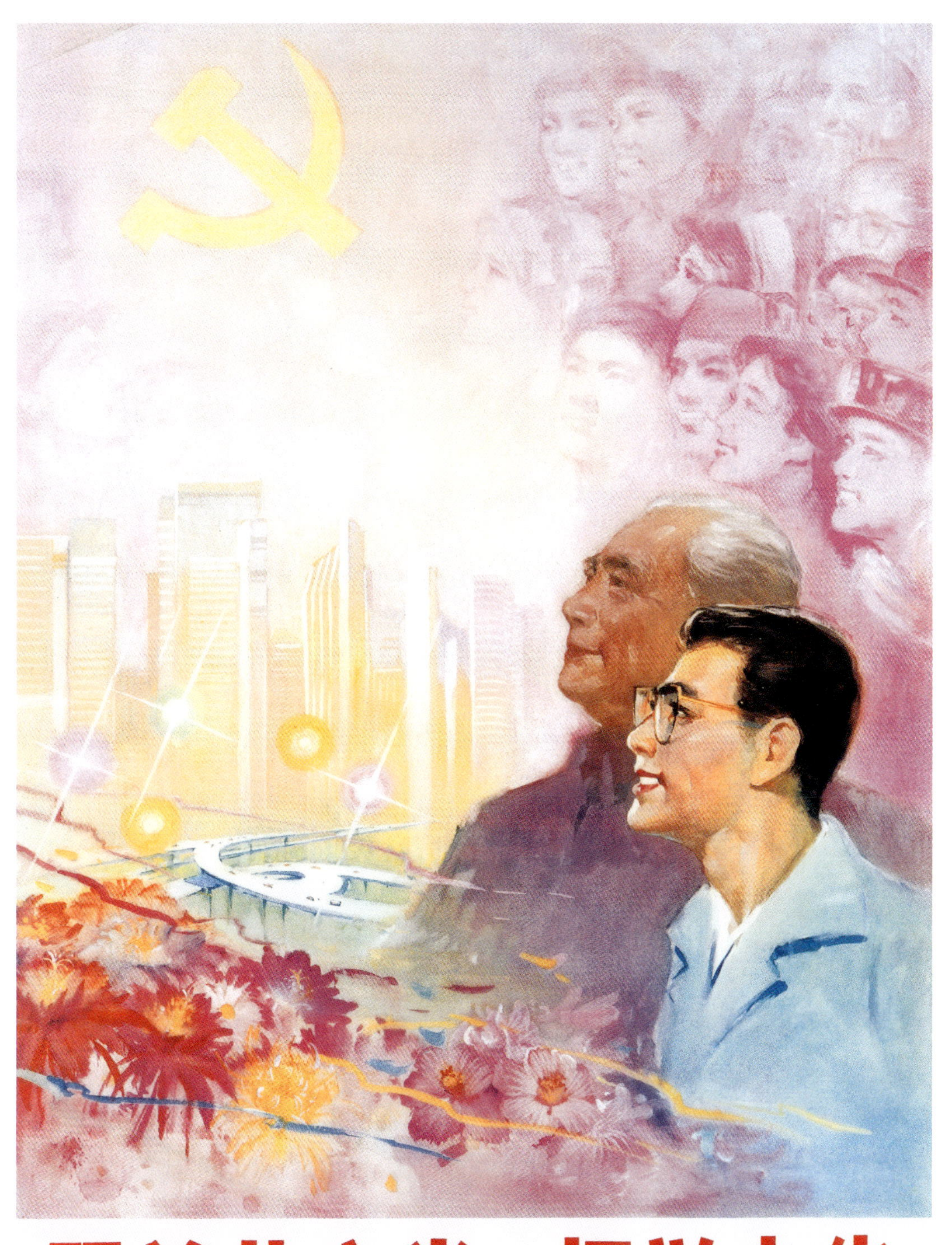

跟着共产党　振兴中华

Long live the Great Chinese Communist Party *Artists:* Jiang Nanchun and Yao Zhongyu; Shanghai People's Publishing House, 1st edn 1974, 2nd edn 1974 *Print run:* 1,000,001–2,000,000; 0.14 Yuan

Es lebe die große Kommunistische Partei Chinas *Gemalt von* Jiang Nanchun und Yao Zhongyu; Volksverlag Shanghai, 1. Aufl. 1974, 2. Aufl. 1974 *Auflage:* 1 000 001–2 000 000; 0,14 Yuan

Vive le grand Parti communiste chinois *Peintres :* Jiang Nanchun et Yao Zhongyu ; Éditions Populaires de Shanghai, 1ère éd. 1974, 2e éd. 1974 *Tirage :* 1 000 001–2 000 000 ; 0,14 yuan

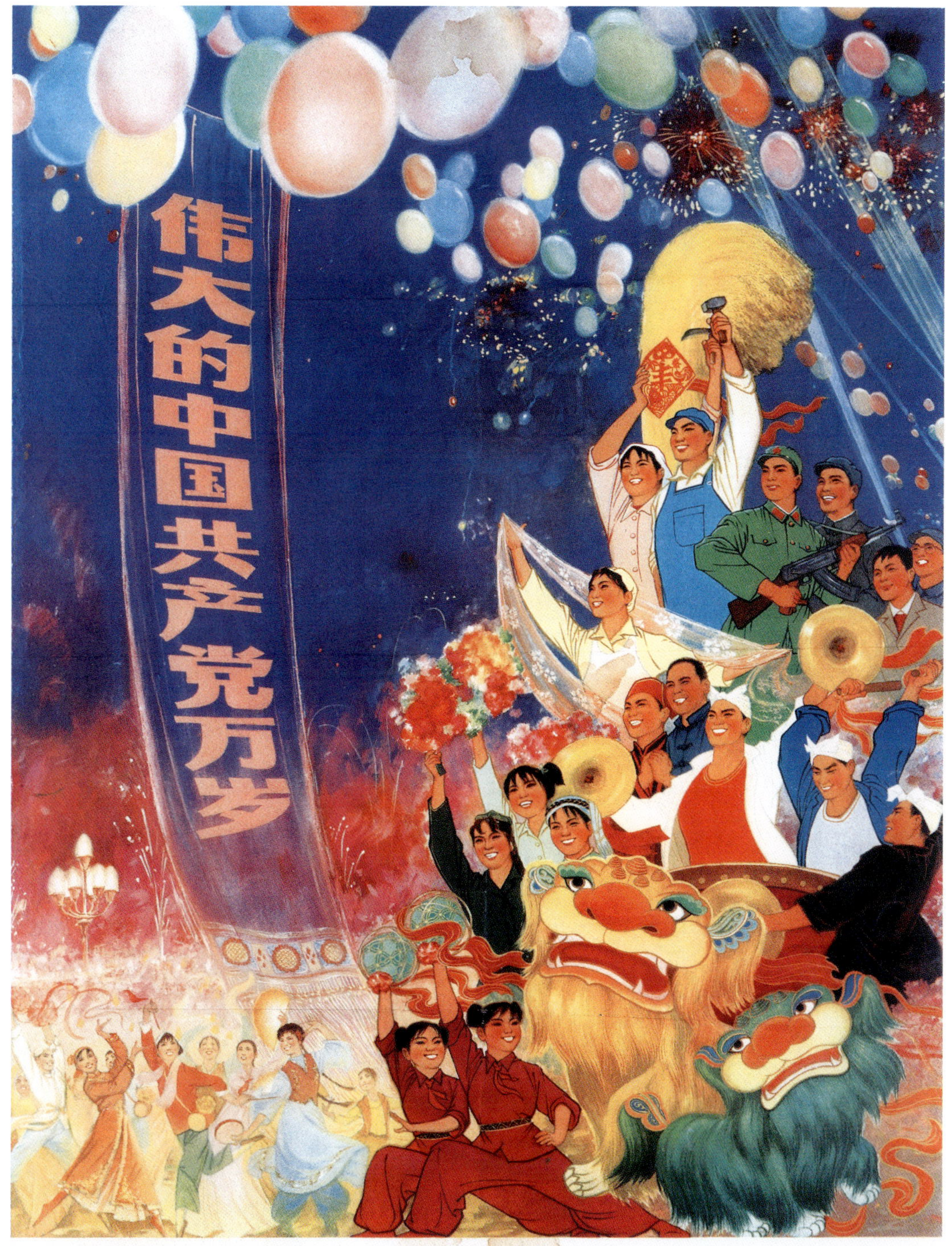

WEI DA DE ZHONG GUO GONG CHAN DANG WAN SUI

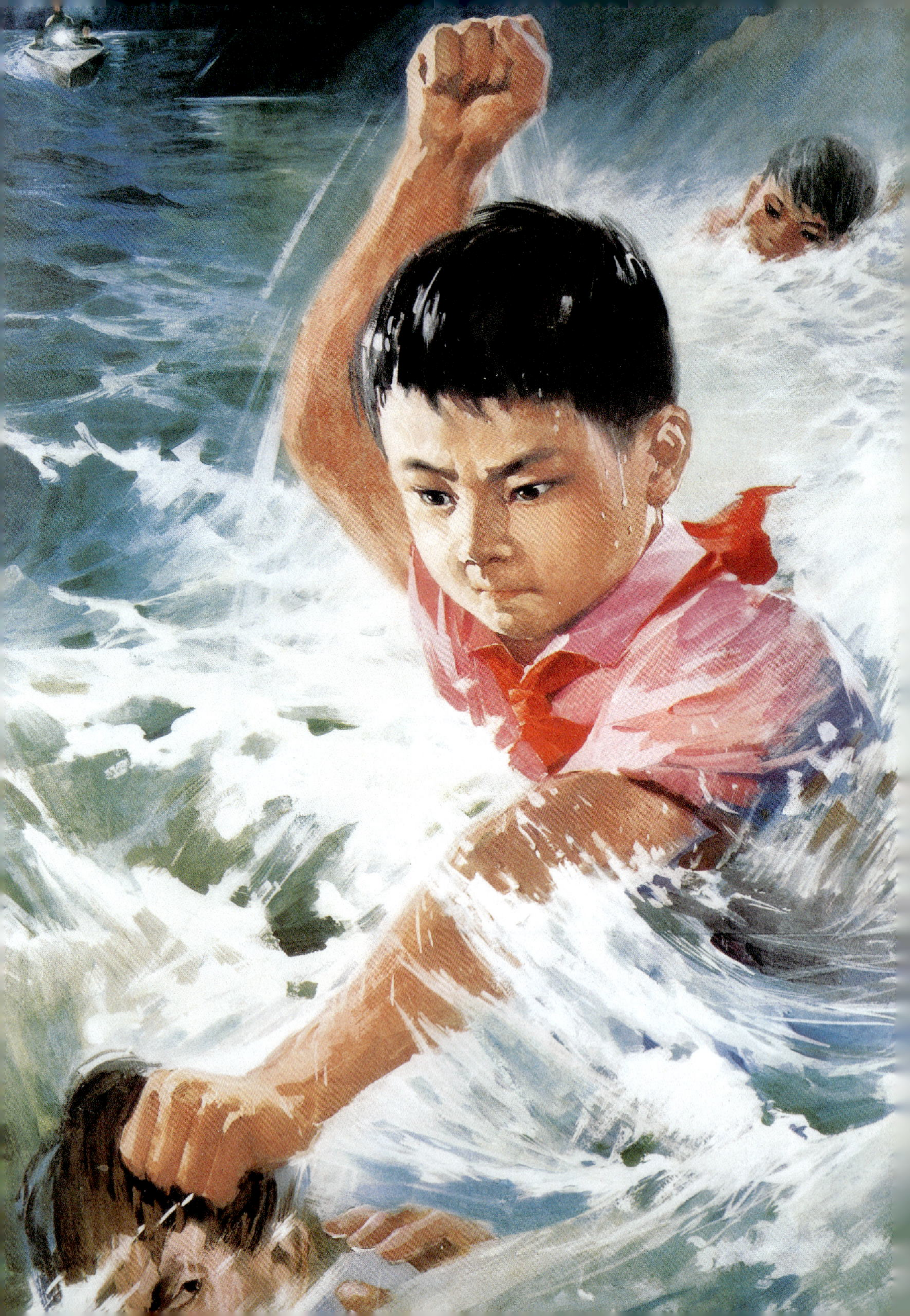

II

CLASSES AND CLASS STRUGGLE

KLASSEN UND KLASSENKAMPF
LES CLASSES ET LA LUTTE DES CLASSES

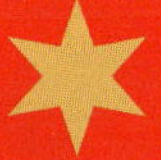

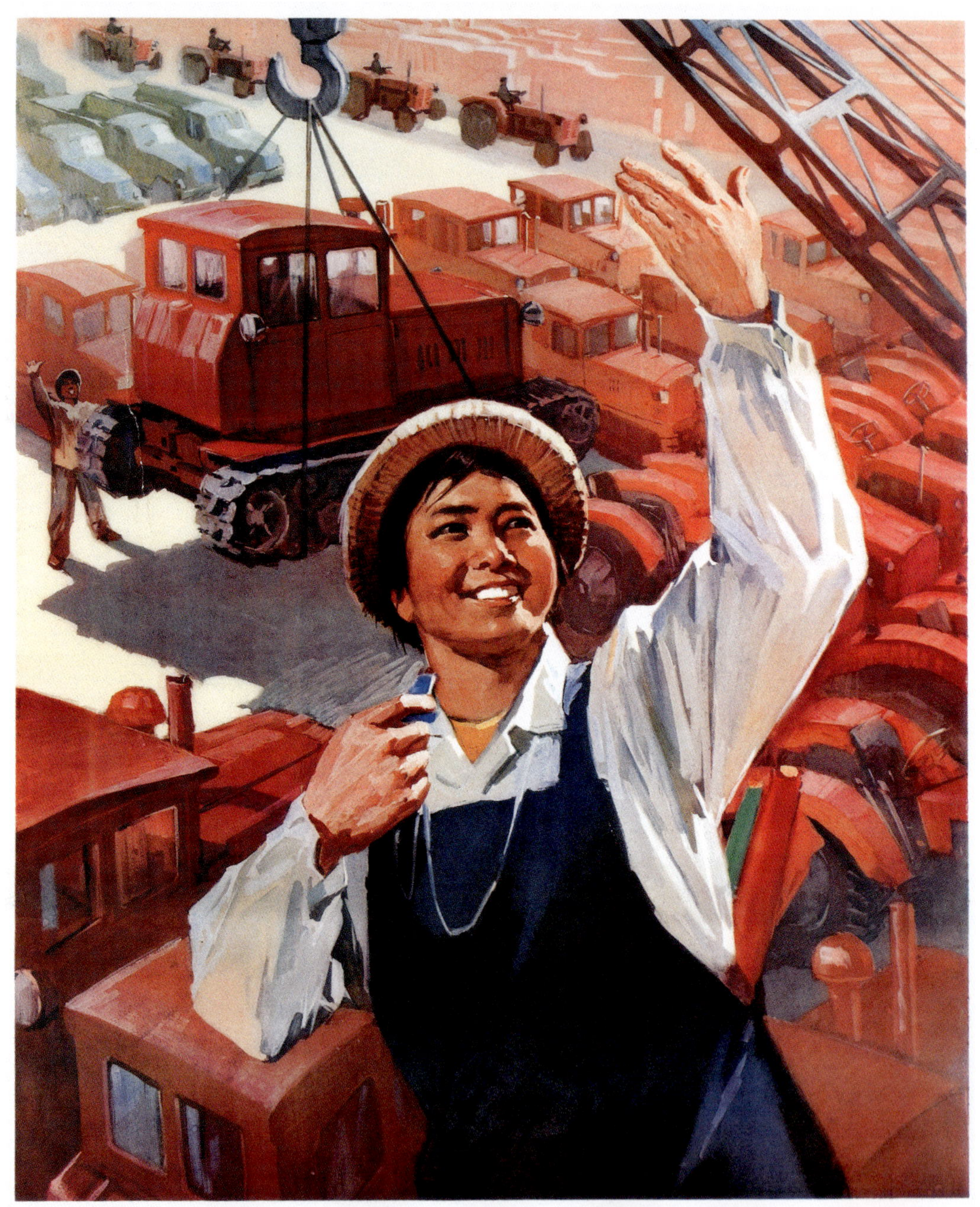
以阶级斗争为纲
为在一九八〇年基本上实现农业机械化而奋斗

Page 84
Bravely fighting the enemy Teaching poster *Artist:* Song Mingyuan; Shanghai Educational Publishing House, 1979 *Print run:* 500,000; 0.12 Yuan

Tapfer gegen den Feind kämpfen Erziehungsplakat *Gemalt von* Song Mingyuan; Erziehungsverlag Shanghai, 1979 *Auflage:* 500 000; 0,12 Yuan

Luttons avec bravoure contre l'ennemi Affiche éducative *Peintre :* Song Mingyuan, Éditions Éducatives de Shanghai, 1979 *Tirage :* 500 000 ; 0,12 yuan

Opposite
Regard the class struggle as the main link in the chain Strive to achieve the greatest possible degree of mechanization in agriculture by 1980 *Artist:* Yang Jincheng *Designed by:* Propaganda Poster Painting Class for Peasants in the Jin district of Liaoning Province, People's Art Publishing House, 1976

Den Klassenkampf als Hauptkettenglied betrachten Für die Mechanisierung der Landwirtschaft in möglichst großem Umfang bis 1980 kämpfen *Gemalt von* Yang Jincheng *Entwurf:* Propagandaplakat-Malkurs für Bauern des Kreises Jin, Provinz Liaoning; Volkskunstverlag, 1976

Voyons dans la lutte des classes le principal maillon de la transformation Luttons, dans toute la mesure du possible, pour la mécanisation de l'agriculture jusqu'en 1980 *Peintre :* Yang Jincheng *Conception :* Affiche de propagande du cours de peinture pour paysans du canton de Jin, province du Liaoning ; Éditions Populaires d'Art, 1976

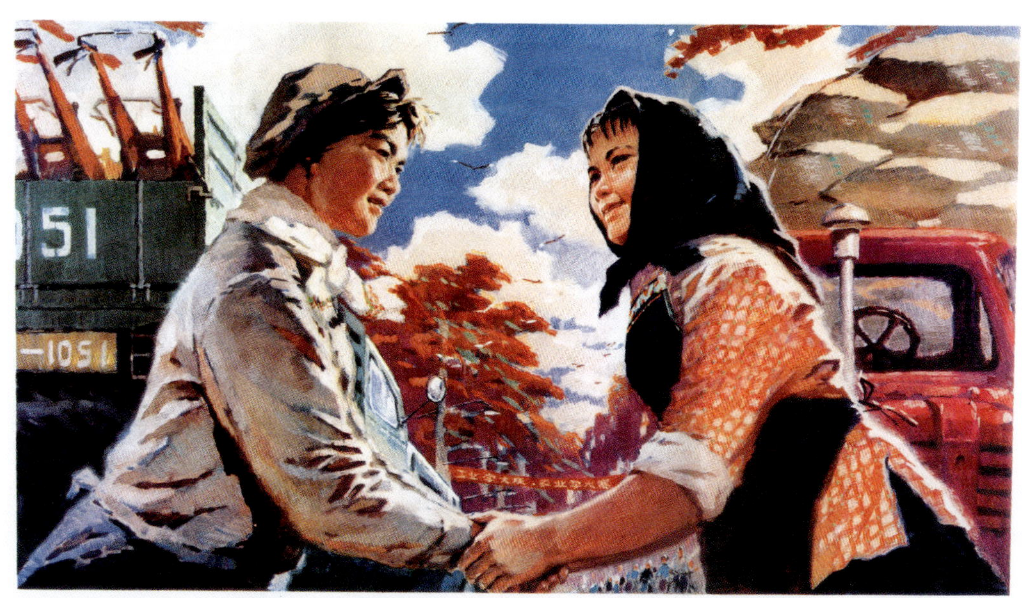

Workers and peasants join hands and advance *Designed by:* Guangzhou Art Studio; People's Art Publishing House, 1977; 0.14 Yuan

Hand in Hand schreiten Arbeiter und Bauern voran *Entwurf:* Kunststudio Guangzhou; Volkskunstverlag, 1977; 0,14 Yuan

Ouvriers et paysans avancent main dans la main *Conception :* Studio d'Art de Guangzhou; Éditions Populaires d'Art, 1977; 0,14 yuan

Revolutionary rebels of the municipal technical training course, unite! *Bottom right:* Designed by the Committee of the Revolutionary Rebels of the Shanghai municipal technical training course *Contact:* Sichuan Zhonglu No. 110, Room 19; Telephone: 215 530–19

Revolutionäre Rebellen der Technischen Ausbildungskurse der Stadt, vereinigt euch! *Unten rechts:* Entworfen von der Leitung der revolutionären Rebellen der Technischen Ausbildungskurse der Stadt Shanghai *Kontakt:* Sichuan Zhonglu Nr. 110, Zimmer 19, Telefon: 215 530–19

Rebelles révolutionnaires des Cours de Formation technique de la ville, unissez-vous ! *En bas à droite :* Conçue par la Direction des Rebelles révolutionnaires des Cours de Formation technique de la ville de Shanghai *Contacts :* Sichuan Zhonglu n° 110, chambre 19, Téléphone : 215 530–19

"Who are our enemies? Who are our friends? This is a question of the first importance for the revolution."

Wer sind unsere Feinde? Wer sind unsere Freunde? Das ist eine Frage, die für die Revolution erstrangige Bedeutung hat. ✶ Quels sont nos ennemis et quels sont nos amis ? C'est là une question d'une importance primordiale pour la révolution.

Pages 90–91
People of the lower class are the most intelligent *Artists:* Wen Gegui and Sun Weipin; Beijing People's Publishing House, 1974; 0.14 Yuan

Menschen von niederem Stand sind am intelligentesten *Gemalt von* Wen Gegui und Sun Weipin; Volksverlag Peking, 1974; 0,14 Yuan

Les gens de condition inférieure sont les plus intelligents *Peintres :* Wen Gegui et Sun Weipin; Éditions Populaires de Pékin, 1974 ; 0,14 yuan

Pages 92–93
We ask the worker, our dear comrade, to teach us his trade *On wall newspaper, left:* Never forget class and the class struggle People's Art Publishing House, 1977 *Print run:* 100,000; 0.11 Yuan

Wir bitten den Onkel Arbeiter, uns im Hauptfach Unterricht zu geben *Links auf der Wandzeitung:* Auf keinen Fall die Klassen und den Klassenkampf vergessen; Volkskunstverlag, 1977 *Auflage:* 100 000; 0,11 Yuan

Nous demandons à notre oncle ouvrier de faire cours dans notre matière principale *Sur le journal mural à gauche :* N'oubliez en aucun cas l'existence et la lutte des classes ; Éditions Populaires d'Art, 1977 *Tirage :* 100 000 ; 0,11 yuan

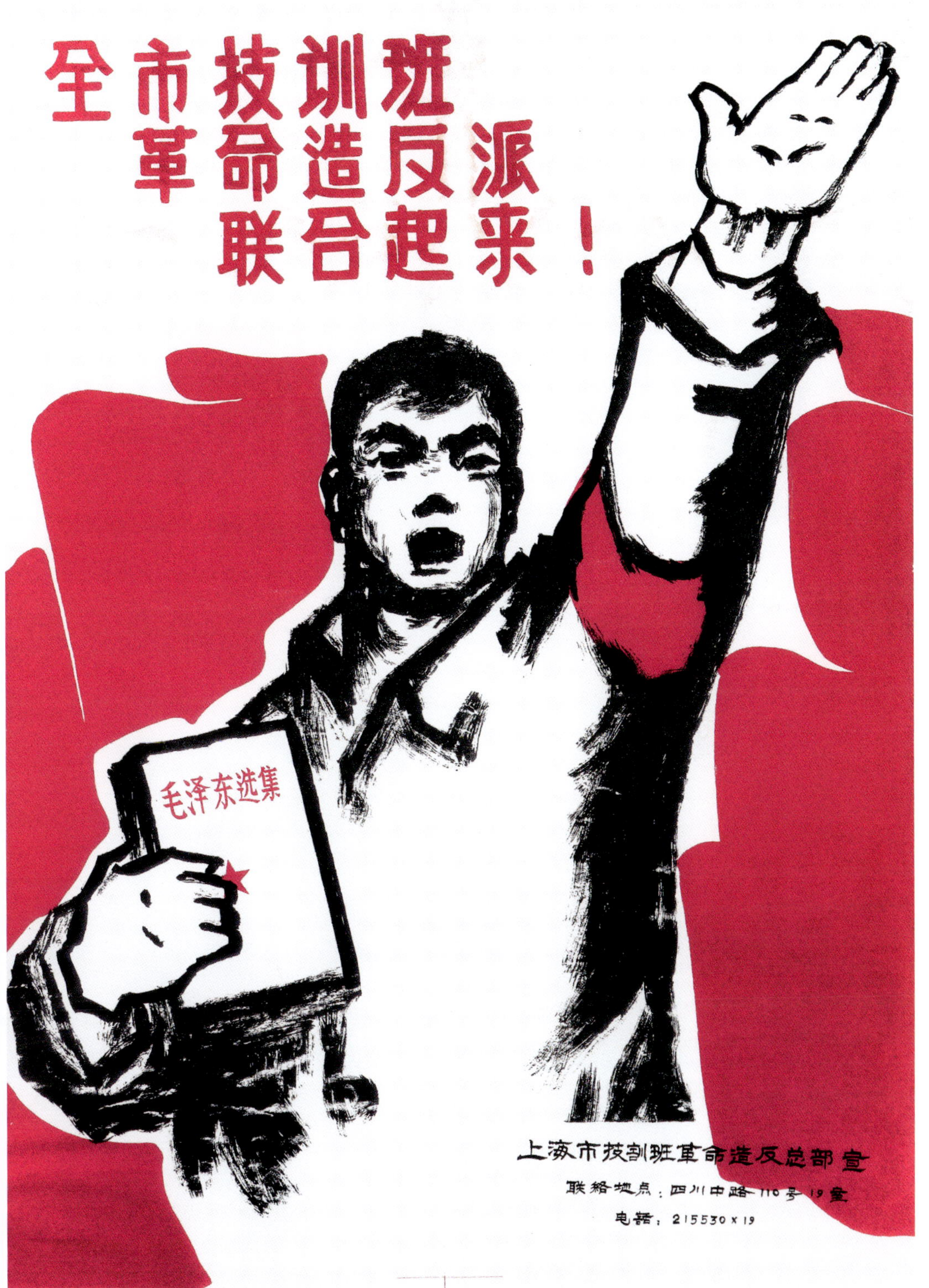
全市技训班
革命造反派
联合起来！
毛泽东选集
上海市技训班革命造反总部宣
联络地点：四川中路110号19室
电話：215530×19

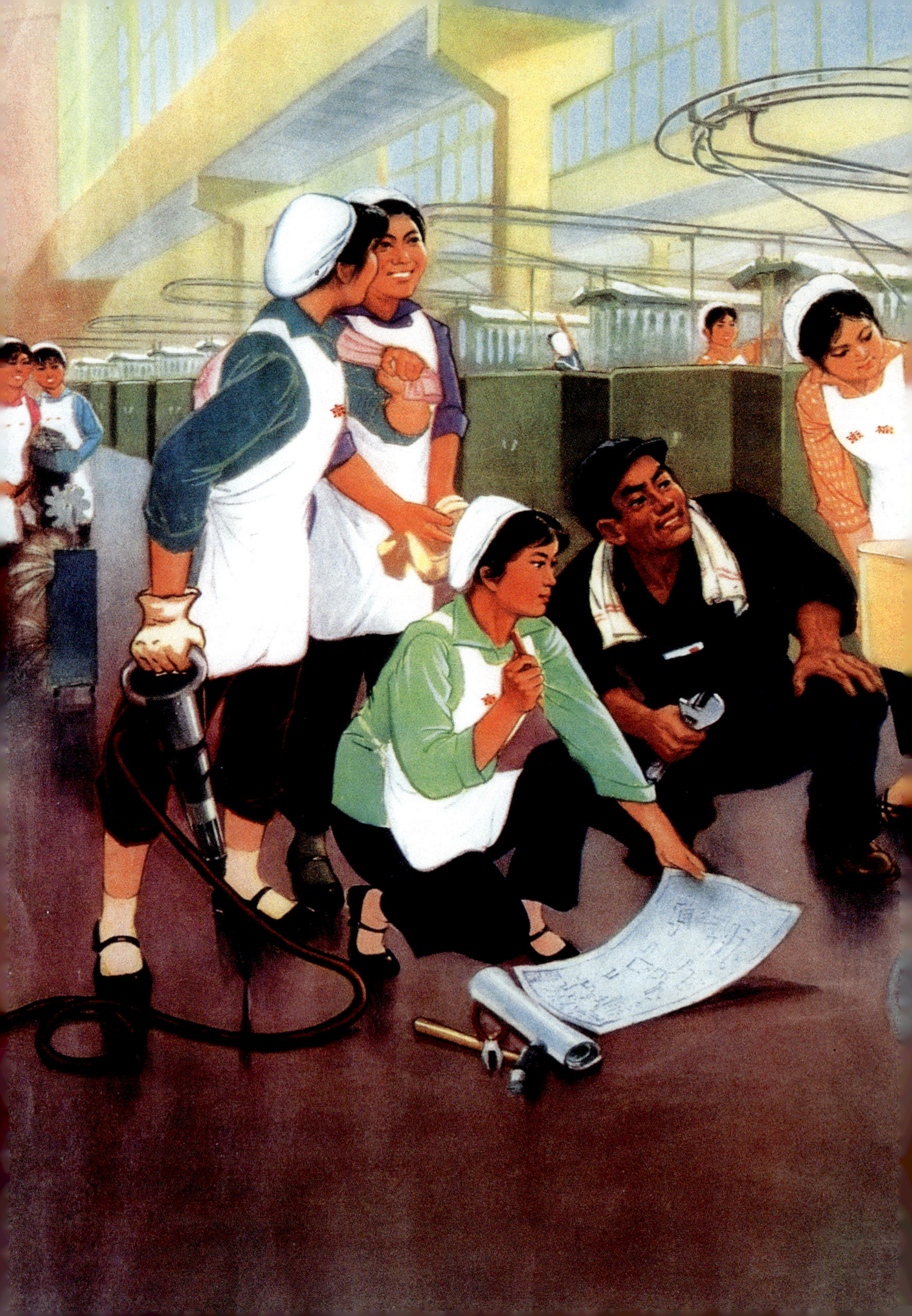

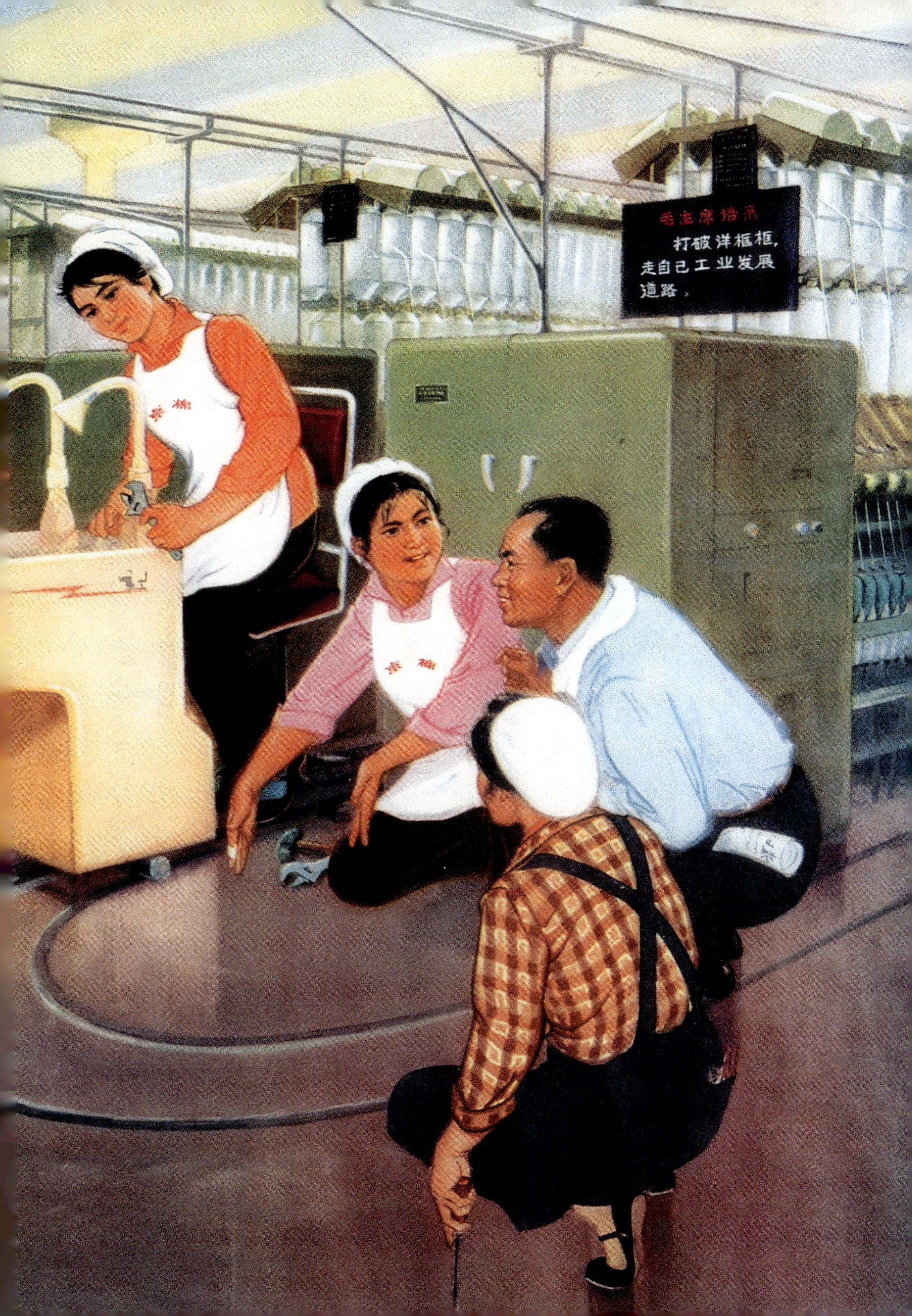
毛主席指示
打破洋框框，
走自己工业发展
道路。

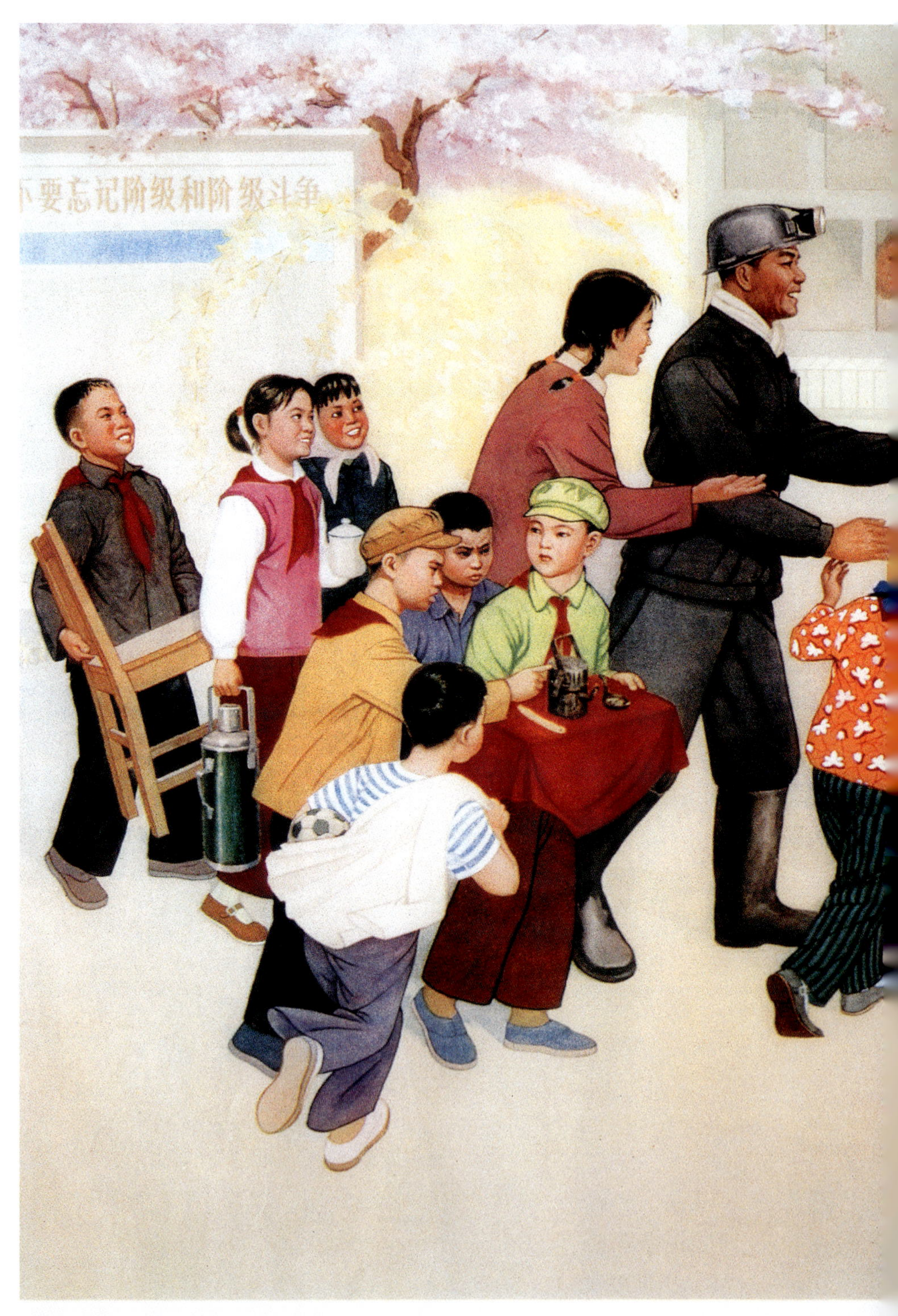

请 工 人

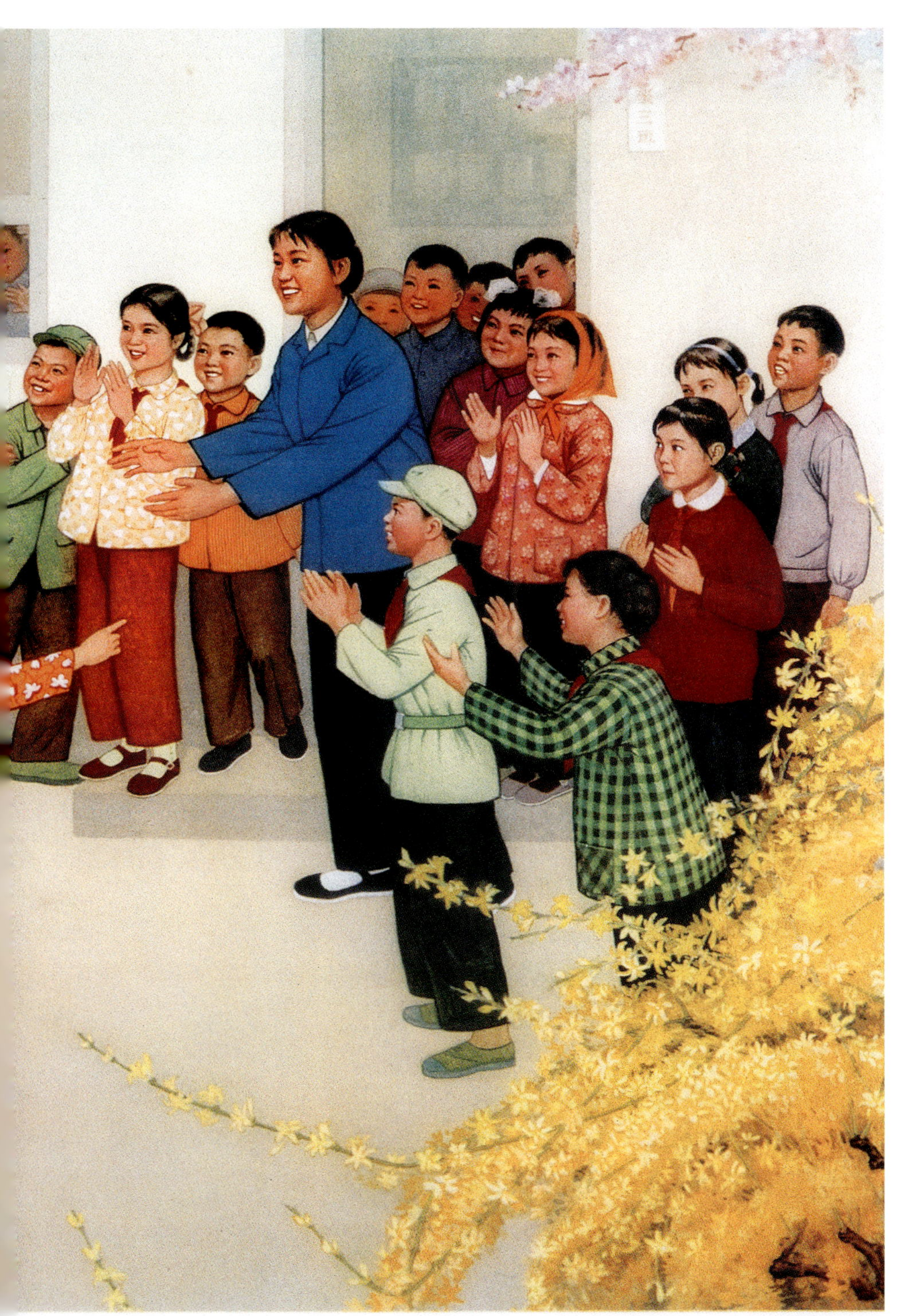

上 主 课

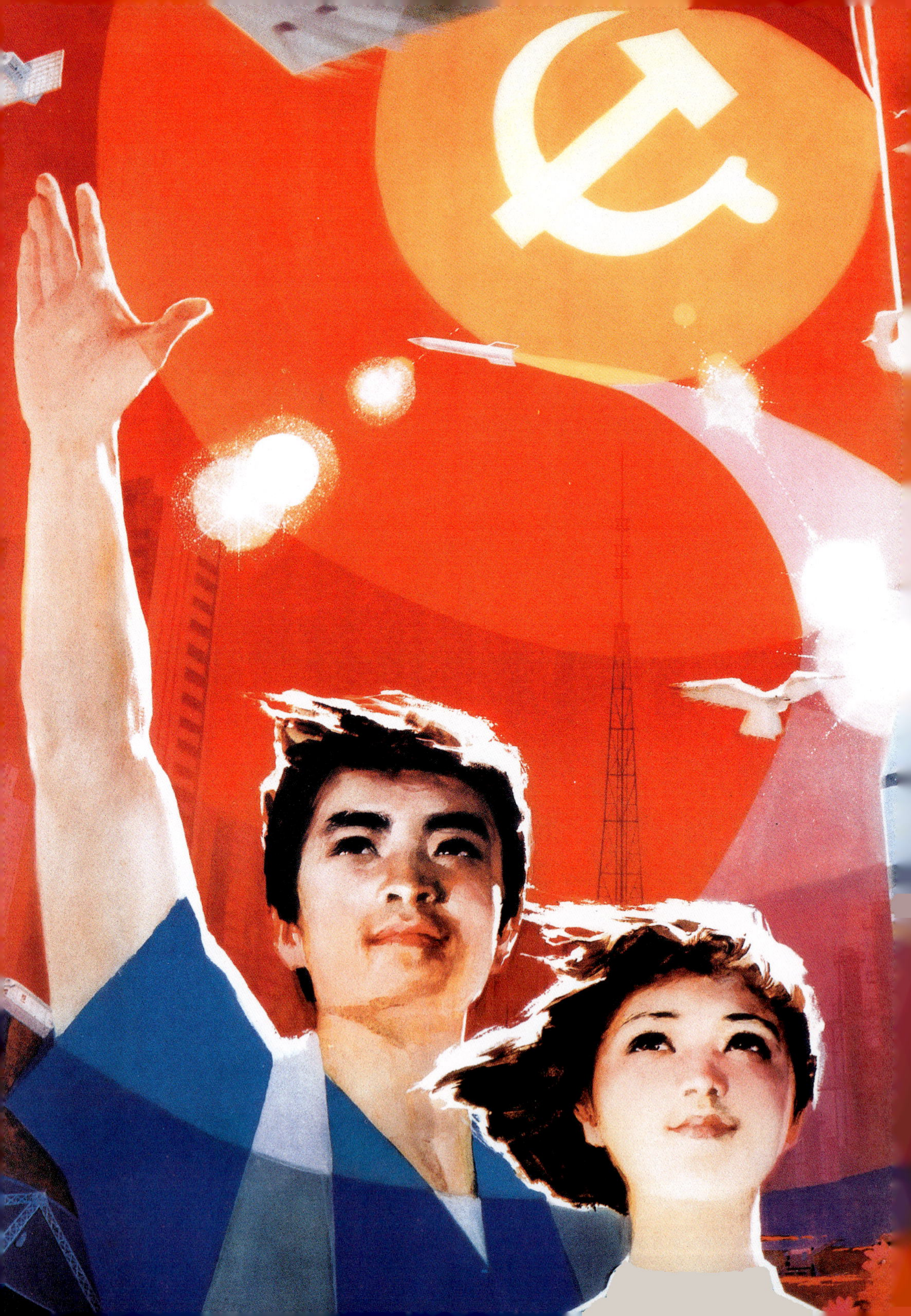

III

SOCIALISM AND COMMUNISM

SOZIALISMUS UND KOMMUNISMUS
LE SOCIALISME ET LE COMMUNISME

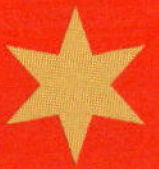

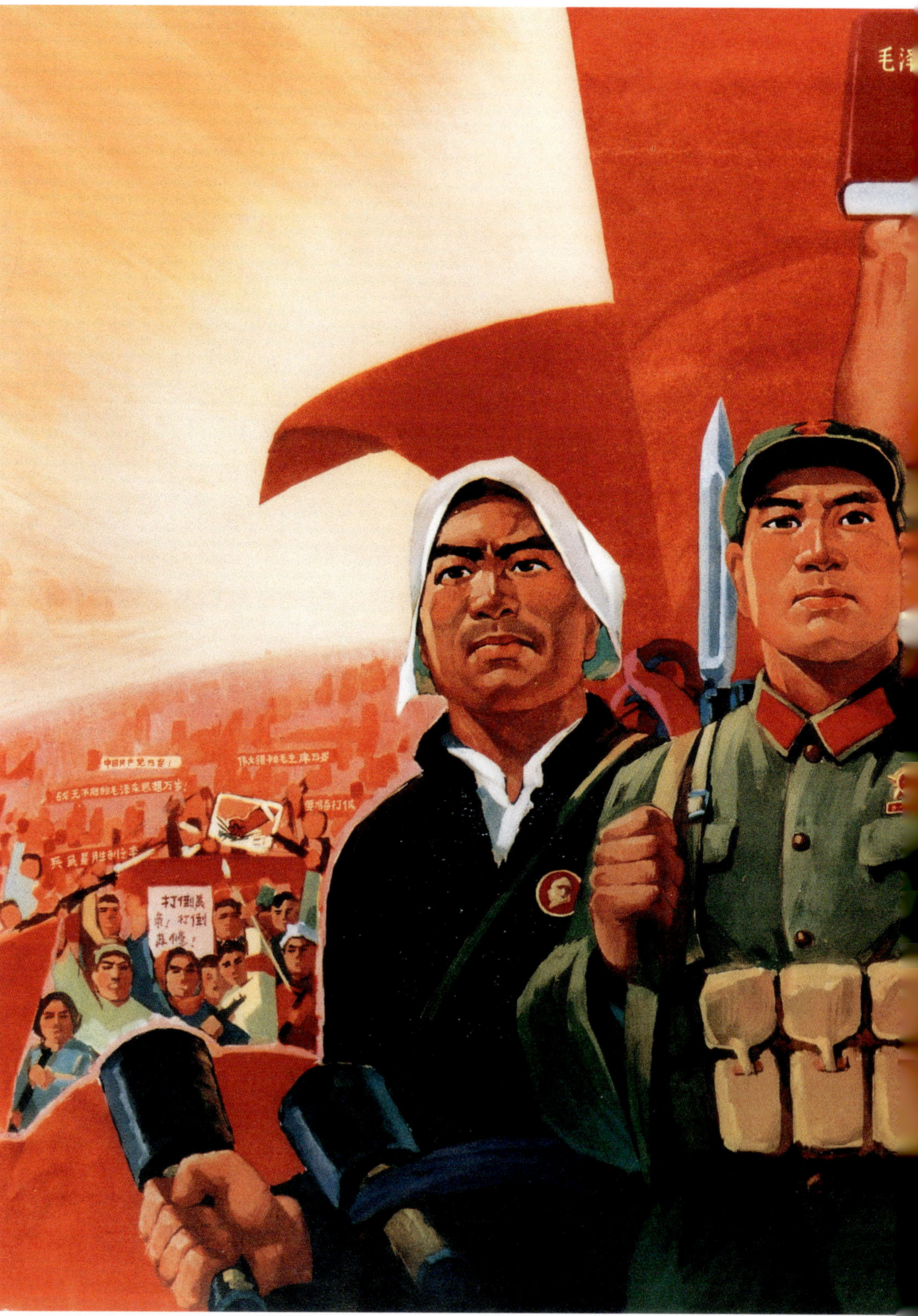
毛泽
中国共产党万岁！
伟大领袖毛主席万岁
战无不胜的毛泽东思想万岁！
兵民是胜利之本
打倒美帝！打倒苏修！

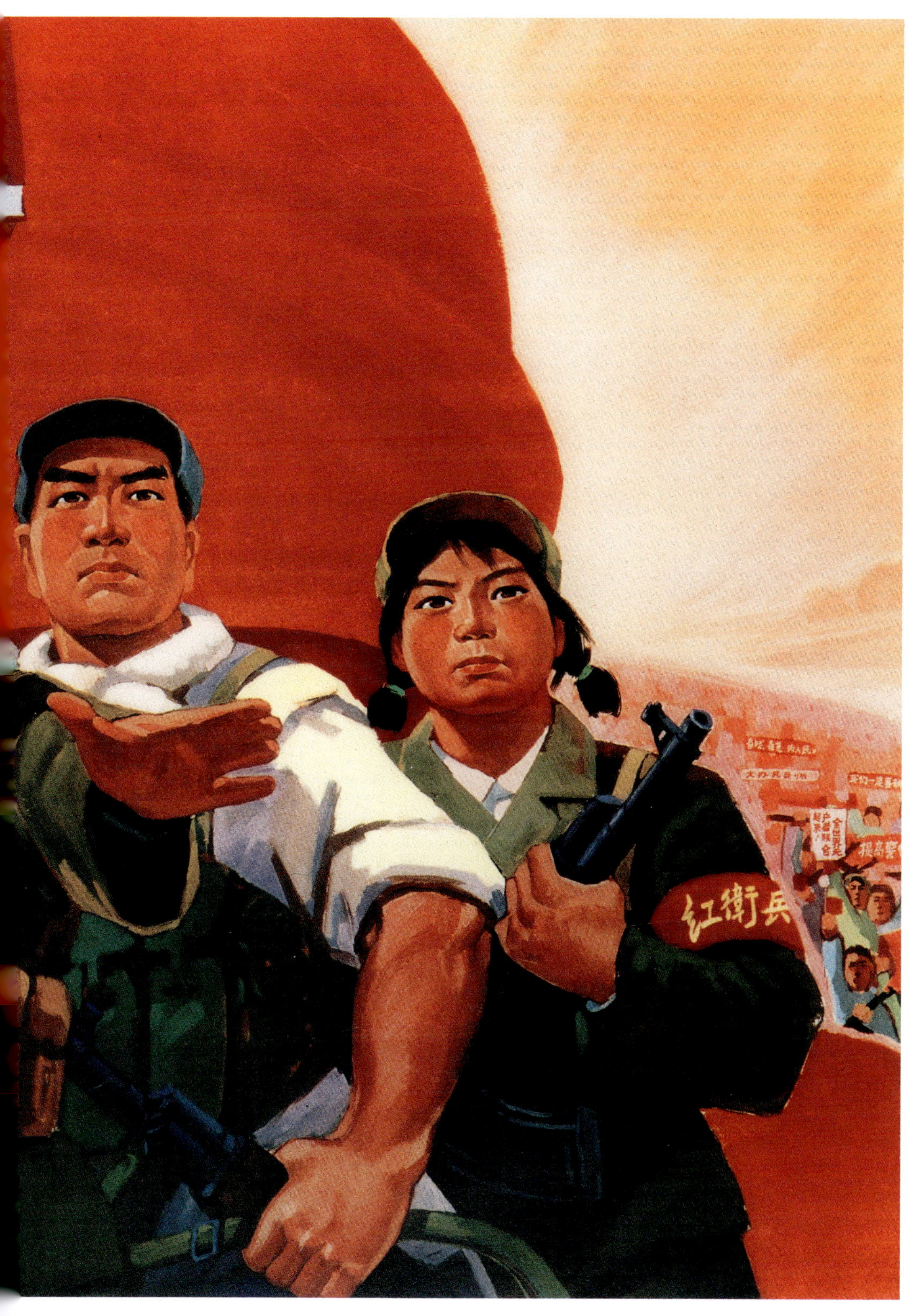
红衛兵

Page 94
Carry out the Four Modernizations* of the Fatherland Strive for even greater glory *Artists:* Qiu Baiping, Chen Zhenxin; People's Art Publishing House, 1981 *Print run:* 30,000; 0.16 Yuan
* The modernizations of agriculture, national defence, industry, and science and technology.

Die Vier Modernisierungen* des Vaterlandes verwirklichen Nach noch größerem Ruhm streben *Gemalt von* Qiu Baiping, Chen Zhenxin; Volkskunstverlag, 1981 *Auflage:* 30 000; 0,16 Yuan
* Die Modernisierung von Landwirtschaft, Industrie, Verteidigung sowie Wissenschaft und Technik.

Réalisons les Quatre modernisations* de la patrie Vers une gloire encore plus éclatante *Peintres :* Qiu Baiping, Chen Zhenxin ; Éditions Populaires d'Art, 1981 *Tirage :* 30 000 ; 0,16 yuan
* La modernisation de l'agriculture, de l'industrie, de la défense et des sciences et techniques.

Pages 96–97
"Threefold Defence"* *Book:* Selected Works of Mao Zedong *Armband (woman):* Red Guard Poster 30 *Designed and published by:* the General Staff of the Chinese People's Liberation Army
* This was a well-known abbreviation at the time: Defence against Nuclear, Chemical, and Biological Warfare or Weapons.

„Dreierschutz"* *Buch:* Ausgewählte Werke Mao Zedongs *Armbinde der Frau:* Rote Garde Plakat 30 *Entwurf und Herausgeber:* Generalstab der Volksbefreiungsarmee Chinas
* Das ist eine allgemein bekannte Abkürzung zu der Zeit: Schutz vor atomaren, chemischen und biologischen Waffen oder Kriegen.

« Triple protection »* *Livre :* Œuvres choisies de Mao Zedong *Brassard (femme) :* Garde Rouge Affiche n° 30 *Conception et éditeur :* l'état-major général de l'Armée de Libération Populaire de Chine
* Il s'agit d'une formule bien connue à l'époque : une protection contre les armes ou les guerres nucléaires, chimiques et biologiques.

Onward, towards an even higher goal *Top left (plaque):* The General Line *Top right (under the man's arm):* Production Tasks *Bottom right:* Race against time, Be ahead of the time! *Bottom:* By exerting every effort *Artist:* Chen Lieyang; Shanghai People's Publishing House, 1959; 0.11 Yuan

Vorwärts, einem noch höheren Ziel entgegen *Links oben (Plakette):* Generallinie *Rechts oben (unter dem Arm des Mannes):* Produktionsaufgaben *Rechts unten:* Wettlauf mit der Zeit, sei der Zeit voraus! *Ganz unten:* Unter Anspannung aller Kräfte *Gemalt von* Chen Lieyang; Volksverlag Shanghai, 1959; 0,11 Yuan

En avant, vers un objectif encore plus élevé *En haut à gauche (macaron) :* Ligne générale *En haut à droite (sous le bras de l'homme) :* Tâches de production *En bas à droite :* Dans la course contre la montre. Il faut devancer son époque ! *Tout en bas :* Mobilisez toutes vos forces *Peintre :* Chen Lieyang ; Éditions Populaires de Shanghai, 1959 ; 0,11 yuan

Pages 100–101
The working class is the major force that will contribute to the acceleration and implementation of the Four Modernizations *Banner, right:* Striving towards the goal of modernizing science and technology *Artist:* Chao Deren; People's Art Publishing House, 1978 *Print run:* 38,000; 0.14 Yuan

Die Arbeiterklasse als Hauptkraft soll ihren Teil dazu beitragen, um die Verwirklichung der Vier Modernisierungen zu beschleunigen *Transparent rechts:* Dem Ziel der Modernisierung von Wissenschaft und Technik zustreben *Gemalt von* Chao Deren; Volkskunstverlag, 1978 *Auflage:* 38 000; 0,14 Yuan

La classe ouvrière, en tant que force vive, doit apporter son concours à l'accélération de la réalisation des Quatre Modernisations *Banderole de droite :* Orientez vos efforts vers la modernisation des sciences et des techniques *Peintre :* Chao Deren; Éditions Populaires d'Art, 1978 *Tirage :* 38 000 ; 0,14 yuan

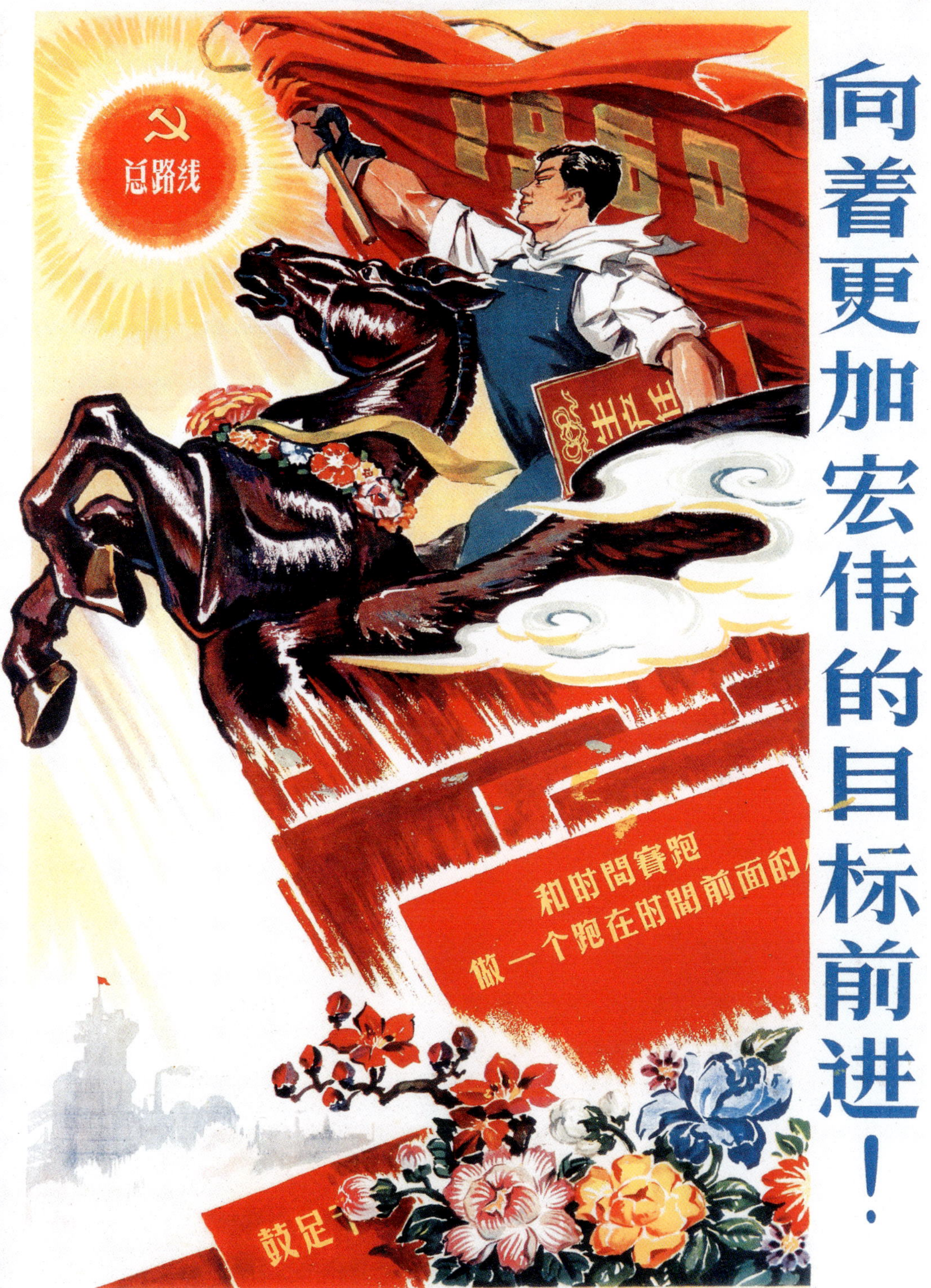

向着更加宏伟的目标前进！
总路线
1960
和时間賽跑
做一个跑在时間前面的
鼓足

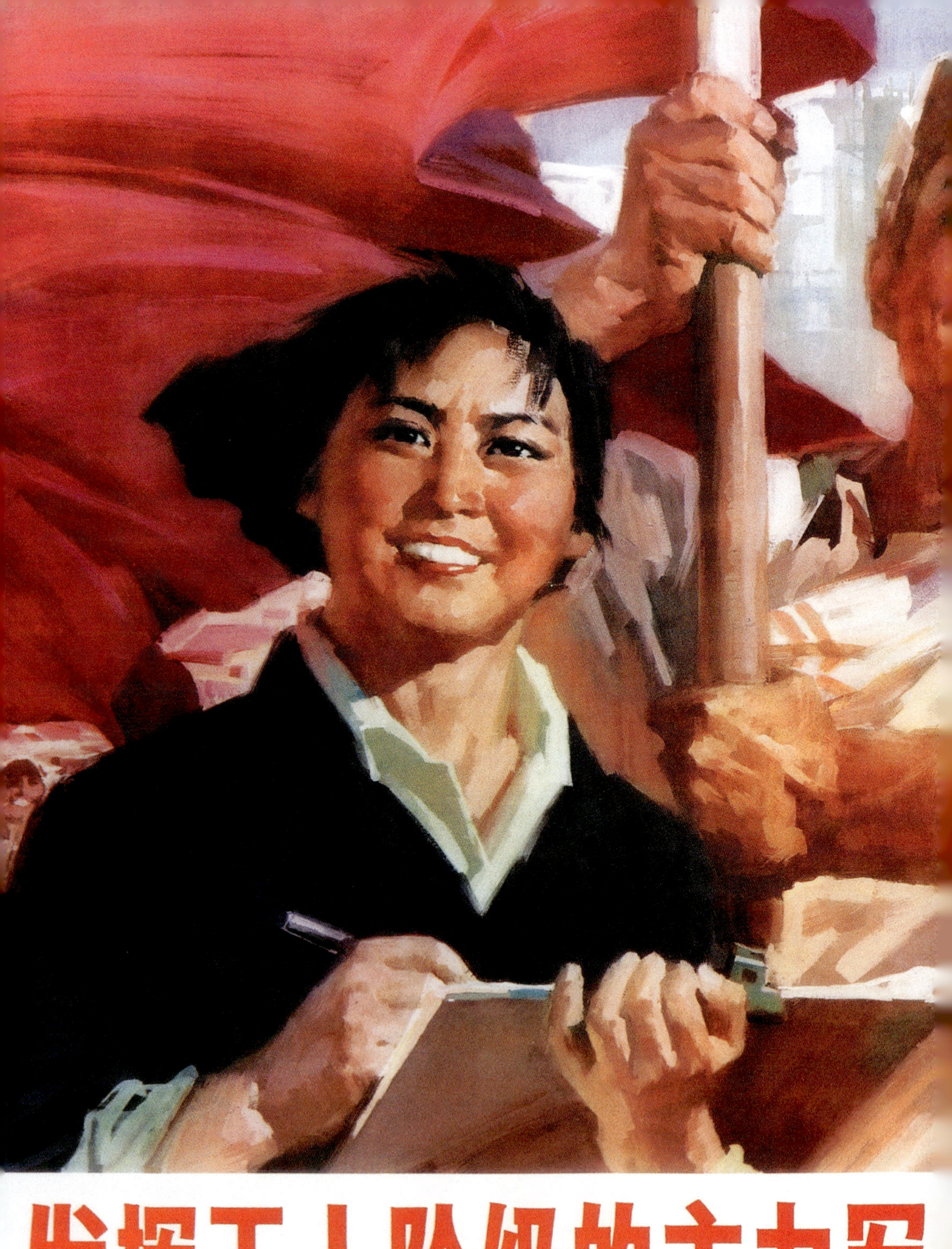

发挥工人阶级的主力军

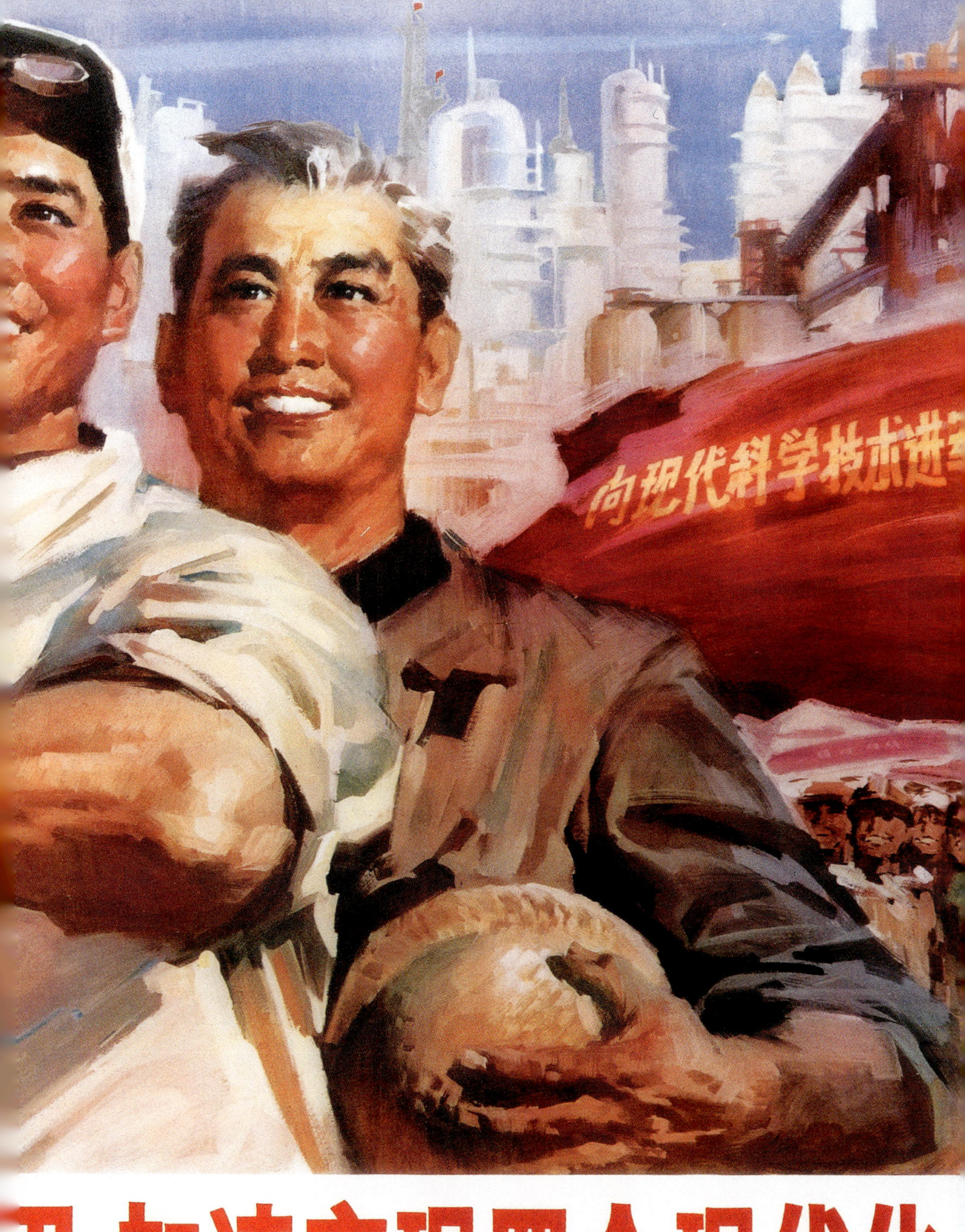

加速实现四个现代化

Opposite

Red lantern *On the lantern:* The People's Commune is good *Above the door:* A family for everyone *Scrolls either side of door:* Eternal happiness in the People's Commune. The east wind brings spring to the whole country *Chinese character held by woman, right:* Happiness *Artist:* Wang Xin; Liaoning People's Publishing House, 1963; 0.16 Yuan

Rote Laterne *Auf der Laterne*: Die Volkskommune ist gut *Über der Tür*: Familie für alle *Schriftrollen an der Tür*: Ewiges Glück in der Volkskommune. Der Ostwind bringt Frühling ins ganze Land. *Schrift in der Hand einer Frau*: Glück *Gemalt von* Wang Xin; Volksverlag Liaoning, 1963; 0,16 Yuan

Lampion rouge *Sur le lampion :* La Commune populaire est quelque chose de bien *Au-dessus de la porte :* Famille pour tous *Rouleaux à côté de la porte :* Bonheur éternel dans la Commune populaire. Le vent d'Est amène le printemps dans tout le pays *Caractères dans la main d'une femme :* Bonheur *Peintre :* Wang Xin ; Éditions Populaires du Liaoning, 1963 ; 0,16 yuan

With full steam ahead, "Peace No. 28" *On the ship:* Peace No. 28 *Slogan on the ship:* With full steam ahead, together we stride forward *Bottom left:* The latest 5,000-ton ocean steamer is launched *Artists:* Wu Shaoyun, Zhang Yuqing, and Lu Zezhi; Shanghai People's Art Publishing House, 1st edn 1958, 3rd edn 1959 *Print run:* 26,001–66,000; 0.12 Yuan

Mit voller Kraft voraus, „Frieden Nr. 28" *Auf dem Schiff:* Frieden Nr. 28 *Parole auf dem Schiff:* Mit voller Kraft voraus, gemeinsam vorwärts schreiten *Links unten:* Der neue 5000-Tonnen-Ozeandampfer läuft vom Stapel *Gemalt von* Wu Shaoyun, Zhang Yuqing und Lu Zezhi; Volkskunstverlag Shanghai; 1. Aufl. 1958, 3. Aufl. 1959 *Auflage:* 26 001–66 000; 0,12 Yuan

De toutes nos forces en avant, « Paix n° 28 » *Sur le bateau :* Paix n° 28 *Slogan sur le bateau :* De toutes nos forces, avançons côte à côte *En bas à gauche :* Le nouveau trans-atlantique de 5000 tonnes est mis à l'eau *Peintres :* Wu Shaoyun, Zhang Yuqing et Lu Zezhi ; Éditions Populaires d'Art de Shanghai, 1ère éd. 1958, 3e éd. 1959 *Tirage :* 26 001–66 000 ; 0,12 yuan

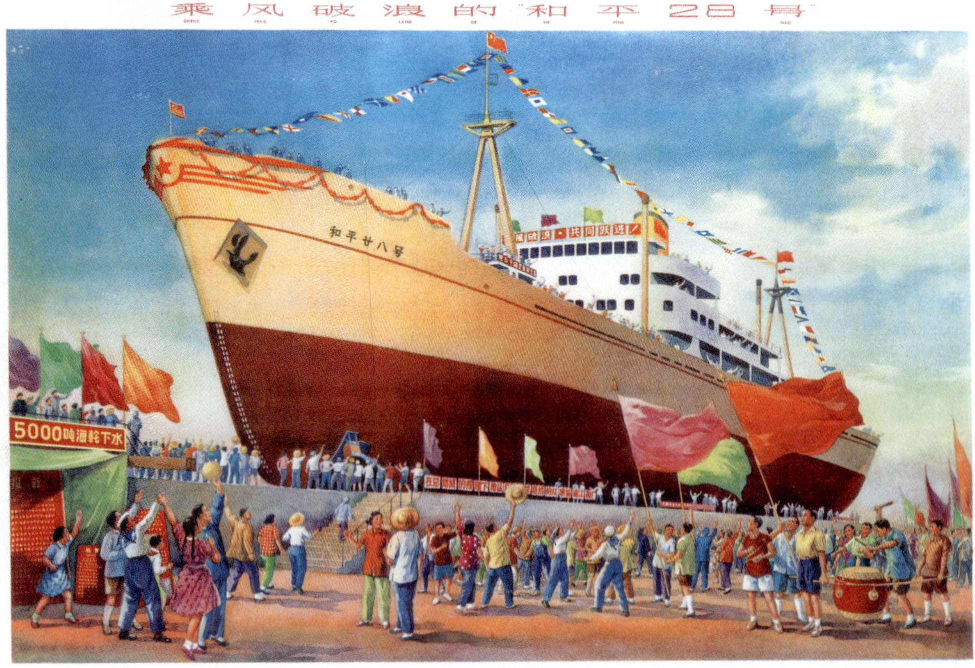

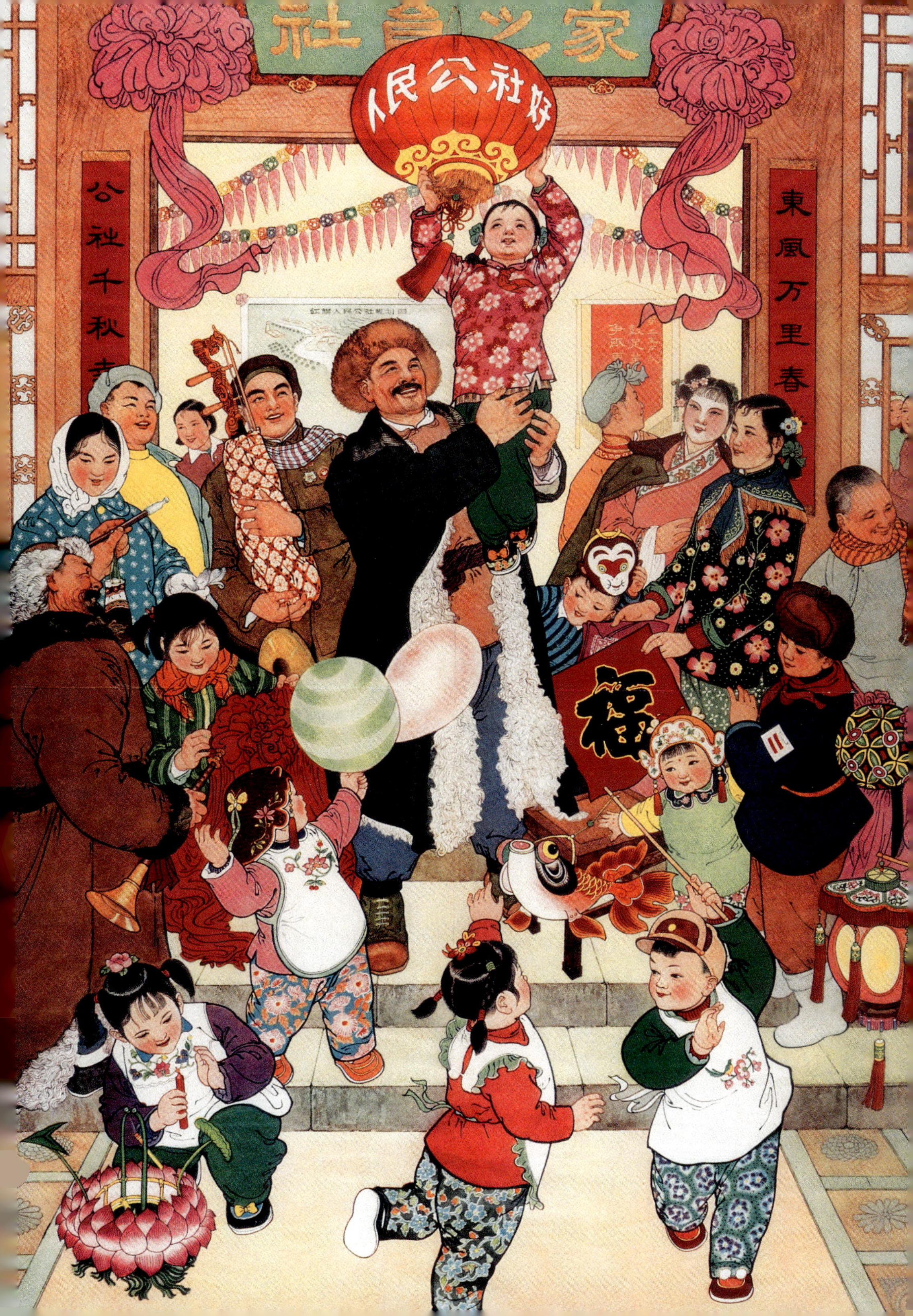

人民公社好
公社千秋
東風万里春
福

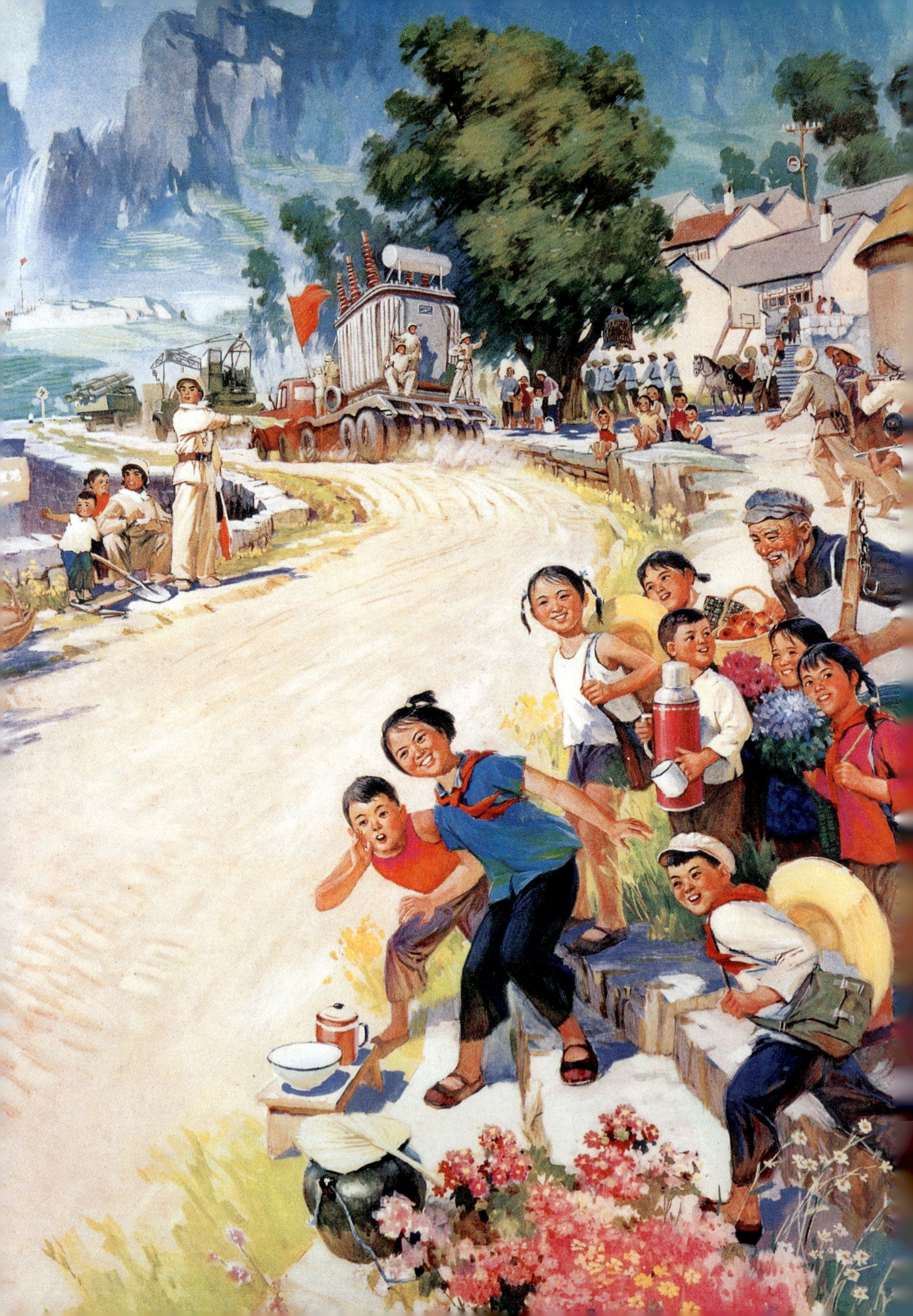

"The ultimate aim for which all communists strive is to bring about a socialist and communist society."

Das Endziel jedoch, das alle Kommunisten anstreben, ist die Verwirklichung der sozialistischen und kommunistischen Gesellschaft. ✶ Le but final de tout communiste, et pour lequel il doit lutter de toutes ses forces, c'est l'instauration définitive d'une société socialiste et communiste.

Life is exciting in a mountain village *Artist:* Zhang Chengsi; Liaoning People's Publishing House, 1973 *Print run:* 318,000; 0.11 Yuan

Das aufregende Leben in einem Bergdorf *Gemalt von* Zhang Chengsi; Volksverlag Liaoning, 1973 *Auflage:* 318 000; 0,11 Yuan

Les joies de la vie dans un village de montagne *Peintre :* Zhang Chengsi ; Éditions Populaires du Liaoning, 1973 *Tirage :* 318 000 ; 0,11 yuan

Opposite
Festival of sport in the mountain village *Flag, bottom right:* Toughen the body and develop the socialist rural regions; dedicated by the "Solidarity" brigade; People's Sports Publishing House, 1976 *Print run:* 100,000; 0.11 Yuan

Sportfest im Bergdorf *Fahne rechts unten:* Den Körper stählen und die ländlichen Regionen des Sozialismus aufbauen, gewidmet von der Brigade „Solidarität"; Volkssportverlag, 1976 *Auflage:* 100 000; 0,11 Yuan

Fête du sport au village de montagne *Drapeau en bas à droite :* Aguerrissons nous et édifions les régions rurales du socialisme, dédicace de la brigade « Solidarité » ; Éditions Populaires sportives, 1976 *Tirage :* 100 000 ; 0,11 yuan

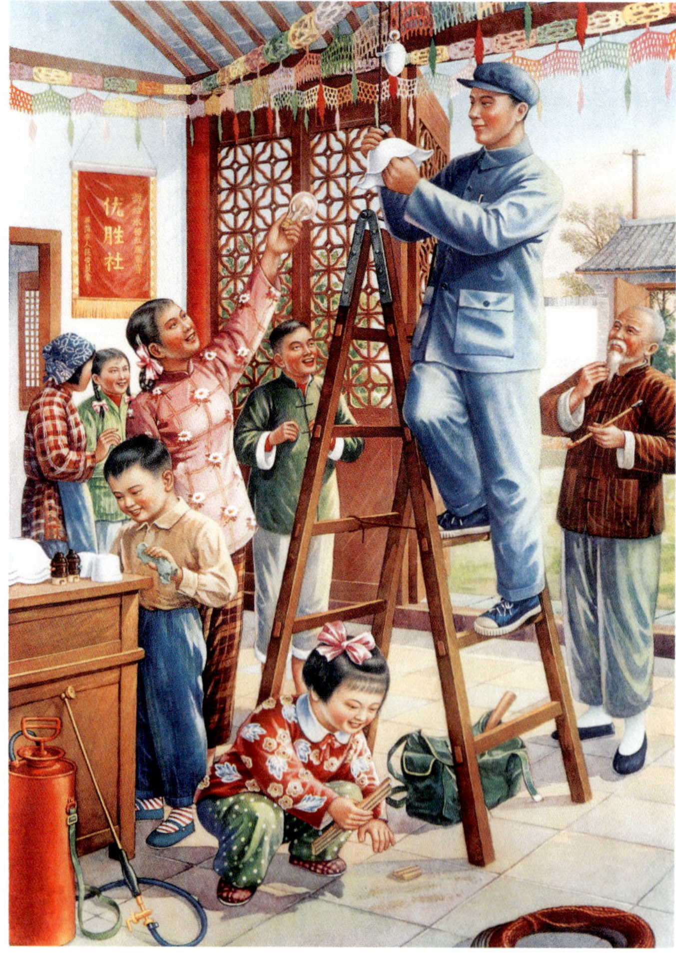

Through co-operation the electric light was fixed *Banner on the wall:* Co-operation for victory *Artist:* Zhang Yuqing; Shanghai Picture Publishing House, 1957 *Print run:* 10,000; 0.13 Yuan

In der Genossenschaft wird die elektrische Lampe angebracht *Banner an der Wand:* Siegesgenossenschaft *Gemalt von* Zhang Yuqing; Bilderverlag Shanghai, 1957 *Auflage:* 10 000; 0,13 Yuan

Installation de la lumière électrique à la coopérative *Bannière au mur :* Coopérative de la victoire *Peintre :* Zhang Yuqing ; Éditions des Images de Shanghai, 1957 *Tirage :* 10 000 ; 0,13 yuan

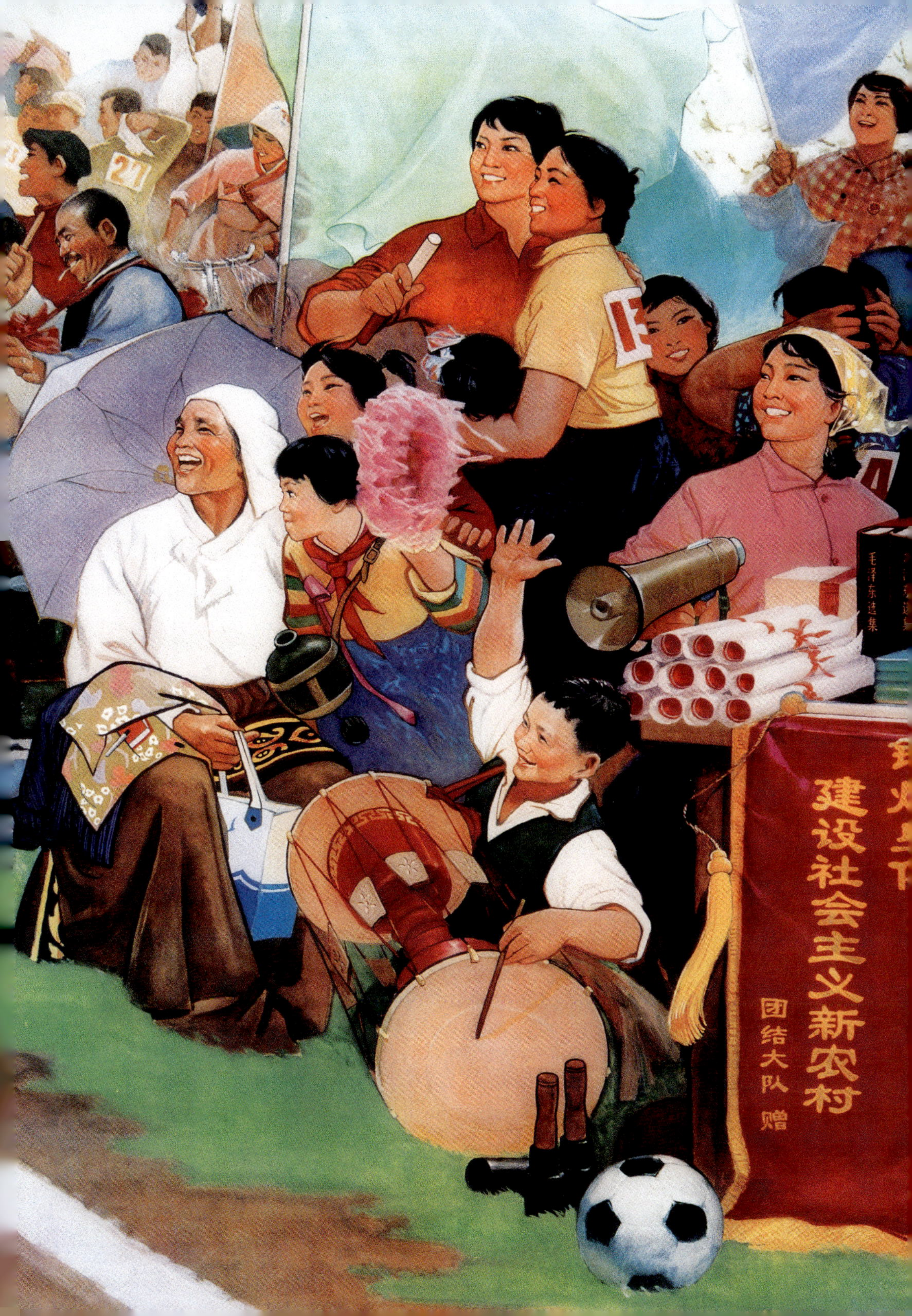

27
13
毛泽东选集
建设社会主义新农村
团结大队
赠

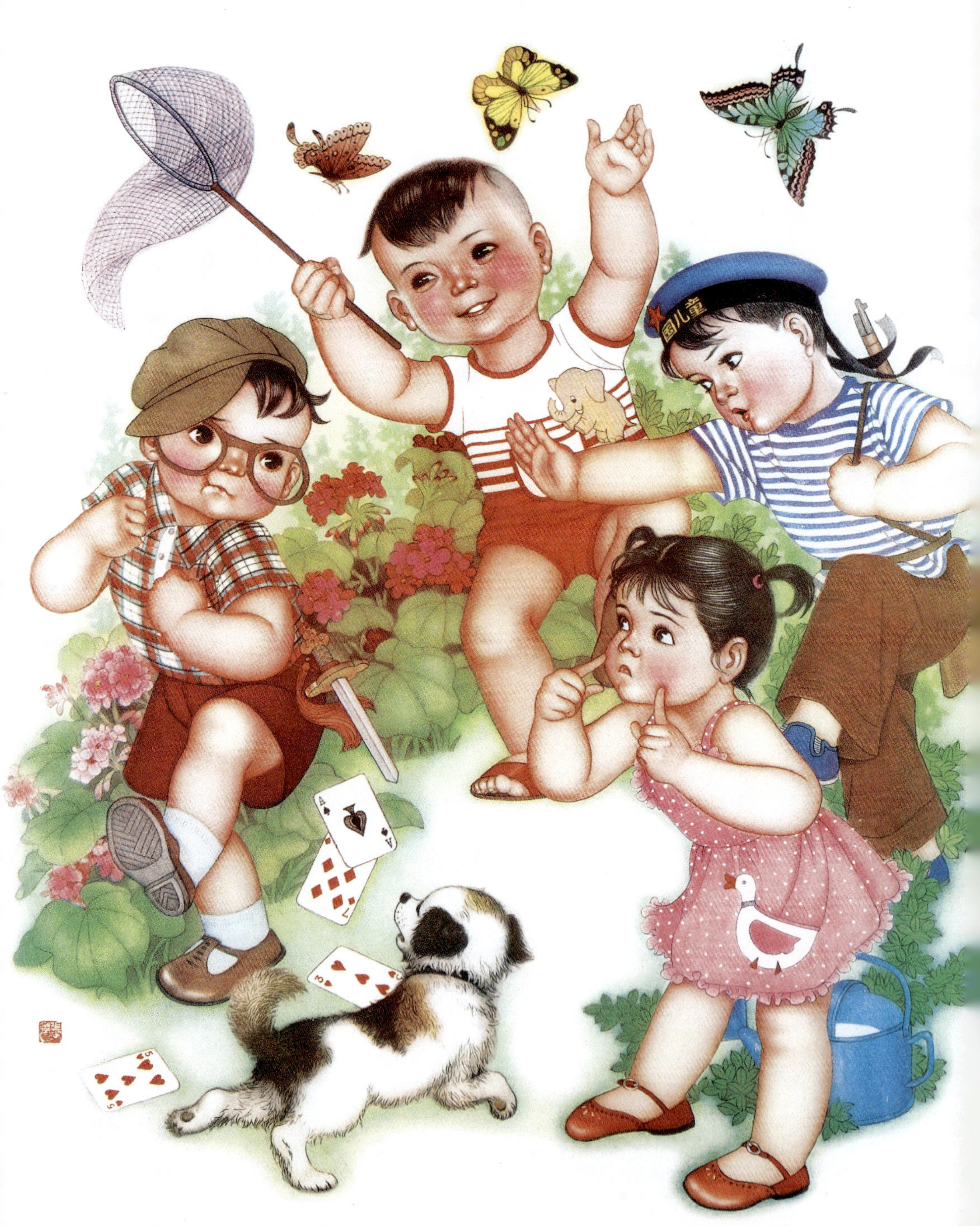

不学他的样

IV

THE CORRECT HANDLING OF CONTRADICTIONS AMONG THE PEOPLE

DIE RICHTIGE BEHANDLUNG DER WIDERSPRÜCHE IM VOLKE
LA JUSTE SOLUTION DES CONTRADICTIONS AU SEIN DU PEUPLE

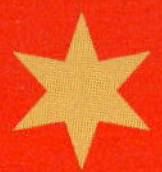

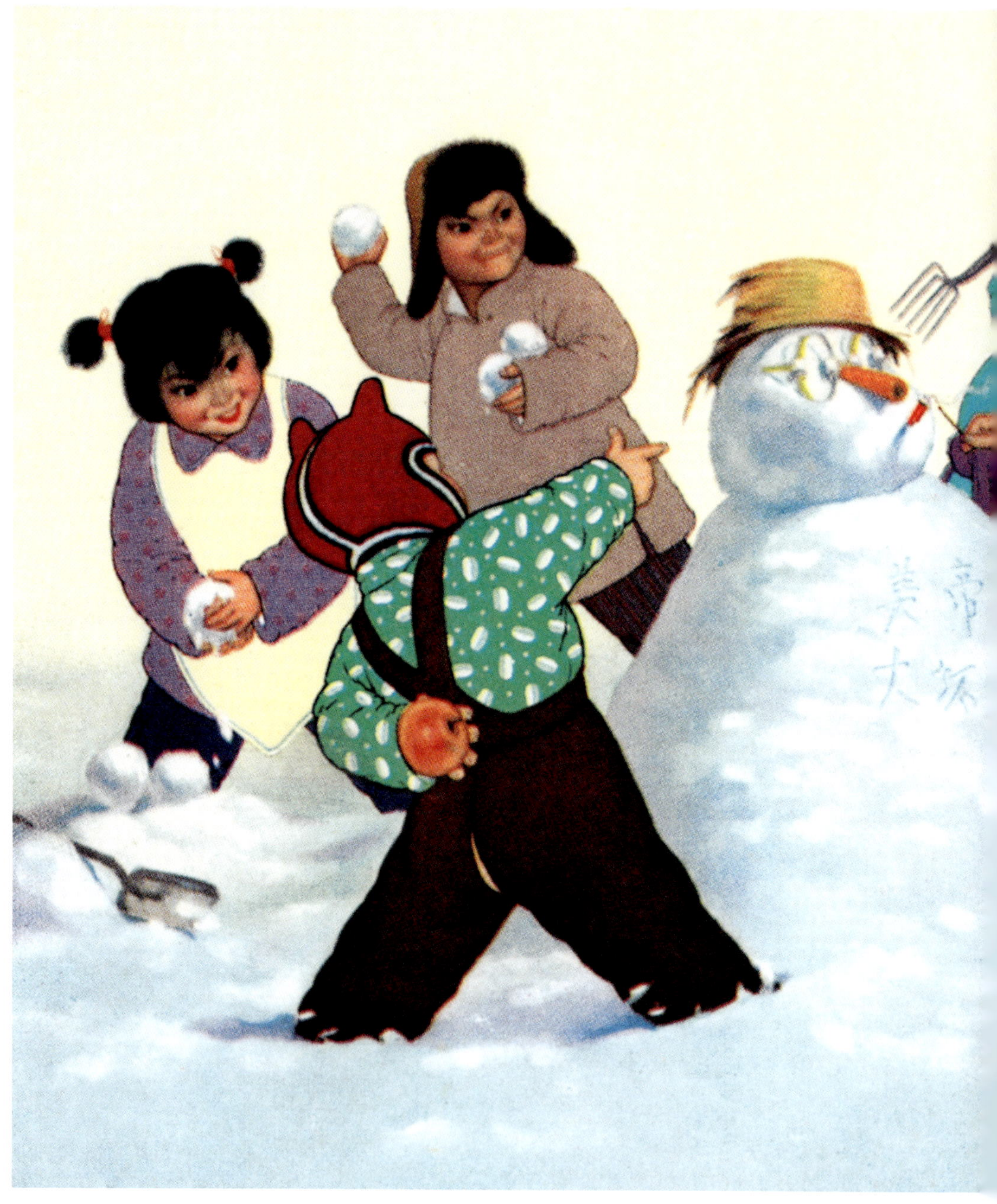

Page 108
Don't copy him *Artist:* Zhang Luan; Tianjin People's Art Publishing House, 1962
Print run: 250,000; 0.18 Yuan

Macht ihn nicht nach *Gemalt von* Zhang Luan; Volkskunstverlag Tianjin, 1962
Auflage: 250 000; 0,18 Yuan

Ne faites pas comme lui *Peintre :* Zhang Luan ; Éditions Populaires d'Art de Tianjin, 1962
Tirage : 250 000 ; 0,18 yuan

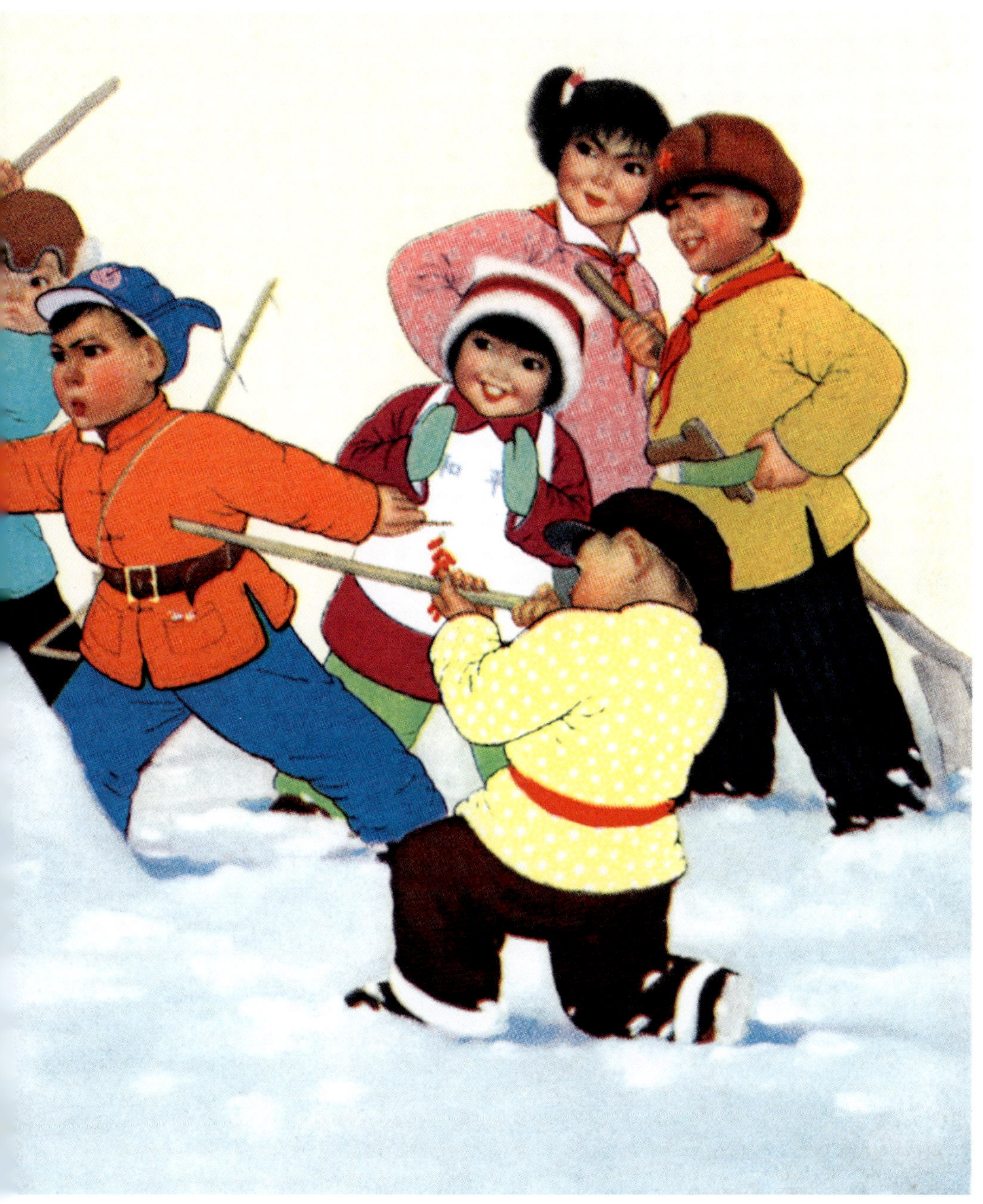

Punish the rascal! *Designed by:* House of Culture of the Xiong District of Hebei province, amended by Ren Jixue; Hebei People's Publishing House, 1966; 0.03 Yuan

Schlagt den Bösewicht! *Entwurf:* Kulturhaus des Kreises Xiong, Provinz Hebei, verbessert von Ren Jixue; Volksverlag Hebei, 1966; 0,03 Yuan

Frappez cette crapule ! *Conception :* Maison de la Culture du canton de Xiong, province du Hebei, affiche retravaillée par Ren Jixue ; Éditions Populaires d'Art du Hebei, 1966 ; 0,03 yuan

"Contradiction and struggle are universal and absolute, but the methods of resolving contradictions, that is, the forms of struggle, differ according to the differences in the nature of the contradictions."

Die Widersprüche und der Kampf sind allgemein, absolut, doch die Methoden zur Lösung der Widersprüche, das heißt die Formen des Kampfes, sind je nach dem Charakter der Widersprüche verschieden. ✶ La contradiction et la lutte sont universelles, absolues, mais les méthodes pour résoudre les contradictions, c'est-à-dire les formes de lutte, varient selon le caractère de ces contradictions.

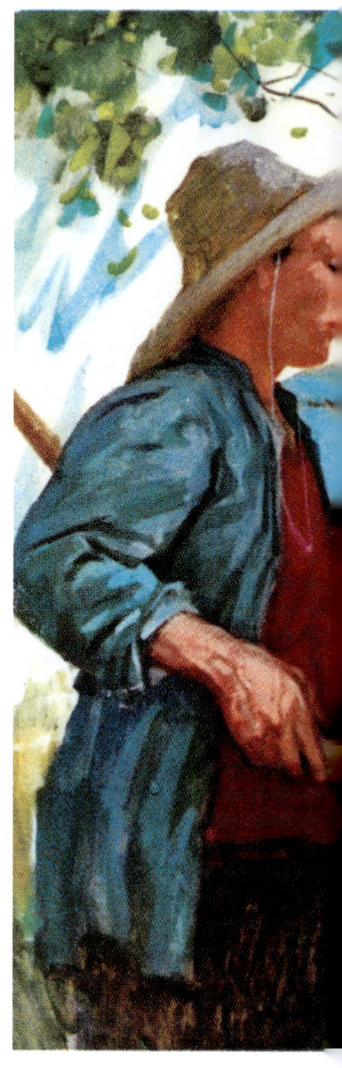

A bad element is publicly criticized, 1960s

Ein schlechtes Element wird öffentlich kritisiert, 1960er Jahre

Un mauvais élément fait l'objet d'une critique publique, années 1960

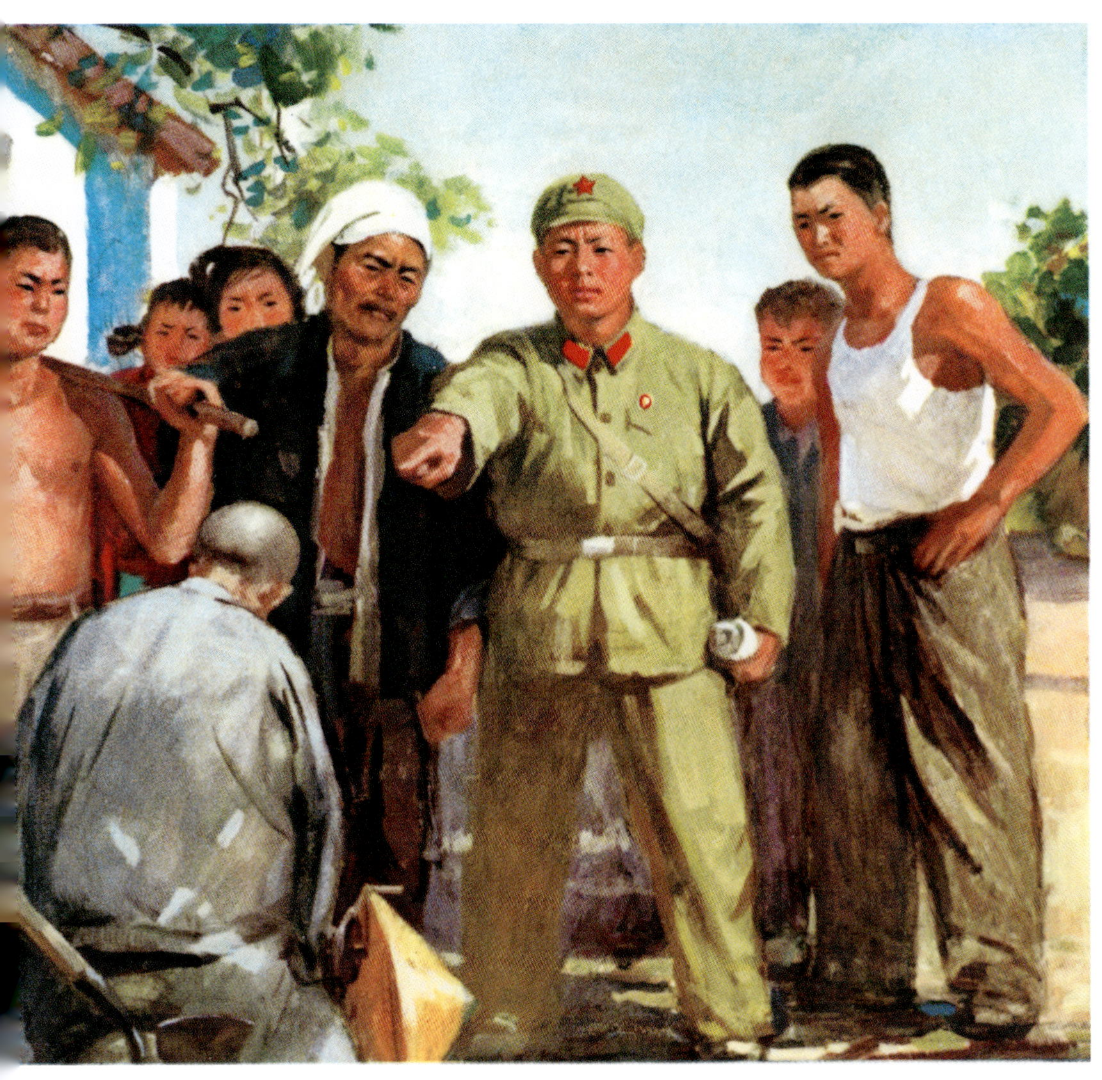

Pages 114–115

Study Marx and Lenin; think clearly *Book in woman's hand:* Lenin's State and Revolution *Book on the desk:* Selected Works of Mao Zedong *Magazine on the desk:* Red Flag *Wall newspaper in the background:* Make an intensive study of the theory of the dictatorship of the proletariat *Artist:* Zhang Daxin; Shanghai People's Publishing House, 1975; 0.11 Yuan

Marx und Lenin studieren, einen klaren Kopf haben *Buch in der Hand der Frau:* Staat und Revolution von Lenin *Buch auf dem Tisch:* Ausgewählte Werke Mao Zedongs *Zeitschrift auf dem Tisch:* Rote Fahne *Auf der Wandzeitung im Hintergrund:* Die Theorie der Diktatur des Proletariats intensiv studieren *Gemalt von* Zhang Daxin; Volksverlag Shanghai, 1975; 0,11 Yuan

Étudions Marx et Lénine pour avoir des idées claires *Livre dans la main de la femme :* « État et Révolution » de Lénine *Livre sur la table :* Œuvres choisies de Mao Zedong *Périodique sur la table :* Drapeau rouge *Sur le journal mural au fond :* Étudions scrupuleusement la théorie de la dictature du prolétariat *Peintre :* Zhang Daxin ; Éditions Populaires de Shanghai, 1975 ; 0,11 yuan

学好无产阶级专政的理论

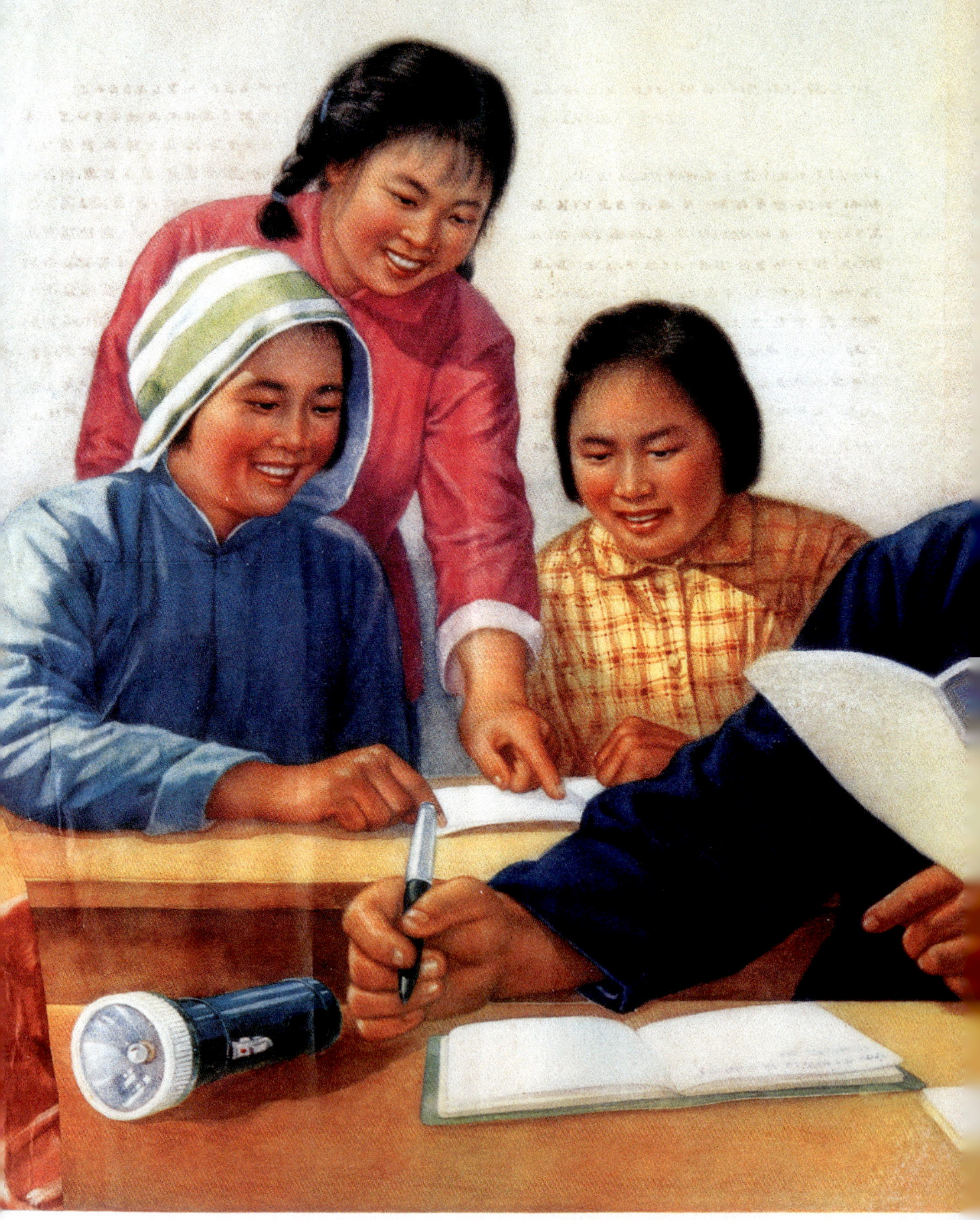

学习马列 眼明心亮

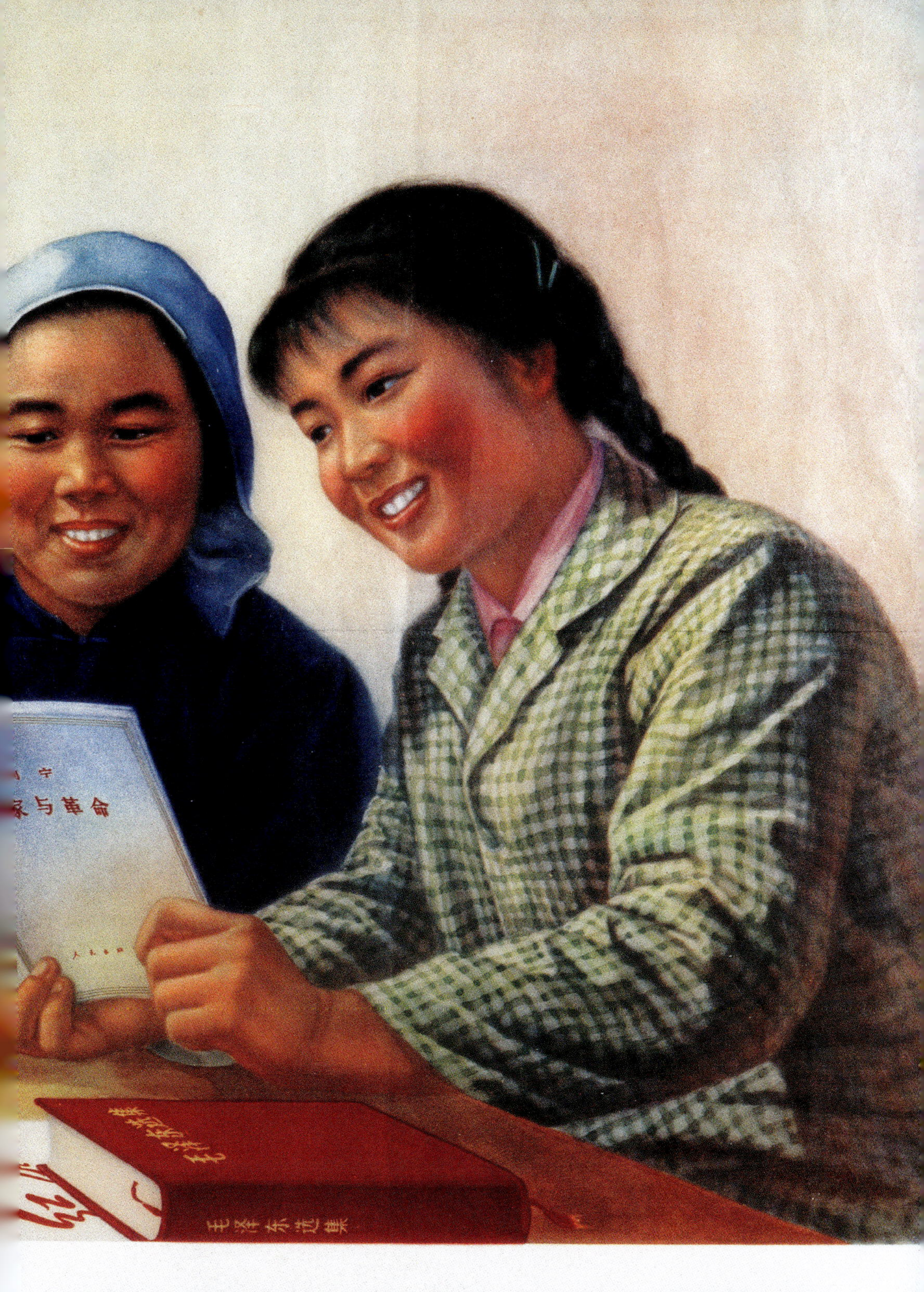
家与革命
毛泽东选集

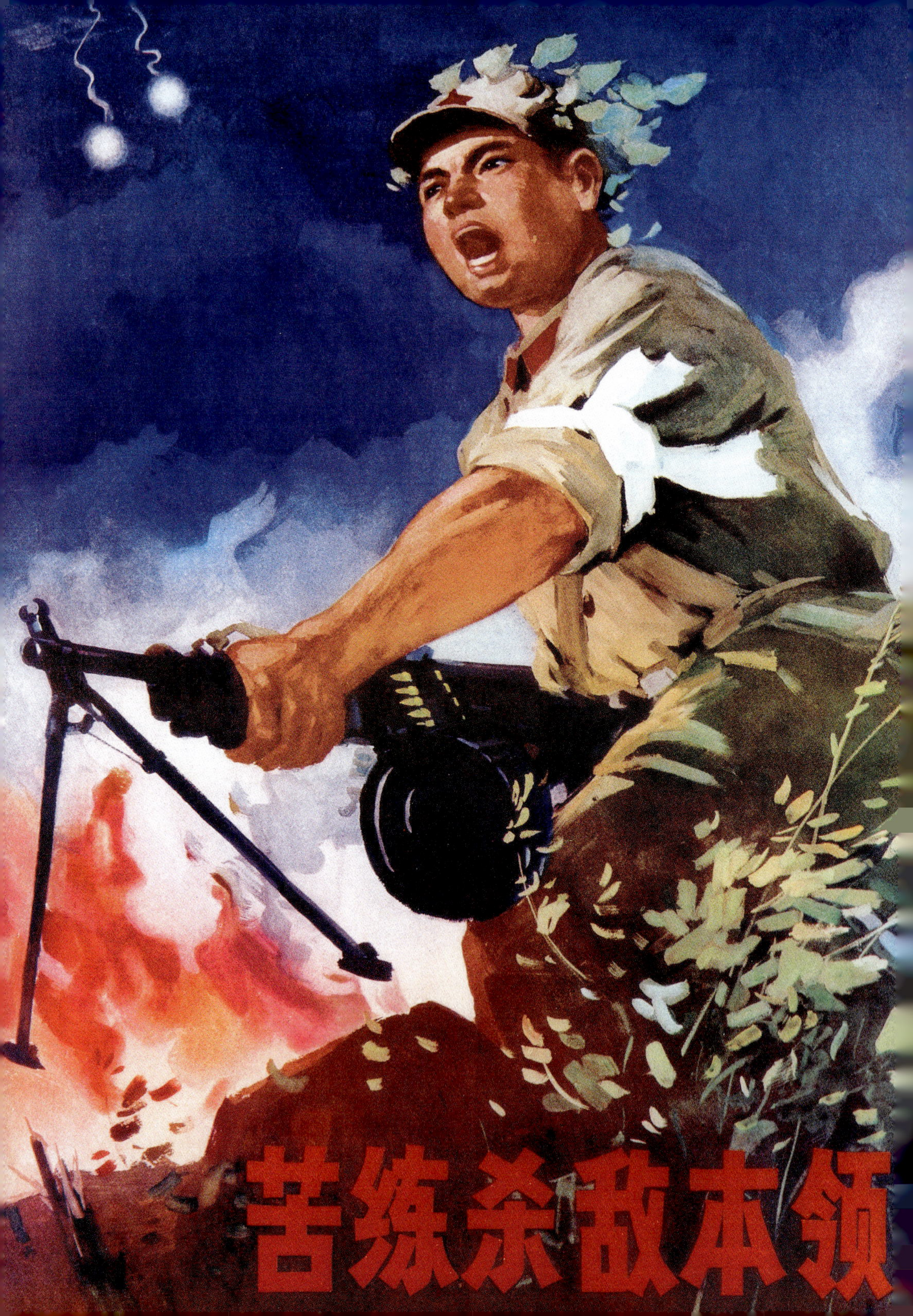
苦练杀敌本领

V

WAR AND PEACE

KRIEG UND FRIEDEN
LA GUERRE ET LA PAIX

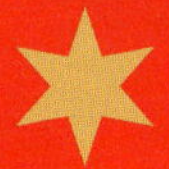

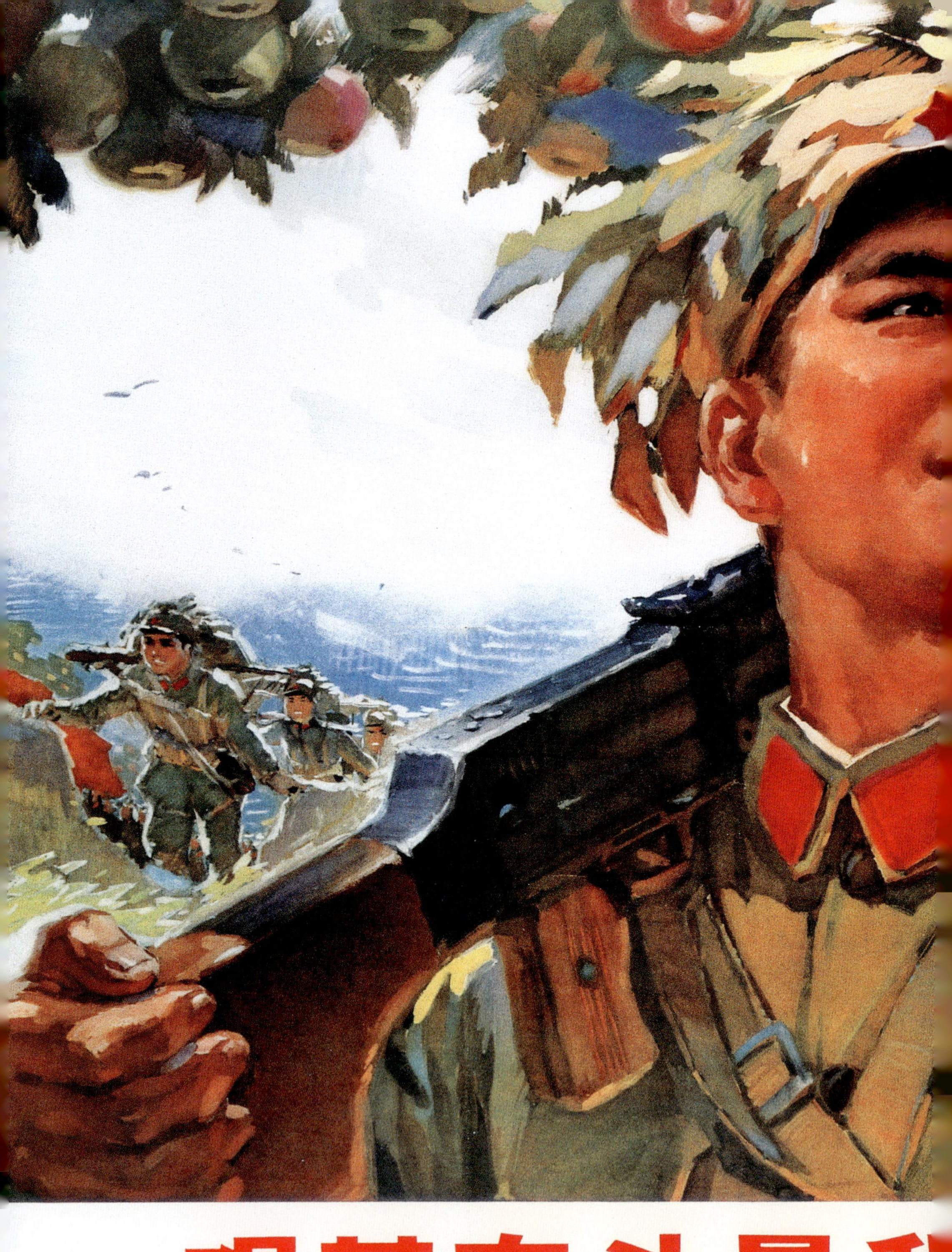

艰苦奋斗是我

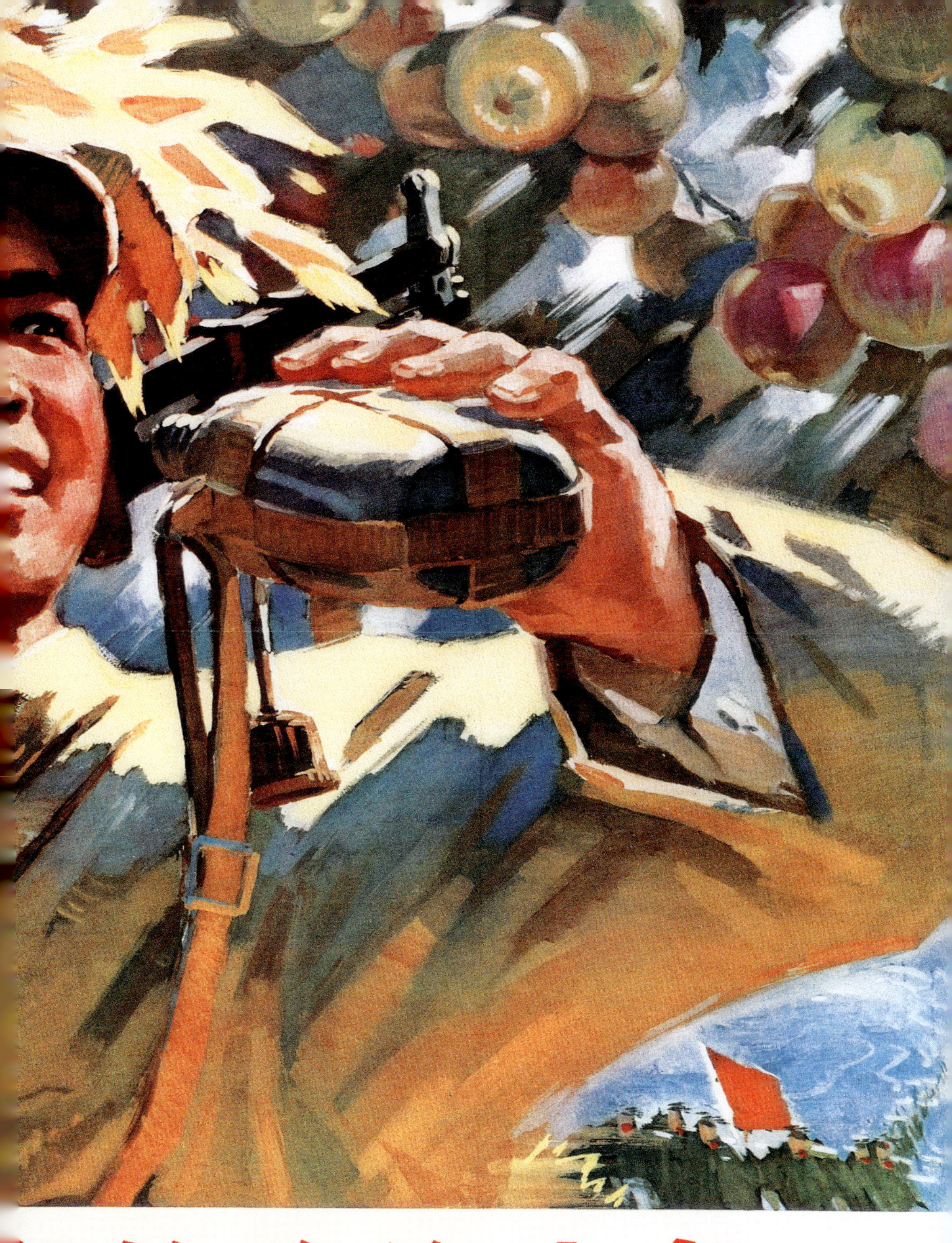

门的政治本色

Page 116
Submit to rigorous military training *Artist:* Zhao Guangtao; Tianjin People's Art Publishing House, 1972; 0.11 Yuan

Sich einer harten Kampfausbildung unterziehen *Gemalt von* Zhao Guangtao; Volkskunstverlag Tianjin, 1972; 0,11 Yuan

Soumettons-nous à un entraînement militaire intensif *Peintre :* Zhao Guangtao ; Éditions Populaires d'Art de Tianjin, 1972 ; 0,11 yuan

Pages 118–119
Fighting hard is a characteristic of our politics *Designed by:* Guangzhou Party Committee, Propaganda Department *Published by:* People's Art Publishing House, 1973; 0.22 Yuan

Hart kämpfen gehört zu unseren politischen Eigenschaften *Entwurf:* Propaganda-Abteilung des Parteikomitees Guangzhou *Herausgeber:* Volkskunstverlag, 1973; 0,22 Yuan

L'ardeur au combat fait partie de nos qualités politiques *Conception :* Département de la Propagande du Comité du Parti de Guangzhou *Éditeur :* Éditions Populaires d'Art, 1973 ; 0,22 yuan

Defend and develop the island together *Artist:* a soldier in the People's Liberation Army Navy; Zhejiang People's Publishing House, 3rd edn 1973 *Print run:* 1,320,001–2,180,000; 0.14 Yuan

Gemeinsam die Insel verteidigen und aufbauen *Gemalt von* einem Soldaten der Marine der Volksbefreiungsarmee; Volksverlag Zhejiang, 3. Aufl. 1973 *Auflage:* 1 320 001–2 180 000; 0,14 Yuan

Ensemble, défendons et construisons l'île *Peintre :* un soldat de la marine de l'Armée de Libération Populaire ; Éditions Populaires de Zhejiang, 1973 *Tirage :* 320 001–2 180 000 ; 0,14 yuan

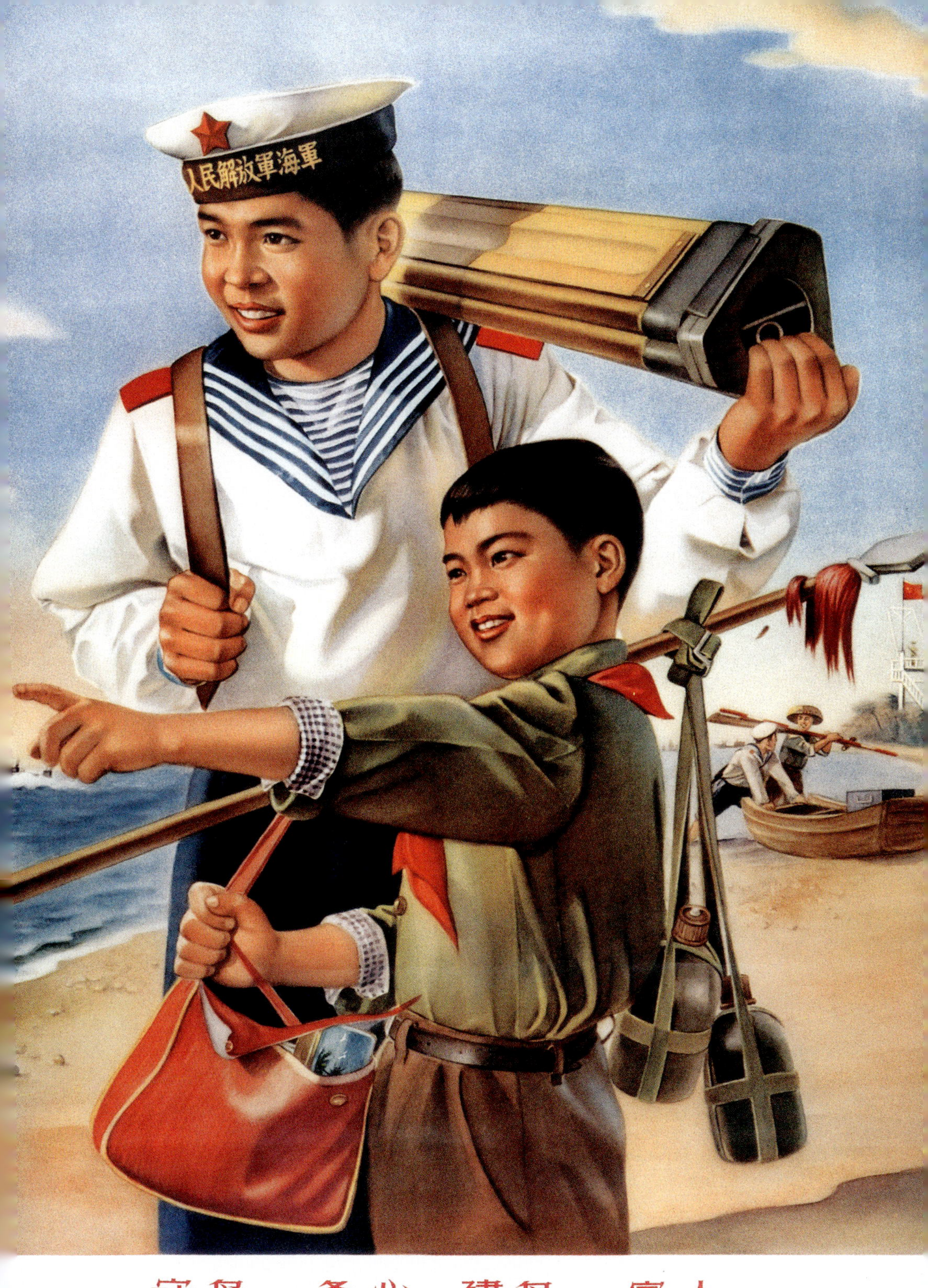

守岛一条心　建岛一家人

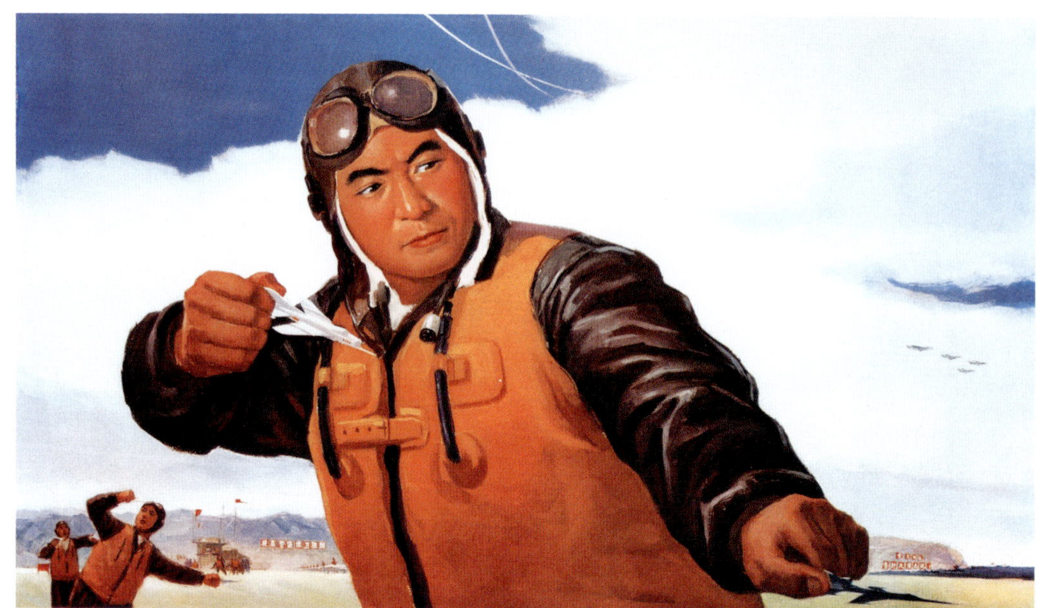

常备不懈务歼入侵之敌

Maintain constant vigilance, destroy the invading enemy *Banner in the distance, left:* Increase vigilance and defend the fatherland *Artist:* Jia Haijiang, a soldier in a Navy unit stationed in Shanghai; Shanghai People's Publishing House; 4th edn 1972

Beständige Wachsamkeit bewahren, die eindringenden Feinde vernichten *Transparent in der Ferne links:* Die Wachsamkeit erhöhen und das Vaterland verteidigen *Gemalt von* Jia Haijiang, einem Soldaten einer in Shanghai stationierten Einheit der Marine; Volksverlag Shanghai, 4. Aufl. 1972

Soyons constamment vigilants face à l'envahisseur, anéantissons l'ennemi *Banderole au fond à gauche :* Augmentons la vigilance pour défendre la patrie *Peintre :* Jia Hiajiang, soldat d'une unité de la marine stationnée à Shanghai, Éditions Populaires de Shanghai, 4e éd. 1972

Everyone is a soldier in defence of the fatherland Reporting for duty whenever called, trained for every form of action, always victorious in battle *Artist:* Weng Yizhi; Shanghai People's Publishing House, 1968; 0.30 Yuan

Jeder ein Soldat, das Vaterland zu verteidigen Bei jedem Appell sofort zur Stelle, zu jedem Kampfeinsatz befähigt, im Kampf immer siegreich *Gemalt von* Weng Yizhi; Volksverlag Shanghai, 1968; 0,30 Yuan

Que chacun soit un soldat prêt à défendre la patrie *En haut :* Présent dès que sonne l'heure du rassemblement, prêt à entrer en ligne à chaque opération militaire, toujours victorieux au combat *Peintre :* Weng Yizhi ; Éditions Populaires de Shanghai, 1968 ; 0,30 yuan

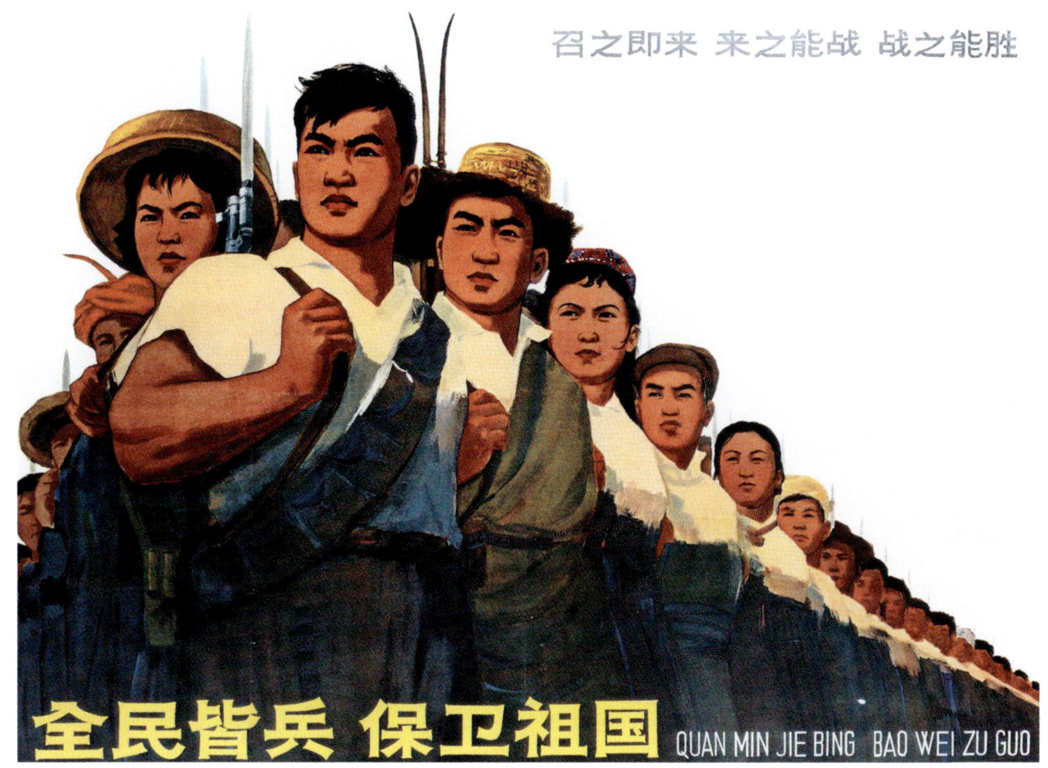

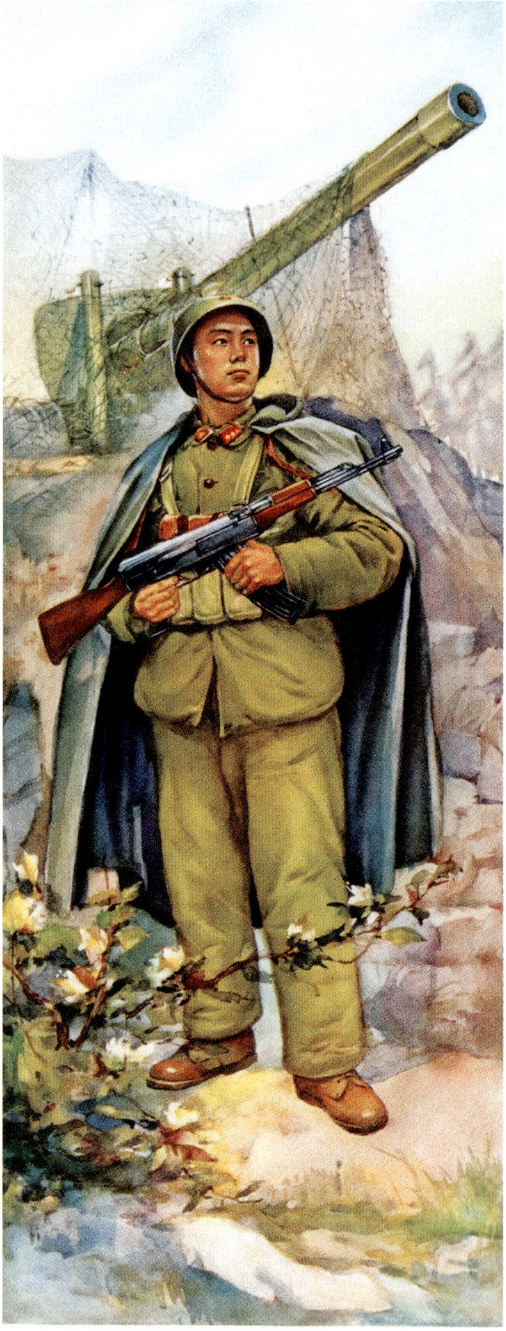

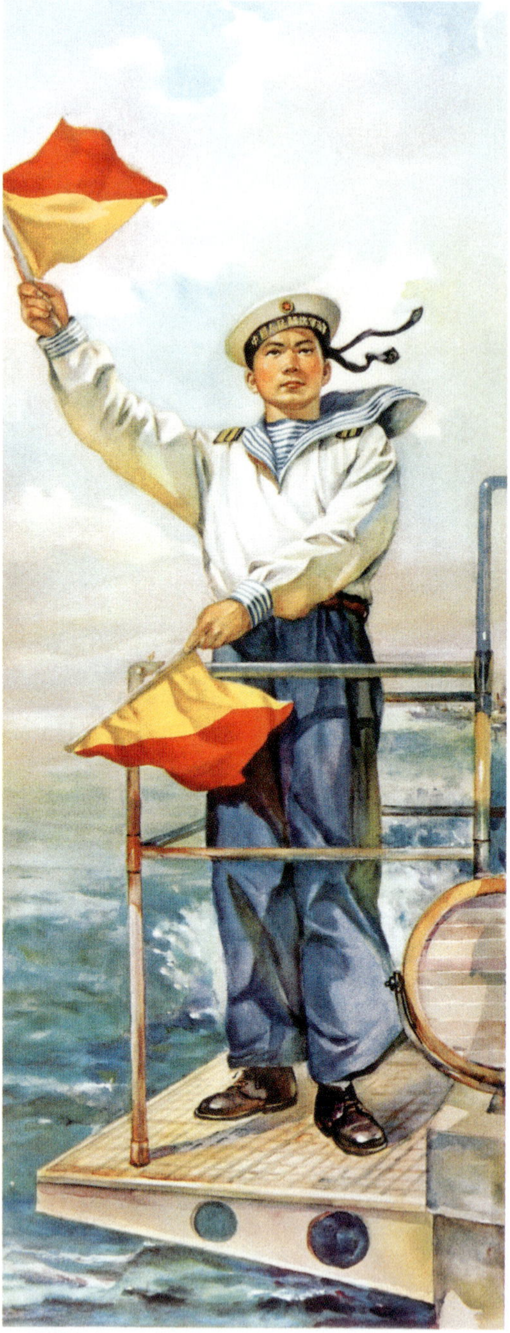

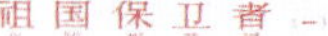

Defender of the fatherland (No. 1)
Verteidiger des Vaterlandes (Nr. 1)
Défenseur de la patrie (n° 1)

祖国保卫者

Defender of the fatherland (No. 2)
Verteidiger des Vaterlandes (Nr. 2)
Défenseur de la patrie (n° 2)

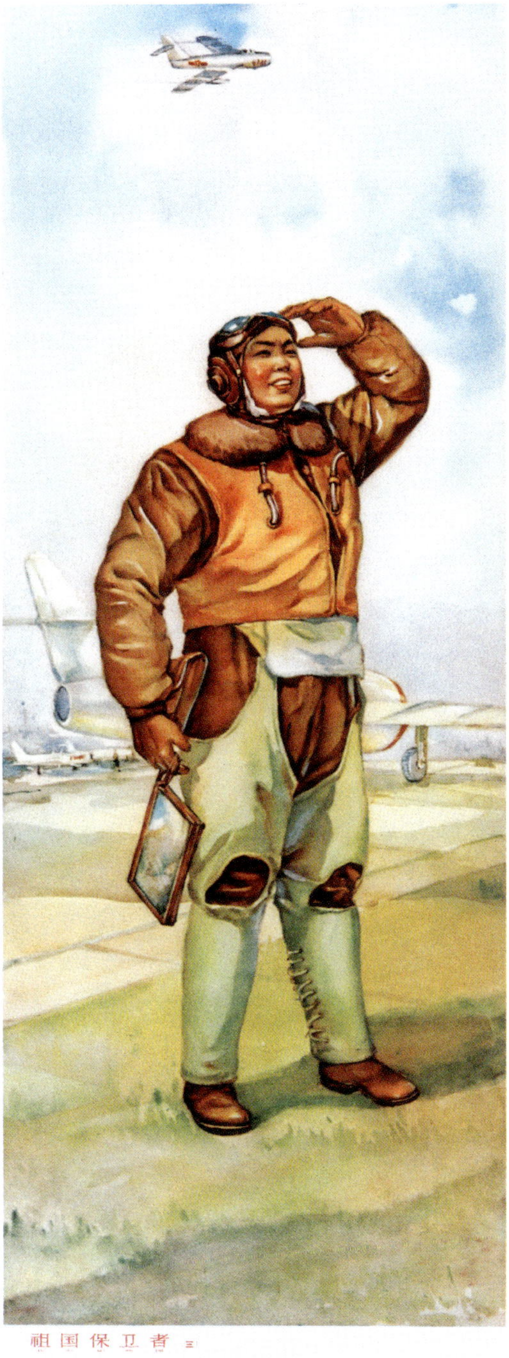

祖国保卫者 三

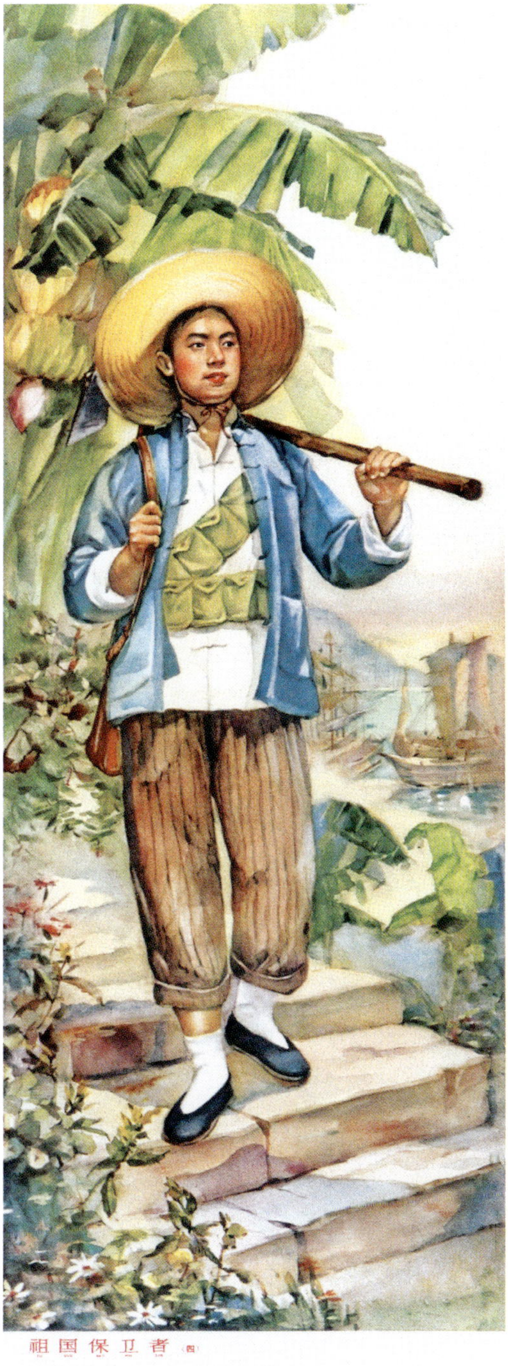

祖国保卫者 四

Defender of the fatherland (No. 3)
Verteidiger des Vaterlandes (Nr.3)
Défenseur de la patrie (n° 3)

Defender of the fatherland (No. 4)
Verteidiger des Vaterlandes (Nr.4)
Défenseur de la patrie (n° 4)

Mobilize to prepare for the event of war *Poster left:* Increase vigilance, defend the fatherland (Mao Zedong) *Poster right:* In the interest of the people stock up on grain to prepare for war or natural catastrophe (Mao Zedong) *Bottom border:* Chairman Mao teaches us that "It is very important there are frequent political campaigns urging mobilization in the event of war. Victory in war depends on this. There should be regular ideological education in preparation for the event of war with reference to the current situation and task, as well as the masses' ideological tendency. Permanent readiness must be firmly anchored in all heads in order that we be well prepared for an aggressive war from imperialism and social imperialism." *Published by:* War Preparation Office of Tianjin City Revolutionary Committee, 1971

Mobilisierung zur Vorbereitung auf einen Kriegsfall *Plakat links:* Die Wachsamkeit erhöhen, das Vaterland verteidigen (Mao Zedong) *Plakat rechts:* Im Interesse des Volkes Getreidevorräte für den Fall eines Krieges oder einer Naturkatastrophe anlegen (Mao Zedong) *Unterer Rand:* Der Vorsitzende Mao lehrt uns: „Es ist sehr wichtig, die politische Mobilisierung zum Krieg als eine häufige Kampagne durchzuführen. Ob man in einem Krieg siegen kann, hängt davon ab. Es soll, auf die aktuelle Lage und Aufgabe sowie die ideologische Tendenz der Massen bezugnehmend, regelmäßig die ideologische Erziehung zur Vorbereitung auf einen Kriegsfall durchgeführt werden. Die permanente Bereitschaft muss fest im Kopf verankert sein, damit wir auf einen Aggressionskrieg des Imperialismus und Sozialimperialismus gut vorbereitet sind." *Herausgeber:* Kriegsvorbereitungsbüro des Revolutionskomitees der Stadt Tianjin, 1971

Mobilisation de préparation à une guerre éventuelle *Affiche à gauche :* Intensifiez la vigilance, défendez la patrie. (Mao Zedong) *Affiche à droite :* Dans l'intérêt du peuple, stockez des céréales au cas où surviendrait une guerre ou une catastrophe naturelle. (Mao Zedong) *Marge inférieure :* Le président Mao nous enseigne : « Il est très important que la mobilisation politique en vue de la guerre prenne la forme insistante d'une campagne. La possibilité de vaincre en dépend. Tout en nous référant à la situation et à l'objectif actuels ainsi qu'à la tendance idéologique des masses, l'éducation idéologique de préparation à une éventuelle guerre est à faire de façon régulière. La disponibilité permanente doit être fermement ancrée dans les esprits si nous voulons être bien préparés à une guerre d'agression de la part de l'impérialisme et de l'impérialisme social. » *Éditeur :* Bureau de préparation à la guerre du Comité révolutionnaire de la ville de Tianjin, 1971

Pages 128–129

We love peace *Artist:* Li Mubai; Shanghai Picture Publishing House, 1st edn 1951, 10th edn 1955 *Print run:* 355,001–735,900; 0.15 Yuan

Wir lieben Frieden *Gemalt von* Li Mubai; Bilderverlag Shanghai, 1951, 10. Aufl. 1955 *Auflage:* 355 001–735 900; 0,15 Yuan

Nous aimons la paix *Peintre :* Li Mubai ; Éditions des Images de Shanghai, 1ère éd. 1951, 10e éd. 1955 *Tirage :* 355 001–735 900 ; 0,15 yuan

战备思想教育

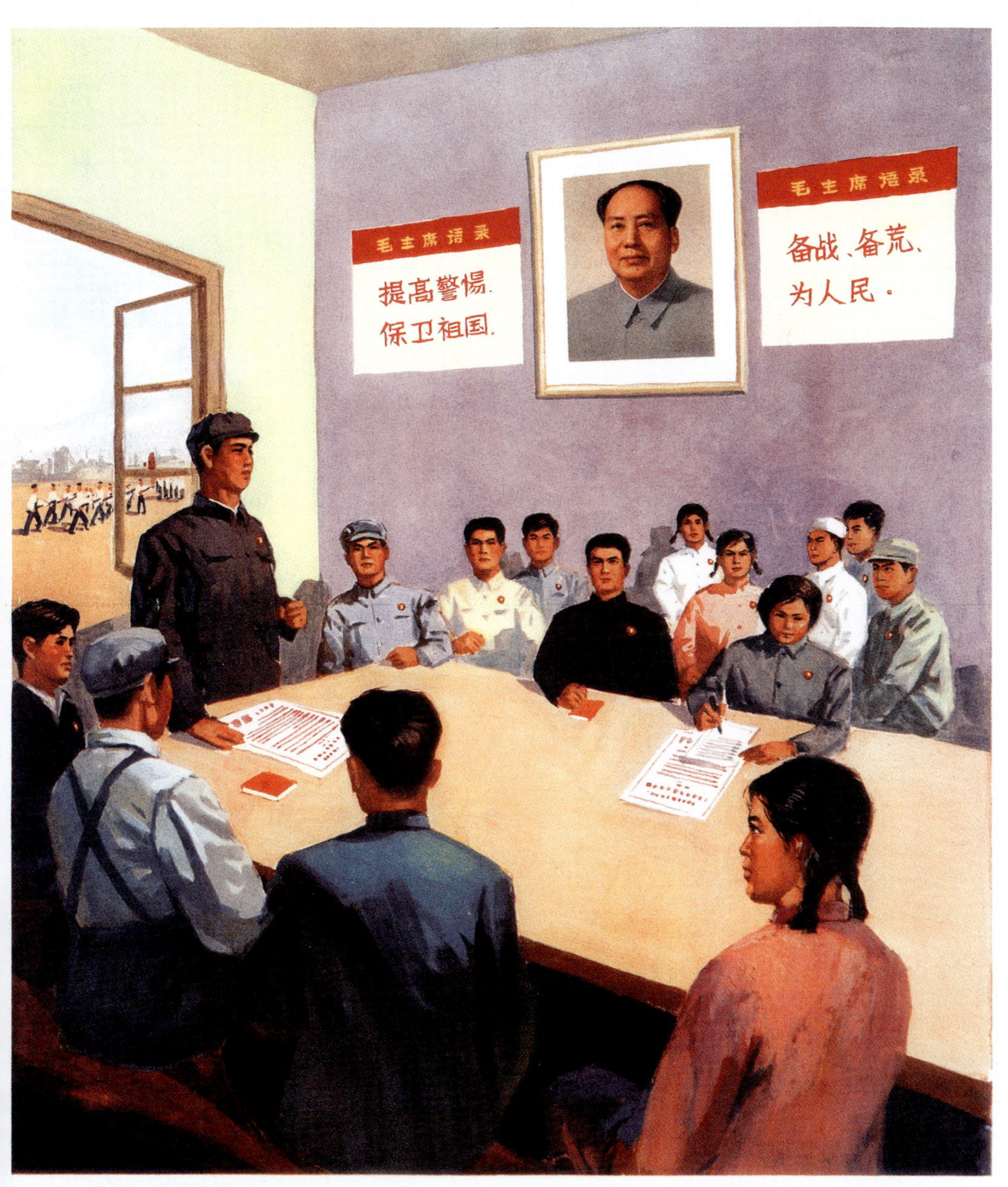

毛主席教导说："把战争的政治动员，变成经常的运动。这是一件绝大的事，战争首先要靠它取得胜利。"要结合形势、任务和群众的思想，进行经常性的战备思想教育，牢固树立常备不懈的思想，做好防御帝国主义、社会帝国主义侵略的准备。

我 們 熱

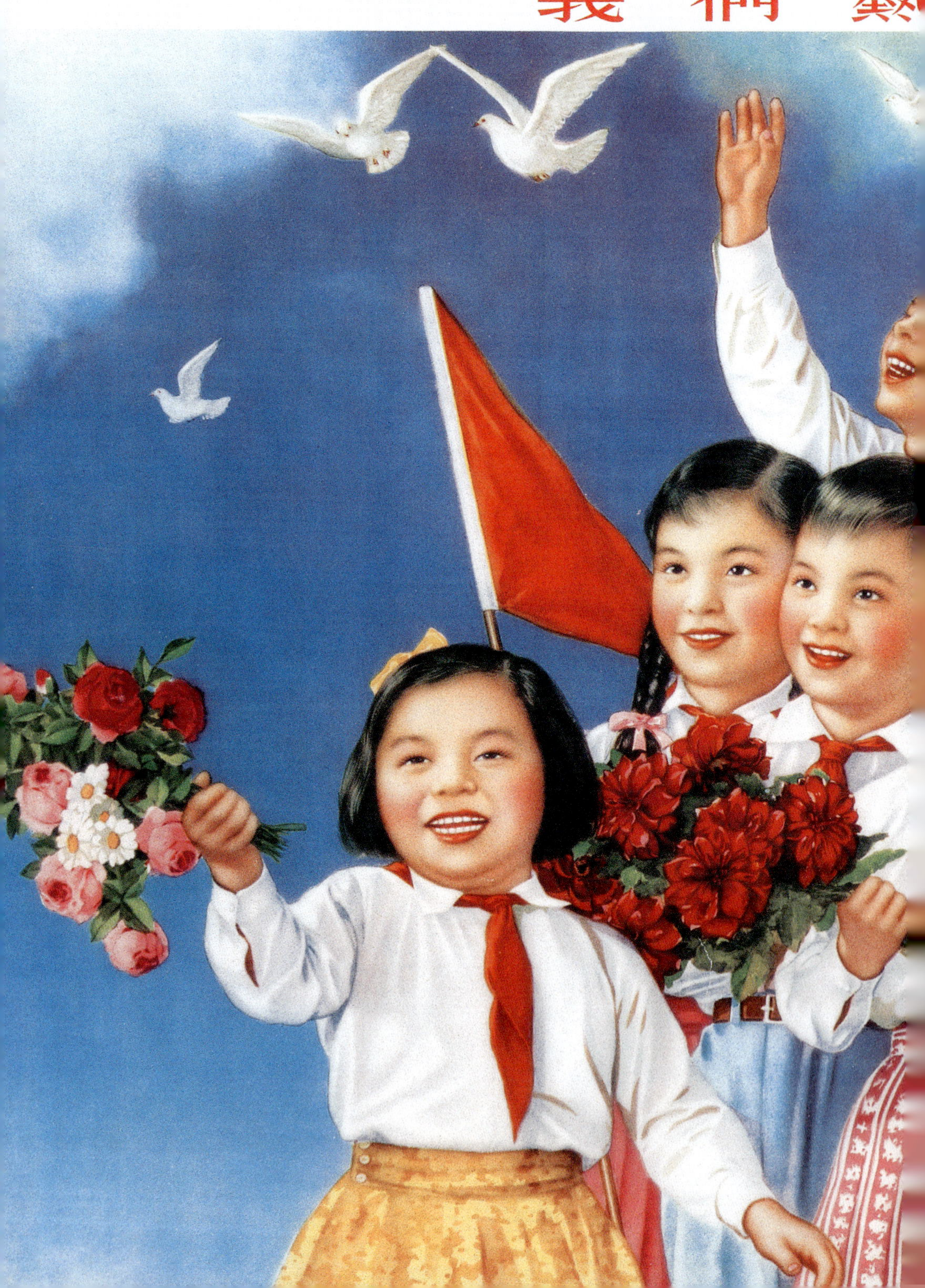

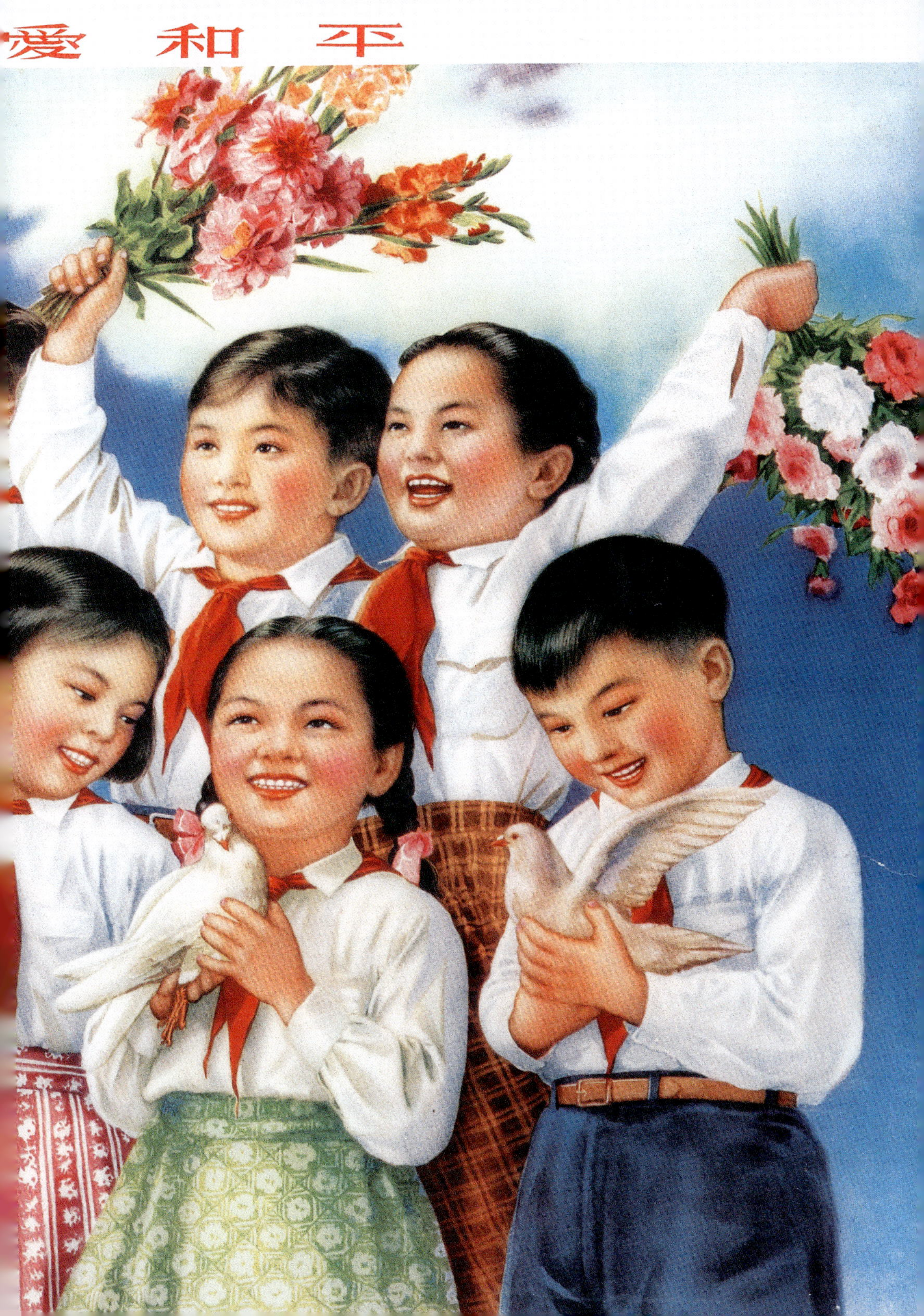
爱 和 平

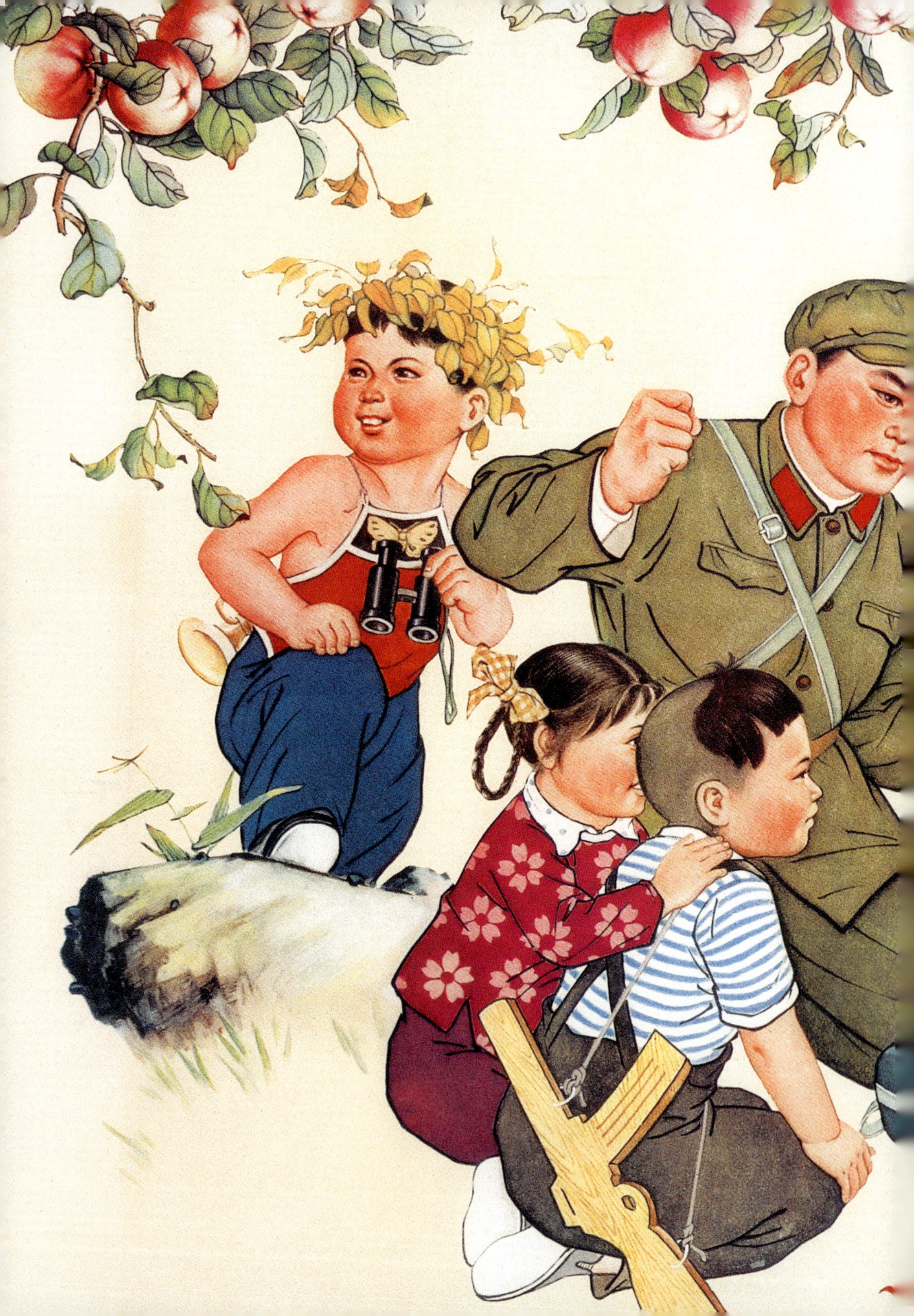

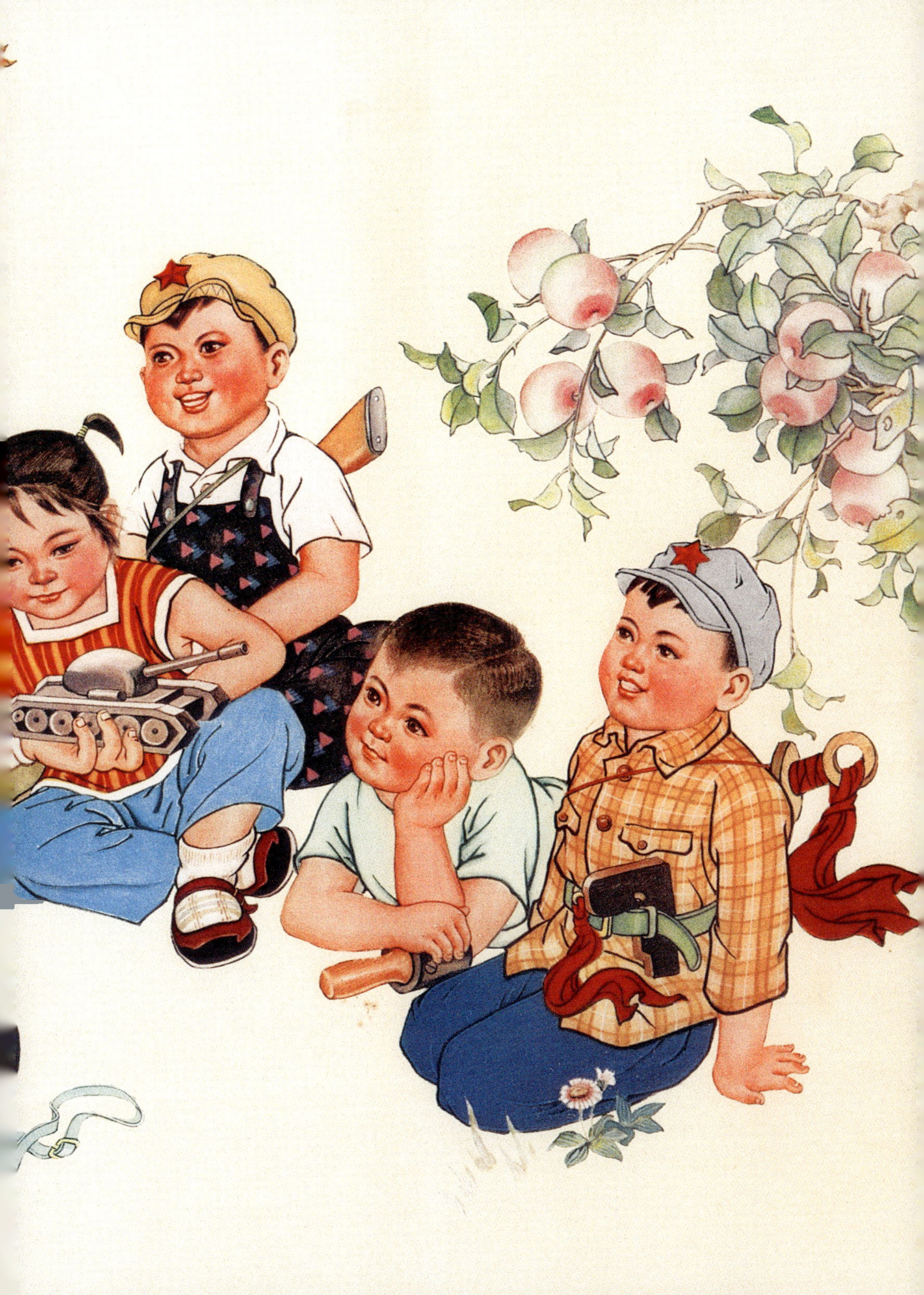

Pages 130–131

The story of Damansky Island* *Artists:* Hou Zemin, Cheng Hongye, and Hou Shuxun; Shanxi People's Publishing House, 1974; 0.14 Yuan
* An island in the Ussury River between China and the former Soviet Union and claimed by both countries. In 1969 there were several gun battles that Chinese media referred to as a "counter-attack in defence of Damansky Island."

Die Geschichte von der Damanskiinsel* *Gemalt von* Hou Zemin, Cheng Hongye und Hou Shuxun; Volksverlag Shanxi, 1974; 0,14 Yuan
* Eine Insel im Grenzfluss Ussuri zwischen China und der Sowjetunion, um die es 1969 mehrere Feuergefechte gab. In den chinesischen Medien wurde dies als „Gegenangriff zur Selbstverteidigung auf der Damanskiinsel" bezeichnet.

L'histoire de l'île Damanski* *Peintres :* Hou Zemin, Cheng Hongye et Hou Shuxun ; Éditions Populaires du Shanxi, 1974 ; 0,14 yuan
* Île de la rivière Ussuri entre la Chine et l'Union Soviétique à cause de laquelle plusieurs coups de feu furent échangés en 1969. Dans les médias chinois cet événement fut qualifié de « contre-offensive de légitime défense ».

Learning how to prepare for war *On the wall:* Study for the Revolution *On the wall poster:* Criticize Lin Biao's* capitalist military strategy *Artist:* Chao Dezhao, Northern District House of Culture; Tianjin People's Art Publishing House, 1972; 0.11 Yuan
* Lin Biao (1907–1971) is the one-time successor to Mao. He died in a plane crash while fleeing the country after a failed putsch in 1971.

Unterricht im Fach Vorbereitung auf den Kriegsfall *An der Wand:* Für die Revolution lernen *Auf dem Plakat an der Tafel:* Lin Biaos* kapitalistische Militärlinie verurteilen *Gemalt von* Chao Dezhao, Kulturhaus des Nordbezirks; Volkskunstverlag Tianjin, 1972; 0,11 Yuan
* Lin Biao (1907–1971) war der Nachfolger Maos, der bei der Flucht nach einem gescheiterten Putsch 1971 mit dem Flugzeug abgestürzt und umgekommen ist.

Enseignement de la discipline « Préparation à la guerre » *Au mur :* Instruisons-nous pour la révolution *Sur l'affiche au tableau :* Condamnons la ligne militaire capitaliste de Lin Biao* *Peintre :* Chao Dezhao, Maison de la Culture du quartier nord ; Éditions Populaires de Tianjin, 1972 ; 0,11 yuan
* Lin Biao (1907–1971), le successeur initial de Mao, mourut dans un crash d'avion tandis qu'il s'enfuyait après l'échec d'un putsch en 1971.

Pages 134–135

Red flowers blossom on the former battleground *Artist:* Zhang Enliang; Liaoning People's Publishing House, 1972; 0.12 Yuan

Rote Blumen blühen auf dem ehemaligen Schlachtfeld *Gemalt von* Zhang Enliang; Volksverlag Liaoning, 1972; 0,12 Yuan

Des fleurs rouges poussent sur l'ancien champ de bataille *Peintre :* Zhang Enliang ; Éditions Populaires du Liaoning, 1972 ; 0,12 yuan

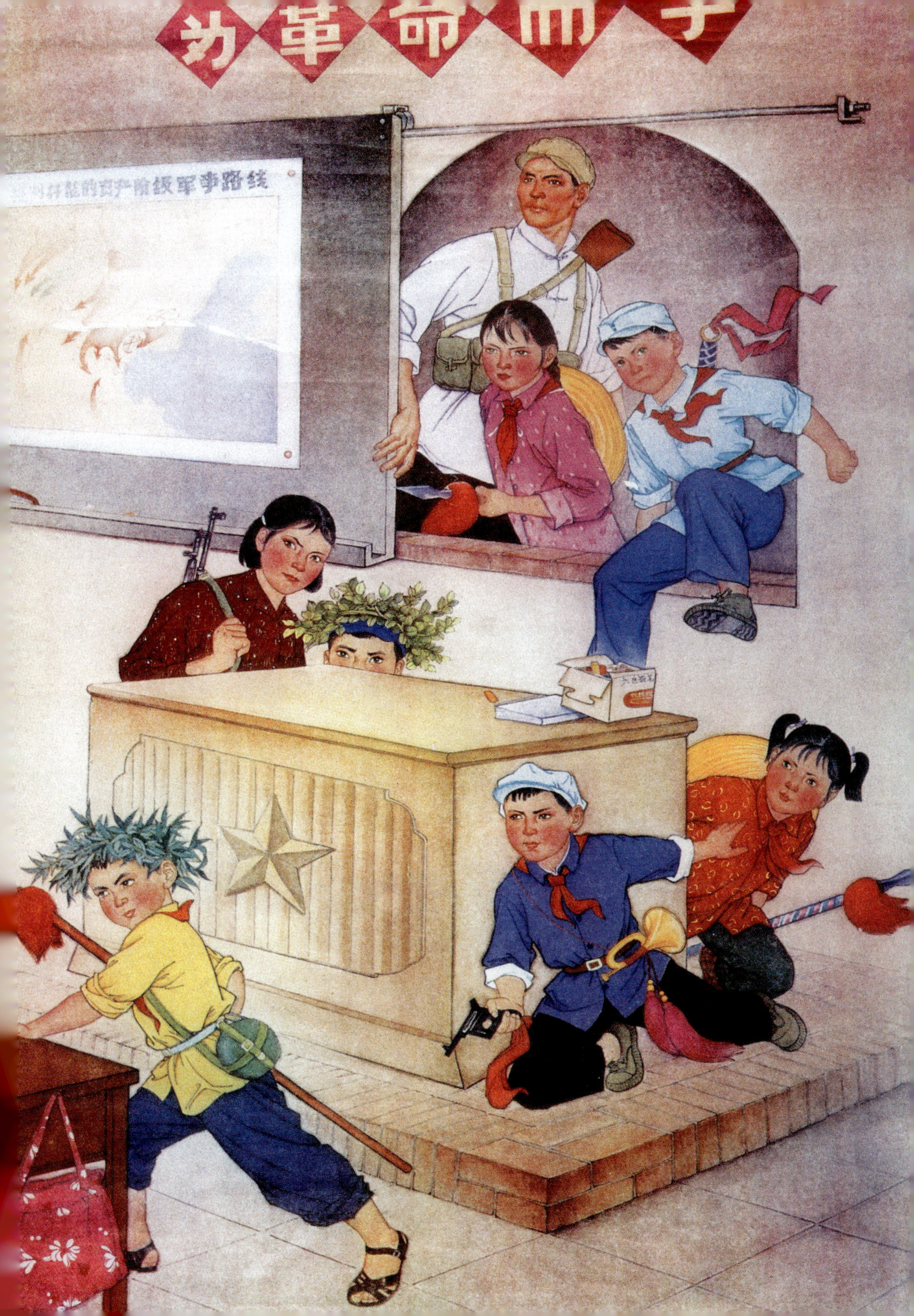
革命
林彪的资产阶级军事路线

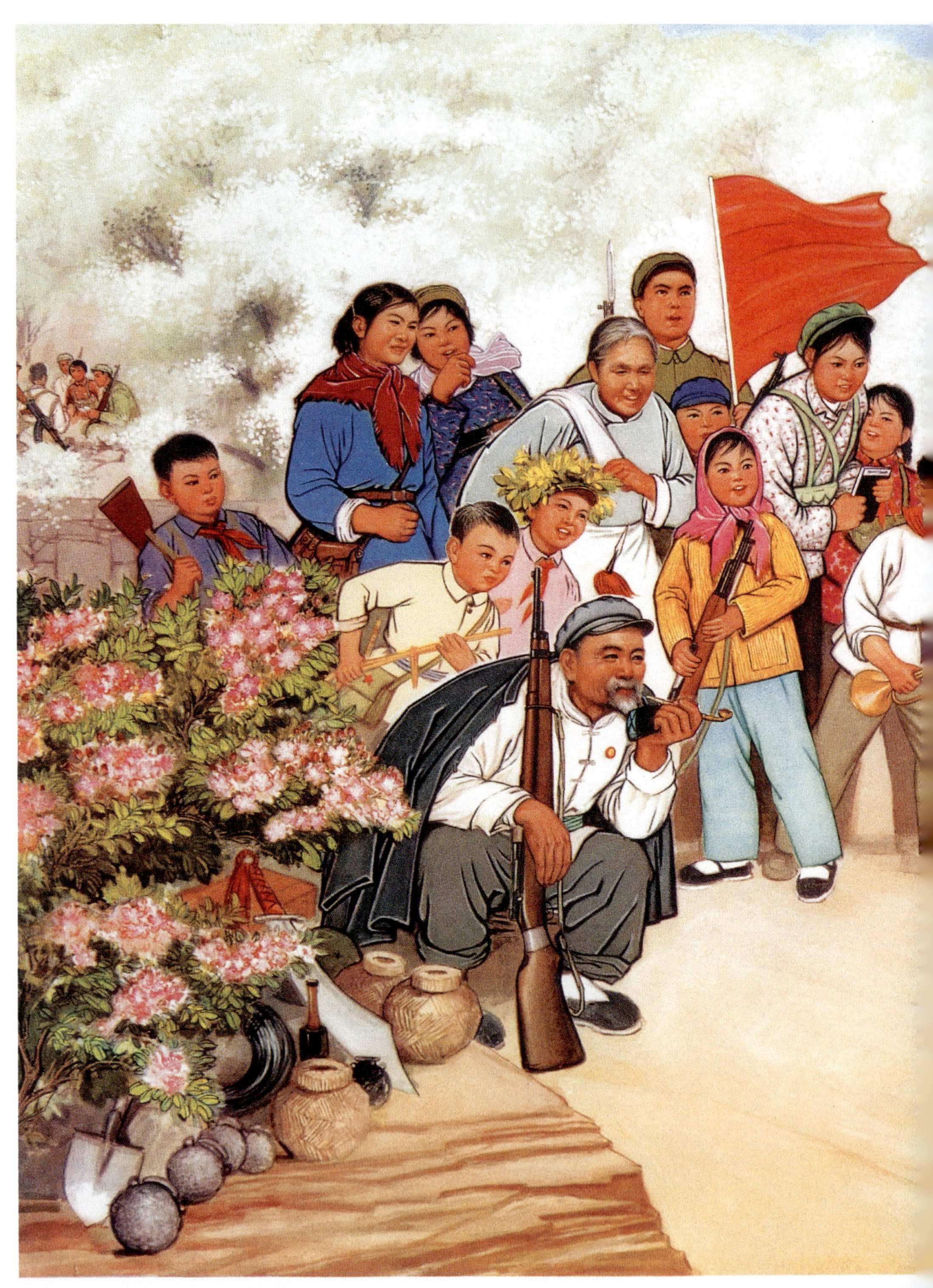

当年战场开红花

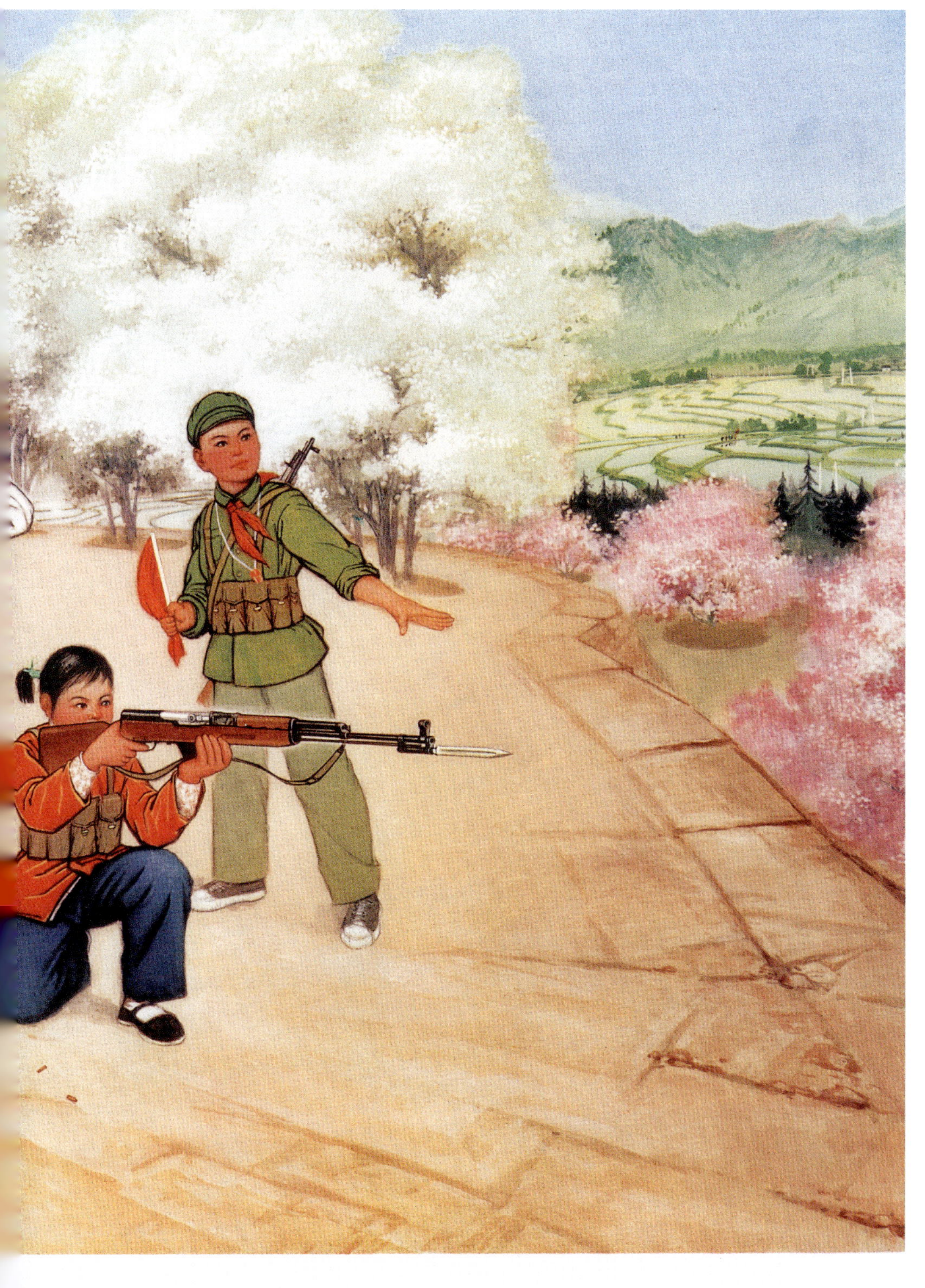

和 平

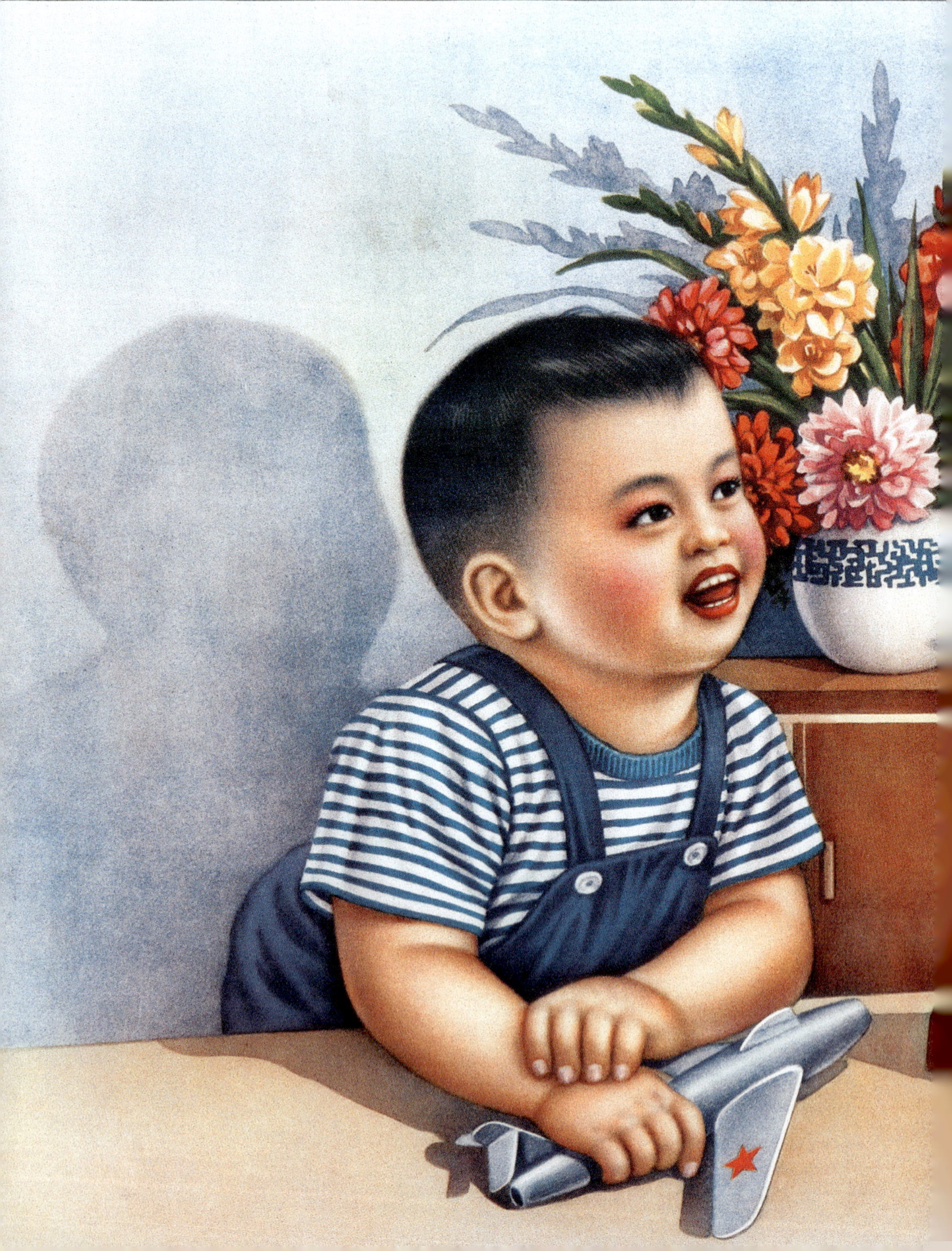

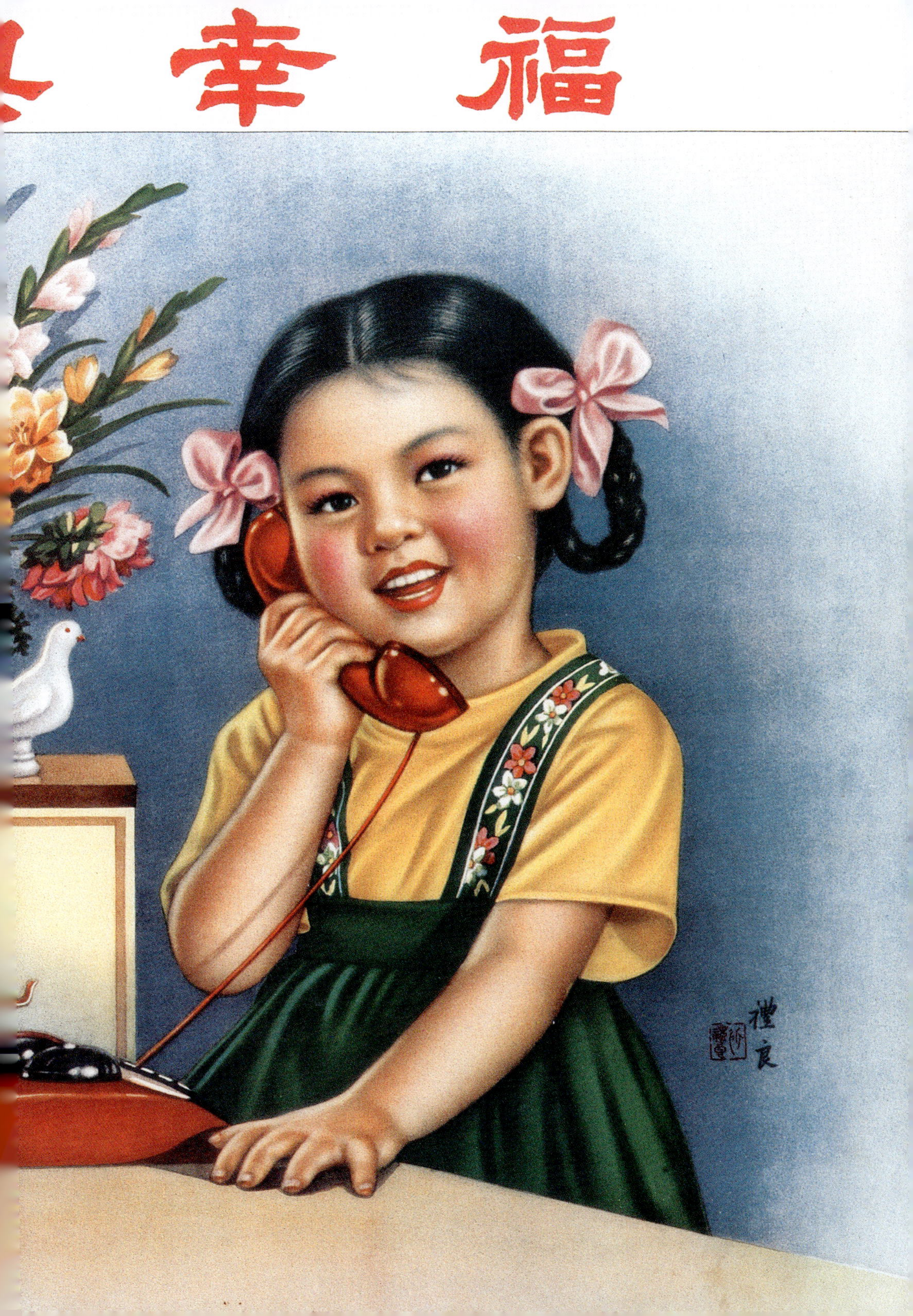

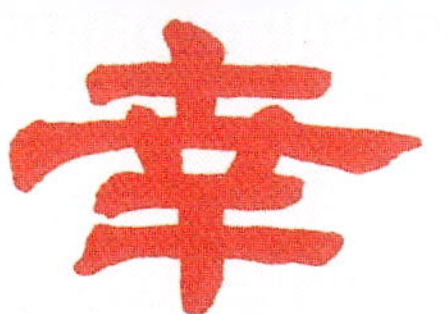
幸
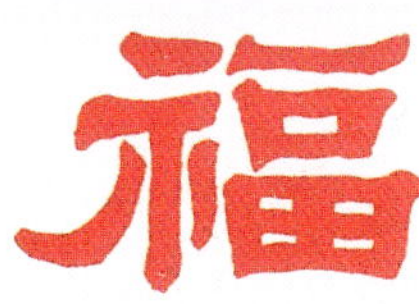
福

Pages 136–137
Peace and happiness *Artist:* Xin Liliang *Published and distributed by:* Shanghai Picture Publishing House, 1st new edn, 5th edn 1954 *Print run:* 100,001–1,130,000; 1.80 Yuan

Frieden und Glück *Gemalt von* Xin Liliang *Herausgeber und Vertrieb:* Bilderverlag Shanghai, 1. neue Ausgabe, 5. Aufl. 1954 *Auflage:* 100 001–130 000; 1,80 Yuan

La paix et le bonheur *Peintre :* Xin Liliang *Éditeur et distributeur :* Éditions des Images de Shanghai, 1ère nouvelle éd., 5e éd. 1954 *Tirage :* 100 001–130 000 ; 1,80 yuan

"It can therefore be said that politics is war without bloodshed while war is politics with bloodshed."

Man kann deshalb sagen: Die Politik ist Krieg ohne Blutvergießen, der Krieg ist Politik mit Blutvergießen. ✶ C'est pourquoi l'on peut dire que la politique est une guerre sans effusion de sang et la guerre une politique avec effusion de sang.

Nuclear civil defence measures *Quotation above the title:* "People of the world unite! Revolt against any war of aggression by imperialism and social imperialism, particularly against a nuclear war of aggression! In the event of such a war, the people of the world should destroy the war of aggression with the help of a revolutionary war. From now on we must be prepared for this!" Mao Zedong *Published and printed by:* the People's Air Raid Commando of the City of Qingdao's Revolutionary Committee, 1970

Schutzmaßnahmen gegen Atomwaffen *Zitat über der Überschrift:* „Völker der ganzen Welt, vereinigt euch! Lehnt euch gegen jeden Aggressionskrieg des Imperialismus und Sozialimperialismus auf, insbesondere gegen einen atomaren Aggressionskrieg! Sollte sich ein solcher Krieg ereignen, müssen Völker der ganzen Welt mithilfe eines revolutionären Krieges den Aggressionskrieg vernichten. Ab jetzt muss man darauf vorbereitet sein!" Mao Zedong *Herausgegeben und gedruckt vom* Volksluftschutzkommando des Revolutionskomitees der Stadt Qingdao, 1970

Mesures de protection contre les armes nucléaires « Peuples du monde entier, unissez-vous ! Insurgez-vous contre cette guerre d'agression de l'impérialisme et de l'impérialisme social-démocrate, en particulier contre une guerre nucléaire ! Si ce genre de guerre devait se produire, les peuples du monde entier devraient terrasser cette guerre d'agression par une guerre révolutionnaire. À partir de maintenant, il faut nous tenir prêts à cette éventualité ! » Mao Zedong *Affiche éditée et imprimée par* l'état-major de Défense antiaérienne populaire du Comité révolutionnaire de la ville de Qingdao, 1970

全世界人民团结起来，反对任何帝国主义，社会帝国主义发动的侵略战争，特别要反对以原子弹为武器的侵略战争！如果这种战争发生，全世界人民就应以革命战争消灭侵略战争，从现在起就要有所准备！

毛泽东

原子武器的防护

原子弹爆炸时，产生冲击波、光幅射、贯穿幅射和放射性沾染杀伤（破坏）因素。

原子弹在空中爆炸时、出现极亮的闪光，在数十公里以外都能看到。

火球迅速扩大，开始上升。

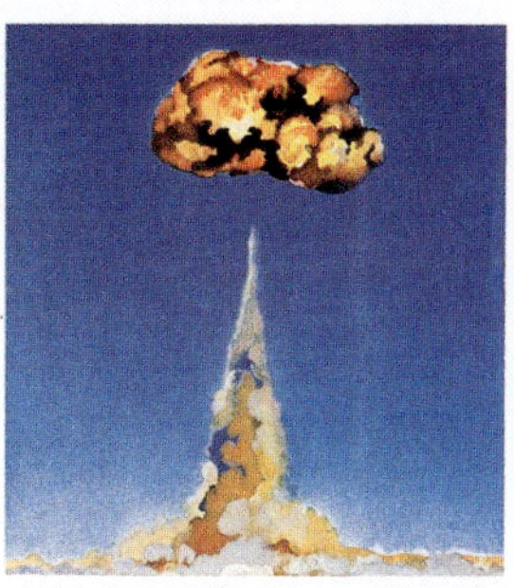

火球冷却后，变成一团烟云，并迅速扩大和升高。

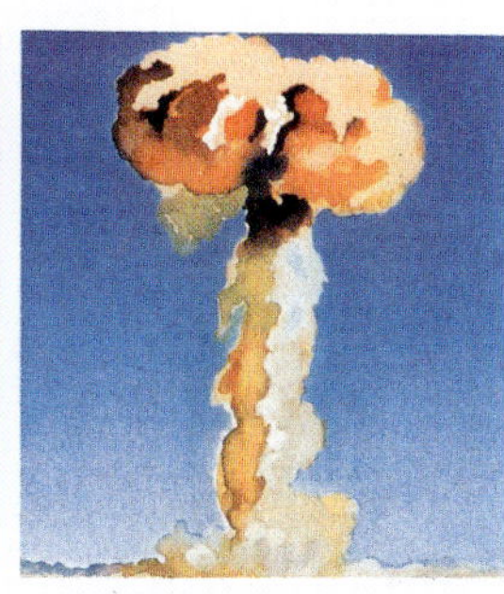

烟云能上升到10—15公里以上的高度。然后逐渐散开而消失。

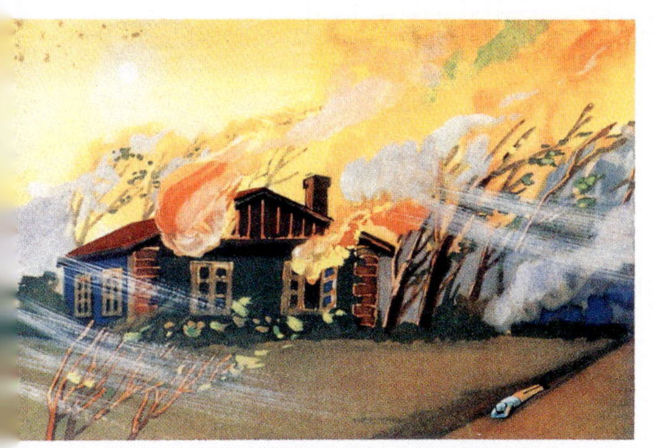

一、光幅射，就是核爆炸时，高温火球所产生出来的强烈光线。用它来烧焦、烧着或溶化物质。人体的外露部分也会被灼伤。

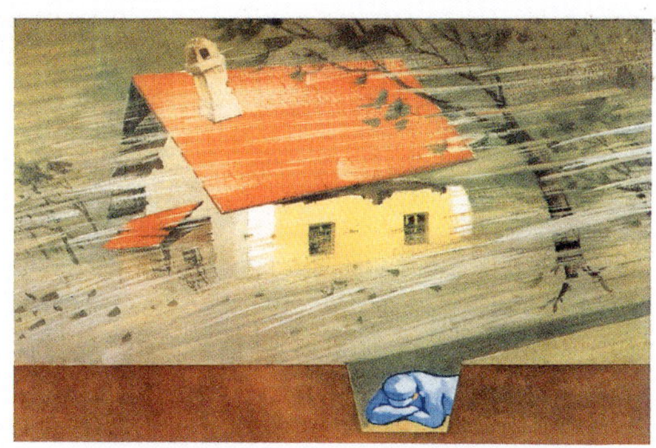

二、冲击波，就是核爆炸后产生的，最强劲的高速空气流。用以摧毁工事、建筑物，同时借以伤害人员。

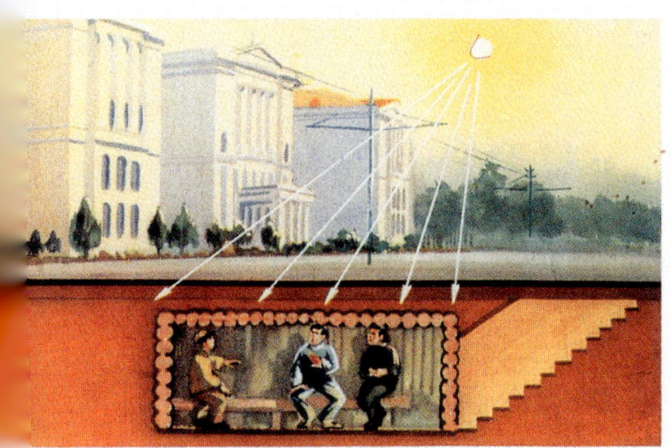

三、贯穿幅射，是一种看不见，感觉不到的杀伤因素。它有非常强的穿透能力，能使无掩蔽人员或掩蔽效果不好的人员患射线病。

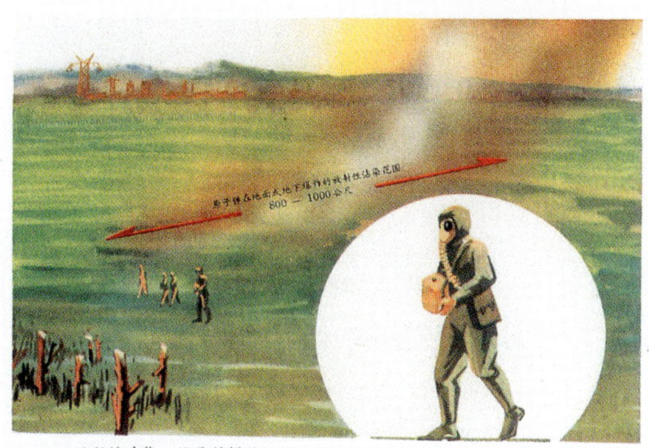

四、放射性沾染，就是核爆炸以后，掉下来的放射性物质。它是一种持续时间较长的杀伤因素，放射性物质可侵入人体内部，使人患放射线病。

对原子、化学、細菌
武器的防护常識挂圖

美军細菌武器

共14張 第13号

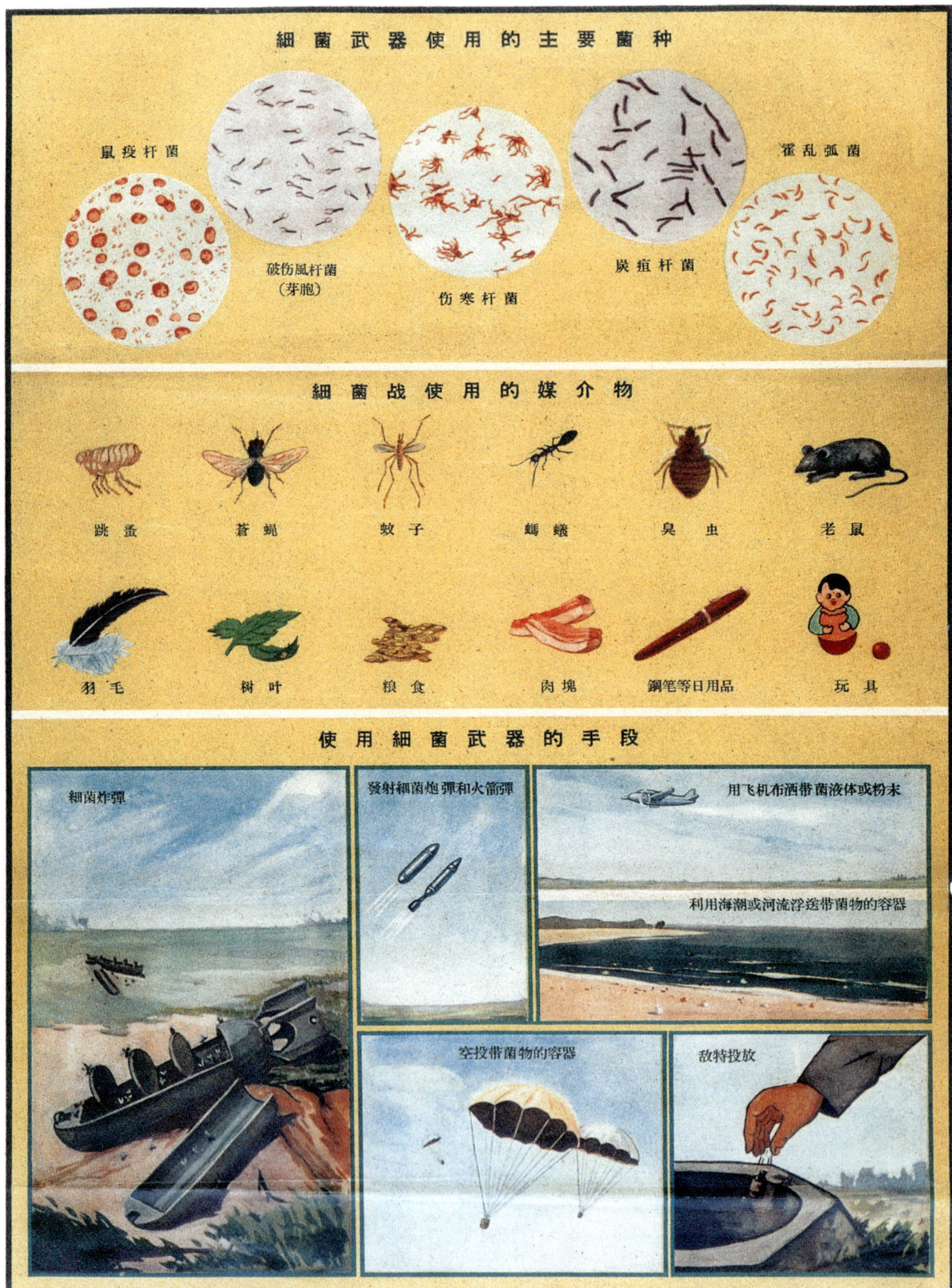

中国人民解放軍总参謀部出版部出版

一九六〇年六月

Opposite
Basic information about protection from atomic, chemical, and biological weapons
No. 13 in a series of 14 posters: Biological agents used by the American army *Published by:* Publishing House of the General Staff of the Chinese People's Liberation Army, June 1960

Grundwissen über den Schutz vor atomaren, chemischen und biologischen Waffen
Nr. 13 von insgesamt 14 Plakaten: Biologische Kampfstoffe der amerikanischen Armee *Herausgeber:* Verlag des Generalstabs der Volksbefreiungsarmee Chinas, Juni 1960

Ce qu'il faut savoir pour se protéger des armes nucléaires, chimiques et biologiques
N° 13 d'un ensemble de 14 affiches : Armes biologiques de l'armée américaine *Éditeur :* Éditions de l'état-major général de l'Armée de Libération Populaire de Chine, Juin 1960

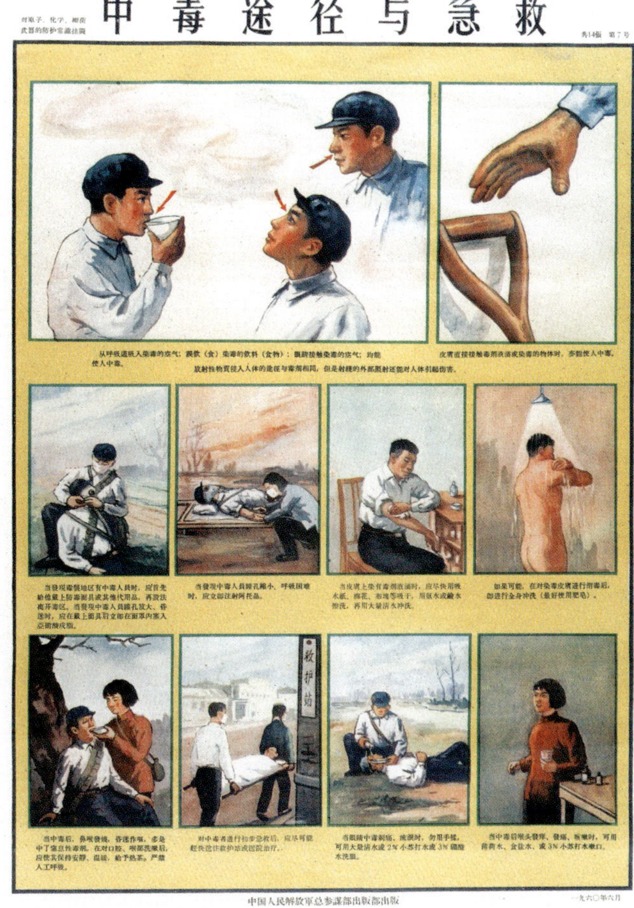

Basic information about protection from atomic, chemical, and biological weapons
No. 7 in a series of 14 posters: How poison can enter the body and first aid *Published by:* Publishing House of the General Staff of the Chinese People's Liberation Army, June 1960

Grundwissen über den Schutz vor atomaren, chemischen und biologischen Waffen
Nr. 7 von insgesamt 14 Plakaten: Vergiftungswege und Erste Hilfe *Herausgeber:* Verlag des Generalstabs der Volksbefreiungsarmee Chinas, Juni 1960

Ce qu'il faut savoir pour se protéger des armes nucléaires, chimiques et biologiques
N° 7 d'un ensemble de 14 affiches : Voies d'intoxication et premiers secours *Éditeur :* Éditions de l'état-major général de l'Armée de Libération Populaire de Chine, Juin 1960

Opposite
Basic information about protection from atomic, chemical, and biological weapons
No. 6 in a series of 14 posters: Protection for livestock *Published by:* Publishing House of the General Staff of the Chinese People's Liberation Army, June 1960

Grundwissen über den Schutz vor atomaren, chemischen und biologischen Waffen
Nr. 6 von insgesamt 14 Plakaten: Schutz für das Vieh *Herausgeber:* Verlag des Generalstabs der Volksbefreiungsarmee Chinas, Juni 1960

Ce qu'il faut savoir pour se protéger des armes nucléaires, chimiques et biologiques
N° 6 d'un ensemble de 14 affiches : Protection du bétail *Éditeur :* Éditions de l'état-major général de l'Armée de Libération Populaire de Chine, Juin 1960

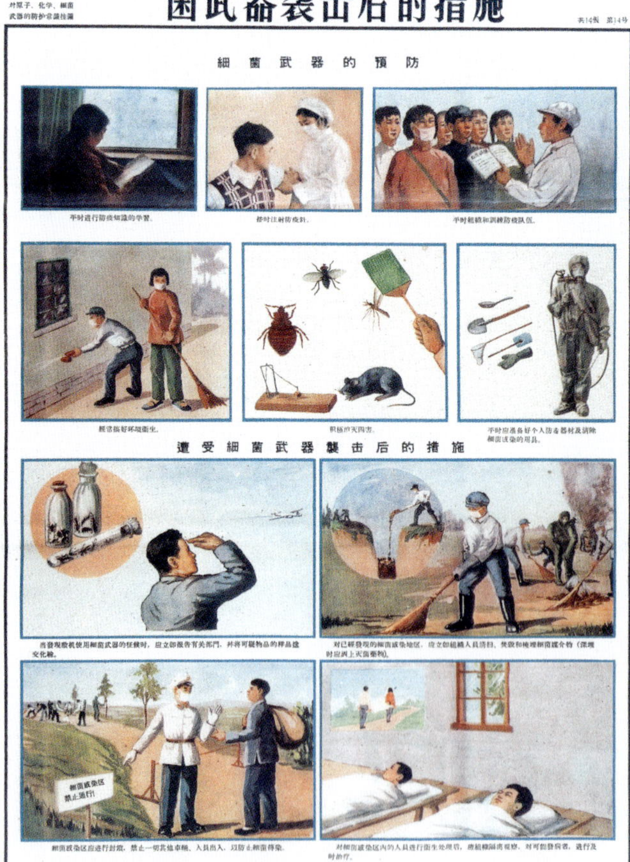

Basic information about protection from atomic, chemical and biological weapons
No. 3 in a series of 14 posters: Biological agents used by the American army *Published by:* Publishing House of the General Staff of the Chinese People's Liberation Army, June 1960

Grundwissen über den Schutz vor atomaren, chemischen und biologischen Waffen
Nr. 3 von insgesamt 14 Plakaten: Biologische Kampfstoffe der amerikanischen Armee *Herausgeber:* Verlag des Generalstabs der Volksbefreiungsarmee Chinas, Juni 1960

Ce qu'il faut savoir pour se protéger des armes nucléaires, chimiques et biologiques
N° 3 d'un ensemble de 14 affiches : Armes biologiques de l'armée américaine *Éditeur :* Éditions de l'état-major général de l'Armée de Libération Populaire de Chine, Juin 1960

对原子、化学、細菌
武器的防护常識挂圖

牲 畜 防 护

共14張 第6号

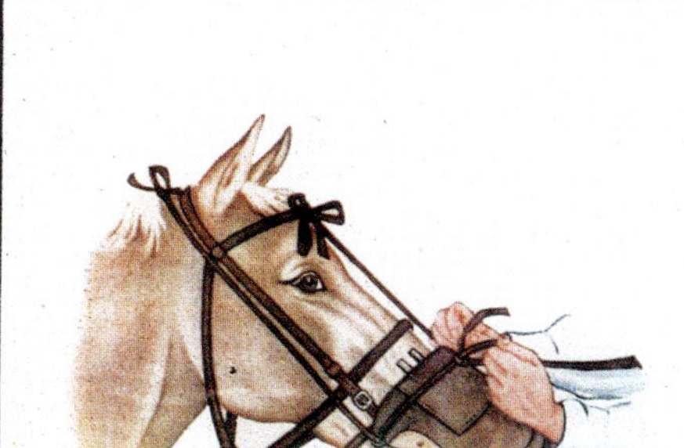

給馬匹佩戴制式的潮湿面具。

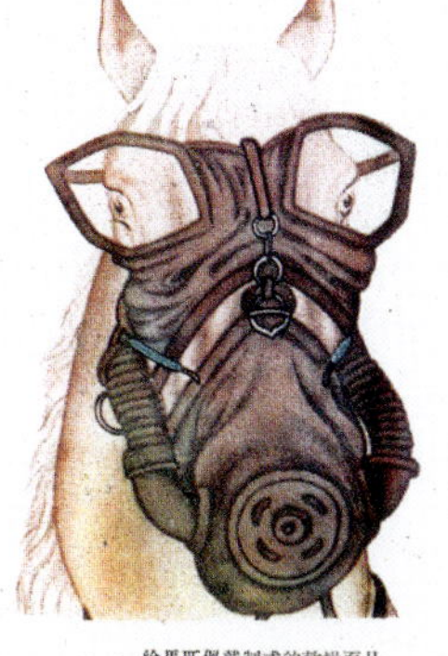

給馬匹佩戴制式的乾燥面具。

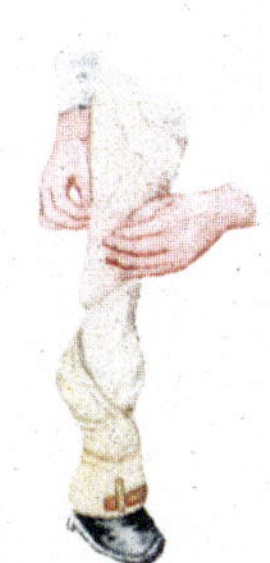

制式的馬用裹腿

毒剂、放射性物質和細菌，同样能够通过呼吸道、皮膚和飼料，使牲畜受到伤害。因此，对牲畜应当特别注意呼吸道、皮膚和腿的防护；防止牲畜食用染毒、沾染或感染細菌的飼料和水。

牲畜的集体防护場所，可以設在有頂棚的地方。在頂棚下面的牲畜，仍应注意呼吸道的防护。

利用麻布、油布、帆布等，遮盖馬头、馬身和裹好馬腿，可使馬匹得到防护。

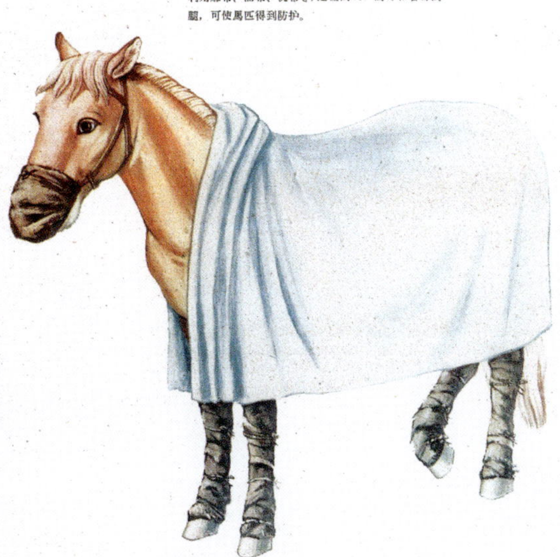

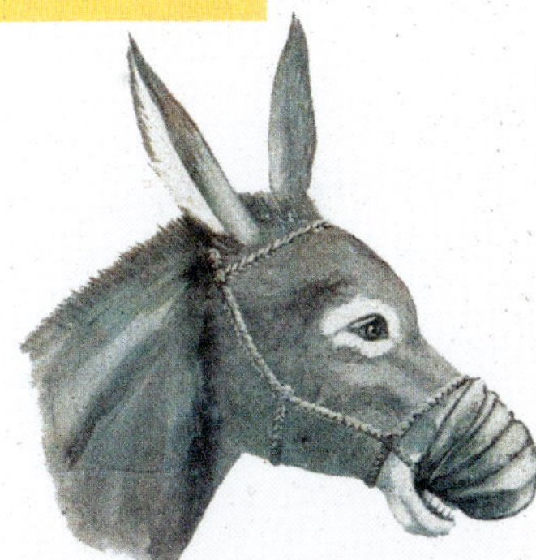

浸过藥水或水的麻布可做为潮湿面具的代用品。

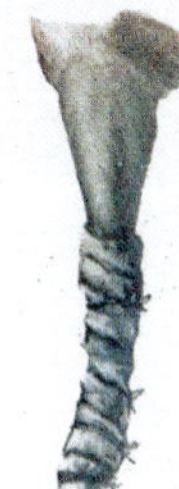

利用麻布、油布、布等代用品做成的防毒裹腿。

中国人民解放軍总参謀部出版部出版

一九六〇年六月

人員局部和

人員进行局部消除沾染时，主要应消除身体暴露部分的放射性沾染。

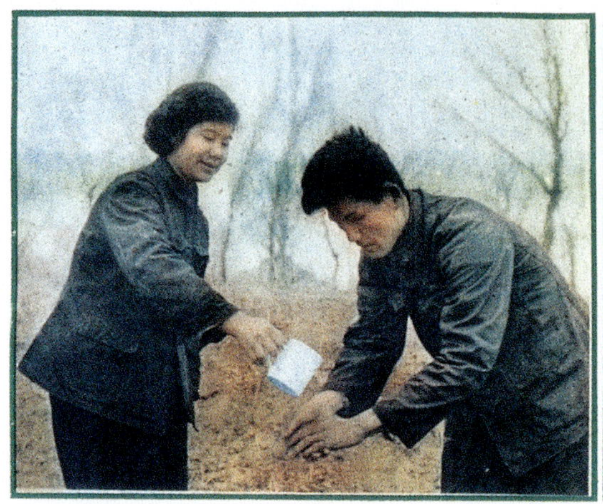

用未沾染的水洗滌身体的暴露部分（脸、頸、手）及漱口。

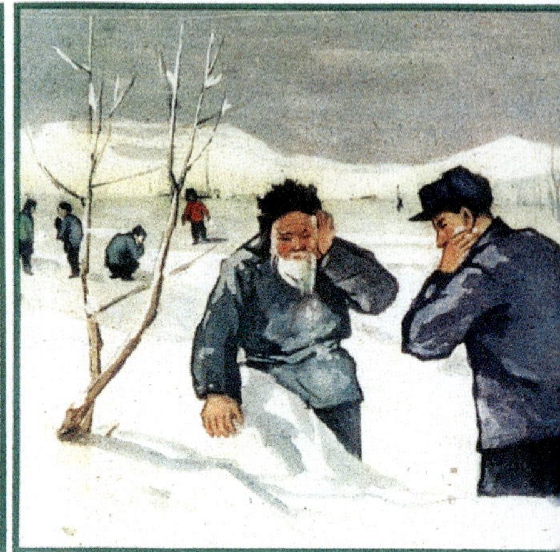

在冬季缺水的情况下，也可用干淨的雪擦洗脸、頸、
部份。

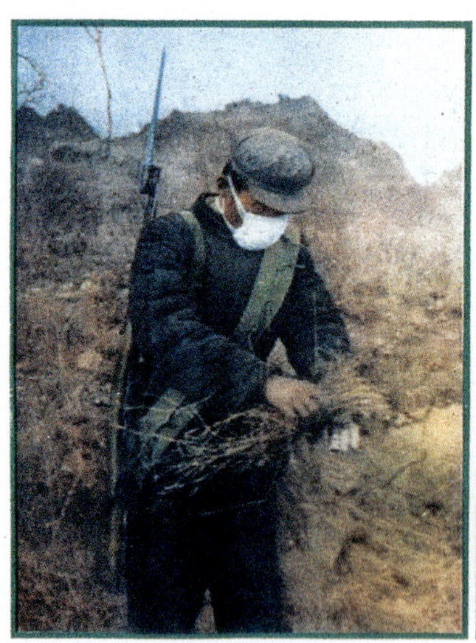

在万不得已的情况下，在离开沾染地域后可用草、树叶等来擦拭。

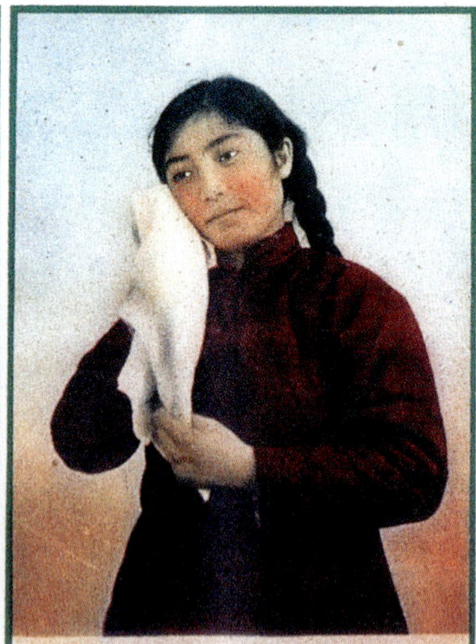

可用毛巾来擦拭身体的暴露部份，擦淨后毛巾应用水洗淨。

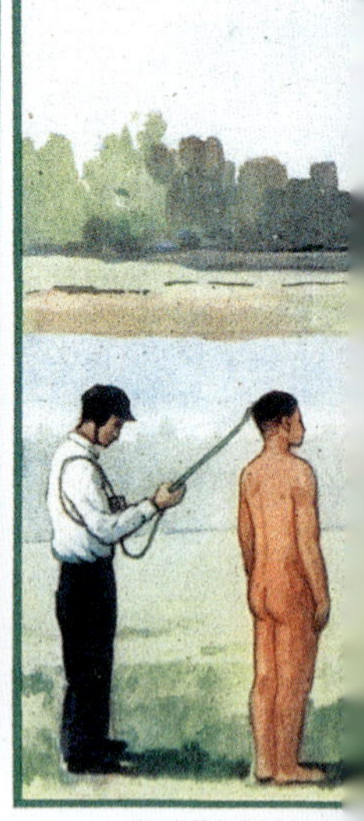

夏天可在潔淨的河
游，洗澡前应在洗澡
除沾染，然后将其轉
若有沾染程度检查仪

部消除沾染

人員进行全部消除沾染时，应对全身、眼睛、鼻孔、口腔消除放射性沾染。

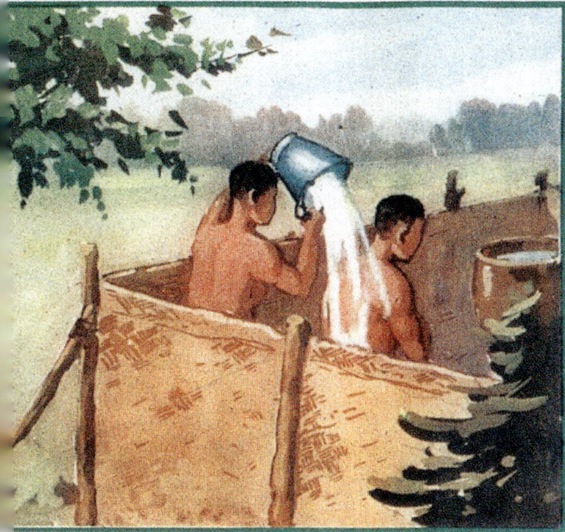

人員全部消除沾染，夏天可在室外进行。用水进行冲洗，最好用热水和肥皂。

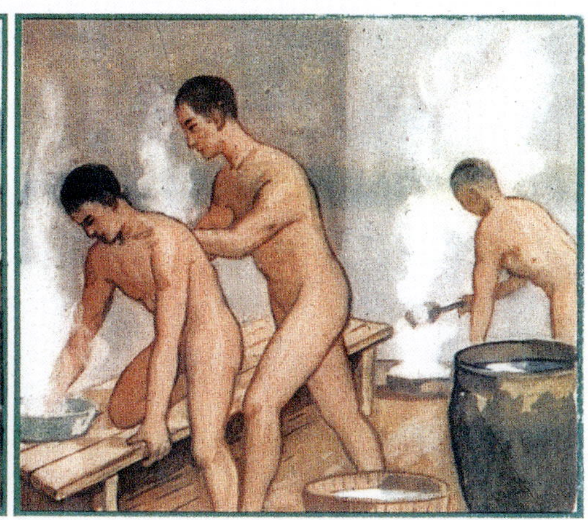

冷天可在室内进行全部消除沾染。

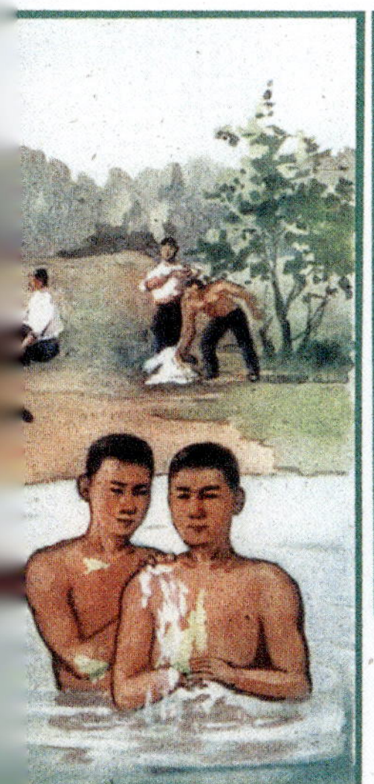

澡，地点应在居民地下地上，对服装、装具消淨場地上。洗澡完畢，查。

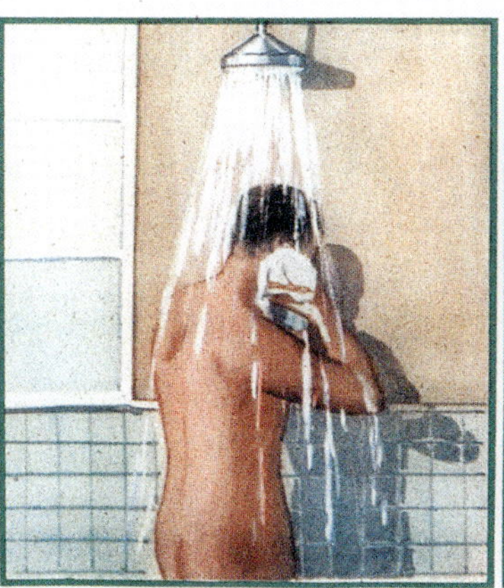

利用浴室、澡堂进行全部消除沾染(用淋浴)。

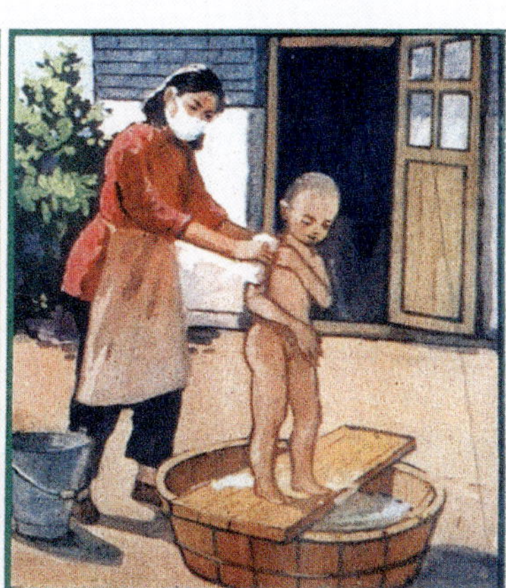

应当即时的替兒童进行全部消除沾染。

全部消除沾染，必需在沾染地域外进行

出版部出版

一九六〇年六月

对原子、化学、細菌
武器的防护常識挂圖

对武器、器材、车
局部消毒

对武器、車輛和服裝、裝具的局部消毒和消除沾染，一有可能，卽应
毒或沾染地域后实施。

服装和裝具的局部

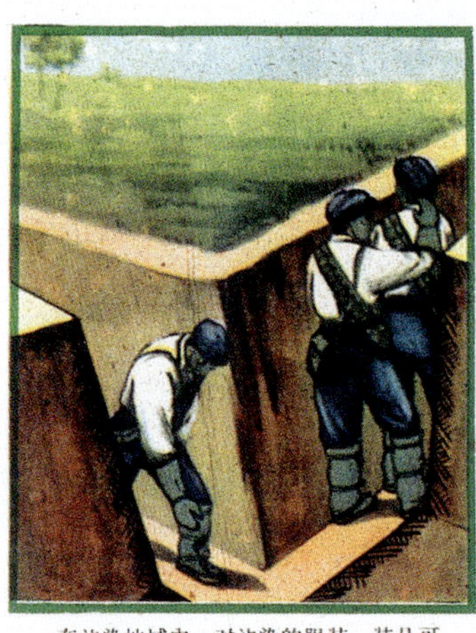

在沾染地域內，对沾染的服装、装具可用抖拂和扫除法局部消除。如染有毒剂时，可用人員消毒包局部消毒。但不得卸下装具。

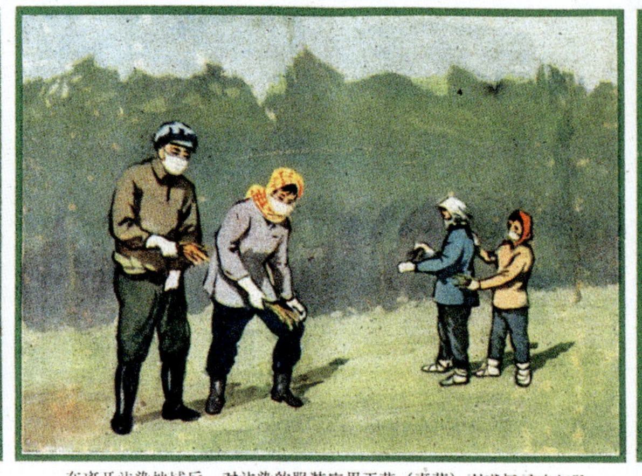

在离开沾染地域后，对沾染的服装应用干草（青草）束或扫帚来扫除。
在离开染毒地域后，染毒的服装一有可能就应当脫掉，更换干淨的服装。

武器和車輛的局

对武器和車輛局部消毒或消除沾染时，应消除

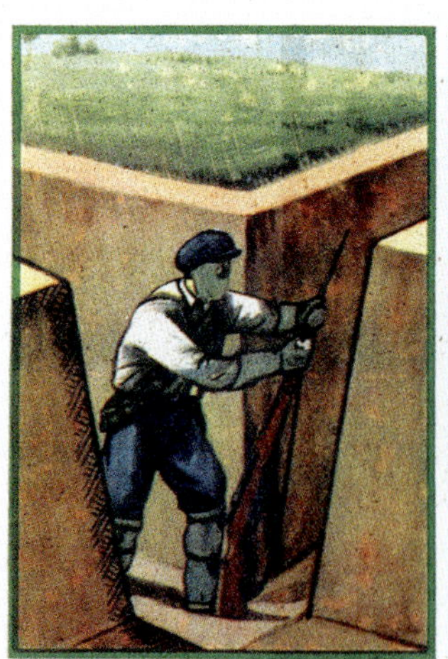

局部消除沾染时，用蘸有水（溶剂）的麻屑团或布团擦拭步槍的外部。擦拭时，应自上而下，并不断地轉动麻屑团或布团，但不得分解武器。局部消毒的方法相同，但需使用漂白粉浆或鹼水、溶剂。

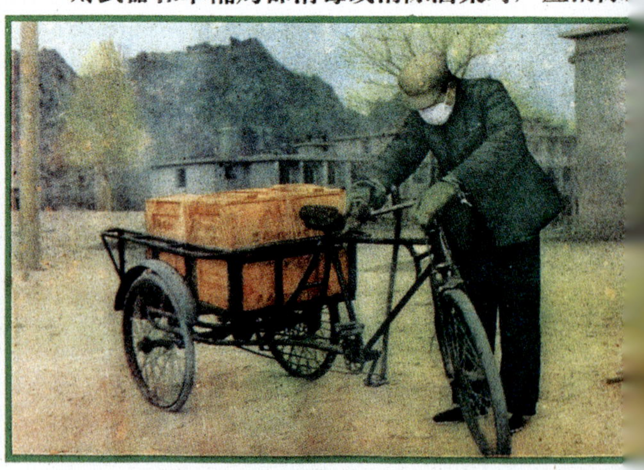

用蘸有水（消毒剂）的破布擦拭人員經常接触的部位，如車把、座垫、手閘等。
有可能时再进行全部消毒。

武器和車輛的局部消毒或消除沾染完畢后，人員应再一次进

中国人民解

两和服装、装具的
消除沾染

共14張 第9号

員的决定，直接在染毒或沾染地域（輻射級超过0.1 倫/时）內或离开染

和 消 除 沾 染

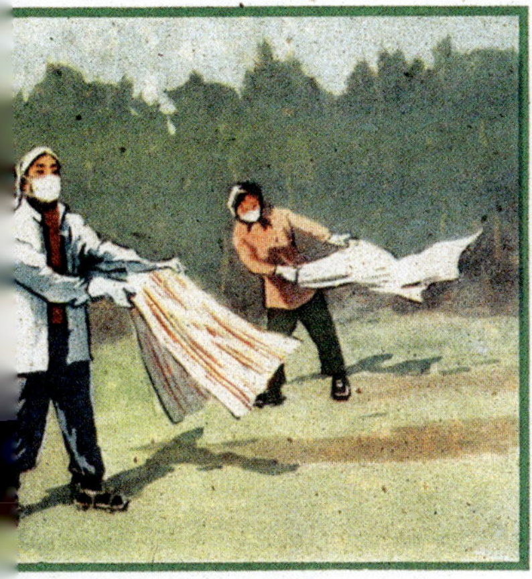

地域外，当时間許可时，应仔細地抖拂服装和

在沾染地域外，当情况許可时，应用棍子、树枝拍打服装和装具。

毒 和 消 除 沾 染

用时需要接触的部位上的毒剂或放射性沾染。

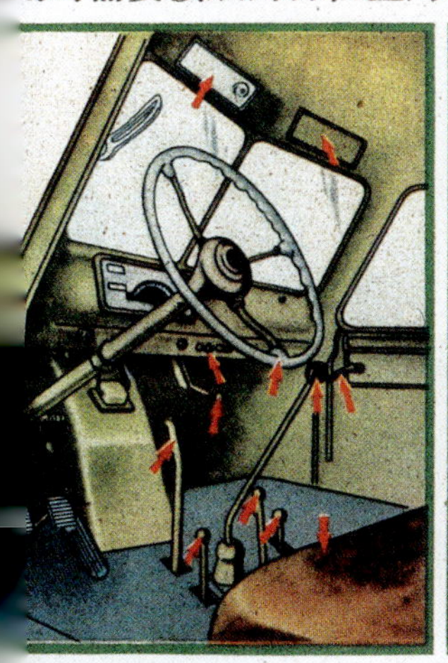

有水、汽油或消毒剂的破布擦拭駕內表面以及操縱杆和坐位（箭头所方）。

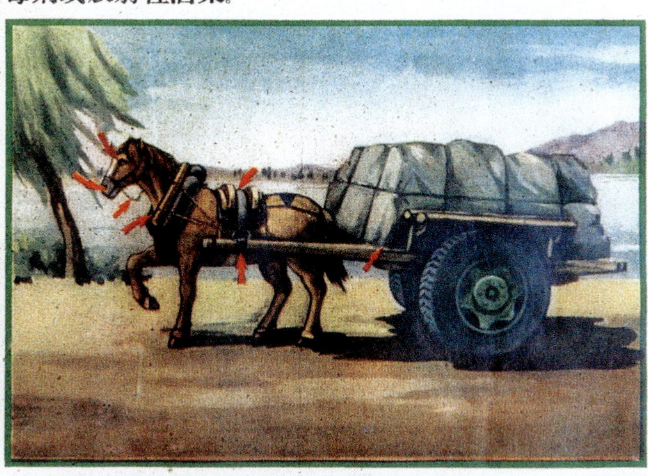

用蘸有水或消毒剂的破布擦拭馬匹的头部（鼻孔、眼、嘴）、韁繩、車轅、鞍具和坐位等部位（箭头所指的地方）。对馬匹头部局部消毒时，最好用淡鹼水或馬用消毒包。馬車的局部消毒可用漂白粉浆或鹼水擦拭。

消除沾染，并对服装、装具及防毒器材进行局部消毒或消除沾染。

出版部出版

一九六〇年六月

对原子、化学、細菌
武器的防护常識挂圖

对武器、器材、车
全部消毒

对武器、器材、車輛和朋
染，只能在未染毒（沾染）北
地上实施。

若情况許可，并經上級首
域撤出，实施全部消毒和消除

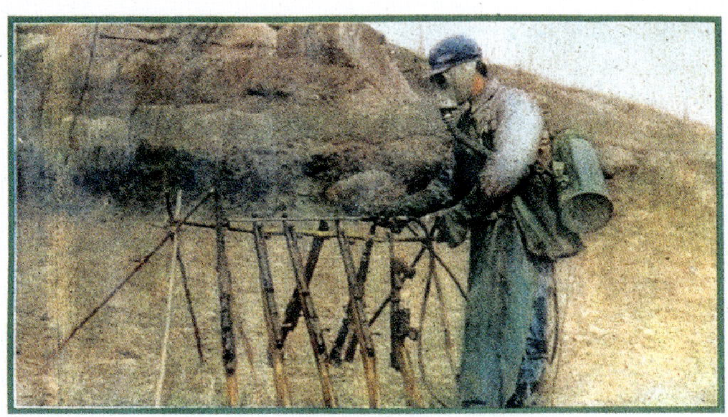

对步枪全部消除沾染时，可用背囊式洗消器或消毒汽車，以水冲洗。冬季使用背囊式洗消器时，应注入汽油或煤油等防冻剂。消除沾染后，应将武器擦干，并上油。对枪背带的消除沾染，应單独实施（可用洗滌法）。对步枪消毒时，用消毒剂实施。

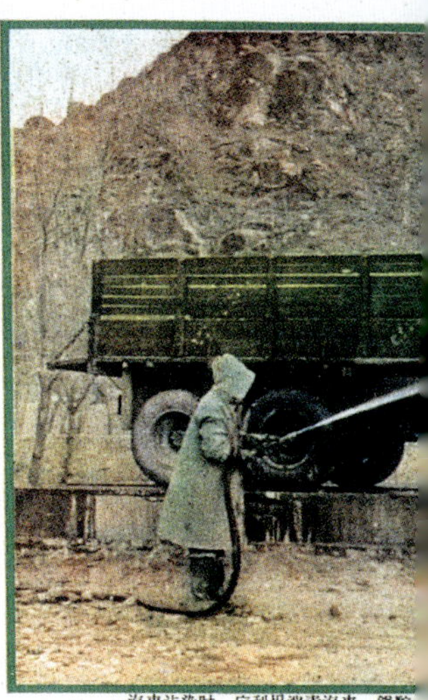

汽車沾染时，应利用消毒汽車、鍋駝
的水柱，实施全部消除放射性沾染。染
代用品如石灰水、鹼[illegible]等）或汽油等溶

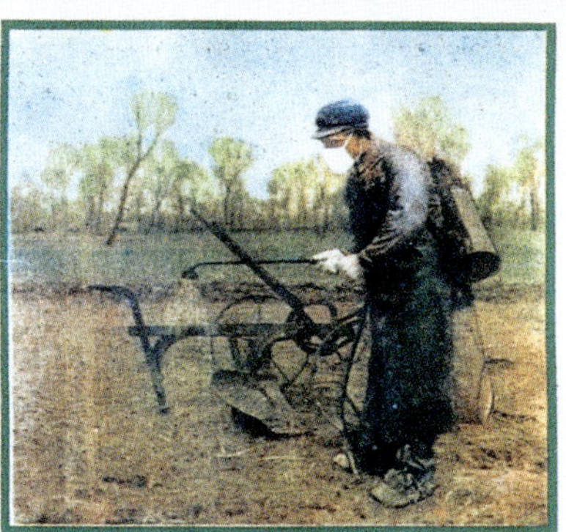

用噴霧器装上消毒剂（或鹼水、石灰水）可以对农具消毒；装上水可以对农具消除沾染。

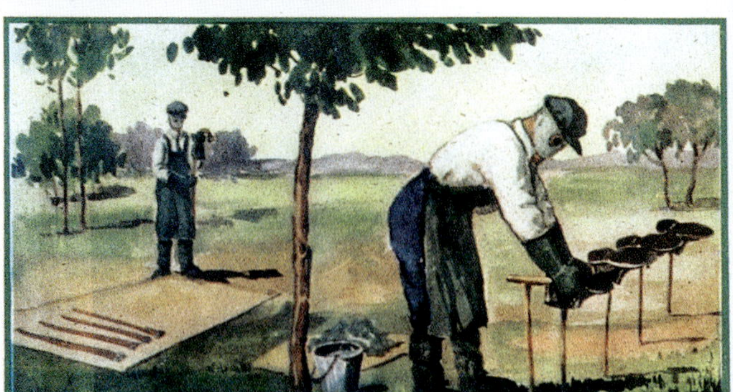

对靴鞋和装具全部消除沾染时，可用浸有水的破布擦拭。靴鞋和装具的消毒可用日光晒和通風法消毒。最好用热空气法消毒（使密閉的容器内保持 60°C 以上的温度和一定的水分，将靴、鞋、装具等放在这种容器内消毒 6 小时左右）。

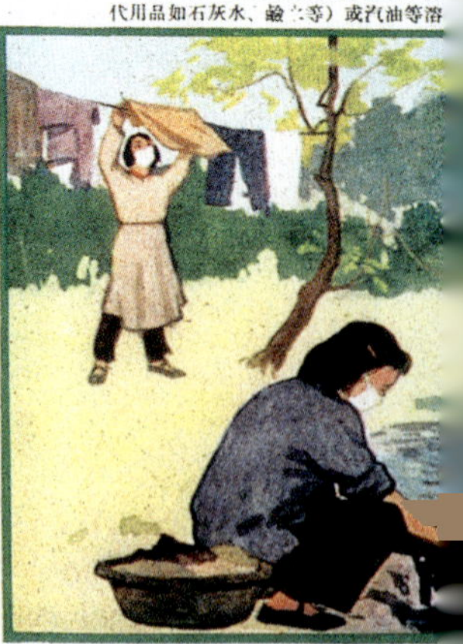

沾染的服装、装具，可以用水洗滌
洗滌时，应当注意选擇不是飲用的水

和服装、装具的
消除沾染

的全部消毒和消除沾
站内或在專設的場

可从染毒(沾染)地

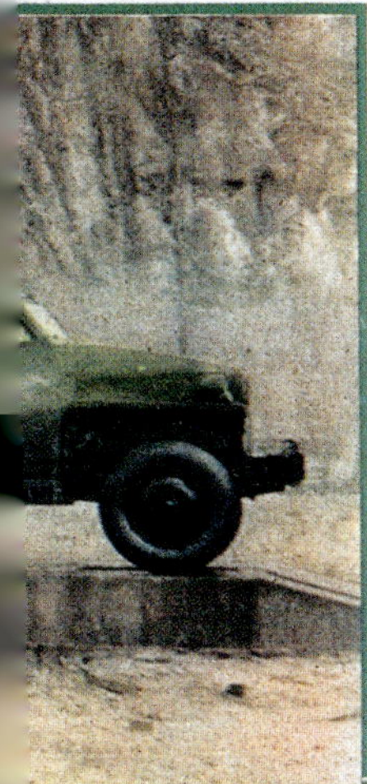

抽水和压水装置所压出
毒汽車装上消毒剂（或

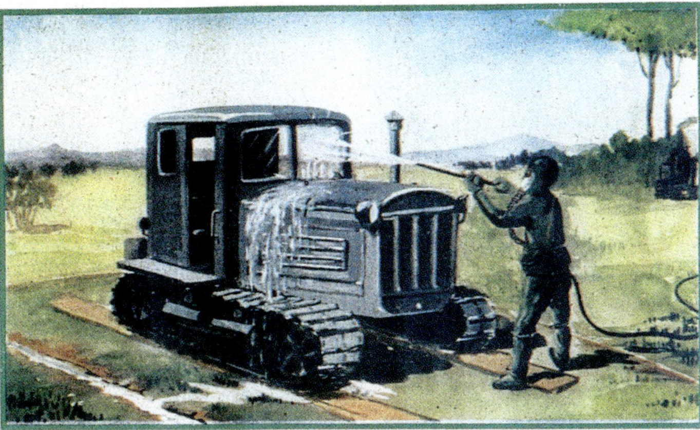

拖拉机沾染时，应利用消毒汽車、鍋駝机（带水泵）、水泵等抽水和压水装置所压出的水柱来消除沾染。染毒时可利用喷雾器或消毒汽車装上消毒剂（或代用品如石灰水、鹼水等）或煤油等溶剂来消毒。

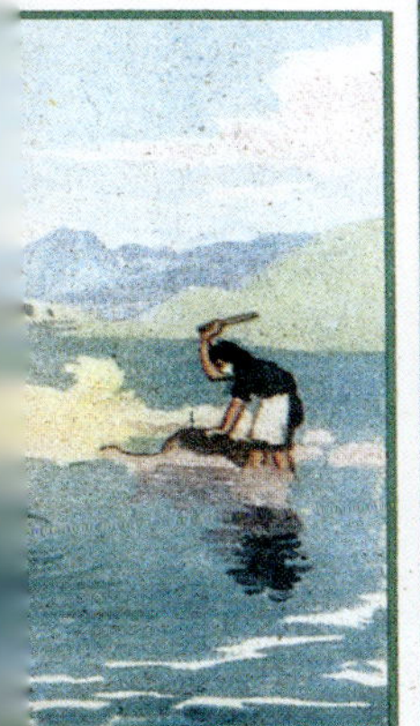

皂。当利用水池或河流
飲用的地方。

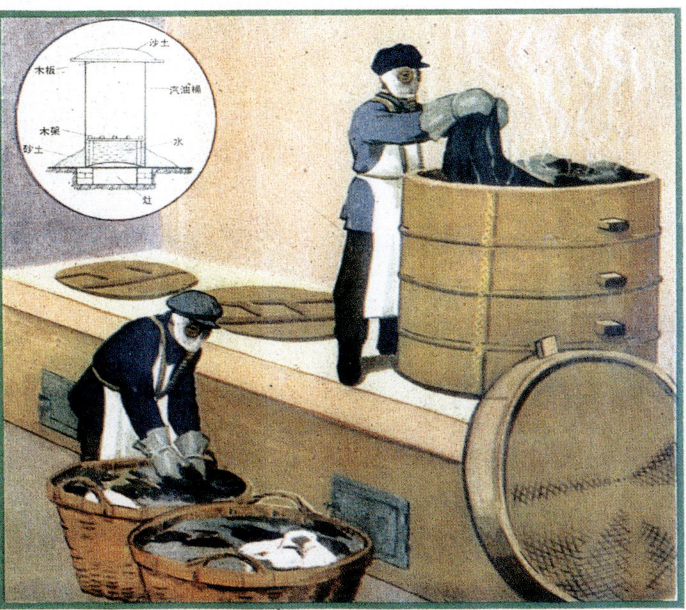

染毒的服装可以用鹼水蒸煮消毒。普通的汽油桶可以改装成蒸汽消毒鍋（左上圖）。蒸煮过的服装应当擰干、晾晒，并进行檢查。未消毒澈底应再消毒。

版部出版　　一九六〇年六月

个别地段、道路、阵地和建筑物的消毒和消除沾染

沾染放射性物質的程度，若超过下列容許标准时，才进行消除沾染。

——当地面沾染程度每分鐘在每平方厘米面积上超过 500,000 个 蜕变数并且輻射級又超过 1 倫/时 时，应对个别地段和道路消除沾染（在沒有繞行路的情况下）；

——当陣地或建筑物沾染放射性物質后，輻射級超过 0.1 倫/时 时，应当消除沾染（在必須繼續使用的情况下）。

必須繼續使用的个别地段、道路、陣地、建筑物染毒时，应进行消毒。

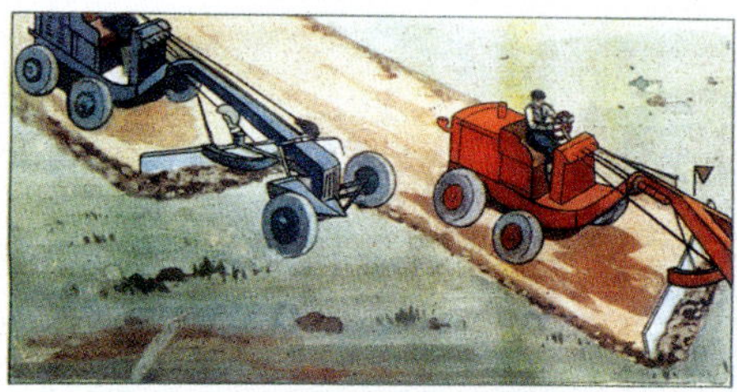

用鏟除沾染土壤（雪）的方法在染毒或沾染地域內开辟通路。
鏟除厚度：軟土 5–7 厘米；硬土 3–4 厘米；松雪 20–25 厘米。

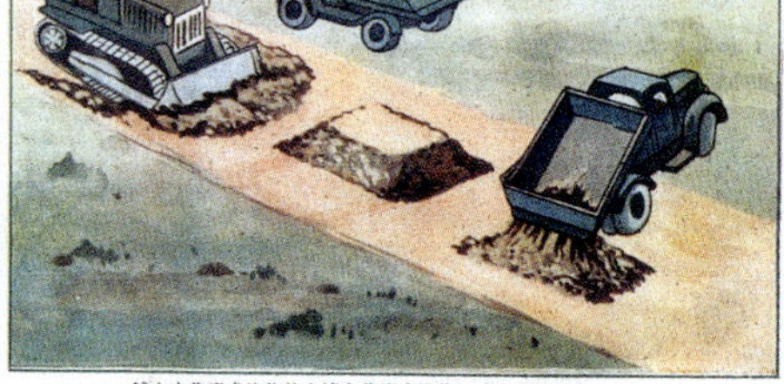

鋪上未染毒或沾染的土壤在染毒或沾染地域內开辟通路。
在一般地面上鋪上未染毒或沾染的土壤的厚度不得少于 8—10 厘米。

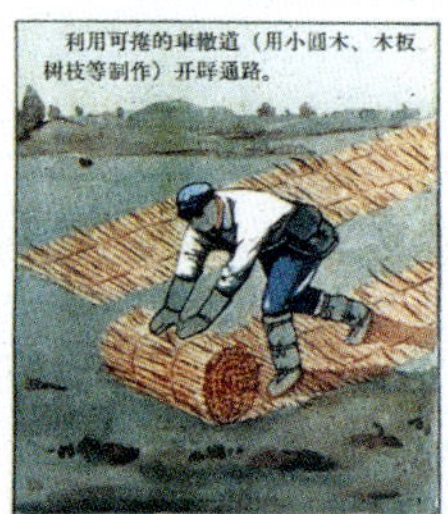

利用可捲的車轍道（用小圓木、木板树枝等制作）开辟通路。

染毒、沾染和細菌感染地域的标志和指标

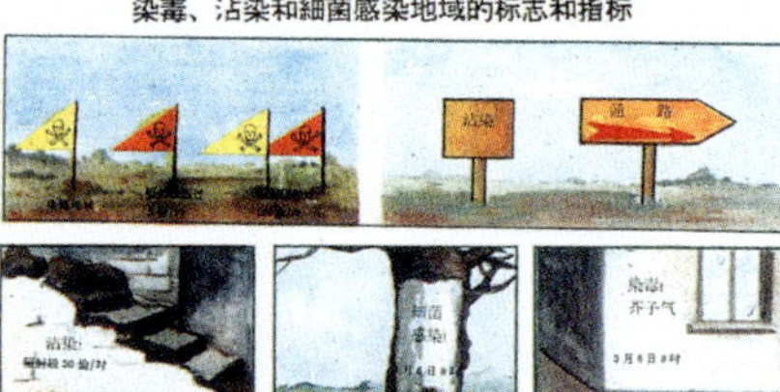

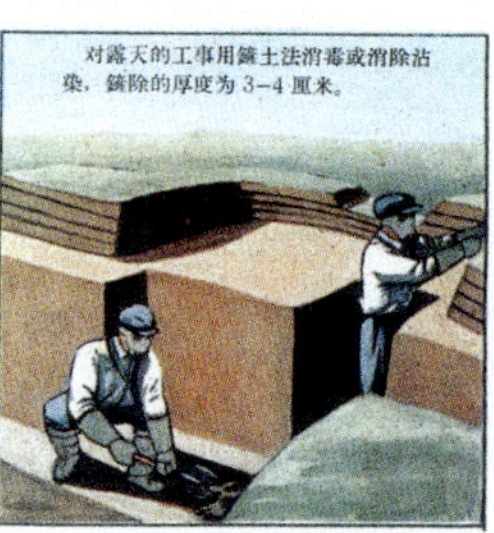

对露天的工事用鏟土法消毒或消除沾染，鏟除的厚度为 3–4 厘米。

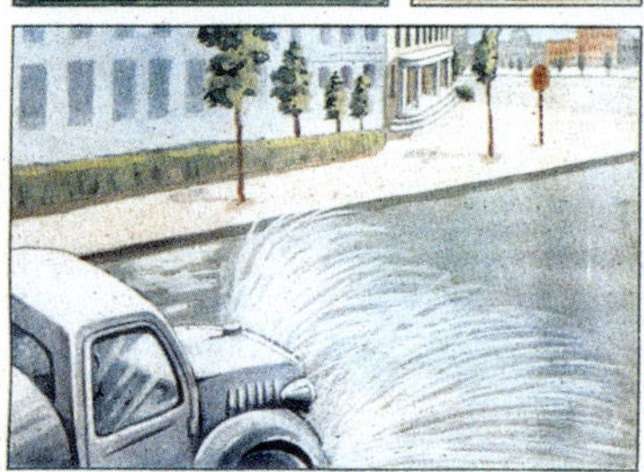

消毒汽車或洒水車装上消毒剂就可对染毒道路进行消毒；装上水就可对沾染的柏油（水泥）路面消除沾染。漂白粉也可用来对道路消毒（每平方米半公斤漂白粉）。

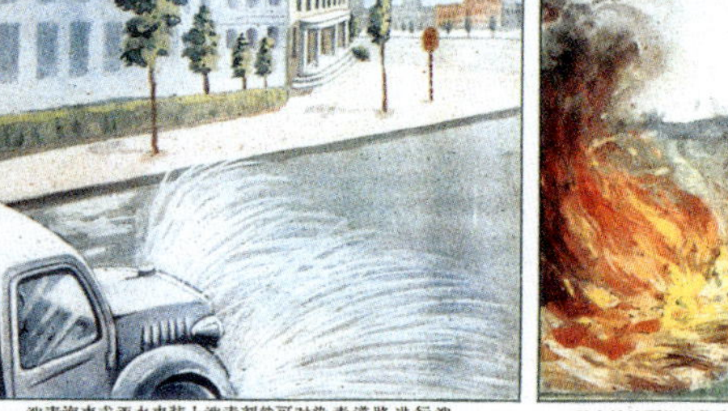

用火燒法可以对染毒的道路消毒。
树枝、干草、秫楷都可做为燃料。

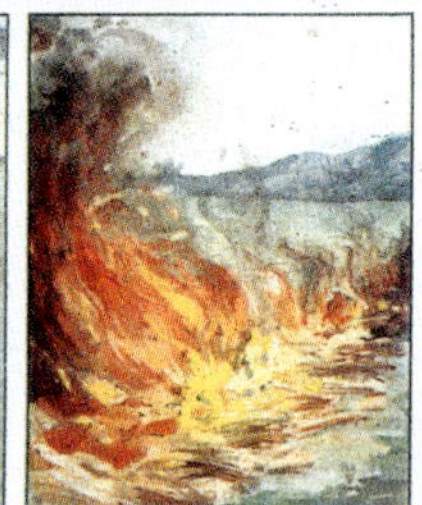

对个别地段地面上的放射性物質或毒剂，可用拖拉机犂地的方法将它翻到地下面，耕犂的深度不得少于 20 厘米。

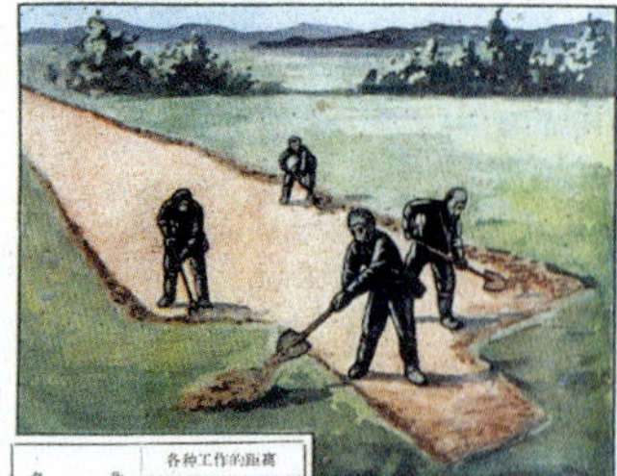

名　称	各种工作的距离		
	鏟土时	清扫时	鏟雪时
每人清除的宽度（米）	0.5	1—1.2	0.8—0.9
每人之間的距离（步）	2–3	5—6	5—6

用人工鏟土法对个别地段消毒或消除沾染（当輻射級不超过 10倫/时，必須使用的地段上）。

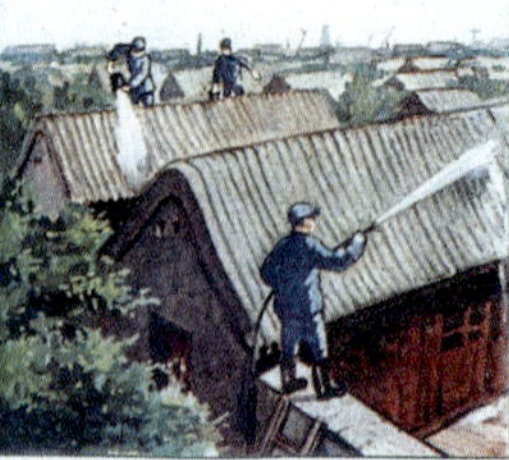

用水桶、水龙对建筑物冲洗的方法来消除沾染。建筑物外部的消毒，可用石灰水或鹼水洗刷。

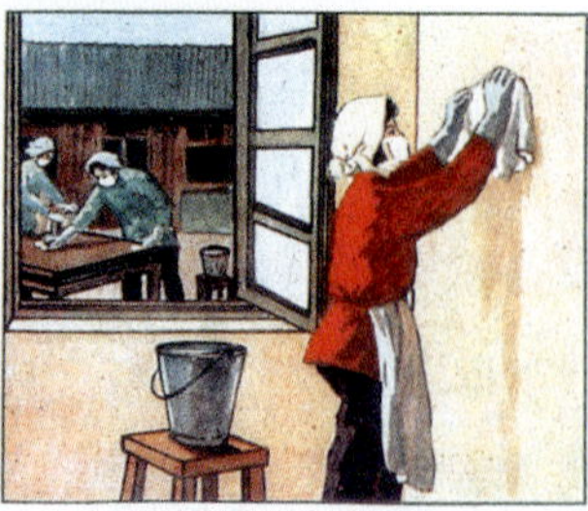

对建筑物内部消除沾染时，視情况可用干刷或水洗方法实施。室內的用具应搬到室外洗刷来消除沾染。室內的毒气可用通風法消毒。用具应当拿到室外通風日晒消毒。如果染有毒剂液滴时可用鹼水或石灰水、漂白粉浆消毒。

中国人民解放軍总参謀部出版部出版　　一九六〇年六月

Pages 144–145

Basic information about protection from atomic, chemical, and biological weapons
No. 8 in a series of 14 posters: Decontamination of individual parts of the body and the whole body *Published by:* Publishing House of the General Staff of the Chinese People's Liberation Army, June 1960

Grundwissen über den Schutz vor atomaren, chemischen und biologischen Waffen
Nr. 8 von insgesamt 14 Plakaten: Entseuchung einzelner Körperteile und des ganzen Körpers *Herausgeber:* Verlag des Generalstabs der Volksbefreiungsarmee Chinas, Juni 1960

Ce qu'il faut savoir pour se protéger des armes nucléaires, chimiques et biologiques
N° 8 d'un ensemble de 14 affiches : Désinfection et décontamination, de parties du corps et du corps entier. *Éditeur :* Éditions de l'état-major général de l'Armée de Libération Populaire de Chine, Juin 1960

Pages 146–147

Basic information about protection from atomic, chemical, and biological weapons
No. 9 in a series of 14 posters: Disinfection and decontamination of individual parts of weapons, equipment, vehicles, clothing, and containers *Published by:* Publishing House of the General Staff of the Chinese People's Liberation Army, June 1960

Grundwissen über den Schutz vor atomaren, chemischen und biologischen Waffen
Nr. 9 von insgesamt 14 Plakaten: Desinfizierung und Entseuchung einzelner Teile von Waffen, Geräten, Fahrzeugen, Kleidung und Behältern *Herausgeber:* Verlag des Generalstabs der Volksbefreiungsarmee Chinas, Juni 1960

Ce qu'il faut savoir pour se protéger des armes nucléaires, chimiques et biologiques
N° 9 d'un ensemble de 14 affiches : Désinfection et décontamination, de parties des armes, outils, vêtements et récipients *Éditeur :* Éditions de l'état-major général de l'Armée de Libération Populaire de Chine, Juin 1960

Pages 148–149

Basic information about protection from atomic, chemical, and biological weapons
No. 10 in a series of 14 posters: Disinfection and decontamination of weapons, equipment, vehicles, clothing, and containers *Published by:* Publishing House of the General Staff of the Chinese People's Liberation Army, June 1960

Grundwissen über den Schutz vor atomaren, chemischen und biologischen Waffen
Nr. 10 von insgesamt 14 Plakaten: Desinfizierung und Entseuchung von Waffen, Geräten, Fahrzeugen, Kleidung und Behältern *Herausgeber:* Verlag des Generalstabs der Volksbefreiungsarmee Chinas, Juni 1960

Ce qu'il faut savoir pour se protéger des armes nucléaires, chimiques et biologiques
N° 10 d'un ensemble de 14 affiches : Désinfection et décontamination des armes, outils, véhicules, vêtements et récipients *Éditeur :* Éditions de l'état-major général de l'Armée de Libération Populaire de Chine, 1960

Basic information about protection from atomic, chemical and biological weapons
No. 11 in a series of 14 posters: Disinfection and decontamination of individual districts, streets, military positions and buildings *Published by:* Publishing House of the General Staff of the Chinese People's Liberation Army, June 1960

Grundwissen über den Schutz vor atomaren, chemischen und biologischen Waffen
Nr. 11 von insgesamt 14 Plakaten: Desinfizierung und Entseuchung von einzelnen Gebieten, Straßen, Stellungen und Gebäuden *Herausgeber:* Verlag des Generalstabs der Volksbefreiungsarmee Chinas, Juni 1960

Ce qu'il faut savoir pour se protéger des armes nucléaires, chimiques et biologiques
N° 11 d'un ensemble de 14 affiches : Désinfection et décontamination des zones, rues, positions et bâtiments particuliers *Éditeur :* Éditions de l'état-major général de l'Armée de Libération Populaire de Chine, 1960

Pages 152–153

Basic information about protection from atomic, chemical, and biological weapons
No. 12 in a series of 14 posters: Disinfection and decontamination of grain and foodstuffs *Published by:* Publishing House of the General Staff of the Chinese People's Liberation Army, June 1960

Grundwissen über den Schutz vor atomaren, chemischen und biologischen Waffen
Nr. 12 von insgesamt 14 Plakaten: Desinfizierung und Entseuchung von Getreide und Lebensmitteln *Herausgeber:* Verlag des Generalstabs der Volksbefreiungsarmee Chinas, Juni 1960

Ce qu'il faut savoir pour se protéger des armes nucléaires, chimiques et biologiques
N° 12 d'un ensemble de 14 affiches : Désinfection et décontamination des céréales et des produits alimentaires *Éditeur :* Éditions de l'état-major général de l'Armée de libération populaire de Chine, Juin 1960

对原子、化学、細菌
武器的防护常識挂圖

粮秣、食品消

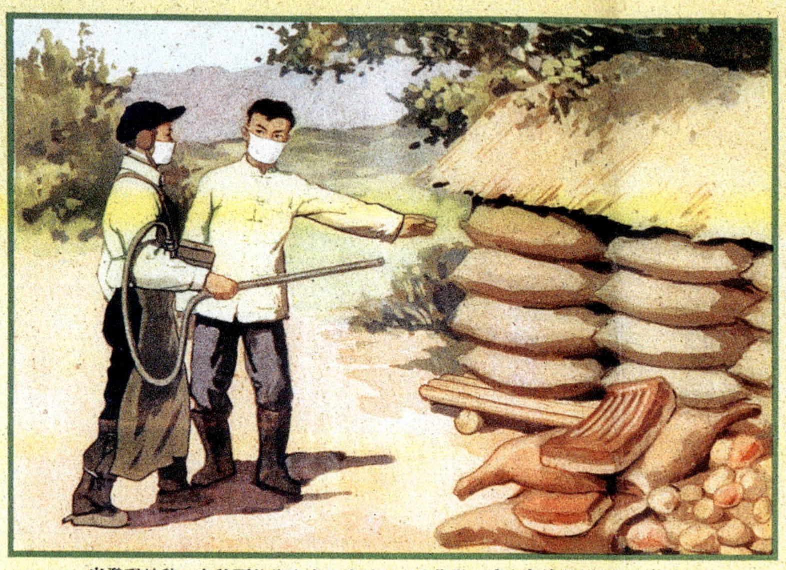

当發現粮秣、食物可能染毒或沾染时，应搜集样品送交有关單位化驗（檢查）或請有关單位派人前来化驗（檢查），以便确定处理方法。

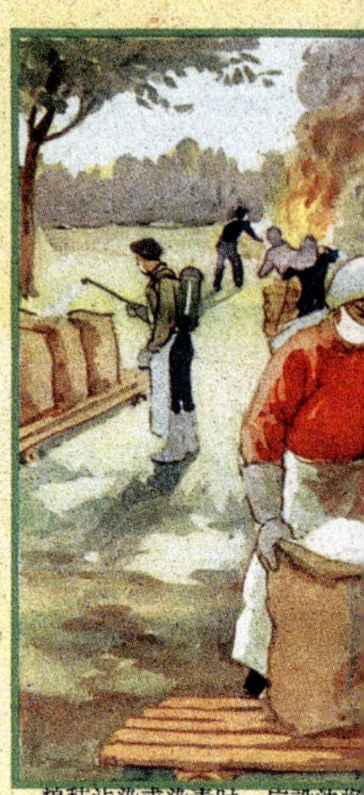

粮秣沾染或染毒时，应設法将
除去的粮秣燒毁或掩埋掉。剩下
理沾染的粮秣时，在更换容器前
湿，以防止放射性物質飞揚起来
换下的容器应当根据情况消毒

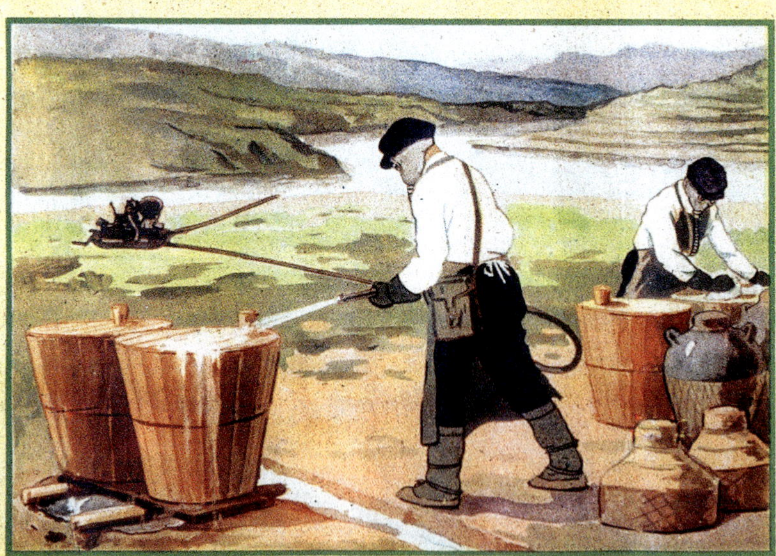

对装有調味品或飲料的密封木桶、罎子等容器消除沾染时，只需用水洗刷2—3次就可以了。当容器染毒时，可用漂白粉浆（1份水加1份粉），或鹼水消毒，然后用清水洗淨（木桶染毒时，在消毒后最好将桶內的調味品或飲料倒到干淨的桶內）。

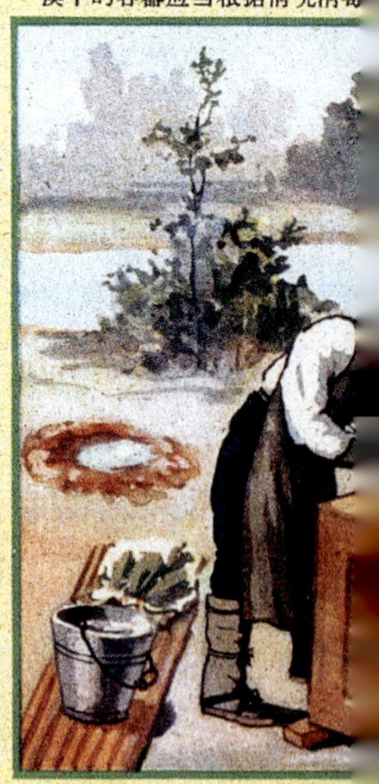

对装有食品的普通木箱等容
水洗刷2—3次。染毒时可用漂
后用淸水洗淨（如果木箱漏水
品取出，将沾染或染毒的部分
入干淨的木箱內，再对原来的

和消除沾染

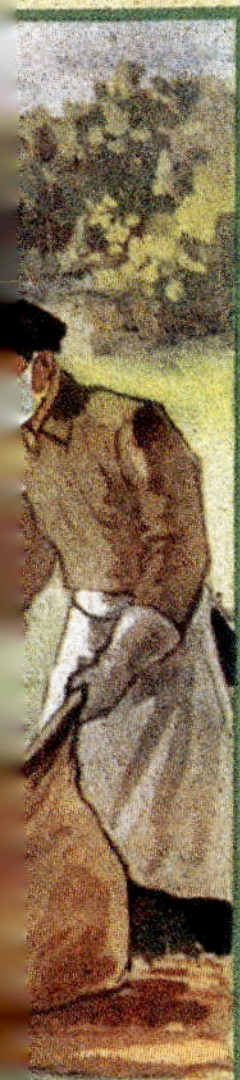

份除去，幷将
更换容器（处
]麻袋表面沾

燒毀。

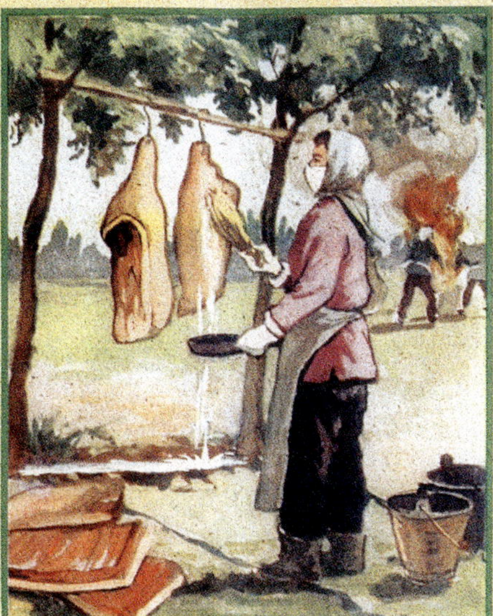

当肉类（魚）染毒时，应将染毒的部分切去，幷燒毀或掩埋。沾染的肉类（魚）可以用水洗刷，直到沾染程度低于容許标准时为止（沾染的魚应除去魚鱗洗刷）。

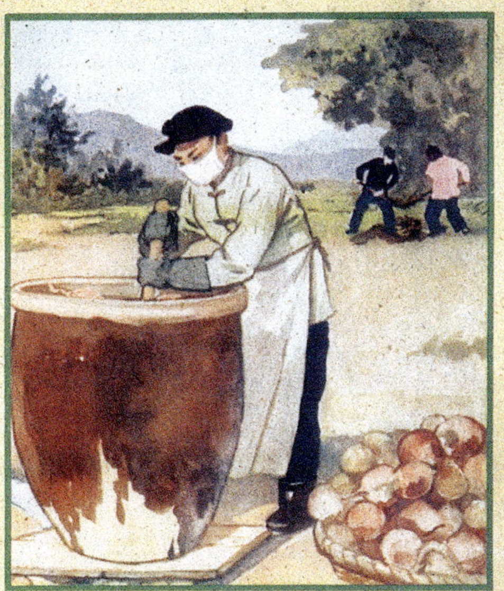

染毒的蔬菜应当燒毀或掩埋。沾染的蔬菜可以用水多次洗滌，直到低于容許标准时为止。

应用
然
的食
的放
毒）。

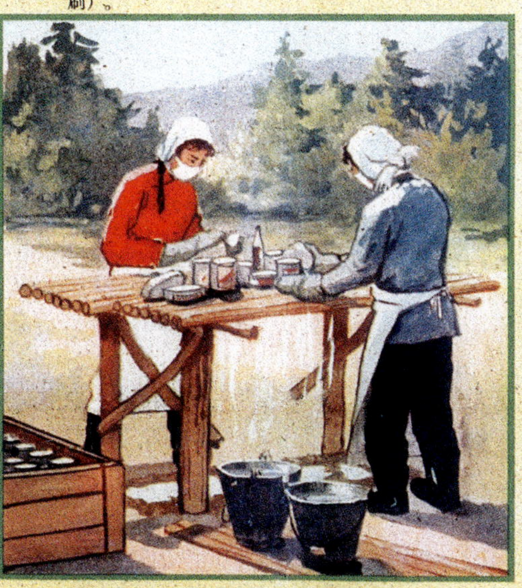

对装有食品或飲料的罐头、瓶子消除沾染时，应用水擦洗 2—3 次。染毒时，应用漂白粉浆、鹼水或煤油等溶剂消毒，消毒后，用清水洗刷一次就行了。

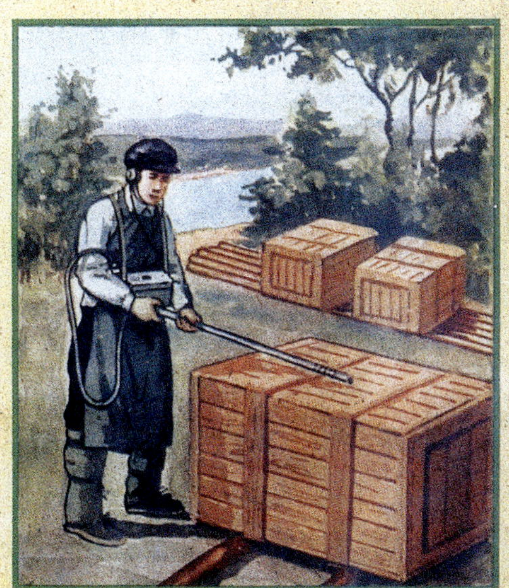

对粮秣、食物、及各种装有食物、飲料的容器消除沾染或消毒后，均应进行化驗或沾染檢查。只有当消除沾染或消毒合乎标准时才能食用。对多次处理仍不合乎标准的可以銷毀。

出版部出版 一九六〇年六月

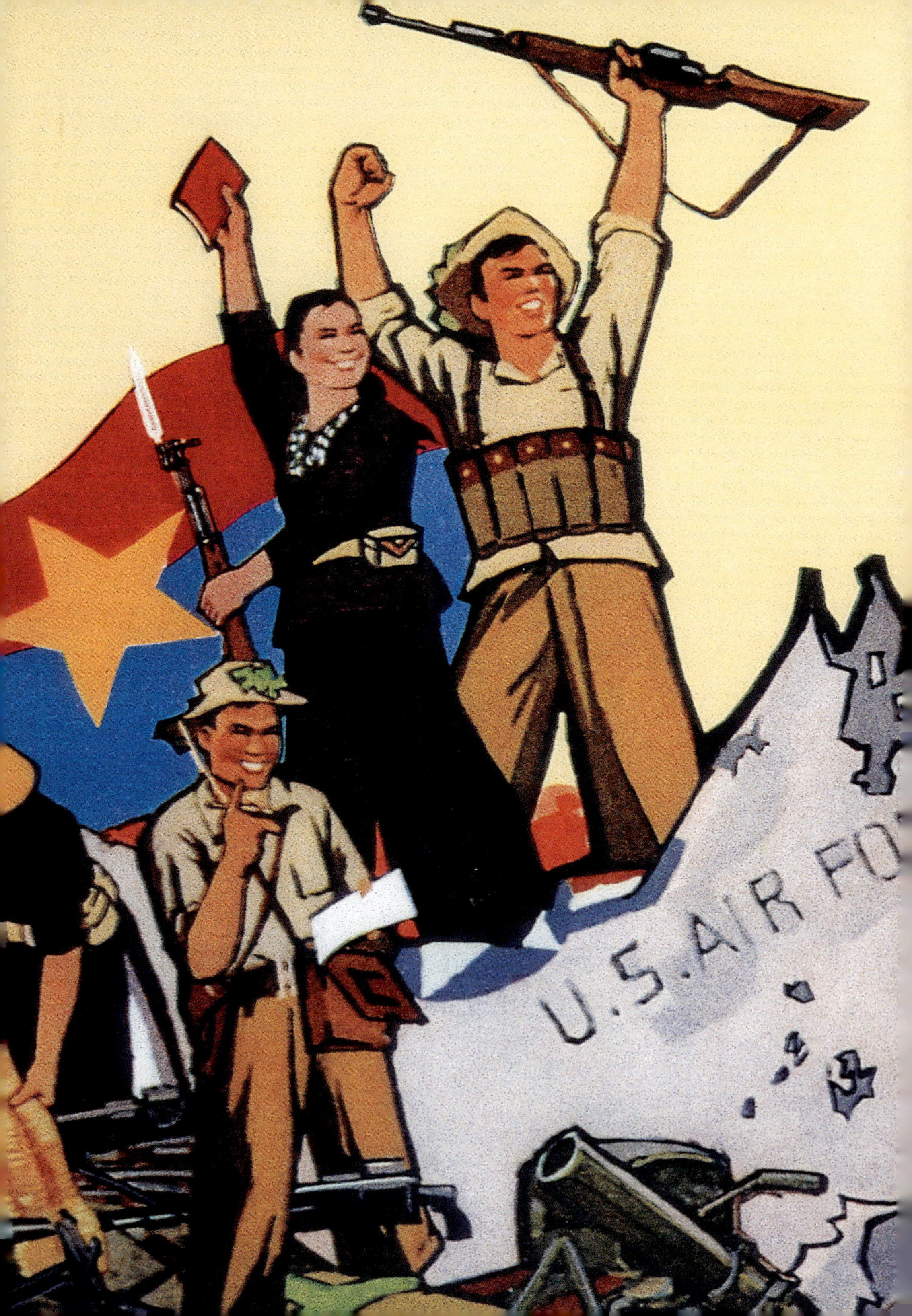

VI

IMPERIALISM AND ALL REACTIONARIES ARE PAPER TIGERS

DER IMPERIALISMUS UND ALLE REAKTIONÄRE SIND PAPIERTIGER

L'IMPÉRIALISME ET TOUS LES RÉACTIONNAIRES SONT DES TIGRES DE PAPIER

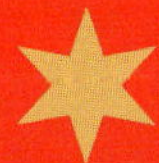

突出政治、练好

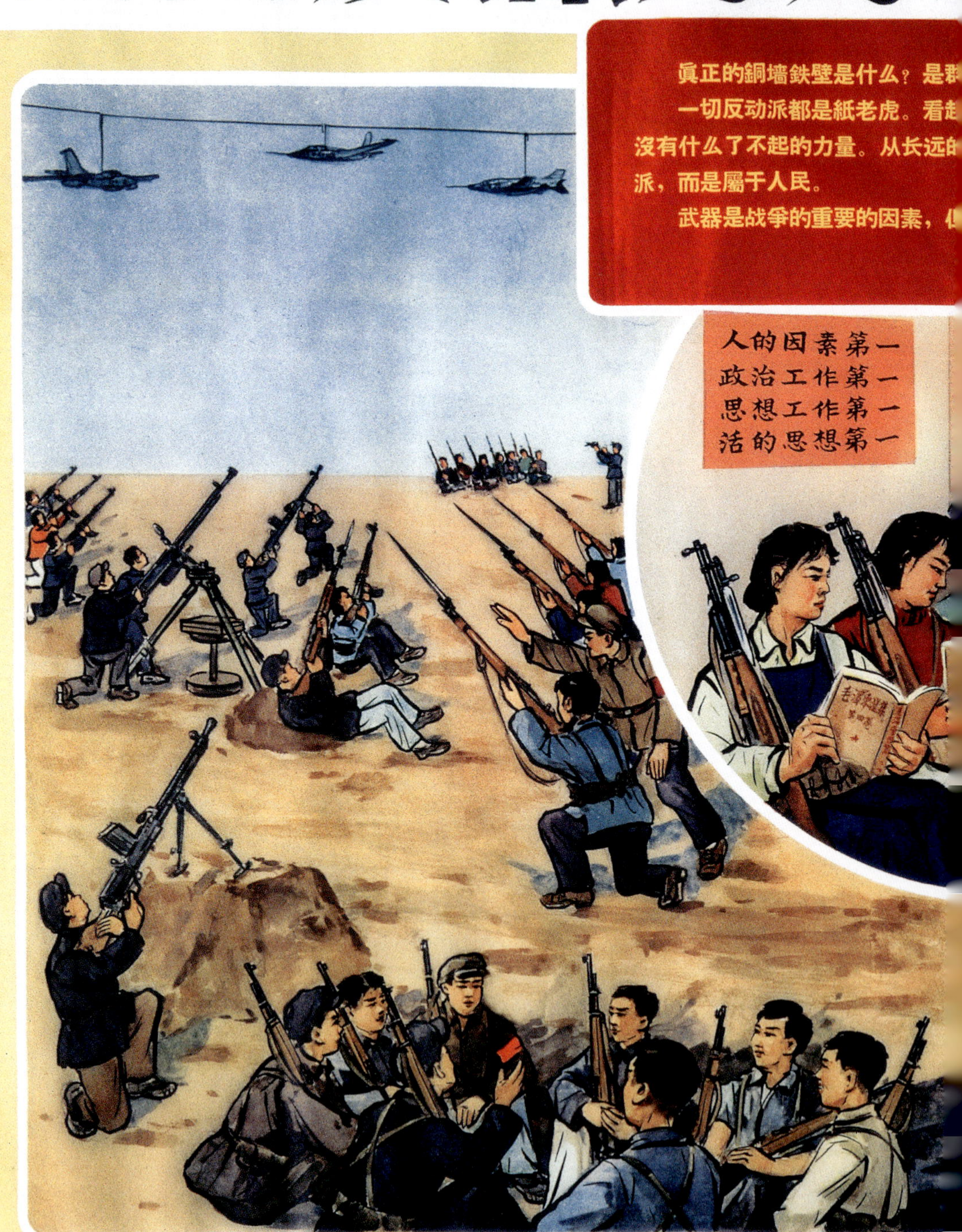

民兵防空訓练挂图之一

领、打击侵略者

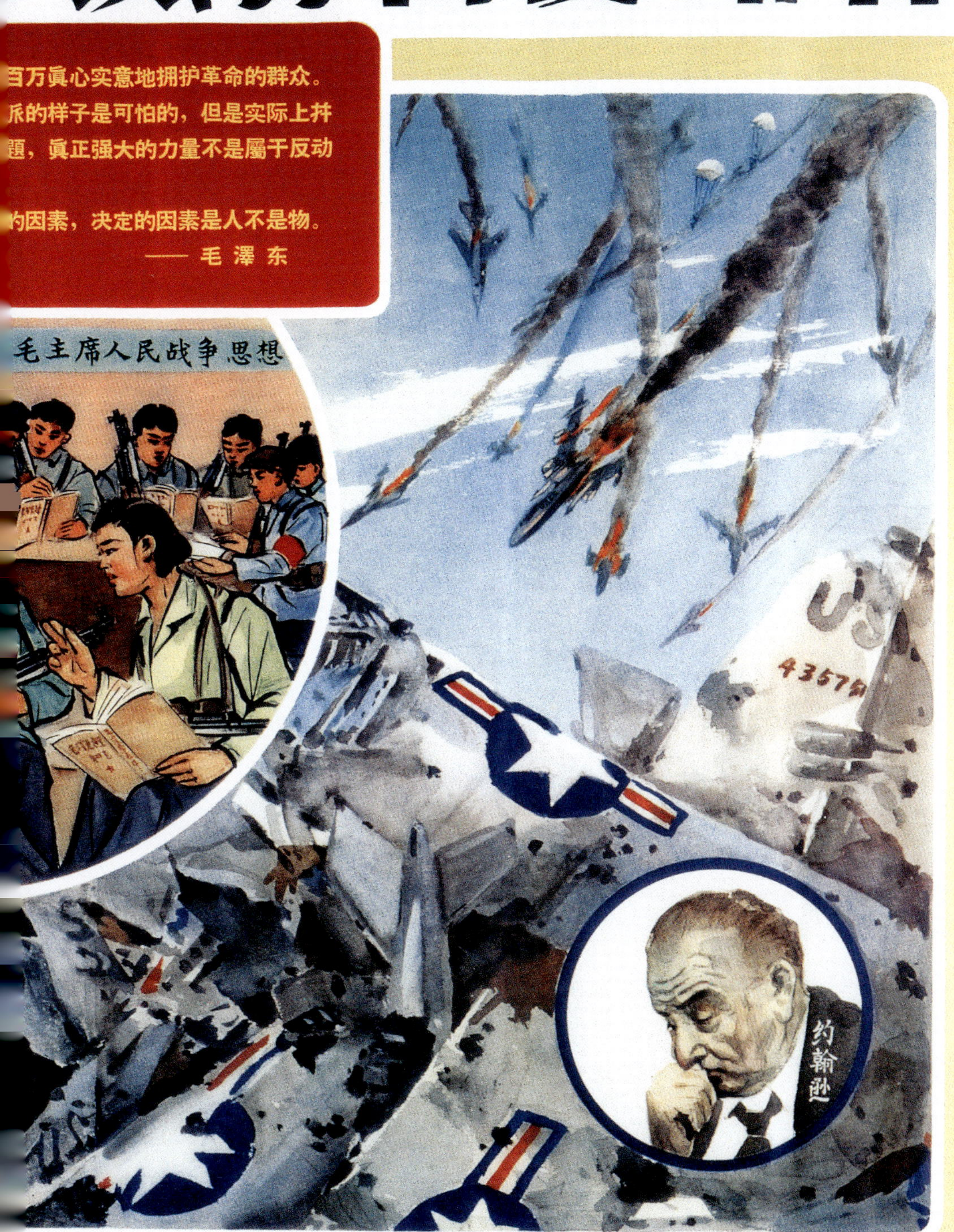

中国人民解放军总参谋部编印　一九六五年

Page 154
"All reactionaries are paper tigers. In appearance, the reactionaries are terrifying, but in reality they are not so powerful. From a long-term point of view, it is not the reactionaries but the people who are really powerful." Mao Zedong Poster shown at the "Long Live the Victory of Chairman Mao's Revolutionary Line" exhibition; Shanghai Revolutionary Educational Publishing House, 1968; 0.11 Yuan

„Alle Reaktionäre sind Papiertiger. Dem Aussehen nach sind sie Furcht erregend, aber in Wirklichkeit sind sie nicht gar so mächtig. Auf lange Sicht haben nicht die Reaktionäre, sondern hat das Volk eine wirklich große Macht." Mao Zedong Ein Exponat der Ausstellung „Es lebe der Sieg der revolutionären Linie des Vorsitzenden Mao"; Revolutionärer Erziehungsverlag Shanghai, 1968; 0,11 Yuan

« Tous les réactionnaires sont des tigres de papier. En apparence, ils sont terribles, mais en réalité, ils ne sont pas si puissants. À long terme, c'est le peuple qui est vraiment puissant, et non les réactionnaires. » Mao Zedong Affiche montrée à l'exposition « Vive la victoire de la ligne révolutionnaire du président Mao » ; Éditions Éducatives Révolutionnaires de Shanghai, 1968 ; 0,11 yuan

Pages 156–157 and opposite
Keep up to date with political thinking; perfect your fighting skills; destroy enemy invaders *Rectangular box:* What is a true bastion of iron? It is the masses, millions upon millions of people who genuinely and sincerely support the revolution. All reactionaries are paper tigers. In appearance, the reactionaries are terrifying, but in reality they are not so powerful. From a long-term point of view, it is not the reactionaries but the people who are really powerful. Weapons are an important factor in war, but not the decisive factor. It is people, not things, that are decisive. Mao Zedong *In round box, left:* Most important is the human factor, political work, ideological work, and living ideology *In round box, right:* Study Mao Zedong's ideas on the People's War *Designed and printed by:* the General Staff of the Chinese People's Liberation Army, 1965

Auf dem Vorrang der Politik beharren, Kampffähigkeiten beherrschen, einfallende Feinde vernichten *Rechteckiger Rahmen:* Wer bildet in Wirklichkeit die uneinnehmbare Festung? Die Massen, Hunderte und Tausende von Menschen, die mit ganzem Herzen die Revolution unterstützen. Alle Reaktionäre sind Papiertiger. Dem Aussehen nach sind sie Furcht erregend, aber in Wirklichkeit sind sie nicht gar so mächtig. Auf lange Sicht haben nicht die Reaktionäre, sondern hat das Volk eine wirklich große Macht. Waffen sind ein wichtiger Faktor im Krieg, aber kein entscheidender Faktor. Der entscheidende Faktor ist der Mensch und nicht das Material. Mao Zedong *Im runden Rahmen, links:* An erster Stelle steht: der Faktor Mensch, politische Arbeit, ideologische Arbeit und lebendige Ideologie *Im runden Rahmen, rechts:* Mao Zedongs Ideen über den Volkskrieg studieren *Entworfen und gedruckt vom* Generalstab der Volksbefreiungsarmee Chinas, 1965

Insistons sur le rôle prioritaire de la politique, maîtrisons nos aptitudes à combattre, anéantiseons les ennemis qui nous envahissent
Dans le cadre rectangulaire : Qui forme en réalité la forteresse imprenable ? Les masses, des centaines et des milliers de gens qui soutiennent la révolution de tout leur cœur. Tous les réactionnaires sont des tigres de papier. En apparence, ils sont terribles, mais en réalité, ils ne sont pas si puissants. À long terme, c'est le peuple qui est vraiment puissant, et non les réactionnaires. Les armes sont un facteur important de la guerre, mais non un facteur décisif. Le facteur décisif est l'homme, et non le matériel. Mao Zedong *Dans le cadre rond à gauche :* Se trouvent en première place le facteur humain, le travail politique, le travail idéologique et l'idéologie vivante *À droite :* Étudions les idées de Mao Zedong sur la guerre populaire *Conçu et imprimé par* l'état-major général de l'Armée de libération populaire de Chine, 1965

眞正的銅墻鉄壁是什么？是群众，是千百万眞心实意地拥护革命的群众。

一切反动派都是紙老虎。看起来，反动派的样子是可怕的，但是实际上并沒有什么了不起的力量。从长远的观点看問題，眞正强大的力量不是屬于反动派，而是屬于人民。

武器是战爭的重要的因素，但不是决定的因素，决定的因素是人不是物。

—— 毛澤东

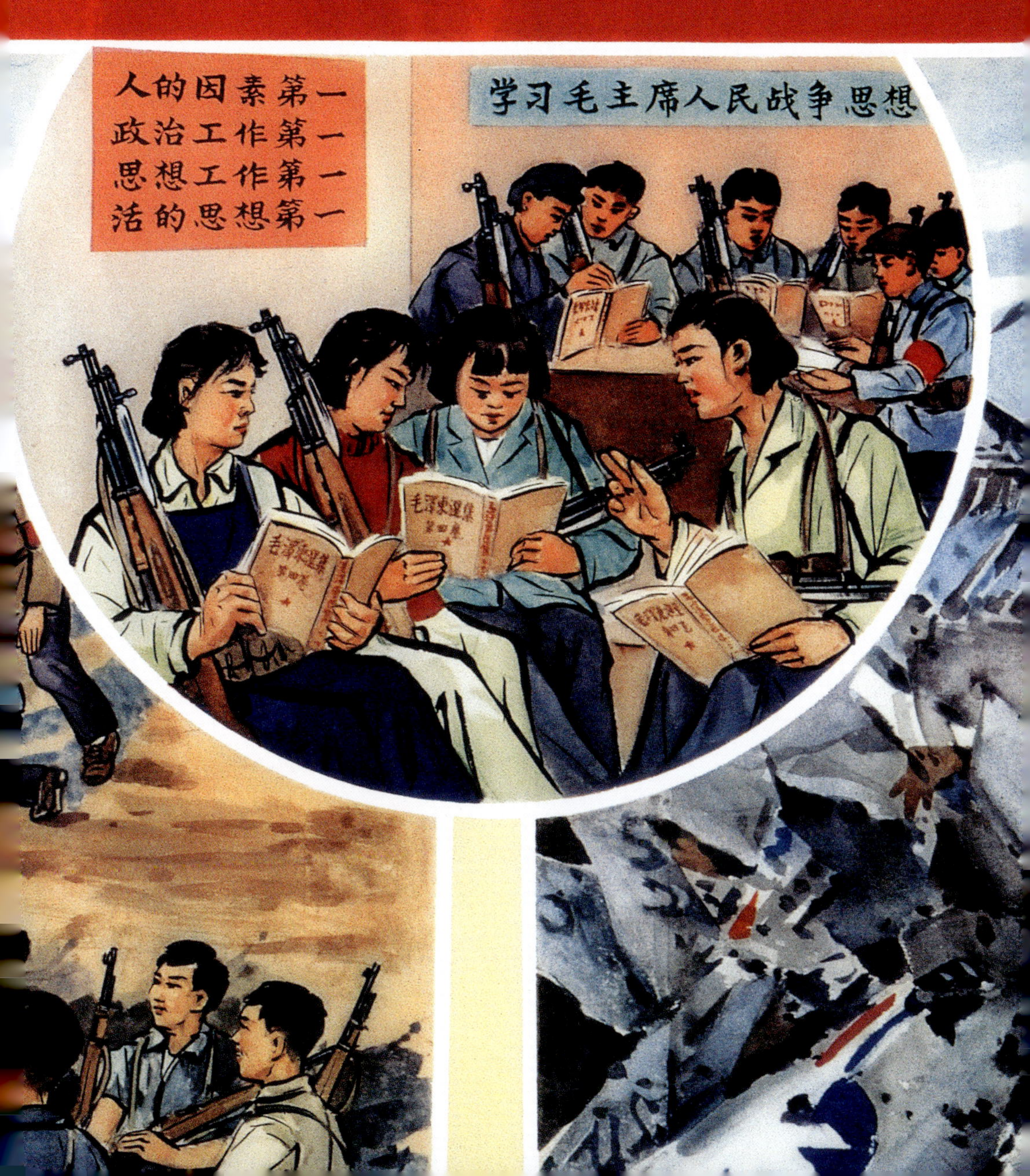

"Imperialism and all reactionaries are paper tigers. Revisionists are also paper tigers." Mao Zedong *Designed by:* People's Air Raid Protection Office of the City of Shanghai; Shanghai People's Publishing House, 1971

„Der Imperialismus und alle Reaktionäre sind Papiertiger. Die Revisionisten sind auch Papiertiger." Mao Zedong *Entwurf:* Volksluftschutzbüro der Stadt Shanghai; Volksverlag Shanghai, 1971

« L'impérialisme et tous les réactionnaires sont des tigres de papier. Les révisionnistes sont eux aussi des tigres de papier. » Mao Zedong *Conception :* Bureau de protection antiaérienne de la ville de Shanghai ; Éditions Populaires de Shanghai, 1971

"The atom bomb is a paper tiger which the U. S. reactionaries use to scare people. It looks terrible, but in fact it isn't."

Die Atombombe ist ein Papiertiger, mit dem die amerikanischen Reaktionäre die Menschen einschüchtern wollen. Sie sieht fürchterlich aus, aber in Wirklichkeit ist sie es nicht. ✶ La bombe atomique est un tigre en papier dont les réactionnaires américains se servent pour effrayer les gens. Elle a l'air terrible, mais en fait, elle ne l'est pas.

Pages 162–163
"All reactionaries are paper tigers" *On the figures:* Imperialists, Revisionists; Shanghai People's Art Publishing House, 1967 *Print run:* 110,000; 0.01 Yuan

"Alle Reaktionäre sind Papiertiger" *Auf den Figuren:* Imperialisten, Revisionisten; Volkskunstverlag Shanghai, 1967 *Auflage:* 110 000; 0,01 Yuan

« Tous les réactionnaires sont des tigres en papier » *Sur les personnages :* Impérialistes, Révisionistes ; Éditions Populaires d'Art de Shanghai, 1967 *Tirage :* 110 000 ; 0,01 yuan

帝国主义和一切反动派都是纸老虎·修正主义者也是纸老虎。 毛泽东

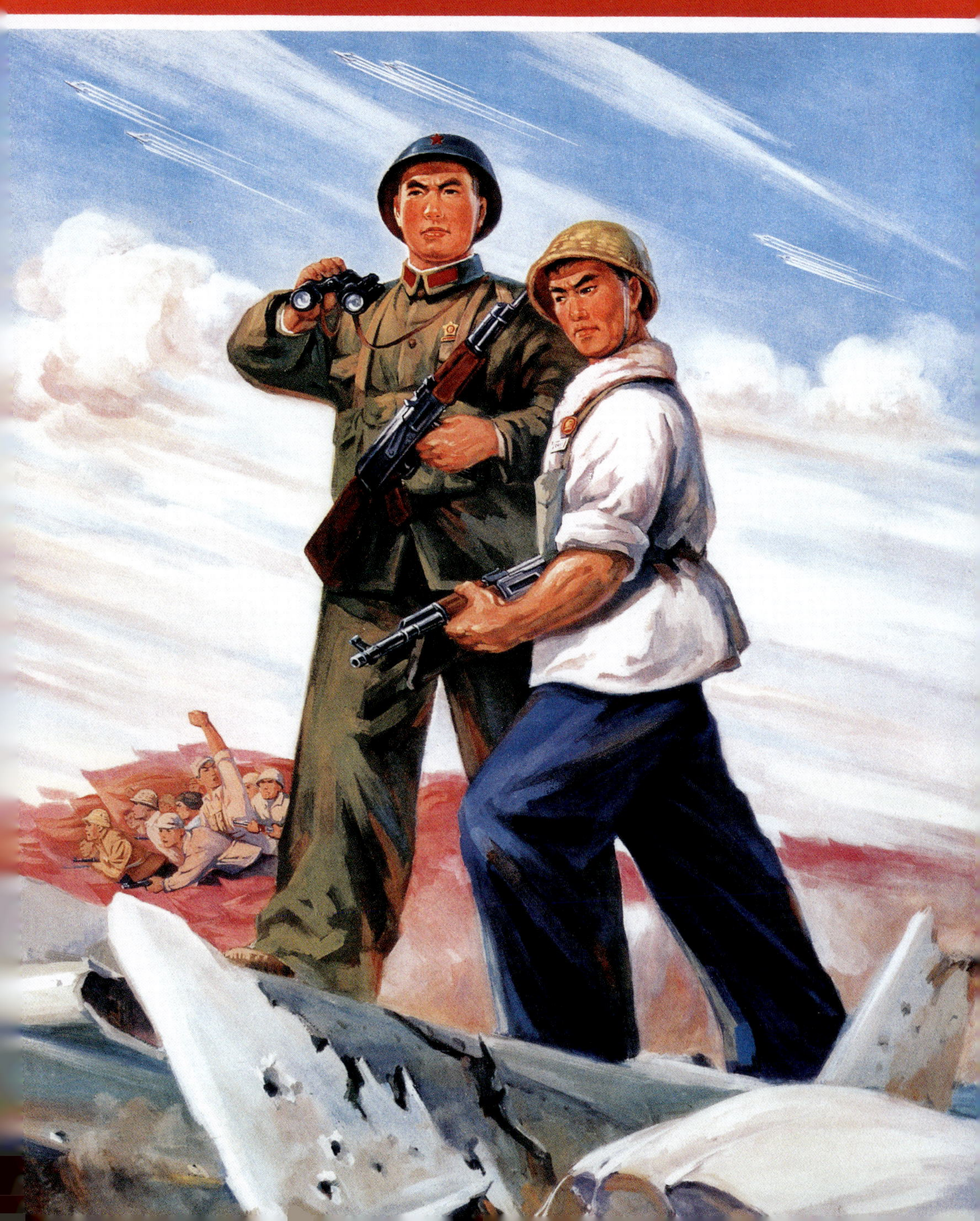

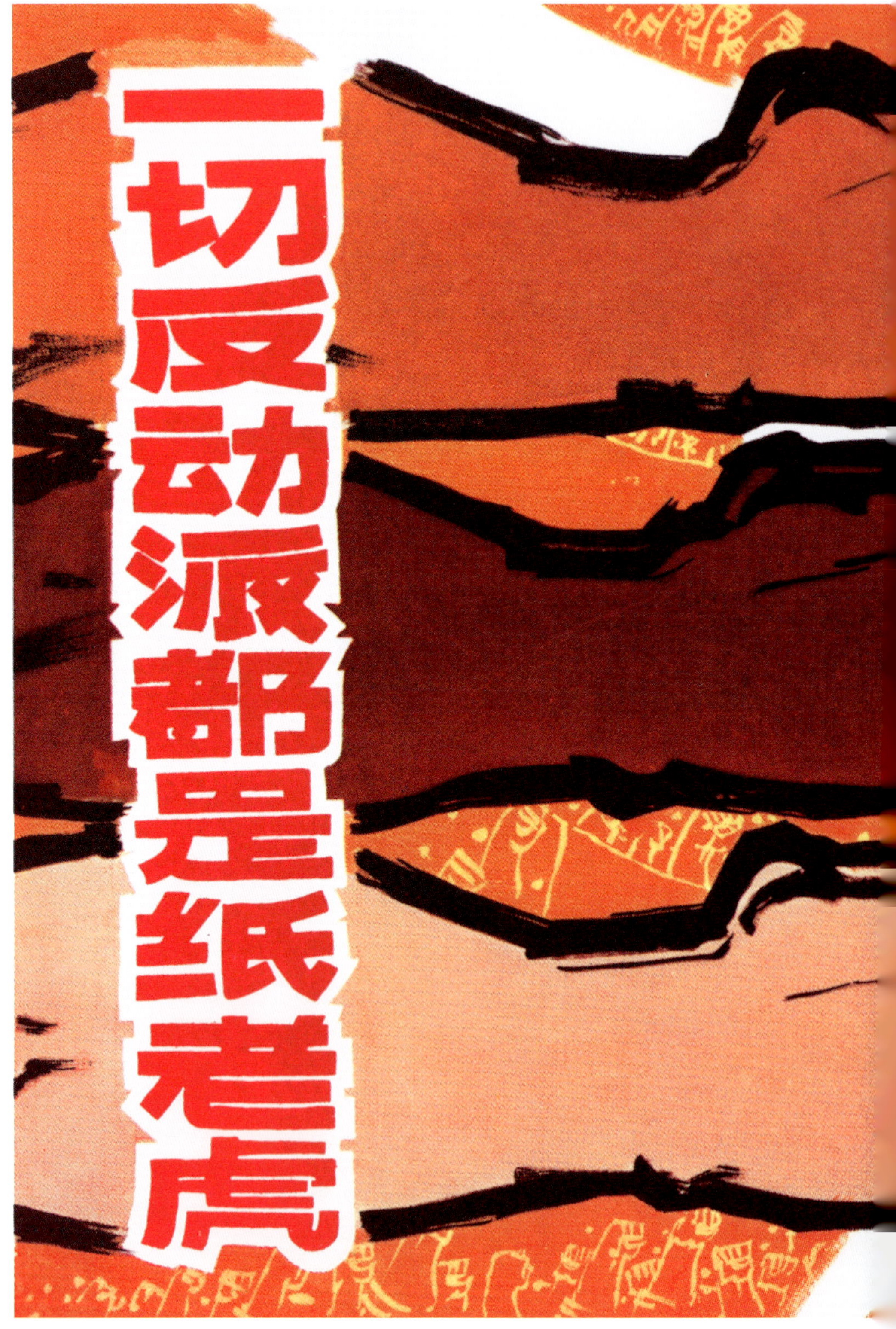
一切反动派都是纸老虎

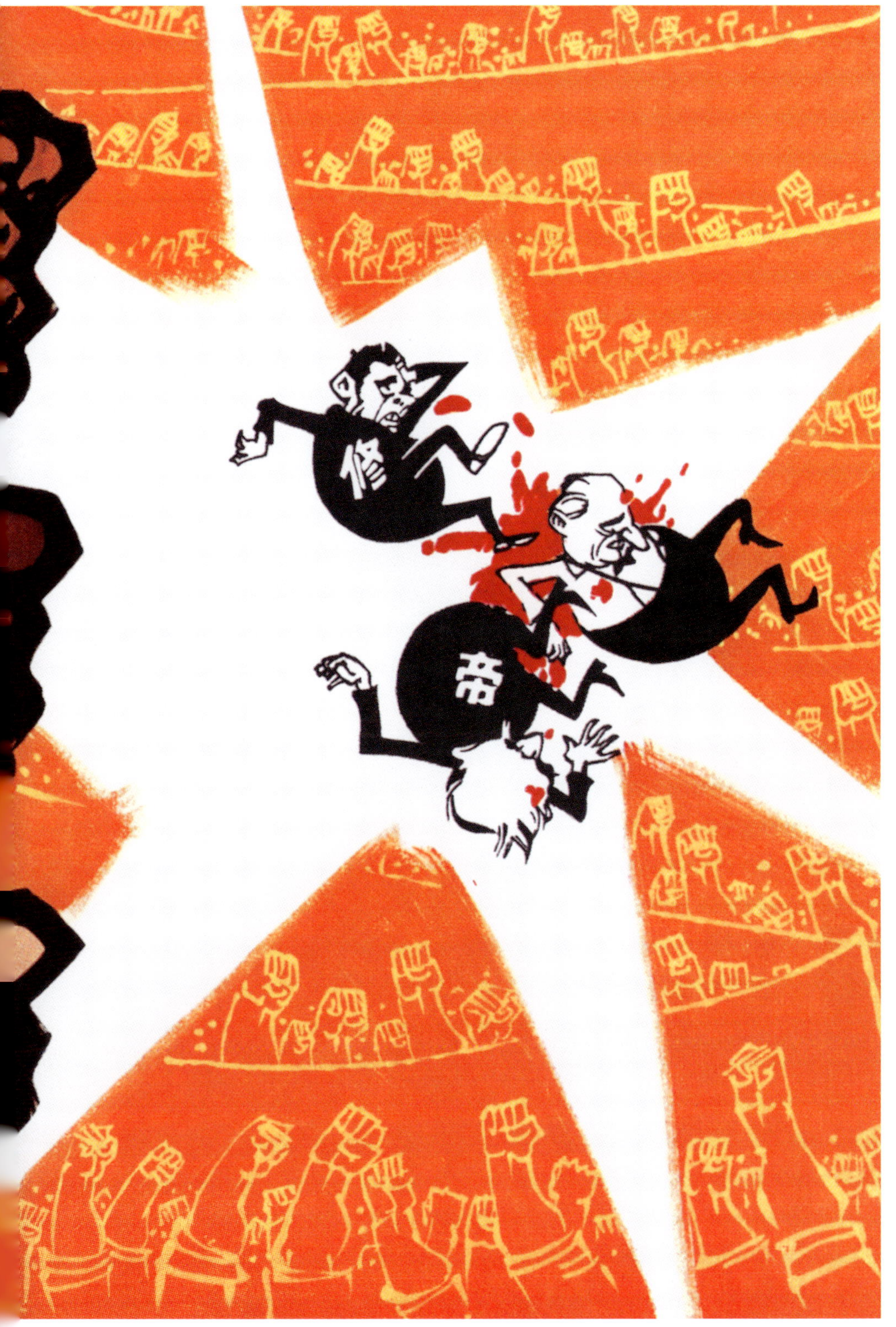
修
帝

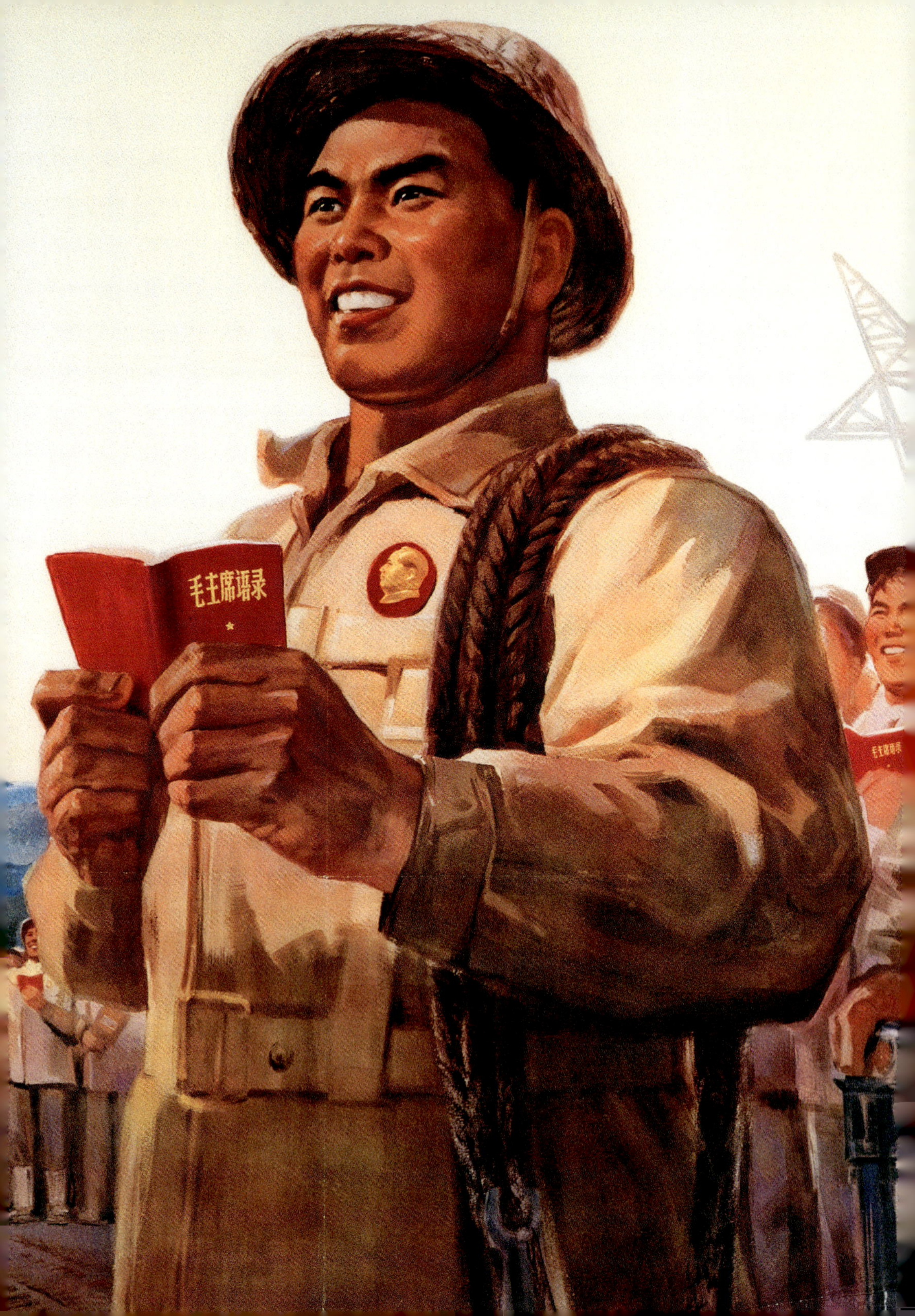
毛主席语录

VII

DARE TO STRUGGLE, DARE TO WIN

HAB MUT ZU KÄMPFEN,
HAB MUT ZU SIEGEN!
OSEZ LUTTER, OSEZ VAINCRE

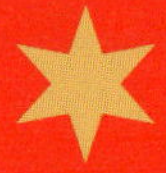

Page 164
Acting in accordance with Chairman Mao's instructions means victory *Booklet:* Quotations of Chairman Mao Zedong

Nach Anweisungen des Vorsitzenden Mao handeln, bedeutet siegen *Büchlein:* Worte des Vorsitzenden Mao Zedong

Agir selon les directives du président Mao est synonyme de victoire *Petit livre :* Citations du président Mao Zedong

"When dark clouds appeared in the sky, we pointed out that they were only temporary, that the darkness would soon pass and the sun break through."

Als sich am Himmel finstere Wolken zeigten, stellten wir fest: Das ist nur eine vorübergehende Erscheinung, die Finsternis wird bald weichen, der Morgen naht. ✶ Lorsque des nuages ont assombri le ciel, nous avons fait remarquer que ces ténèbres n'étaient que temporaires, qu'elles se dissiperaient bientôt et que le soleil brillerait sous peu.

Concentrate your hatred into the soul of your weapon and annihilate the American aggressors!

Konzentriert den Hass in der Seele des Gewehrs und vernichtet die amerikanischen Aggressoren!

Concentrez votre haine dans l'âme du fusil et écrasez les agresseurs américains !

Pages 168–169
Answer the call of Chairman Mao with determination and support the revolution in the countryside *Top left:* "In the interest of the people, lay in stores of grain in case of war or natural disaster." Mao Zedong Shanghai People's Art Publishing House, 1970s

Mit Entschlossenheit dem Aufruf des Vorsitzenden Mao Folge leisten und die Revolution im Landesinneren unterstützen *Oben links:* „Im Interesse des Volkes Getreidevorräte für den Fall eines Krieges oder einer Naturkatastrophe anlegen." Mao Zedong Volkskunstverlag Shanghai, 1970er Jahre

Répondez énergiquement à l'appel du président Mao et soutenez la révolution à l'intérieur du pays. *En haut à gauche :* « Dans l'intérêt du peuple, stockez des céréales au cas où surviendrait une guerre ou une catastrophe naturelle. » Mao Zedong Éditions Populaires d'Art de Shanghai, années 1970

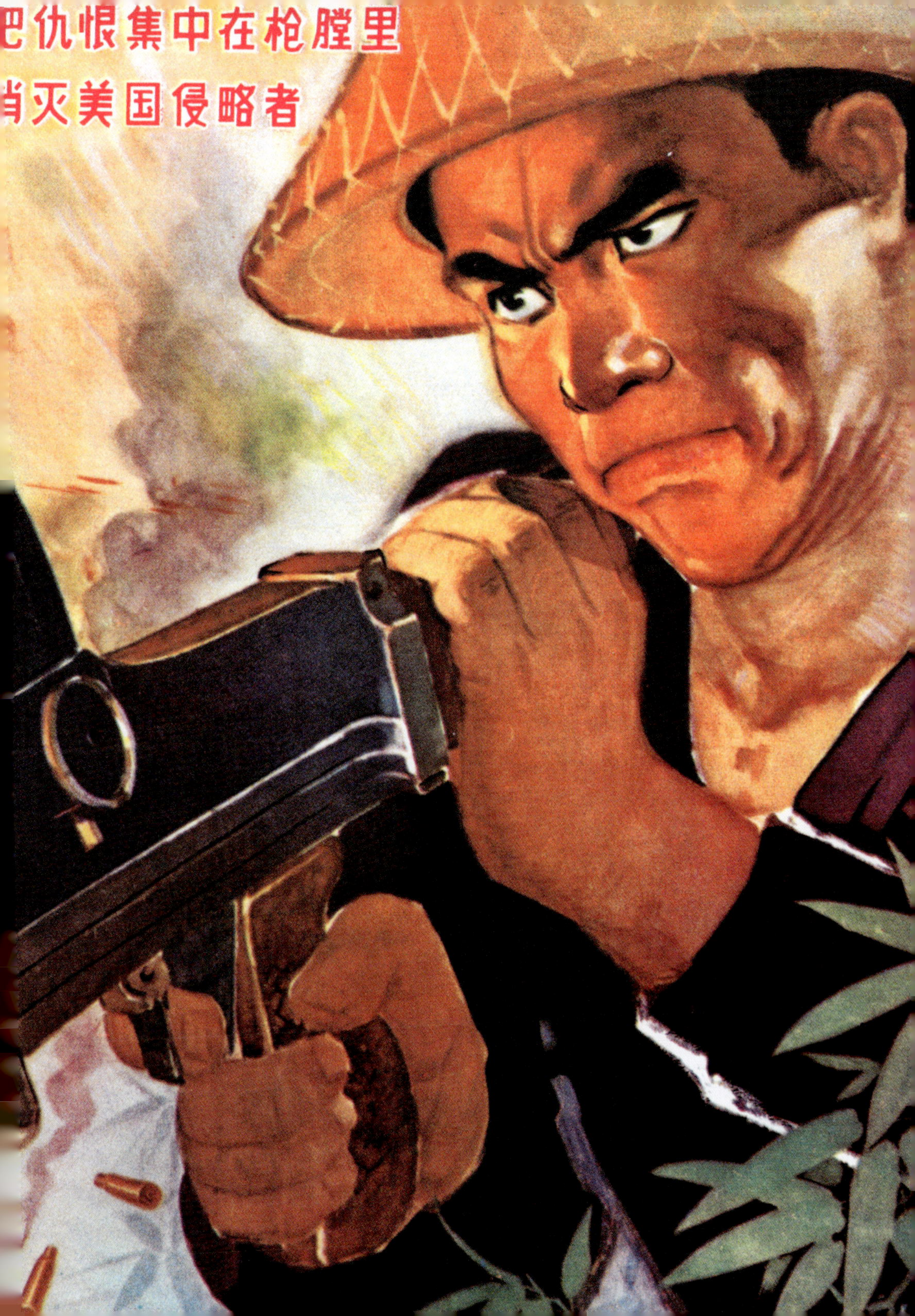
仇恨集中在枪膛里
灭美国侵略者

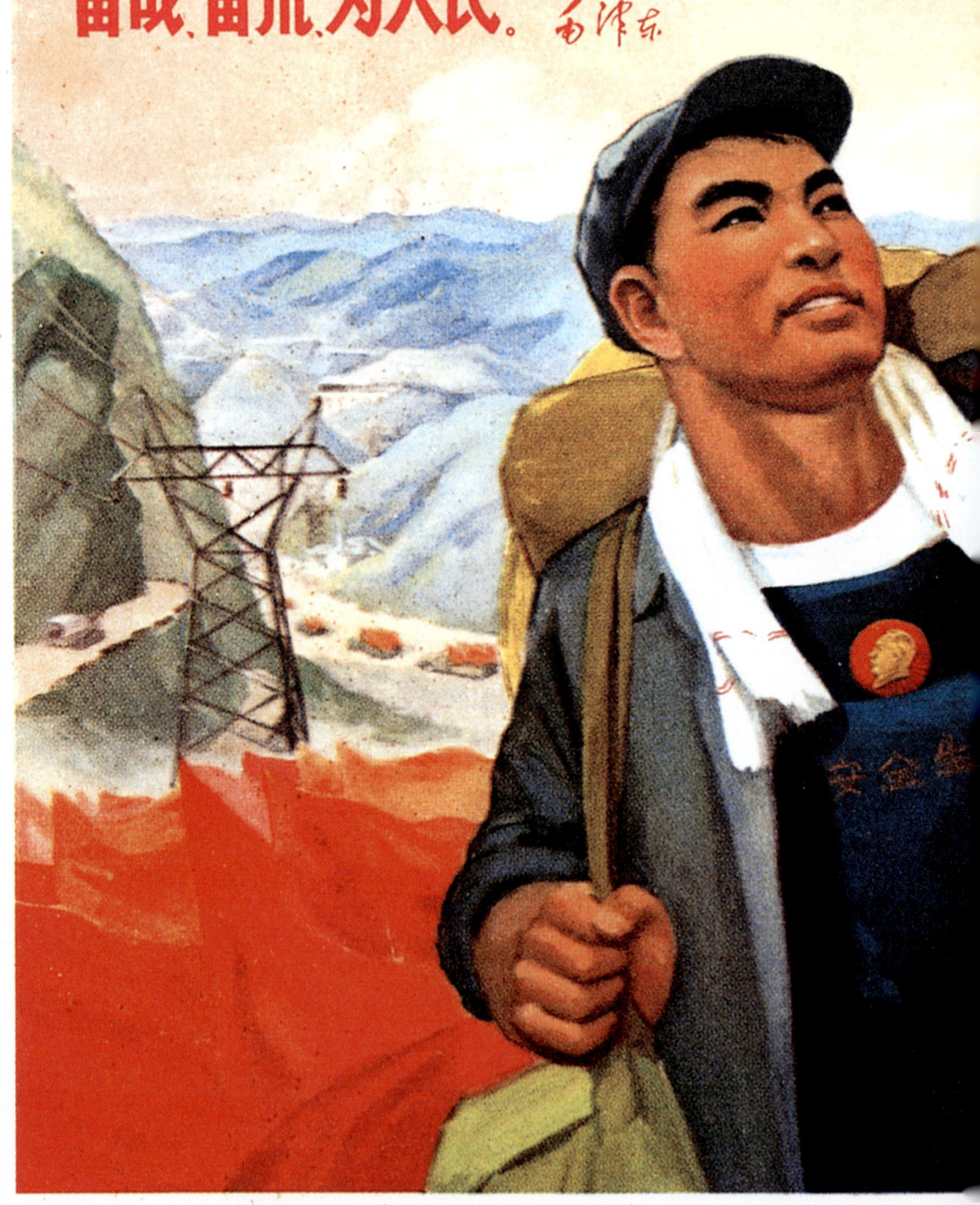
备战、备荒、为人民。
毛泽东
坚决响应毛主席的号

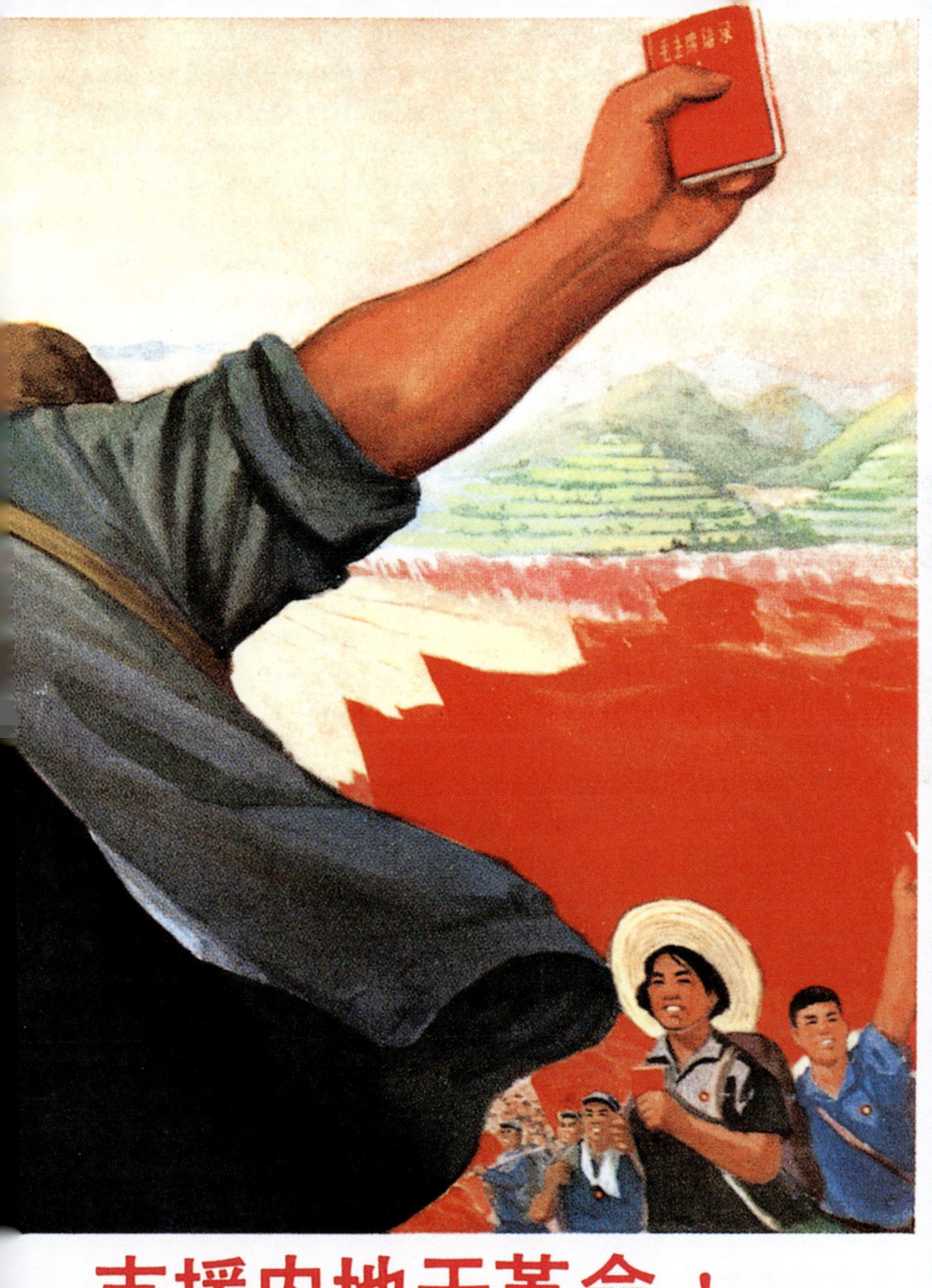
，支援内地干革命！

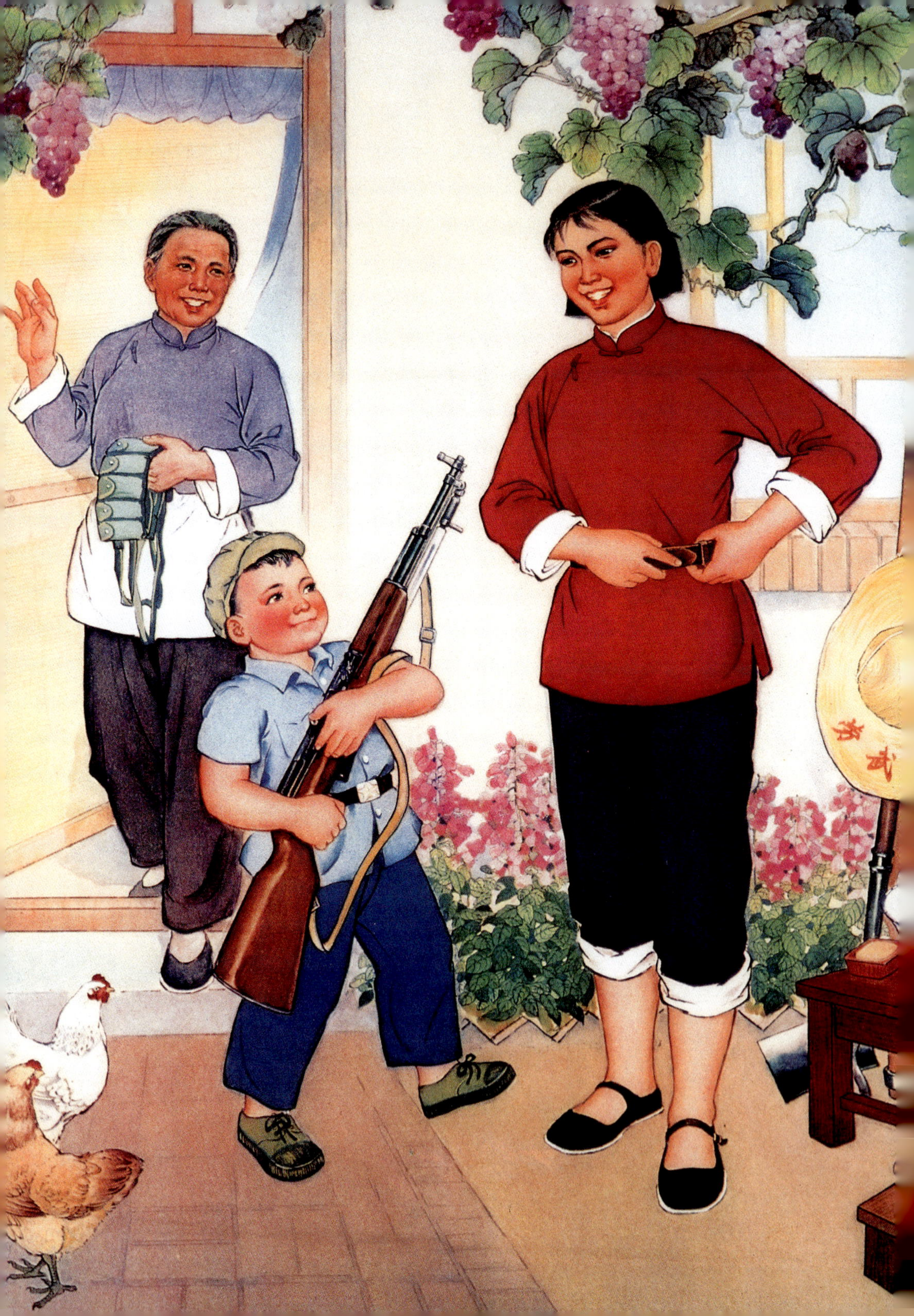
劳武

VIII

PEOPLE'S WAR

DER VOLKSKRIEG
LA GUERRE POPULAIRE

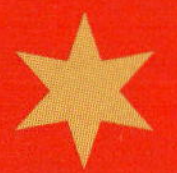

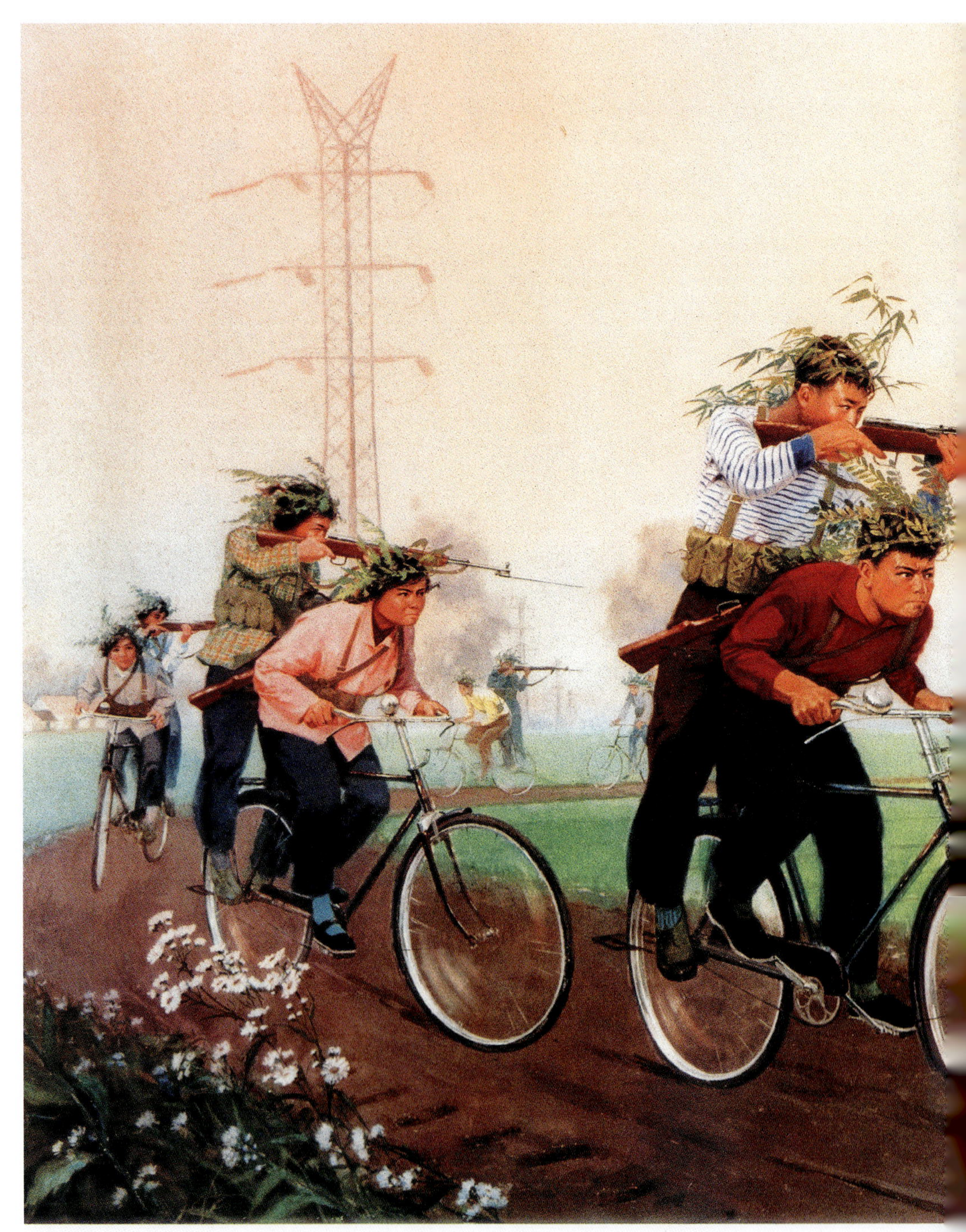

曙光初照演兵场

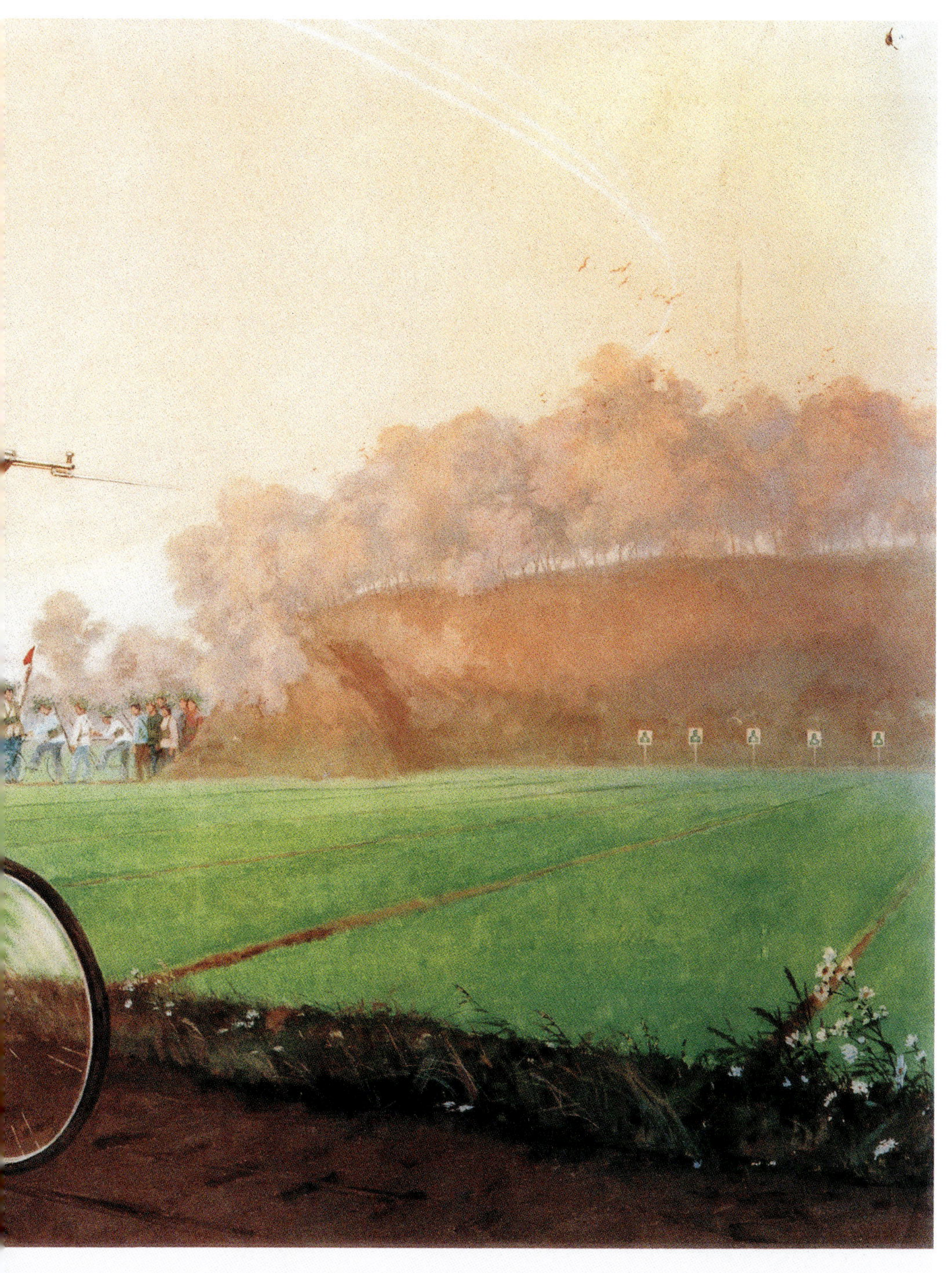

Page 170
Getting ready for military exercises *On straw hat, right:* Combine working the land with military exercises *Artist:* Zhao Jinlong; Tianjin People's Art Publishing House, 1976; 0.11 Yuan

Zur militärischen Übung gehen *Rechts auf dem Strohhut:* Landarbeit mit den militärischen Übungen verbinden *Gemalt von* Zhao Jinlong; Volkskunstverlag Tianjin, 1976; 0,11 Yuan

Je vais à l'entraînement militaire *À droite sur le chapeau de paille :* Le travail agricole et les exercices militaires doivent aller de pair *Peintre :* Zhao Jinlong ; Éditions Populaires d'Art de Tianjin, 1976 ; 0,11 yuan

Pages 172–173
The red dawn lights up our parade ground *Artist:* Yao Zhongyu; Shanghai People's Publishing House, 1974 *Print run:* 300,000; 0.11 Yuan

Morgenröte erleuchtet unseren Exerzierplatz *Gemalt von* Yao Zhongyu; Volksverlag Shanghai, 1974; *Auflage:* 300 000; 0,11 Yuan

L'aurore illumine notre terrain d'exercices *Peintre :* Yao Zhongyu ; Éditions Populaires de Shanghai, 1974 ; *Tirage :* 300 000 ; 0,11 yuan

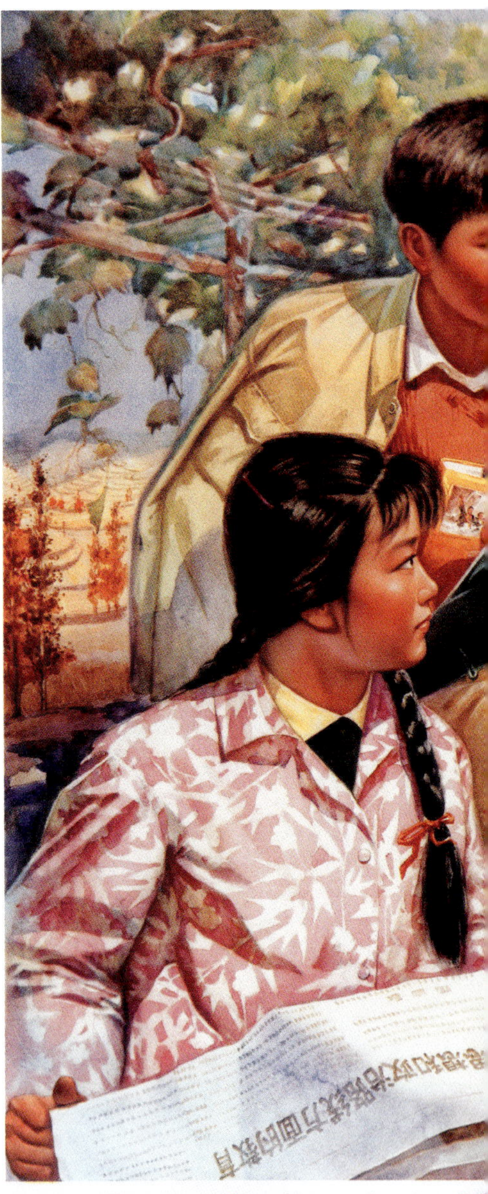

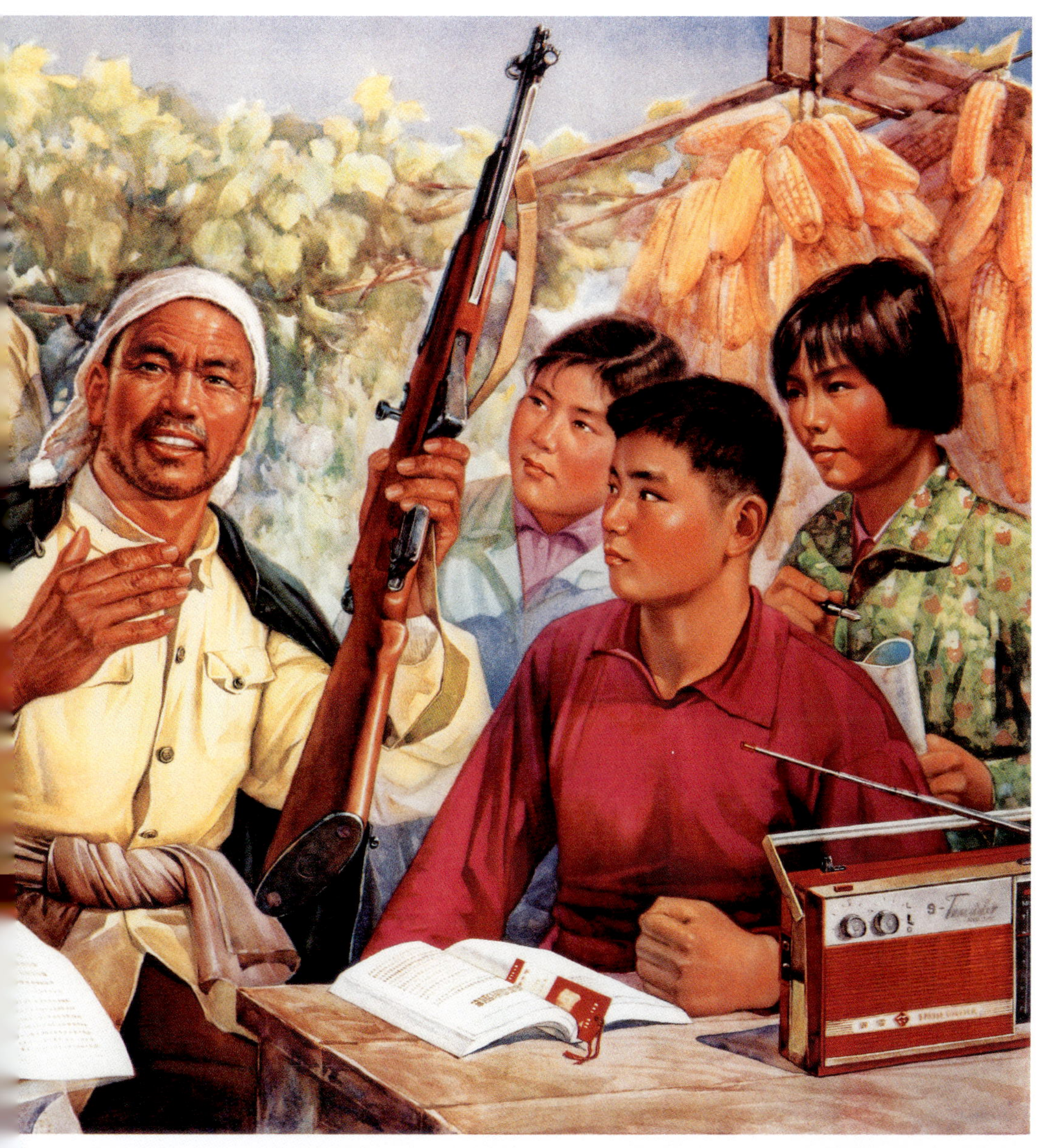

Always keep a firm grip on the rifle *Bottom left, on newspaper:* Provide an education in the spirit of the ideological and political line *Artist:* Yao Zhongyu; Shanghai People's Publishing House, 1st edn 1973, 2nd edn 1974
Print run: 100,001– 1,300,000; 0.11 Yuan

Das Gewehr immer fest in der Hand halten *Unten links auf der Zeitung:* Eine Erziehung im Sinne der ideologischen und politischen Linie durchführen *Gemalt von* Yao Zhongyu; Volksverlag Shanghai, 1. Aufl. 1973, 2. Aufl. 1974
Auflage: 100 001–1 300 000; 0,11 Yuan

Ayez toujours votre fusil bien en main *Sur le journal, en bas à gauche :* Donnez une éducation qui aille dans le sens de la ligne idéologique et politique *Peintre :* Yao Zhongyu ; Éditions Populaires de Shanghai, 1ère éd. 1973, 2e éd. 1974
Tirage : 1 000 001–1 300 000; 0,11 yuan

Carrying out military exercises *Artist:* Zhang Jianhua of the city of Yantai's Print Works; Shandong People's Publishing House, 1976; 0.11 Yuan

Militärische Übungen durchführen *Gemalt von* Zhang Jianhua, Druckerei der Stadt Yantai; Volksverlag Shandong, 1976; 0,11 Yuan

Faisons des exercices militaires *Peintre :* Zhang Jianhua, Presses de la ville de Yantai ; Éditions populaires du Shandong, 1976 ; 0,11 yuan

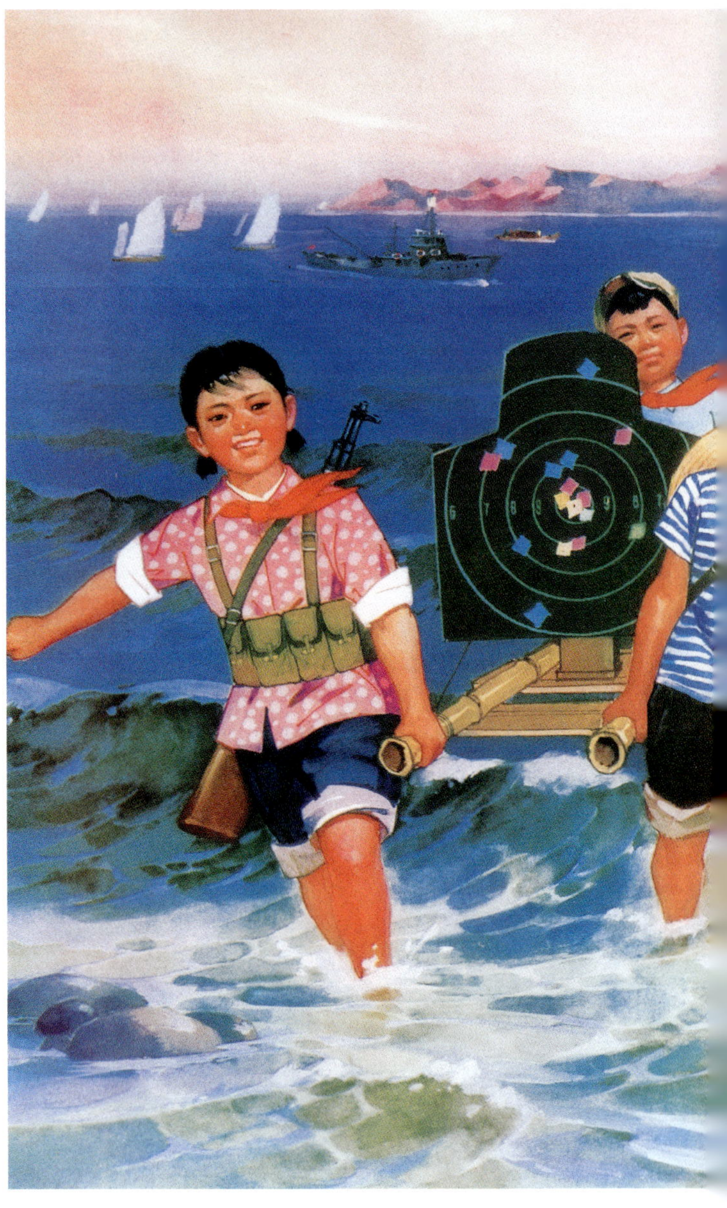

Pages 178–179

In the footsteps of the Red Army *Sign, left:* The struggle of Huang Yangjie *Artist:* Zhang Renlian; Shanghai People's Publishing House, 1st edn 1976, 2nd edn 1976; 0.11 Yuan

Auf dem Weg der Roten Armee *Schild links:* Der Kampf von Huang Yangjie *Gemalt von* Zhang Renlian; Volksverlag Shanghai, 1. Aufl. 1976, 2. Aufl. 1976; 0,11 Yuan

Sur la voie de l'Armée Rouge *Panneau à gauche :* Le combat de Huang Yangjie *Peintre :* Zhang Renlian ; Éditions Populaires de Shanghai, 1ère éd. 1976, 2e éd. 1976 ; 0,11 yuan

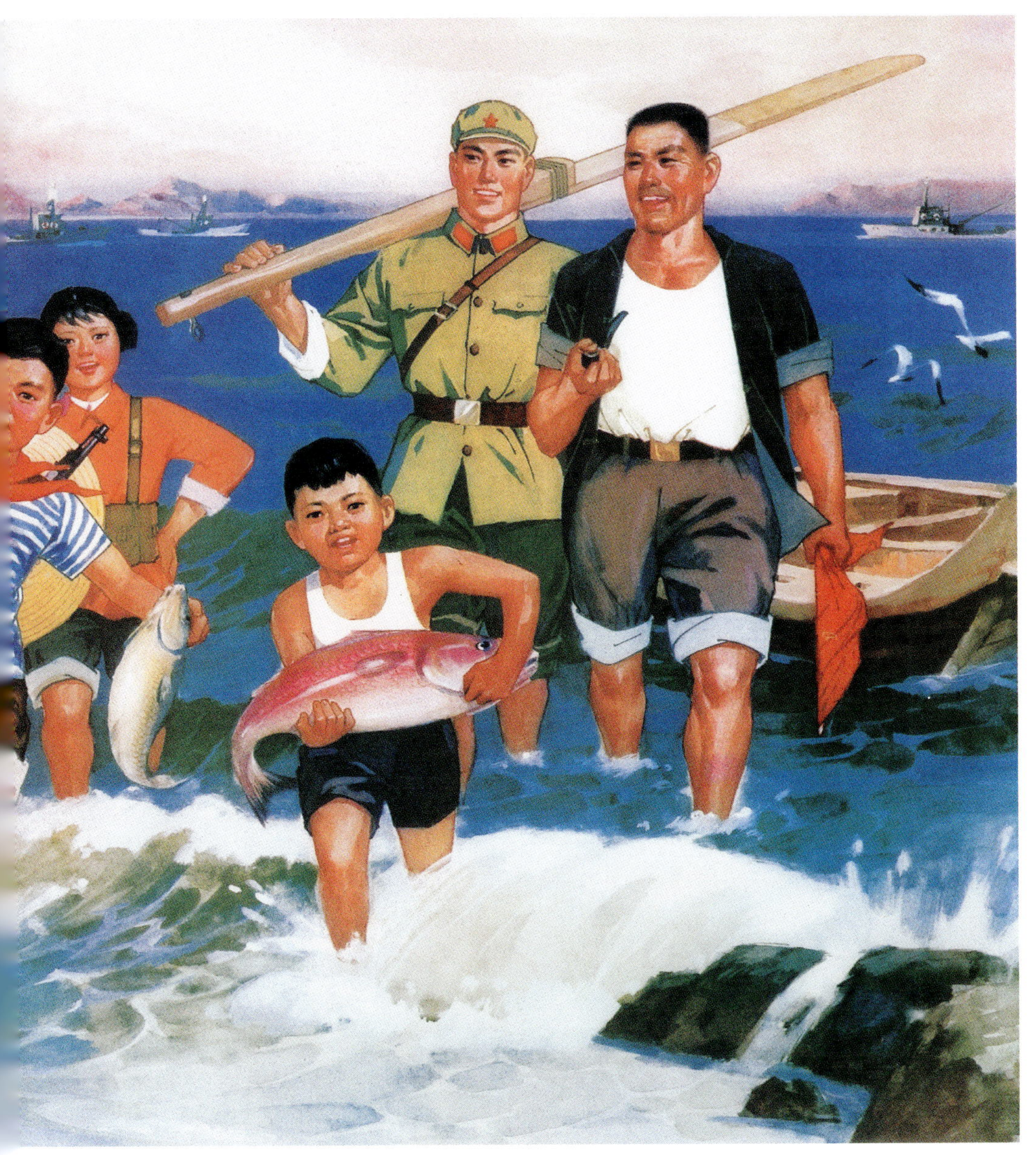

“The richest source of power to wage war lies in the masses of the people.”

Die stärkste Kraftquelle für die Kriegsführung liegt in den Volksmassen. ✶ Les grandes forces de la guerre ont leurs sources profondes dans les masses populaires.

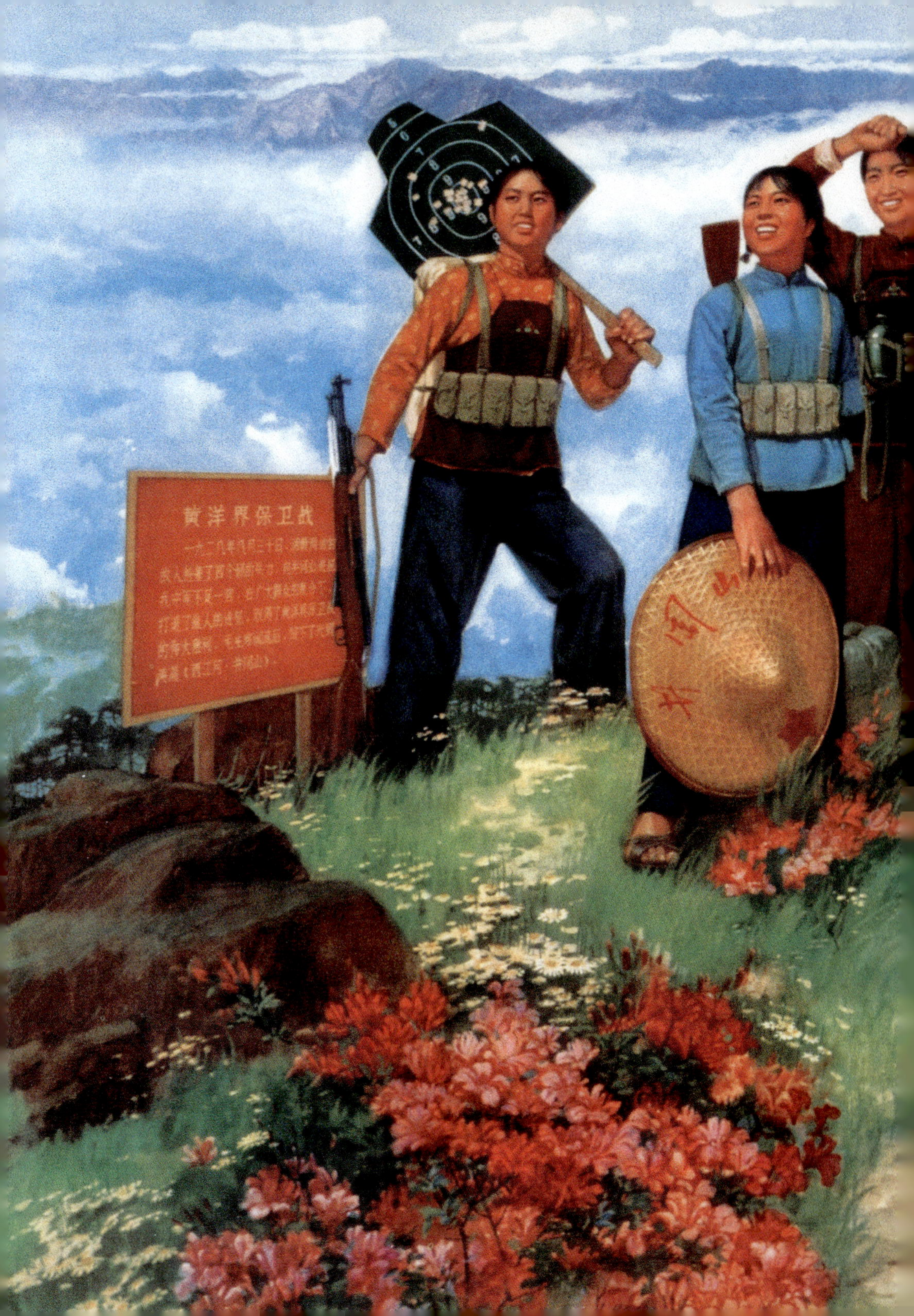
黄洋界保卫战

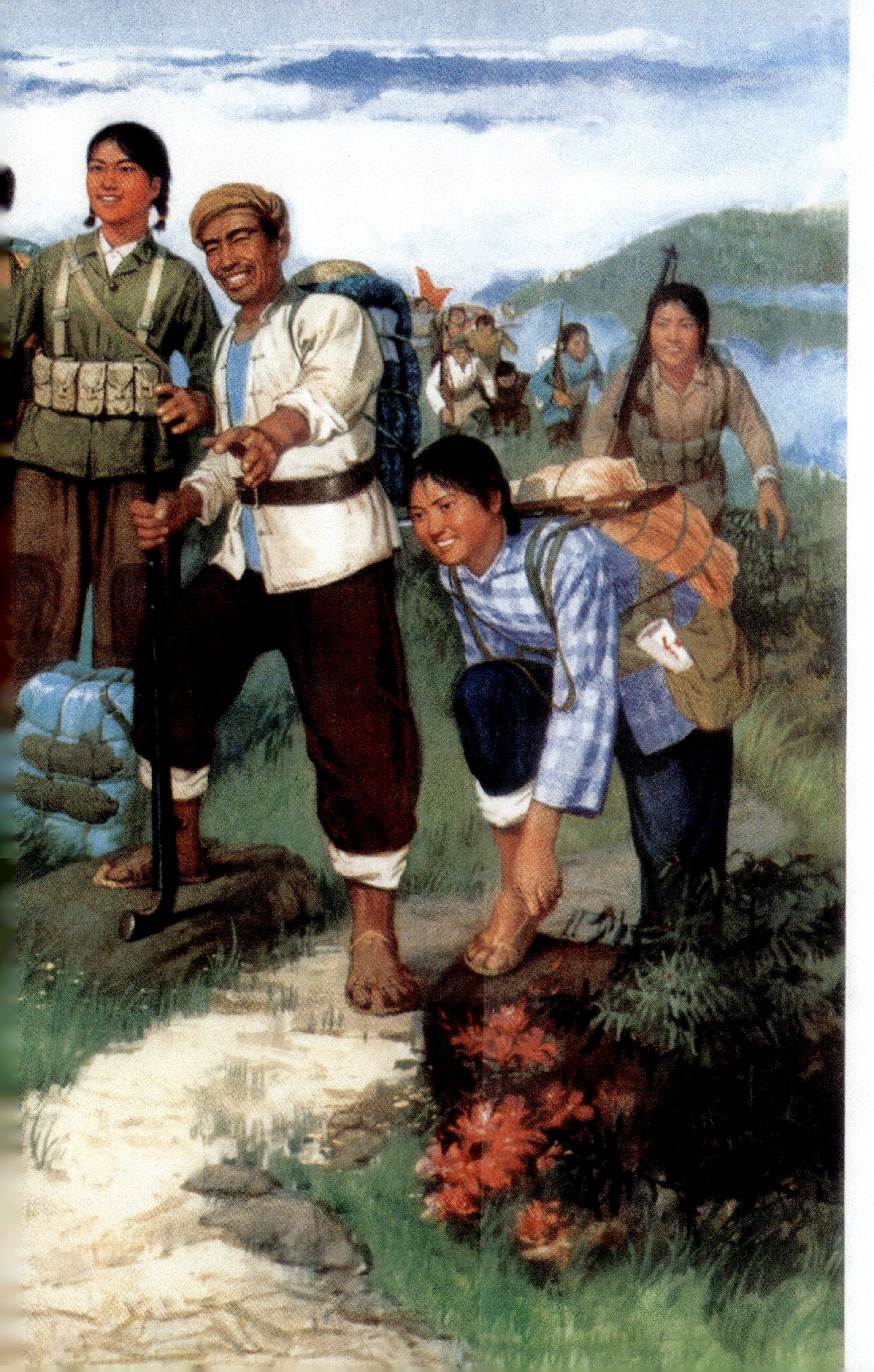

红军路上

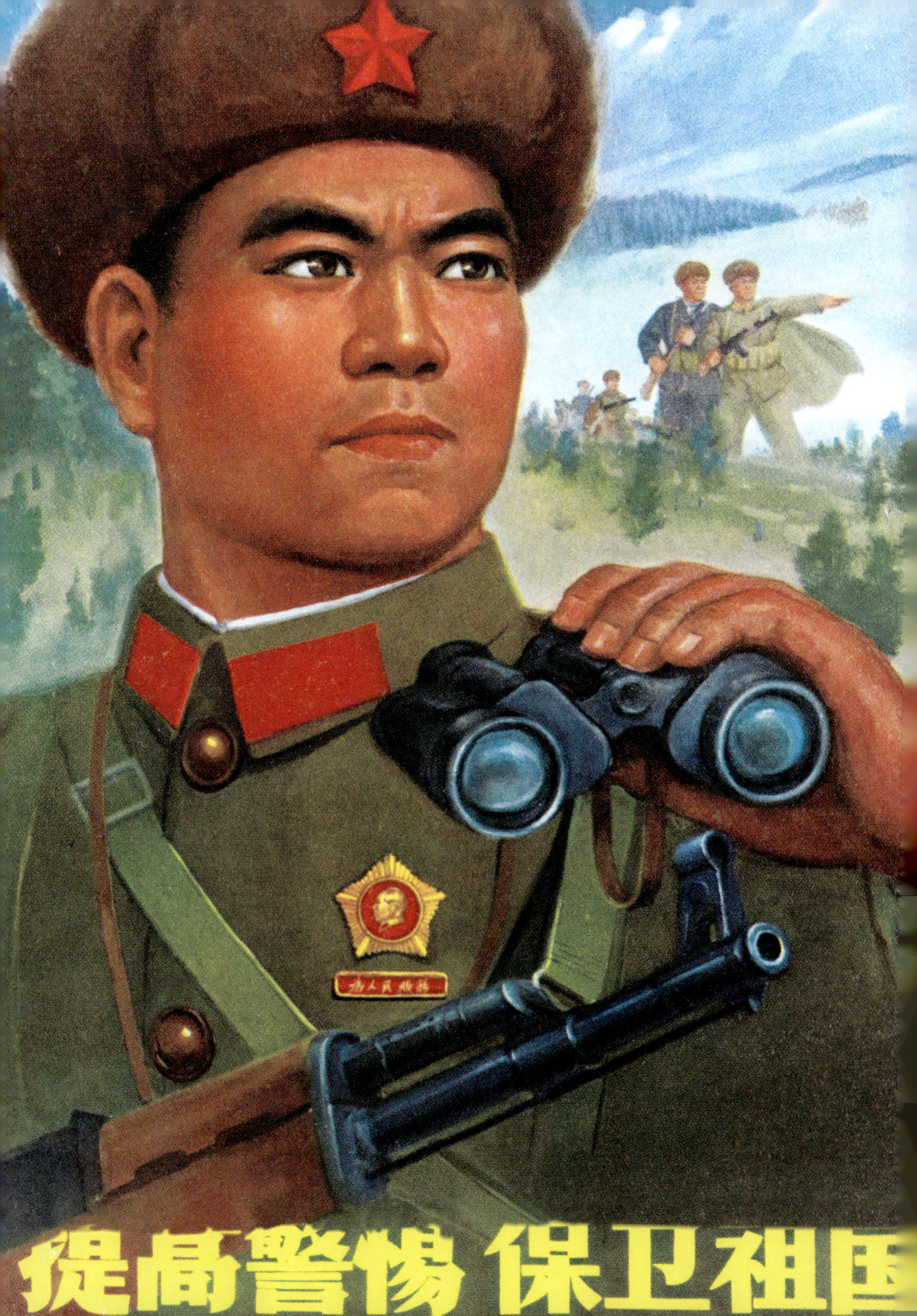
为人民服务
提高警惕 保卫祖国

IX

THE PEOPLE'S ARMY

DIE ARMEE DES VOLKES
L'ARMÉE POPULAIRE

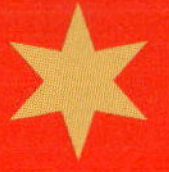

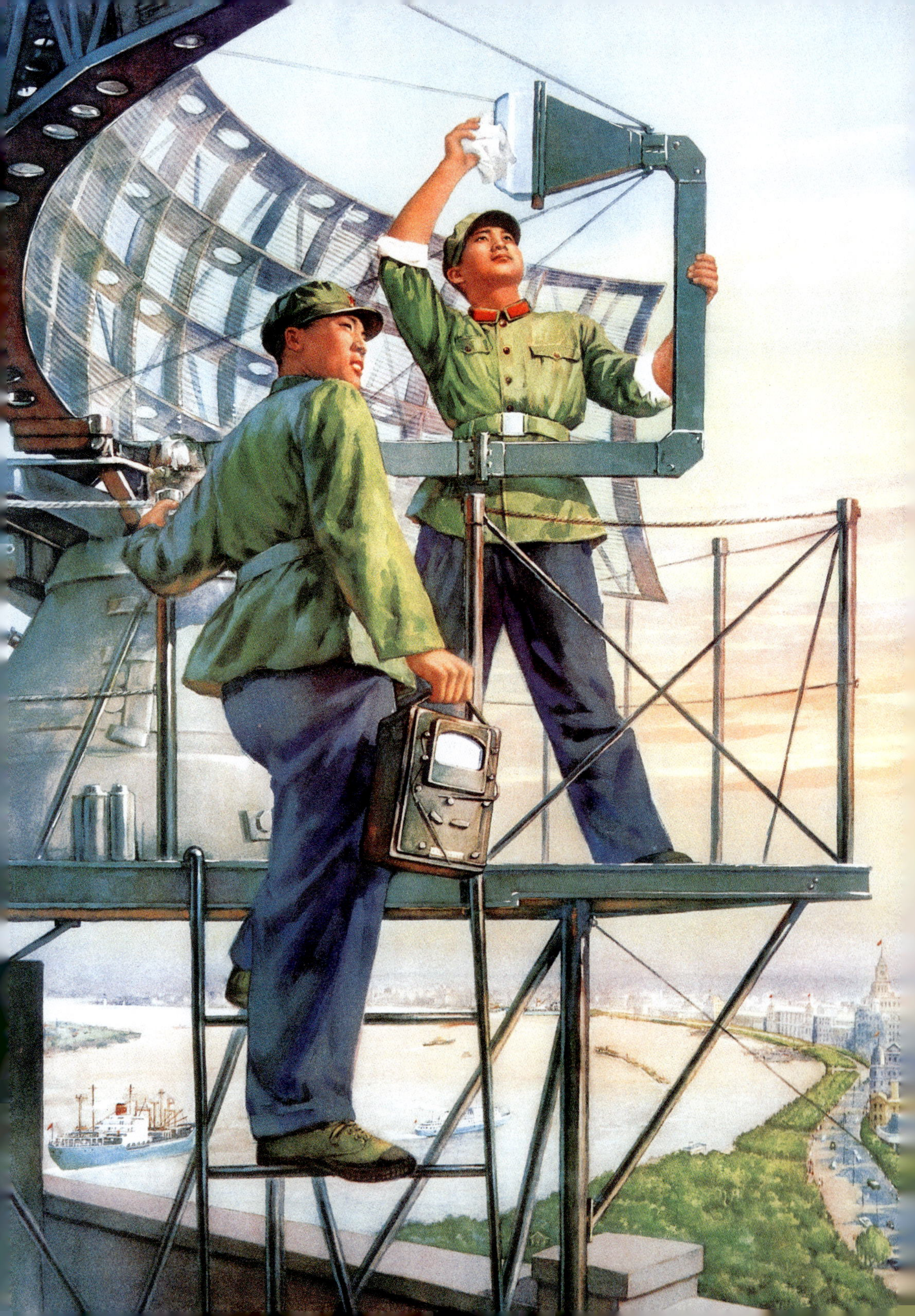

Page 180
Increase vigilance and defend the Fatherland *Artist:* Hong Ying of the Nanjin Regional Airforce; Shanghai People's Publishing House, 1970s; 0.01 Yuan

Erhöht die Wachsamkeit und verteidigt das Vaterland *Gemalt von* Hong Ying von der Luftwaffe des Bezirks Nanjing; Volkskunstverlag Shanghai, 1970er Jahre; 0,01 Yuan

Augmentez la vigilance pour défendre la patrie *Peintre :* Hong Ying de l'Armée de l'air de la région de Nanjing ; Éditions Populaires d'Art de Shanghai, années 1970 ; 0,01 yuan

Keeping our eyes open
Original by: Wang Hongyu, Lin Jianguo, Zhang Diping and Hu Zhenlang *Adapted by:* Xu Yupin; Shanghai People's Publishing House, 1st edn 1974, 2nd edn 1975; *Print run:* 800,000–1,000,000; 0.11 Yuan

Die Augen offen halten
Originalfassung: Wang Hongyu, Lin Jianguo, Zhang Diping und Hu Zhenlang *Adaptation:* Xu Yupin; Volksverlag Shanghai, 1. Aufl. 1974, 2. Aufl. 1975 *Auflage:* 800 000–1 000 000; 0,11 Yuan

Gardons les yeux ouverts
Version originale : Wang Hongyu, Lin Jianguo, Zhang Diping et Hu Zhenlang *Adaptation :* Xu Yupin ; Éditions Populaires de Shanghai, 1ère éd. 1974, 2e éd. 1975 ; *Tirage:* 800 000–1 000 000 ; 0,11 yuan

Pages 184–185
Our dear comrade in the People's Liberation Army is a nice person *Artist:* Shen Shaolun; Shanghai People's Art Publishing House; 0.11 Yuan

Der Onkel von der Volksbefreiungsarmee ist lieb *Gemalt von* Shen Shaolun; Volkskunstverlag Shanghai; 0,11 Yuan

L'oncle de l'Armée de Libération populaire est gentil
Peintre : Shen Shaolun ; Éditions Populaires d'Art de Shanghai ; 0,11 yuan

Pages 186–187
Follow the instructions from the highest level: "Do your best and annihilate the invading enemy!"
1970s

Mit Entschlossenheit die höchste Anweisung befolgen: „Tut euer Bestes und vernichtet die einfallenden Feinde!"
1970er Jahre

Suivez résolument la directive suprême: « Faites de votre mieux pour écraser les envahisseurs ennemis! »
Années 1970

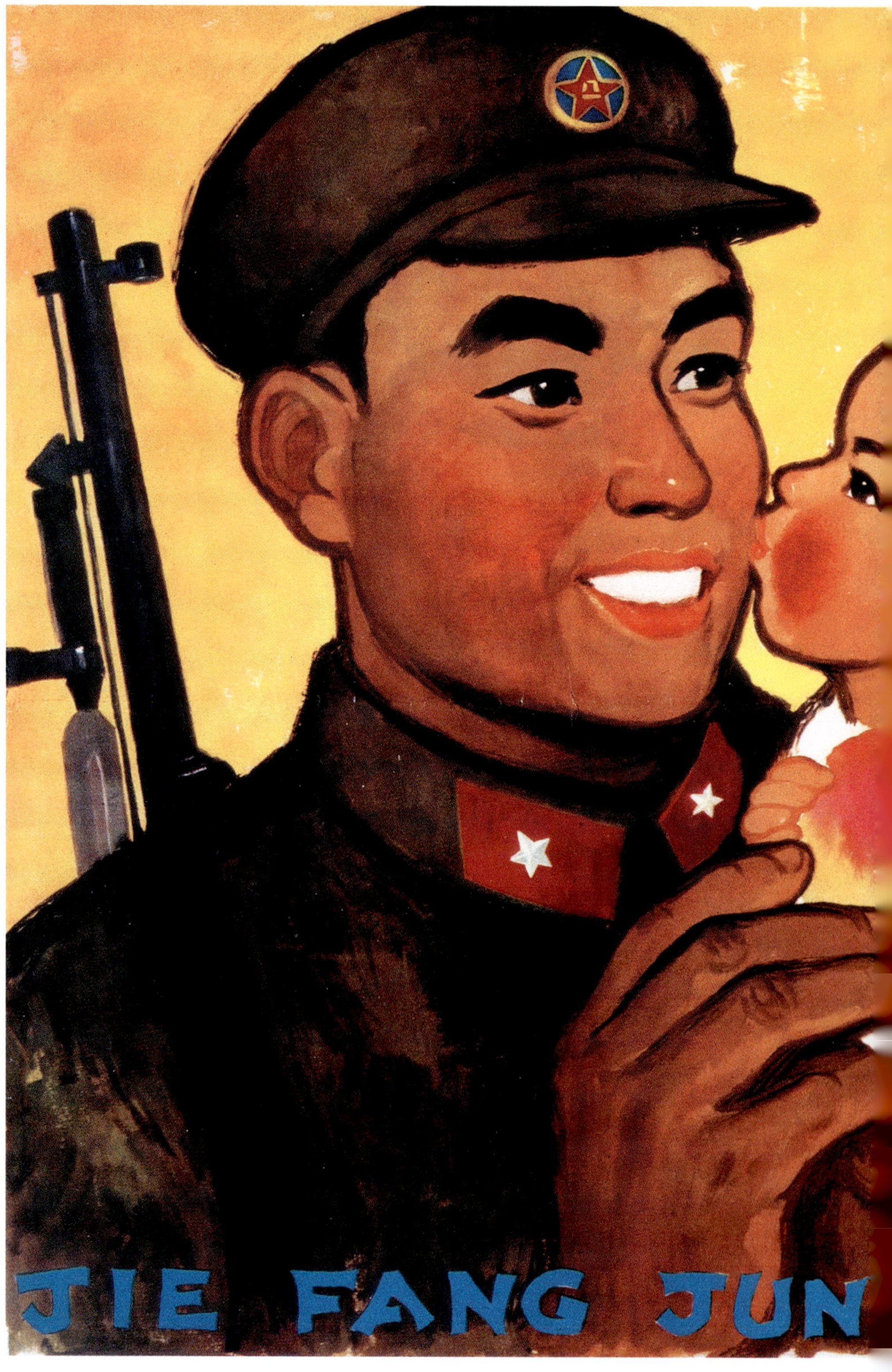
JIE FANG JUN

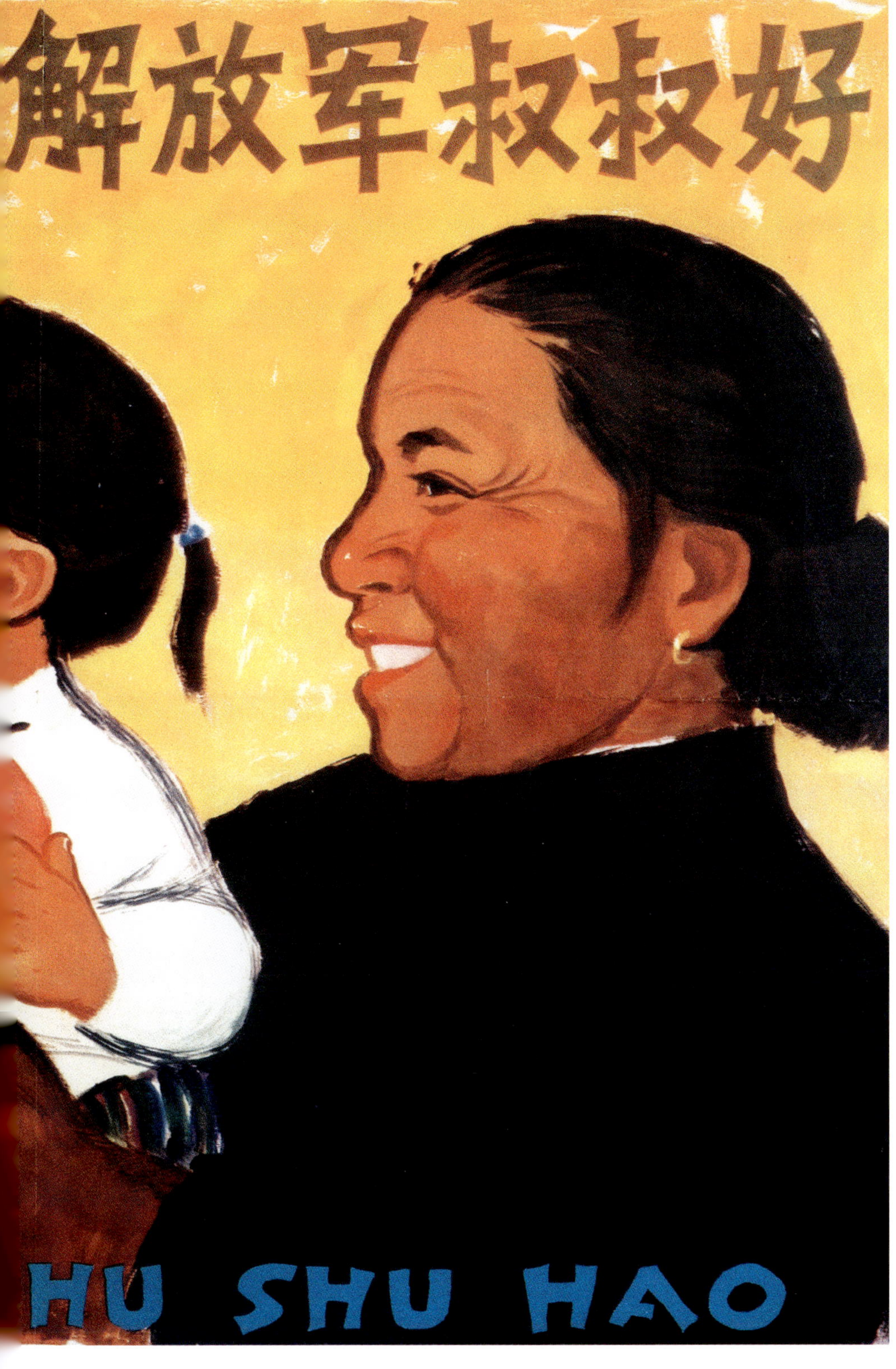
解放军叔叔好
HU SHU HAO

坚决执行最高指示：

全力以赴，殲滅入侵之敵

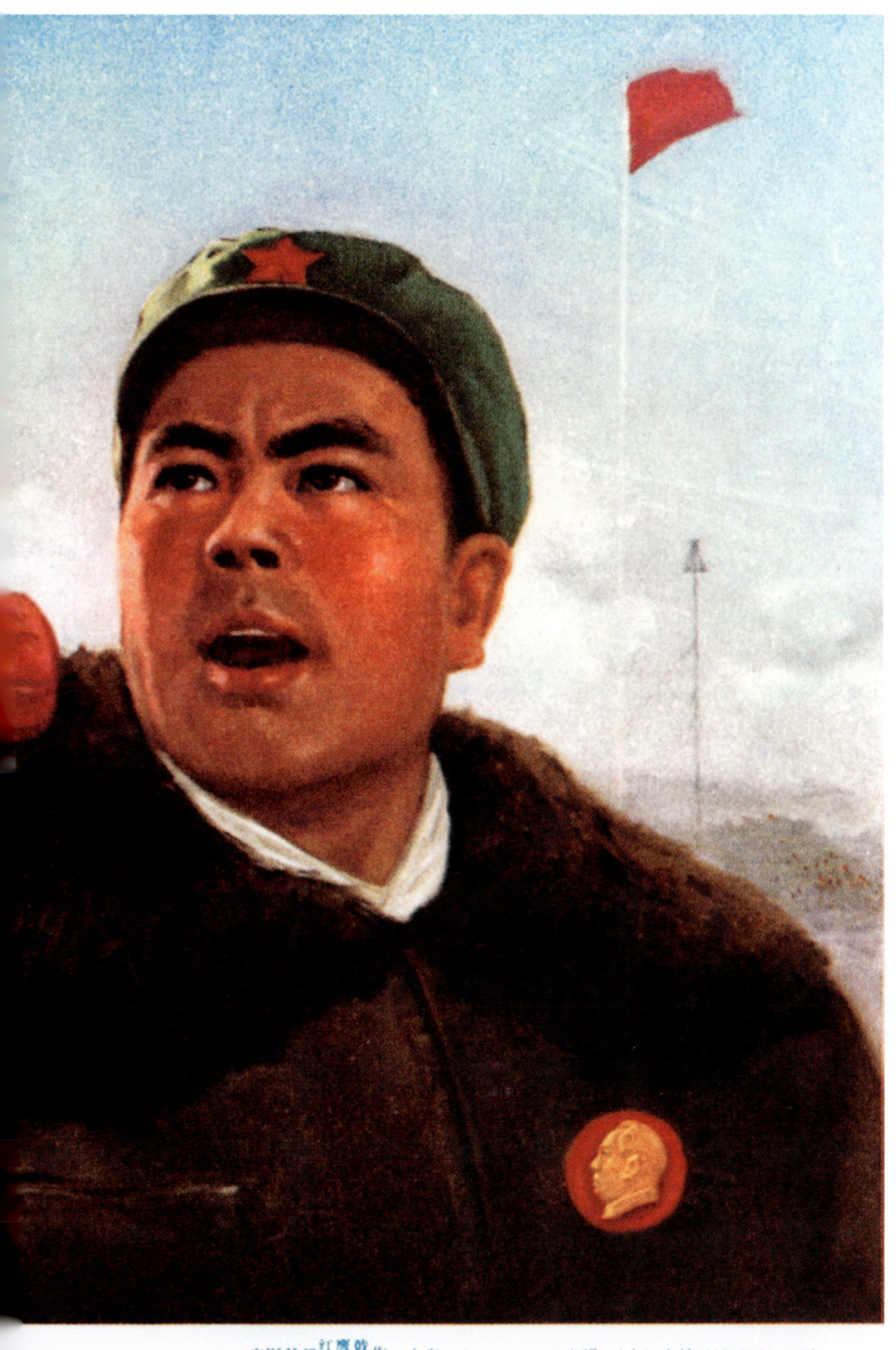

空军某部红鹰战
卫红鹰 作　上海人民美术出版社出版·（1）　书号：69103233 0.01

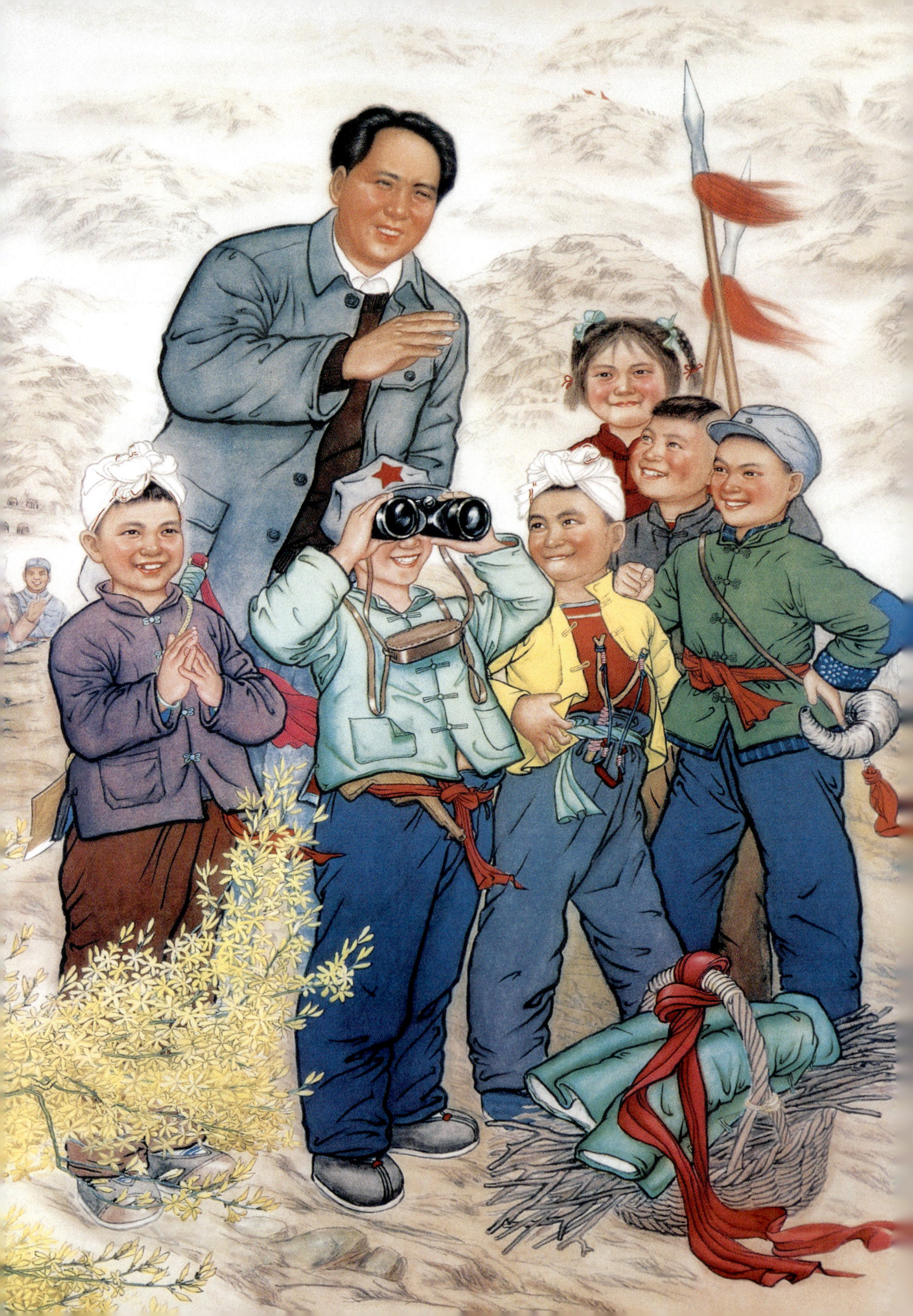

X

LEADERSHIP OF PARTY COMMITTEES

DIE FÜHRUNG DURCH DIE PARTEIKOMITEES
LE RÔLE DIRIGEANT DES COMITÉS DU PARTI

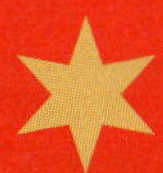

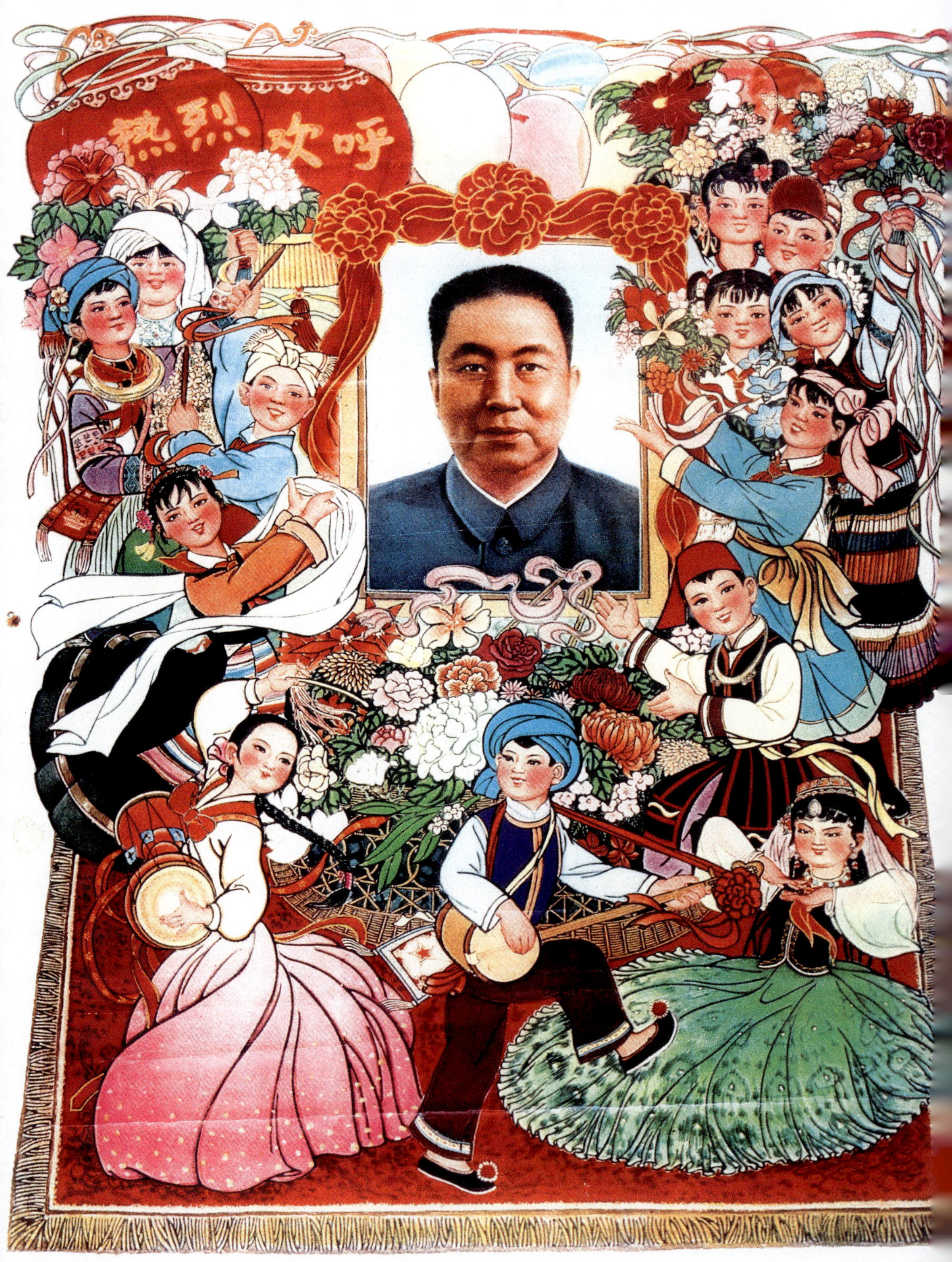

我们热爱华主席

Page 188

Looking into the distance
Artist: Xiang Qijiu, Cultural and Political Department of the Jinan Military District; Shanghai People's Art Publishing House, 1978; 0.14 Yuan

We love Chairman Hua*
On two lanterns, top: A hearty welcome *Artists:* Bu Wanfang, Han Zuyin, and Zheng Kexiang; Tianjin People's Art Publishing House, 1977; 0.14 Yuan
* Mao Zedong's chosen successor (1976–1981).

Ein Blick in die Ferne *Gemalt von* Xiang Qijiu, Kulturabteilung und politische Abteilung des Militärbezirks Jinan; Volkskunstverlag Shanghai, 1978; 0,14 Yuan

Wir lieben den Vorsitzenden Hua* *Auf den Laternen oben:* Herzlich begrüßen *Gemalt von* Bu Wanfang, Han Zuyin und Zheng Kexiang; Volkskunstverlag Tianjin, 1977; 0,14 Yuan
* Der von Mao Zedong selbst erwählte Nachfolger (1976–1981).

Voyons ce qui se passe au loin
Peintre : Xiang Qijiu, Département de la Culture et Département politique du quartier militaire de Jinan ; Éditions Populaires d'Art de Shanghai, 1978 ; 0,14 yuan

Nous aimons le président Hua*
Sur deux lampions, en haut : Salutations cordiales *Peintres :* Bu Wanfang, Han Zuyin et Zheng Kexiang ; Éditions Populaires d'Art de Tianjin, 1977 ; 0,14 yuan
* L'homme désigné par Mao lui-même comme son successeur (1976–1981).

Opposite

Celebrating with great joy and enthusiasm the publication of the constitution of the People's Republic of China
Artist: Yu Yunjie; Guangdong People's Art Publishing House, 1954 *Print run:* 140,000; 1.60 Yuan

Mit großer Freude und Begeisterung die Veröffentlichung der Verfassung der VR China feiern
Gemalt von Yu Yunjie; Volkskunstverlag Guangdong, 1954 *Auflage:* 140 000; 1,60 Yuan

Célébrons dans l'allégresse et l'enthousiasme la publication de la constitution de la République Populaire de Chine
Peintre : Yu Yunje ; Éditions Populaires d'Art du Guangdong, 1954 *Tirage :* 140 000 ; 1,60 yuan

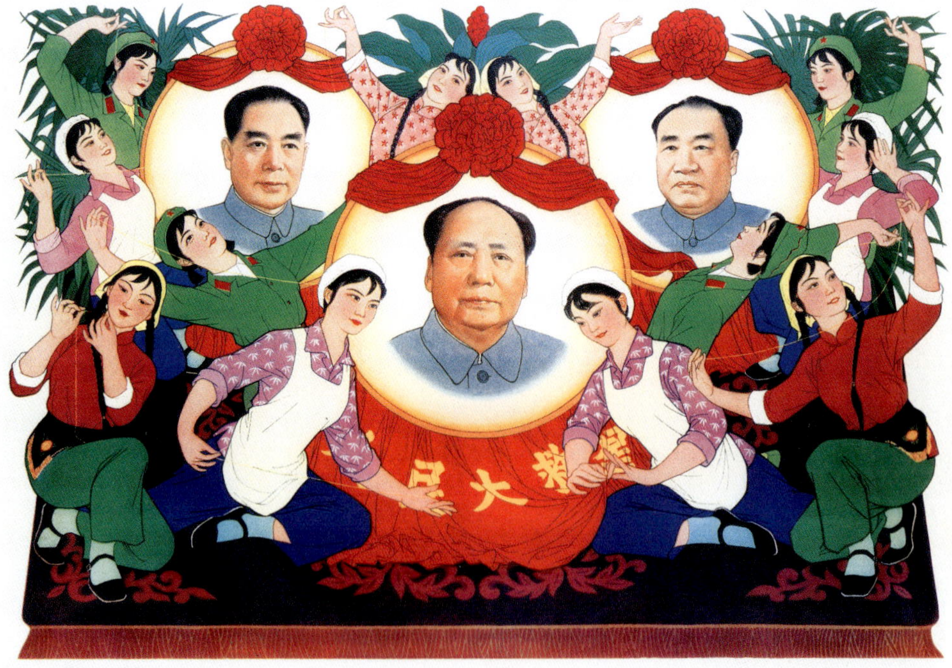

Embroidering pictures of silk
Below portrait of Mao: The People's Great Saviour *Artist:* Lu Hongen; Shandong People's Publishing House, 1978; 0.14 Yuan

Seidene Bilder besticken
Unter dem Mao-Porträt: Großer Retter des Volkes *Gemalt von* Lu Hongen; Volksverlag Shandong, 1978; 0,14 Yuan

Brodons des images sur soie
Sous le portrait de Mao : Le grand sauveur du peuple *Peintre :* Lu Hongen ; Éditions Populaires du Shandong, 1978 ; 0,14 yuan

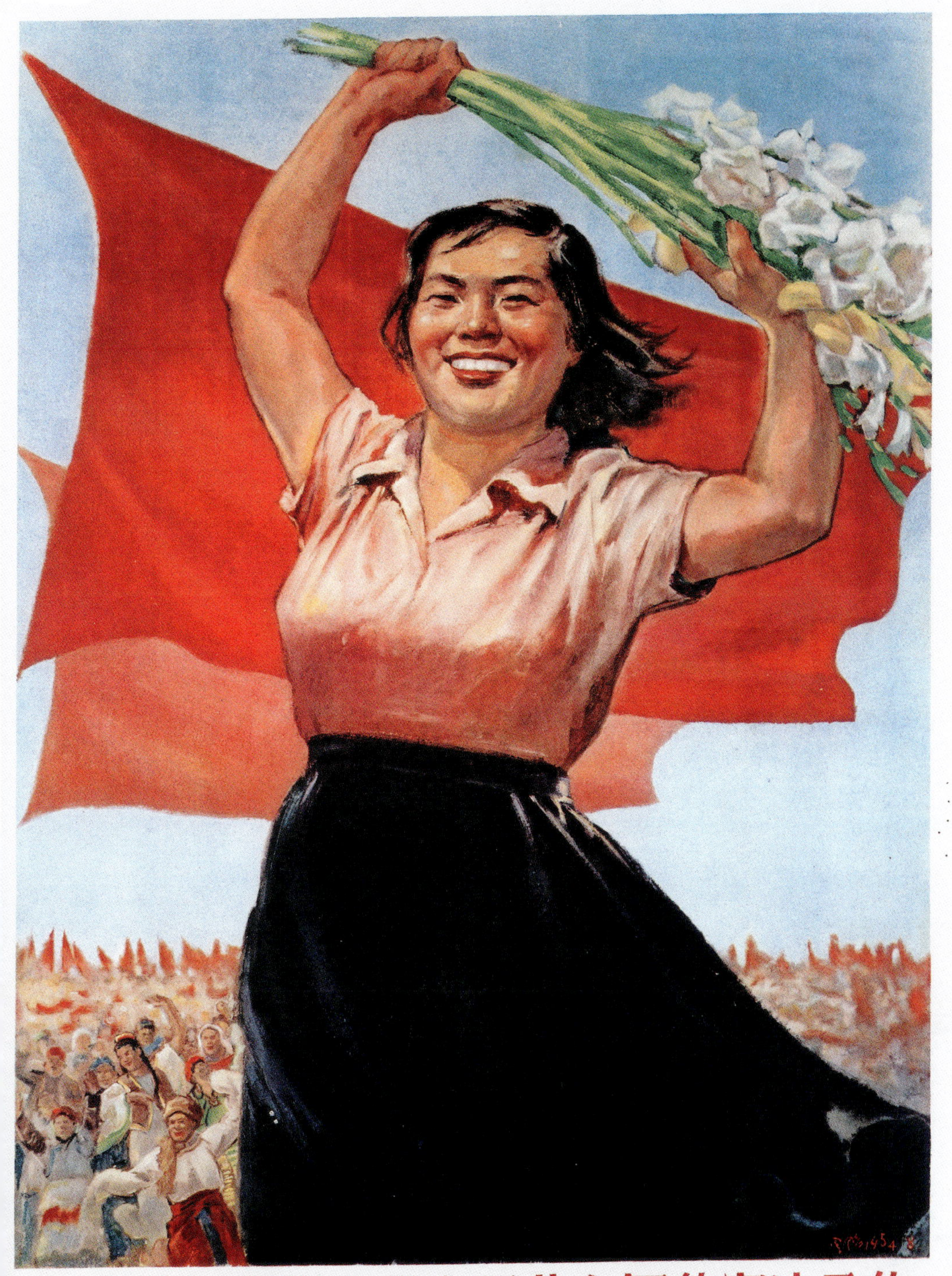

歡欣鼓舞慶祝中華人民共和國的憲法公佈

俞雲階作

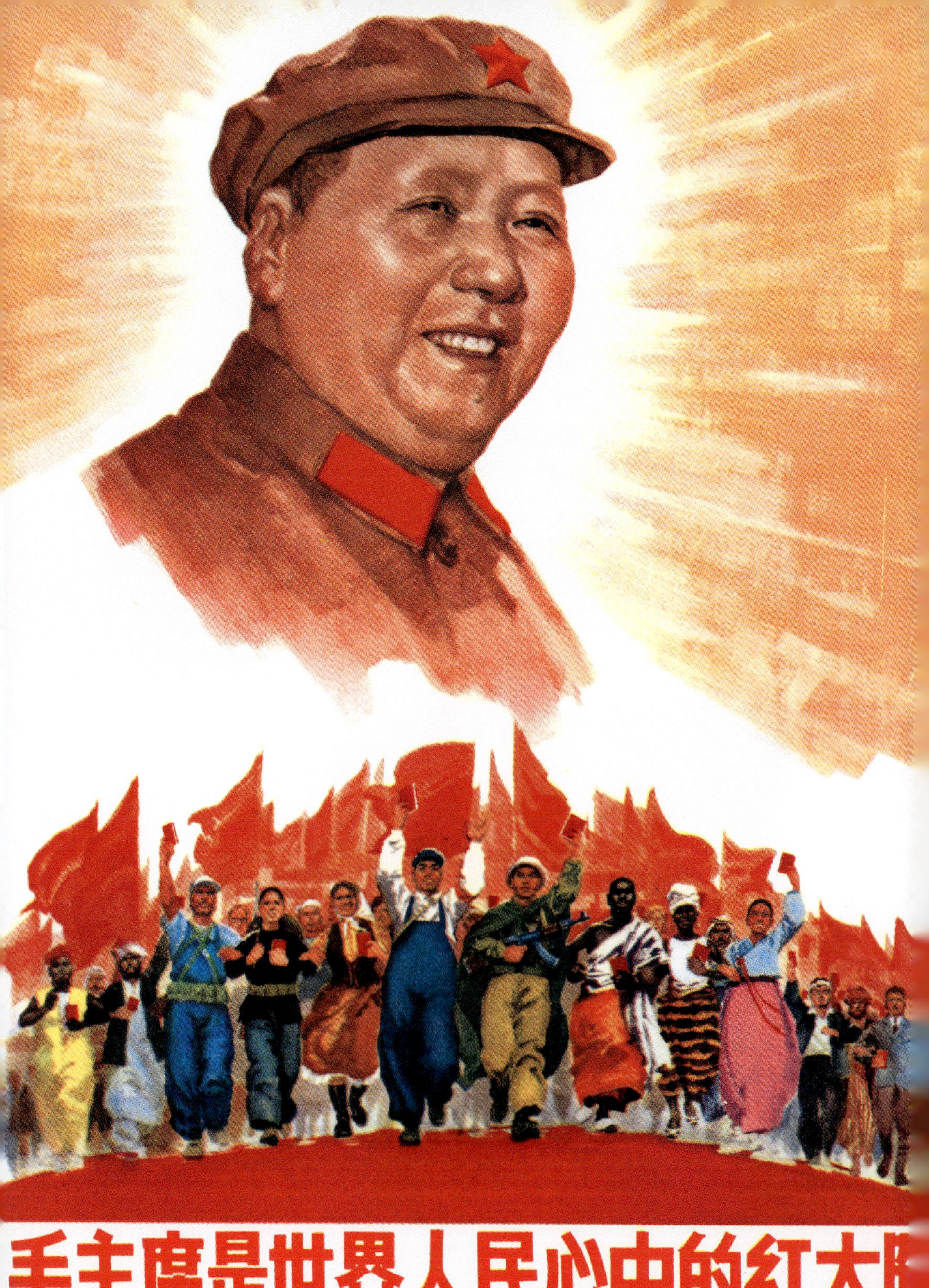
毛主席是世界人民心中的红太

XI

THE MASS LINE

DIE MASSENLINIE
LA LIGNE DE MASSE

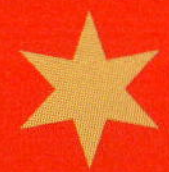

Page 194

Chairman Mao is the red sun in the hearts of the people of every land *Published by:* Shanghai People's Art Publishing House, 1967

Der Vorsitzende Mao ist die rote Sonne im Herzen der Völker aller Länder *Herausgeber:* Volkskunstverlag Shanghai, 1967

Le président Mao est le soleil rouge qui brille dans le cœur des peuples de tous les pays *Éditeur :* Éditions Populaires d'Art de Shanghai, 1967

Supporting the will of the people Fearlessly striding forward by exerting all our efforts Joyfully we celebrate the successful opening of the 5th National Congress *Artist:* Zhang Ruwei; Tianjin People's Art Publishing House, 1978; 0.14 Yuan

Den Willen des Volkes vertreten Unter Anspannung aller Kräfte unerschrocken vorwärts schreiten Mit Freude die erfolgreiche Eröffnung des 5. Nationalen Volkskongresses feiern *Gemalt von* Zhang Ruwei; Volkskunstverlag Tianjin, 1978; 0,14 Yuan

Représentons la volonté du peuple Mobilisons sans peur toutes les forces du pays pour aller de l'avant Célébrons dans l'allégresse l'ouverture du 5e Congrès National Populaire *Peintre :* Zhang Ruwei ; Éditions Populaires d'Art de Tianjin, 1978 ; 0,14 yuan

Pages 198–199

Long live victory in the People's War *Artist:* Wang Tongren; Peking Publishing House, 1966; 0.03 Yuan

Es lebe der Sieg des Volkskrieges *Gemalt von* Wang Tongren; Peking-Verlag, 1966; 0,03 Yuan

Vive la victoire de la guerre populaire *Peintre :* Wang Tongren ; Éditions de Pékin, 1966 ; 0,03 yuan

Pages 200–201

At the side of Chairman Mao *Red flag:* Victorious *Yellow flag:* First Production Brigade of the "The East is Red" People's Commune *Artist:* Liu Wenxi; People's Art Publishing House, 1st edn 1961, 2nd edn 1962 *Print run:* 25,001–170,000; 0.25 Yuan

An der Seite des Vorsitzenden Mao *Rote Fahne oben:* Siegreich *Gelbe Fahne:* Die erste Produktionsbrigade, die Volkskommune „Der Osten ist rot" *Gemalt von* Liu Wenxi; Volkskunstverlag, 1. Aufl. 1961, 2. Aufl. 1962 *Auflage:* 25 001–170 000; 0,25 Yuan

Aux côtés du président Mao *Drapeau rouge en haut :* Vainqueurs *Drapeau jaune :* La première brigade de production de la Commune populaire, « L'Est est rouge » *Peintre :* Liu Wenxi ; Éditions Populaires d'Art, 1ère éd. 1961, 2e éd. 1962 *Tirage :* 25 001–170 000 ; 0,25 yuan

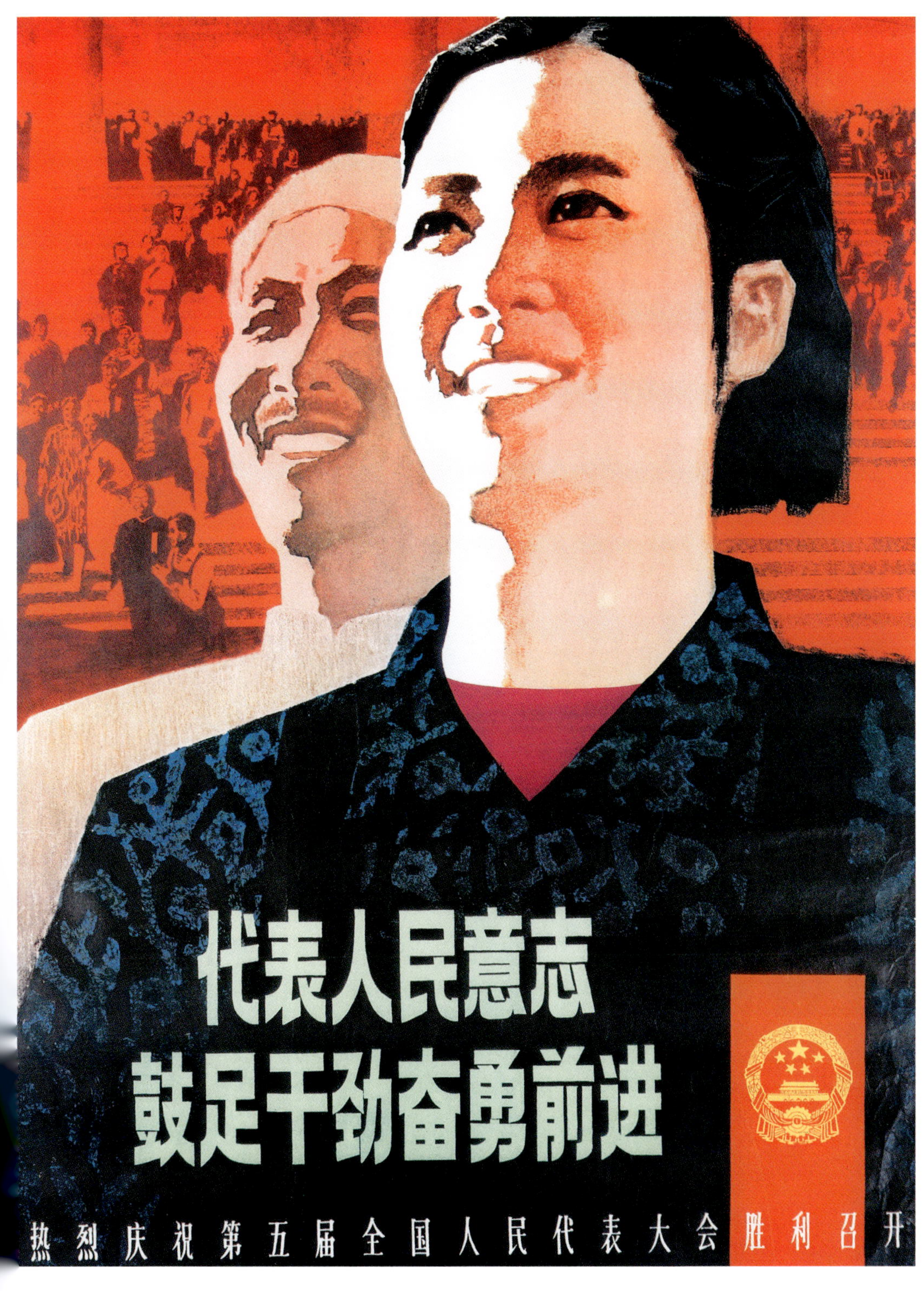
代表人民意志
鼓足干劲奋勇前进
热烈庆祝第五届全国人民代表大会胜利召开

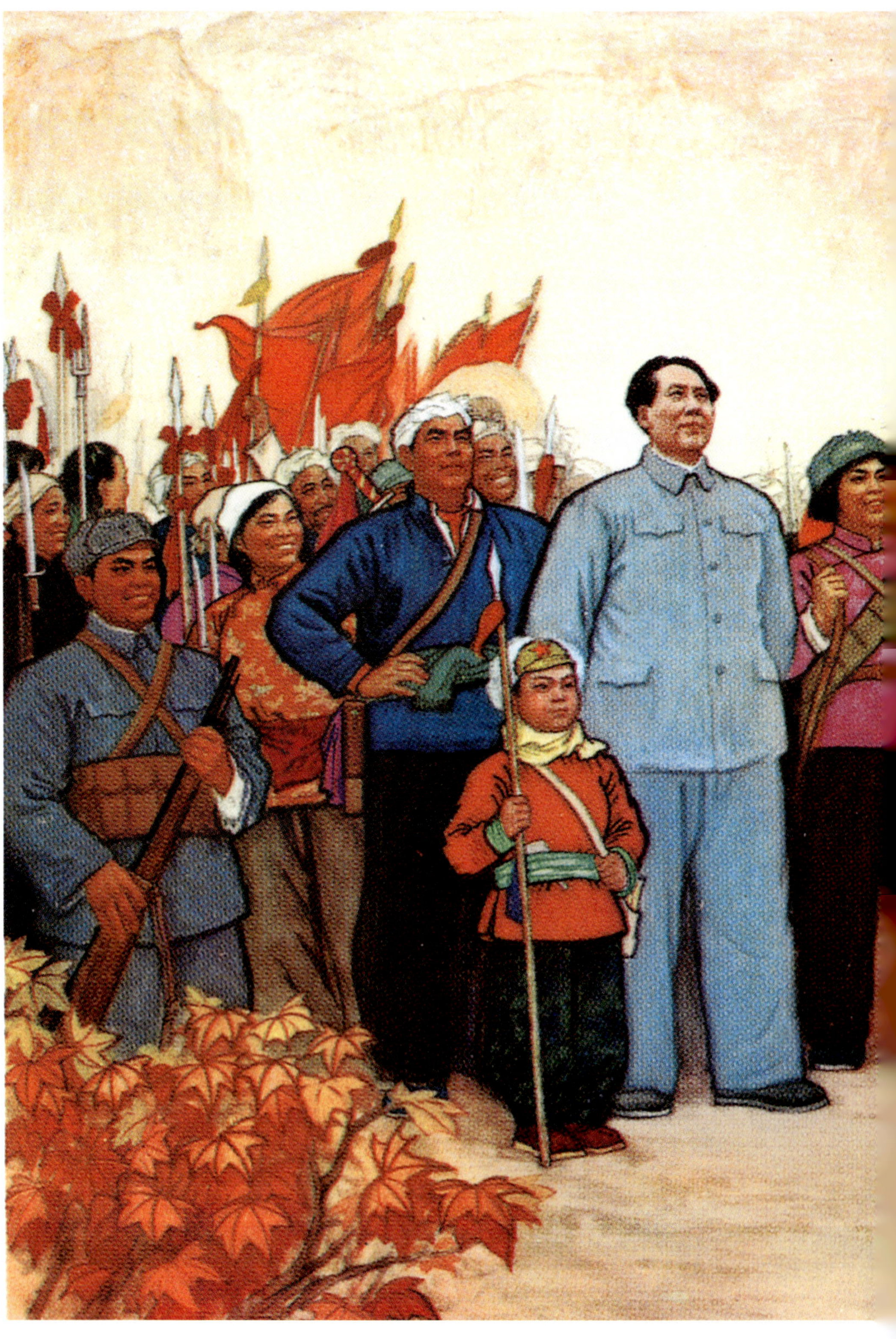

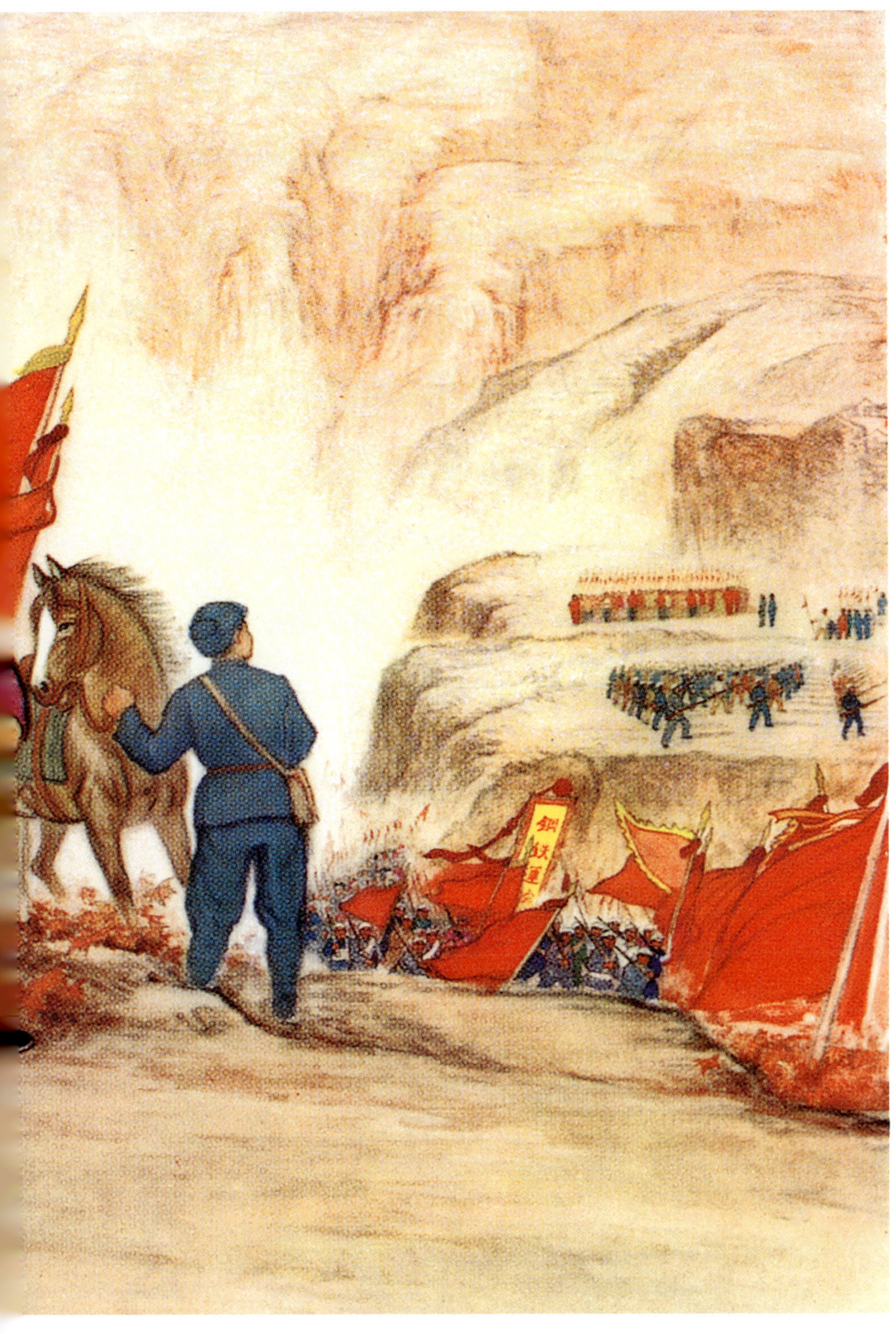

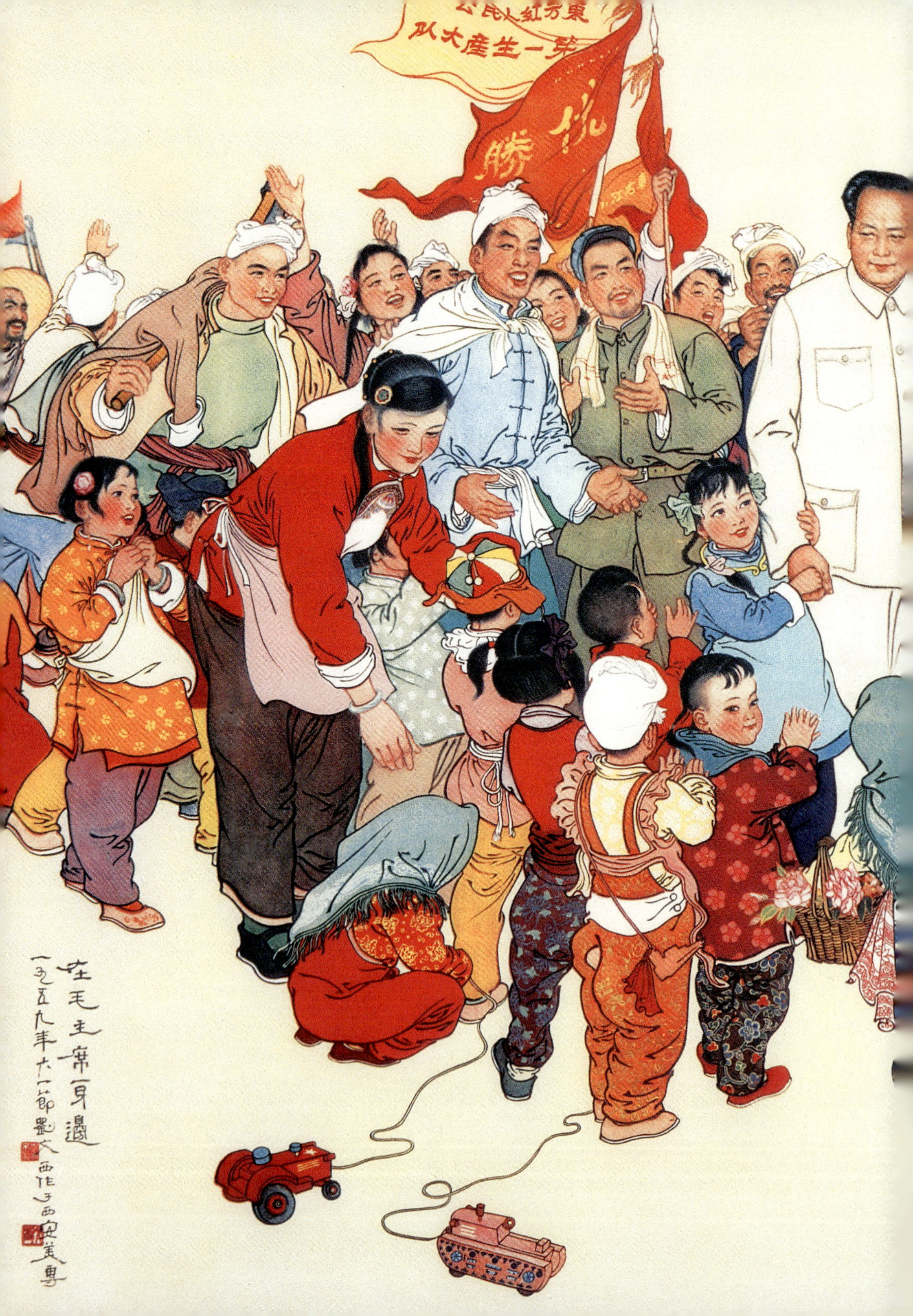
東方紅人民公
第一生產大队
优勝
在毛主席身邊
一九五九年六一節 劉文西作于西安美專

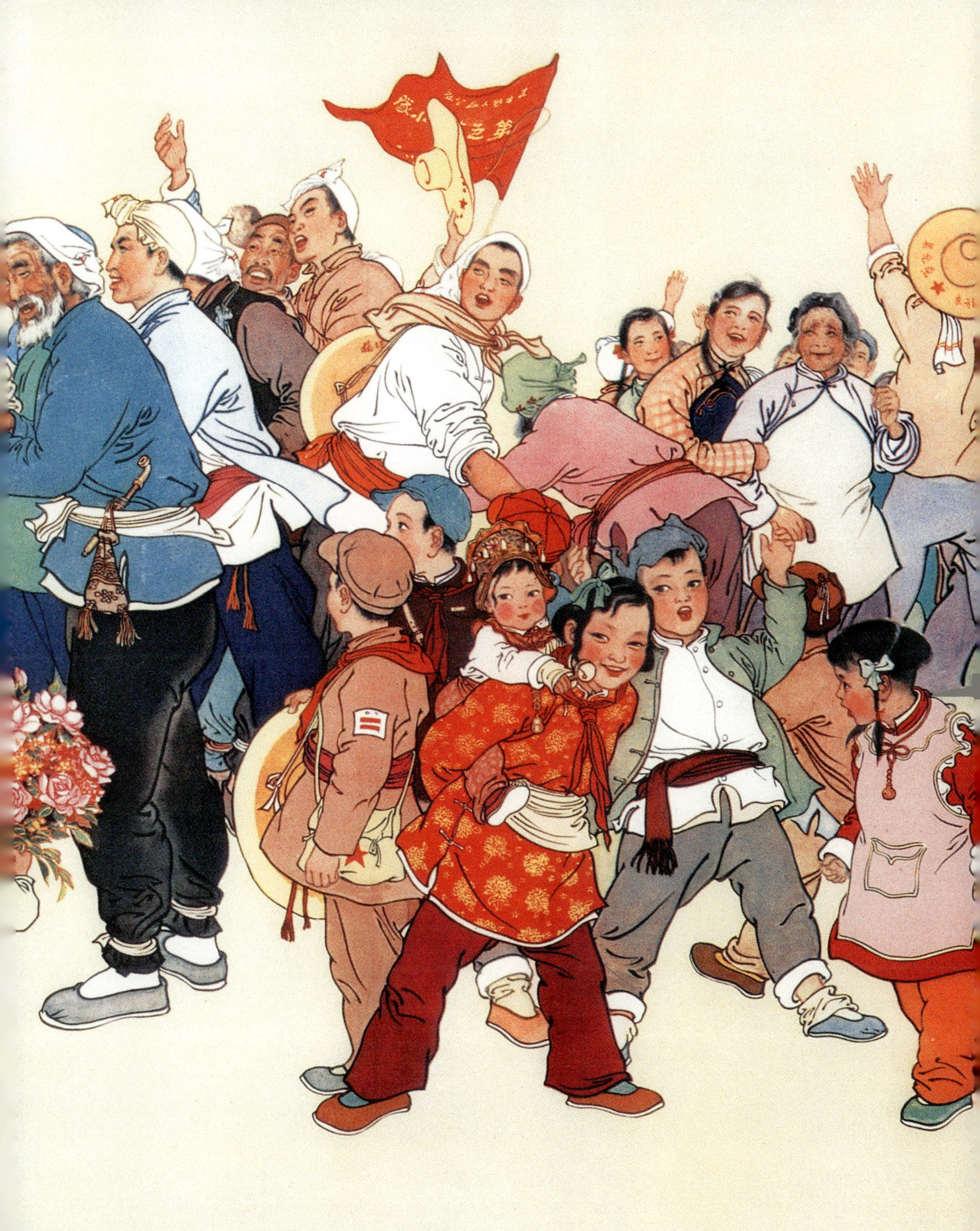

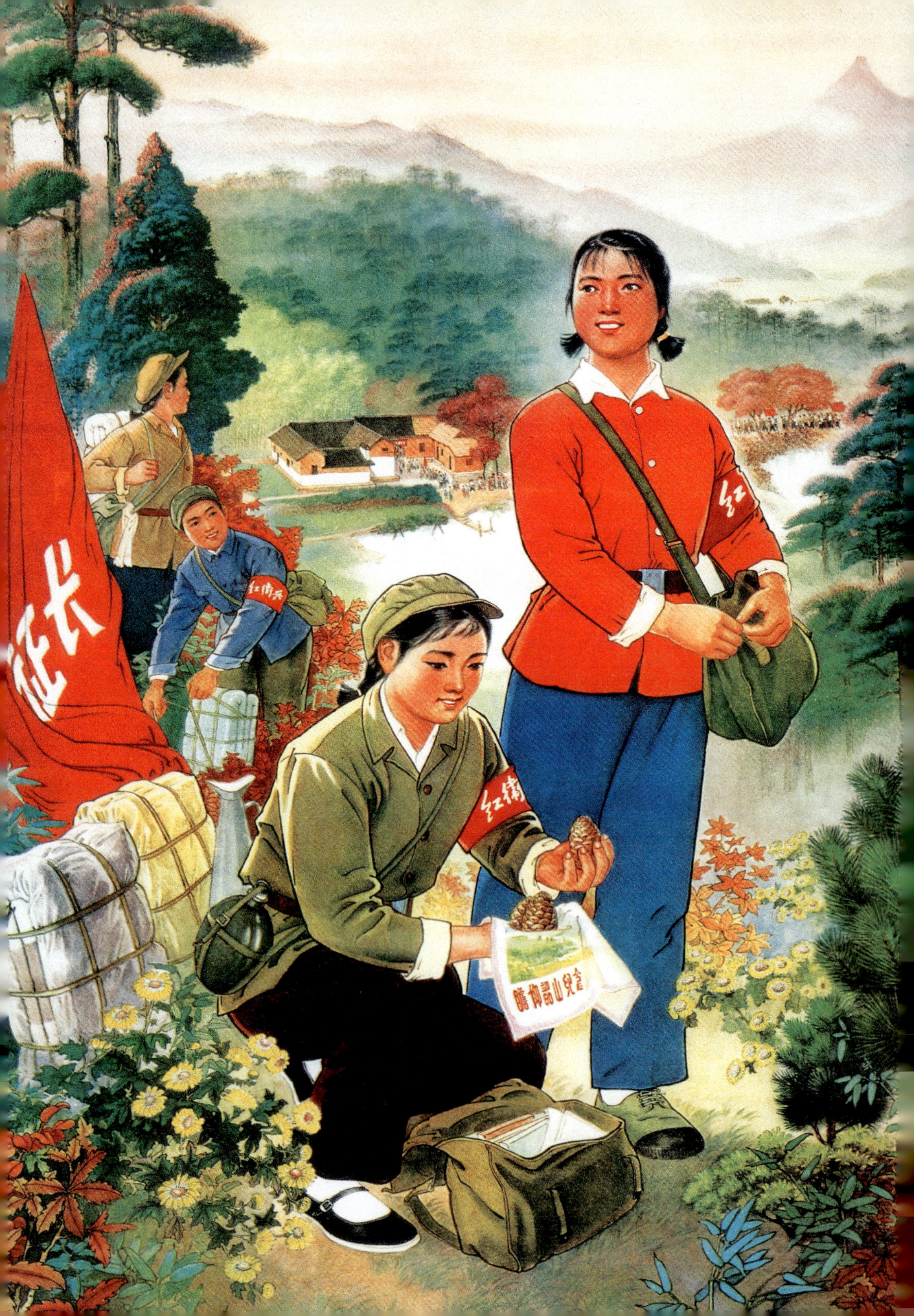

长征
红衛兵
红衛
红
瞻仰韶山纪念

XII
POLITICAL WORK

DIE POLITISCHE ARBEIT
LE TRAVAIL POLITIQUE

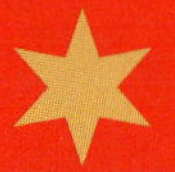

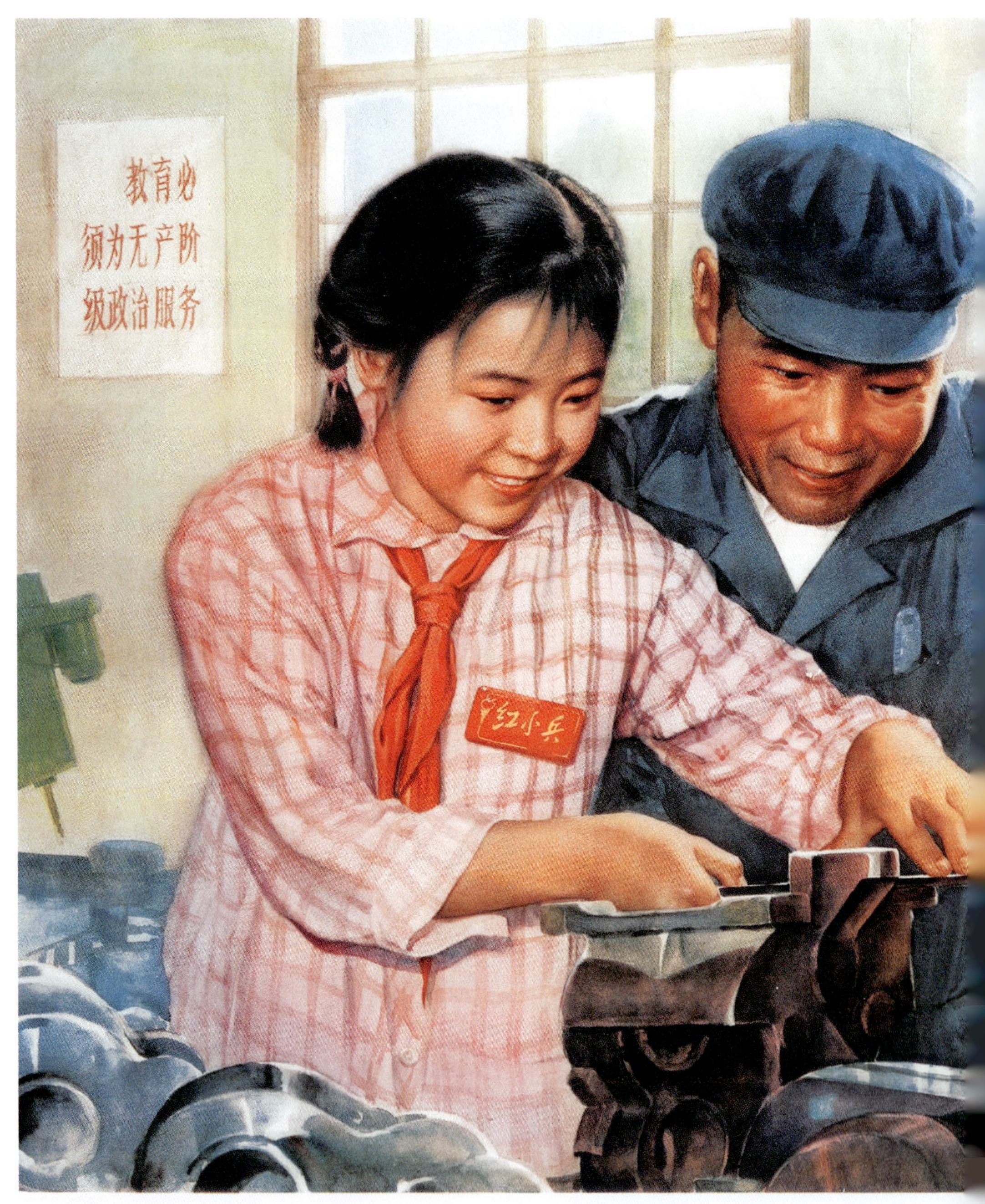

红小兵学工

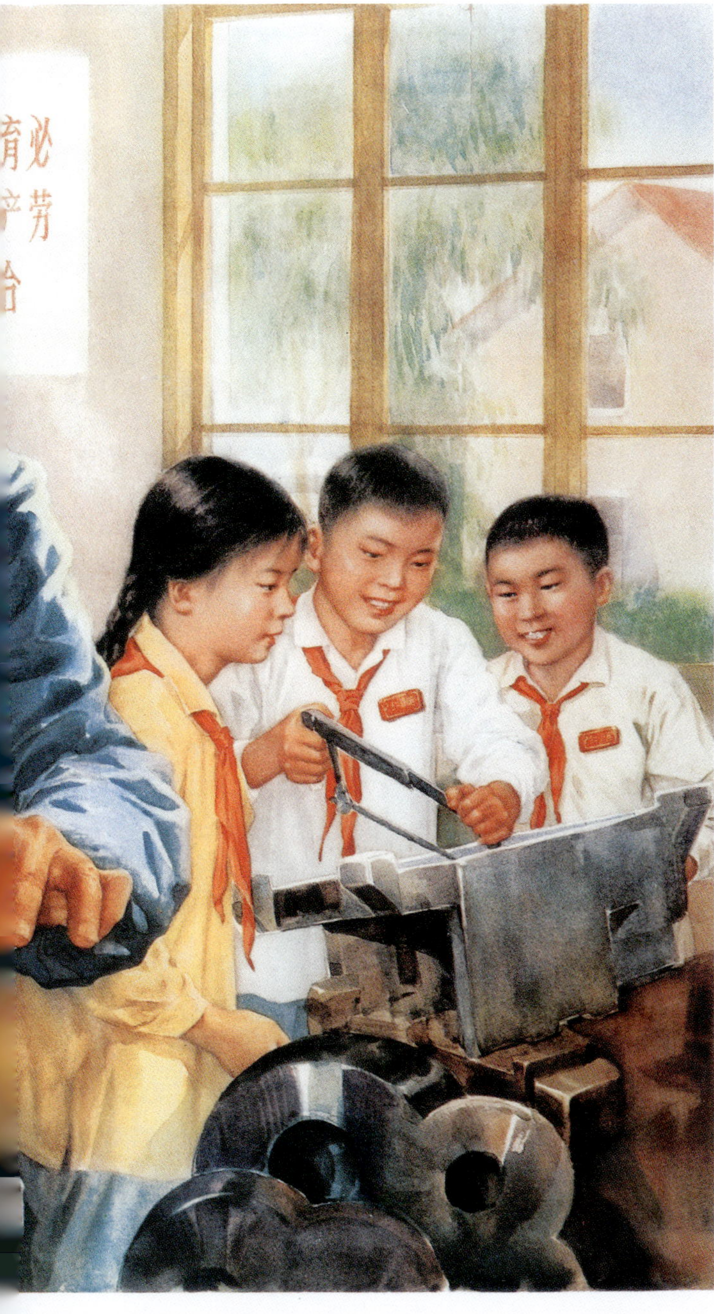

Page 202
Pines and cypresses on Mount Shaoshan (Mao Zedong's birthplace) *Red flag, left:* Long March *Armbands:* Red Guard *Artist:* Wang Xin; Hebei People's Publishing House, 1975 *Print run:* 725,000; 0.14 Yuan

Kiefern und Zypressen auf dem Berg von Shaoshan (Geburtsort Mao Zedongs) *Auf der Fahne links:* Langer Marsch *Armbinden:* Rote Garde *Gemalt von* Wang Xin; Volksverlag Hebei, 1975; *Auflage:* 725 000; 0,14 Yuan

Pins et cyprès sur la montagne de Shaoshan (lieu de naissance de Mao Zedong) *Sur le drapeau, à gauche :* Longue marche *Brassards :* Garde Rouge *Peintre :* Wang Xin ; Éditions Populaires du Hebei, 1975 ; *Tirage :* 725 000 ; 0,14 yuan

Young Red Guards learn from the workers *Poster, left:* Education must serve proletarian policy *Poster, center:* Education must be linked to productive work *Artist:* Xie Mulian; Shanghai People's Publishing House, 1974 *Print run:* 400,000; 0.11 Yuan

Junge Rotgardisten lernen von den Arbeitern *Plakat links:* Die Erziehung muss der proletarischen Politik dienen *Plakat Mitte:* Die Erziehung muss mit der produktiven Arbeit verbunden sein *Gemalt von* Xie Mulian; Volksverlag Shanghai, 1974 *Auflage:* 400 000; 0,11 Yuan

De jeunes gardes rouges s'instruisent auprès des ouvriers *Affiche de gauche :* L'éducation doit servir la politique prolétarienne *Affiche du milieu :* L'éducation doit être liée au travail de production *Peintre :* Xie Mulian ; Éditions Populaires de Shanghai, 1974 *Tirage :* 400 000 ; 0,11 yuan

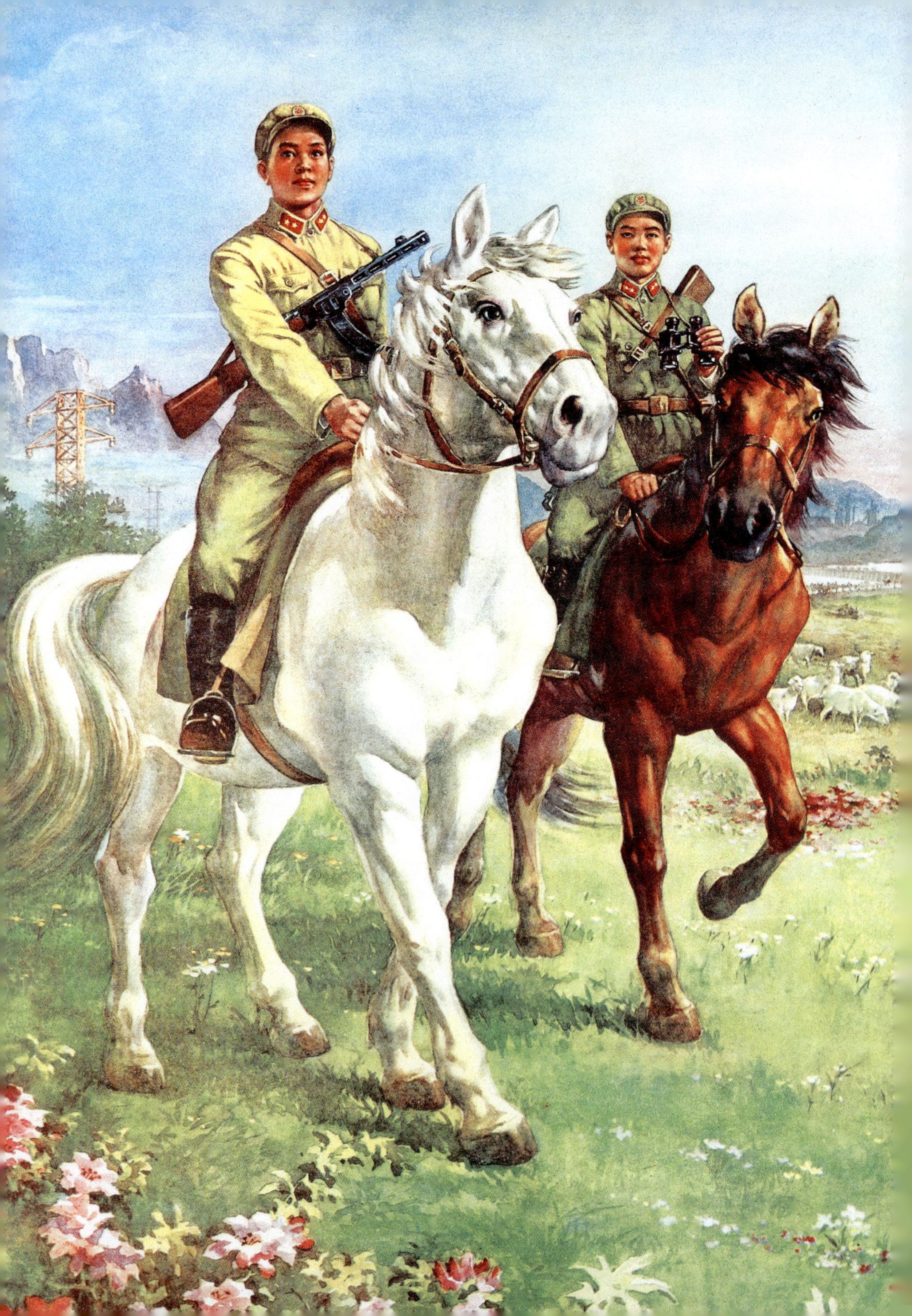

XIII

RELATIONS BETWEEN OFFICERS AND MEN

DIE BEZIEHUNGEN ZWISCHEN OFFIZIEREN UND MANNSCHAFTEN

LES RAPPORTS ENTRE OFFICIERS ET SOLDATS

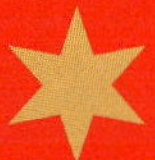

Page 206
Light cavalry *Artist:* Zhang Biwu; Shanghai People's Art Publishing House, 1960

Leichte Kavallerie *Gemalt von* Zhang Biwu; Volkskunstverlag Shanghai, 1960

Cavalerie légère *Peintre :* Zhang Biwu ; Éditions Populaires d'Art de Shanghai, 1960

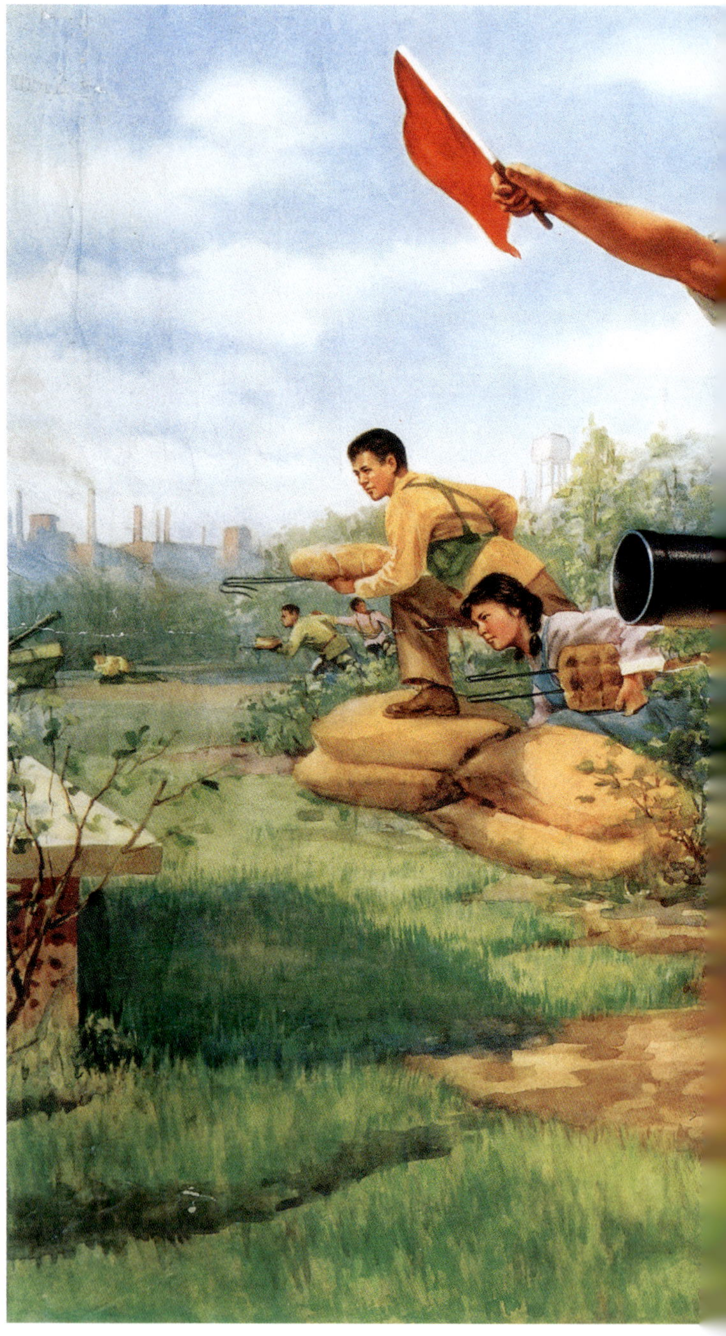

Soldiers and members of the People's Militia on a joint exercise *Artist:* Luo Weiqing of the People's Liberation Army's Unit 83 305; Shanghai People's Publishing House, 1977; 0.11 Yuan

Soldaten und Volksmiliz üben gemeinsam *Gemalt von* Luo Weiqing der Truppe 83 305 der Volksbefreiungsarmee; Volksverlag Shanghai, 1977; 0,11 Yuan

Les soldats et la milice populaire œuvrent en commun *Peintre :* Luo Weiqing, de la compagnie 83 305 de l'Armée de Libération Populaire ; Éditions Populaires de Shanghai, 1977 ; 0,11 yuan

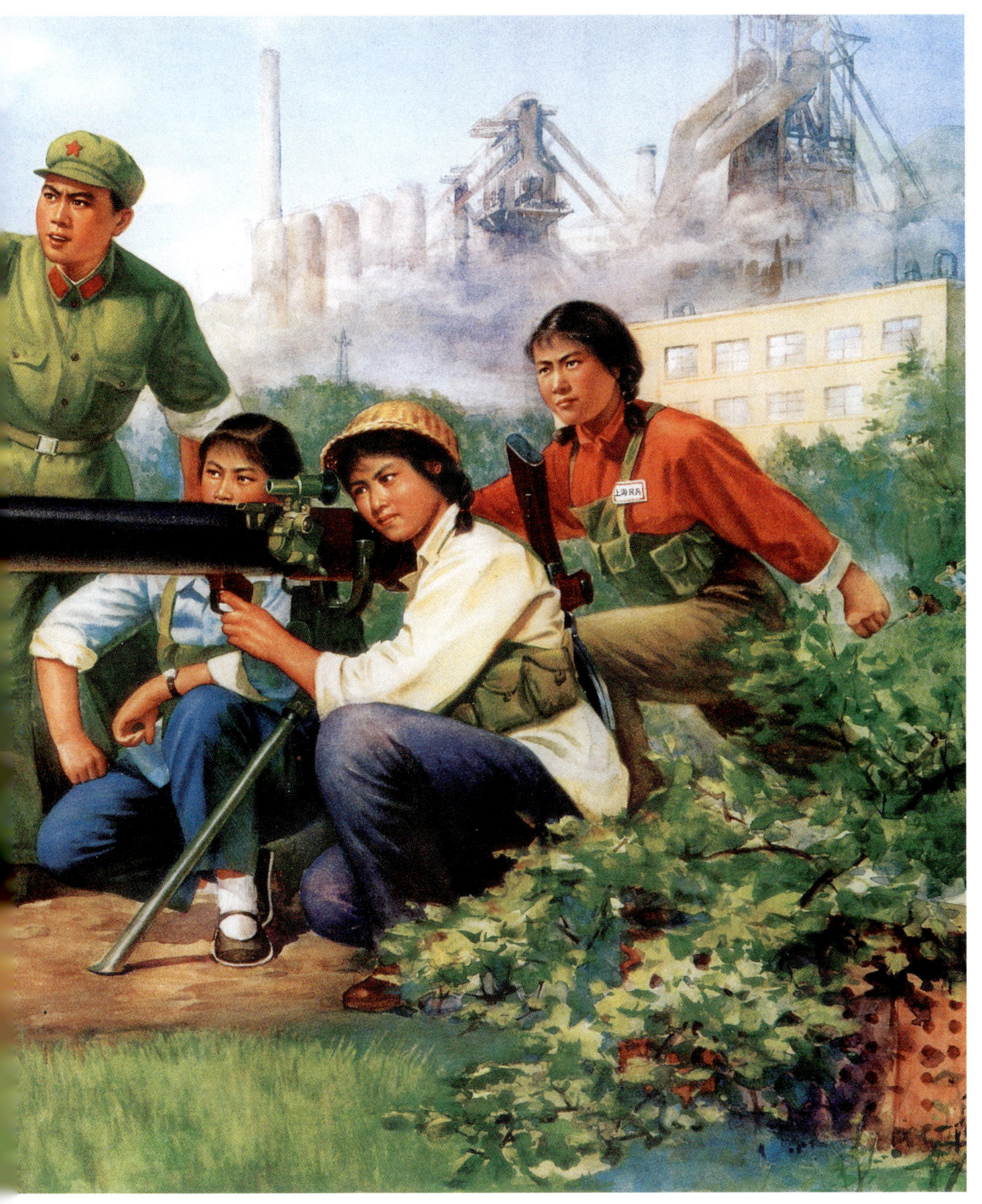
上海民兵

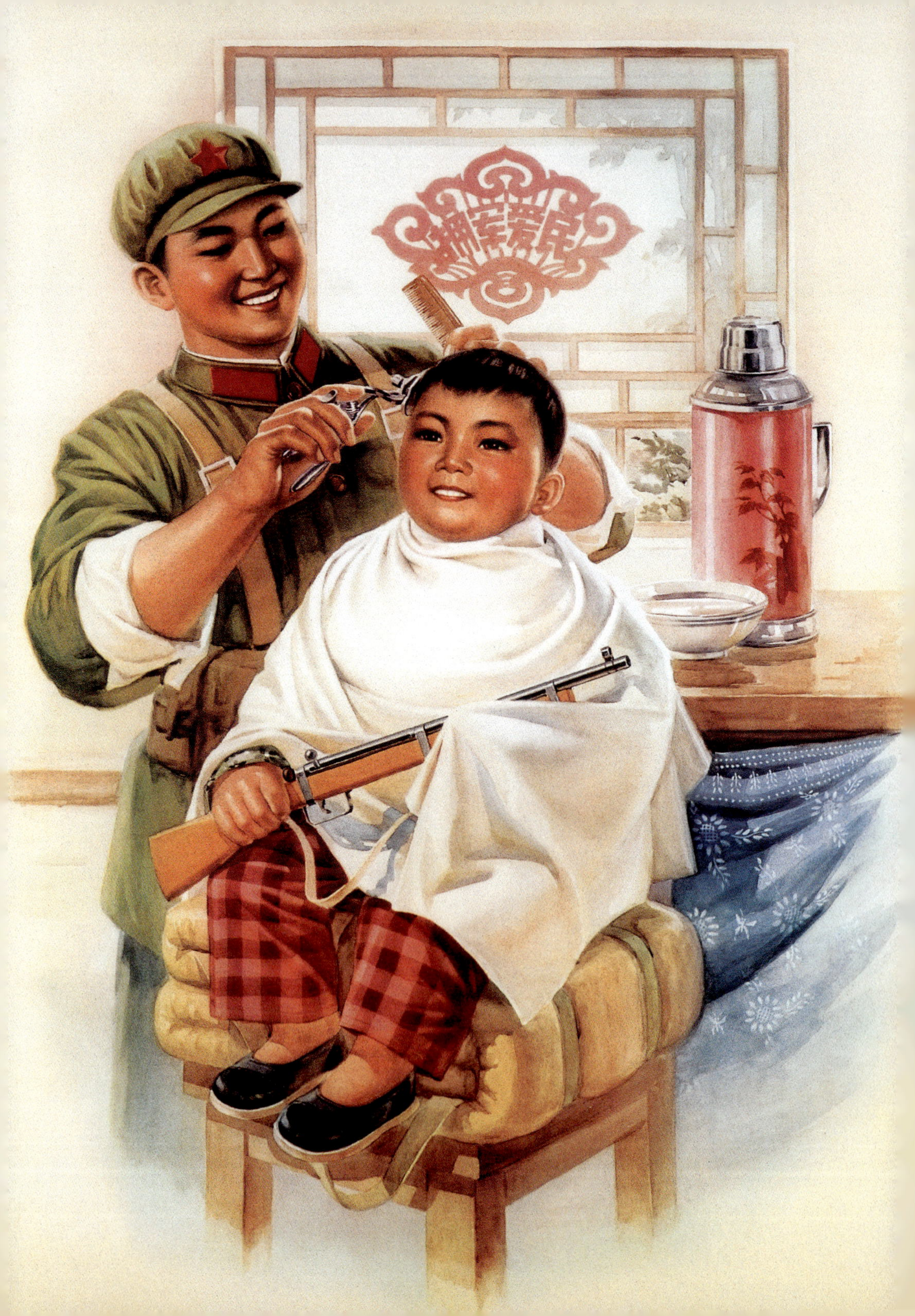
拥军爱民

XIV

RELATIONS BETWEEN THE ARMY AND THE PEOPLE

DIE BEZIEHUNGEN ZWISCHEN ARMEE UND VOLK
LES RAPPORTS ENTRE L'ARMÉE ET LE PEUPLE

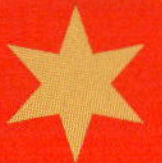

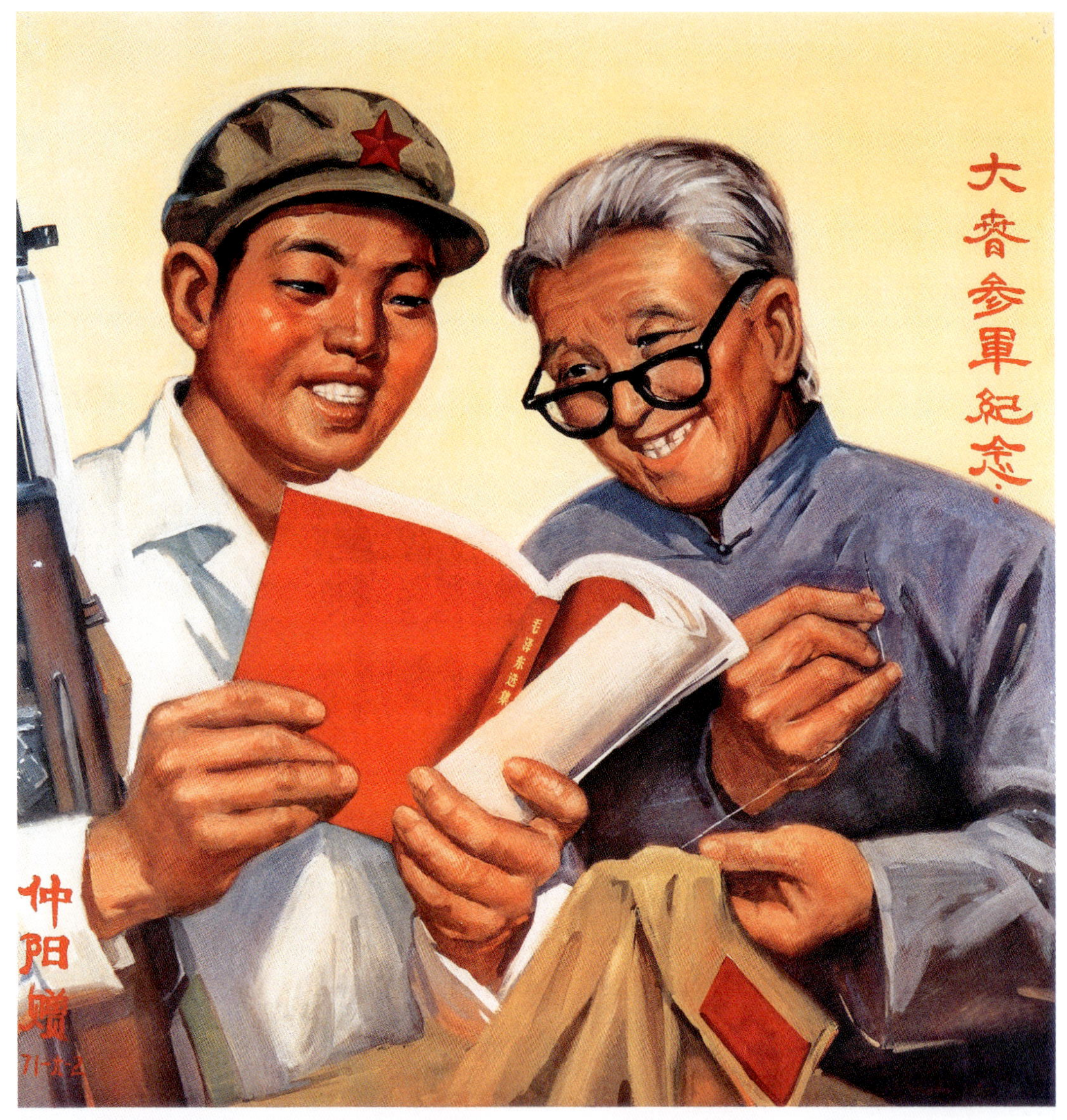

拥军 爱民

一人参軍　全家光荣

Page 210
The army and the people are all one family *In window:* The army supports and takes care of the people *Artist:* Han Guangxu; People's Art Publishing House, 1975; 0.11 Yuan

Armee und Volk sind wie eine Familie *Am Fenster:* Die Armee unterstützen und für das Volk sorgen *Gemalt von* Han Guangxu; Volkskunstverlag, 1975; 0,11 Yuan

L'armée et le peuple sont comme une même famille *À la fenêtre :* Soutenons l'armée et œuvrons pour le peuple *Peintre :* Han Guangxu ; Éditions Populaires d'Art, 1975 ; 0,11 yuan

Opposite
Support the army and look after the people When one person joins the armed forces, the whole family takes credit *Top right:* In memory of the day Da Chun joined the army *Bottom left:* Dedicated by Zhong Yang *Designed by:* the Revolutionary Committee of Nanjing Textile Factory *Published and distributed by:* The Revolutionary Committee of Jiangsu Province, 1976; 0.12 Yuan

Die Armee unterstützen und für das Volk sorgen Tritt einer in den Militärdienst ein, genießt die ganze Familie diese Ehre *Rechts oben:* Zur Erinnerung an den Armeebeitritt von Da Chun *Links unten:* gewidmet von Zhong Yang *Entwurf:* Revolutionskomitee der Textilfabrik Nanjing *Herausgeber und Vertrieb:* Revolutionskomitee der Provinz Jiangsu, 1976; 0,12 Yuan

Soutenons l'armée et œuvrons pour le peuple Quand quelqu'un fait son service militaire, l'honneur en rejaillit sur toute sa famille *En haut à droite :* En souvenir de l'engagement dans l'armée de Da Chun *En bas à gauche :* Hommage de Zhong Yang *Conception :* Comité révolutionnaire de l'usine de textile de Nanjing *Éditeur et distributeur :* Comité révolutionnaire de la province du Jiangsu, 1976 ; 0,12 yuan

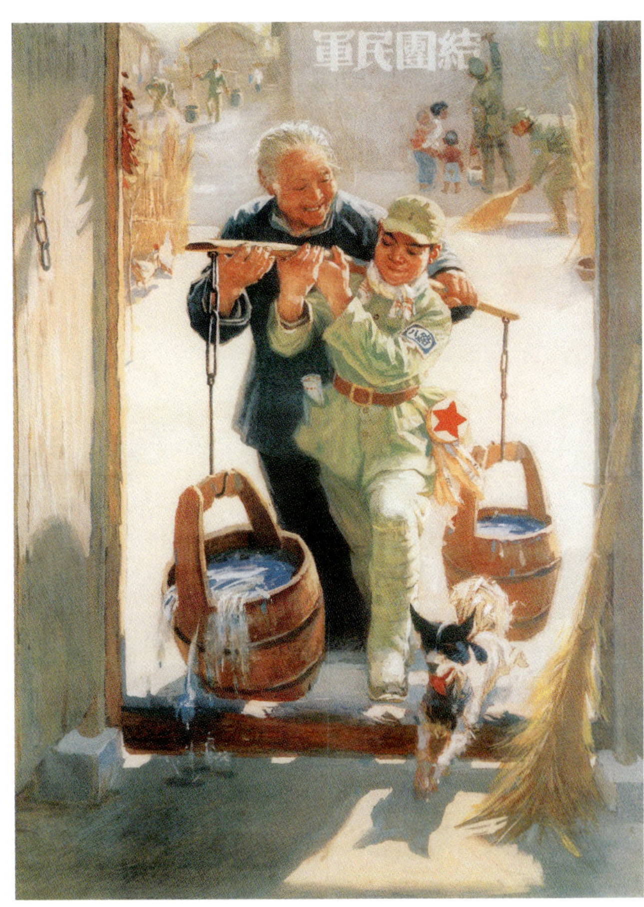

The young soldier helps to carry water (basic exercise 4)
Wall in background: Solidarity between the armed forces and civilians *Soldier's armband:* Eighth Road Army Poster used as a teaching aid with the textbook *Chinese for Primary Schools*, Book 5; Shanghai Educational Publishing House

Der junge Soldat hilft beim Wassertragen (Grundübung 4)
Mauer im Hintergrund: Solidarität zwischen Armee und Zivilisten *Armbinde des Soldaten:* Die Achte Route-Armee Unterrichtsplakat zum Lehrbuch *Chinesisch für Grundschulen*, Band 5; Erziehungsverlag Shanghai

Le jeune soldat aide à porter de l'eau (exercice de base n° 4)
Mur du fond : Solidarité entre l'armée et les civils *Brassard du soldat :* Huitième armée itinérante Affiche pédagogique accompagnant le volume 5 du manuel de chinois des écoles primaires ; Éditions Éducatives de Shanghai

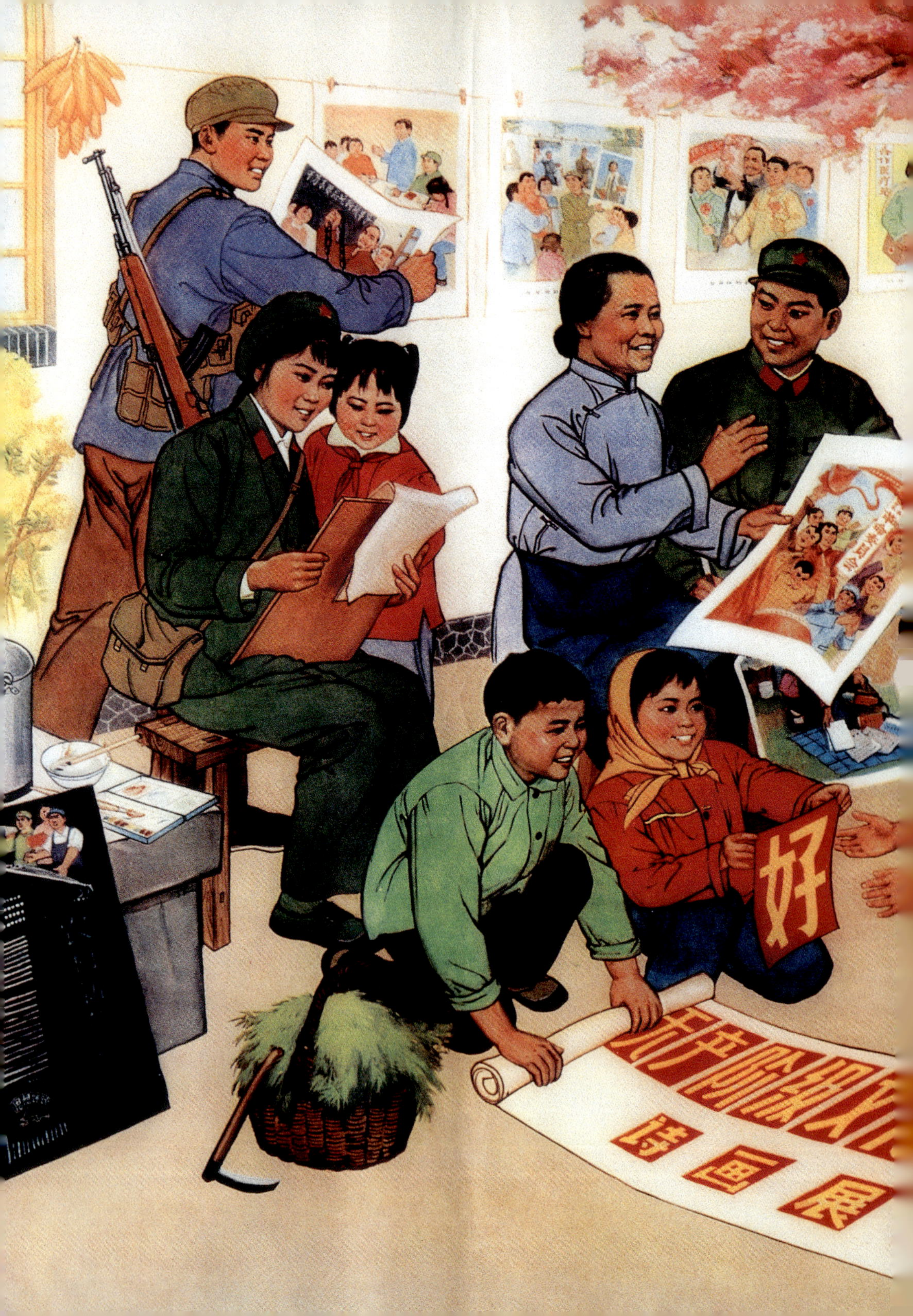
好
诗画展

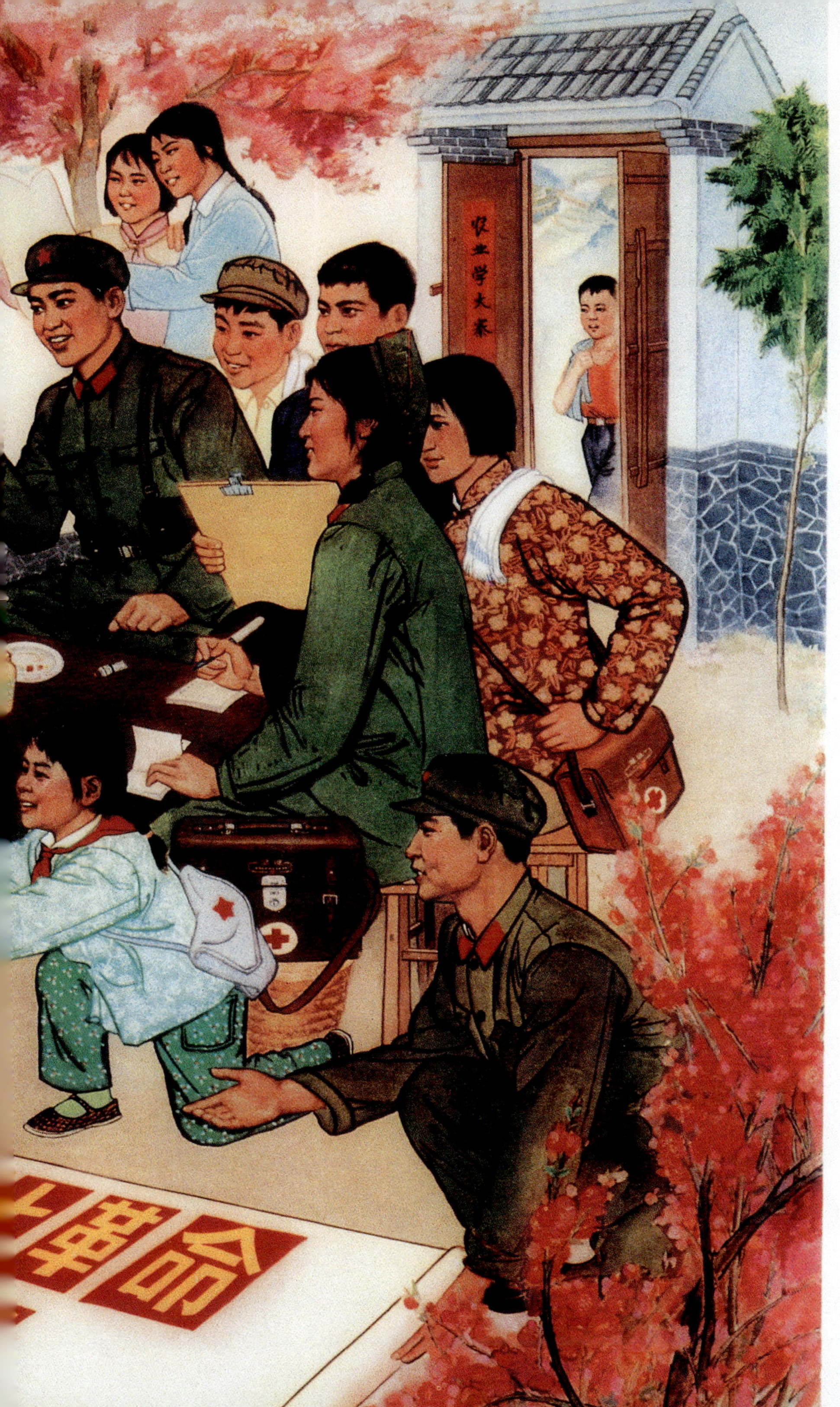

满园春色

Pages 214–215
The whole garden blossoms in the colors of spring *Banner on the floor:* Exhibition of Poetry and Painting about the Great Proletarian Cultural Revolution *Chinese character in girl's hand:* "Good" *Scroll beside the door:* In agriculture, learn from Dazhai! *Artist:* Unit 54 811 of the People's Liberation Army, Jinan Military District; Shanghai People's Publishing House, 1977; 0.11 Yuan

Der ganze Garten blüht in Frühlingsfarben *Transparent auf dem Boden:* Gedichte- und Gemälde-Ausstellung über die Große Proletarische Kulturrevolution *Schriftzeichen in der Hand des Mädchens:* „Gut" *Schriftrolle an der Tür:* Lernt in der Landwirtschaft von Dazhai! *Gemalt von* der Truppe 54 811 der Volksbefreiungsarmee, Militärbezirk Jinan; Volksverlag Shanghai, 1977; 0,11 Yuan

Le jardin entier se pare de couleurs printanières *Banderole sur le sol :* Exposition de poèmes et de tableaux sur la Grande Révolution culturelle prolétarienne *Dans la main de la petite fille :* « Bien » *Sur la porte :* Instruisez-vous de l'expérience agricole de Dazhai ! *Peintre :* la compagnie 54 811 de l'Armée de Libération Populaire, quartier militaire de Jinan ; Éditions Populaires de Shanghai, 1977 ; 0,11 yuan

Goodbye, dear comrade from the People's Liberation Army! *Artist:* Zhou Guojun; Liaoning People's Publishing House, 1976 *Print run:* 450,000; 0.11 Yuan

Auf Wiedersehen, Onkel von der Volksbefreiungsarmee! *Gemalt von* Zhou Guojun; Volksverlag Liaoning, 1976 *Auflage:* 450 000; 0,11 Yuan

Au revoir, oncle de l'Armée de Libération Populaire ! *Peintre :* Zhou Guojun ; Éditions Populaires du Liaoning, 1976 *Tirage :* 450 000 ; 0,11 yuan

"The army must become one with the people so that they see it as their own army."

Die Armee muss mit dem Volk zu einem Ganzen verschmelzen, so dass sie vom Volk als seine eigene Armee angesehen wird. ✶ L'armée doit ne faire qu'un avec le peuple, afin qu'il voie en elle sa propre armée.

Pages 218–219
The soldiers pass by the apple orchard. The peasants kindly offer the soldiers some apples. The soldiers adhere strictly to the "Three Main Rules of Discipline" and the "Eight Points for Attention" and will not accept a single apple. Poster used as a teaching aid with the textbook *Chinese for Primary Schools; Artist:* Fang Shicong *Published by:* Shanghai People's Publishing House; 1974 *Print run:* 65,000; 0.16 Yuan

Die Soldaten gehen am Apfelgarten vorbei: Die Bauern bieten den Soldaten freundlich Äpfel an. Die Soldaten halten sich streng an die „Drei Hauptregeln der Disziplin und die Acht Punkte zur Beachtung" und wollen keinen einzigen Apfel annehmen. Unterrichtsplakat zum Lehrbuch *Chinesisch für Grundschulen; Gemalt von* Fang Shicong *Herausgeber:* Volksverlag Shanghai, 1974 *Auflage:* 65 000; 0,16 Yuan

Les soldats passent devant la pommeraie. Les paysans offrent des pommes aux soldats en signe d'amitié. Les soldats s'en tiennent rigoureusement aux « Trois grandes règles de la discipline et aux Huit recommandations » et ne veulent pas accepter la moindre pomme. Affiche pédagogique accompagnant le manuel de chinois des écoles primaires *Peintre :* Fang Shicong *Éditeur :* Éditions Populaires de Shanghai ; 1974 *Tirage :* 65 000 ; 0,16 yuan

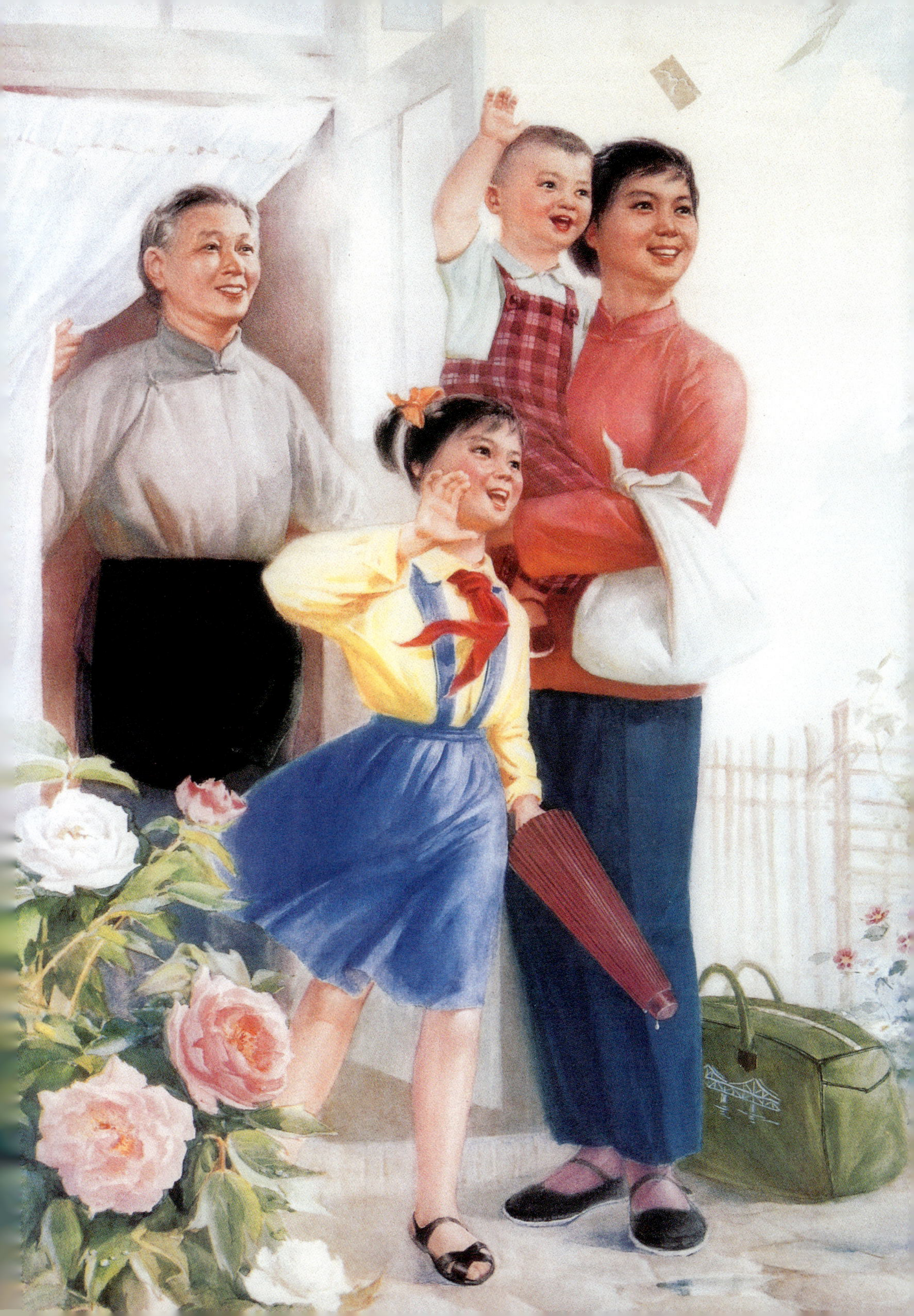

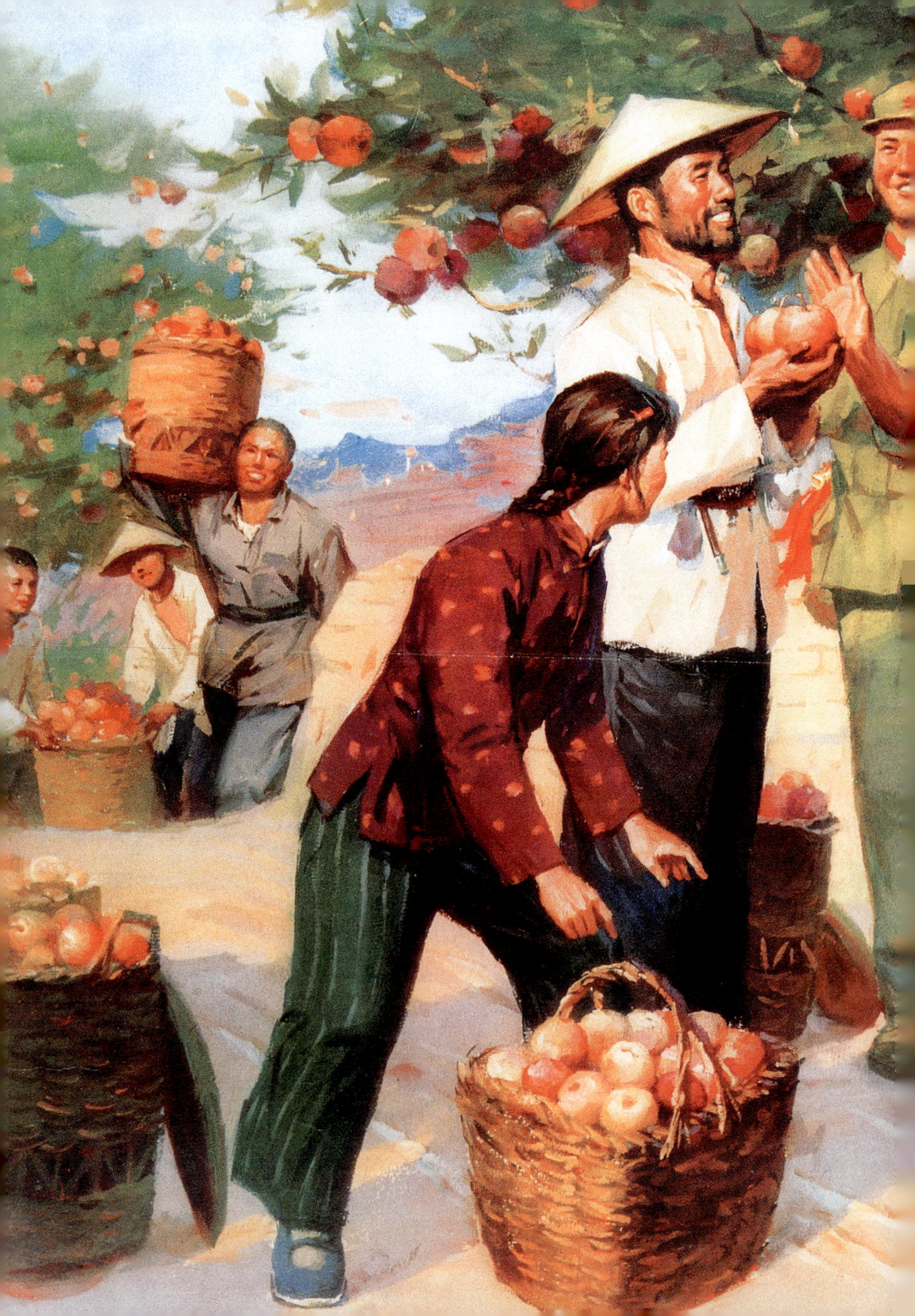

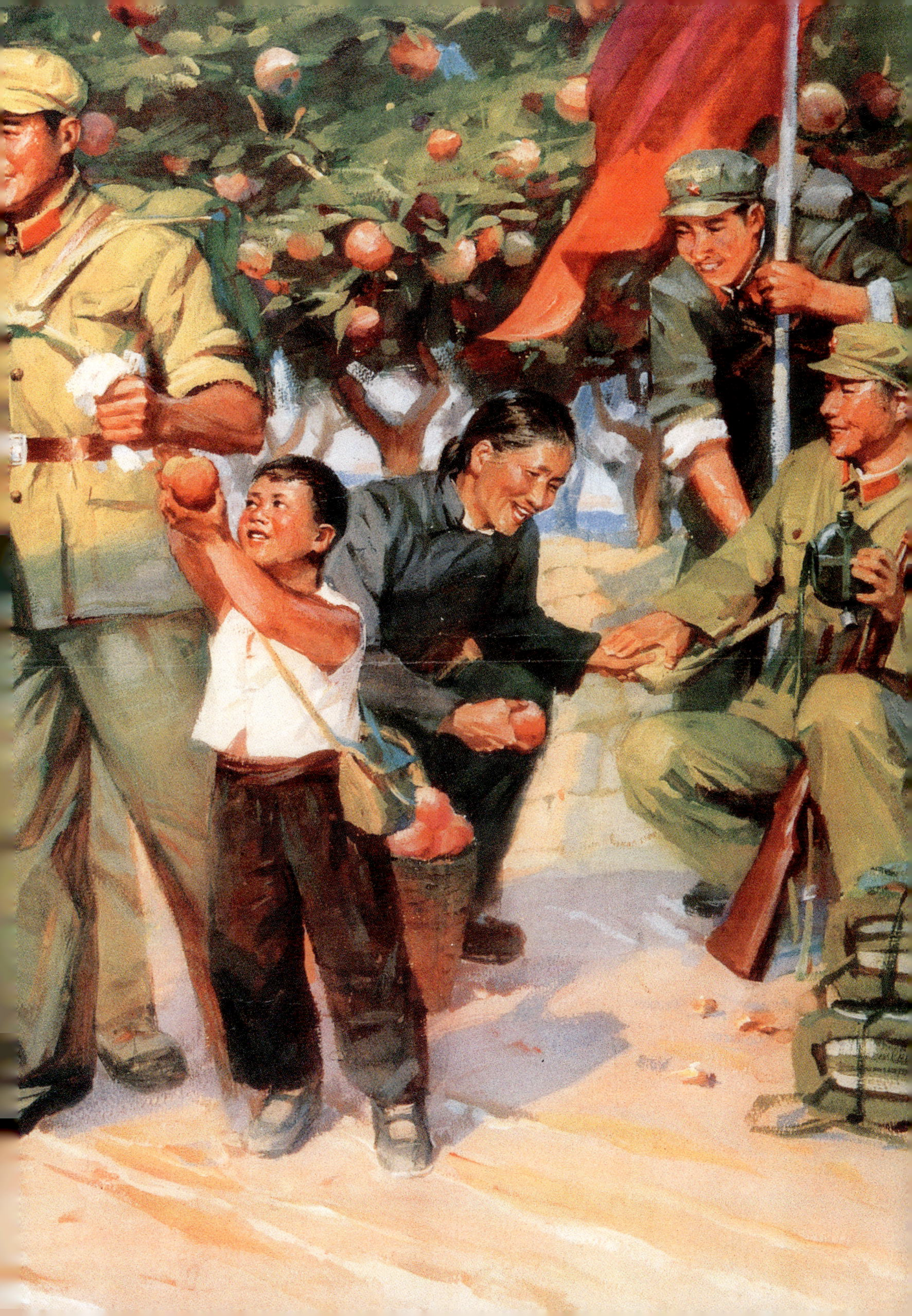

The "Uncles" of the People's Liberation Army are on active service *Artist:* Xiang Qijiu; Shanghai People's Art Publishing House, 1st edn 1978, 2nd edn 1978; 0.11 Yuan

Die Onkel von der Volksbefreiungsarmee sind im Einsatz *Gemalt von* Xiang Qiji; Volkskunstverlag Shanghai, 1. Aufl. 1978, 2. Aufl. 1978; 0,11 Yuan

Les oncles de l'Armée de Libération Populaire sont entrés en action *Peintre :* Xiang Qijiu ; Éditions Populaires d'Art de Shanghai, 1ère éd. 1978, 2e éd. 1978 ; 0,11 yuan

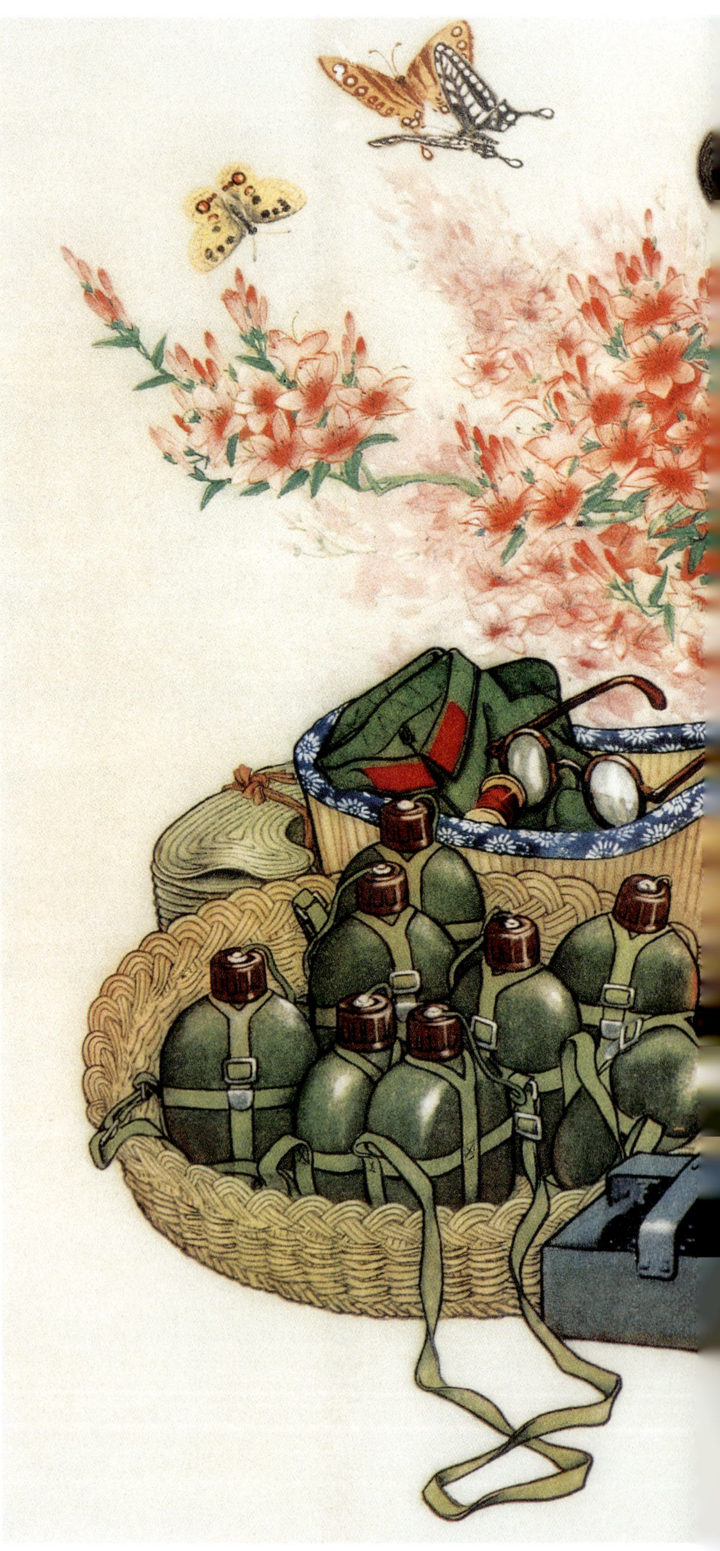

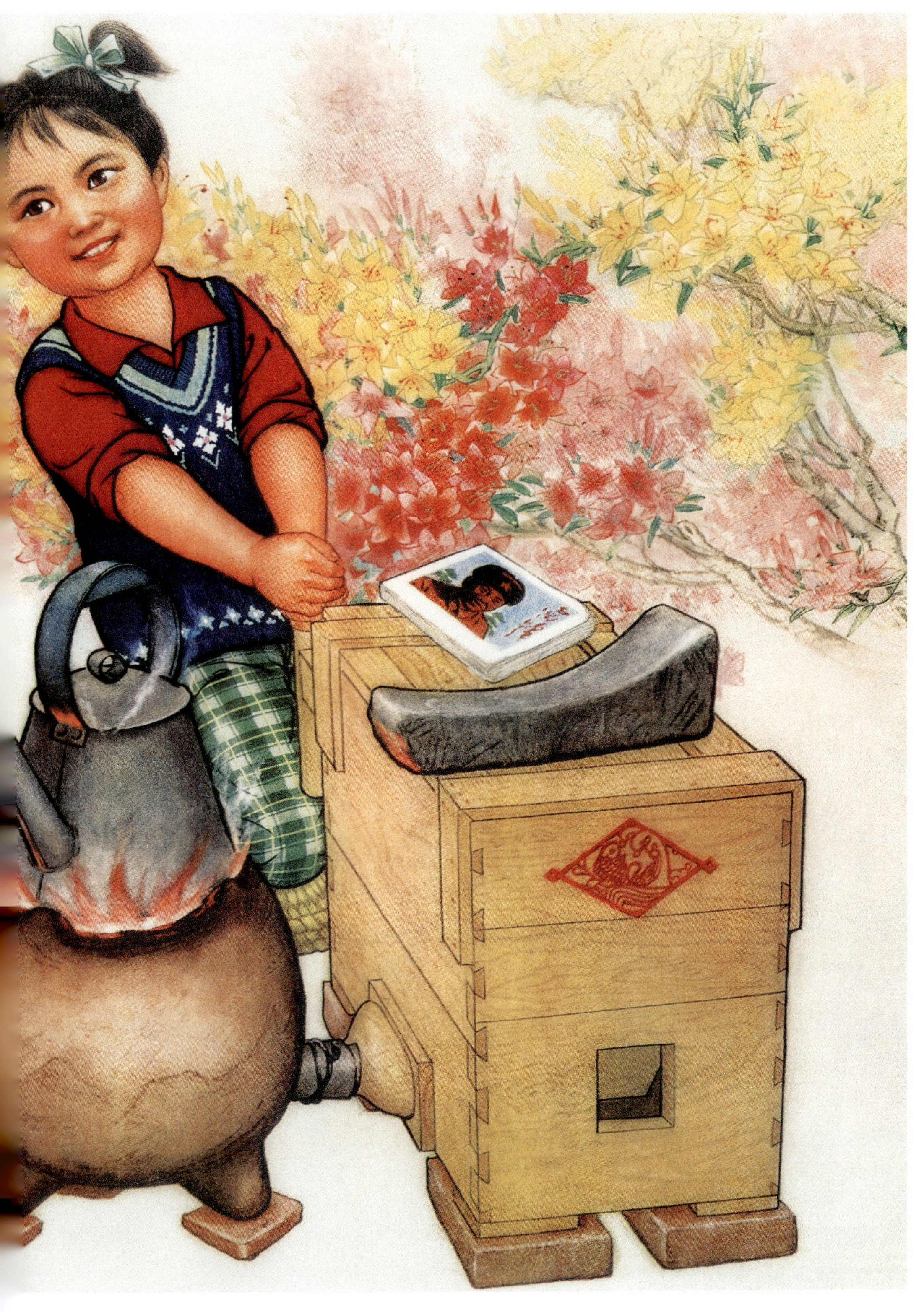

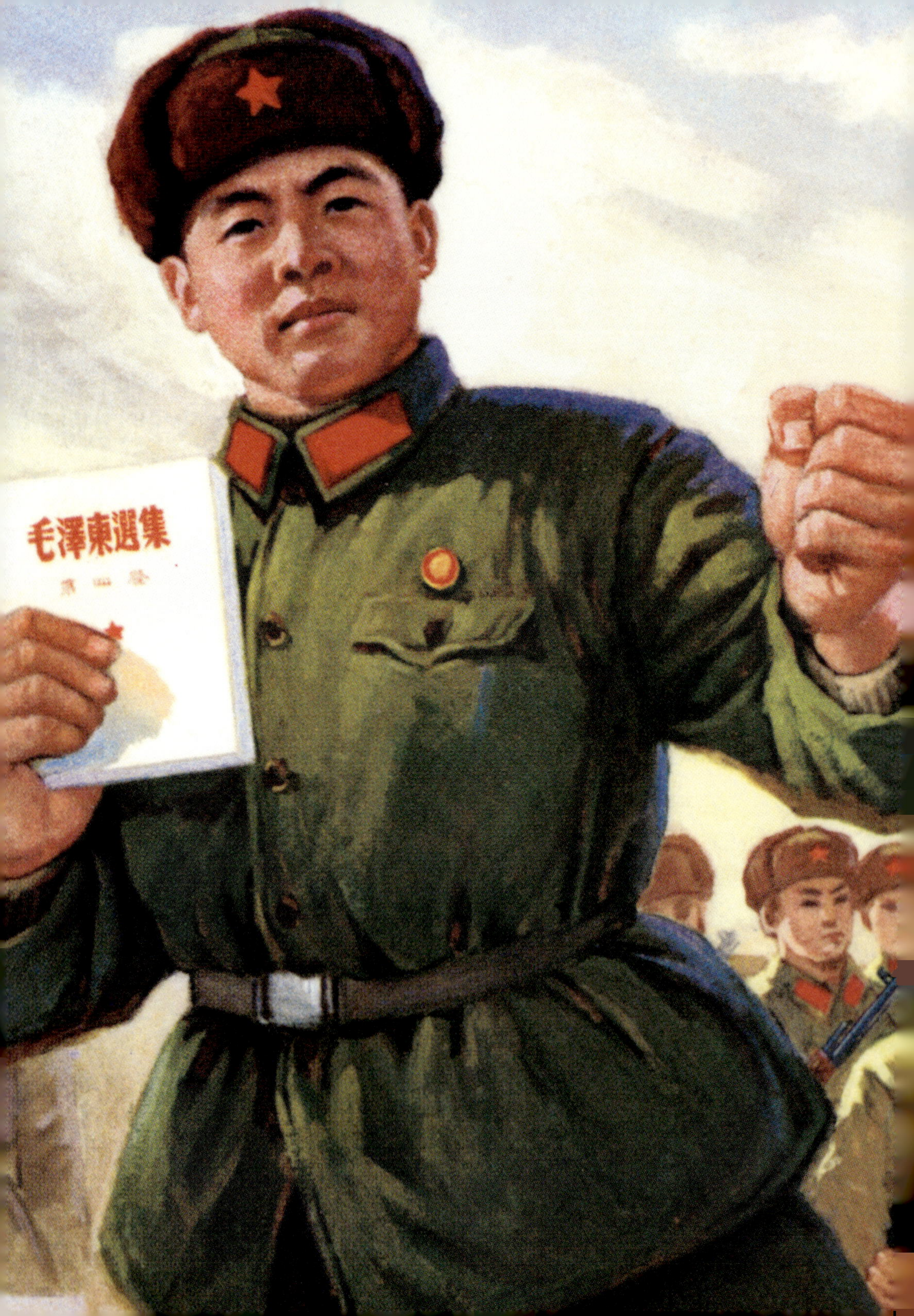
毛澤東選集

XV

DEMOCRACY IN THE THREE MAIN FIELDS

DIE DEMOKRATIE IN DEN DREI HAUPTBEREICHEN
LES « TROIS DÉMOCRATIES »

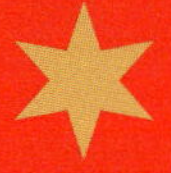

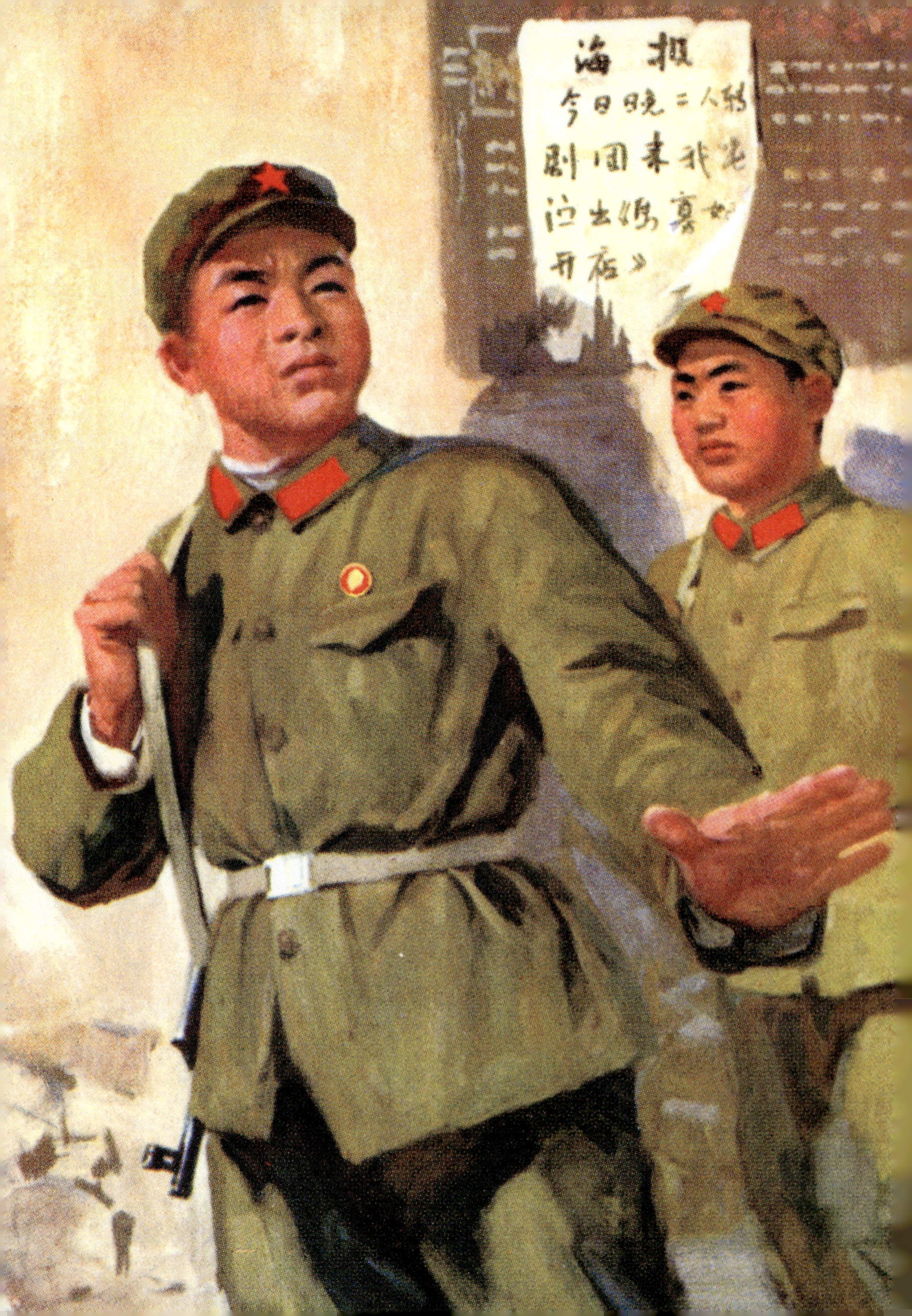
海报
今日晚二人影
剧团来我

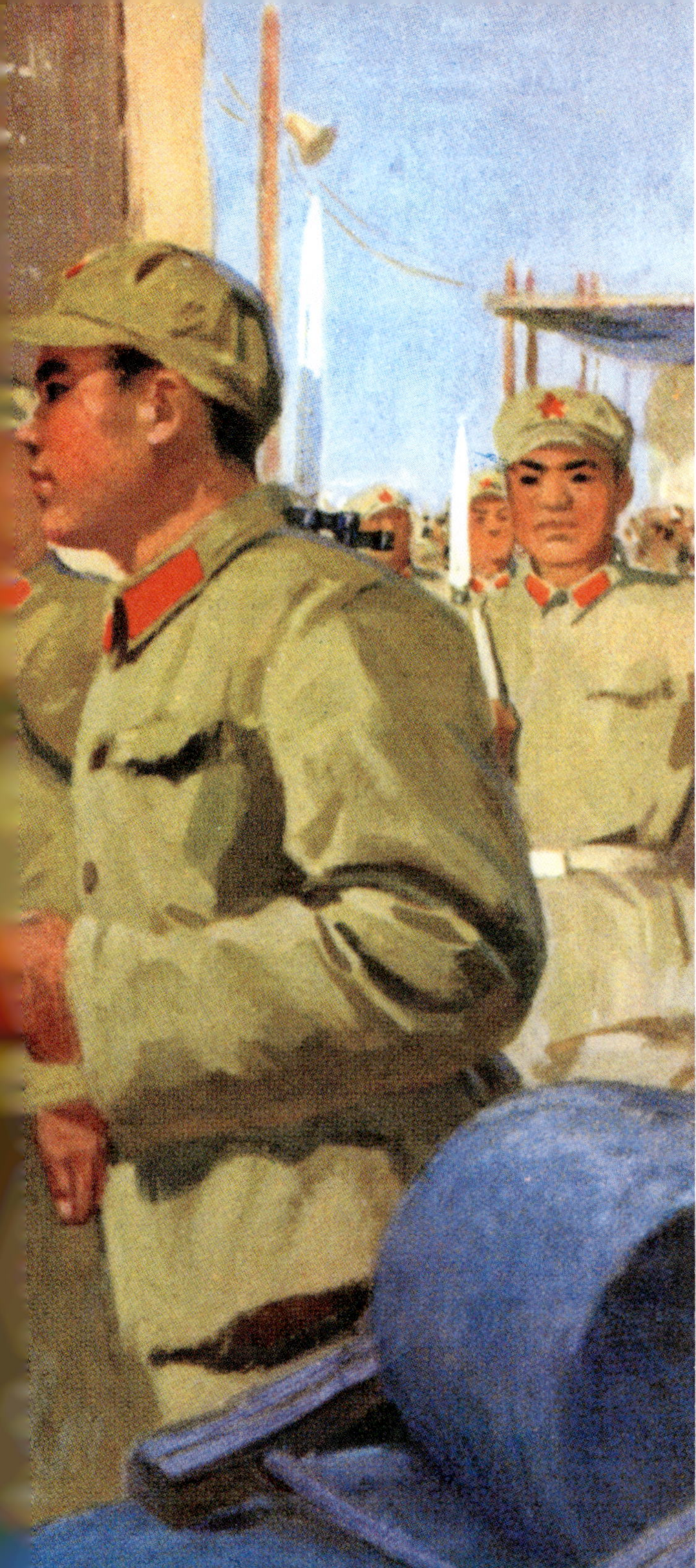

Page 222
Ruthlessly criticize the bourgeoisie *Book:* Selected Works of Mao Zedong, 1970s

Die Bourgeoisie radikal verurteilen *Buch:* Ausgewählte Werke Mao Zedongs, 1970er Jahre

Condamnez la bourgeoisie de façon radicale
Livre : Œuvres choisies de Mao Zedong, années 1970

Democracy in the three main sectors: Soldiers take part in planning operations, 1960s

Demokratie in den drei Hauptbereichen: Die Soldaten nehmen an der Planung von Aktionen teil, 1960er Jahre

Les « trois démocraties » : Les soldats prennent part à la planification d'opérations, années 1960

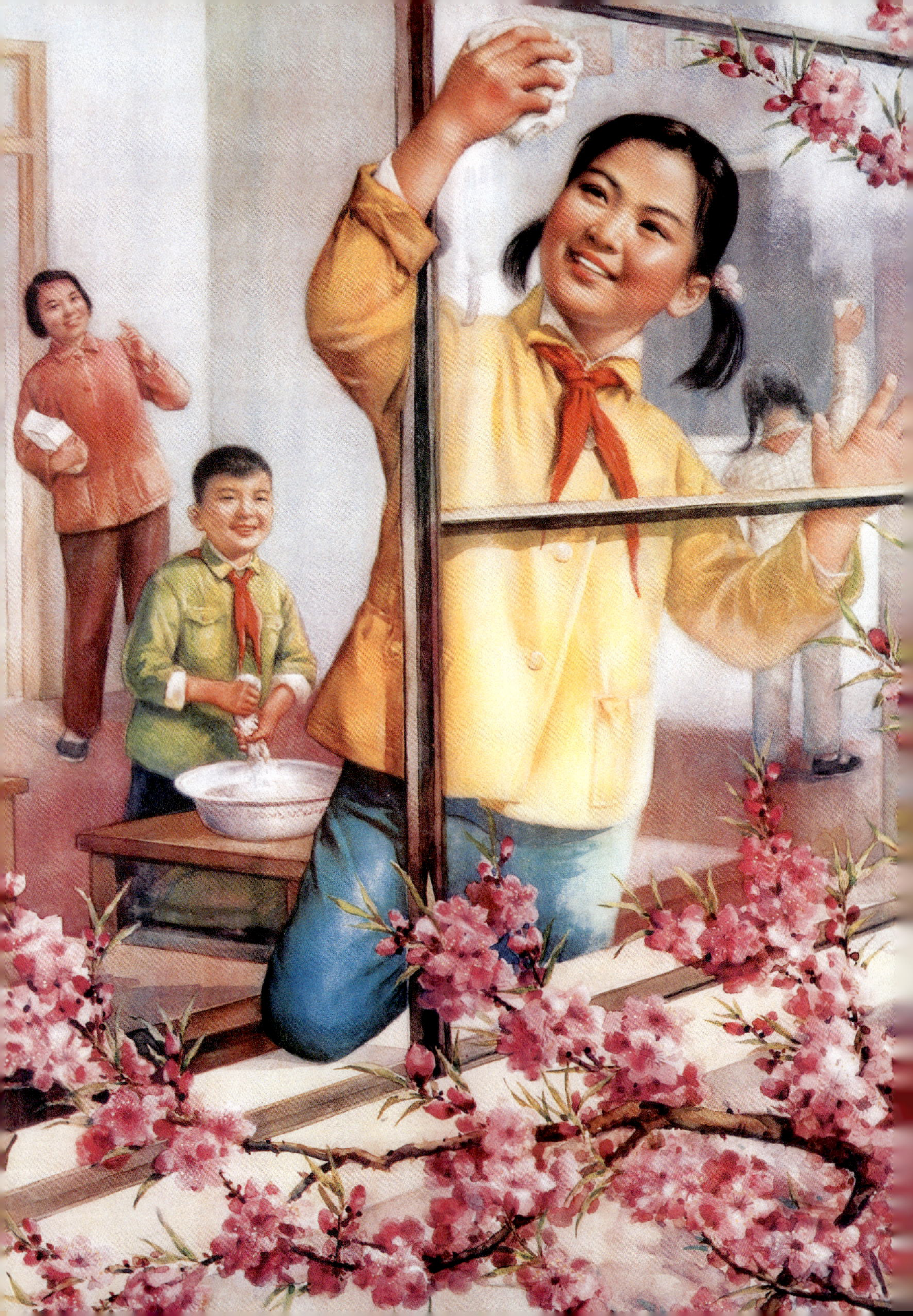

XVI

EDUCATION AND THE TRAINING OF TROOPS

ERZIEHUNG UND AUSBILDUNG
L'ÉDUCATION ET L'ENTRAÎNEMENT DES TROUPES

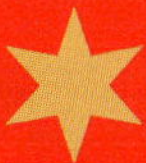

Page 226
We love cleanliness *Artist:* Xu Jiping; Shanghai People's Art Publishing House, 1978; 0.11 Yuan

Wir lieben die Sauberkeit *Gemalt von* Xu Jiping; Volkskunstverlag Shanghai, 1978; 0,11 Yuan

Nous aimons la propreté *Peintre :* Xu Jiping ; Éditions Populaires d'Art de Shanghai, 1978 ; 0,11 yuan

Opposite
Please give it back to the owner! *Artist:* Jiang Feng; Shanghai People's Art Publishing House, 1950s; 0.15 Yuan

Bitte, geben Sie ihn dem Besitzer wieder! *Gemalt von* Jiang Feng; Volkskunstverlag Shanghai, 1950er Jahre; 0,15 Yuan

Rendez-le s'il-vous-plaît à son propriétaire *Peintre :* Jiang Feng ; Éditions Populaires d'Art de Shanghai, années 1950 ; 0,15 yuan

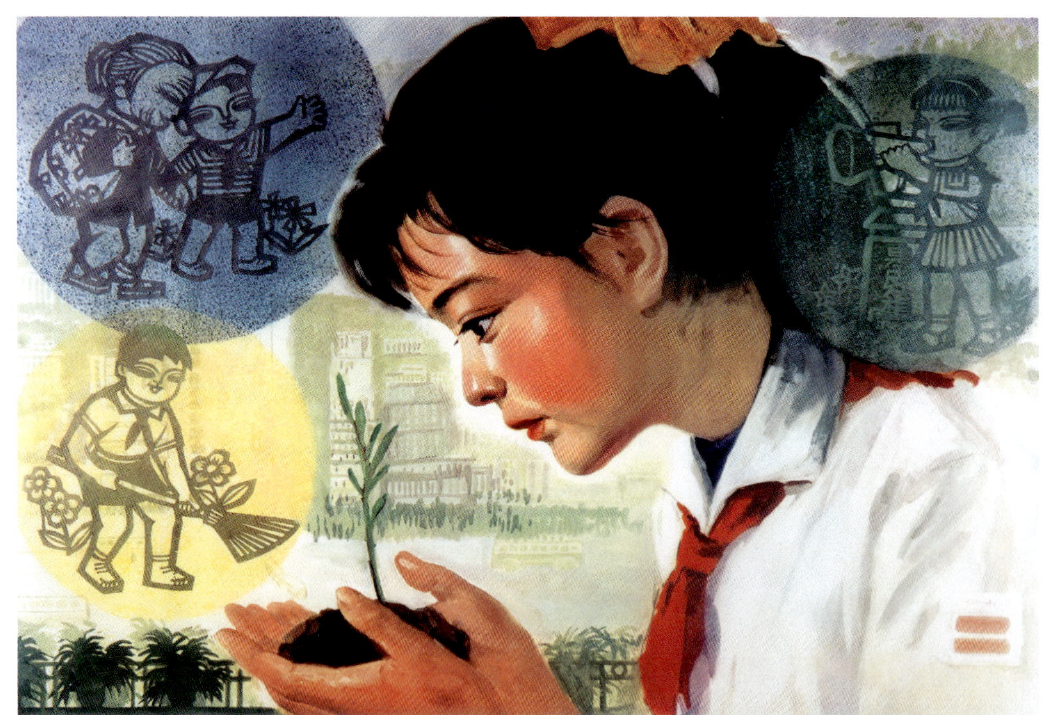

Encourage good manners and politeness; brighten up your surroundings with plants *Artists:* Lu Ping and Xin Zhang; Chongqing Publishing House, 1982 *Print run:* 41,000; 0.16 Yuan

Kultiviertheit und Höflichkeit fördern, die Umgebung bepflanzen und verschönern *Gemalt von* Lu Ping und Xin Zhang; Verlag Chongqing, 1982 *Auflage:* 41 000; 0,16 Yuan

Cultivés et polis, faisons pousser des plantes pour embellir notre environnement *Peintres :* Lu Ping et Xin Zhang ; Éditions de Chongqing, 1982 *Tirage :* 41 000 ; 0,16 yuan

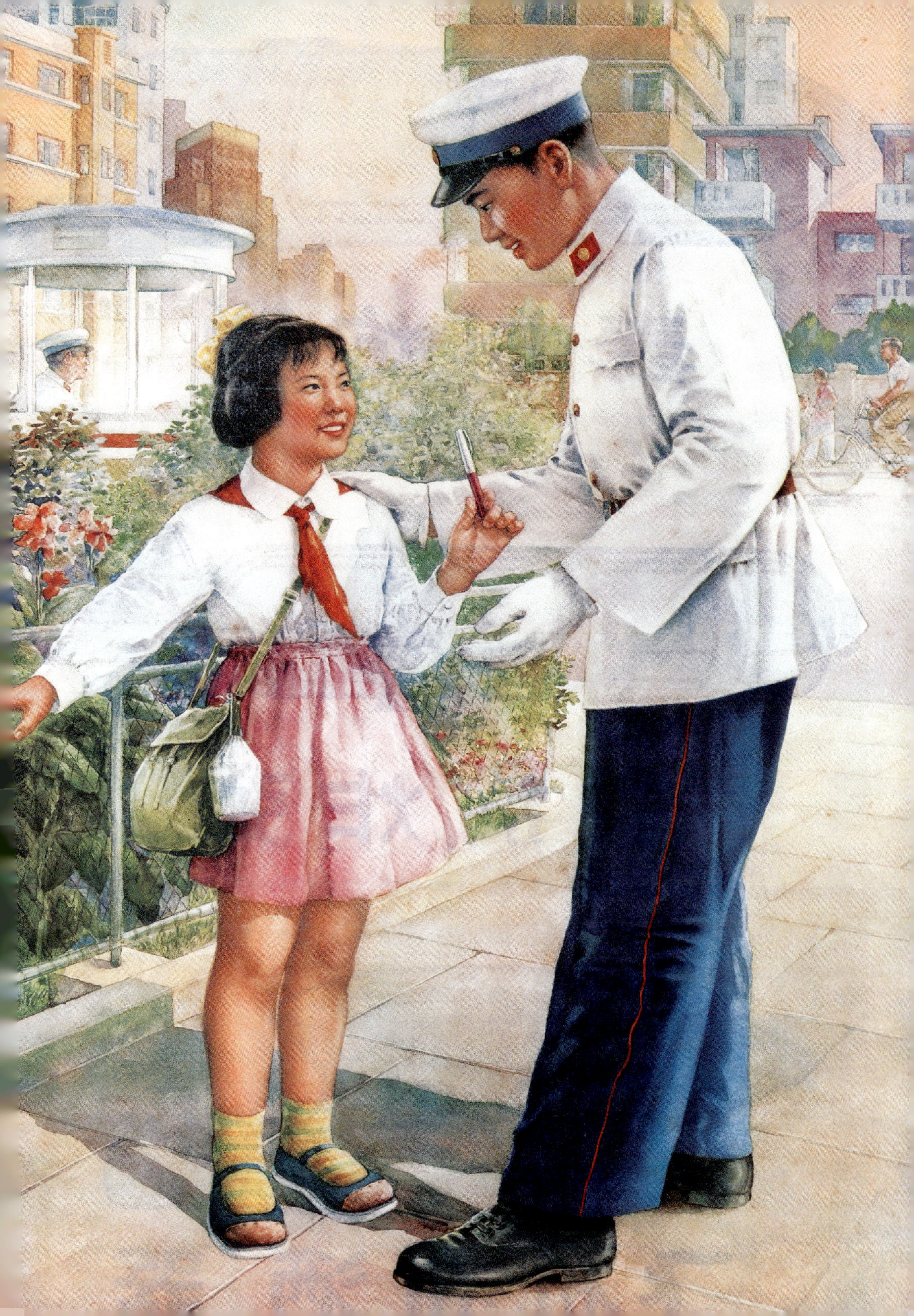

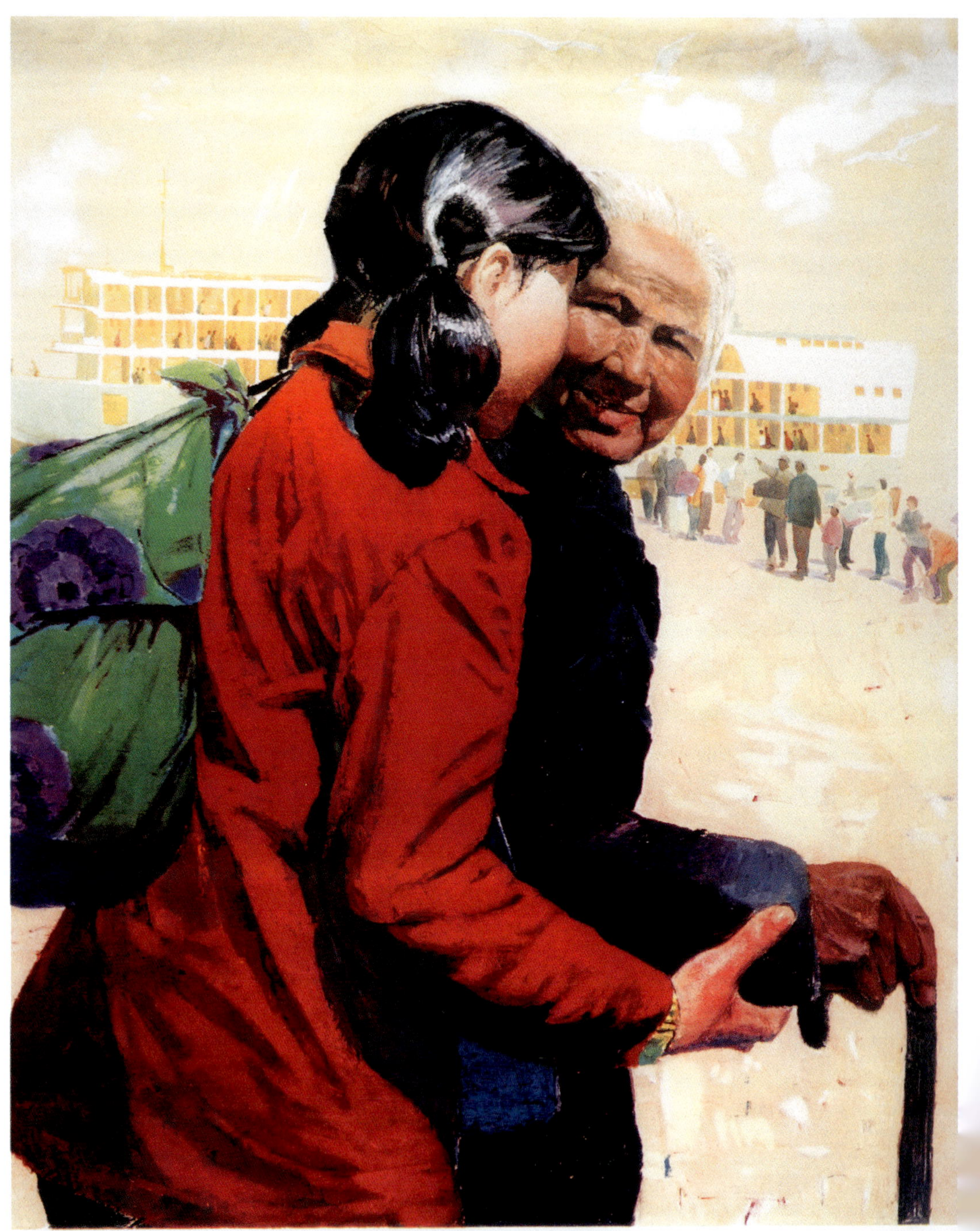

ZHU REN WEI LE 助人为乐

Opposite
Take pleasure from helping others *Artist:* Zhou Ruizhuang; Shanghai People's Art Publishing House 1st edn 1981, 2nd edn 1981 *Print run:* 10,001–183,000; 0.16 Yuan

Freude daran haben, anderen zu helfen *Gemalt von* Zhou Ruizhuang; Volkskunstverlag Shanghai, 1. Aufl. 1981, 2. Aufl. 1981 *Auflage:* 10 001–183 000; 0,16 Yuan

Ayez de la joie à aider les autres *Peintre :* Zhou Ruizhuang ; Éditions Populaires de Shanghai, 1ère éd. 1981, 2e éd. 1981 *Tirage :* 10 001–183 000 ; 0,16 yuan

Give up your seat to the elderly (basic exercise 2) Checked and passed by the National Teaching Materials Commission (syllabus) for Primary and Middle Schools Poster used as a teaching aid with the textbook *Chinese for Primary Schools*, Book 2, for sixth-year classes *Artists:* Ni Fanghua and Ma Hongdao; Shanghai Educational Publishing House

Älteren Menschen den eigenen Platz anbieten (Grundübung 2) Überprüft und genehmigt von der Prüfkommission für Unterrichtsmaterial (Lehrstoffe) der Grund- und Mittelschulen des ganzen Landes, Unterrichtsplakat (Teil 1) zum Lehrbuch *Chinesisch für Grundschulen*, Band 2 für das sechste Schuljahr *Gemalt von* Ni Fanghua und Ma Hongdao; Erziehungsverlag Shanghai

Offrez votre place aux personnes âgées (Exercice fondamental n° 2) Revu et agréé par la Commission de contrôle du matériel d'enseignement des écoles primaires et secondaires de l'ensemble du pays, affiche pédagogique (1ère partie) accompagnant le volume 2 du manuel de chinois des écoles primaires (6e année scolaire) *Peintres :* Ni Fanghua et Ma Hongdao ; Éditions Éducatives de Shanghai

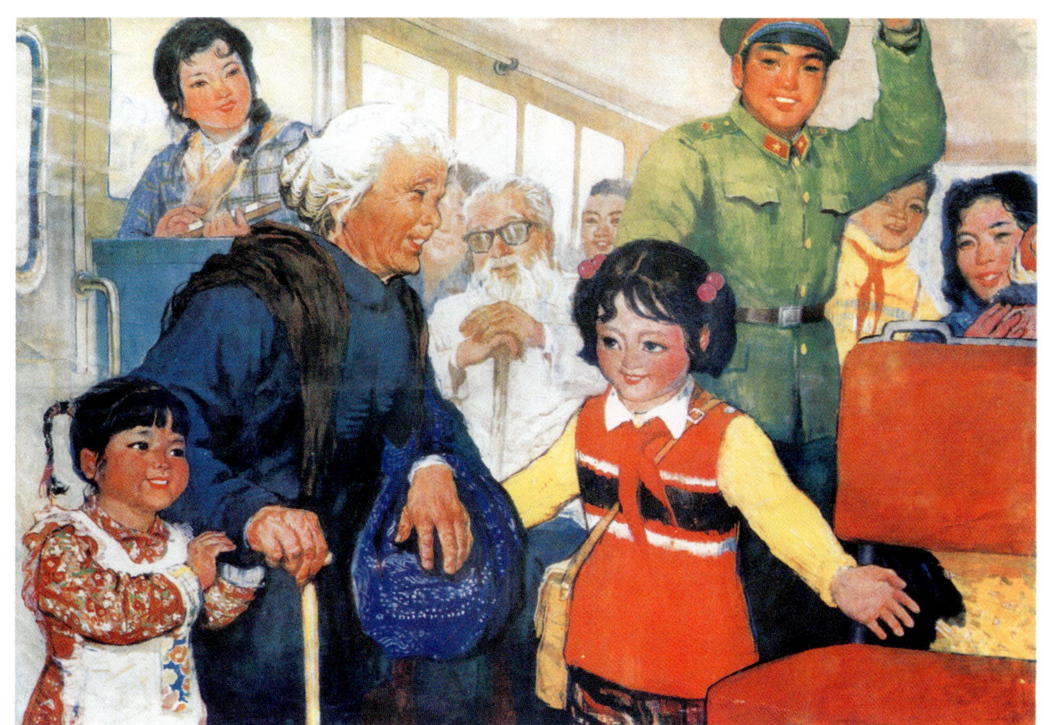

Opposite
Be a good child of the Party
Captions on the wall newspaper: The red star lights our way in our struggle. Learn from Pan Dongzi* to be a good child of the Party *On blackboard:* The dictatorship of the proletariat is good. Agitation unit *Artists:* Shan Lianxiao and Qi Daoyan, Dalian Porcelain Isolator Factory; Liaoning People's Publishing House, 1976; 0.14 Yuan
* The young protagonist of *Sparkling Red Stars* (1974), a film about a peasant boy who bravely fought against the enemy during the Second Revolutionary Civil War (1927–1937) and eventually became a soldier with the Red Army.

Ein gutes Kind der Partei sein
Überschriften der Wandzeitung: Der rote Stern leuchtet uns beim Kampf. Von Pan Dongzi* lernen, ein gutes Kind der Partei zu sein *Auf der Tafel:* Die Diktatur des Proletariats ist gut, Agitationsgruppe *Gemalt von* Shan Lianxiao und Qi Daoyan, Porzellanisolator-Fabrik Dalian; Volksverlag Liaoning, 1976; 0,14 Yuan
* Der junge Protagonist in dem 1974 gedrehten Spielfilm „Der leuchtende rote Stern". Es handelt sich um einen Bauernjungen, der im 2. Revolutionären Bürgerkrieg (1927–1937) tapfer gegen die Feinde kämpft und schließlich ein Soldat der Roten Armee wird.

Soyez de bons enfants du Parti
Légendes du journal mural : L'étoile rouge nous éclaire pendant le combat. Retenez la leçon de Pan Dongzi* pour être de bons enfants du Parti *Sur le tableau :* La dictature du prolétariat est une bonne chose, groupe d'agitation *Peintres :* Shan Lianxiao et Qi Daoyan, usine de porcelaine de Dalian ; Éditions Populaires du Liaoning, 1976 ; 0,14 yuan
* Le jeune protagoniste du film « La lumière de l'étoile rouge », tourné en 1974. Il s'agit d'un jeune paysan qui, pendant la 2e guerre civile révolutionnaire (1927–1937), se bat avec bravoure contre les ennemis et finit par devenir un soldat de l'Armée Rouge.

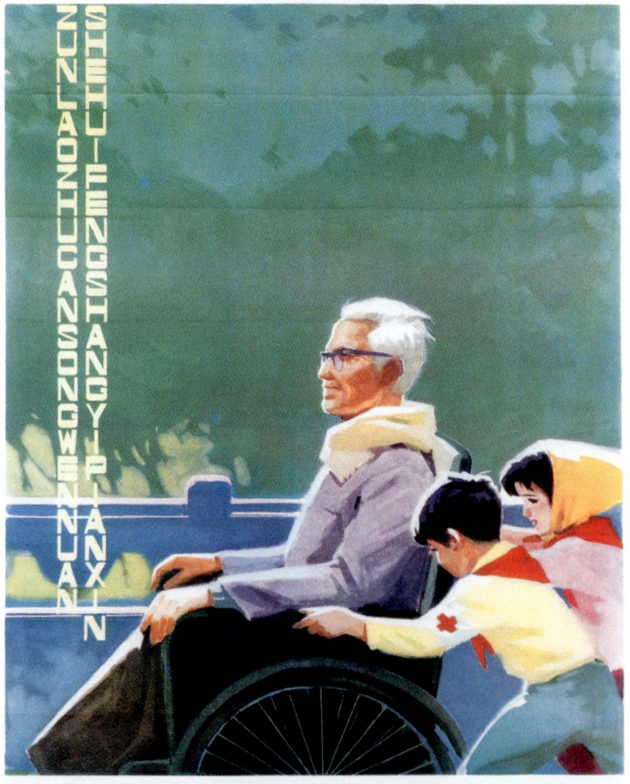

Respect your elders; help the handicapped; be kind to other people; create new social customs *Artists:* Jin Putang and Yang Jingzhi *Published by:* the Chinese Red Cross, 1983

Ältere achten, Behinderten helfen, Mitmenschen Wärme geben, neue gesellschaftliche Sitten schaffen *Gemalt von* Jin Putang und Yang Jingzhi *Herausgeber:* Chinesisches Rotes Kreuz, 1983

Respectez les personnes âgées, aidez les handicapés, donnez de la chaleur à vos semblables, créez de nouveaux usages sociaux *Peintres :* Jin Putang et Yang Jingzhi *Éditeur :* Croix-Rouge chinoise, 1983

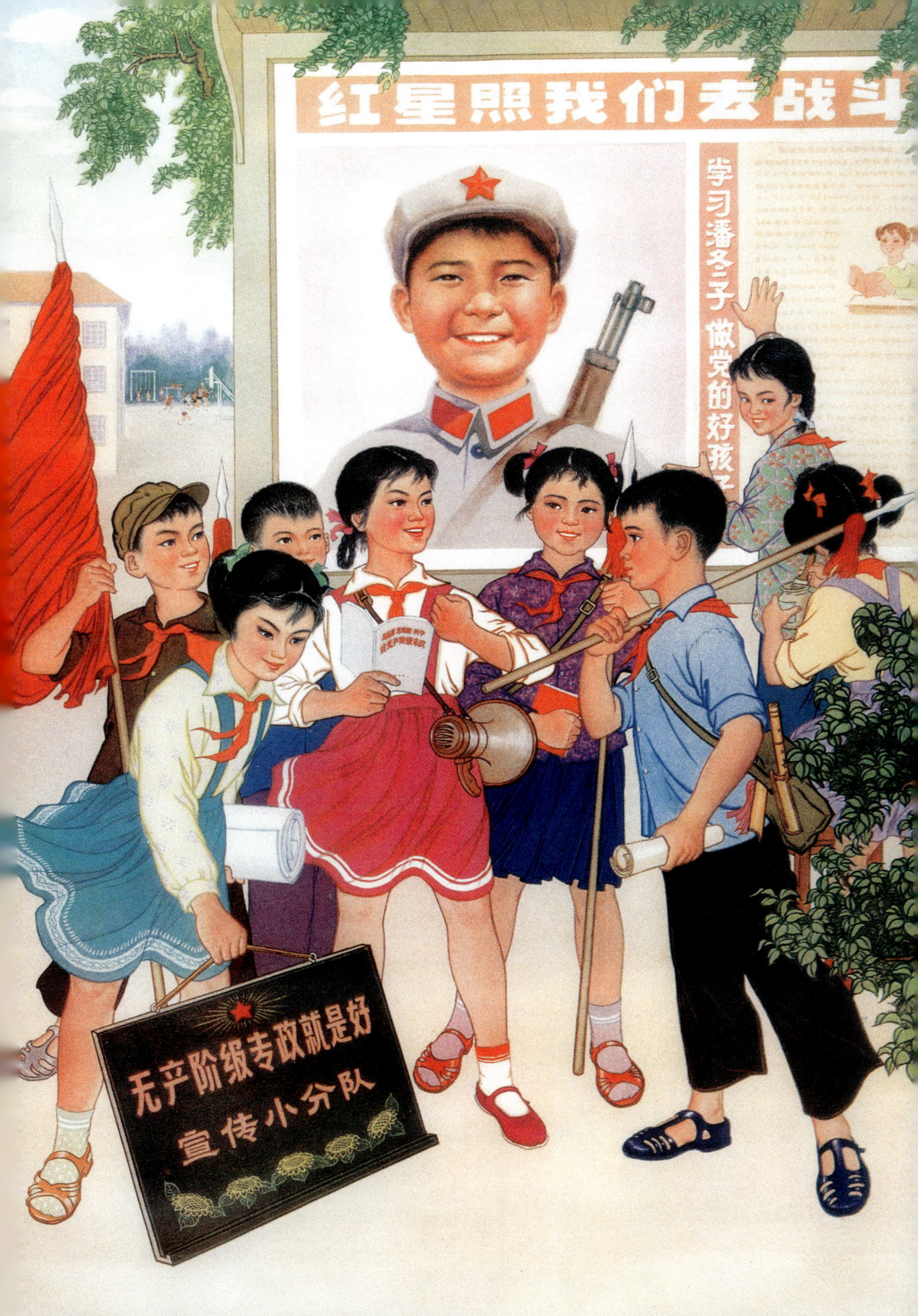
红星照我们去战斗
学习潘冬子 做党的好孩子
无产阶级专政就是好
宣传小分队

fēi jī
飞机
wèi xīng
卫星
fān bǎn
帆板
jī qiāng
机枪
huǒ jiàn
火箭
qián shuǐ tǐng
潜水艇
tuō lā jī
拖拉机
kuài tǐng
快艇
tuī tǔ jī
推土机
diàn chē
电车
dà pào
大炮
qì chē
汽车
zhuāng jiǎ chē
装甲车
tǎn kè
坦克
lún chuán
轮船
huǒ chē
火车

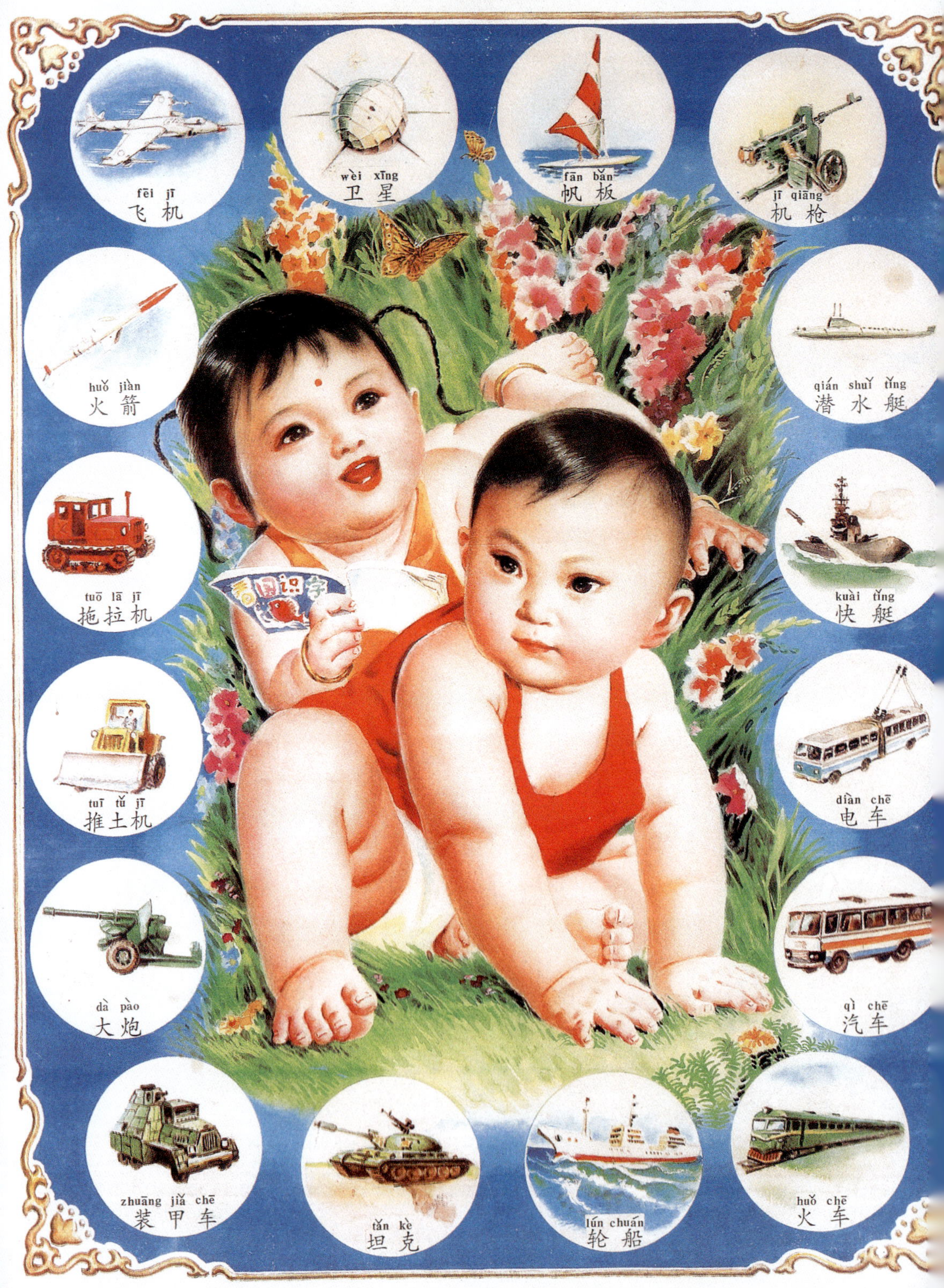

宝宝识字图

"Our educational policy must enable everyone who receives an education to develop morally, intellectually, and physically and become a worker with both socialist consciousness and culture."

Unser Kurs auf dem Gebiet des Bildungswesens muss gewährleisten, dass jeder, der eine Ausbildung erhält, sich moralisch, geistig und körperlich entwickelt und ein gebildeter Werktätiger mit sozialistischem Bewusstsein wird. ✶ Notre politique dans le domaine de l'éducation doit permettre à ceux qui la reçoivent de se former sur le plan moral, intellectuel et physique pour devenir des travailleurs cultivés, ayant une conscience socialiste.

Little treasure learns to read* *Artist:* Lin Lin; Shandong Art Publishing House, 1987; 0.27 Yuan
* The image depicts the characters for each respective object.

Schätzchen lernt lesen* *Gemalt von* Lin Lin; Kunstverlag Shandong, 1987; 0,27 Yuan
* Auf dem Bild sind die Schriftzeichen der jeweiligen Gegenstände zu sehen.

Les petits bouts de choux apprennent à lire* *Peintre :* Lin Lin ; Éditions d'Art du Shandong, 1987 ; 0,27 yuan
* Pour chaque objet figure sur l'image la façon dont il s'écrit.

Study hard! Make progress every day! *Badges:* Red Guard Youth Section *Designed by:* Lintong and Yuxin Middle School; Shanghai People's Publishing House, 1972; 0.11 Yuan

Lernt fleißig! Macht täglich Fortschritte! *Brosche:* Junge Rote Garde *Entwurf:* Mittelschule Lintong und Yuxin; Volksverlag Shanghai, 1972; 0,11 Yuan

Appliquez-vous à l'étude ! Faites chaque jour des progrès ! *Insigne :* Jeune Garde Rouge *Conception :* Collège de Lintong et Yuxin ; Éditions Populaires de Shanghai, 1972 ; 0,11 yuan

Pages 238–239

Pay attention to hygiene, do more sports and exercise; improve public health *Posters:* It is important to combine sport and hygiene. Eradicate the four pests (mosquitoes, flies, rats and bed bugs) and pay attention to hygiene; Sport and Hygiene Plan; Shanghai People's Hygiene Propaganda Office

Auf die Hygiene achten, das Sporttraining verstärken, das Niveau des Gesundheitswesens erhöhen *Plakate:* Es ist wichtig, Sport und Hygiene zu verbinden, Die vier Schädlinge (Mücken, Fliegen, Ratten und Wanzen) ausrotten und auf die Hygiene achten; Sport- und Hygieneplan; Volkshygiene-Propagandastation Shanghai

Surveillez l'hygiène, renforcez l'entraînement sportif, améliorez le niveau de santé publique *Affiches :* Il est important de lier le sport et l'hygiène. Exterminez les quatre parasites (moustiques, mouches, rats et punaises) et surveillez l'hygiène ; Plan de sport et d'hygiène ; Service de propagande d'hygiène populaire de Shanghai

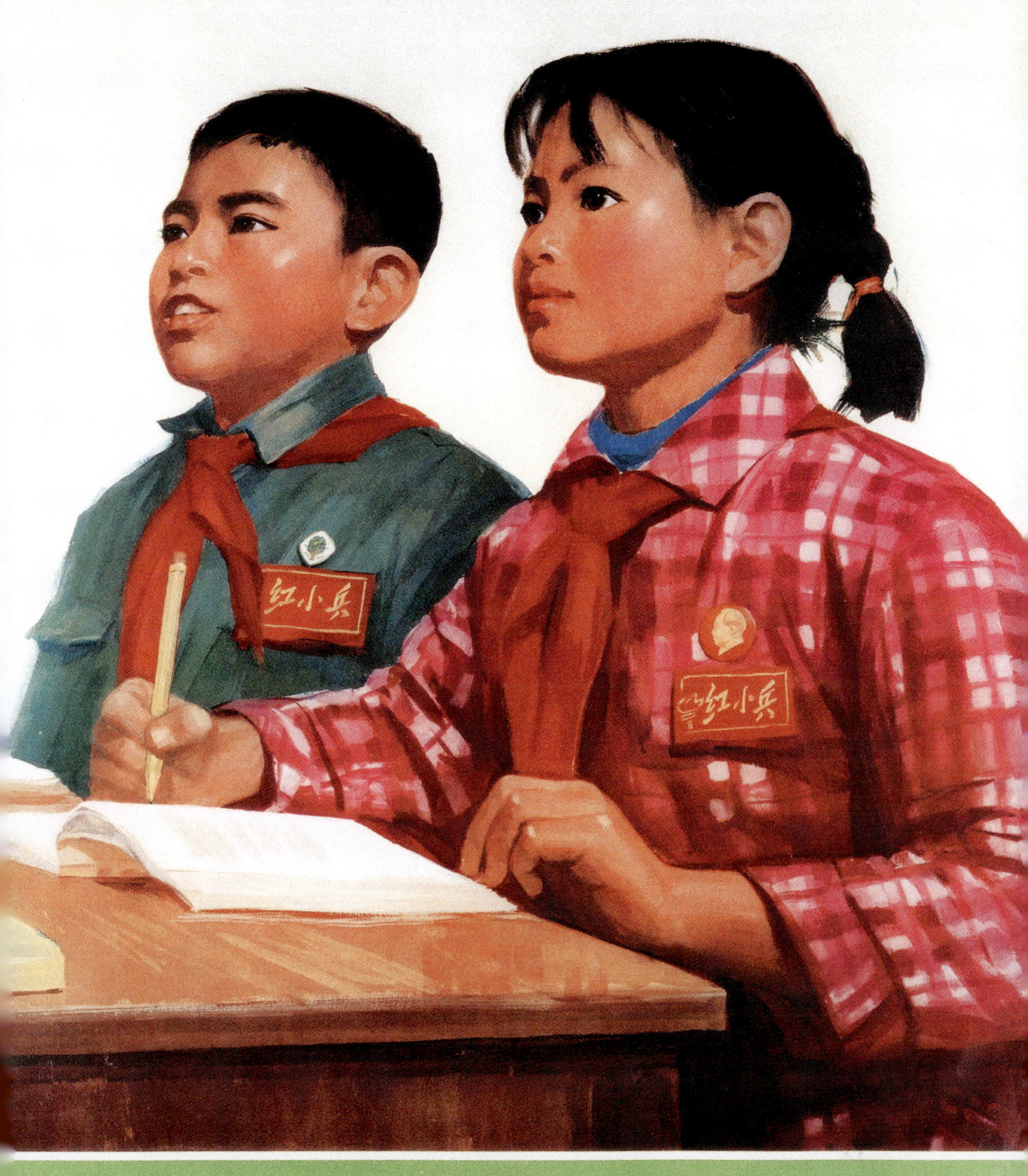

好好学习 天天向上

AO HAO XUE XI TIAN TIAN XIANG SHANG

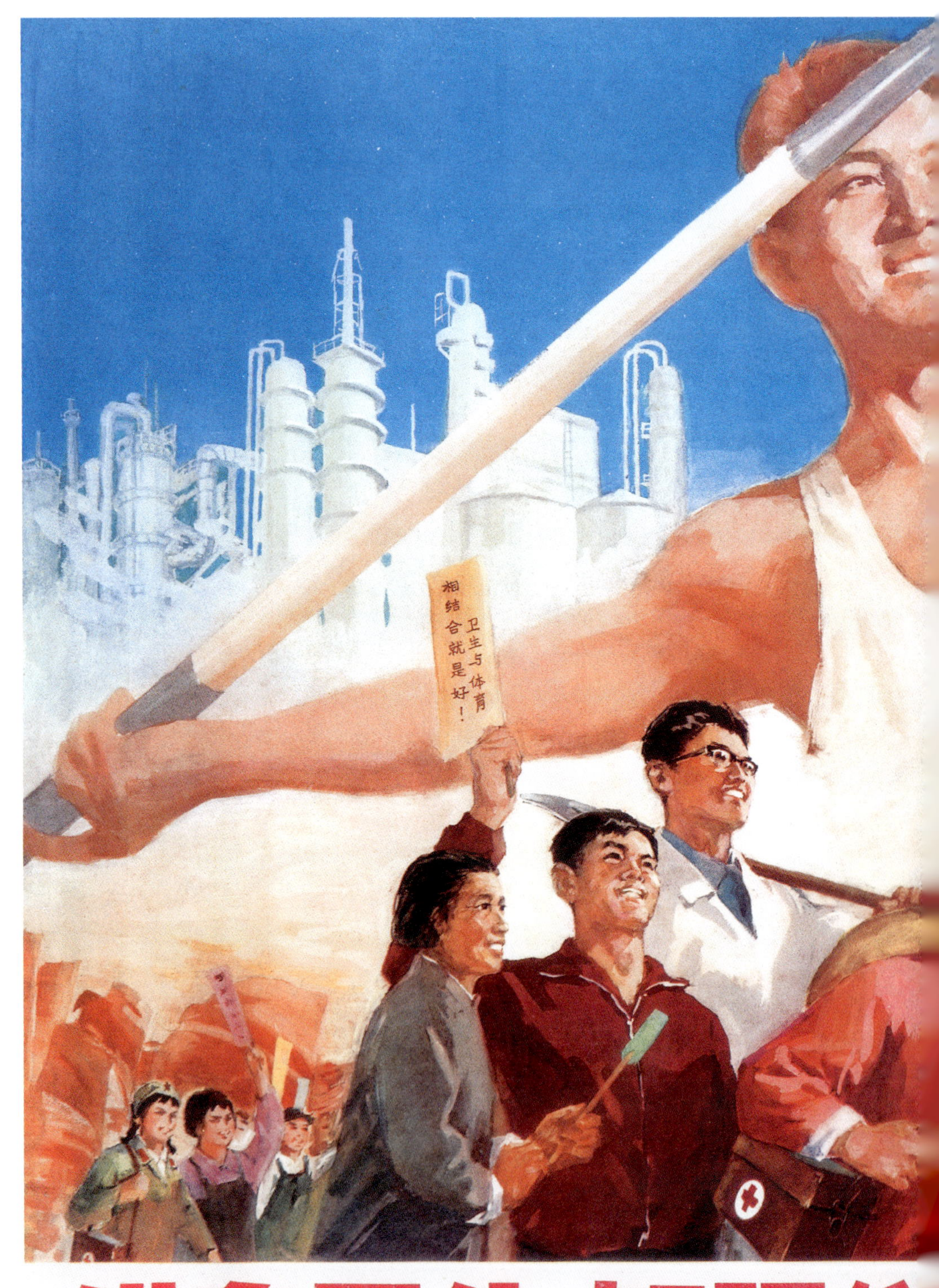

讲究卫生 加强锻

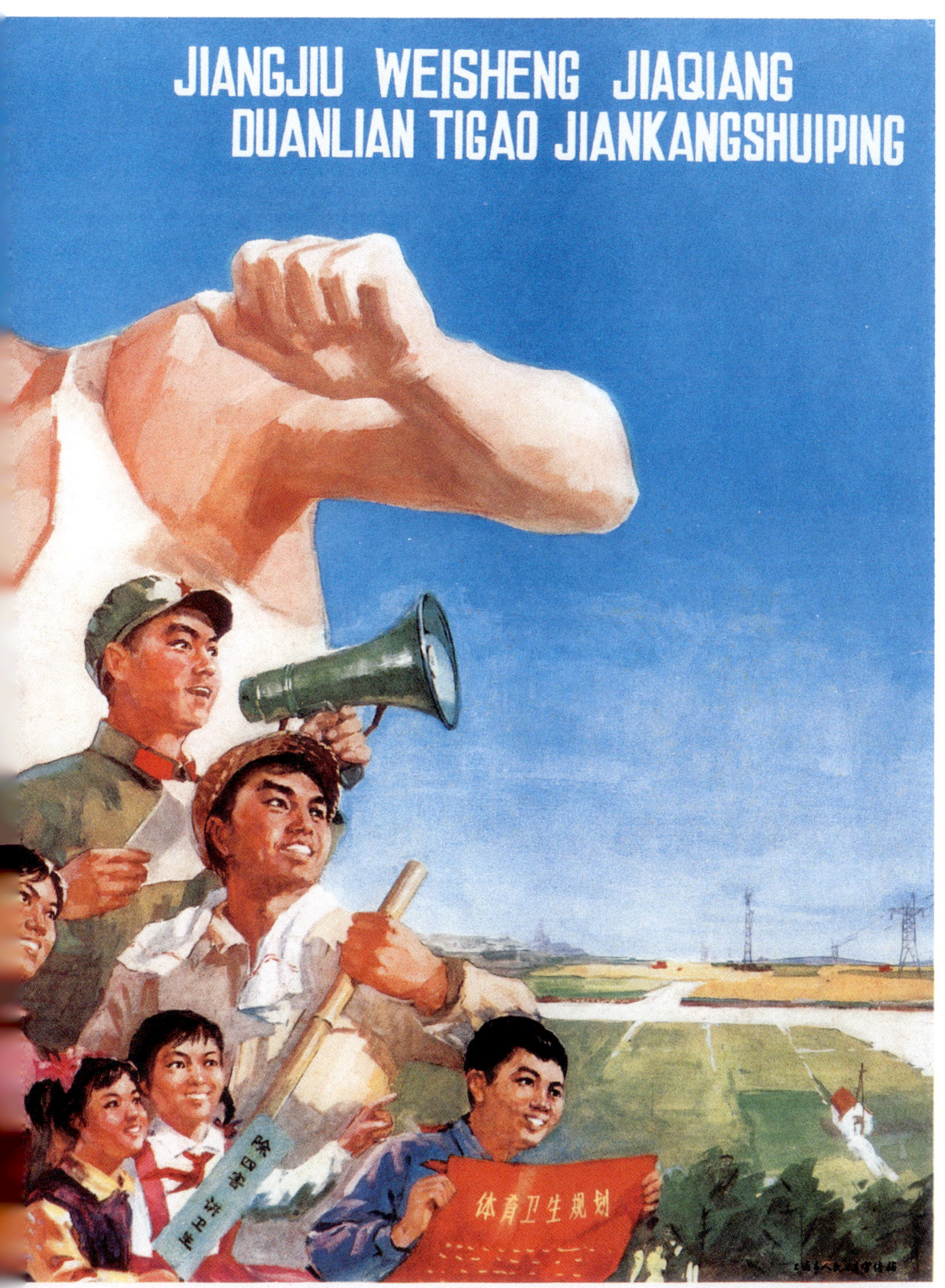
JIANGJIU WEISHENG JIAQIANG
DUANLIAN TIGAO JIANKANGSHUIPING
体育卫生规划
提高健康水平

Opposite

The story of the carrying pole *Artist:* Xin Liliang; Shanghai People's Publishing House, 1st edn 1975, 3rd edn 1976; 0.14 Yuan

Die Geschichte von der Tragestange *Gemalt von* Xin Liliang; Volksverlag Shanghai, 1. Aufl. 1975, 3. Aufl. 1976; 0,14 Yuan

L'histoire du bâton de porteur *Peintre :* Xin Liliang ; Éditions Populaires de Shanghai, 1ère éd. 1975, 3e éd. 1976 ; 0,14 yuan

Learn from Pan Dongzi and be a good child of the Party *Book, top:* Lei Feng *Book, bottom:* Marx, Engels, and Lenin on the dictatorship of the proletariat *Artist:* a worker in the Dalian Electronics Factory; People's Art Publishing House, 1976

Von Pan Dongzi lernen und ein gutes Kind der Partei sein *Buch oben:* Lei Feng *Buch unten:* Marx, Engels und Lenin über die Diktatur des Proletariats *Gemalt in* der Elektrofabrik Dalian; Volkskunstverlag, 1976

Retenez la leçon de Pan Dongzi et soyez de bons enfants du Parti *Livre du haut :* Lei Feng *Livre du bas :* Marx, Engels et Lénine sur la dictature du prolétariat *Peint dans* l'usine d'appareils électriques de Dalian ; Éditions Populaires d'Art, 1976

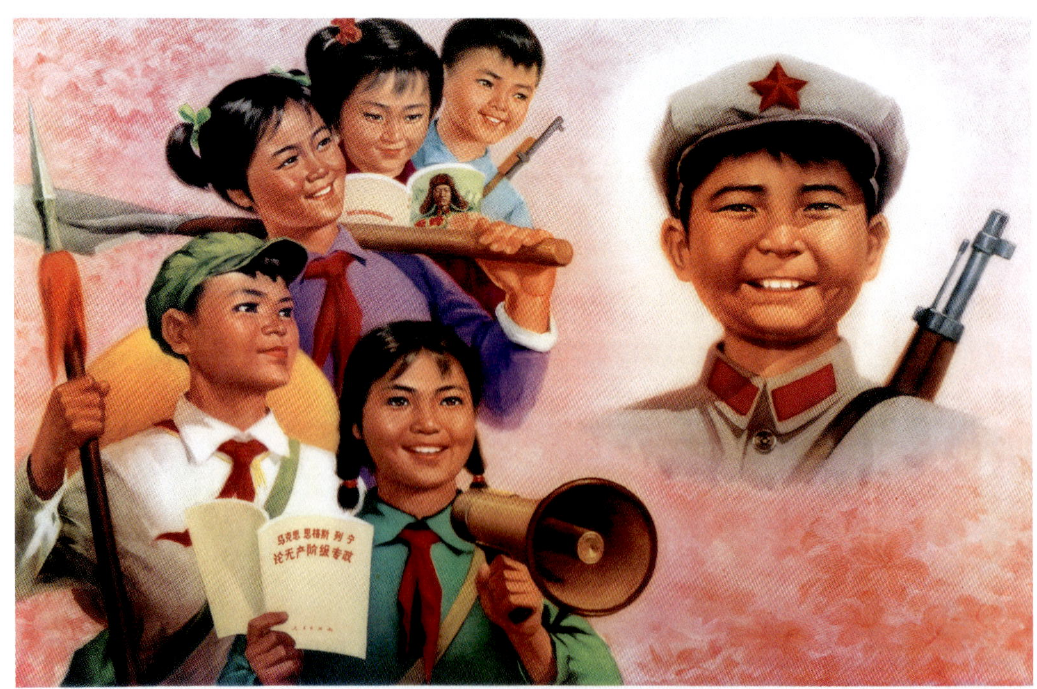

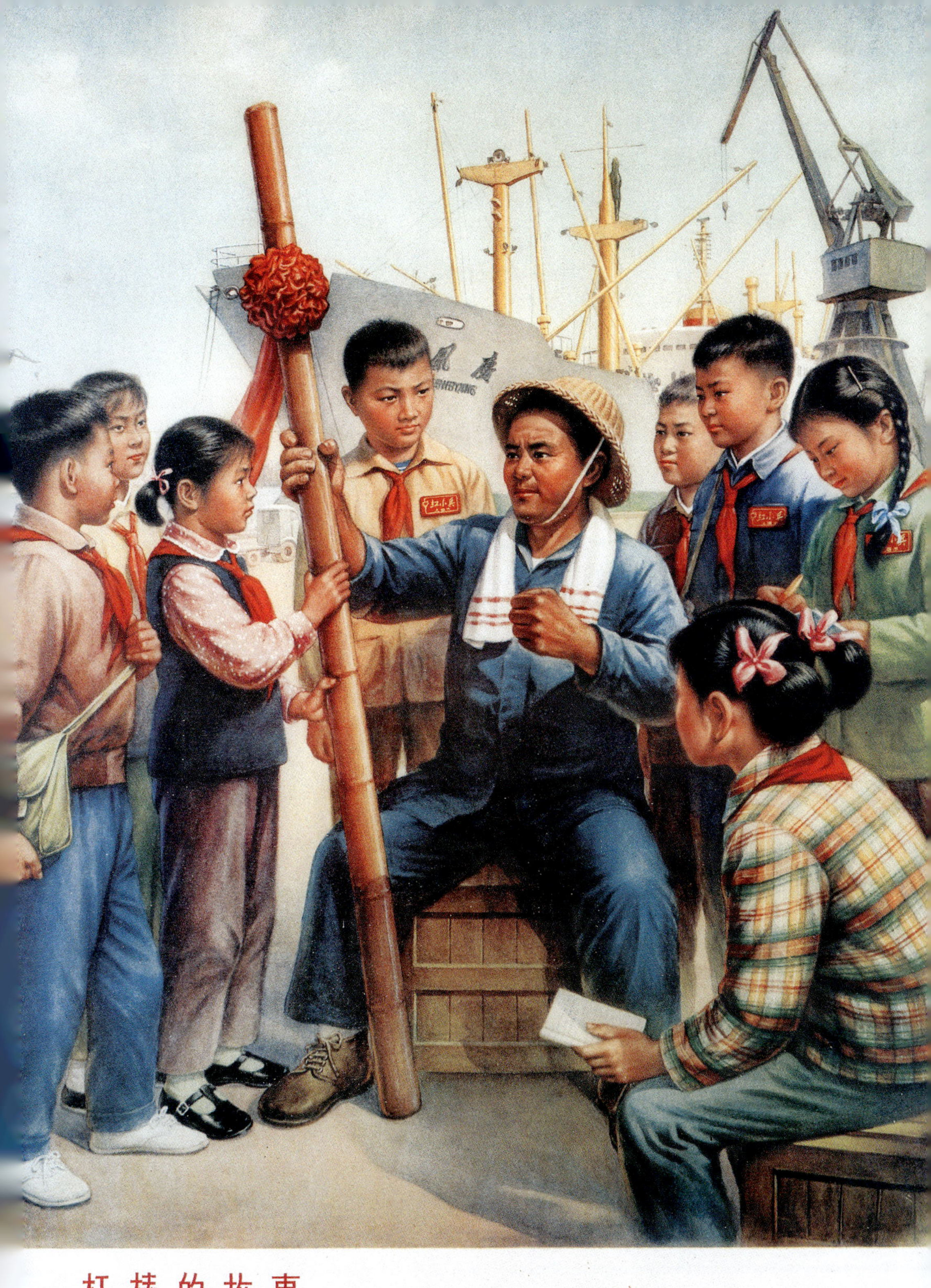

杠棒的故事

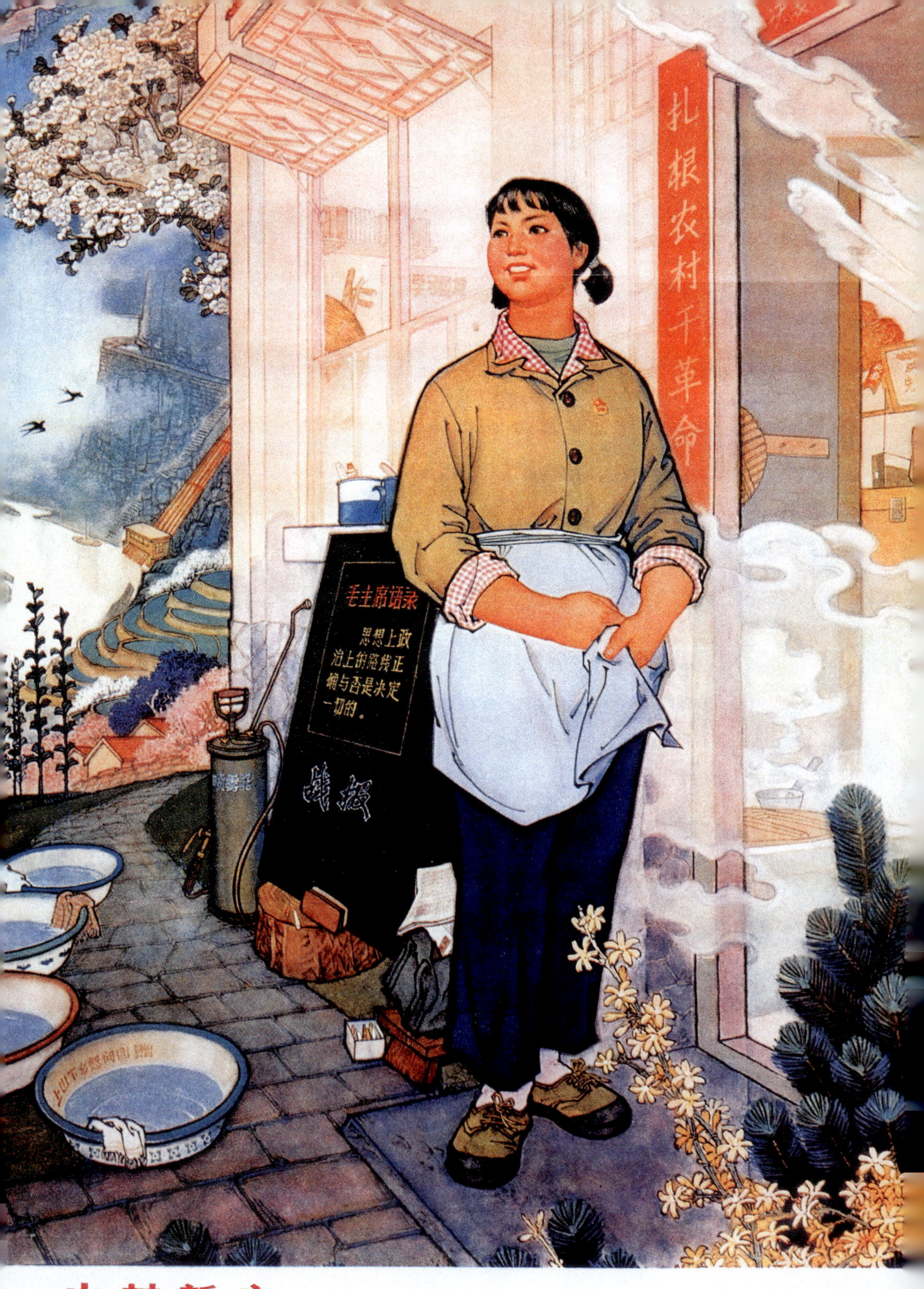

山村新户

Opposite
Setting up a new home in a mountain village *On blackboard:* The correctness or otherwise of the ideological and political line decides everything. Mao Zedong *Above the door:* Break with traditional ideas *Beside the door:* Put down roots in the countryside and bring about the revolution *Artist:* Chen Youji; Shanghai People's Publishing House, 1st edn 1975, 2nd edn 1975; 0.11 Yuan

Ein neuer Haushalt im Bergdorf *Auf der Tafel:* Ob die ideologische und politische Linie richtig ist, ist entscheidend. Mao Zedong *Über der Tür:* Mit den traditionellen Ideen brechen *Neben der Tür:* Wurzeln auf dem Land schlagen und die Revolution durchführen *Gemalt von* Chen Youji; Volksverlag Shanghai, 1. Aufl. 1975, 2. Aufl. 1975; 0,11 Yuan

Un nouveau foyer dans le village de montagne *Citation de Mao sur le tableau :* Savoir si la ligne idéologique et politique est bonne est déterminant. *Au-dessus de la porte :* Rompez avec les idées traditionnelles *Sur le côté de la porte :* Prenez racine à la campagne et faites la révolution *Peintre :* Chen Youji ; Éditions Populaires de Shanghai, 1ère éd. 1975, 2e éd. 1975 ; 0,11 yuan

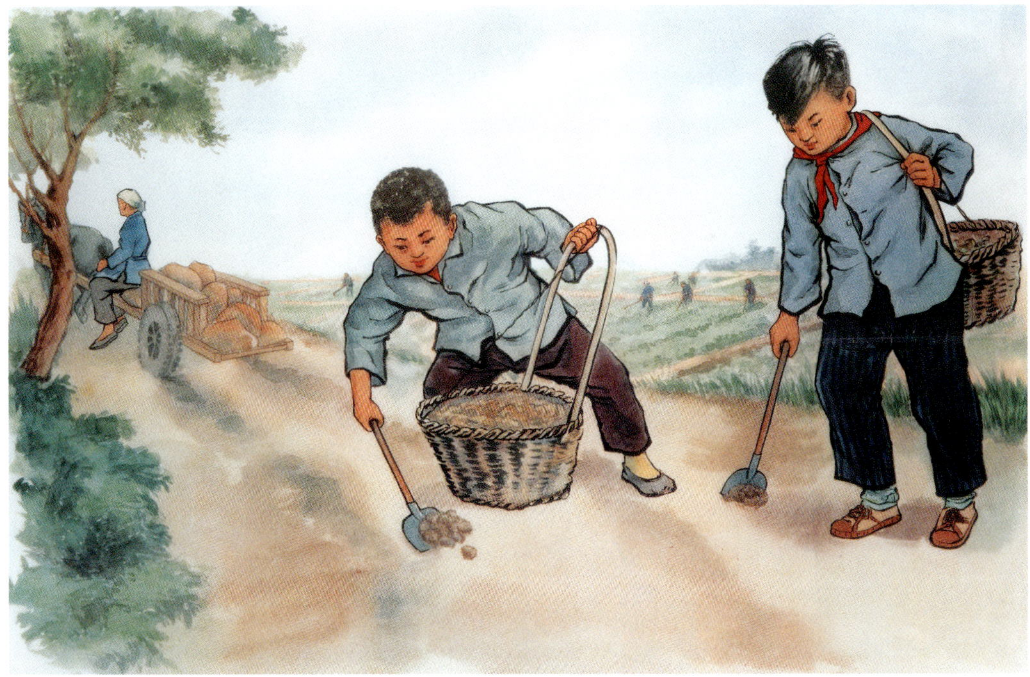

Gathering manure Practising spoken language with the help of pictures, exercise 3, picture 4; Poster used as teaching aid with the textbook *Chinese for Primary Schools*, Book 2, for early primary classes *Artist:* Ma Diexian *Published by:* Shanghai Educational Publishing House *Designed by:* The People's Educational Publishing House, 1959

Dünger sammeln Mithilfe von Bildern sprechen üben, Übung 3, Bild 4; Unterrichtsplakat zum Lehrbuch *Chinesisch für Grundschulen*, Band 2 für die Unterstufe *Gemalt von* Ma Diexian *Herausgeber:* Erziehungsverlag Shanghai *Entwurf:* Volkserziehungsverlag, 1959

Ramassez ce qui peut servir d'engrais Entraînez-vous à parler à l'aide d'images, exercice n° 3, image n° 4 Affiche pédagogique accompagnant le 2e volume du manuel de chinois du cours préparatoire des écoles primaires *Peintre :* Ma Diexian *Éditeur :* Éditions Éducatives de Shanghai, *Conception :* Éditions d'Éducation Populaire, 1959

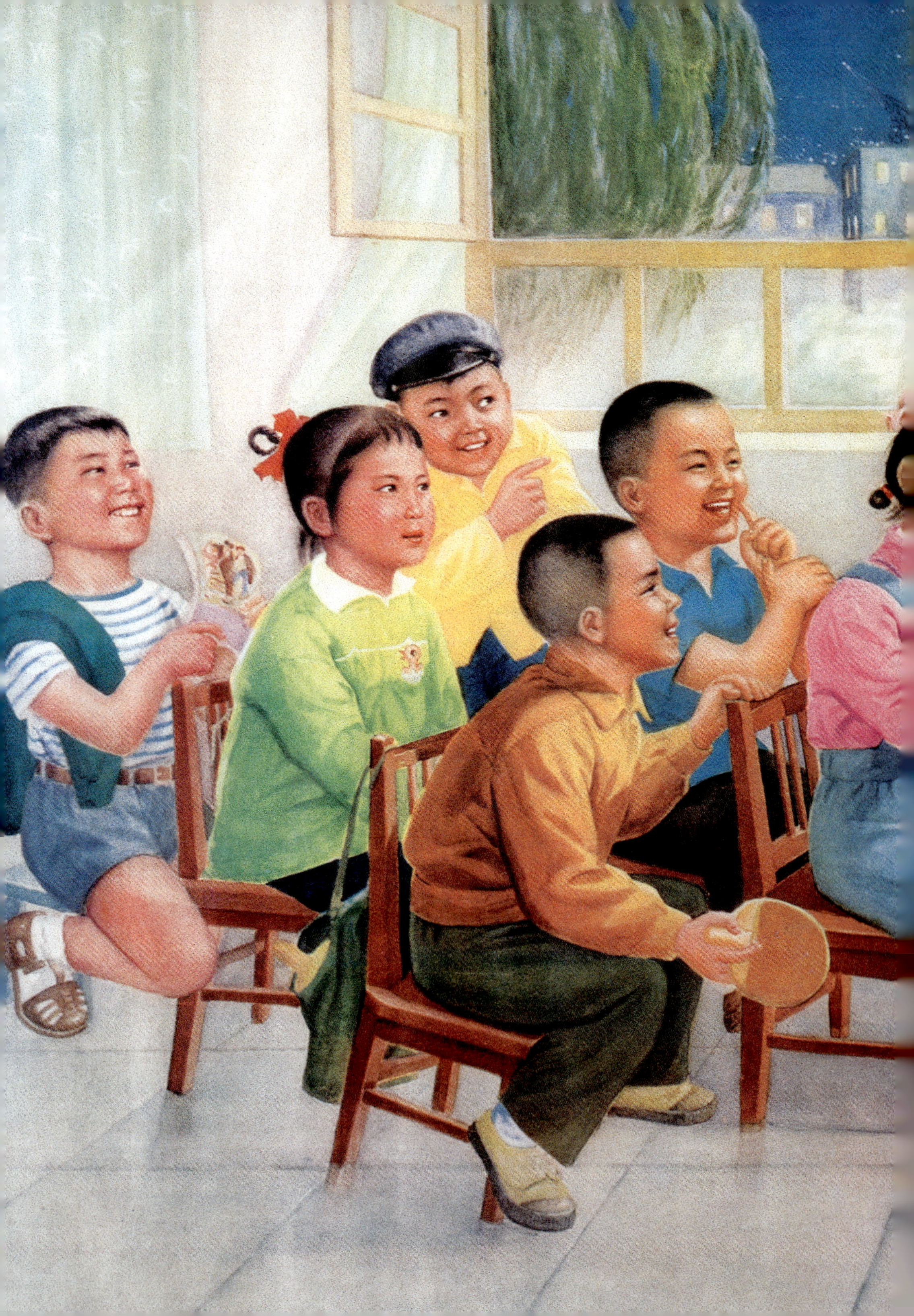

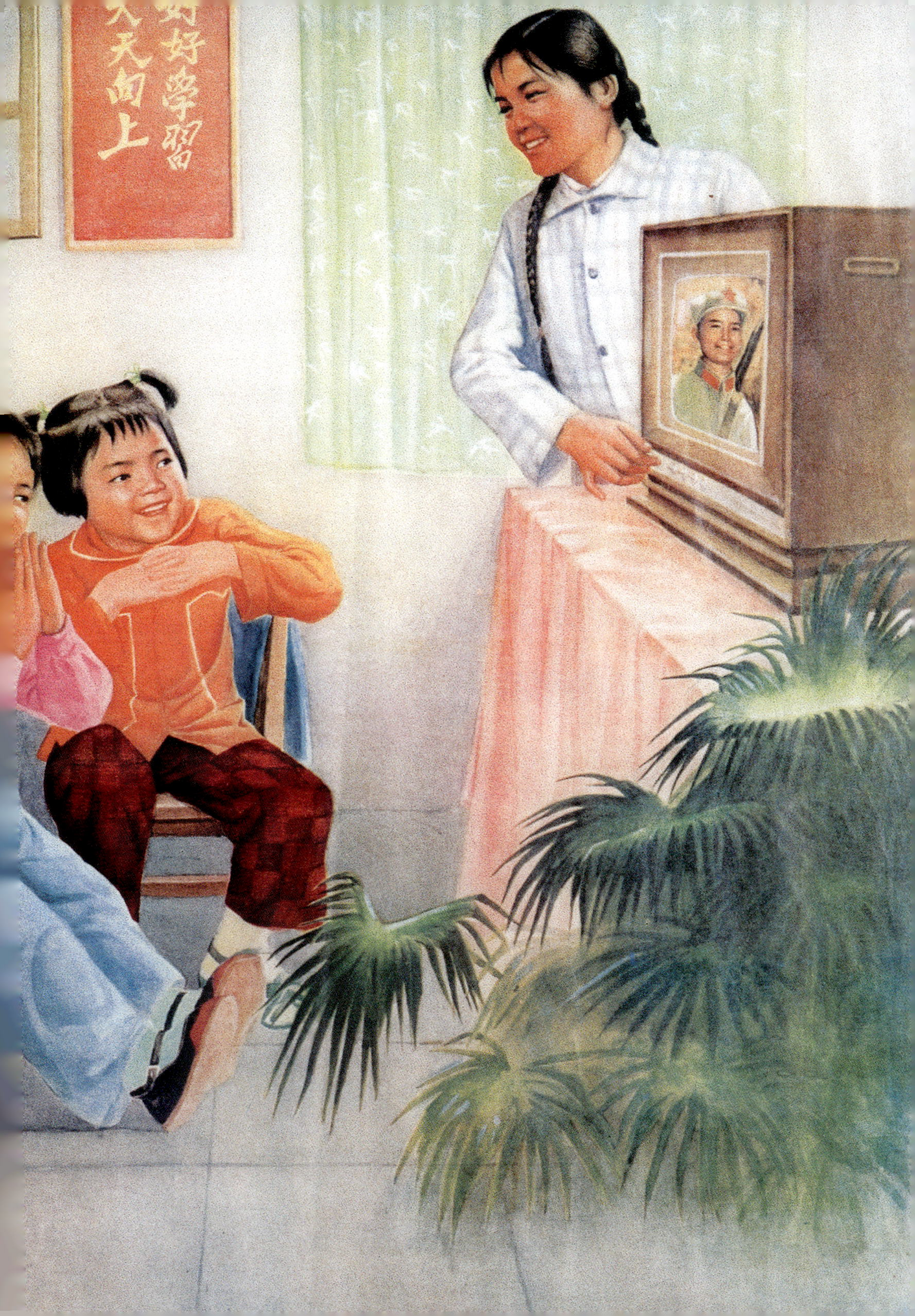
好學習
天向上

Pages 244–245
Learn from Pan Dongzi to be a good child of the Party *Poster next to the window:* Work hard at school! Make daily progress! *Artist:* Nie Wensheng, Linfeng District Exhibition Hall; Shanxi People's Publishing House, 1975; 0.12 Yuan

Lerne von Pan Dongzi und sei ein gutes Kind der Partei *Plakat neben dem Fenster:* Lernt fleißig! Macht täglich Fortschritte! *Gemalt von* Nie Wensheng, Ausstellungshalle Bezirk Linfeng; Volksverlag Shanxi, 1975; 0,12 Yuan

Instruis-toi de l'expérience de Pan Dongzi et sois un bon enfant du Parti *Affiche près de la fenêtre :* Appliquez-vous à l'étude ! Faites chaque jour des progrès ! *Peintre :* Nie Wensheng, Maison des Expositions du canton de Linfeng ; Éditions Populaires du Shanxi, 1975 ; 0,12 yuan

"There is in fact no such thing as art for art's sake, art that stands above classes, art that is detached from or independent of politics."

Eine Kunst um der Kunst willen, eine über den Klassen stehende Kunst, eine Kunst, die neben der Politik einherginge oder unabhängig von ihr wäre, gibt es in Wirklichkeit nicht. ✶ Il n'existe pas, dans la réalité, d'art pour l'art, d'art au-dessus des classes, ni d'art qui se développe en dehors de la politique ou indépendamment d'elle.

Different types of birds, Knowledge in Pictures *Artist:* He Yimei *Published and distributed by:* Yihui Poster Company, West Beijing Street, Lane 240. No. 3, Shanghai, 1953 *Print run:* 10,000

Verschiedene Arten von Vögeln, Bilder des Wissens *Gemalt von* He Yimei *Herausgeber und Vertrieb:* Plakatgeschäft Yihui, Westliche Pekinger Straße, Gasse 240, Nr. 3, Shanghai, 1953 *Auflage:* 10 000

Différentes espèces d'oiseaux, Images du savoir *Peintre :* He Yimei *Éditeur et distributeur :* Magasin d'affiches Yihui, partie ouest de la rue de Pékin, ruelle 240, n° 3, Shanghai, 1953 *Tirage :* 10 000

種禽鳥 **百鳥圖** 知識圖畫

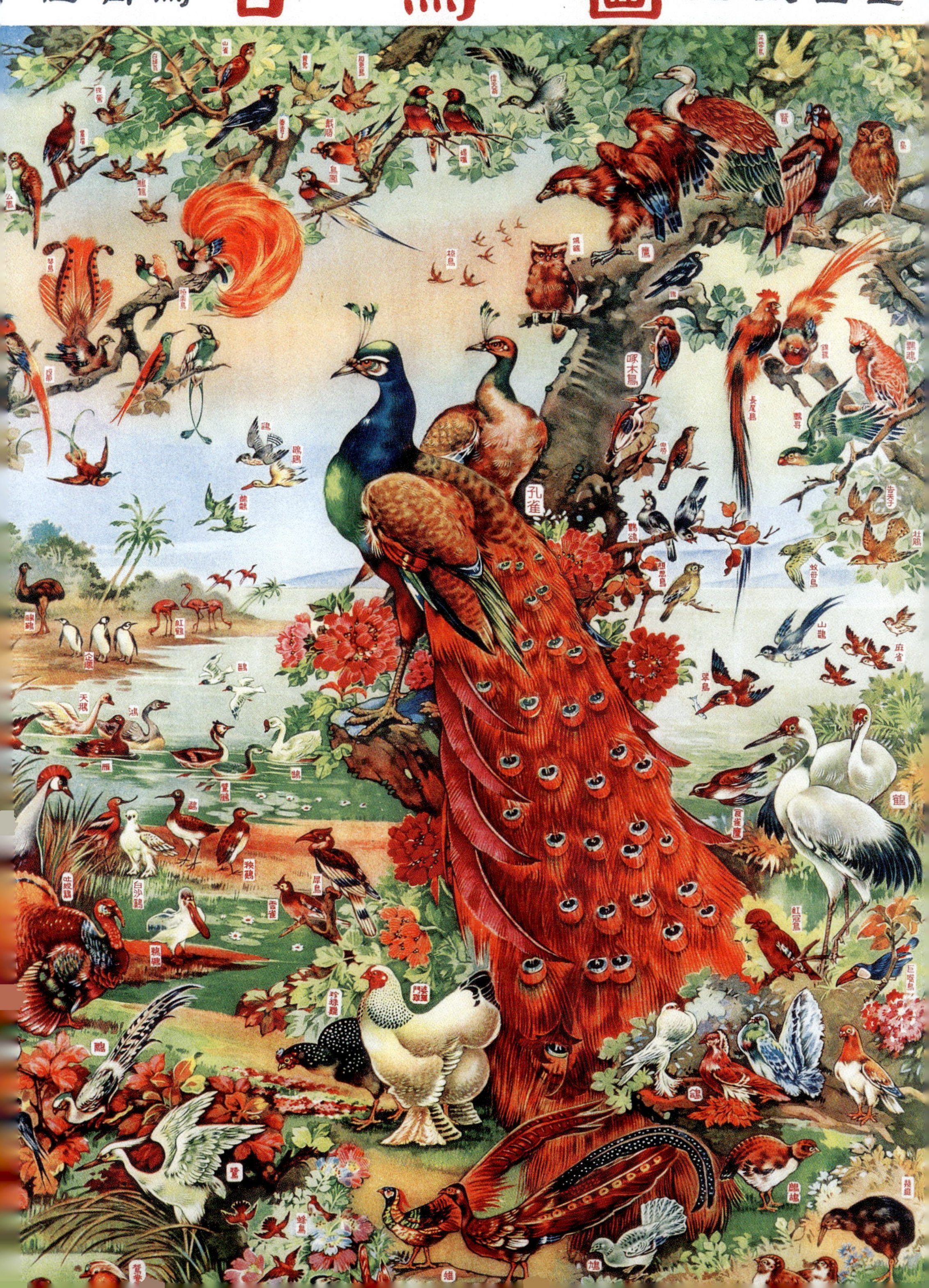

MIAN XIANG NONG CUN WEI WU YI NONG MIN FU WU

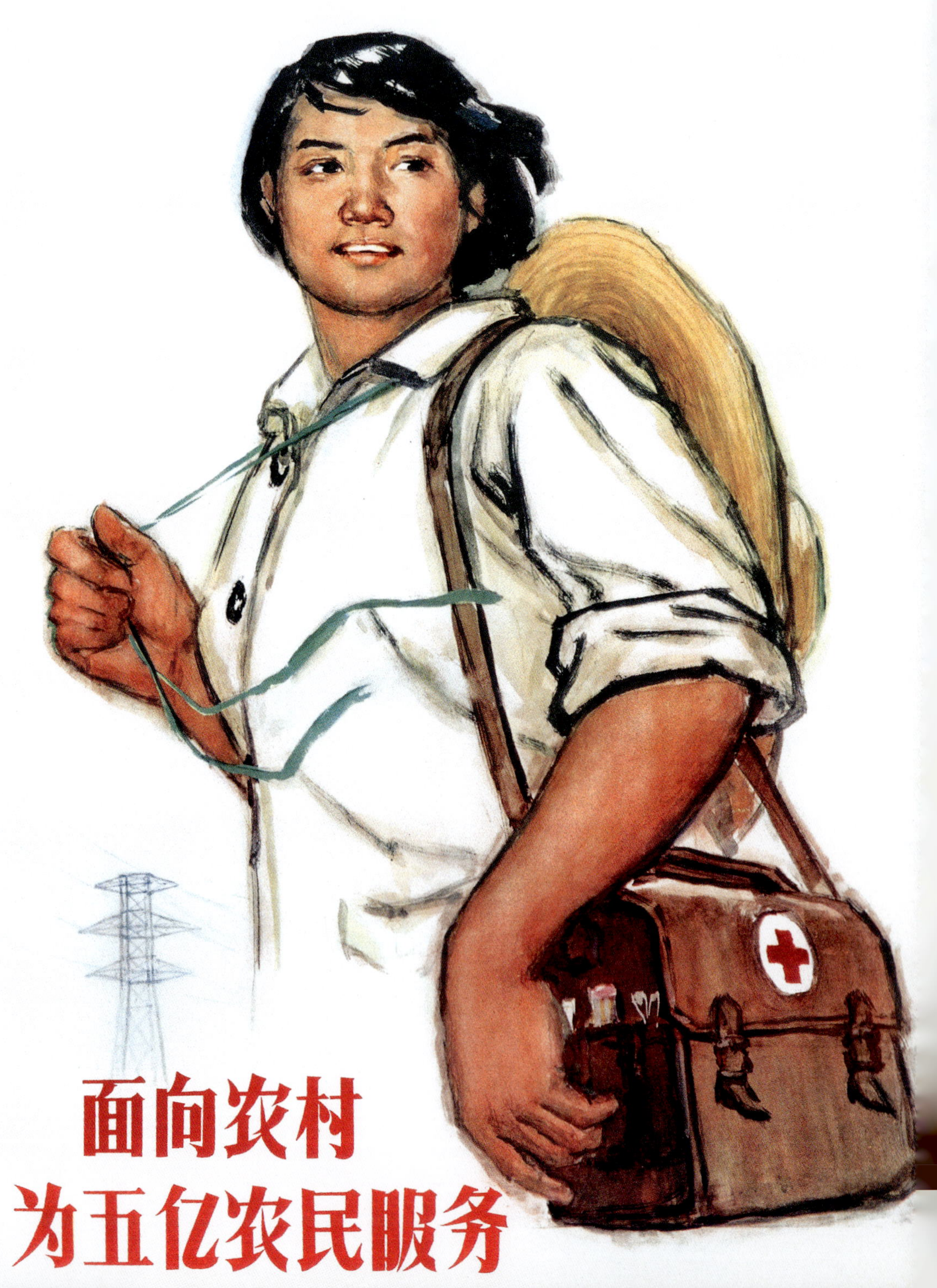

XVII

SERVING THE PEOPLE

DEM VOLKE DIENEN
SERVIR LE PEUPLE

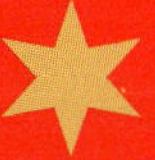

Page 248

Support the rural population and serve 500 million peasants

Sich für die Landbevölkerung einsetzen und den 500 Millionen Bauern dienen

Investissez-vous en faveur de la population rurale et soyez au service des 500 millions de paysans

"We should be modest and prudent, guard against arrogance and rashness, and serve the Chinese people heart and soul …"

Wir müssen bescheiden und umsichtig sein, uns vor Überheblichkeit und Unbesonnenheit in Acht nehmen und mit Leib und Seele dem chinesischen Volke dienen … ✶ Nous devons être modestes et prudents, nous garder de toute imprudence, et de toute précipitation, et servir le peuple chinois de tout notre cœur …

Improve the quality of goods, serve the people with body and soul *Flag, top right:* Raise the red flag *Artist:* Zhang Yongdian; People's Art Publishing House, 1978 *Print run:* 10,000; 0.14 Yuan

Warenqualität erhöhen, mit Leib und Seele dem Volk dienen *Fahne rechts oben:* Mobile rote Fahne *Gemalt von* Zhang Yongdian; Volkskunstverlag, 1978 *Auflage:* 10 000; 0,14 Yuan

Améliorez la qualité des produits, soyez corps et âme au service du peuple *Drapeau en haut à droite :* Drapeau rouge mobile *Peintre :* Zhang Yongdian ; Éditions Populaires d'Art 1978 *Tirage :* 10 000 ; 0,14 yuan

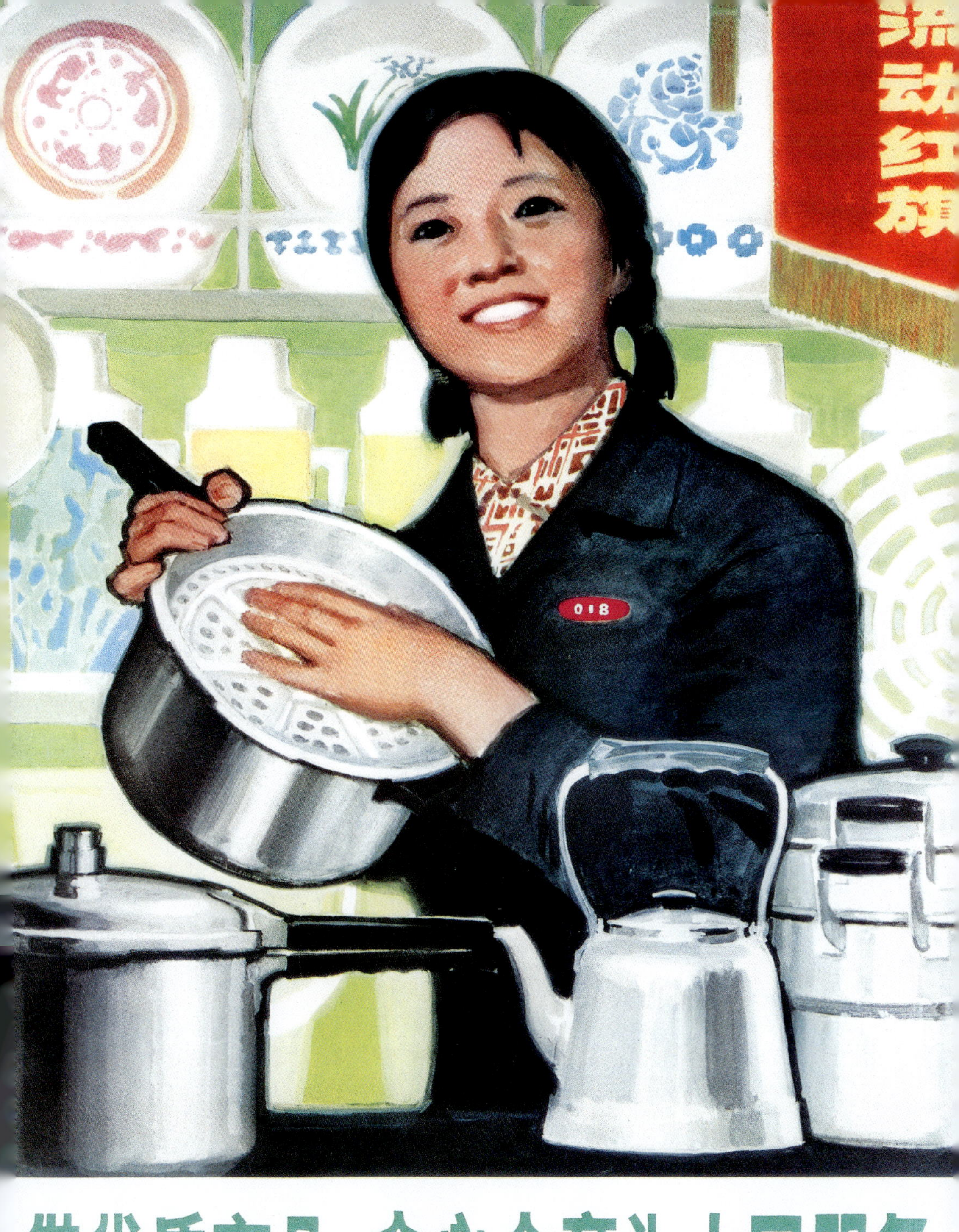

供优质产品 全心全意为人民服务

ONG YOUZHI CHANPIN QUANXINQUANYI WEIRENMIN FUWU

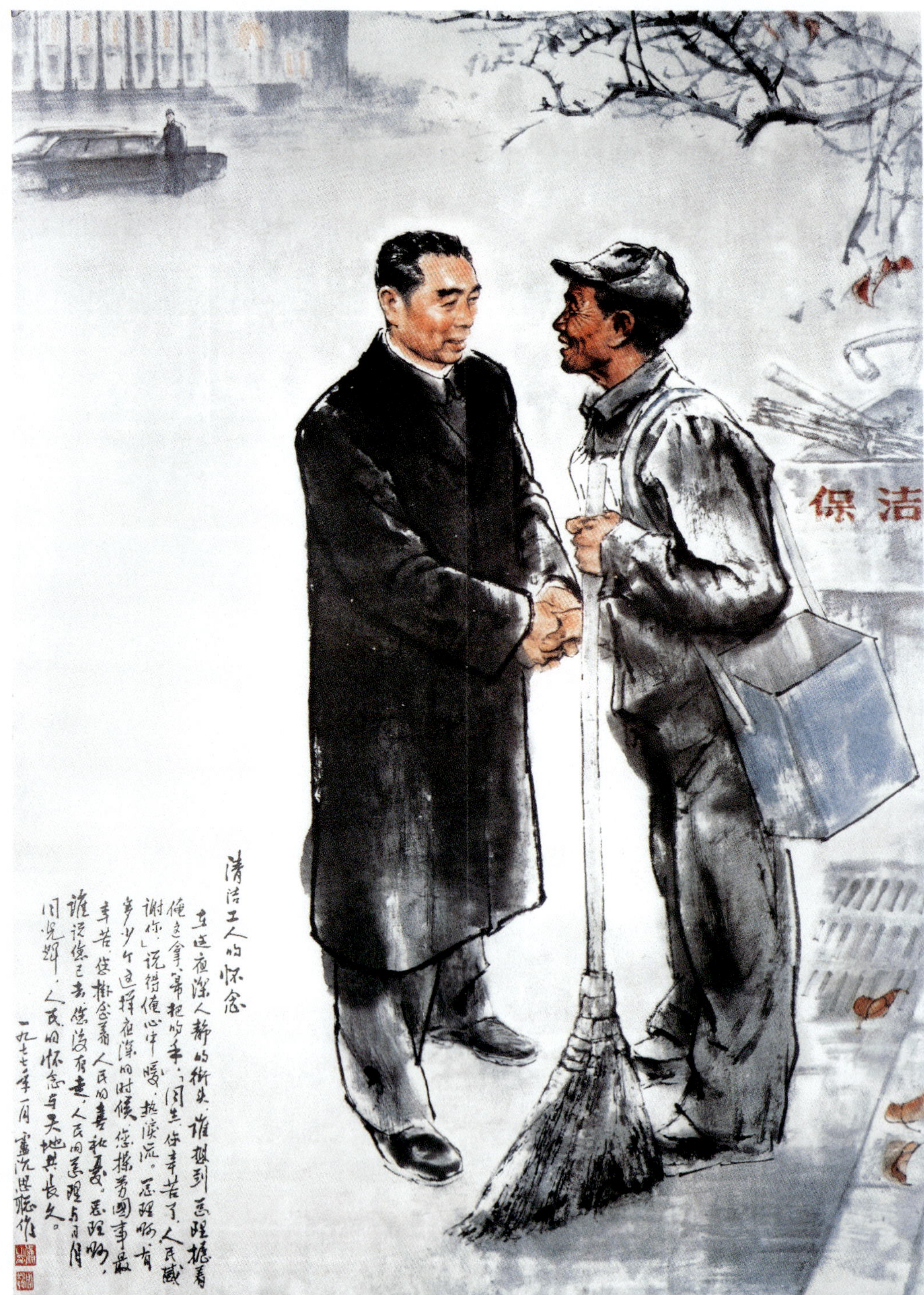
保洁
清洁工人的怀念
在这夜深人静的街头，谁想到总理握着
俺这拿帚把的手，「同志，你辛苦了，人民感
谢你」。说得俺心中暖，热泪流。总理啊，有
多少个这样夜深的时候，您操劳国事最
辛苦，您挂念着人民的喜和忧。总理啊，
谁说您已去，您没有走，人民的总理与日月
同光辉，人民的怀念与天地共长久。
一九七七年一月

温 暖

Warm feelings *Bottom left:* A road-sweeper remembers
On that peaceful night the Prime Minister Zhou Enlai* took me by the hand and said: "Comrade, the people are grateful for your hard work!" Warm feelings flowed through my heart and tears came to my eyes. Dear Prime Minister, how many times did you work through peaceful nights like this on important affairs of state? You always looked after the interests of the people. Dear Prime Minister, who says you have gone away? You have not left us. The people's Prime Minister shines for ever like the sun and moon; the people's memory will last as long as heaven and earth. Si Cong (the artist), January 1977 Poster used as teaching aid with textbook *Chinese for Primary Schools*; Book 3, for sixth-year primary classes; *Artists:* Lu Chen and Si Cong, Shanghai Educational Publishing House
* Prime Minister Zhou Enlai died on 8 January 1976.

Wärme *Links unten:* Erinnerung eines Straßenreinigers
In jener stillen Nacht hielt Premierminister Zhou* meine Hand und sagte: „Genosse, das Volk bedankt sich für deine Mühe!" Ein warmer Strom floss durch mein Herz und meine Augen wurden feucht. Lieber Premierminister, in wie vielen solchen stillen Nächten haben Sie für wichtige Angelegenheiten des Landes durchgearbeitet? Stets kümmerten Sie sich um die Belange des Volkes. Lieber Premierminister, wer sagt, Sie seien fort? Sie sind nicht von uns gegangen. Der Premierminister des Volkes glänzt auf ewig wie Sonne und Mond; die Erinnerung des Volkes existiert so lange wie Himmel und Erde.
Im Januar 1977, Si Cong Unterrichtsplakat zum Lehrbuch *Chinesisch für Grundschulen*, Band 3 für das sechste Schuljahr *Gemalt von* Lu Chen und Si Cong; Erziehungsverlag Shanghai
* Der Premierminister Zhou Enlai starb am 8. Januar 1976.

Chaleur *En bas à gauche :* Souvenirs d'un balayeur
Dans le silence de cette nuit-là, le Premier ministre Chou* tint ma main dans la sienne et me dit : « Camarade, le peuple t'est reconnaissant de ta peine ! » Un flot de chaleur envahit mon cœur et mes yeux devinrent humides. Cher Premier ministre, combien de ces nuits silencieuses avez-vous passées à travailler sur les affaires importantes du pays ? Vous vous êtes toujours soucié des intérêts du peuple. Cher Premier ministre, qui donc dit que vous êtes parti ? Vous ne nous avez pas quittés. Le Premier ministre du peuple brillera d'un éclat éternel comme le soleil et la lune ; il restera dans la mémoire du peuple aussi longtemps qu'existeront le ciel et la terre. Janvier 1977, Si Cong Affiche pédagogique accompagnant le volume 3 du manuel de chinois des écoles primaires (6e année scolaire) *Peintres :* Lu Chen et Si Cong ; Éditions Éducatives de Shanghai
* Le Premier ministre Chou En-lai mourut le 8 janvier 1976.

Opposite
Make good-quality products and brighten up life *On the medal in the background:* Good quality *Artist:* Shen Shaolun; Shanghai People's Art Publishing House, 1982 *Print run:* 50,000; 0.18 Yuan

Produkte guter Qualität schaffen und das Leben verschönern *Auf der Medaille im Bild:* Gute Qualität *Gemalt von* Shen Shaolun; Volkskunstverlag Shanghai, 1982 *Auflage:* 50 000; 0,18 Yuan

Faites des produits de bonne qualité pour rendre la vie plus belle *Sur la médaille :* Bonne qualité *Peintre :* Shen Shaolun; Éditions Populaires d'Art de Shanghai, 1982 *Tirage :* 50 000; 0,18 yuan

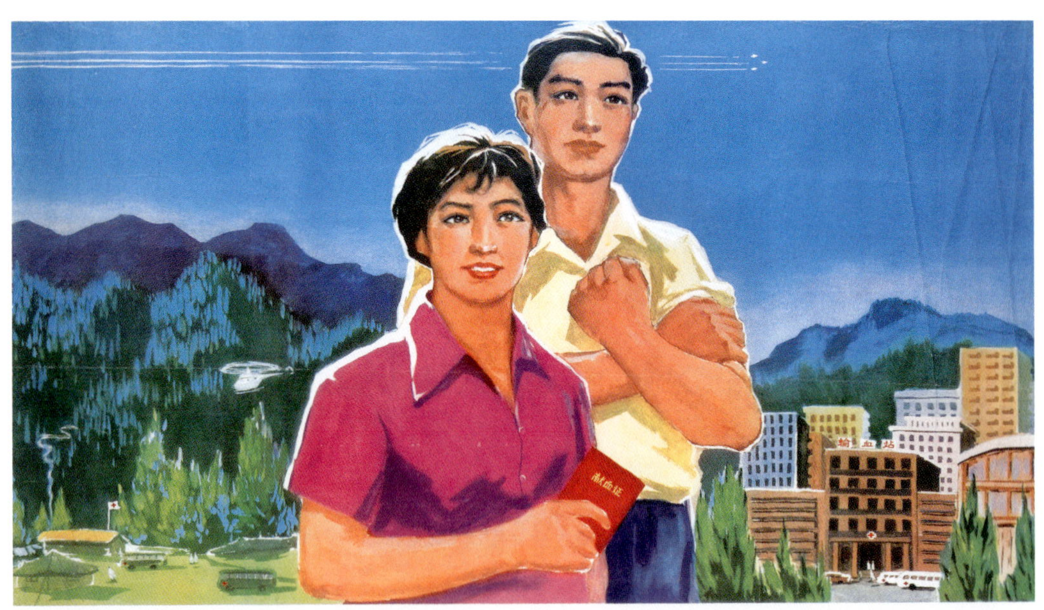

To give blood is the citizen's honorable duty
On top of the building at the front of the picture: Blood donation station *Artist:* Zhang Bingyao *Published by:* Chinese Red Cross, 1980

Blutspenden ist die ehrenvolle Pflicht des Bürgers
Im Bild rechts auf dem vorderen Haus: Blutspendestation *Gemalt von* Zhang Bingyao *Herausgeber:* Rotes Kreuz China, 1980

Donner son sang est pour le citoyen un honneur et un devoir
À droite sur le bâtiment du premier plan : Service de don du sang *Peintre :* Zhang Bingyao *Éditeur :* Croix-Rouge chinoise, 1980

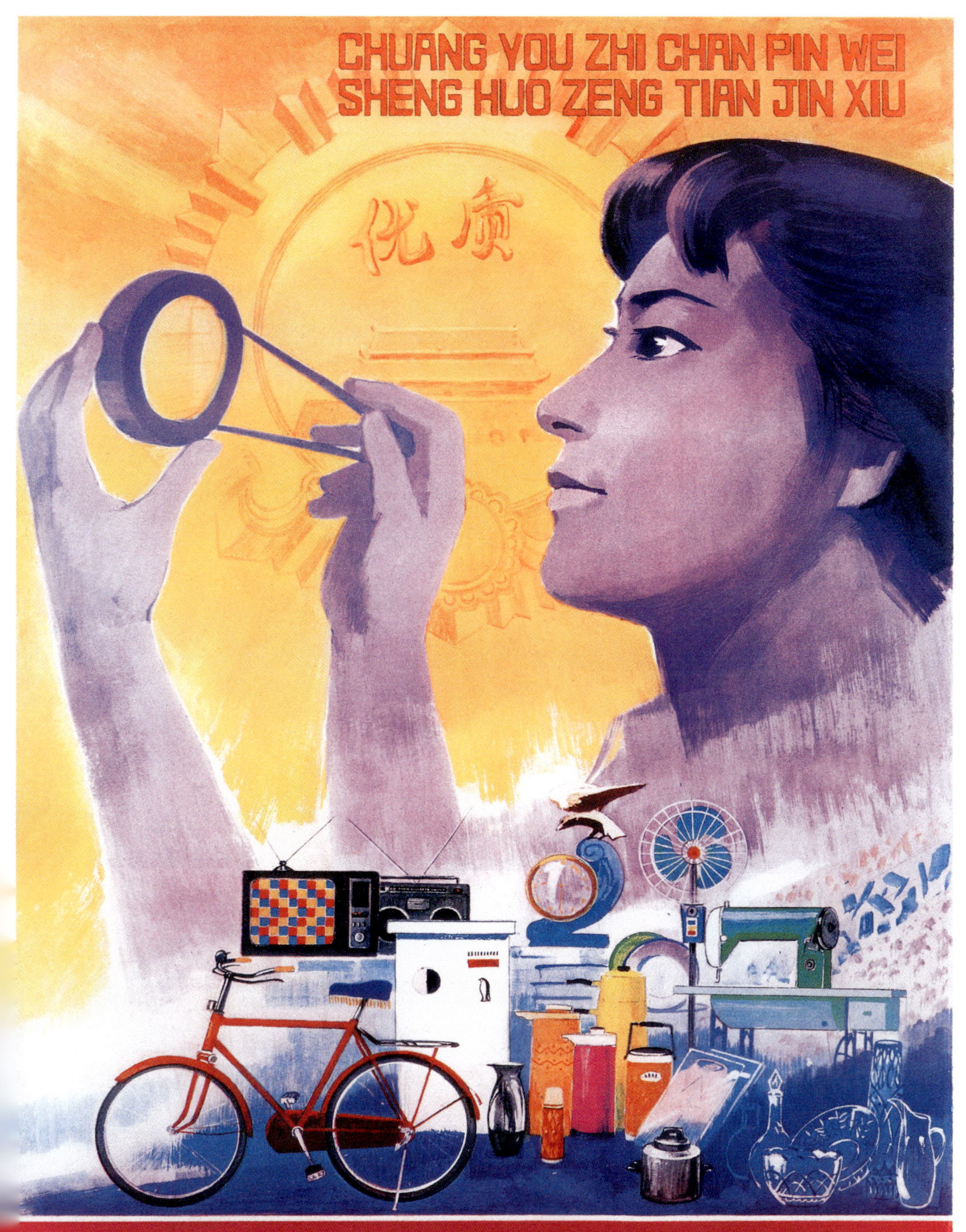

创优质产品为生活增添锦绣

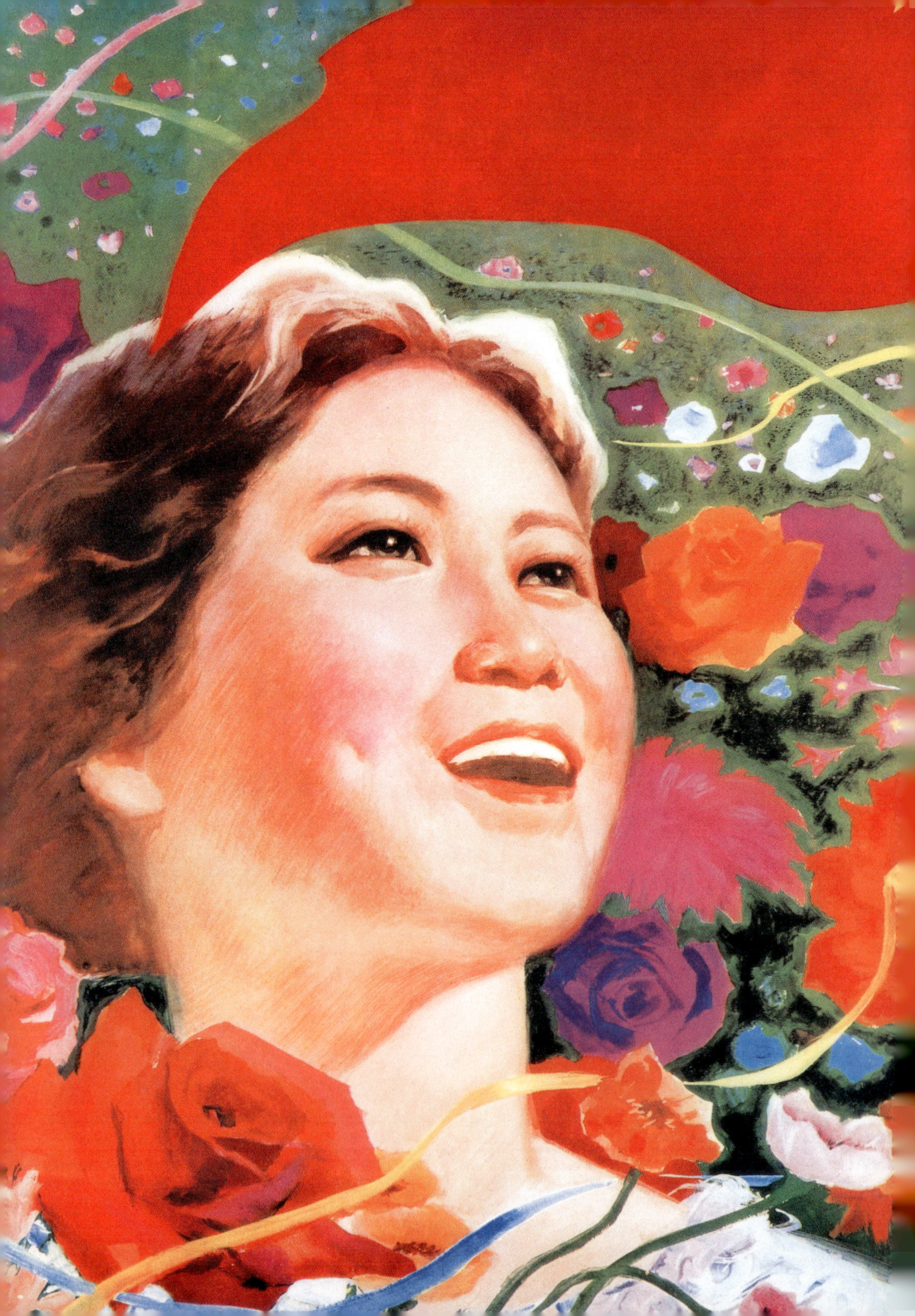

XVIII

PATRIOTISM AND INTERNATIONALISM

PATRIOTISMUS UND INTERNATIONALISMUS
LE PATRIOTISME ET L'INTERNATIONALISME

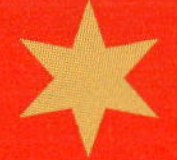

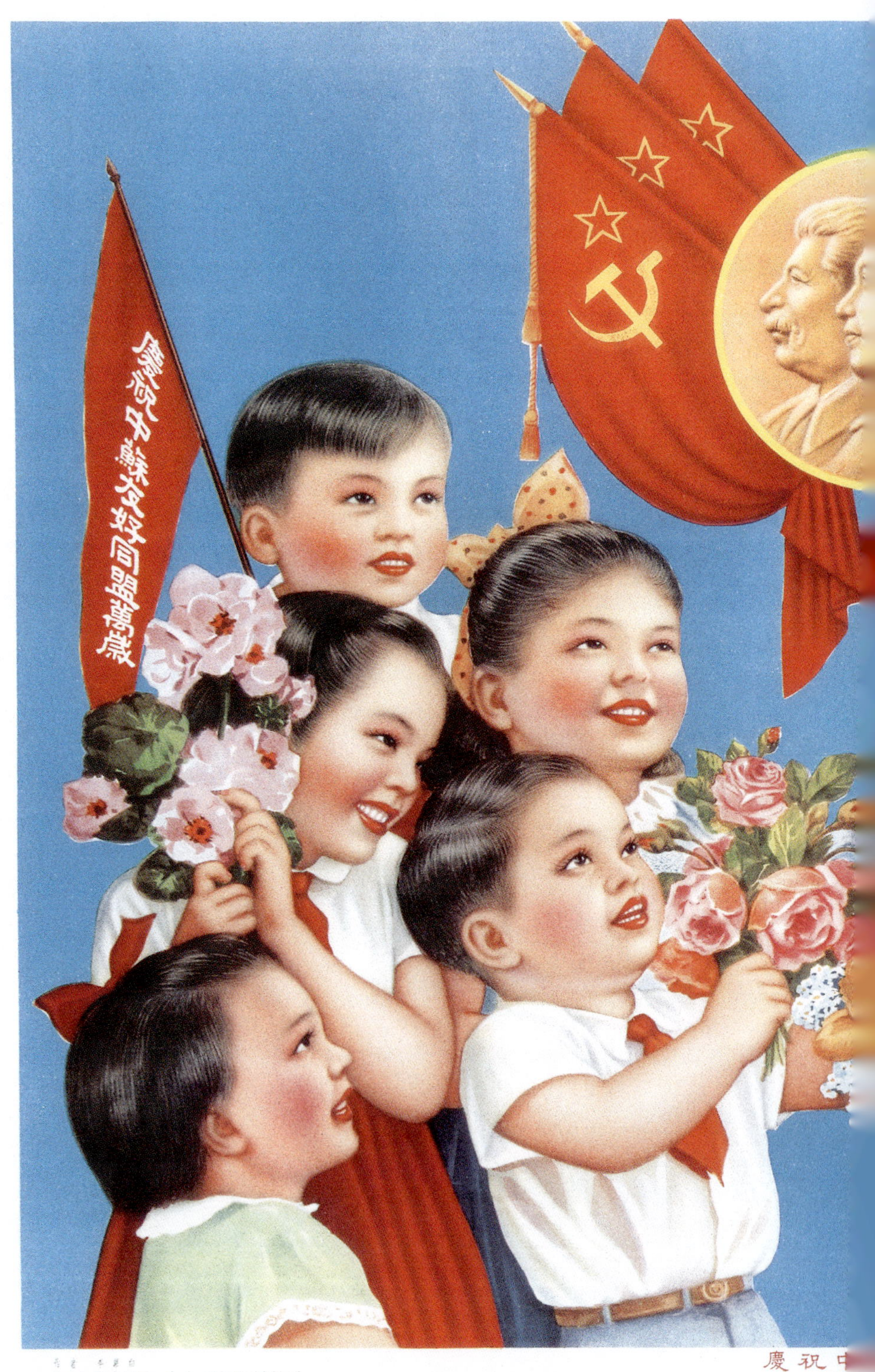
慶祝中蘇友好同盟萬歲
慶祝中

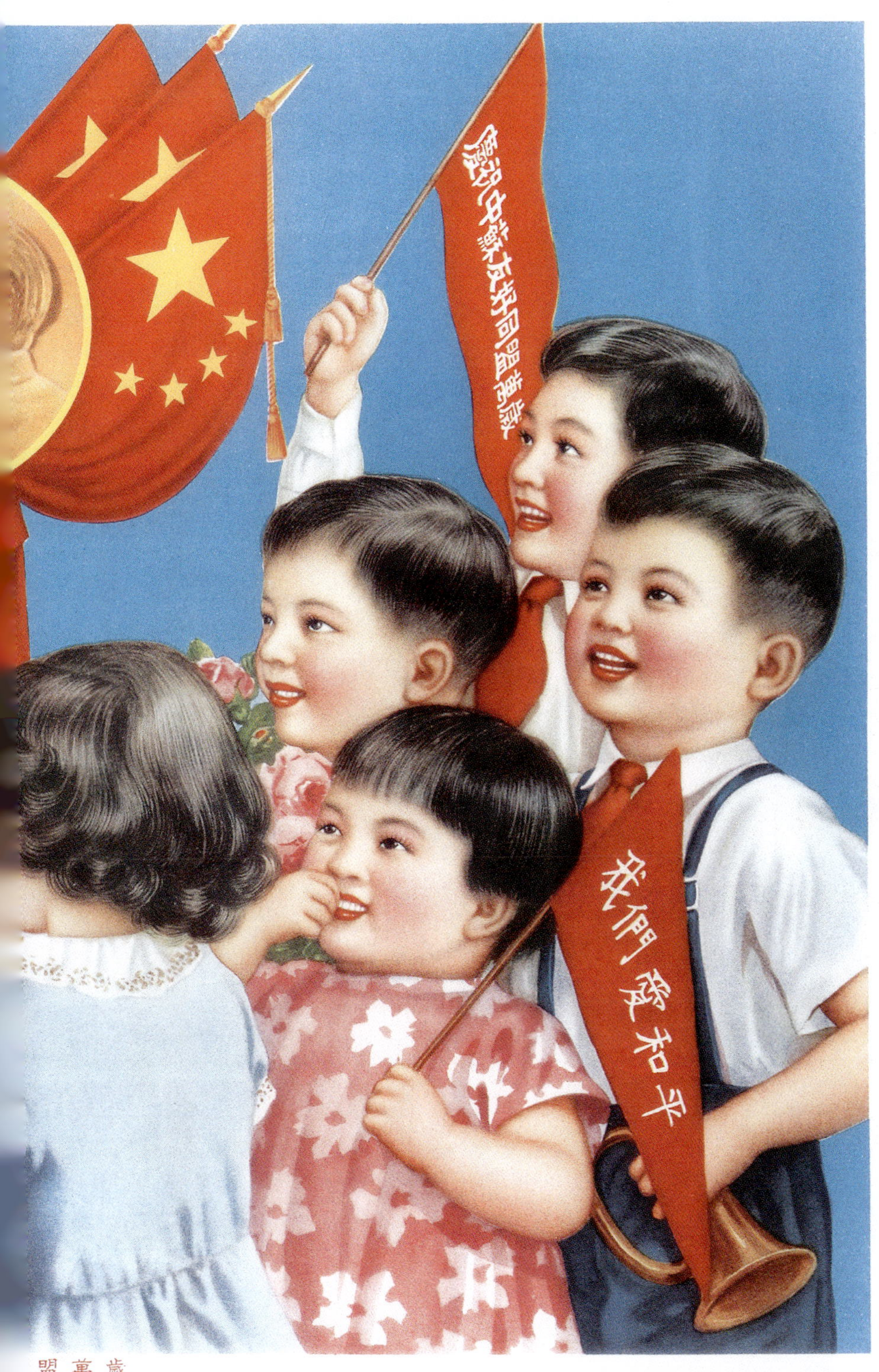

盟萬歲

Page 256
All across the great fatherland magnificent flowers are in bloom Joyfully celebrating the 30th Anniversary of the Founding of the People's Republic of China *Artist:* Zhang Ruwei; Tianjin People's Art Publishing House, 1979; 0.14 Yuan

Im großen Vaterland blühen überall prachtvolle Blumen Mit großer Freude den 30. Gründungstag der VR China feiern *Gemalt von* Zhang Ruwei; Volkskunstverlag Tianjin, 1979; 0,14 Yuan

Dans notre grande patrie fleurissent partout des fleurs magnifiques Célébrons dans l'allégresse le 30e anniversaire de la fondation de la République Populaire de Chine *Peintre :* Zhang Ruwei ; Éditions Populaires d'Art de Tianjin, 1979 ; 0,14 yuan

Pages 258–259
Celebrating the longevity of the friendly alliance between China and the Soviet Union *Small flags:* Celebrating the longevity of the friendly alliance between China and the Soviet Union; We love peace *Artist:* Li Mubai *Published by:* Lushan Picture Publishing House, Shanghai, 1952

Die Langlebigkeit des Freundschaftsbündnisses zwischen China und der UdSSR feiern *Fähnchen:* Die Langlebigkeit des Freundschaftsbündnisses zwischen China und der UdSSR feiern; Wir lieben Frieden *Gemalt von* Li Mubai *Herausgeber:* Lushan-Bilderverlag, Shanghai, 1952

Célébrons la longévité du pacte d'amitié entre la Chine et l'Union Soviétique *Fanions :* Célébrons la longévité du pacte d'amitié entre la Chine et l'Union Soviétique ; Nous aimons la paix *Peintre :* Li Mubai *Éditeur :* Éditions d'Images Lushan, Shanghai, 1952

"People of the world unite and defeat the US aggressors and all their running dogs! People of the world, be courageous, and dare to fight, defy difficulties and advance wave upon wave. Then the whole world will belong to the people. Monsters of all kinds shall be destroyed." Mao Zedong Shown at the exhibition "Long Live the Victory of Chairman Mao's Revolutionary Line"; Revolutionary Educational Publishing House, Shanghai, 1968; 0.11 Yuan

„Völker der ganzen Welt, vereinigt euch, besiegt die USA-Aggressoren und alle ihre Lakaien! Völker der ganzen Welt, seid mutig, habt Mut zu kämpfen, fürchtet keine Schwierigkeiten, stürmt Welle für Welle vorwärts und die ganze Welt wird den Völkern gehören. Alle finsteren Mächte werden restlos vernichtet werden." Mao Zedong Ein Exponat der Ausstellung „Es lebe der Sieg der revolutionären Linie des Vorsitzenden Mao"; Revolutionärer Erziehungsverlag Shanghai, 1968; 0,11 Yuan

« Peuples du monde entier, unissez-vous, pour abattre les agresseurs américains et leurs laquais ! Que les peuples n'écoutent que leur courage, qu'ils osent livrer combat, qu'ils bravent les difficultés, qu'ils avancent par vagues successives, et le monde entier leur appartiendra. Les monstres seront tous anéantis. » Mao Zedong Affiche montrée à l'exposition « Vive la victoire de la ligne révolutionnaire du président Mao » ; Éditions Éducatives Révolutionnaires de Shanghai, 1968 ; 0,11 yuan

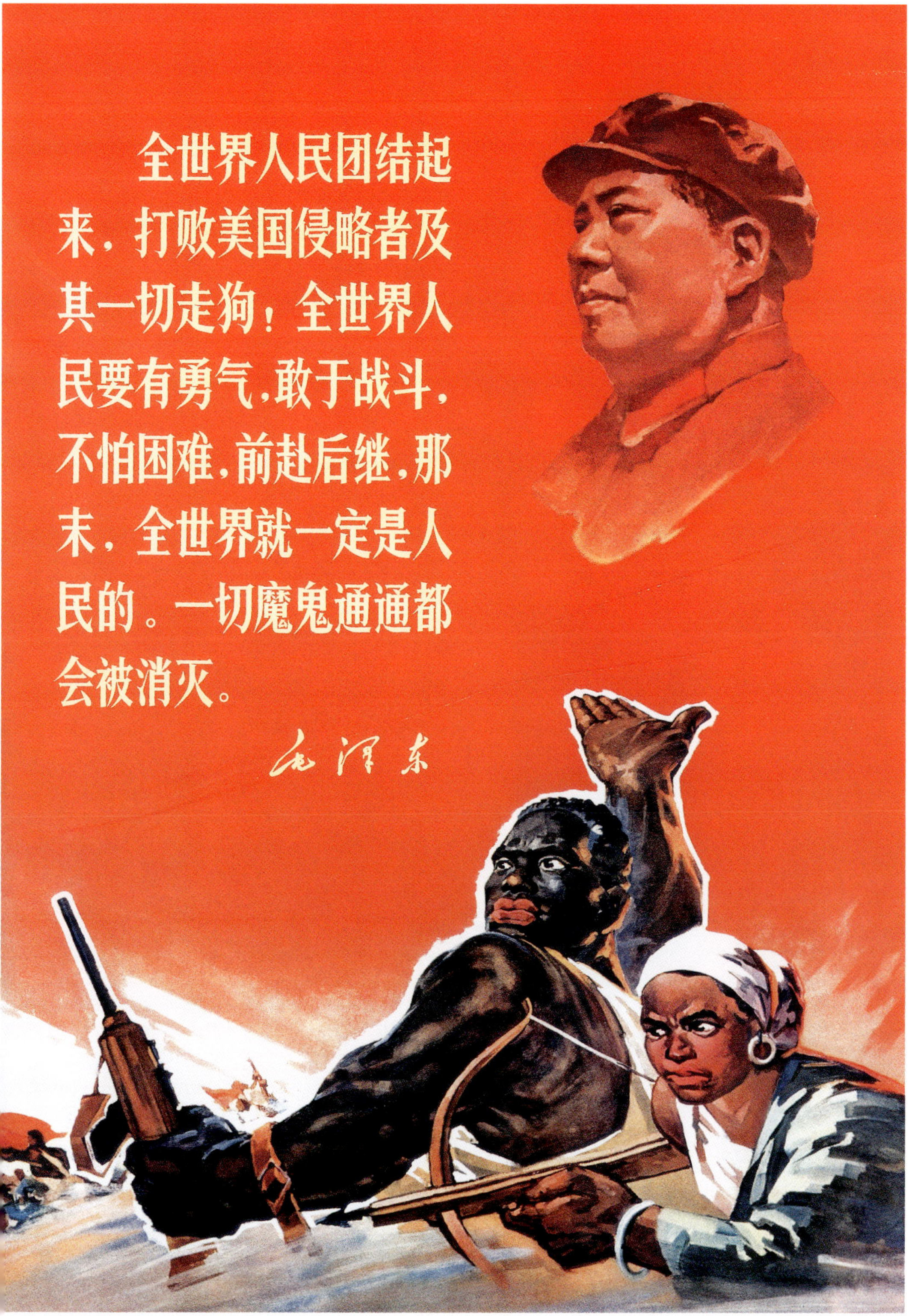

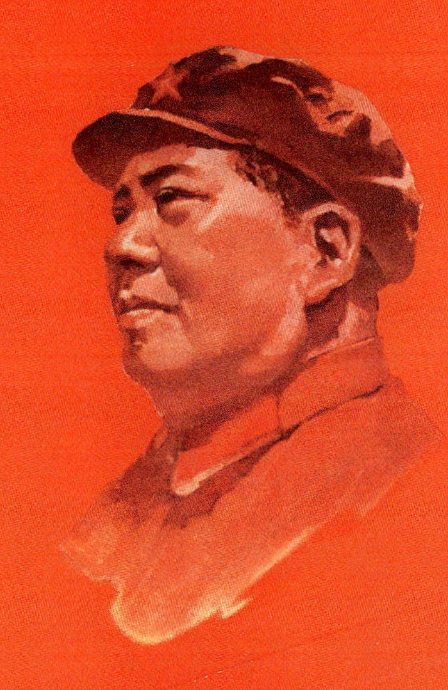

全世界人民团结起来，打败美国侵略者及其一切走狗！全世界人民要有勇气，敢于战斗，不怕困难，前赴后继，那末，全世界就一定是人民的。一切魔鬼通通都会被消灭。

毛泽东

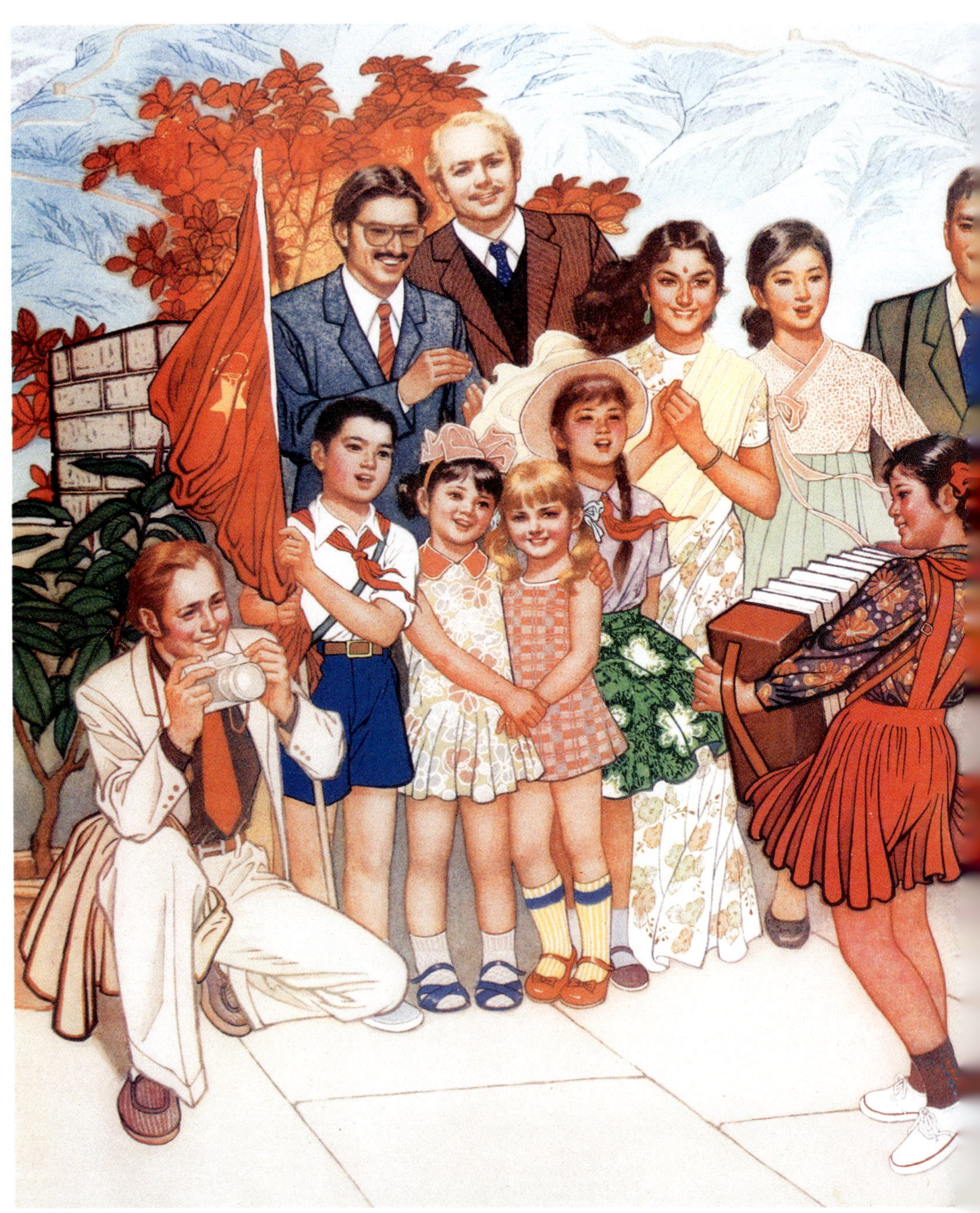

The song of friendship
Artists: Wang Meifang and Zhao Guojing; Tianjin Art Publishing House, 1979 *Print run:* 240,000; 0.11 Yuan

Das Lied der Freundschaft
Gemalt von Wang Meifang und Zhao Guojing; Kunstverlag Tianjin, 1979 *Auflage:* 240 000; 0,11 Yuan

Le chant de l'amitié
Peintres : Wang Meifang et Zhao Guojing ; Éditions d'Art de Tianjin, 1979 *Tirage :* 240 000 ; 0,11 yuan

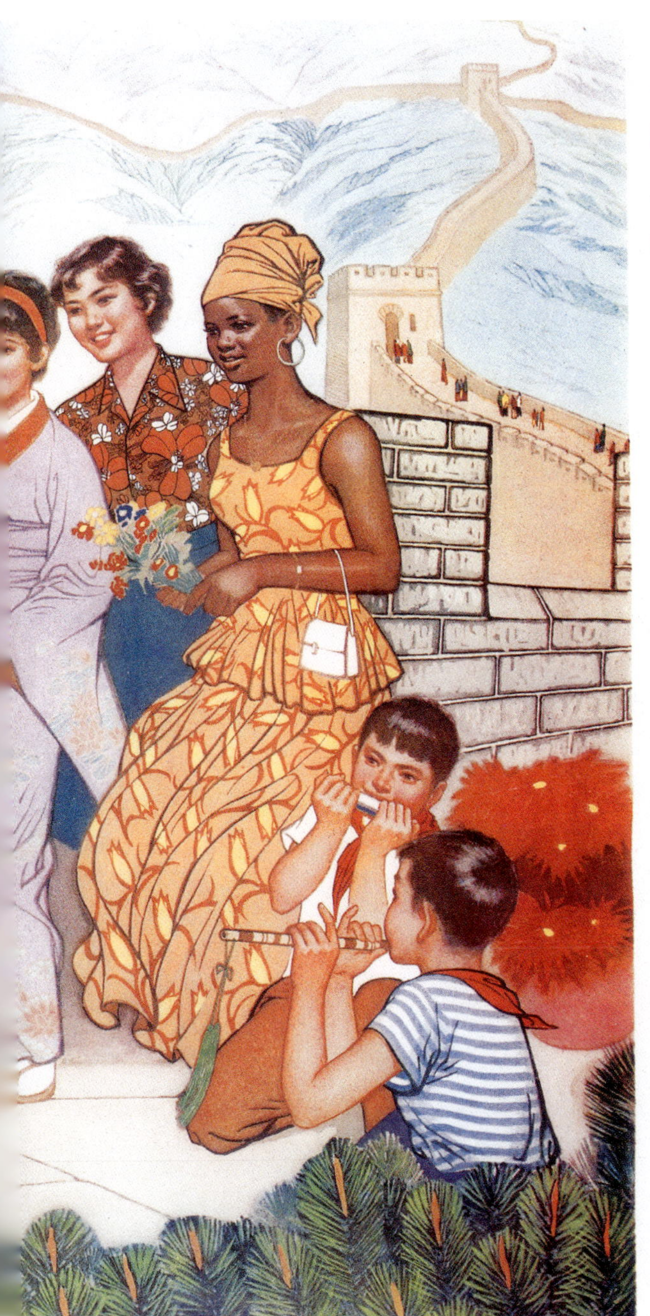

友
谊
之
歌

Pages 264–265
Long live the revolutionary and comradely friendship between the Parties and peoples of China and Albania! *Banners:* Proletarians of all nations unite! Defend Marxism and Leninism! Down with the revisionism of the present! *Artists:* Wang Qingsheng and Shu Chuanxi *Published by:* Revolutionary Committee of the Zhejiang Province Art College for Workers, Peasants, and Soldiers; Zhejiang People's Art Publishing House, 1969; 0.15 Yuan

Es lebe die revolutionäre und kameradschaftliche Freundschaft der Parteien und Völker Chinas und Albaniens!
Transparente: Proletarier aller Länder, vereinigt euch! Verteidigt den Marxismus und Leninismus! Nieder mit dem Revisionismus der Gegenwart! *Gemalt von* Wang Qingsheng und Shu Chuanxi *Herausgeber:* Revolutionskomitee der Hochschule der bildenden Kunst für Arbeiter, Bauern und Soldaten, Provinz Zhejiang; Volkskunstverlag Zhejiang, 1969; 0,15 Yuan

Vive l'amitié révolutionnaire des partis et des peuples camarades de Chine et d'Albanie !
Banderoles : Prolétaires de tous les pays, unissez-vous ! Défendez le marxisme-léninisme ! À bas le révisionnisme ambiant ! *Peintres :* Wang Qingsheng et Shu Chuanxi *Éditeur :* Comité révolutionnaire de l'École des Beaux-Arts pour ouvriers, paysans et soldats, province du Zhejiang ; Éditions Populaires d'Art du Zhejiang, 1969 ; 0,15 yuan

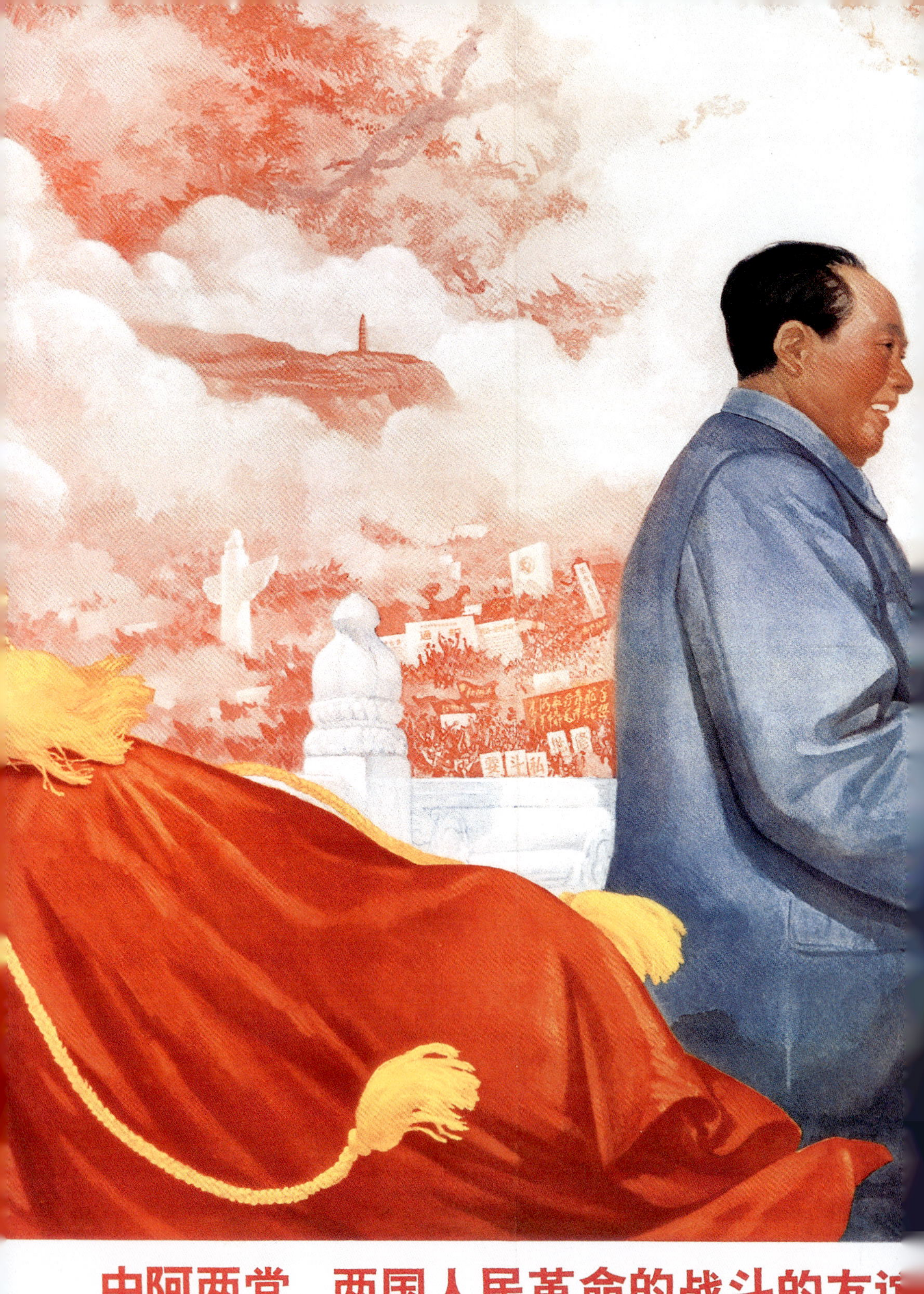

中阿两党、两国人民革命的战斗的友

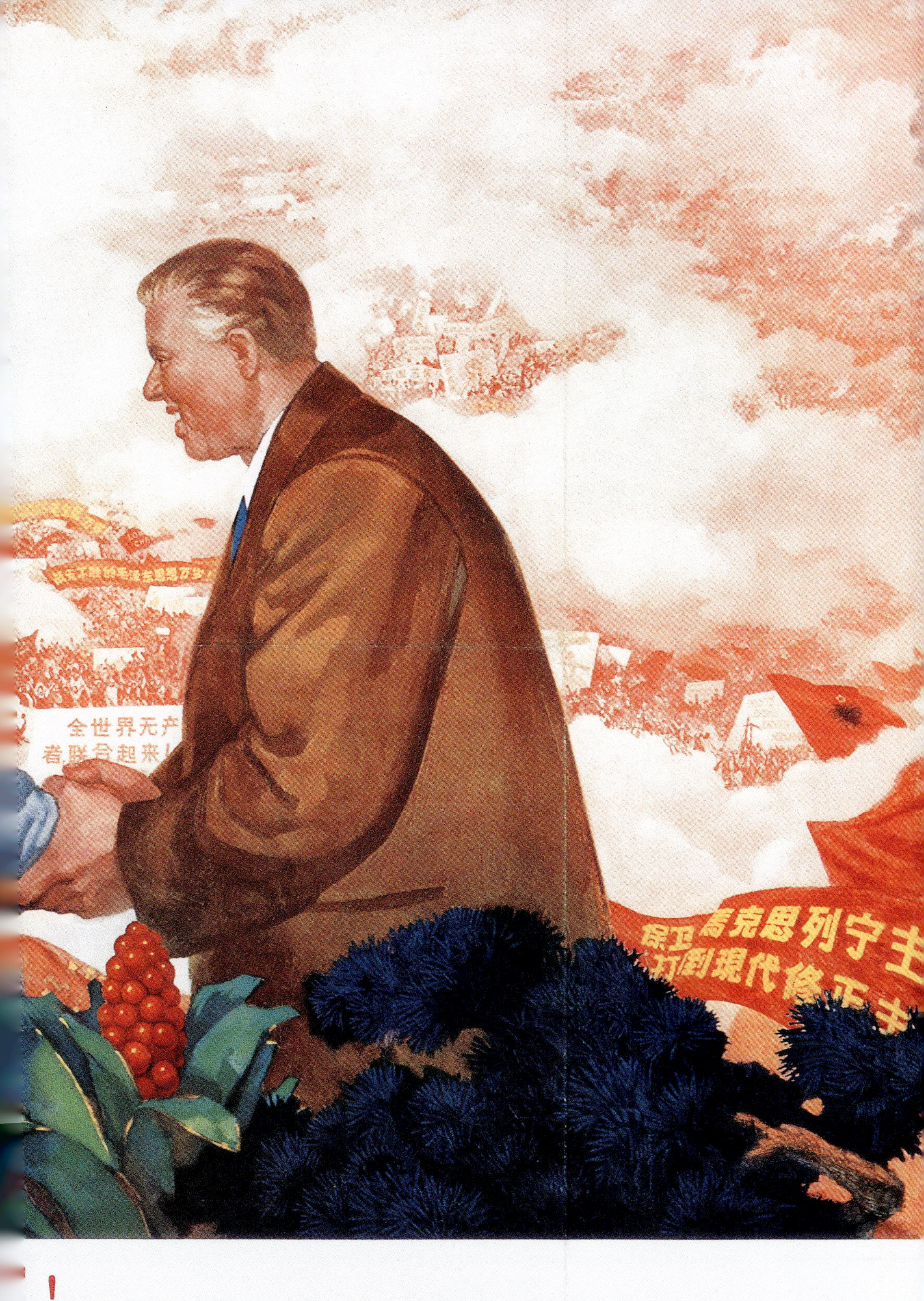
全世界无产
者联合起来！
保卫马克思列宁主
打倒现代修正主
!

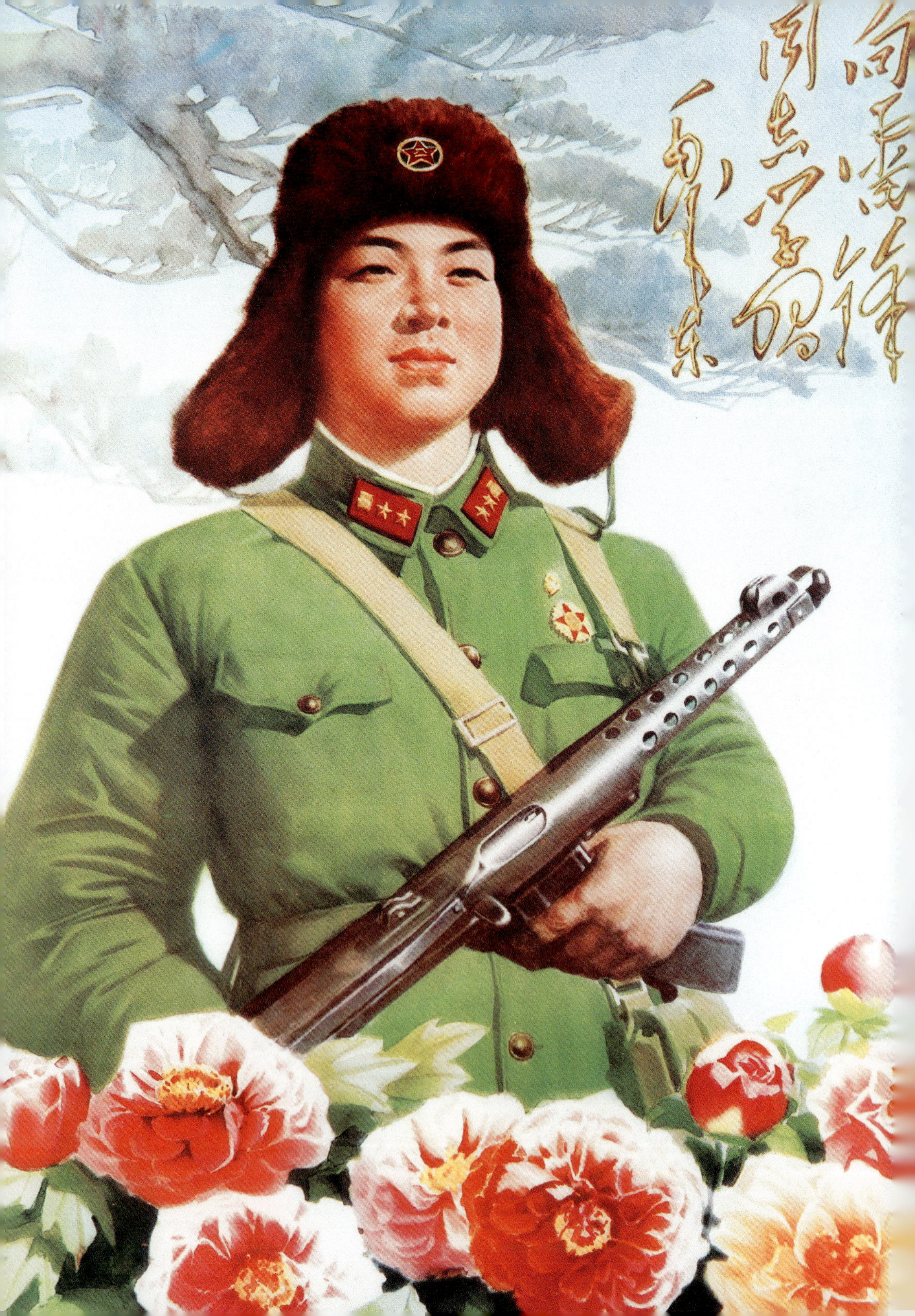
向雷锋同志学习
毛泽东

XIX

REVOLUTIONARY HEROISM

REVOLUTIONÄRER HEROISMUS
L'HÉROÏSME RÉVOLUTIONNAIRE

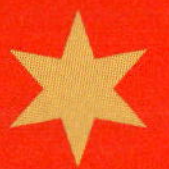

Page 266
Learn from Comrade Lei Feng *Top right, Mao's dedication:* Learn from Comrade Lei Feng, Mao Zedong *Artist:* Wu Huamin; Sichuan People's Publishing House, 1983 *Print run:* 392,600; 1.60 Yuan

Vom Genossen Lei Feng lernen *Rechts oben Maos Widmung:* Vom Genossen Lei Feng lernen, Mao Zedong *Gemalt von* Wu Huamin; Volksverlag Sichuan, 1983 *Auflage:* 392 600; 1,60 Yuan

Instruisez-vous de l'expérience de Lei Feng *Dédicace de Mao en haut à droite :* Instruisez-vous de l'expérience de Lei Feng, Mao Zedong *Peintre :* Wu Huamin ; Éditions Populaires du Sichuan, 1983 *Tirage :* 392 600 ; 1,60 yuan

"Be resolute, fear no sacrifice and surmount every difficulty to win victory."

Fest entschlossen sein, keine Opfer scheuen und alle Schwierigkeiten überwinden, um den Sieg zu erringen. ✶ Prendre sa résolution, ne reculer devant aucun sacrifice, surmonter toutes les difficultés pour remporter la victoire.

Learn from Comrade Wang Guofu!* "Pull forward the revolutionary cart and do not stop until we have achieved Communism." 1970
* Wang Guofu (1921–1969): former Party Secretary of a village south of Beijing. Like many heroes of the time he too was a model communist and conscientious person who never spared a thought for his own interests and, without regard for his health, worked for his village until his death. The above quotation is his. After his death he became a celebrated national hero.

Vom Genossen Wang Guofu* lernen! „Den revolutionären Karren unaufhörlich vorwärts ziehen, bis wir den Kommunismus erreicht haben." 1970
* Wang Guofu (1921–1969): ehemaliger Parteisekretär eines südlich von Peking gelegenen Dorfes. Wie viele andere Helden der damaligen Zeit war auch er ein vorbildlicher Kommunist und verantwortungsbewusster Mensch, der nie an sein eigenes Interesse dachte und ohne Rücksicht auf seine Gesundheit bis zum Tod hart für sein Dorf arbeitete. Das obige Zitat stammt von ihm. Nach seinem Tod wurde er als Held und Vorbild im ganzen Land gerühmt.

Instruisez-vous de l'expérience du camarade Wang Guofu* ! « Tirons inlassablement la charrette révolutionnaire en avant, jusqu'à ce que nous ayons atteint le communisme. » 1970
* Wang Guofu (1921–1969) : ancien secrétaire du Parti d'un village situé au sud de Pékin. Comme beaucoup d'autres héros de cette époque, il fut lui aussi un communiste modèle et un homme responsable qui ne pensait jamais à son intérêt particulier et, sans égards pour sa santé, œuvra durement jusqu'à sa mort pour son village. La citation ci-dessus est de lui. Après sa mort, il connut dans tout le pays une gloire de héros et de modèle.

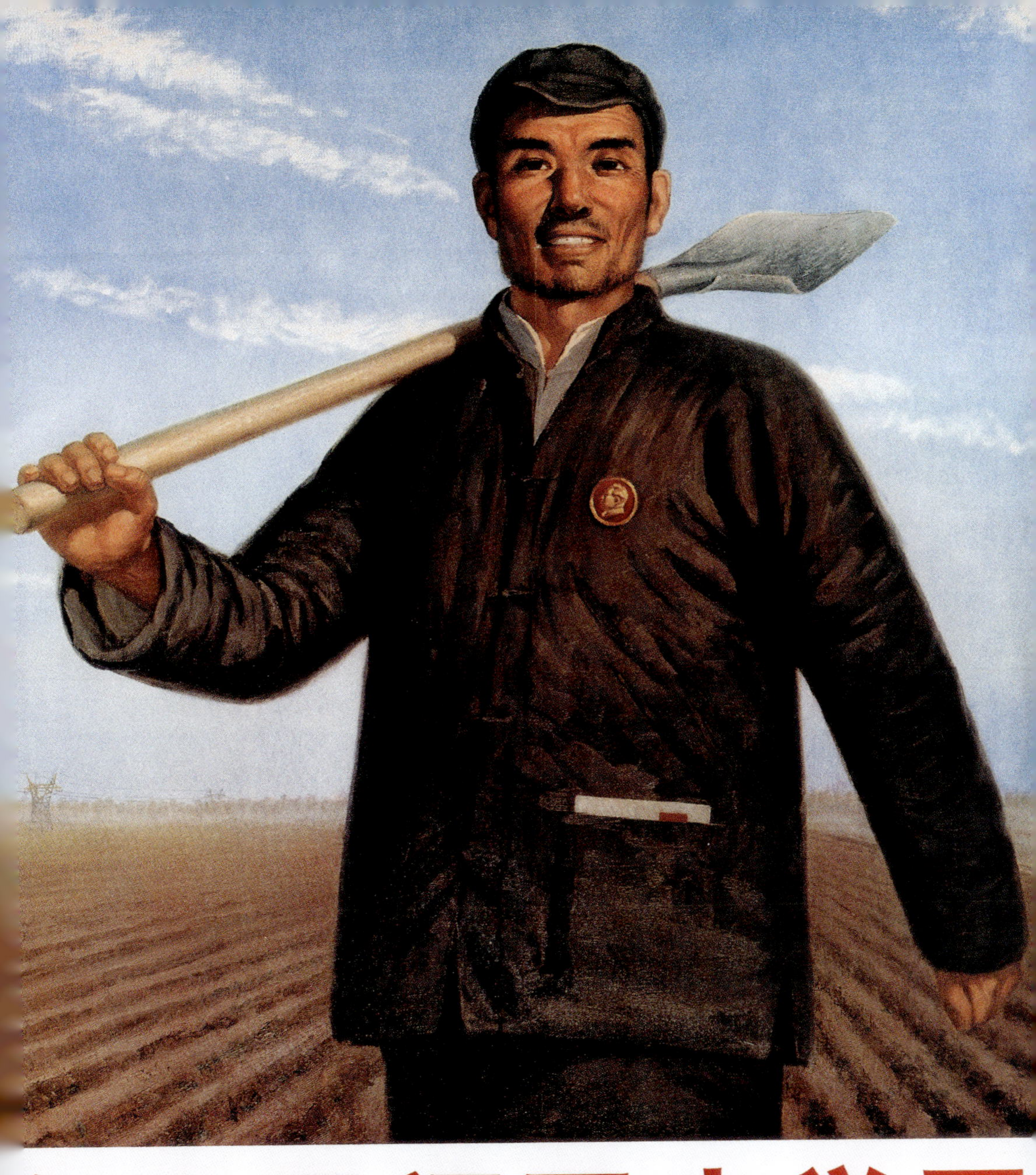

向王国福同志学习

“拉革命车不松套，
一直拉到共产主义”

Left
Young heroes, poster 11
Under the portrait: Long Junjue
Long Junjue, a member of the Dong ethnic group, was born into a poor peasant family in Guizhou Province. In 1957 he was employed by the army as a technical adviser to a workers' detachment. During the war against the USA and while building a railway, Long Junjue was awarded the Order of Merit Second Class once and the Order of Merit Third Class twice. In order to save the railway, construction materials, and equipment belonging to Geological Excavation Brigade 509, he took part in a courageous attempt to fight a forest fire in Fujian Province and died a hero at the age of 26. *Artist:* Li Yuchang

Right
Young heroes, poster 12
Under the portrait: Xiang Xiuli
Xiang Xiuli was born in 1933 into a poor working-class family in Guangzhou. At 13, she found work in the crèche of a pharmaceuticals factory. In December 1958 fire broke out in the factory. The presence of inflammable sodium meant that the blaze quickly spread. In order to save her comrades and state property, Xiang Xiuli bravely fought the flames, suffering severe burns. After 33 days, she lost her battle for life. *Artist:* Mao Fengde

Linkes Bild
Junge Helden, Plakat 11
Unter dem Porträt: Long Junjue
Long Junjue, Nationalität Dong, wurde in einer armen Bauernfamilie in der Provinz Guizhou geboren. 1957 wurde er Angestellter der Armee und übernahm den Posten des technischen Beraters bei einer Arbeitergruppe. Im antiamerikanischen Krieg und beim Bau einer Eisenbahnlinie erhielt Long Junjue einmal den Verdienstorden Zweiter Klasse und zweimal den Verdienstorden Dritter Klasse. Um das Eisenbergwerk und Materialien sowie Geräte der geologischen Schürfungsbrigade 509 zu retten, nahm er am 9. November 1958 tapfer an der Bekämpfung eines Waldbrandes in der Provinz Fujian teil und starb heldenhaft mit 26 Jahren. *Gemalt von* Li Yuchang

Rechtes Bild
Junge Helden, Plakat 12
Unter dem Porträt: Xiang Xiuli
Xiang Xiuli wurde 1933 in einer armen Angestelltenfamilie in Guangzhou geboren. Mit 13 Jahren fand sie Arbeit in der Kindergruppe in einer Pharmafabrik. Im Dezember 1958 kam es zu einem Brand in der Fabrik. Das Feuer breitete sich aufgrund des explosiven Natriums schnell aus. Um die anderen Genossen und das Eigentum des Staates zu retten, kämpfte Xiang Xiuli tapfer gegen die Flammen und erlitt schwere Brandverletzungen. Nach 33 Tagen verlor sie den Kampf um ihr Leben. Xiang Xiuli starb. *Gemalt von* Mao Fengde

Image de gauche
Jeunes héros, affiche n° 11
En dessous du portrait : Long Junjue
Long Junjue, de nationalité dong, est né dans une famille paysanne pauvre de la province de Guizhou. Il entra en 1957, il devint employé de l'armée et occupa le poste de conseiller technique auprès d'un groupe d'ouvriers. Dans la guerre anti-américaine et au cours de la construction d'un réseau ferré, Long Junjue fut décoré une fois de l'Ordre du mérite de première classe et deux fois de l'Ordre du mérite de troisième classe. Le 9 novembre 1958, il participa à l'extinction d'un incendie de forêt dans la province de Fujian pour sauver la mine de fer ainsi que du matériel de la brigade de fouilles géologiques 509. Il mourut en héros à l'âge de 26 ans. *Peintre :* Li Yuchang

Image de droite
Jeunes héros, affiche n° 12
En dessous du portrait : Xiang Xiuli
Xiang Xiuli est née en 1933 à Guangzhou dans une famille paysanne pauvre. À 13 ans, elle s'occupait d'enfants dans une usine de produits pharmaceutiques. En décembre 1958 survint un incendie dans l'usine. Le feu se propagea rapidement en raison de la présence de sodium explosif. Afin de sauver les autres camarades et la propriété d'État, Xiang Xiuli lutta vaillamment contre les flammes et fut grièvement brûlée. Au bout de 33 jours, elle dut s'avouer vaincue : Xiang Xiuli mourut. *Peintre :* Mao Fengde

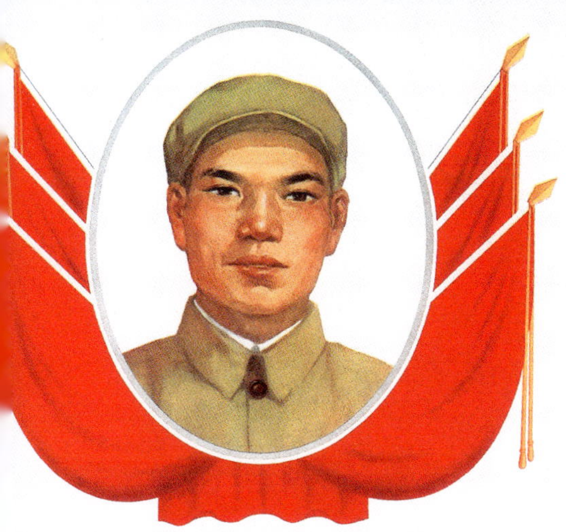

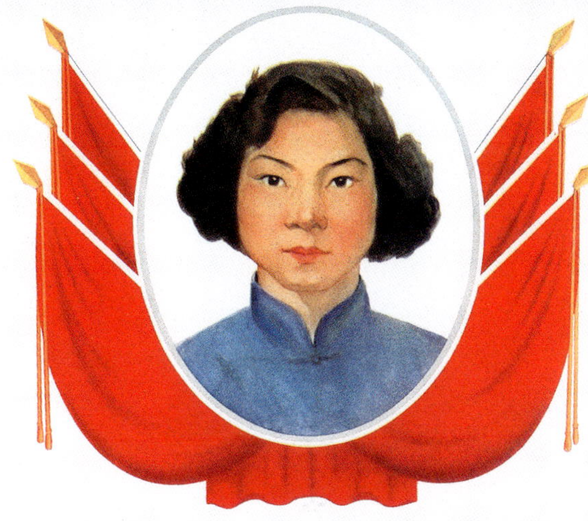

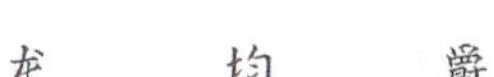

龙　均　爵

龙均爵，侗族人，生长在贵州省錦屛县一个貧农家庭。1951年参加中国人民志願；归国后，分派在鉄道兵部队。1953年加入中国新民主主义青年团，1956年加入中共产党。他在部队里历任战士、班长，1957年改为随軍职工，担任民工分队的技术导。龙均爵在抗美援朝斗爭和修建鹰厦鉄路中先后立二等功一次，三等功两次。58年11月9日他在福建省漳平县大深地方，为扑灭山火，救护鉄矿和509地質队物資器材仓库，壮烈牺牲，时年二十六岁。

向　秀　丽

向秀丽，1933年出生在广州市一个貧苦店員工人家庭。七岁在地主家当丫头，十三岁入药厂当童工。解放后，向秀丽在党的教育下，积极参加工会工作，被选为厂工会組織委員和区工会女工委員。1954年加入中国新民主主义青年团，1958年参加中国共产党，为預备党員。他在工作中多次受到表揚，被評为先进生产者。当时，她所在的厂是私营企业，她曾在党的領导下，积极向不法資本家进行斗爭。1958年12月，因制药时酒精发生燃烧，火势将蔓延到爆炸性很强的金屬鈉，向秀丽为搶救同志們生命和国家财产，舍身扑火，被烈火严重燒伤，党多方設法搶救，延續生命三十三天后，終于牺牲。1959年，中国共产党广州市中区委員会特追認为正式党員。

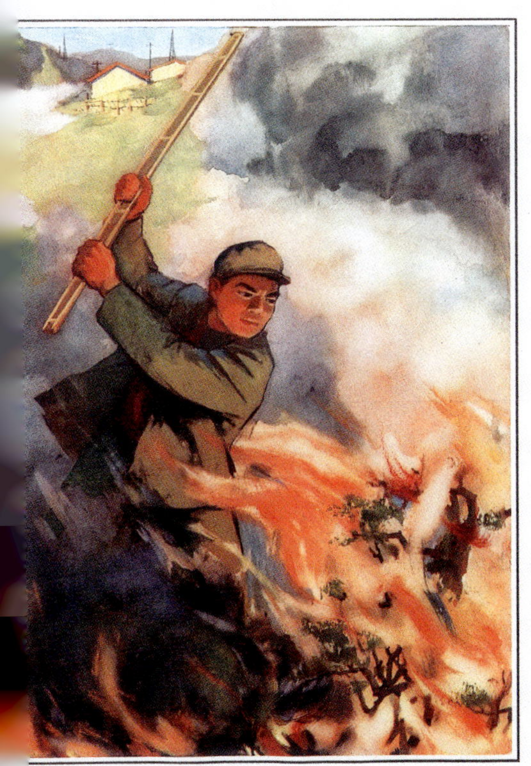

青年英雄挂图（十一）

李玉昌 画

青年英雄挂图（十二）

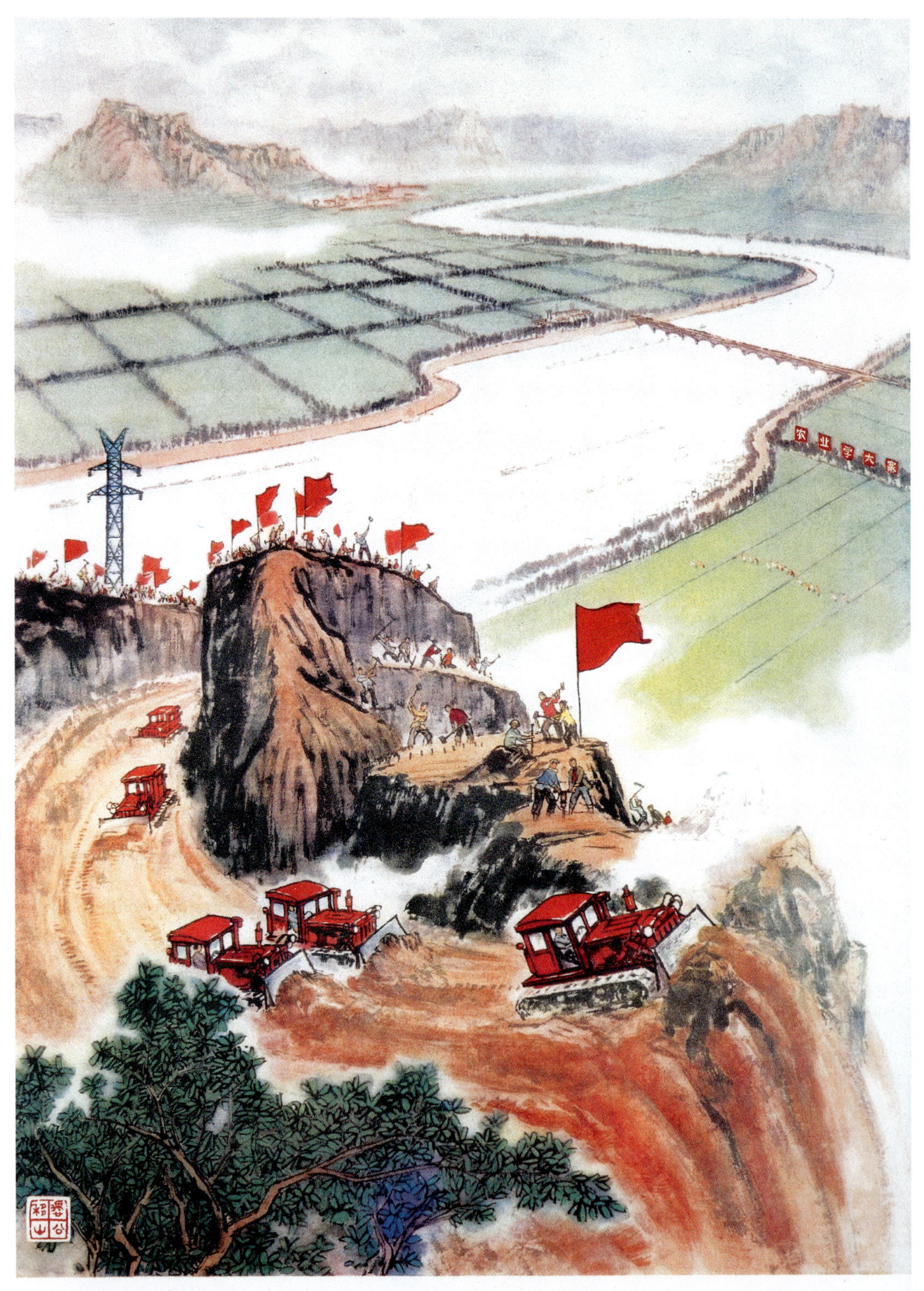

学大寨 挖山不止

Learn to move mountains from the example set by Dazhai* *Artists:* Yu Taichang, Pi Zhixian, Che Tiande, and Wang Jiahua; Shandong People's Publishing House, 1976; 0.11 Yuan
* A model village in Xiyang District, Shanxi Province, which achieved large harvests despite a barren mountainous landscape and the most primitive living and farming conditions. In 1964 Mao Zedong called upon the nation to "Learn from Dazhai's agriculture!"

Von Dazhai* lernen, Berge zu versetzen *Gemalt von* Yu Taichang, Pi Zhixian, Che Tiande und Wang Jiahua; Volksverlag Shandong, 1976; 0,11 Yuan
* Ein Musterdorf im Kreis Xiyang, Provinz Shanxi, das trotz karger bergiger Landschaft und primitivsten Lebens- und Produktionsbedingungen hohe Erträge erzielte. 1964 rief Mao Zedong das ganze Land auf: „Lernt in der Landwirtschaft von Dazhai!"

L'exemple de Dazhai* en tête, soulevons des montagnes *Peintres :* Yu Taichang, Pi Zhixian, Che Tiande et Wang Jiahua ; Éditions Populaires du Shandong, 1976 ; 0,11 yuan
* Village modèle du canton de Xiyang, province de Shanxi, qui, en dépit d'un site montagneux aride et de conditions de vie et de production primitives, atteignit une forte production. En 1964, Mao Zedong proféra : « Retenez l'expérience agricole de Dazhai ! »

Pages 274–275

The spirit of Yan'an* is passed on from generation to generation *On the straw hats:* The spirit of Yan'an will shine for eternity. Maintaining the tradition of the revolution *Artist:* Zuo Jianhua; Tianjin People's Art Publishing House 1974; 0.11 Yuan
* Town in the Shanxi Province (central China); the seat of Mao Zedong's Chinese Communist Party Central Committee from 1937 until March 1947; it is considered an important monument to the Chinese revolution.

Der Geist von Yan'an* wird von Generation zu Generation weitergegeben *Auf den Strohhüten:* Der Geist von Yan'an wird auf ewig strahlen. Die Tradition der Revolution fortsetzen *Gemalt von* Zuo Jianhua; Volkskunstverlag Tianjin, 1974; 0,11 Yuan
* Stadt in der Provinz Shanxi (Zentralchina), von 1937 bis März 1947 Sitz des von Mao Zedong geführten ZK der KPCh, gilt als bedeutende Gedenkstätte der chinesischen Revolution.

L'esprit de Yan'an* se transmet de génération en génération *Sur les chapeaux de paille :* L'esprit de Yan'an rayonnera à jamais, Perpétuons la tradition de la révolution *Peintre :* Zuo Jianhua ; Éditions Populaires d'Art de Tianjin, 1974 ; 0,11 yuan
* Ville dans la province du Shanxi (Chine centrale) ; de 1937 à mars 1947, siège du comité central du Parti communiste chinois dirigé par Mao Zedong ; considéré comme un important lieu de commémoration de la révolution chinoise.

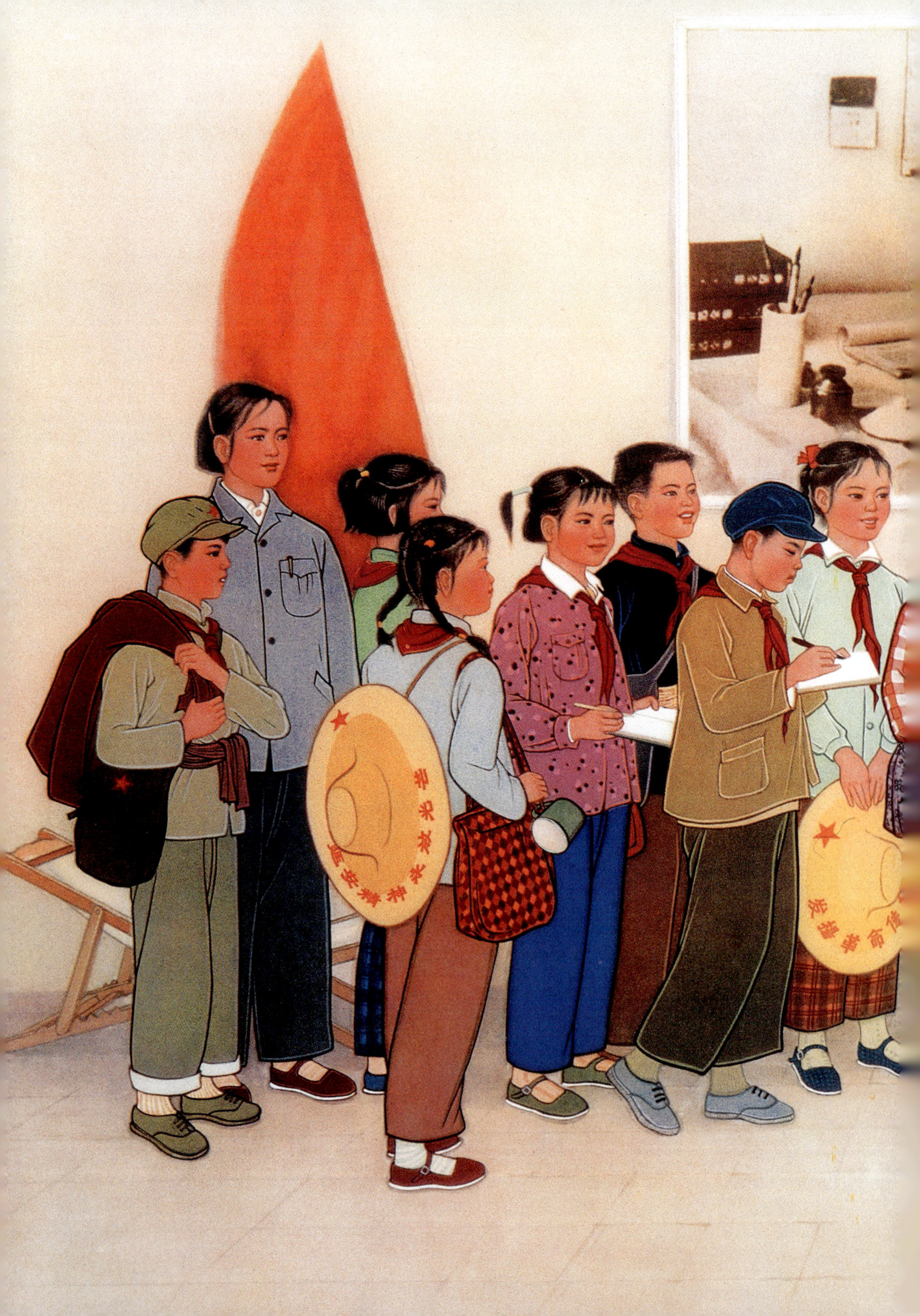

延安精神
发扬革命

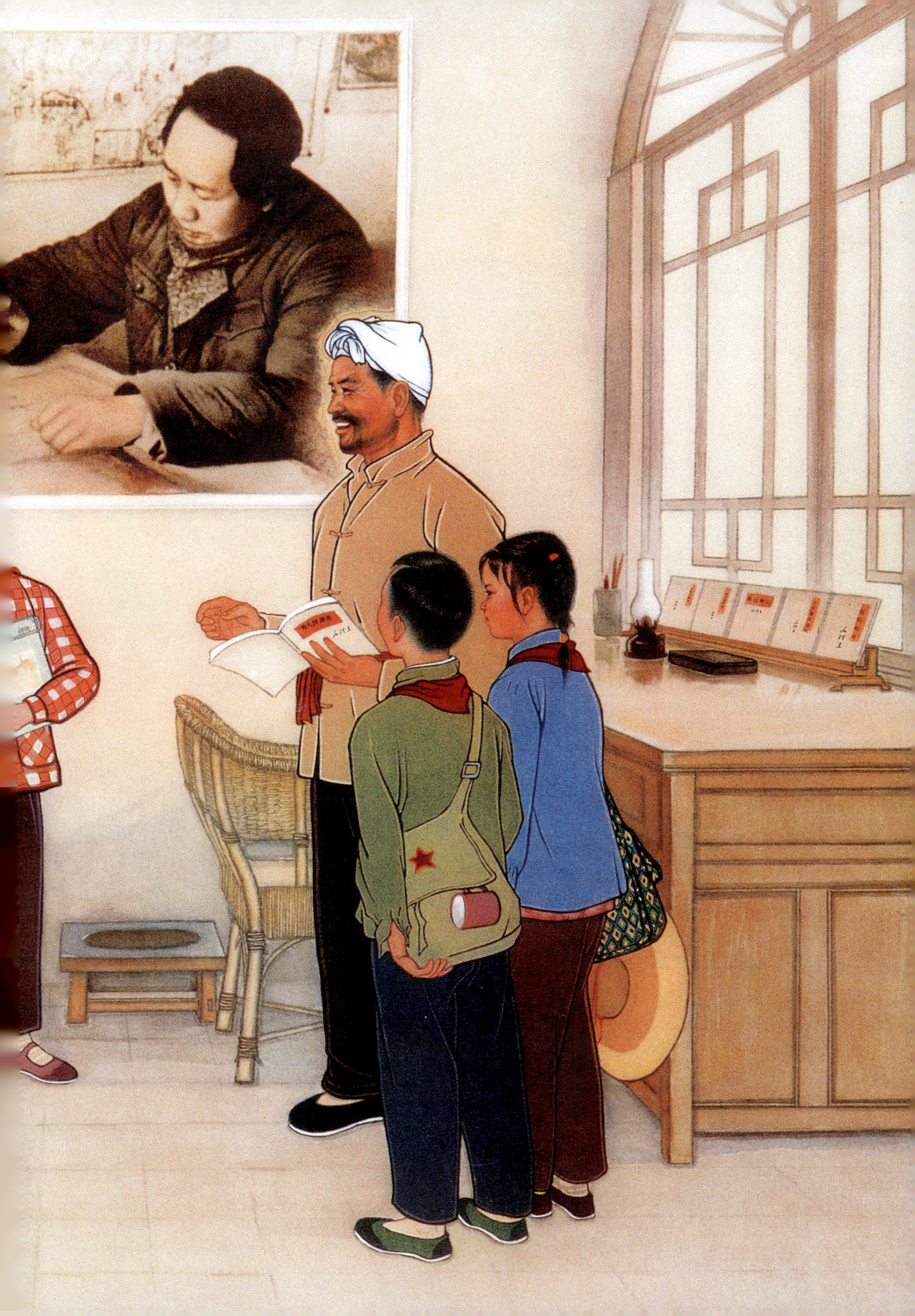

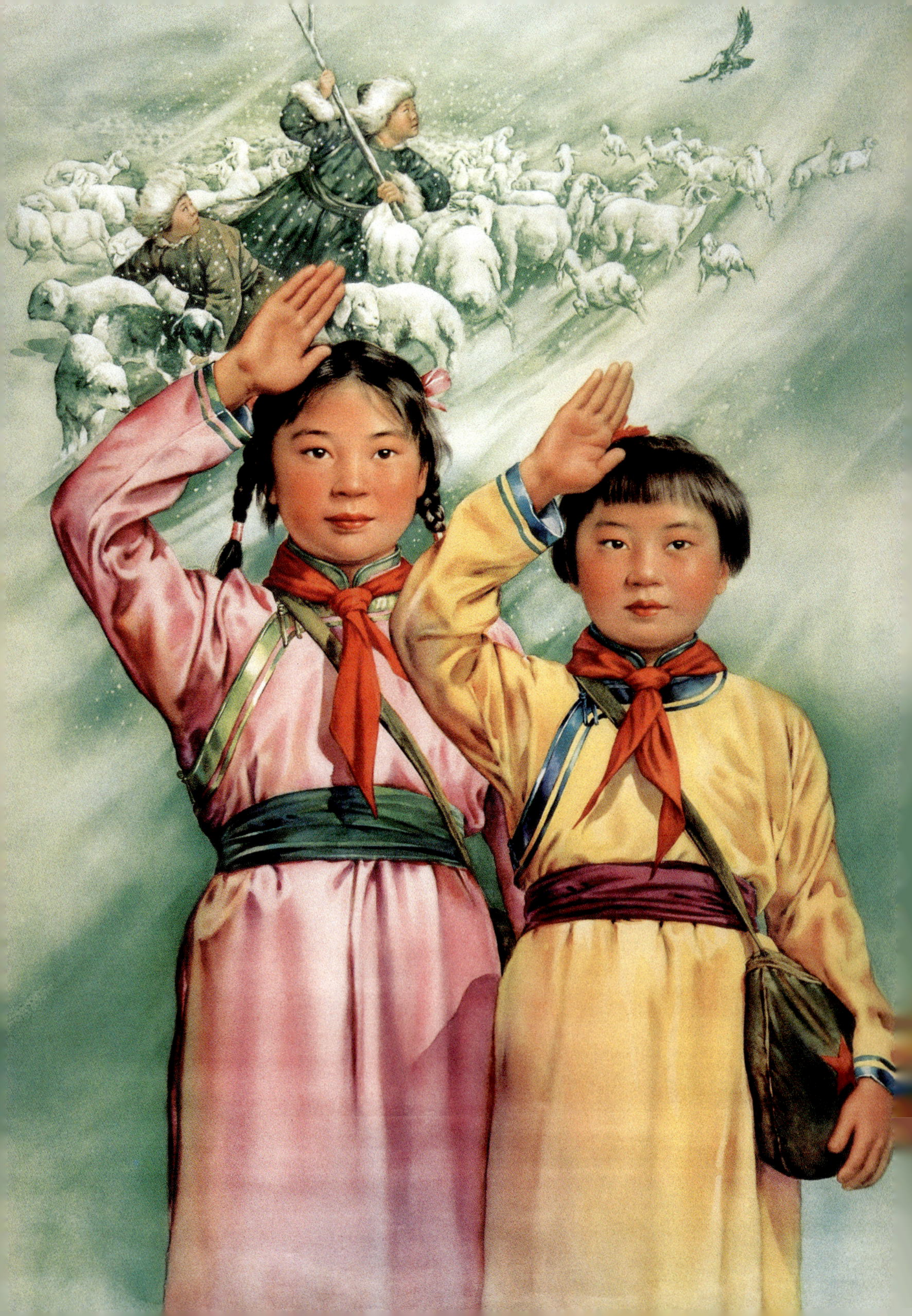

Suddenly there comes news: on earth the tiger has been defeated* *Artist:* Dong Chenqing; Liaoning People's Publishing House 1978 *Print run:* 1,500,000; 0.11 Yuan
* The woman in the white blouse is Mao Zedong's first wife, Yang Kaihui (1901–1930), a member of the Communist Party who was betrayed by the Kuomintang. She was arrested, tortured and in 1930 died a martyr's death in prison. The other female figure is the fairy Chang E, who, according to Chinese mythology, lives on the moon. The caption is a verse from a poem written by Mao Zedong in 1957.

Plötzlich die Nachricht: Auf Erden ist der Tiger bezwungen* *Gemalt von* Dong Chenqing; Volksverlag Liaoning, 1978 *Auflage:* 1 500 000; 0,11 Yuan
* Die Frau in weißer Bluse ist eine der früheren Ehefrauen von Mao Zedong, die Kommunistin Yang Kaihui (1901–1930), die nach Verrat von der Guomindang verhaftet und gefoltert wurde und 1930 im Gefängnis den Märtyrertod starb. Die andere Frau ist die im Mond lebende Fee Chang E aus der chinesischen Mythologie. Die Bildunterschrift ist ein Vers aus einem Gedicht Mao Zedongs von 1957.

Et soudain la nouvelle : sur terre, le tigre est dompté* *Peintre :* Dong Chenqing ; Éditions Populaires du Liaoning, 1978 *Tirage :* 1 500 000 ; 0,11 yuan
* La femme en chemisier blanc est l'une des premières épouses de Mao Zedong, la communiste Yang Kaihui (1901–1930) qui, arrêtée et torturée par le Guomindang à la suite d'une dénonciation, subit le martyre et mourut en prison en 1930. L'autre est Chang E, la fée de la mythologie chinoise qui vit sur la lune. La légende de l'image est un vers extrait d'un poème de Mao Zedong de 1957.

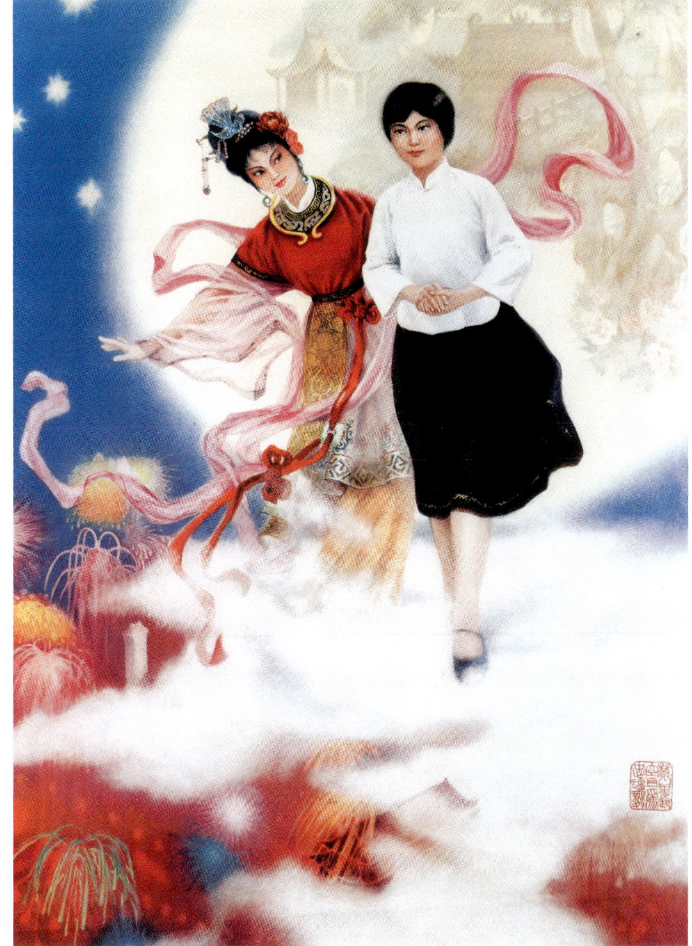

Opposite
Two heroic sisters of the grassland *Artist:* Li Mubai; Shanghai People's Art Publishing House, 1965; 0.15 Yuan

Zwei heldenhafte Schwestern im Grasland *Gemalt von* Li Mubai; Volkskunstverlag Shanghai, 1965; 0,15 Yuan

Deux sœurs héroïques de la prairie *Peintres :* Li Mubai ; Éditions Populaires d'Art de Shanghai, 1965 ; 0,15 yuan

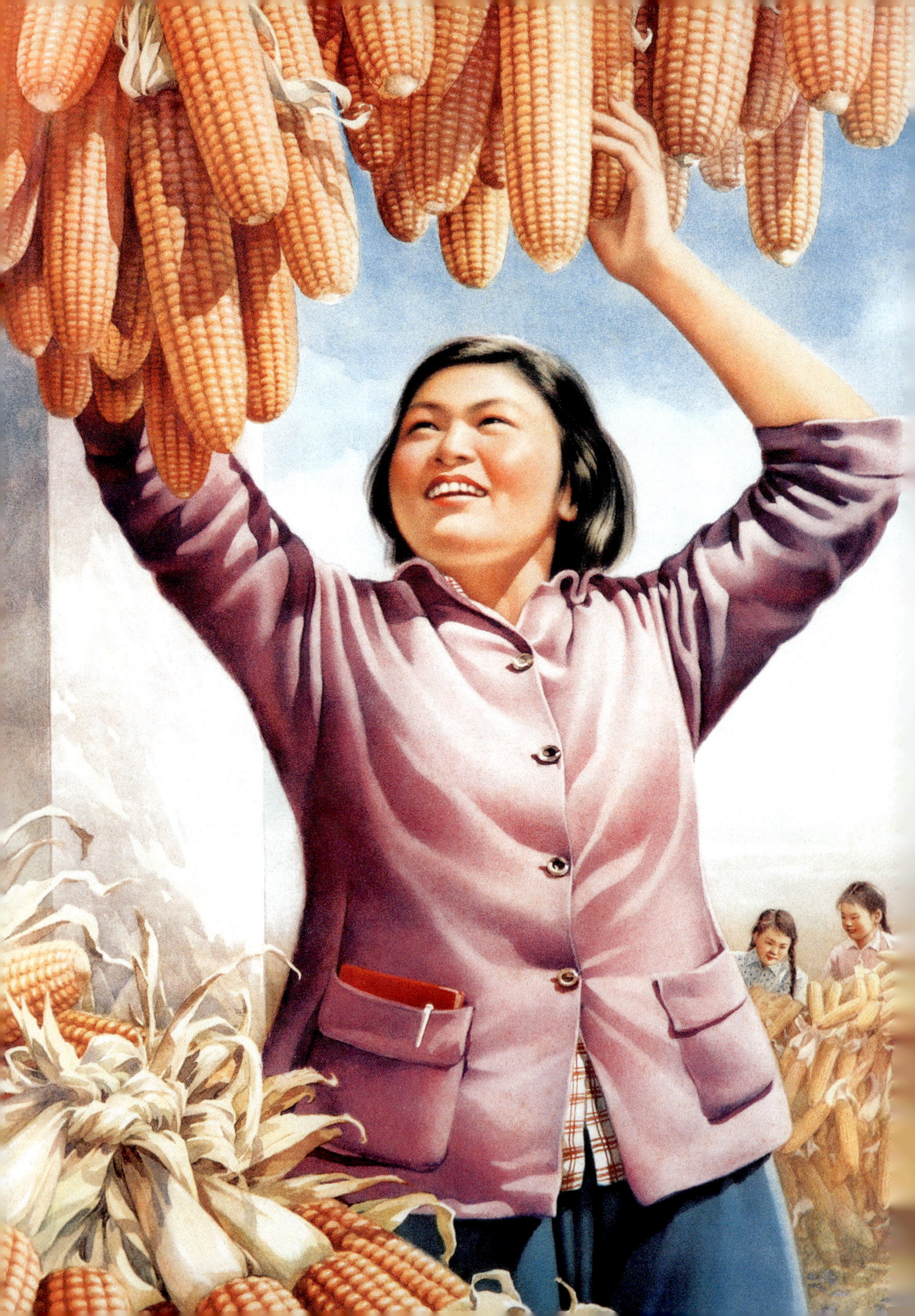

XX

BUILDING OUR COUNTRY THROUGH DILIGENCE AND FRUGALITY

UNSER LAND MIT FLEISS UND GENÜGSAMKEIT AUFBAUEN
ÉDIFIER LE PAYS AVEC DILIGENCE ET ÉCONOMIE

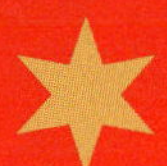

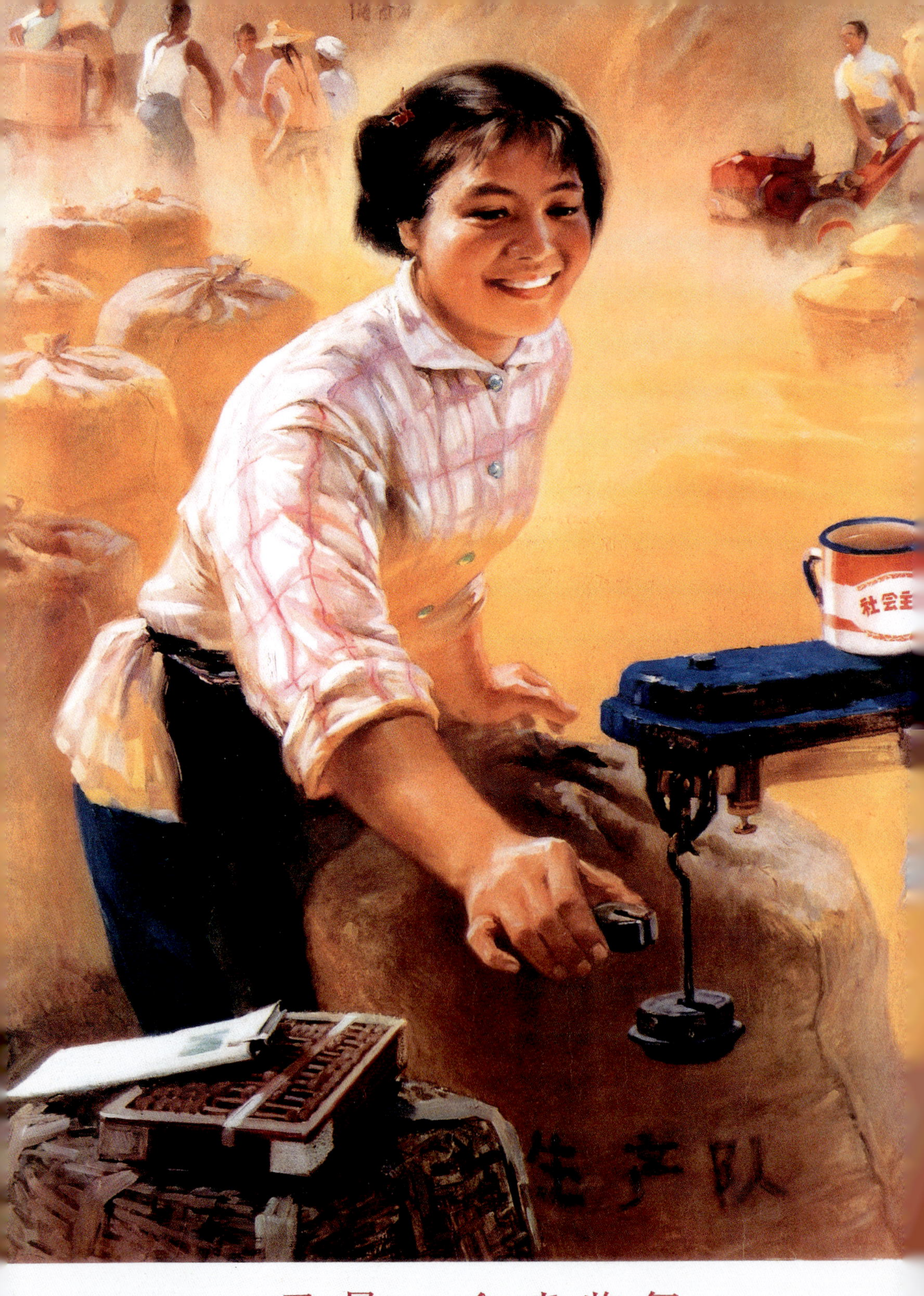

又是一个丰收年

Page 278
Select good seed for increased yields *Artist:* Jin Meisheng; Shanghai People's Publishing House, 1965; 0.15 Yuan

Gute Saaten auswählen, Erträge erhöhen *Gemalt von* Jin Meisheng; Volksverlag Shanghai, 1965; 0,15 Yuan

Choisissez de bonnes semences, augmentez le rendement *Peintre :* Jin Meisheng ; Éditions Populaires de Shanghai, 1965 ; 0,15 yuan

"The principle of diligence and frugality should be observed in everything. This principle of economy is one of the basic principles of socialist economics."

Was auch immer unternommen wird, es muss das Prinzip „Fleiß und Genügsamkeit"eingehalten werden, das heißt das Prinzip der Sparsamkeit, eines der Grundprinzipien der sozialistischen Wirtschaft. ✶ La diligence et l'économie doivent être partout observées. C'est le principe de stricte économie, un des principes fondamentaux de l'économie socialiste.

Another good harvest
On the cup: Socialism is good
On the sack: Production brigade
Artists: Lu Pan and Pan Honghong; People's Art Publishing House, 1972; 0.11 Yuan

Wieder eine gute Ernte
Auf der Tasse: Der Sozialismus ist gut
Auf dem Sack: Produktionsbrigade
Gemalt von Lu Pan und Pan Honghong; Volkskunstverlag, 1972; 0,11 Yuan

De nouveau une bonne récolte
Sur la tasse : Le socialisme, c'est bien
Sur le sac : Brigade de production
Peintres : Lu Pan et Pan Honghong ; Éditions Populaires d'Art, 1972 ; 0,11 yuan

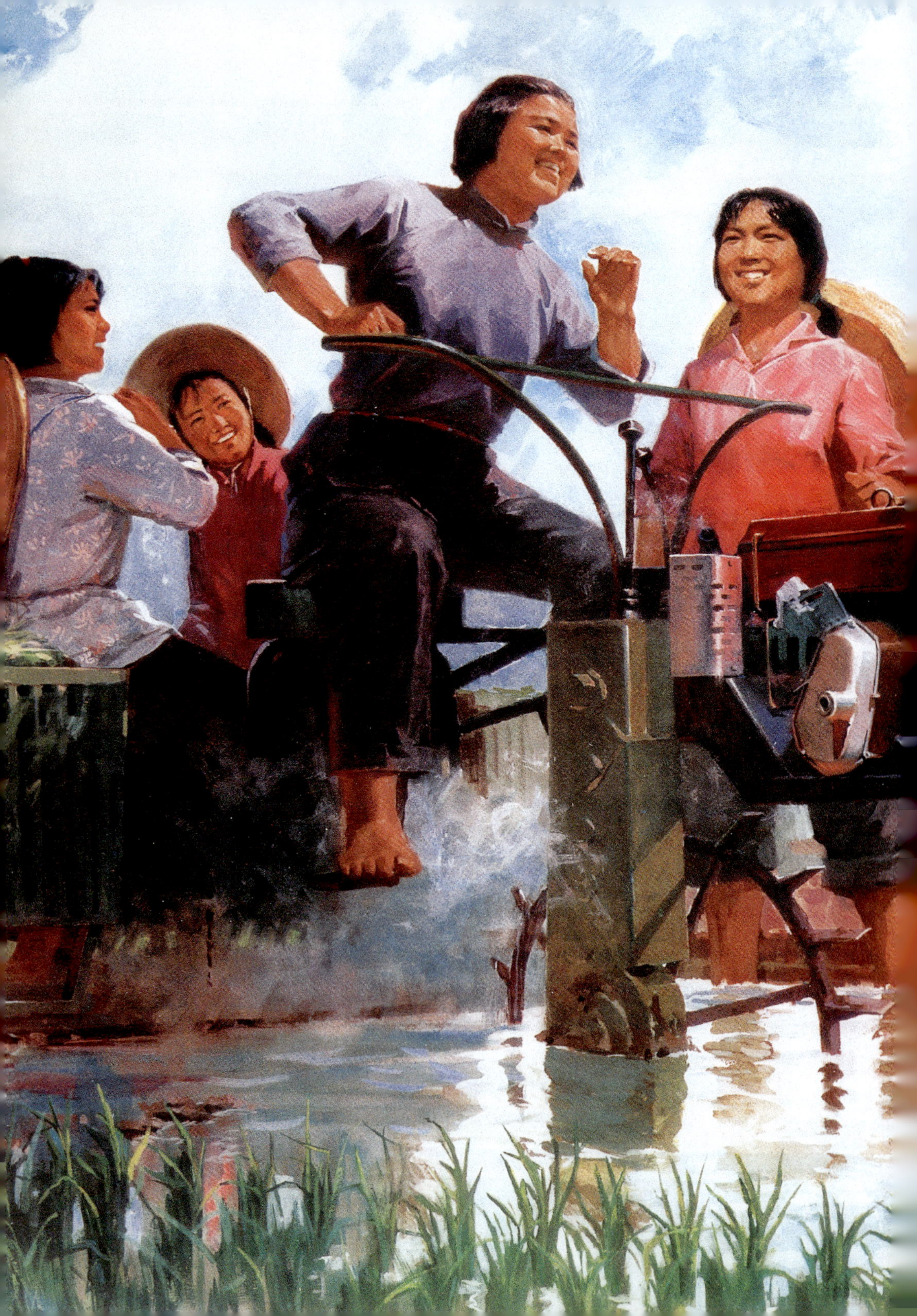

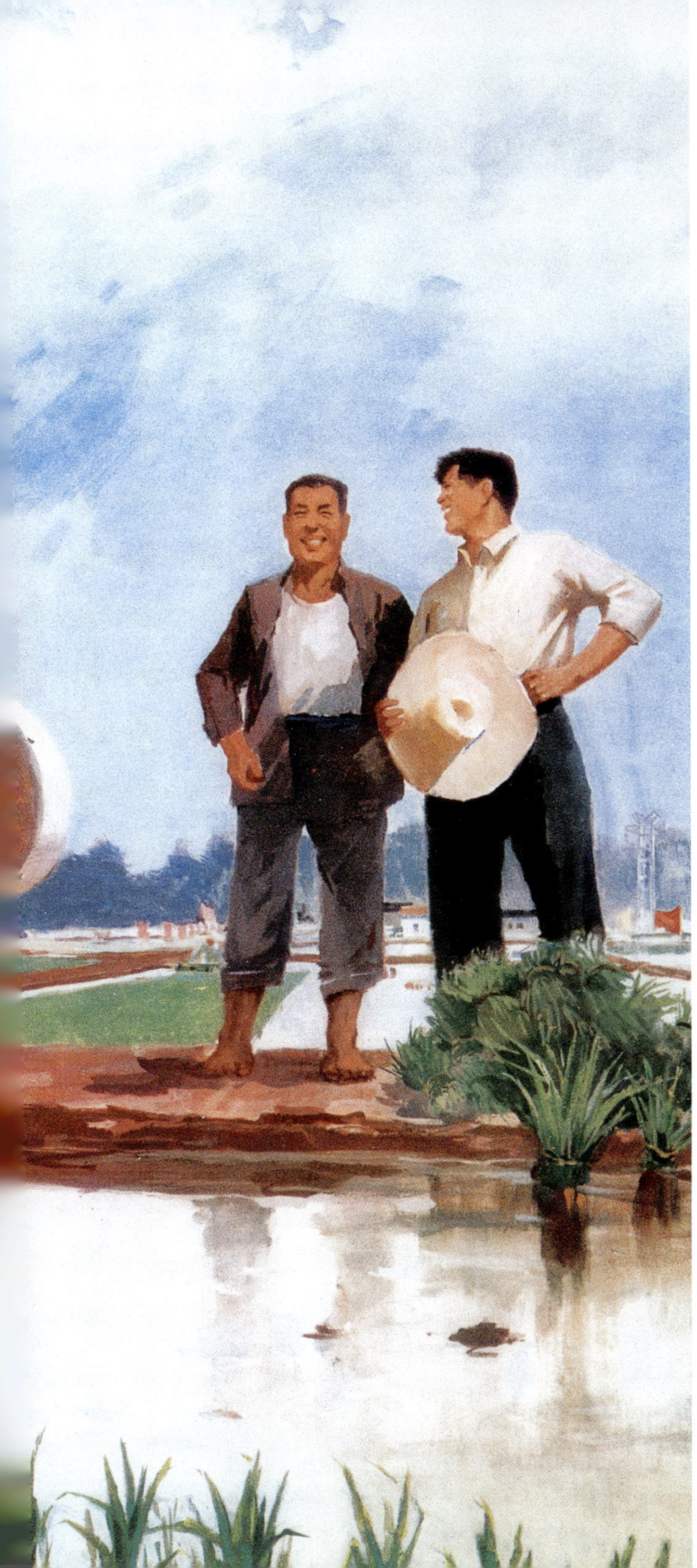

Pages 284–285
Spring rain *Artist:* Zhong Zhaolin; Shanghai People's Publishing House, 1975 *Print run:* 300,000; 0.11 Yuan

Der Frühlingsregen *Gemalt von* Zhong Zhaolin; Volksverlag Shanghai, 1975 *Auflage:* 300 000; 0,11 Yuan

La pluie de printemps *Peintre :* Zhong Zhaolin ; Éditions Populaires de Shanghai, 1975 *Tirage :* 300 000 ; 0,11 yuan

I drive the "iron ox," which is planting rice seedlings *Artist:* Wei Xianqing; Shanghai People's Publishing House, 1977; 0.11 Yuan

Ich treibe den „eisernen Ochsen", der Reissetzlinge pflanzt *Gemalt von* Wei Xianqing; Volksverlag Shanghai, 1977; 0,11 Yuan

Je conduis le « bœuf de fer », qui met en terre des plants de riz *Peintre :* Wei Xianqing; Éditions Populaires de Shanghai, 1977; 0,11 yuan

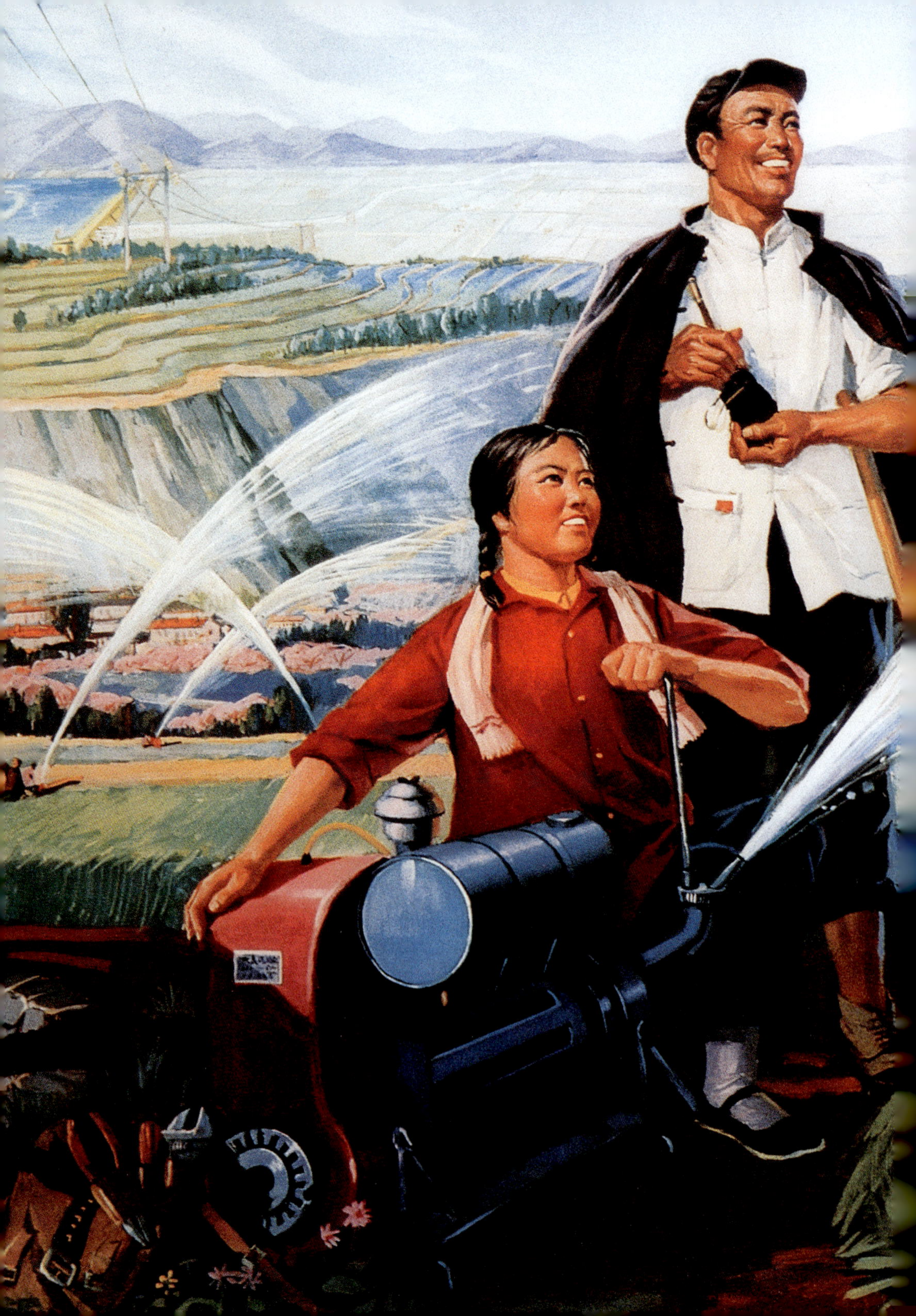

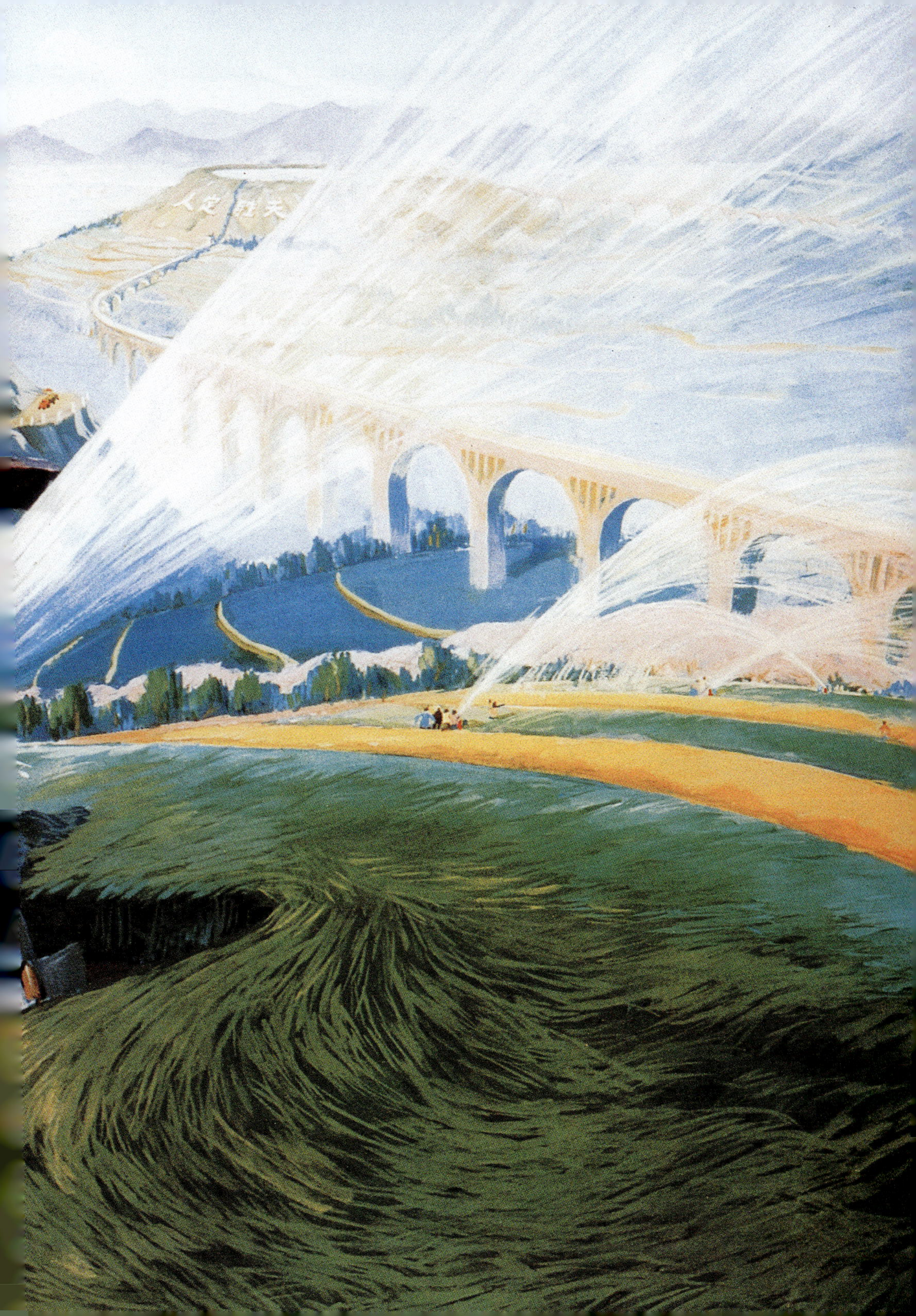

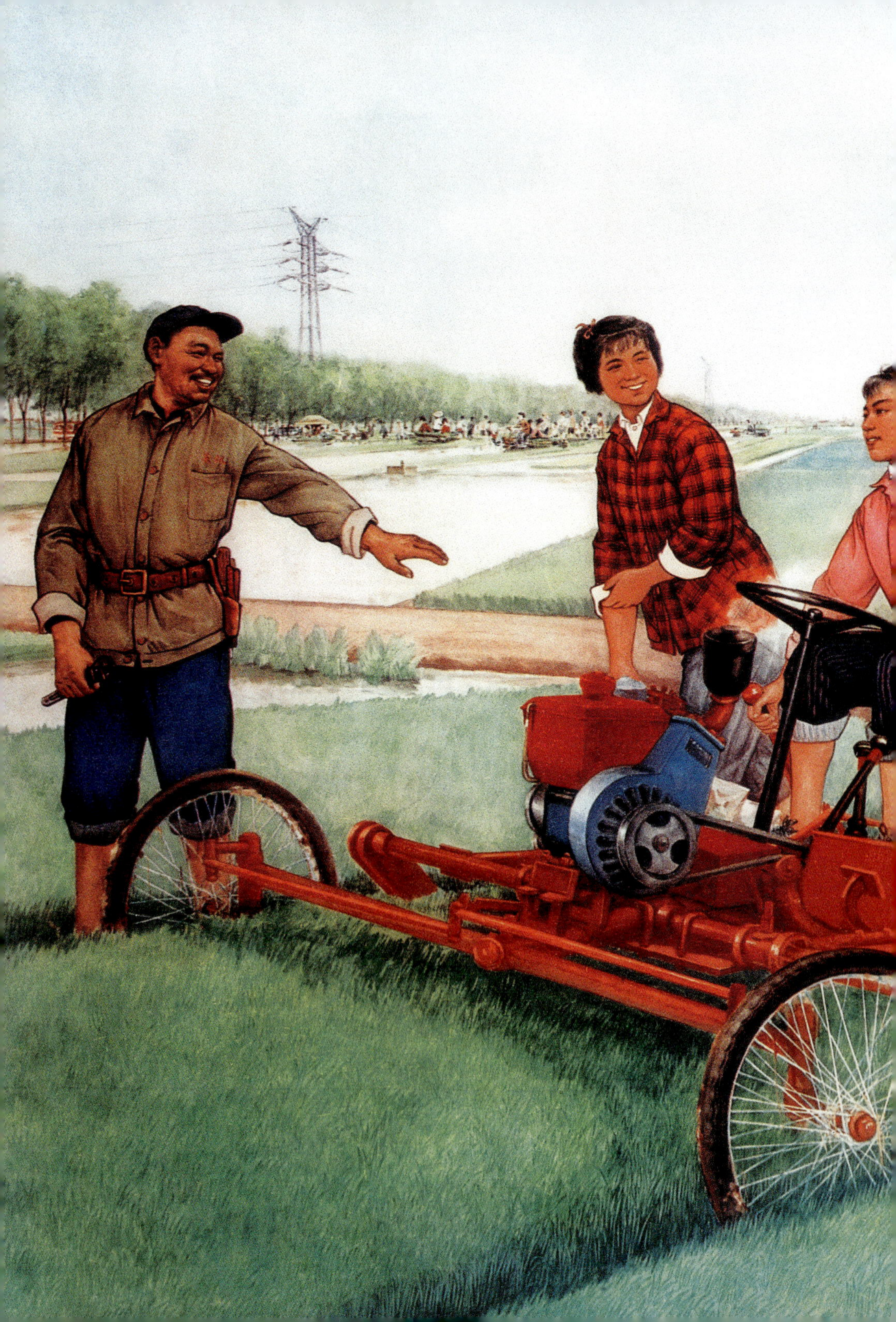

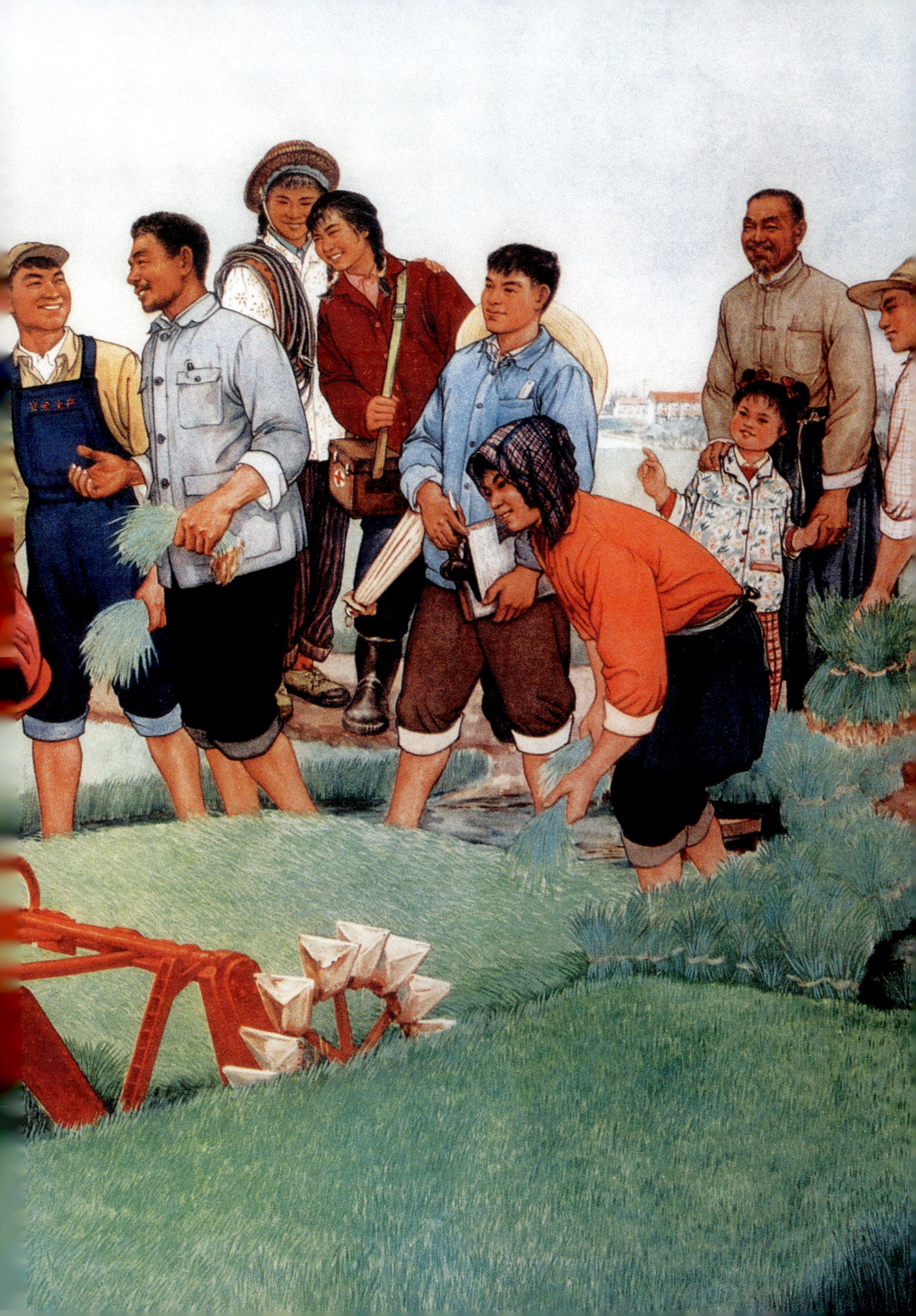

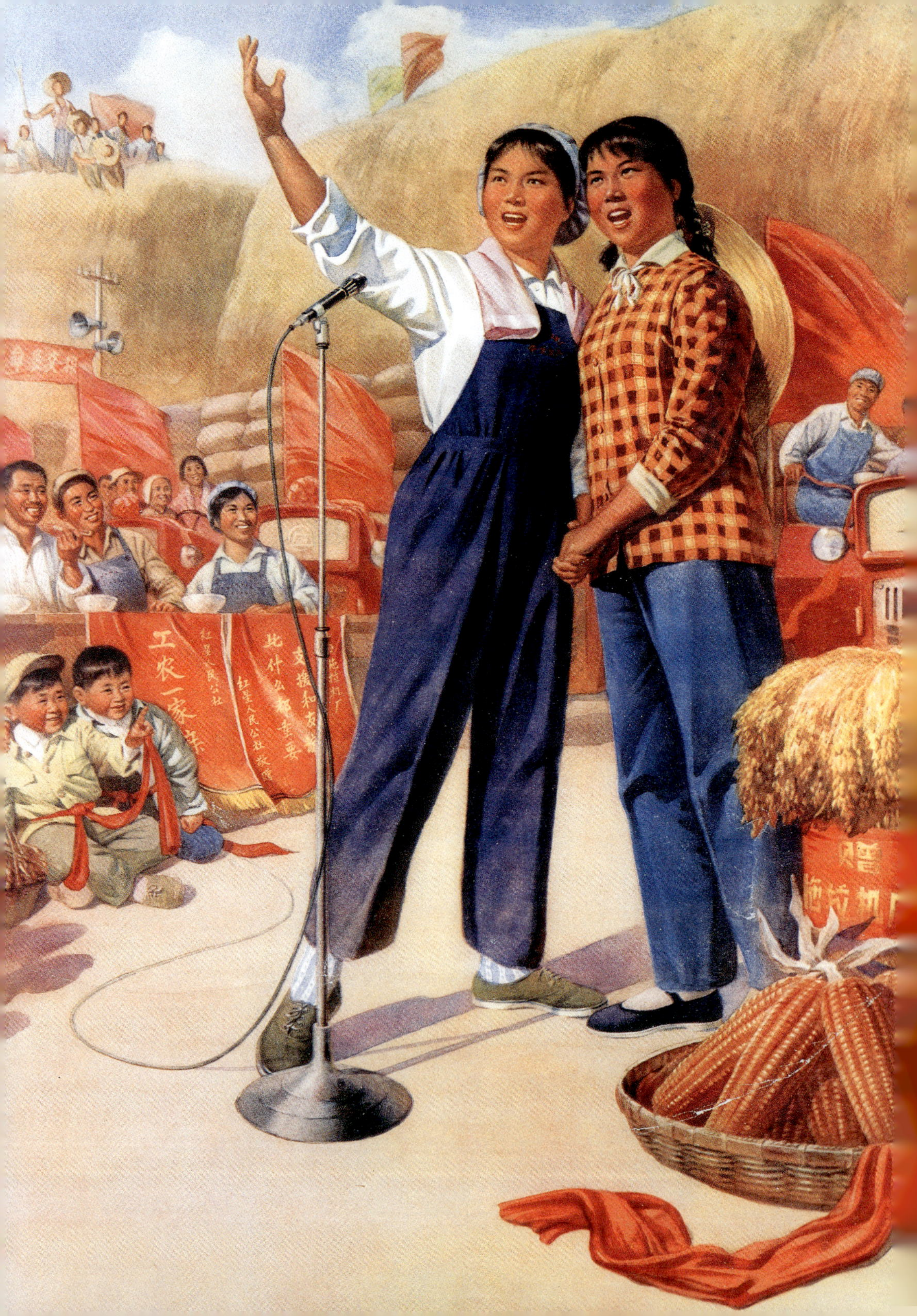
工农一家
红星人民公社
红星人民公社敬赠
支援和友
拖拉机厂

Pages 286–287
What a pleasure it is not to have to bend our backs while planting rice! *Artist:* Wu Guanghua; Shanghai People's Publishing House, 1975; 0.11 Yuan

Welche Freude, dass man sich beim Reispflanzen nicht mehr bücken muss! *Gemalt von* Wu Guanghua; Volksverlag Shanghai, 1975; 0,11 Yuan

Quelle joie de ne plus avoir à se baisser pour planter le riz! *Peintre :* Wu Guanghua ; Éditions Populaires de Shanghai, 1975 ; 0,11 yuan

Opposite
Together the workers and peasants sing the song of the plentiful harvest *Left, on a banner on the table:* Workers and peasants are as one family *Right, on sheaf of grain:* Dedicated to the workers of the tractor factory *Artist:* Chen Kai of the Shanghai Tractor Factory; Shanghai People's Publishing House, 1975; 0.11 Yuan

Arbeiter und Bauern singen gemeinsam das Lied der reichen Ernte *Links auf einer Fahne auf dem Tisch:* Arbeiter und Bauern sind wie eine Familie *Rechts am Getreidebündel*: Den Arbeitern der Traktorenfabrik gewidmet *Gemalt von* Chen Kai, Traktorenfabrik Shanghai; Volksverlag Shanghai, 1975; 0,11 Yuan

Les ouvriers et les paysans chantent ensemble le chant de la riche moisson *À gauche, sur un drapeau posé sur la table :* Les ouvriers et les paysans sont une seule et même famille *Botte de céréales à droite :* Dédié aux ouvriers de l'usine de tracteurs *Peintre :* Chen Kai, de l'usine de tracteurs de Shanghai, Éditions Populaires de Shanghai, 1975 : 0,11 yuan

Planting rice by machine is wonderful *Artist:* Huang Miaofa; Shanghai People's Publishing House, 2nd edn 1973 *Print run:* 200,001–2,000,000; 0.11 Yuan

Mit der Maschine Reis pflanzen ist wunderbar *Gemalt von* Huang Miaofa; Volksverlag Shanghai, 2. Aufl. 1973 *Auflage:* 200 001–2 000 000; 0,11 Yuan

C'est merveilleux de planter du riz à la machine *Peintre :* Huang Miaofa ; Éditions Populaires de Shanghai, 2e éd. 1973 *Tirage :* 200 001–2 000 000 ; 0,11 yuan

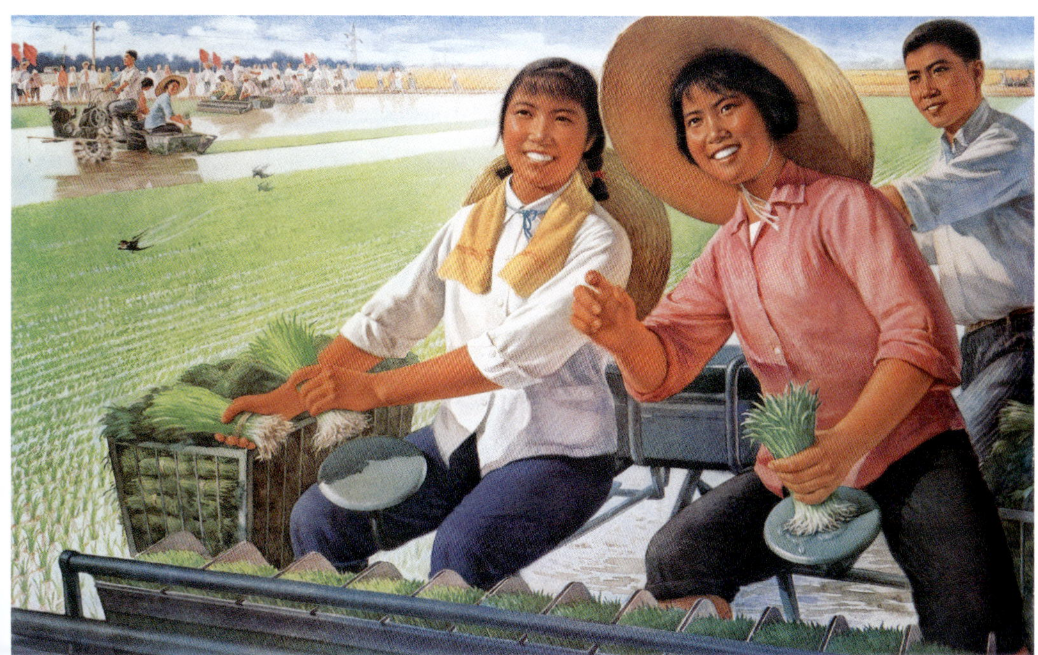

The story of how Yu Qingshou developed and spread a new wheat variety *Designed by:* Shandong Provincial Government, Agriculture, and Forestry Department *Published by:* Shandong People's Publishing House, 1951 *Print run:* 5,000

Die Geschichte, wie Yu Qingshou eine neue Weizenart züchtete und verbreitete *Entwurf:* Abteilung Landwirtschaft und Forst der Provinzregierung Shandong *Herausgeber:* Volksverlag Shandong, 1951 *Auflage:* 5 000

L'histoire de Yu Qingshou qui cultiva des épis de blé et les distribua *Conception :* Département de l'Agriculture et des Eaux et Forêts du gouvernement de la province du Shandong *Éditeur :* Éditions Populaires du Shandong, 1951 *Tirage :* 5 000

Pages 292–293

A rich harvest Poster used as a teaching aid with the textbook *Chinese for Primary Schools*, Book 1, for early primary school *Designed by* The People's Educational Publishing House *Artist:* Zhang Yuejian *Published by:* Shanghai Educational Publishing House 1962 *Print run:* 170,000; 0.19 Yuan

Reiche Ernte Unterrichtsplakat zum Lehrbuch *Chinesisch für Grundschulen*, Band 1 *Entwurf*: Volkserziehungsverlag *Gemalt von* Zhang Yuejian *Herausgeber:* Erziehungsverlag Shanghai, 1962 *Auflage:* 170 000; 0,19 Yuan

Une riche moisson Affiche pédagogique accompagnant le volume 1 du manuel de chinois du cours préparatoire des écoles primaires *Conception :* Éditions d'Éducation Populaire *Peintre :* Zhang Yuejian *Éditeur :* les Éditions Éducatives de Shanghai, 1962 *Tirage :* 170 000 ; 0,19 yuan

于青綬選扁穗小麥的故事

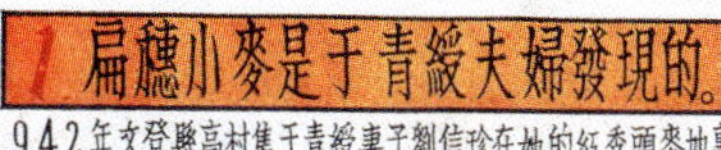

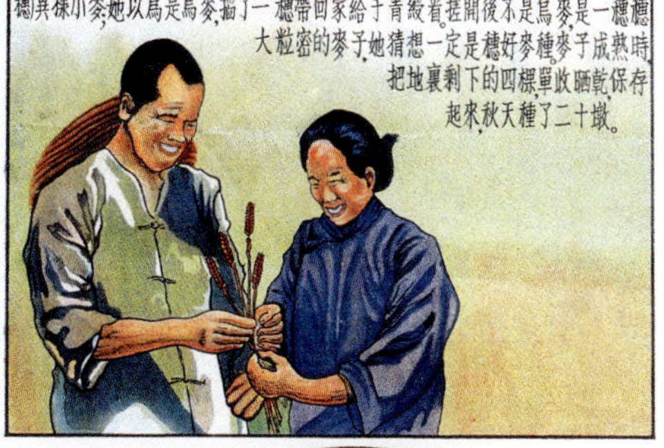

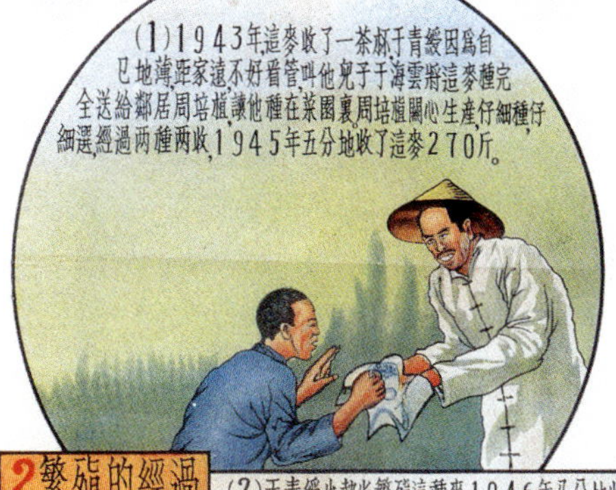

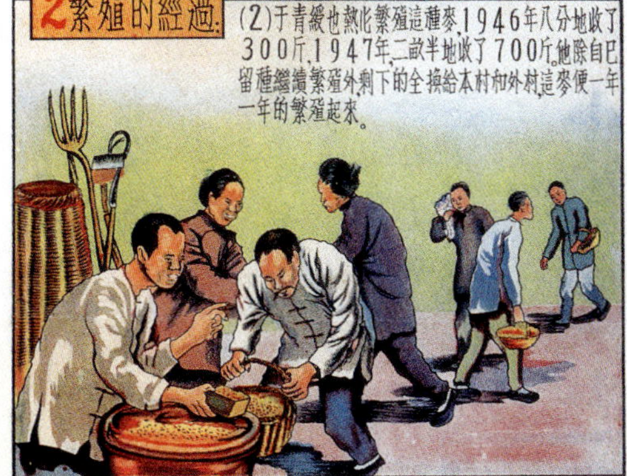

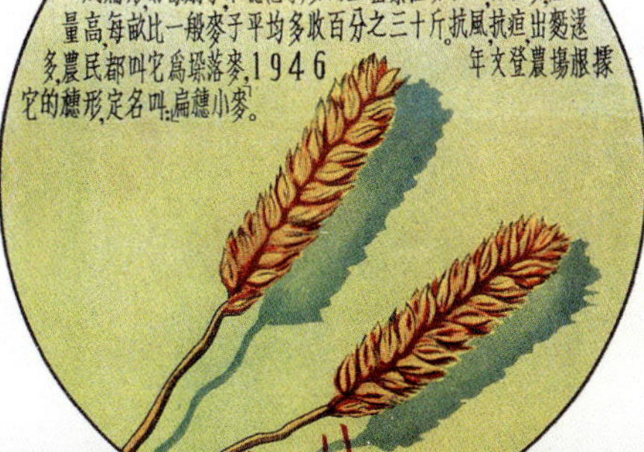

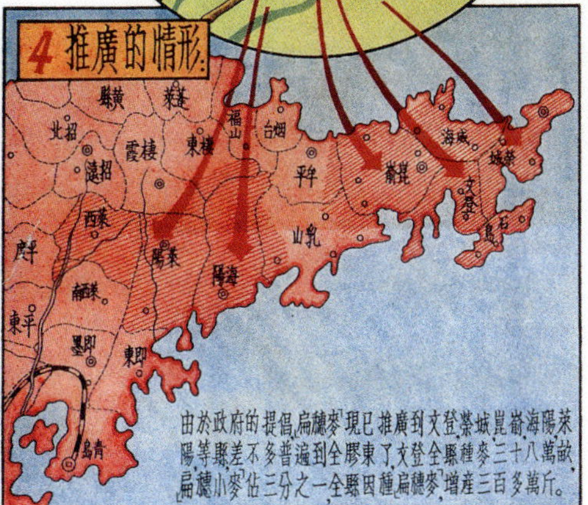

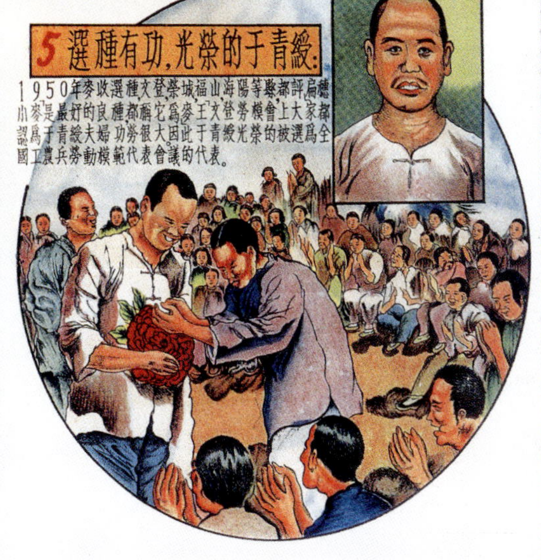

編製者：山東省人民政府農林廳

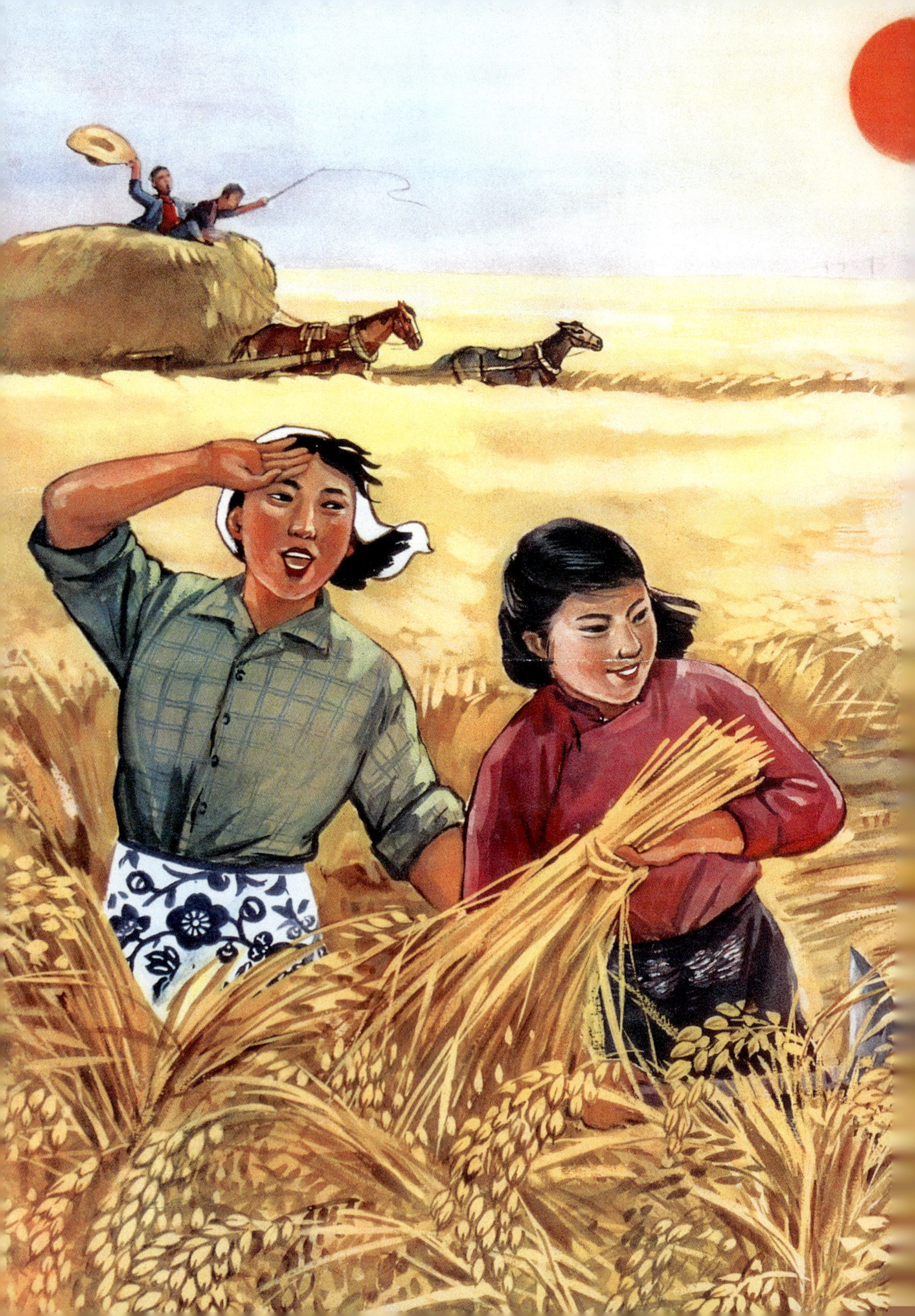

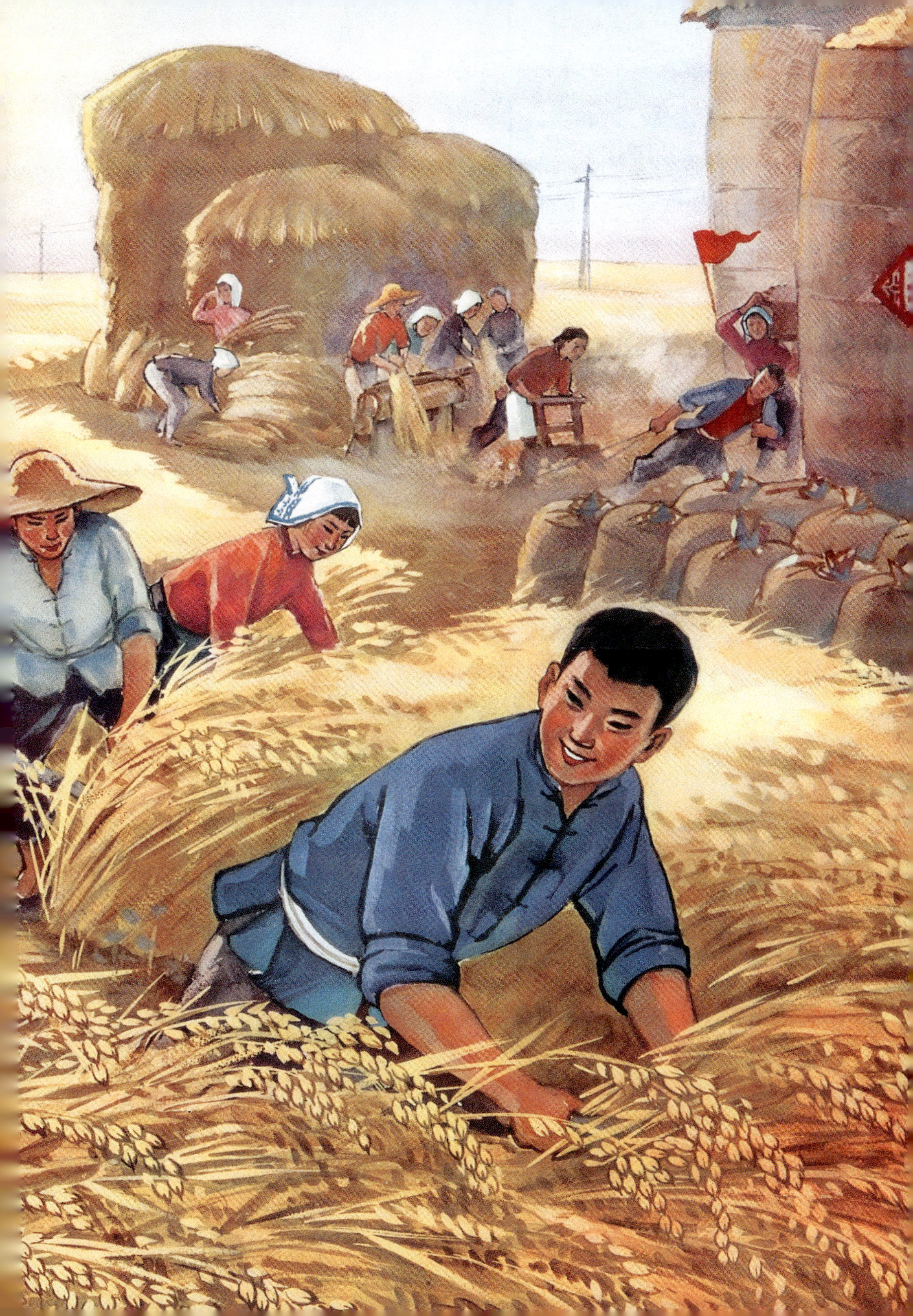

Opposite

Make clouds and rain, and fight for an abundant harvest
Banner in background: Man defeats the sky. Learn from Dazhai's agriculture! *Artist:* Zhang Wuyong, Factory for Optical Equipment; Shanghai People's Publishing House, 1976; 0.14 Yuan

Wolken und Regen zeugen und reiche Ernte erkämpfen
Transparent im Hintergrund: Der Mensch besiegt den Himmel. Lernt in der Landwirtschaft von Dazhai! *Gemalt von* Zhang Wuyong, Fabrik für optische Geräte; Volksverlag Shanghai, 1976; 0,14 Yuan

Faire des nuages et de la pluie et lutter pour de bonnes récoltes
Banderole au fond : L'homme est vainqueur du ciel. Retenez de l'expérience agricole de Dazhai ! *Peintre :* Zhang Wuyong, Usine de matériel optique ; Éditions Populaires de Shanghai, 1976 ; 0,14 yuan

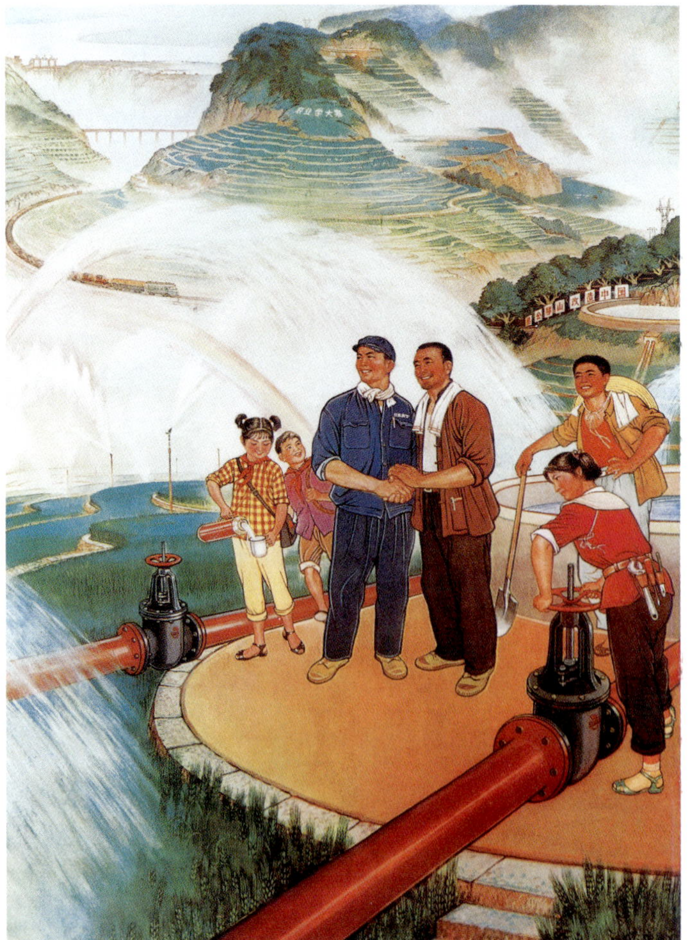

Workers and peasants strive hand in hand for a good harvest
On mountain in background: In agriculture, learn from Dazhai! *Right:* Yu Gong moves mountains, develop China *Artist:* Song Chunmin (peasant); Liaoning People's Publishing House, 1976; 0.11 Yuan

Arbeiter und Bauern kämpfen Hand in Hand für die gute Ernte *Auf dem Berg im Hintergrund:* Lernt in der Landwirtschaft von Dazhai! *Rechts:* Yü Gong versetzt Berge, China aufbauen *Gemalt von* Song Chunmin (Bauer); Volksverlag Liaoning, 1976; 0,11 Yuan

Ouvriers et paysans luttent main dans la main pour avoir une bonne récolte *Sur la montagne, au fond :* Retenez l'expérience agricole de Dazhai ! *À droite :* Yü Gung déplace les montagnes, édifions la Chine *Peintre :* Song Chunmin (paysan) ; Éditions Populaires du Liaoning, 1976 ; 0,11 yuan

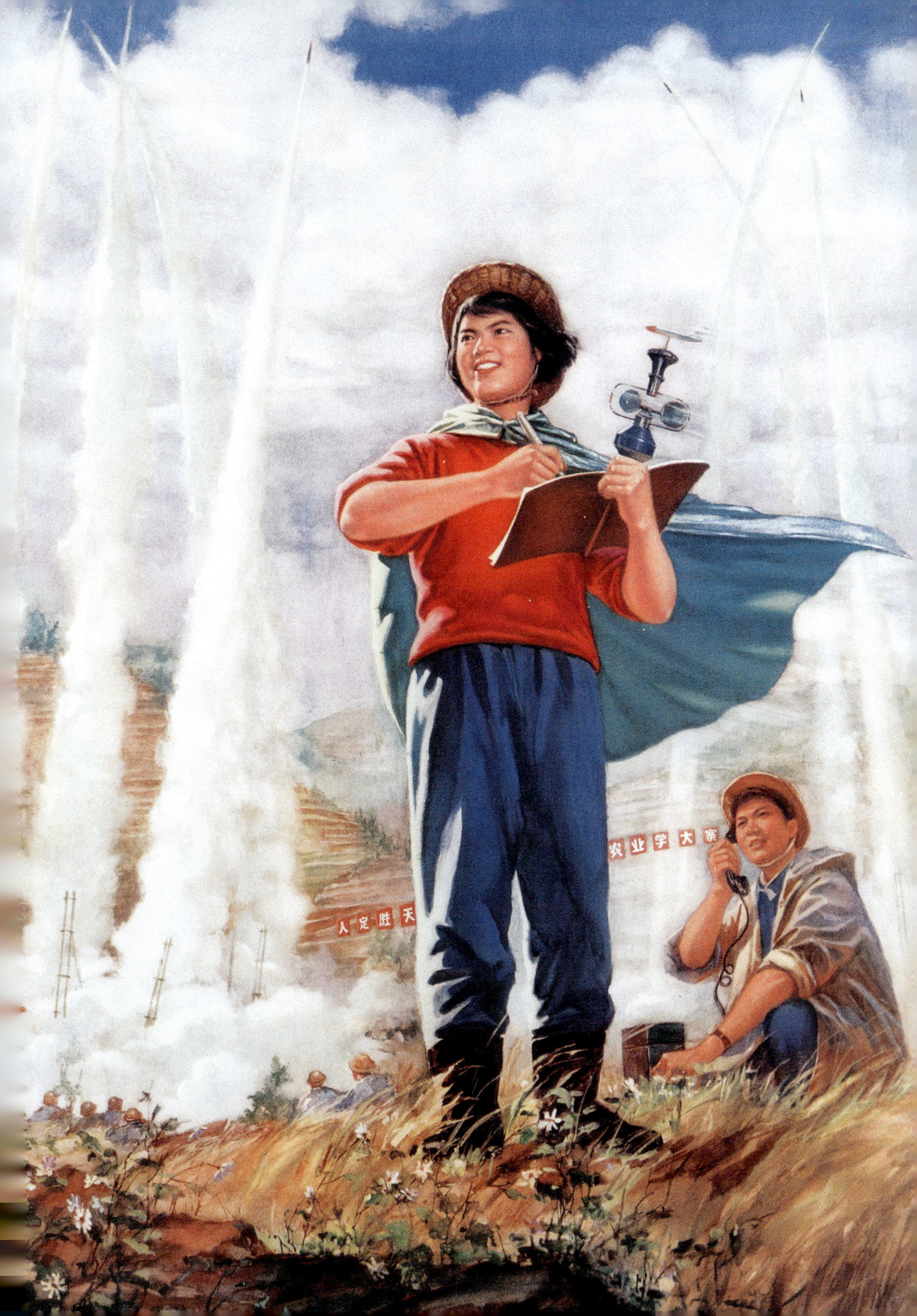
人定胜天
农业学大寨

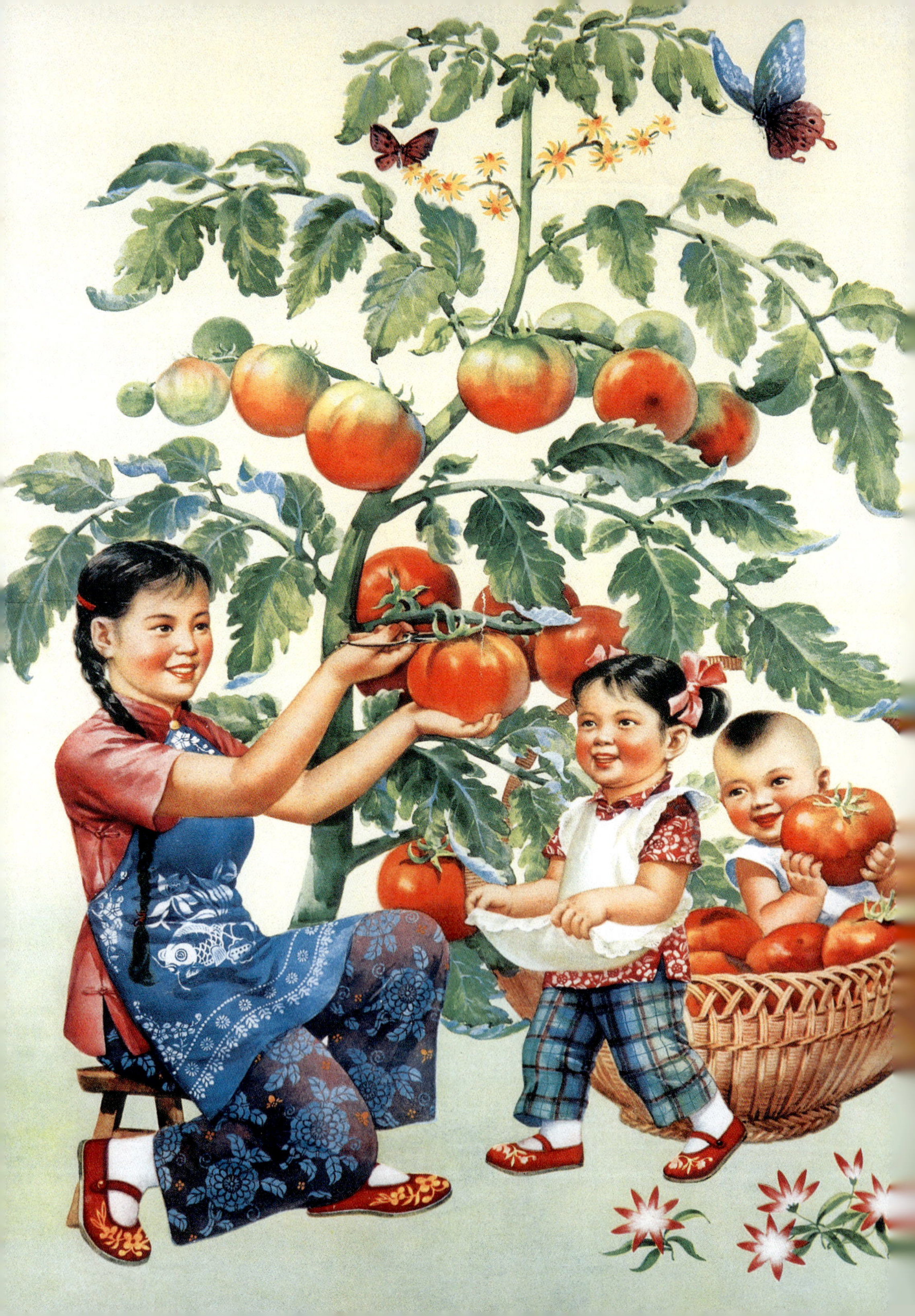

“On the one hand, never be wasteful or extravagant; on the other, actively expand production.”

Einerseits darf es keine Liederlichkeit oder Verschwendung geben, andererseits muss man sich um die Entwicklung der Produktion bemühen. ✶ Gardons-nous de la prodigalité et du gaspillage, tout en développant activement la production.

Picking tomatoes *Artist:* Wang Weishu; Shanghai People's Publishing House, 1st edn 1960, 2nd edn 1960 *Print run:* 160,001–178,000; 0.12 Yuan

Tomaten ernten *Gemalt von* Wang Weishu; Volksverlag Shanghai, 1. Aufl. 1960, 2. Aufl. 1960 *Auflage:* 160 001–178 000; 0,12 Yuan

La cueillette des tomates *Peintre :* Wang Weishu ; Editions Populaires de Shanghai, 1ère éd. 1960, 2e éd. 1960 *Tirage :* 160 001–178 000 exemplares ; 0,12 yuan

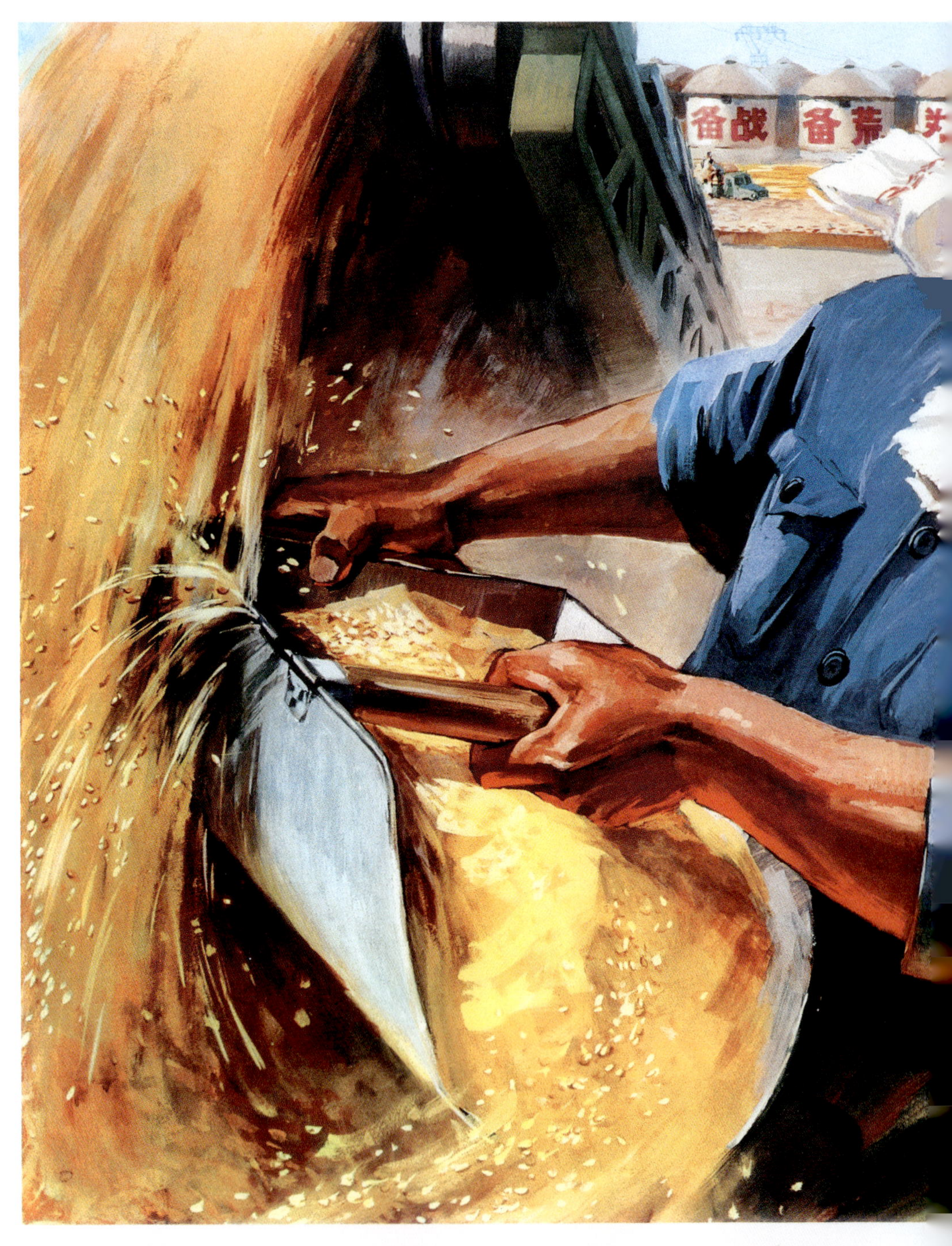

夺丰收

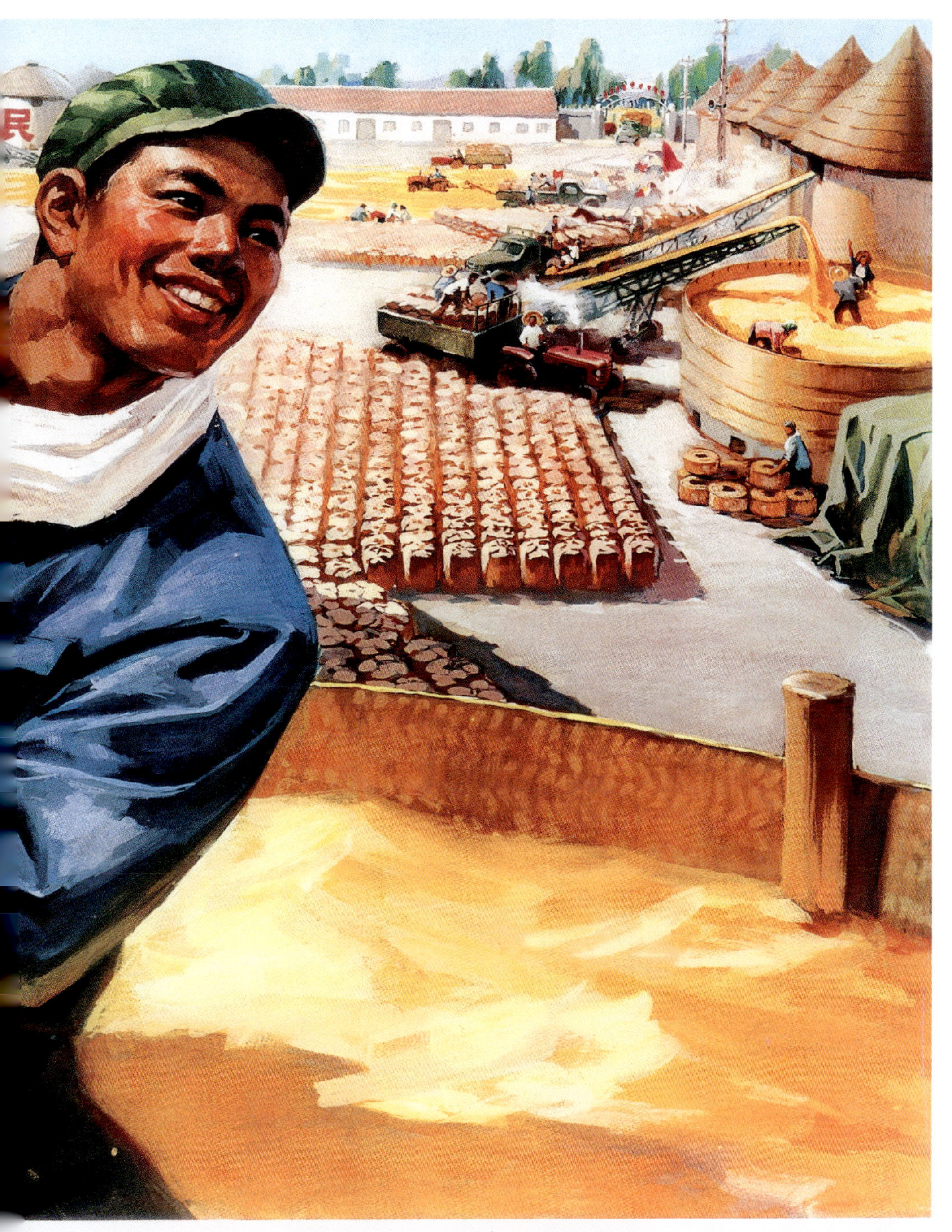

广积粮

Pages 298–299
Fight for rich harvests, store sufficient grain *On the silos in the background:* In the interests of the people, keep stocks of grain in case of war or natural catastrophe *Artists:* Yu Bao and Zhang Fang, Xinjin District Department of Education and Arts and Leisure Center, Liaoning Province; People's Art Publishing House, 1978 *Print run:* 45,000; 0.28 Yuan

Für reiche Ernten kämpfen, ausreichend Getreide speichern *Auf den Speichern im Hintergrund:* Im Interesse des Volkes Getreidevorräte für den Fall eines Krieges oder einer Naturkatastrophe anlegen *Gemalt von* Yu Bao und Zhang Fang, Erziehungsamt und Kulturhaus des Kreises Xinjin, Provinz Liaoning; Volkskunstverlag, 1978 *Auflage:* 45 000; 0,28 Yuan

Luttons pour avoir de riches moissons, stockons des céréales en quantité suffisante *Sur les entrepôts du fond :* Dans l'intérêt du peuple, faisons des provisions de céréales au cas où surviendrait une guerre ou une catastrophe naturelle *Peintres :* Yu Bao et Zhang Fang, Ministère de l'Éducation et Maison de la Culture du canton de Xinjin, province du Liaoning ; Éditions populaires d'Art, 1978 *Tirage :* 45 000 ; 0,28 yuan

As soon as the cockerel crows we start work in the field *Top left:* The east turns red as the cockerel crows; we participate actively in the production process and love our work *Artist:* Yang Furu *Published by:* Shanghai Picture Publishing House, 1st edn 1954, 4th edn 1955 *Print run:* 60,001–70,000; 1.80 Yuan

Sobald der Hahn kräht, gehen wir aufs Feld *Links oben:* Während der Hahn kräht, wird der Osten rot; Man nimmt aktiv an der Produktion teil und liebt die Arbeit *Gemalt von* Yang Furu *Herausgeber:* Bilderverlag Shanghai, 1. Aufl. 1954, 4. Aufl. 1955 *Auflage:* 60 001–70 000; 1,80 Yuan

Dès le chant du coq, nous nous rendons aux champs. *En haut à gauche :* Pendant le chant du coq, l'Orient rougit. On participe activement à la production et on aime le travail *Peintre :* Yang Furu *Éditeur :* Éditions des Images de Shanghai, 1ère éd. 1954, 4e éd. 1955 *Tirage :* 60 001–70 000 ; 1,80 yuan

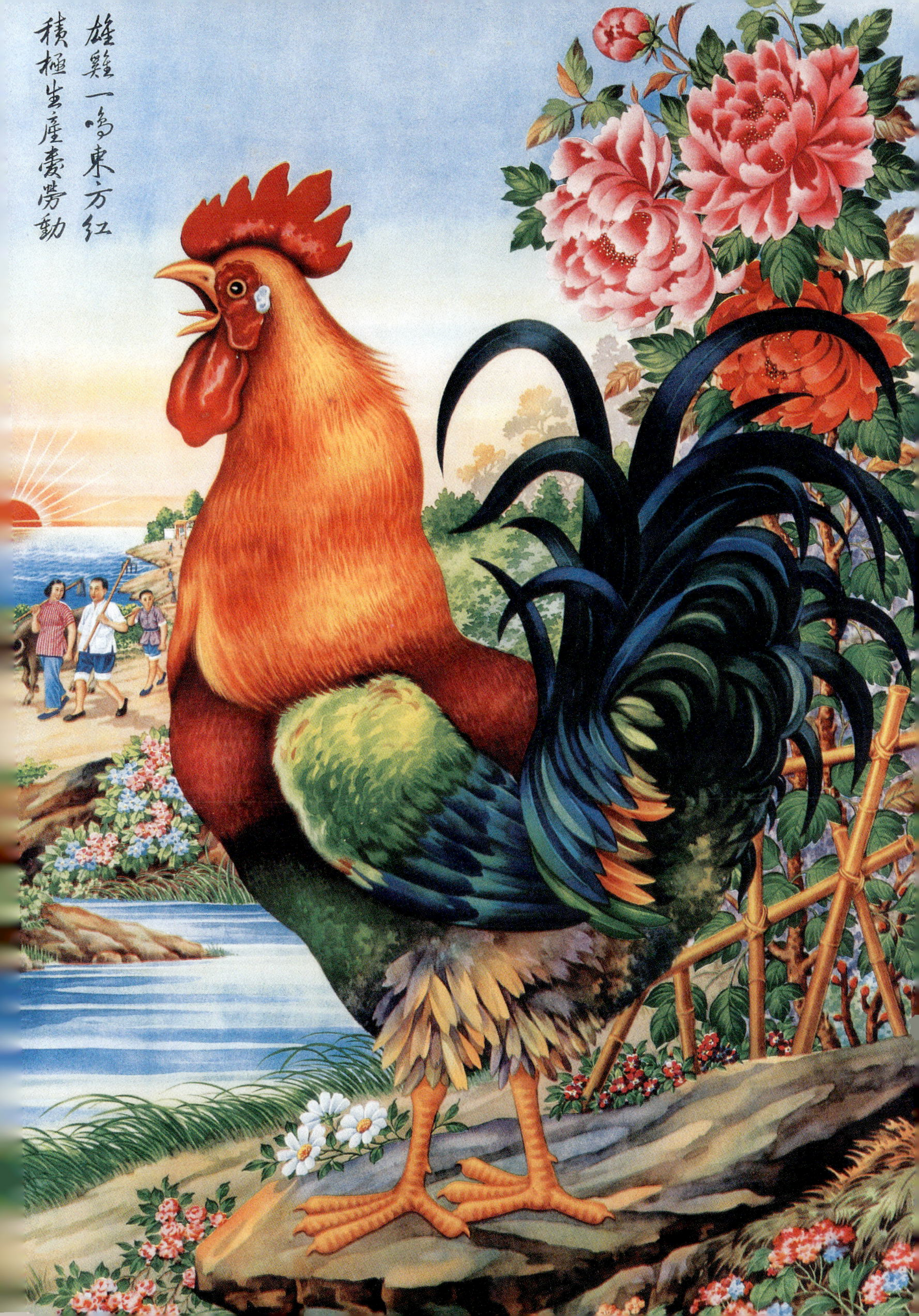
雄雞一鳴東方红
積極生產愛勞動

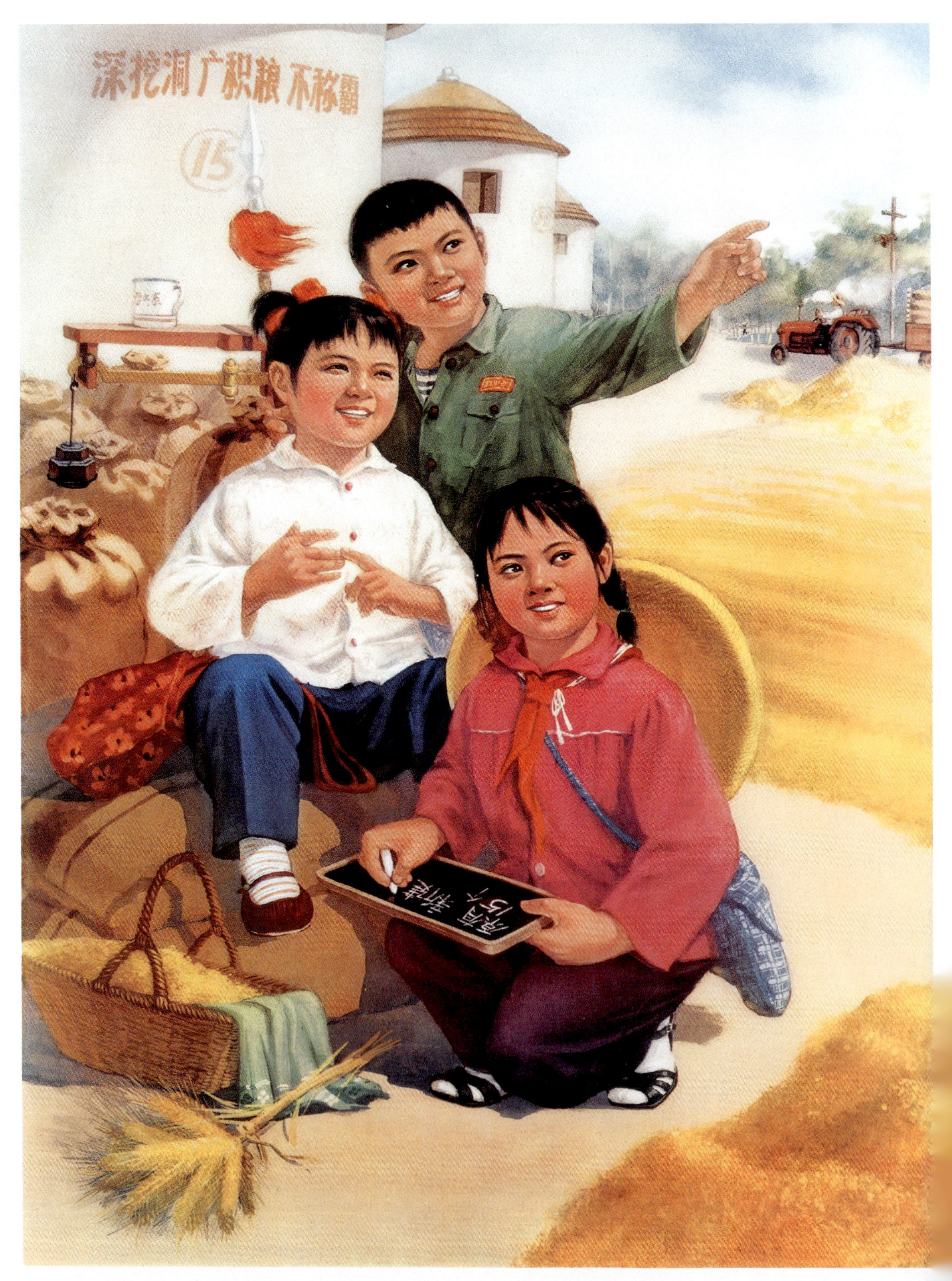

咱 队 又 添 新 粮 仓

Opposite
Our brigade has built another new grain silo *Top left:* Dig a sufficient number of trenches, store sufficient grain, and do not strive for world dominance (Mao Zedong) *Artists:* Liu Jicheng, Zhang Jinping, and Li Chaoxiang; People's Art Publishing House, 1975 *Print run:* 300,000; 0.14 Yuan

In unserer Brigade ist wieder ein neuer Getreidespeicher gebaut worden *Links oben:* Genügend Schutzgräben bauen, ausreichend Getreide speichern und nicht nach Vorherrschaft in der Welt streben (Mao Zedong) *Gemalt von* Liu Jicheng, Zhang Jinping und Li Chaoxiang; Volkskunstverlag, 1975 *Auflage:* 300 000; 0,14 Yuan

Notre brigade a encore construit un nouveau grenier à grain *En haut à gauche :* Construisez assez d'abris, stockez des céréales en quantité suffisante et n'aspirez pas à l'hégémonie mondiale (Mao Zedong) *Peintres :* Liu Jicheng, Zhang Jinping et Li Chaoxiang ; Éditions Populaires d'Art, 1975 *Tirage :* 300 000 ; 0,14 yuan

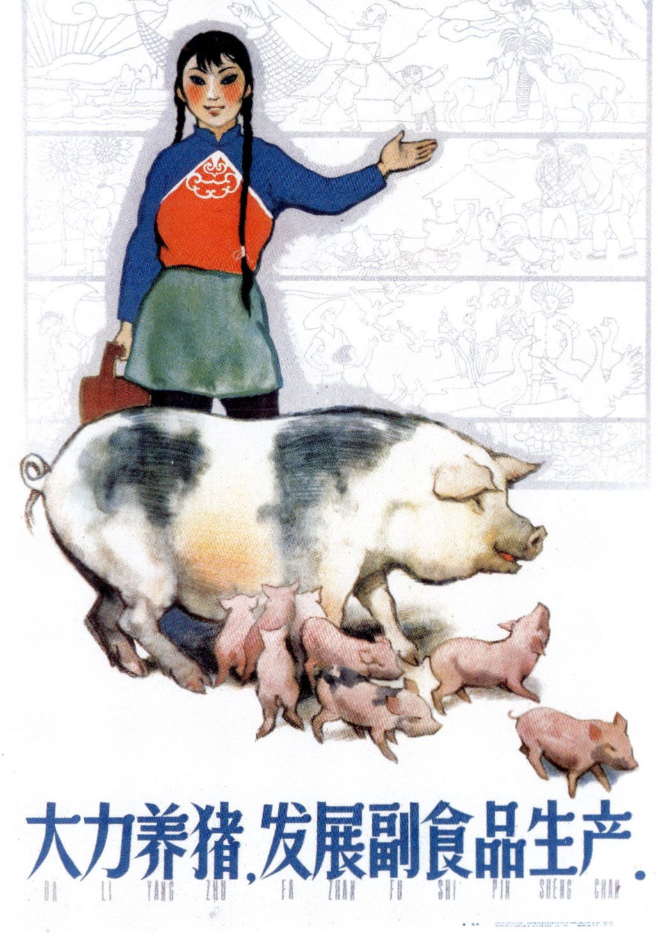

Intensify pig farming and improve food production *Artist:* Han Wu; Shanghai People's Art Publishing House, 1959; 0.11 Yuan

Die Schweinezucht verstärken und die Lebensmittelproduktion verbessern *Gemalt von* Han Wu; Volkskunstverlag Shanghai, 1959; 0,11 Yuan

Intensifions l'élevage porcin et améliorons la production agro-alimentaire *Peintre :* Han Wu ; Éditions Populaires d'Art de Shanghai, 1959 ; 0,11 yuan

Actively supporting pig farming *Artist:* Chen Qingxin; Shanghai People's Publishing House, 1973; 0.11 Yuan

Die Schweinezucht tatkräftig unterstützen *Gemalt von* Chen Qingxin; Volksverlag Shanghai, 1973; 0,11 Yuan

Encourageons activement l'élevage de porcs *Peintre :* Chen Qingxin ; Éditions Populaires de Shanghai, 1973 ; 0,11 yuan

Pages 306–307
Make a special effort to collect kitchen waste and support pig farming *Top left:* In the city kitchen waste is regarded as rubbish. In the country it is a treasure. Left-overs from rice, vegetables, and soup, melon skins and eggshells, old cabbage leaves, chicken and fish bones, and water used for washing rice make good feed for pigs. More pigs produce more manure and more manure produces more grain. For this reason pig farming is very important. *On building, right:* Canteen *On vat, bottom right:* Transform waste into treasure; support pig farming *Border, bottom:* Beijing Cattle Breeding Bureau, 1972

Mit vollem Einsatz Küchenabfälle sammeln und die Schweinezucht unterstützen *Oben links:* In der Stadt gelten Küchenabfälle als Abfall, auf dem Land sind sie ein Schatz. Reste von Reis, Gemüse und Suppen, Melonen- und Eierschalen, alte Gemüseblätter, Hühnerknochen, Gräten sowie Wasser vom Reiswaschen sind gute Grundlagen für Schweinefutter. Mehr Schweine geben mehr Dünger und mehr Dünger mehr Getreide. Deswegen muss hoher Wert auf Schweinezucht gelegt werden. *Rechts am Gebäude:* Kantine *Unten rechts am Krug:* Abfälle in Schätze verwandeln; Schweinezucht unterstützen *Unterer Rand:* Büro der Viehzucht Peking, 1972

Recueillons scrupuleusement les eaux de cuisson pour soutenir l'élevage porcin *En haut à gauche :* L'eau de cuisson est considérée en ville comme un déchet, à la campagne c'est un trésor. Les restes de riz, de légumes et de soupe, les épluchures de melon et les coquilles d'œufs, les vieilles feuilles de légumes, les os de poules, les arêtes ainsi que l'eau de rinçage du riz sont de bons aliments de base pour les porcs. Plus de porcs donnent plus d'engrais, et plus d'engrais plus de céréales. C'est pourquoi nous devons accorder beaucoup d'importance à l'élevage porcin. *Sur le bâtiment de droite :* Cantine *Sur le récipient en bas à droite :* Transformons les déchets en trésors ; soutenons l'élevage porcin *Marge inférieure :* Bureau de l'élevage, Pékin, 1972

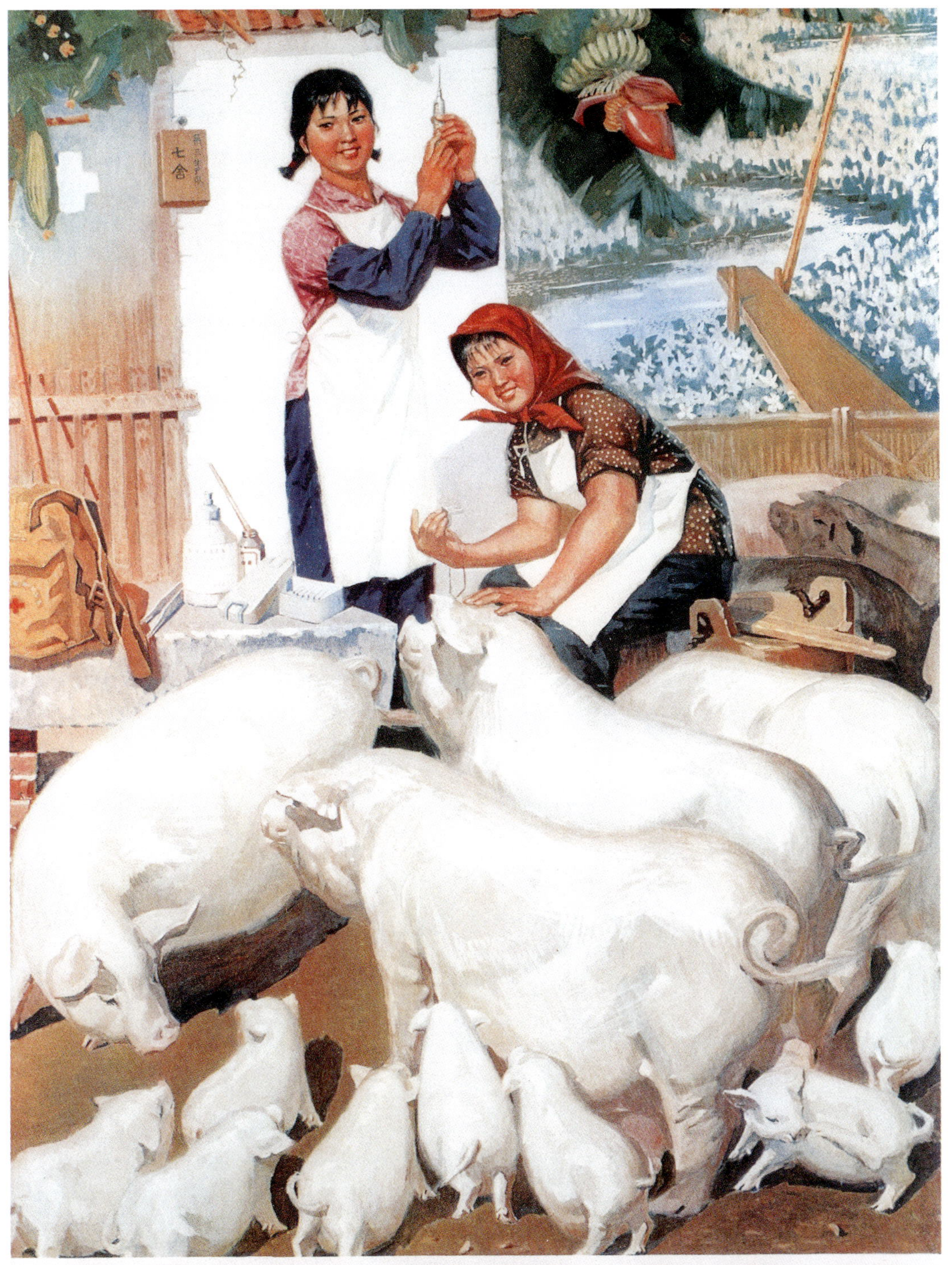

大力发展养猪事业

城市泔水是"废料"，送到农村变为"宝"，

剩饭剩菜米面汤，瓜皮菜叶鸡蛋壳，

鸡骨鱼刺淘米水，都是喂猪好饲料，

猪多肥多粮食多，支农养猪要搞好。

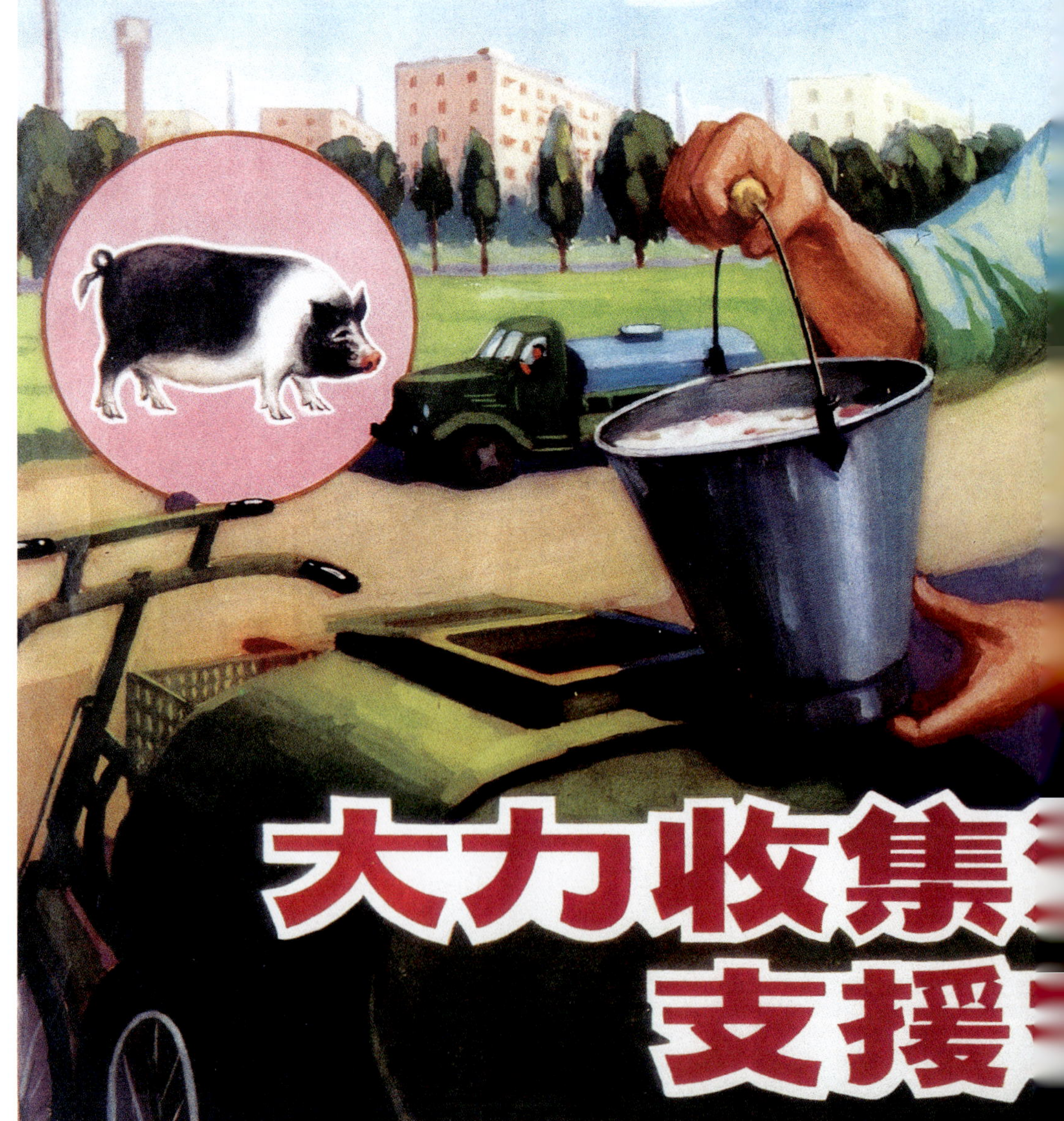

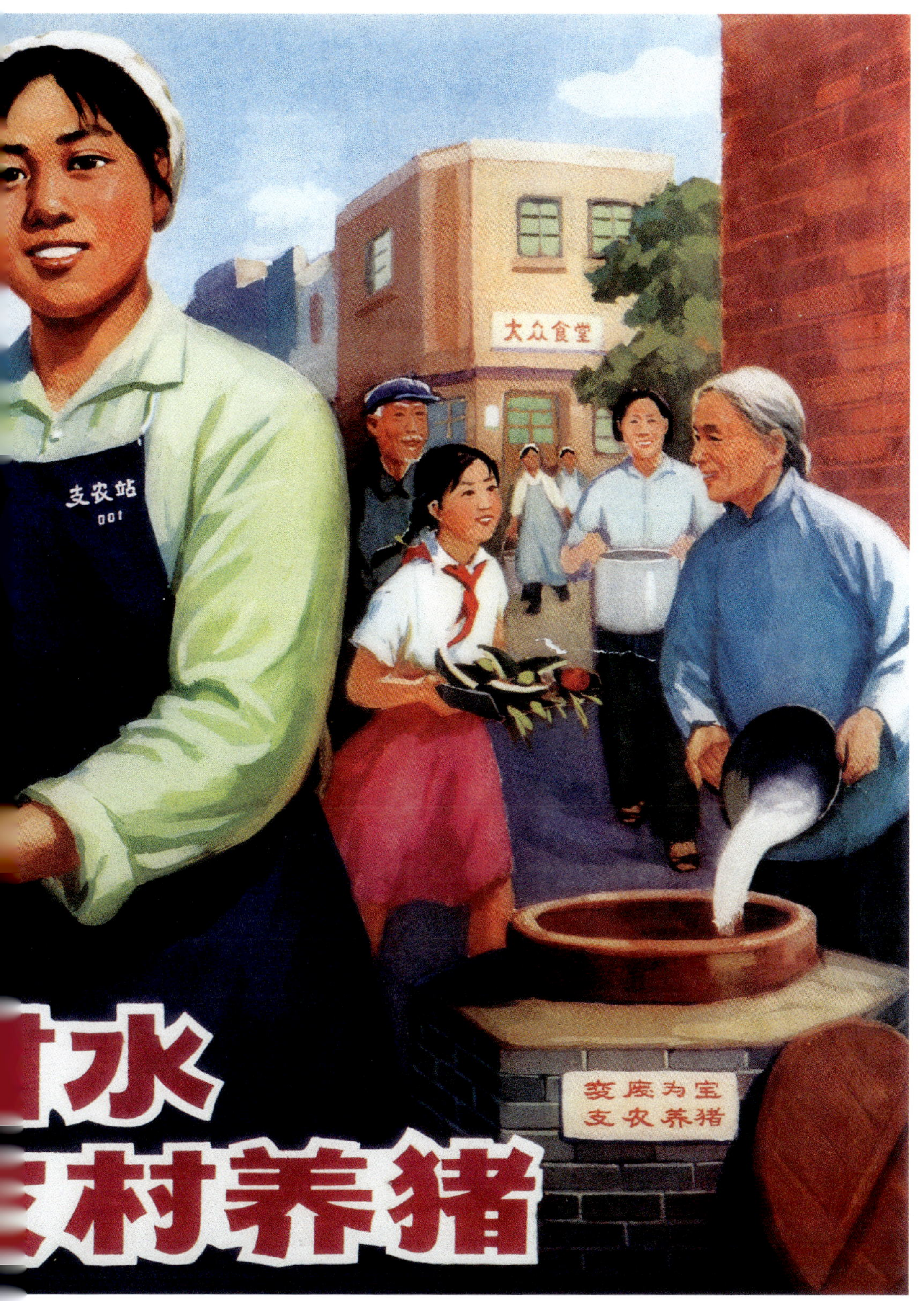
大众食堂
支农站
001
变废为宝
支农养猪
水
村养猪

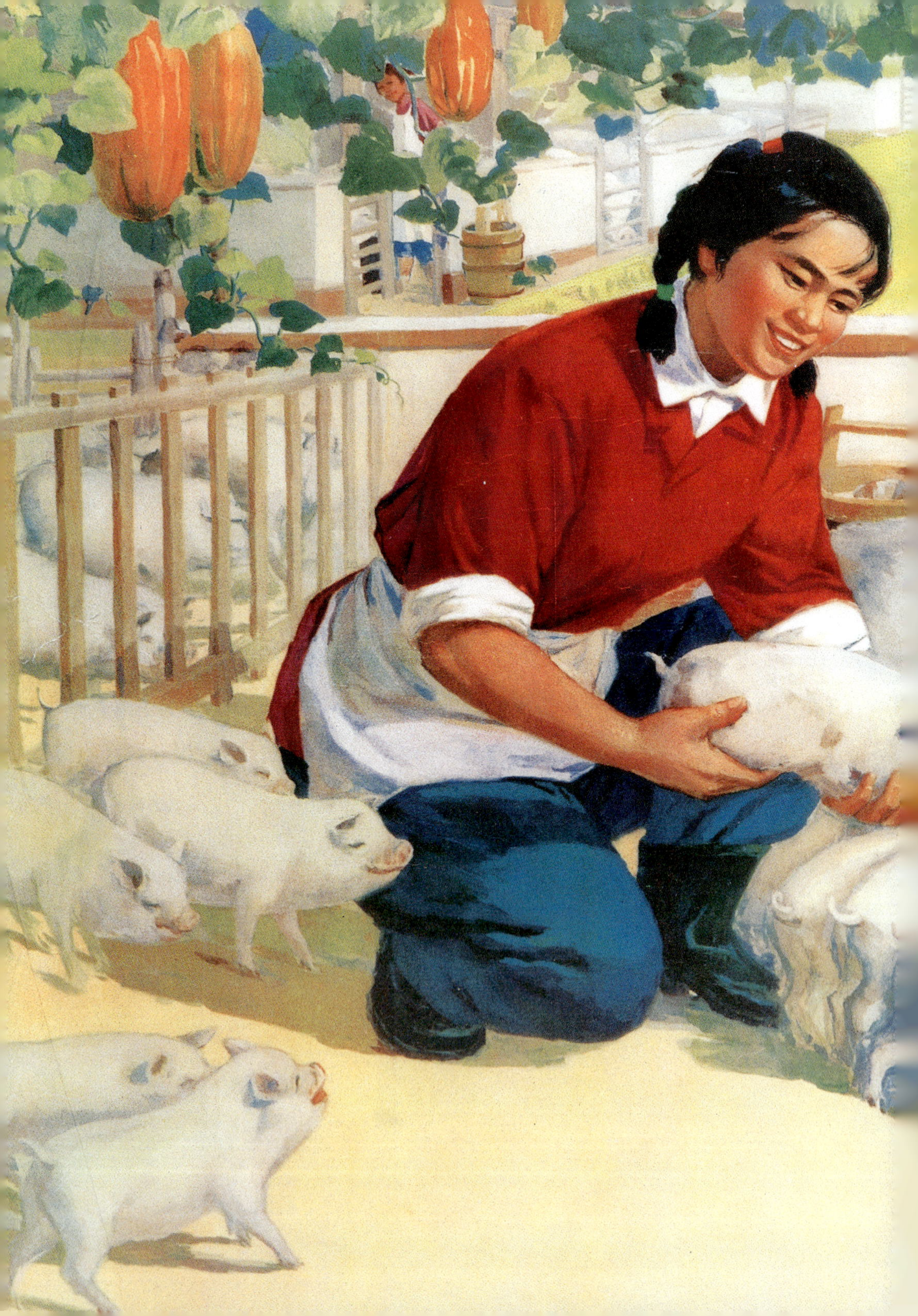

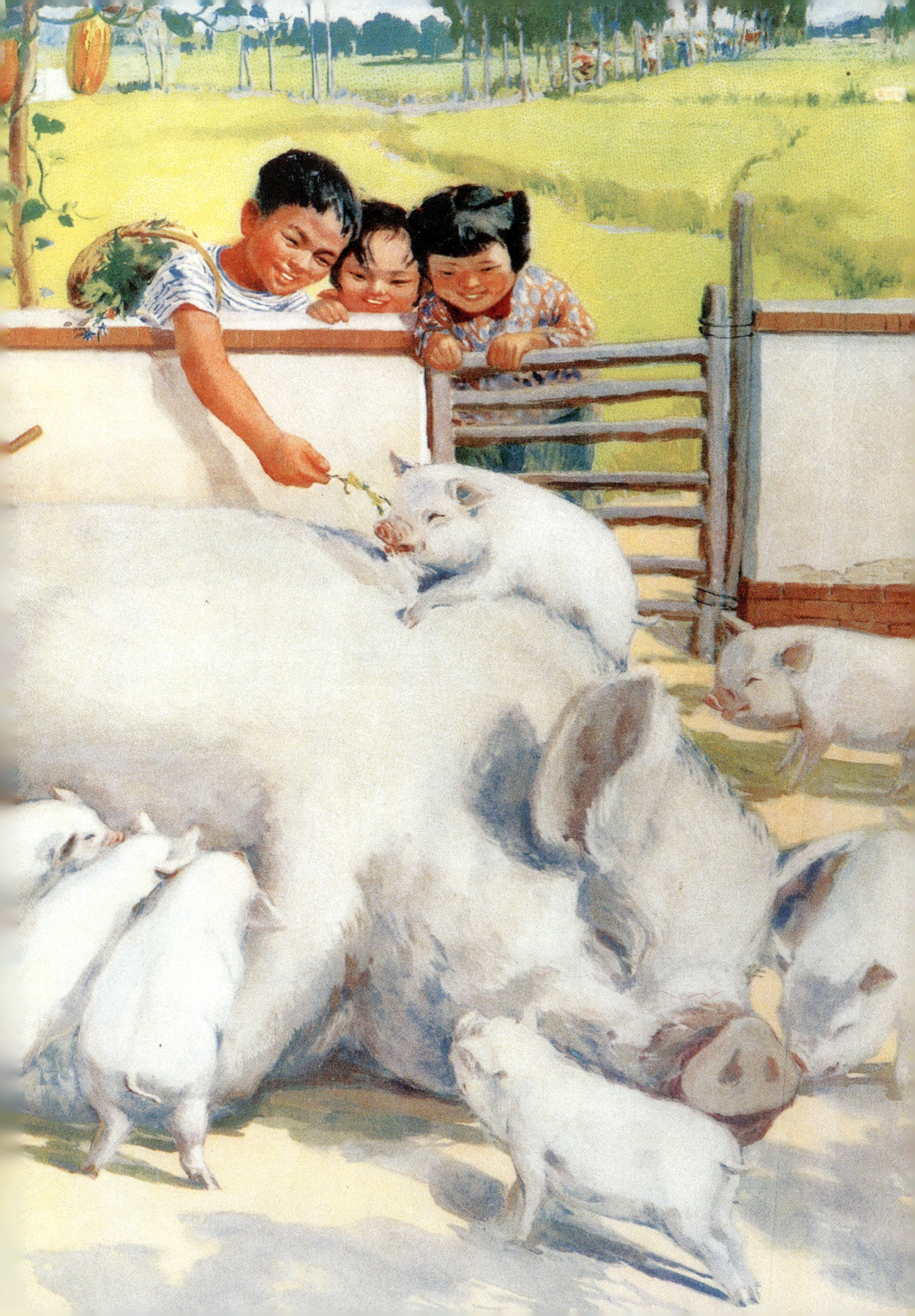

Pages 308–309
Farming pigs for the revolution
Artists: Deng Xiu and Zhang Ruiheng; Tianjin People's Art Publishing House, 1974; 0.14 Yuan

Für die Revolution Schweine züchten *Gemalt von* Deng Xiu und Zhang Ruihen; Volkskunstverlag Tianjin, 1974; 0,14 Yuan

Élevons des porcs pour la révolution *Peintres :* Deng Xiu et Zhang Ruiheng ; Éditions Populaires d'Art de Tianjin, 1974 ; 0,14 yuan

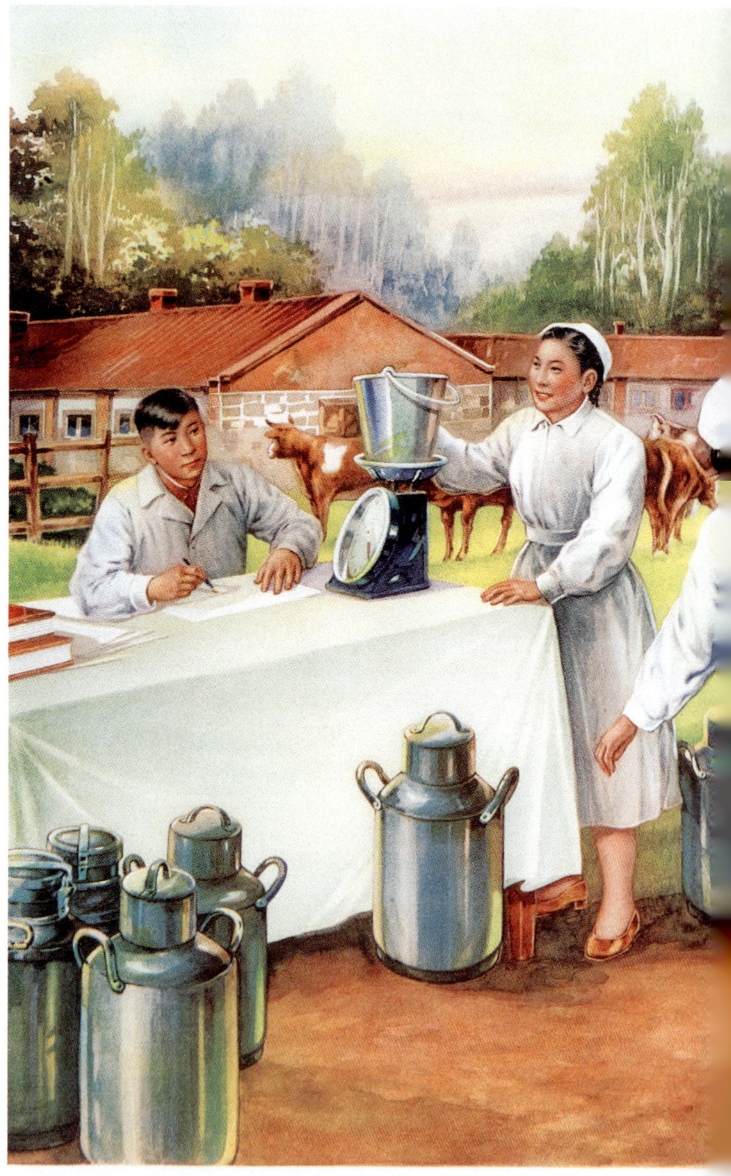

국영목장

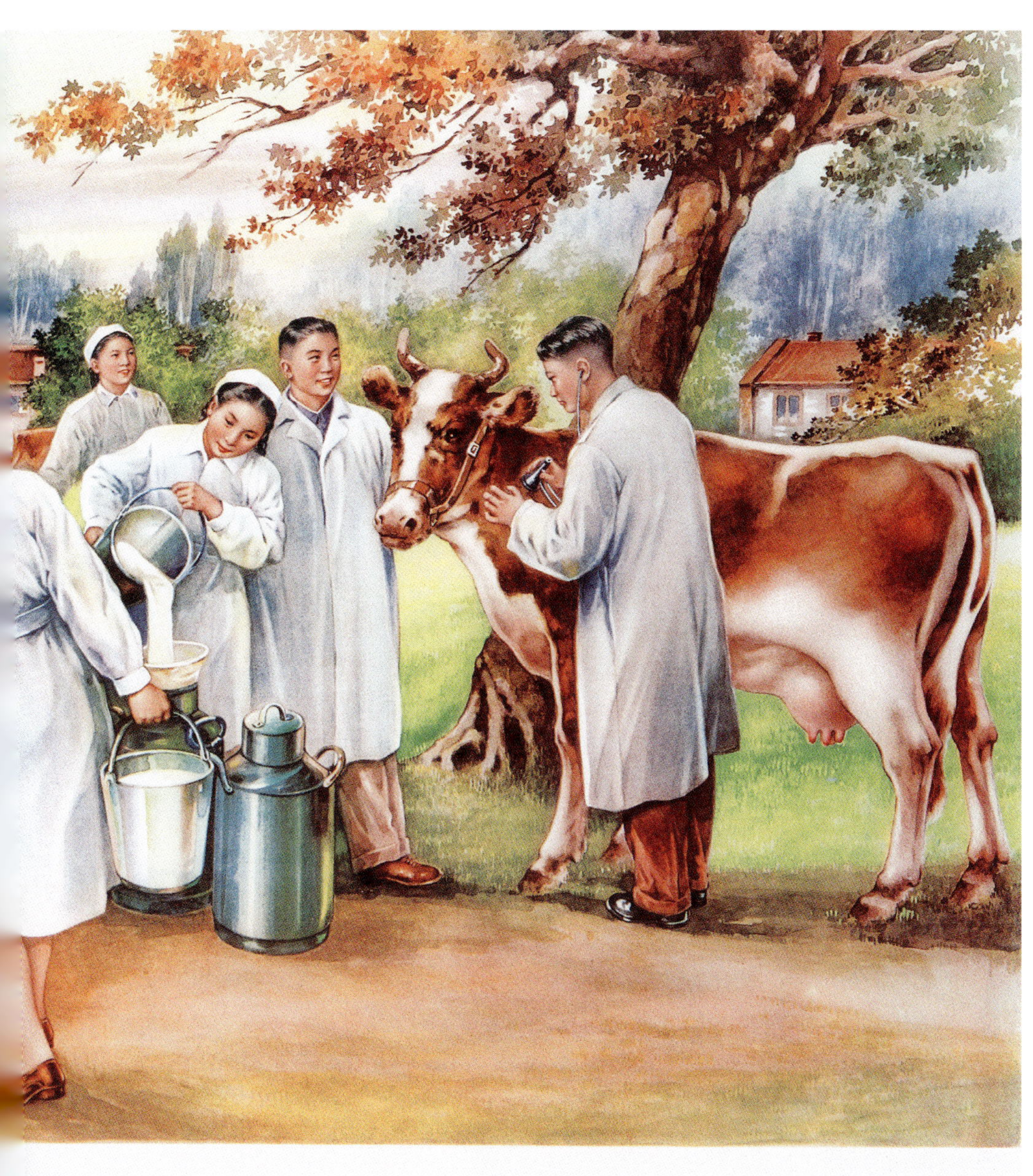

State cattle farm *Artist:* He Yimei; Shanghai Picture Publishing House, 1st edn 1956, 2nd edn 1956 *Print run:* 20,001–25,200

Staatliche Viehzüchterei *Gemalt von* He Yimei; Bilderverlag Shanghai, 1. Aufl. 1956, 2. Aufl. 1956 *Auflage:* 20 001–25 200

Élevage de bétail de l'État *Peintre :* He Yimei ; Éditions des Images de Shanghai, 1ère éd. 1956, 2e éd. 1956 *Tirage :* 20 001–25 200

Opposite
The brigade's deer farm
Artist: Wang Xichang of the Political Department of the Huanghai shipyard, Shandong province; Shandong People's Publishing House, 1976; 0.11 Yuan

Hirschzucht der Brigade
Gemalt von Wang Xichang, Politische Abteilung der Huanghai-Werft, Provinz Shandong; Volksverlag Shandong, 1976; 0,11 Yuan

Élévage de cerfs de la brigade
Peintre : Wang Xichang, du Département politique du chantier naval Huanghai, province du Shandong ; Éditions Populaires du Shandong, 1976 ; 0,11 yuan

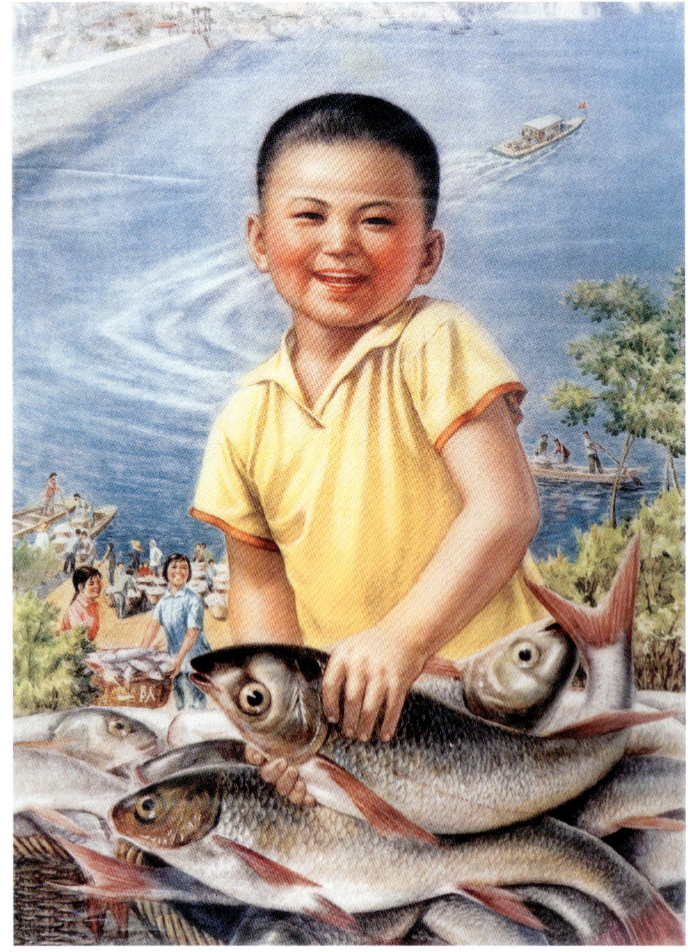

In the gorge there is now a reservoir; rich harvests for grain farming and fisheries, 1978

In der Schlucht entsteht ein Stausee, reiche Ernte im Getreideanbau und in der Fischerei, 1978

Dans la gorge, on aménage un lac de retenue, la culture céréalière et la pêche donnent de bons résultats, 1978

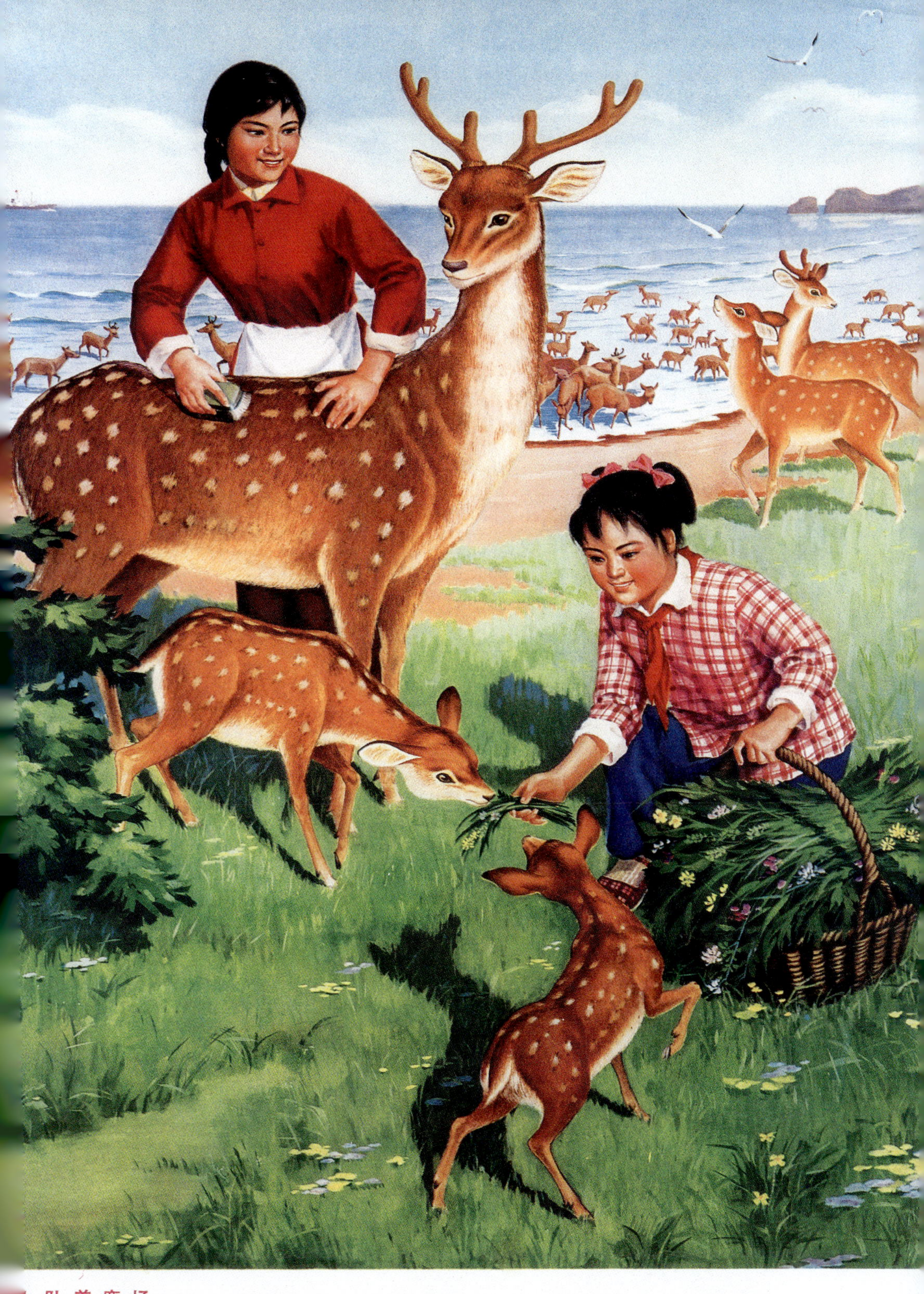

大队养鹿场

The magnificent hydroelectric power station on the Xin'an river* *Artist:* Pang Ka; Shanghai People's Art Publishing House, 1st edn 1964, 2nd edn 1964 *Print run:* 200,000; 0.15 Yuan
* A tributary of the Qiantang River in Zhejiang Province. Construction works for the dam and hydroelectric power station were completed in 1960.

Das prächtige Wasserkraftwerk vom Xin'an-Fluss* *Gemalt von* Pang Ka; Volkskunstverlag Shanghai, 1. Aufl. 1964, 2. Aufl. 1964 *Auflage:* 200 000; 0,15 Yuan
* Ein Nebenfluss des Flusses Qiantang, Provinz Zhejiang. Der Bau des Damms und des Wasserkraftwerks wurde 1960 vollendet.

La prestigieuse centrale hydroélectrique du fleuve Xin'an* *Peintre :* Pang Ka ; Éditions Populaires d'Art de Shanghai, 1ère éd. 1964, 2e éd. 1964 *Tirage :* 200 000 ; 0,15 yuan
* Affluent du fleuve Qiantang, province du Zhejiang. La centrale a été construite en 1960.

Pages 316–317
Fight for even greater iron and steel industry victories by holding aloft the glowing flag of Anshan Iron and Steel Works Combine's industrial constitution *Banner in the picture:* Long live the victory of "Anshan Iron and Steel Works Combine"! *Designed by:* The Art Working Group of the Workers at the No.1 Iron and Steel Works Combine; People's Art Publishing House, 1976; 0.11 Yuan

Die leuchtende Fahne der „Betriebsverfassung des Hüttenkombinats Anshan" hoch tragend größere Siege der Eisen- und Stahlindustrie erkämpfen
Transparent im Bild: Es lebe der Sieg der „Betriebsverfassung des Hüttenkombinats Anshan"! *Entwurf:* Kunst-Arbeitsgruppe der Arbeiter des Hüttenkombinats Nr.1; Volkskunstverlag, 1976; 0,11 Yuan

Brandissons la bannière radieuse du « comité d'entreprise du combinat métallurgique d'An Shan », et remportons de plus grandes victoires dans les secteurs de la sidérurgie et de l'industrie de l'acier
Banderole : Vive la victoire du « comité d'entreprise du combinat métallurgique d'An Shan » ! *Conception :* Groupe de travail artistique des ouvriers du combinat métallurgique n° 1 ; Éditions Populaires d'Art, 1976 ; 0,11 yuan

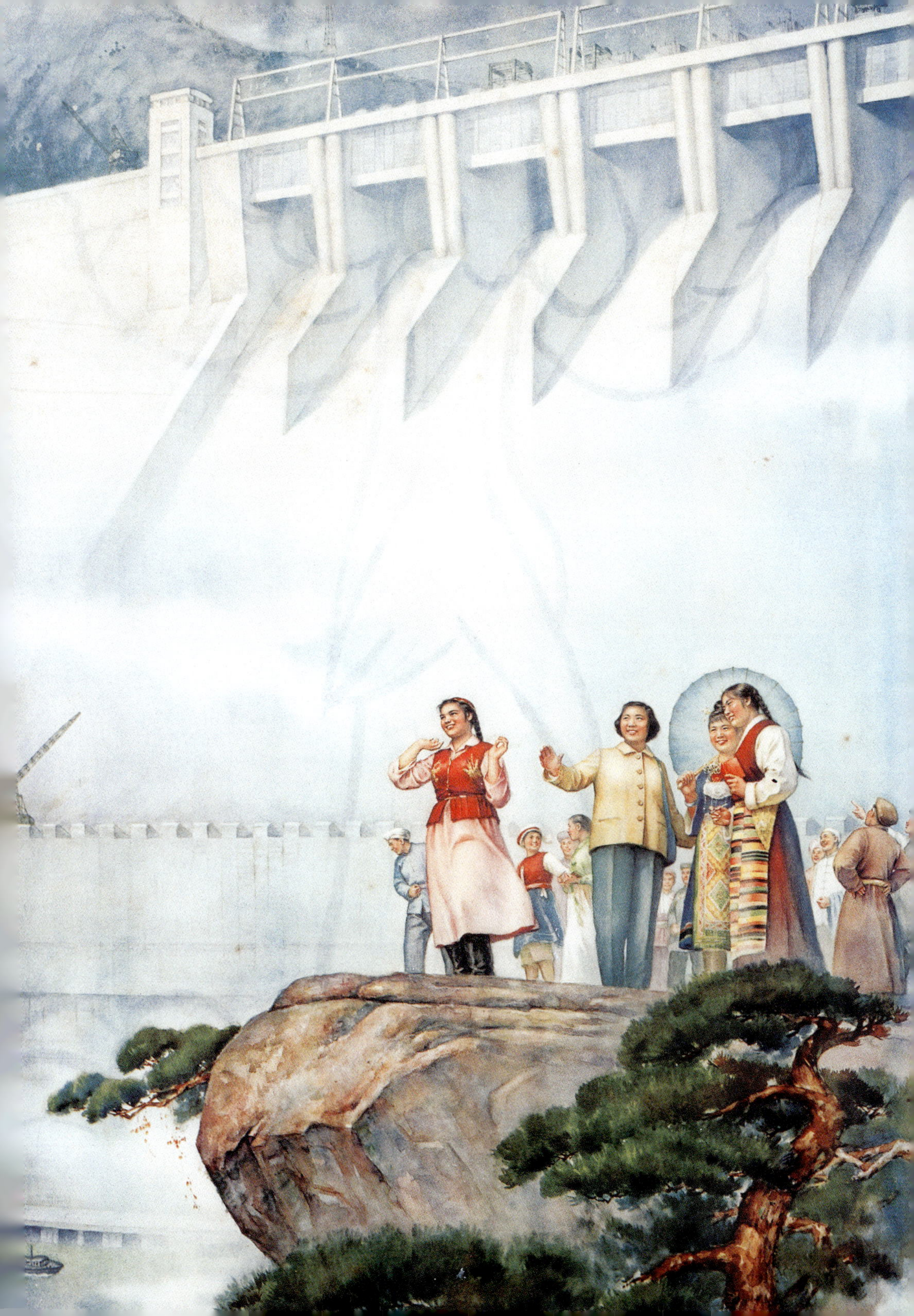

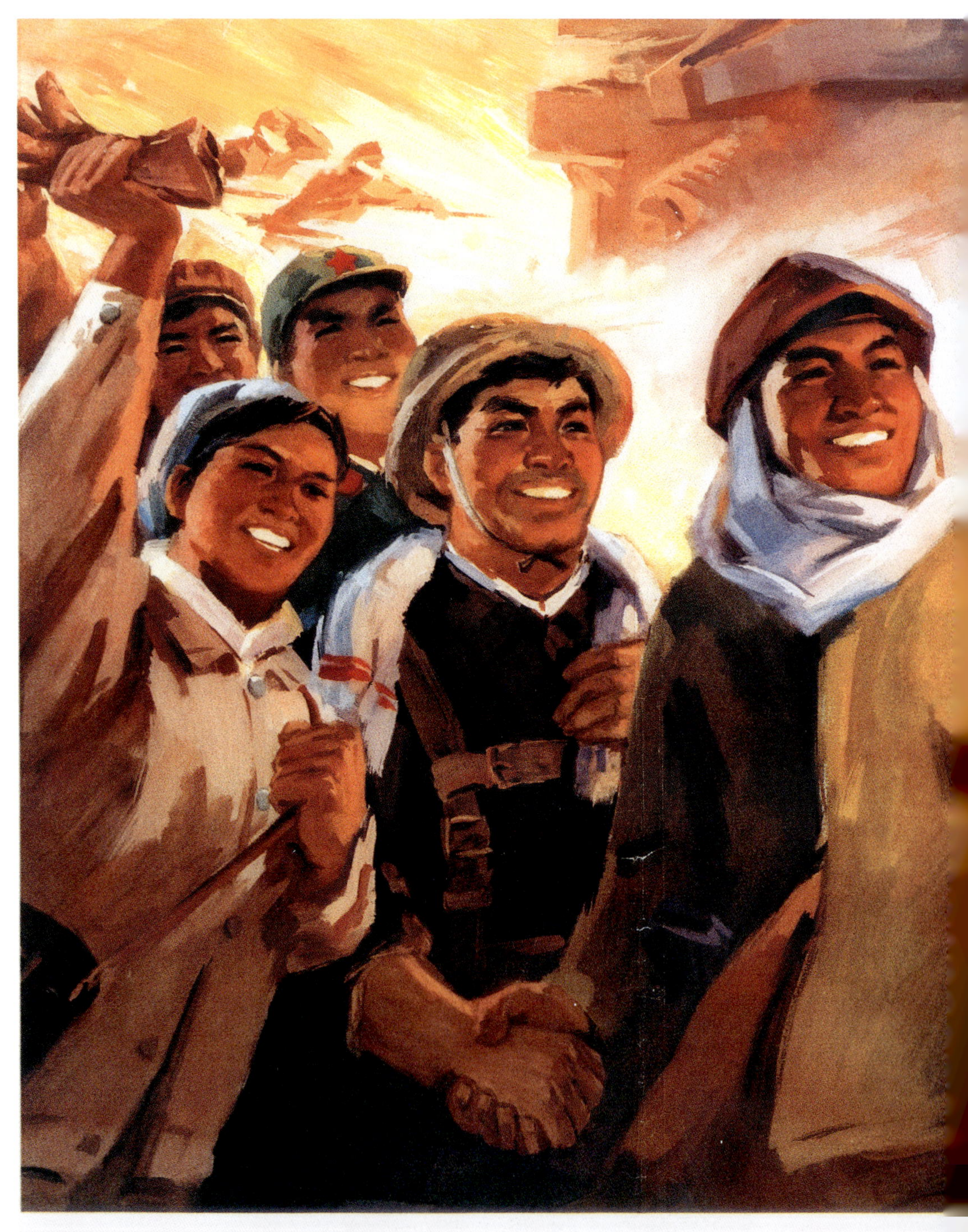

高举《鞍钢宪法》的光辉旗

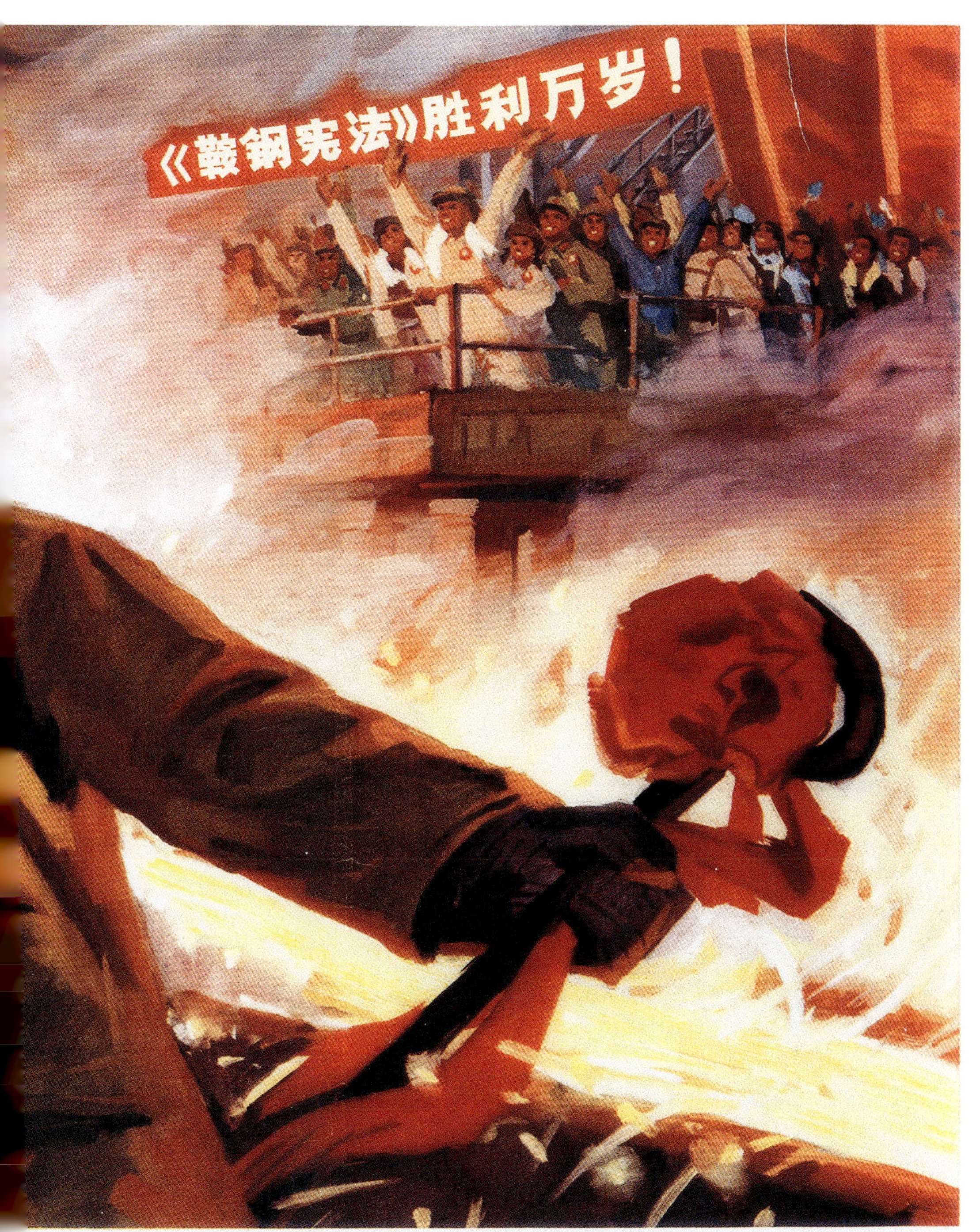

夺取钢铁工业的更大胜利

Opposite

In agriculture, learn from Dazhai and create districts like Dazhai throughout the land *Designed and published by:* Shanghai People's Publishing House, 1st edn 1972, 2nd edn 1973; 0.22 Yuan

In der Landwirtschaft von Dazhai lernen und im ganzen Land Bezirke vom Typ Dazhai aufbauen *Entwurf und Herausgeber:* Volksverlag Shanghai, 1. Aufl. 1972, 2. Aufl. 1973; 0,22 Yuan

Retenons de l'expérience agricole de Dazhai et édifions dans tout le pays des cantons du type de Dazhai *Conception et publication :* Éditions Populaires de Shanghai, 1ère éd. 1972, 2e éd. 1973 ; 0,22 yuan

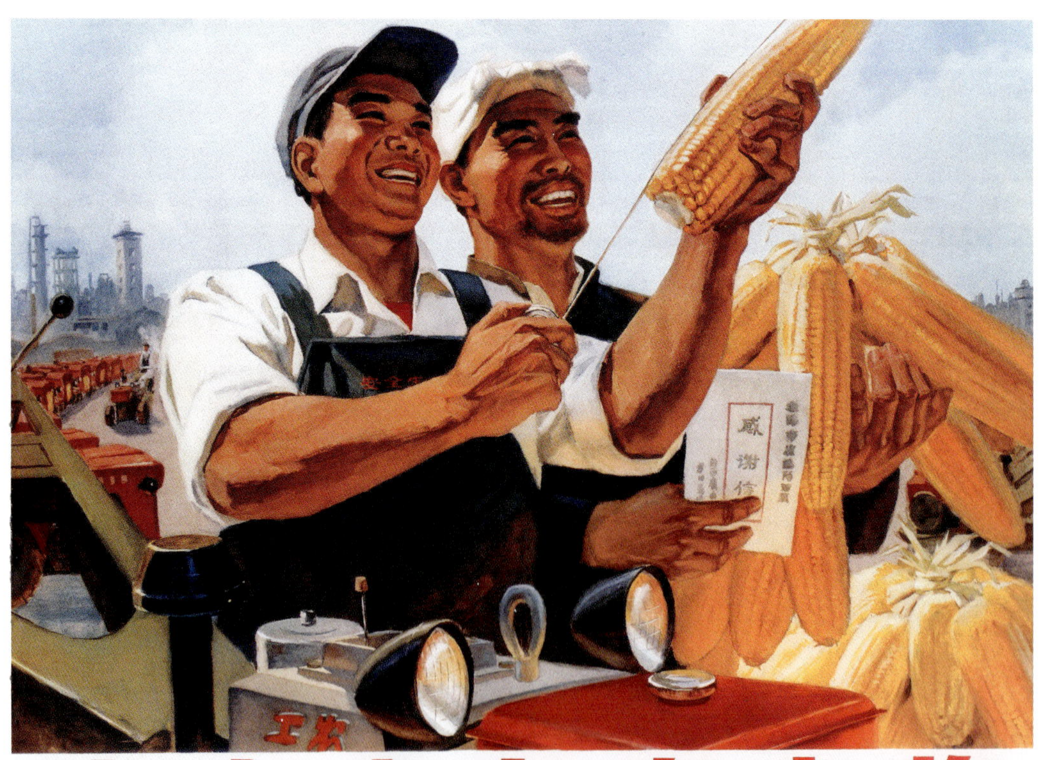

Actively support agriculture to achieve rich harvests *Letter in peasant's hand:* Thank you letter; Shanghai People's Publishing House

Die Landwirtschaft tatkräftig unterstützen, um reiche Ernten einzubringen *Brief in der Hand des Bauers*: Dankesbrief; Volksverlag Shanghai

Soutenons énergiquement l'agriculture pour avoir des récoltes abondantes *Lettre dans la main du paysan :* Lettre de remerciements ; Éditions Populaires de Shanghai

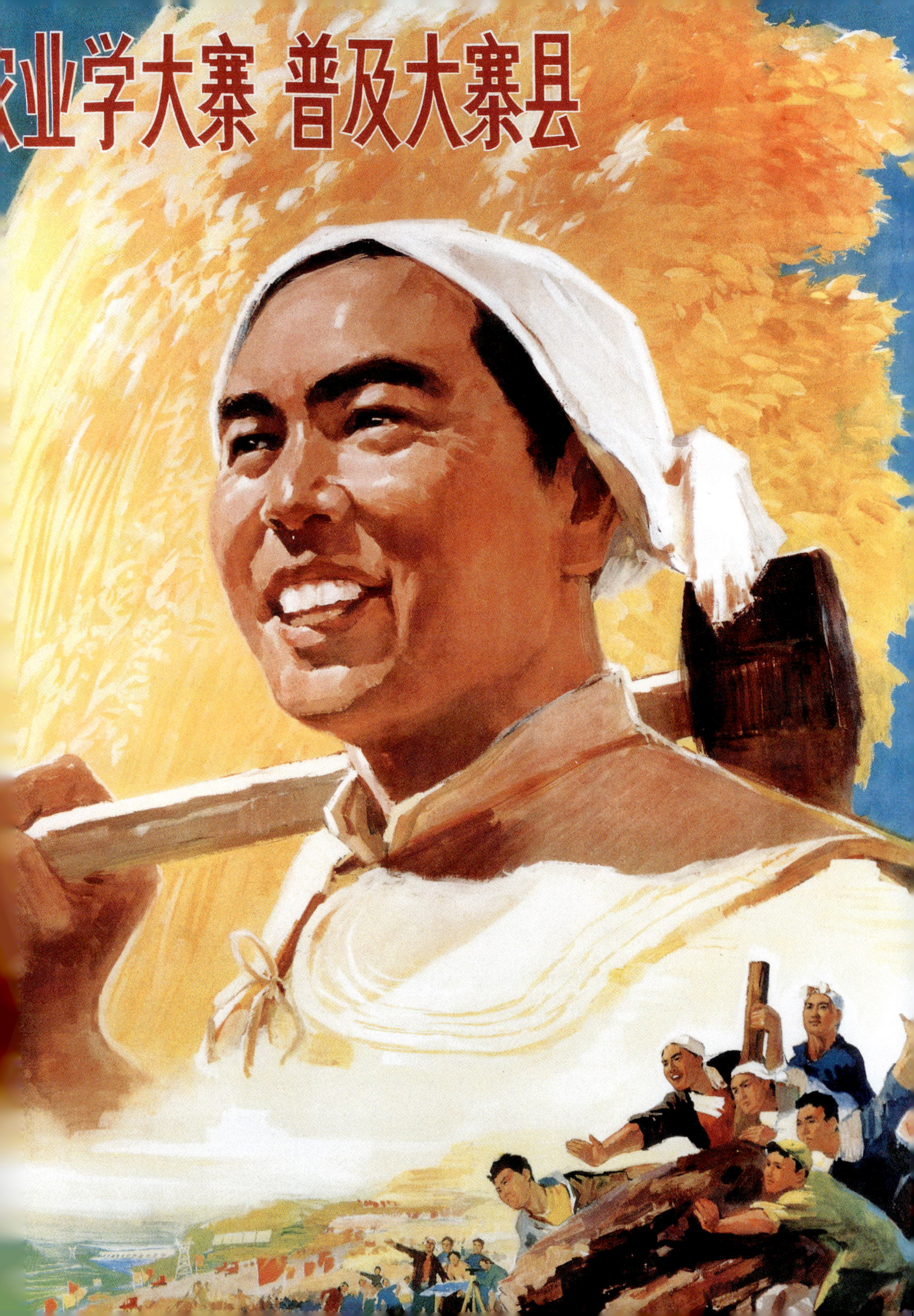
业学大寨 普及大寨县

Taking great strides as we follow the example of Daqing and make new contributions in support of agriculture *Artist:* Mo Shuzi; Shanghai People's Publishing House, 1977; 0.14 Yuan

Mit großen Schritten dem Vorbild Daqing folgen und neue Beiträge zur Unterstützung der Landwirtschaft leisten *Gemalt von* Mo Shuzi; Volksverlag Shanghai, 1977; 0,14 Yuan

Suivons à grands pas l'exemple de Daqing et apportons de nouvelles contributions au soutien de l'agriculture *Peintre :* Mo Shuzi ; Éditions Populaires de Shanghai, 1977 ; 0,14 yuan

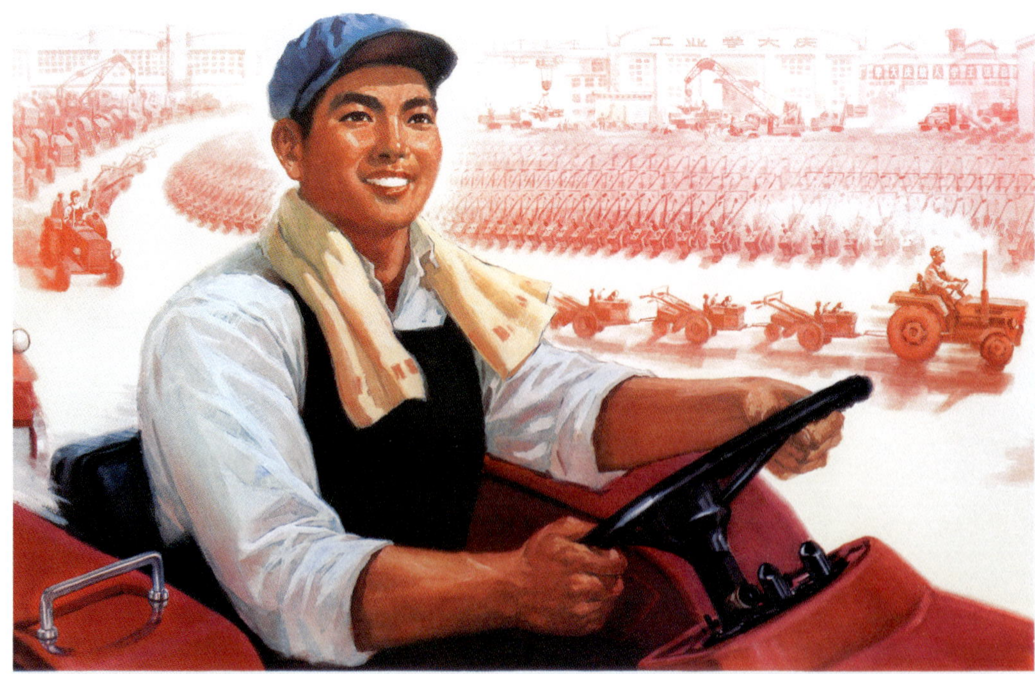

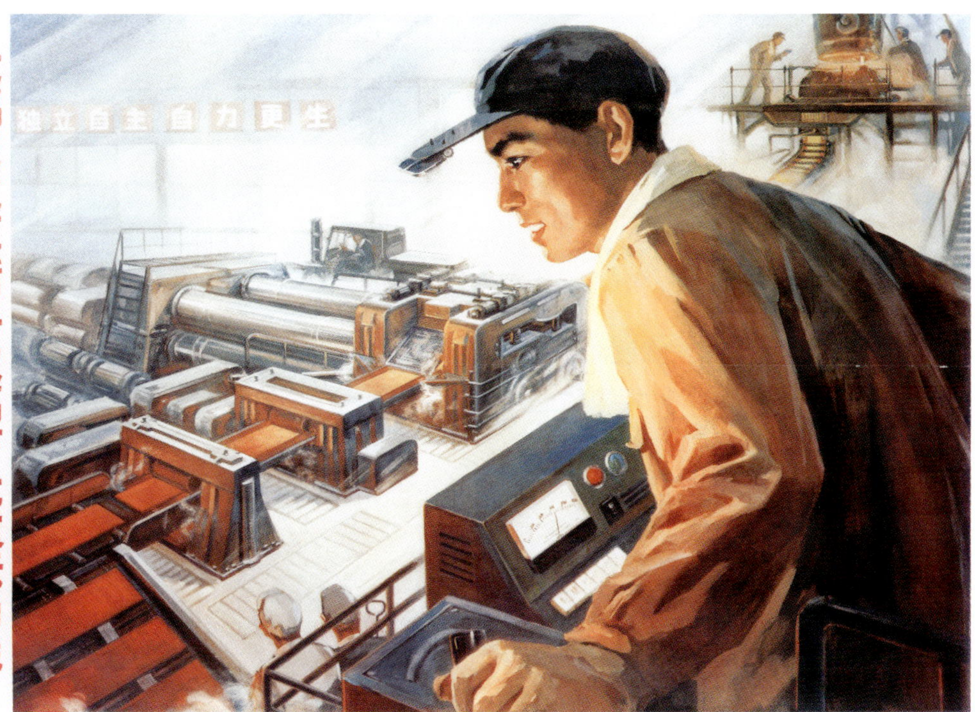

Introduce far-reaching technical innovations, and strive for high quantities, quality and low energy consumption *Banner in background:* Independence and autonomy, faith in our own strength *Artist:* a worker of the Engineering Works, Shanghai; Shanghai People's Publishing House, 1972 *Print run:* 10,000; 0.11 Yuan

Weitgehend technische Neuerungen einführen, nach hoher Quantität und Qualität sowie niedrigem Verbrauch von Energien streben *Transparent im Hintergrund:* Unabhängigkeit und Selbstständigkeit, Vertrauen auf die eigene Kraft *Gemalt* in der Maschinenfabrik Shanghai; Volksverlag Shanghai, 1972 *Auflage:* 10 000; 0,11 Yuan

Introduisons le progrès technique à grande échelle, soucions-nous de quantité et de qualité et veillons à économiser l'énergie *Banderole au fond :* Indépendance et autonomie, ayons confiance en notre propre force *Peint* dans l'usine de construction de machines de Shanghai ; Éditions Populaires de Shanghai, 1972 *Tirage :* 10 000 ; 0,11 yuan

Pages 322–323
Make every effort to develop the coal industry *Top left:* Local industry must find a way to establish an independent system. Mao Zedong; Zhejiang People's Art Publishing House, 1976

Mit vollem Einsatz die Kohlenindustrie entwickeln *Oben links:* Die örtliche Industrie muss einen Weg finden, um ein selbstständiges System zu errichten. Mao Zedong; Volkskunstverlag Zhejiang, 1976

Mettons tout en œuvre pour développer l'industrie houillère *En haut à gauche :* L'industrie locale doit trouver une voie pour ériger un système autonome. Mao Zedong; Éditions Populaires d'Art du Zhejiang, 1976

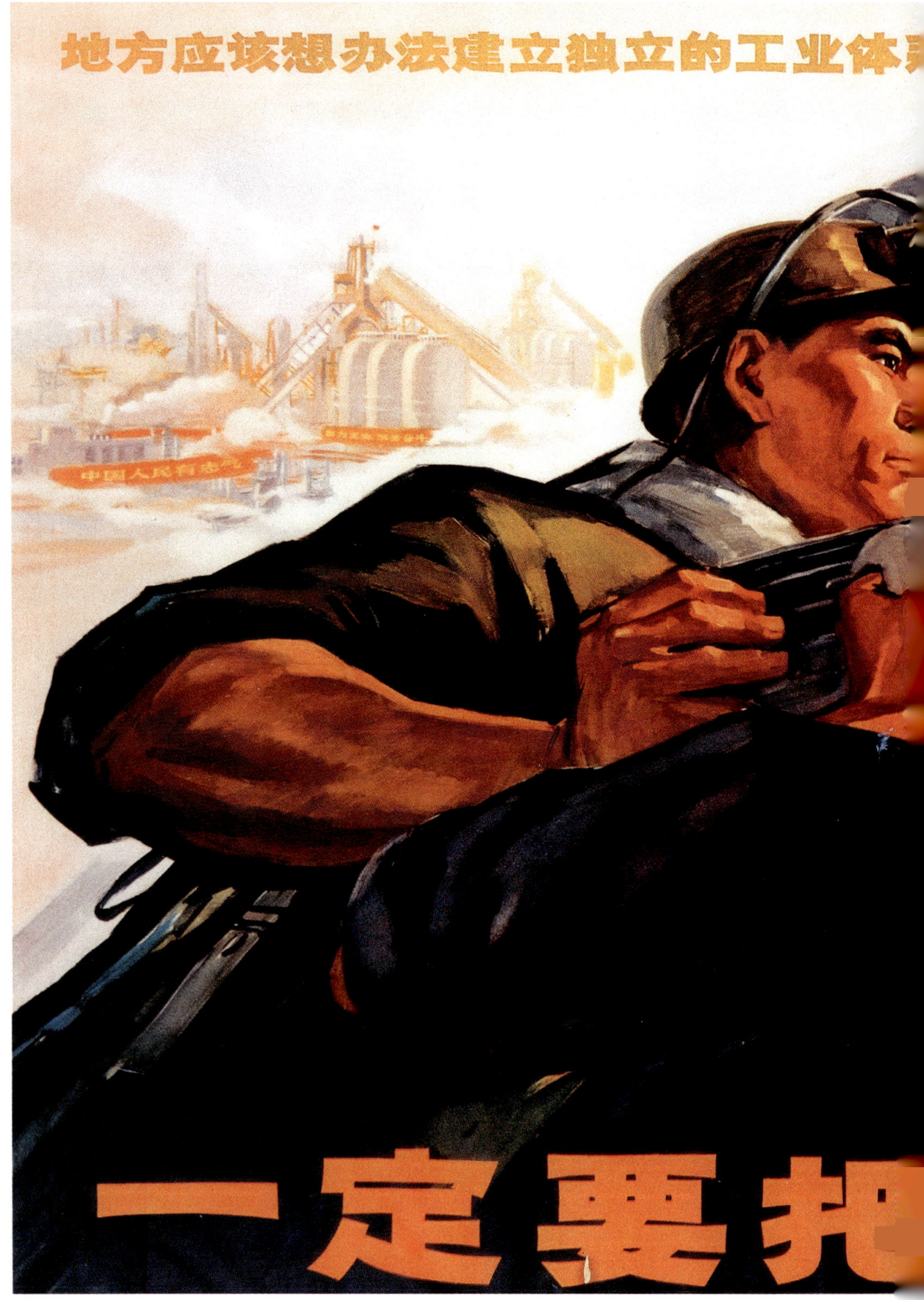
地方应该想办法建立独立的工业体
中国人民有志气
一定要

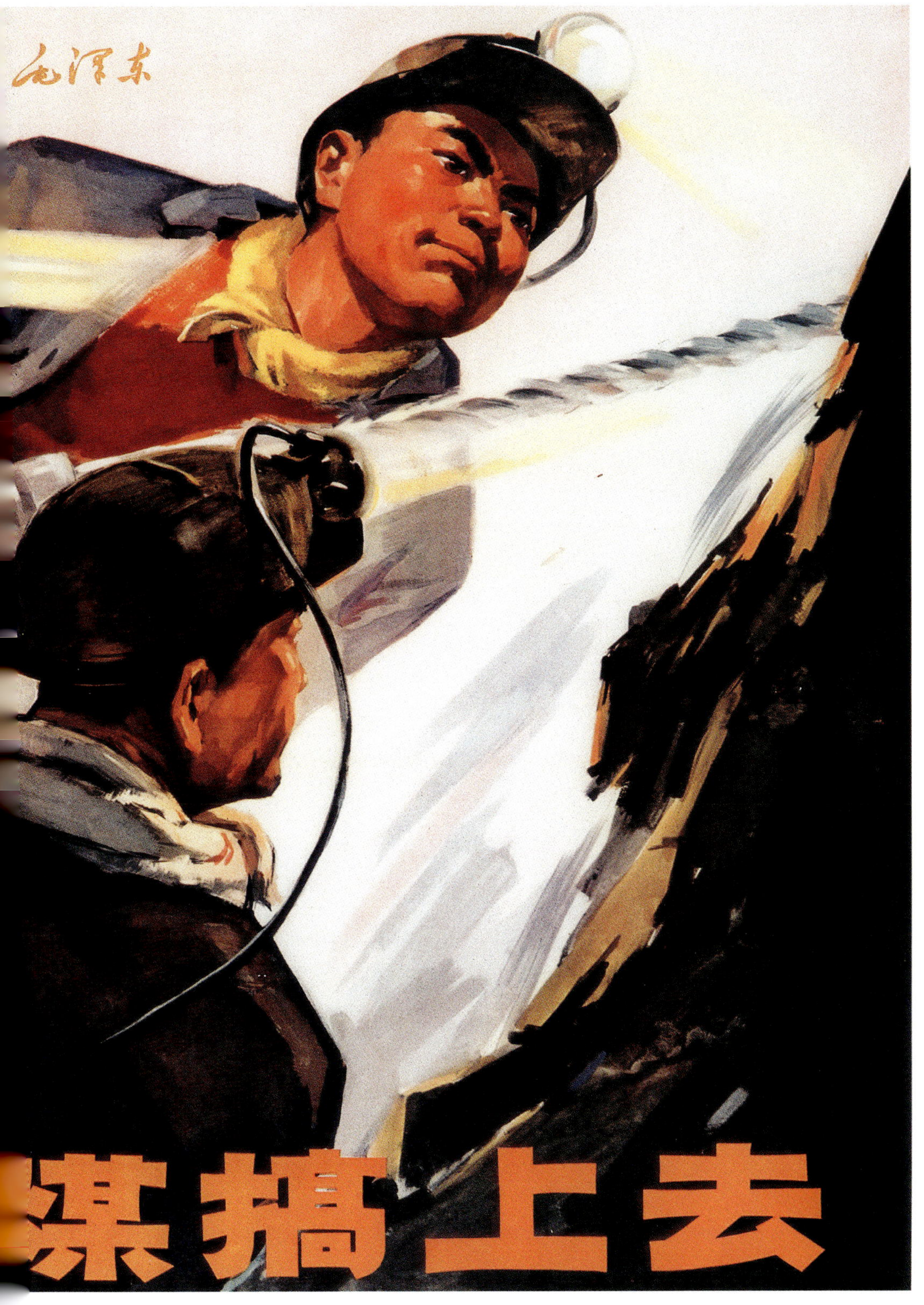
毛泽东
搞上去

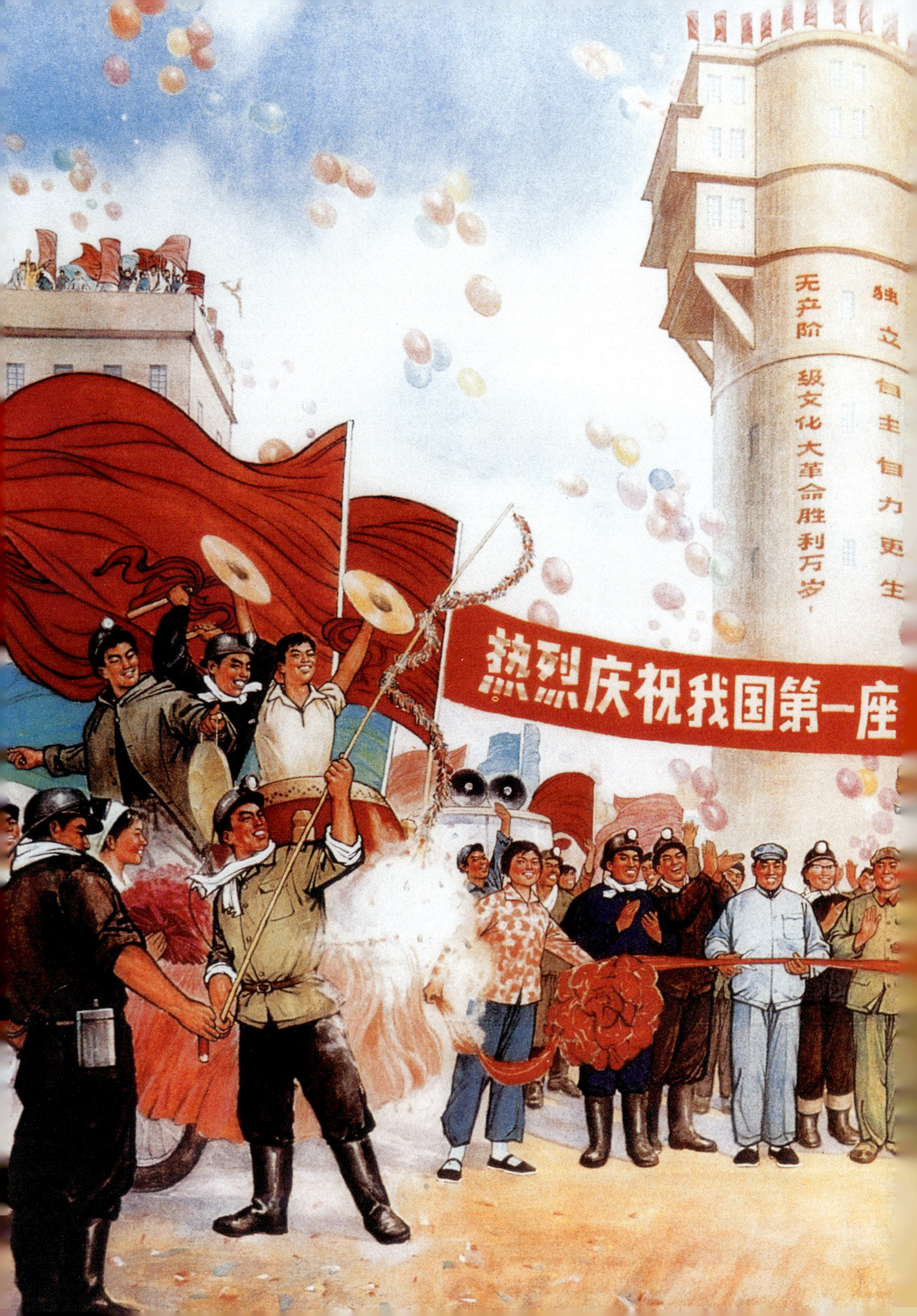
独立自主自力更生
无产阶级文化大革命胜利万岁!
热烈庆祝我国第一座

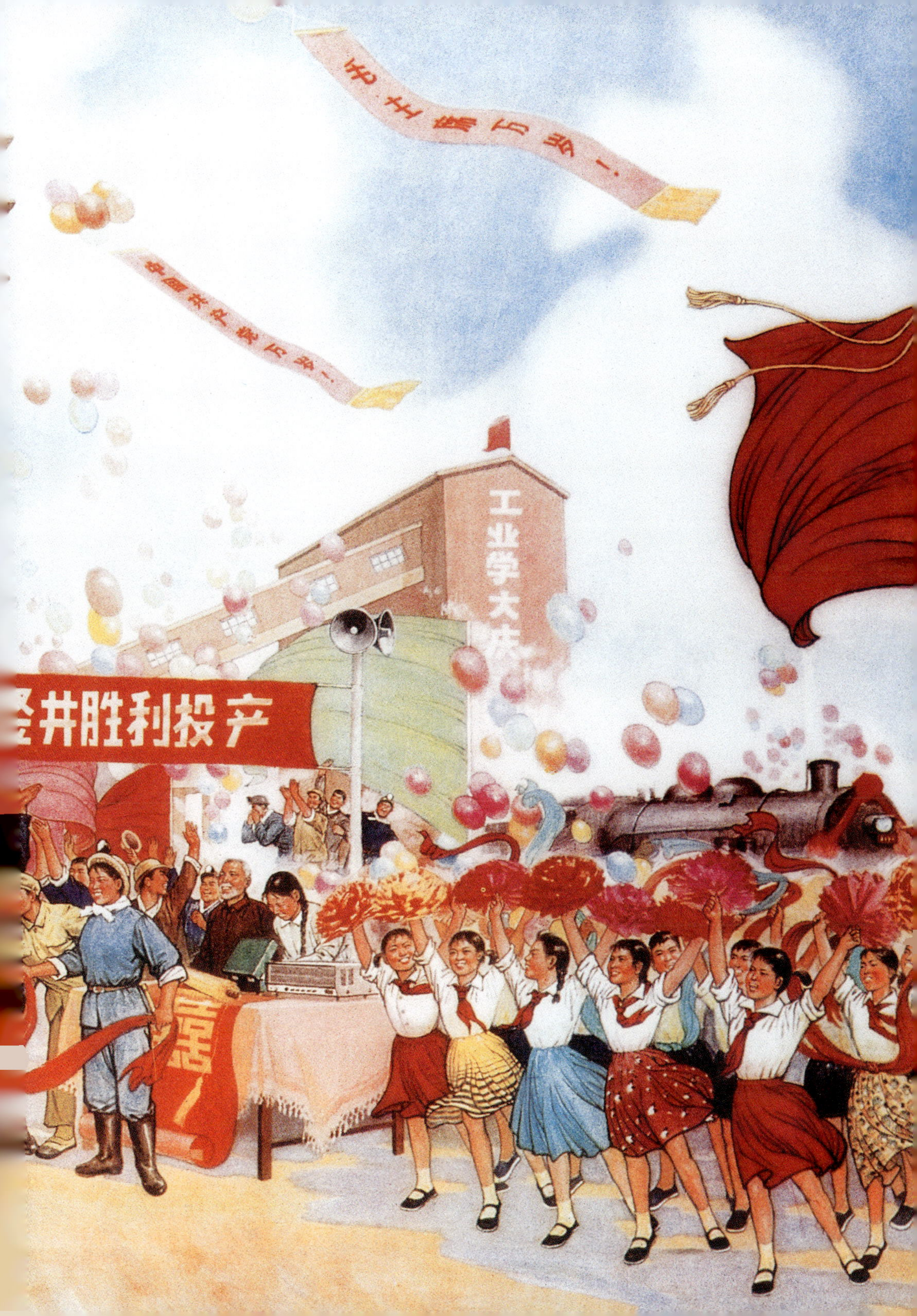
毛主席万岁！
中國共产党万岁！
工业学大庆
井胜利投产

Pages 324–325
A triumphant song ascends to the sky above *Banner, center:* Celebrating with great joy the successful opening of China's first 1,000-metre shaft *On shaft:* Long live the great proletarian cultural revolution! Independence and autonomy, faith in our own strength *On building, right:* Learn from the industry of Daqing! *Artists:* The workers Jin Xiangyin, Zhang Jingtang, Wang Chuntian, Wen Daokuan, and Sun Jiefan; Liaoning People's Publishing House, 1976; 0.11 Yuan

Ein Triumphlied steigt zum Himmel empor *Transparent Mitte*: Mit großer Freude die erfolgreiche Inbetriebnahme des ersten 1000-Meter-Schachtes Chinas feiern *Auf dem Schacht*: Es lebe die Große Proletarische Kulturrevolution! Unabhängigkeit und Selbstständigkeit, Vertrauen auf die eigene Kraft *Auf dem Gebäude rechts*: Lernt in der Industrie von Daqing! *Gemalt von* den Arbeitern Jin Xiangyin, Zhang Jingtang, Wang Chuntian, Wen Daokuan und Sun Jiefan; Volksverlag Liaoning, 1976; 0,11 Yuan

Un chant de triomphe s'élève vers le ciel *Banderole du milieu :* Célébrons dans l'allégresse la mise en exploitation du premier puits de mine de 1000 mètres de Chine *Sur le puits :* Vive la grande révolution culturelle prolétarienne ! Indépendance et autonomie, comptons sur notre propre force *Sur le bâtiment de droite :* Inspirez-vous de l'expérience industrielle de Daqing ! *Peintres :* les ouvriers Jin Xiangyin, Zhang Jingtang ; Wang Chuntian, Wen Daokuan et Sun Jiefan, Éditions Populaires du Liaoning, 1976 ; 0,11 yuan

New flowers bloom magnificently *Artist:* Hu Wenzhi; Hubei People's Publishing House, 1st edn 1974, 2nd edn 1975; 0.14 Yuan

Neue Blumen blühen prächtig *Gemalt von* Hu Wenzhi; Volksverlag Hubei, 1. Aufl. 1974, 2. Aufl. 1975; 0,14 Yuan

Les fleurs nouvelles sont magnifiques *Peintre :* Hu Wenzhi ; Éditions Populaires du Hubei, 1ère éd. 1974, 2e éd. 1975 ; 0,14 yuan

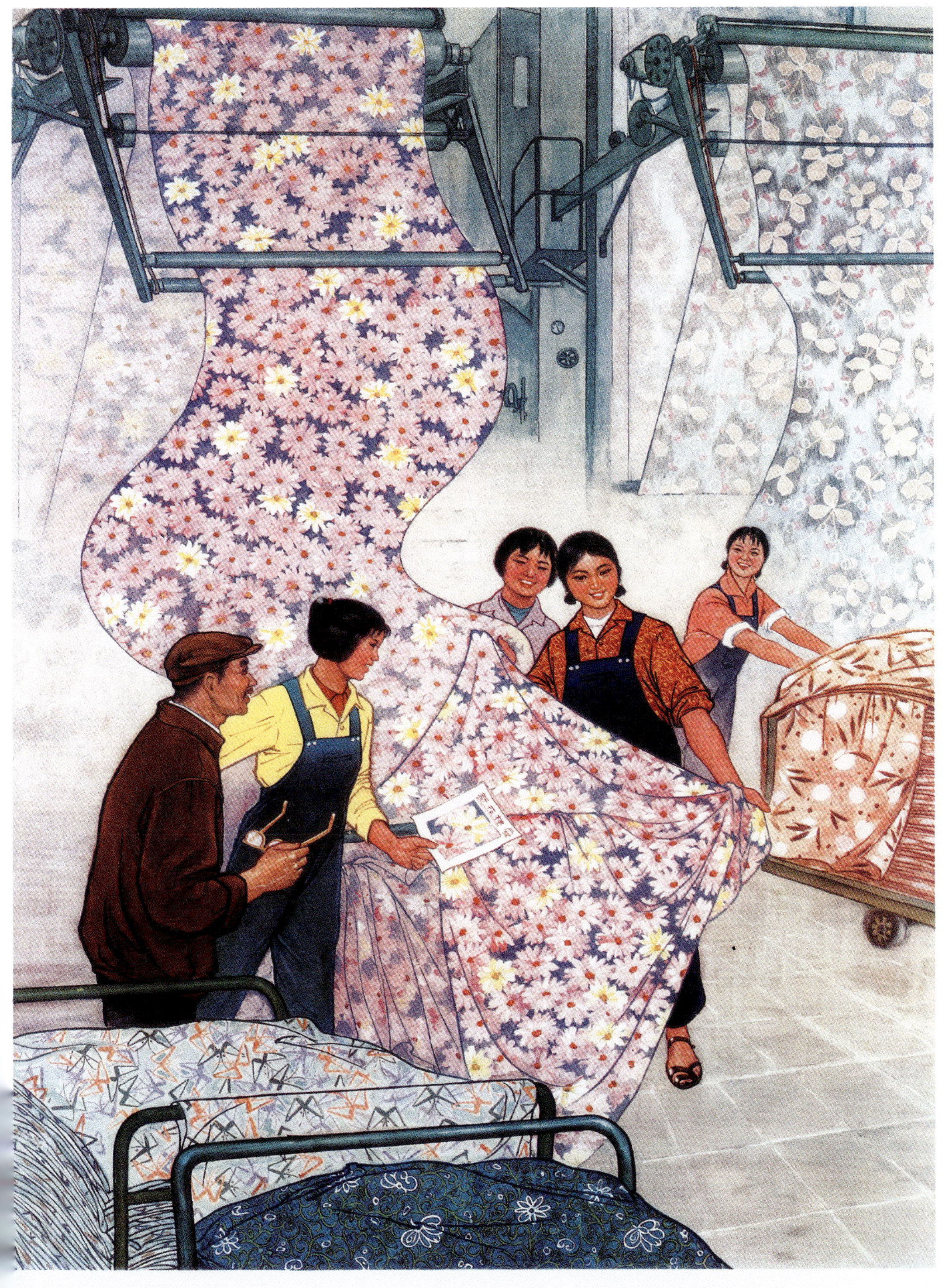

新 花 怒 放

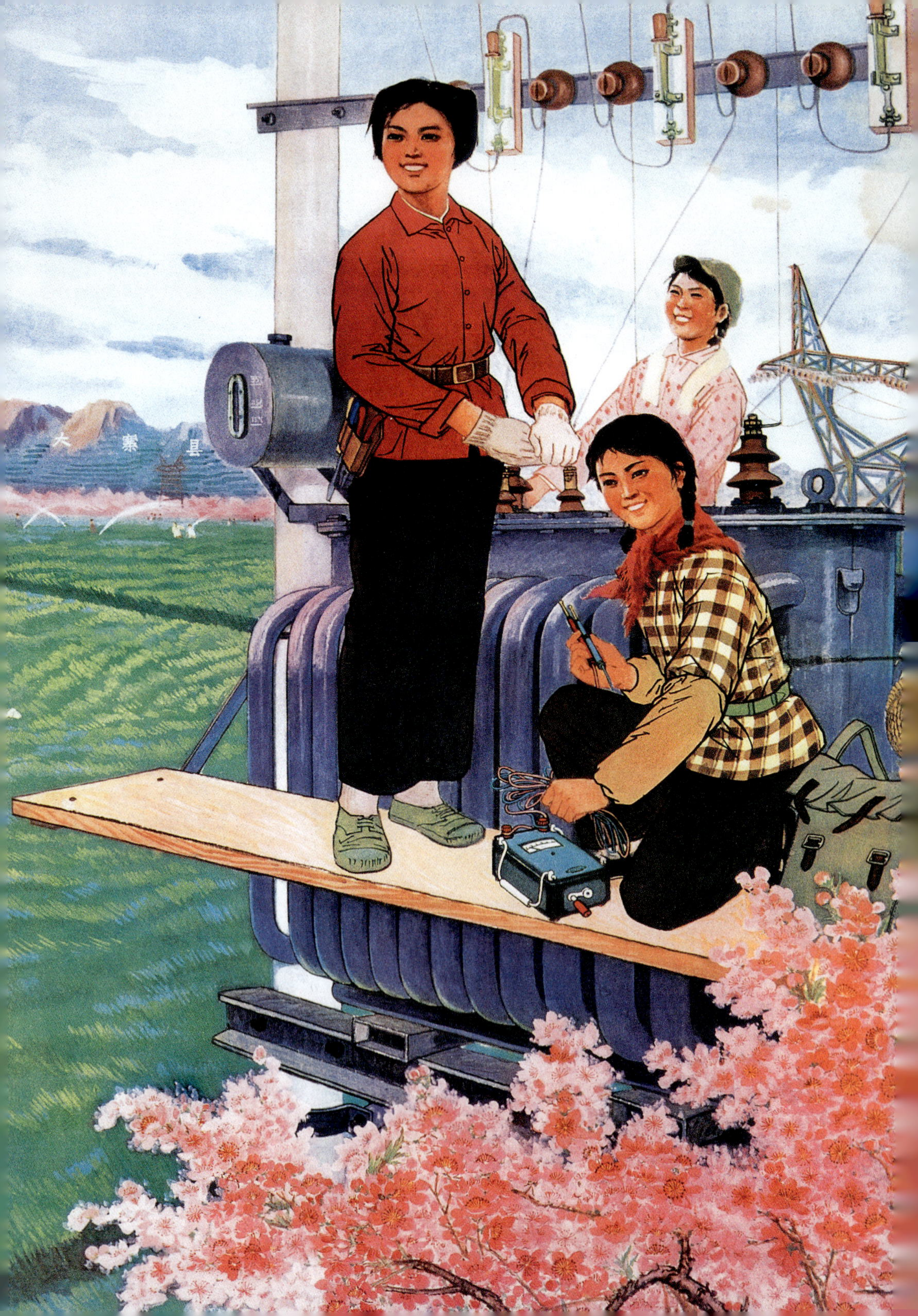
大寨县

Opposite
Joyfully gazing upon the fields of wheat *Artist:* Kang Wensheng (worker); Hebei People's Publishing House, 1976 *Print run:* 35,000; 0.11 Yuan

Mit Freude die Weizenfelder betrachten *Gemalt von* Kang Wensheng (Arbeiter); Volksverlag Hebei, 1976 *Auflage:* 35 000; 0,11 Yuan

Que le spectacle des champs de blé vous enchante *Peintre :* Kang Wensheng (ouvrier) ; Éditions Populaires du Hebei, 1976 *Tirage :* 35 000 ; 0,11 yuan

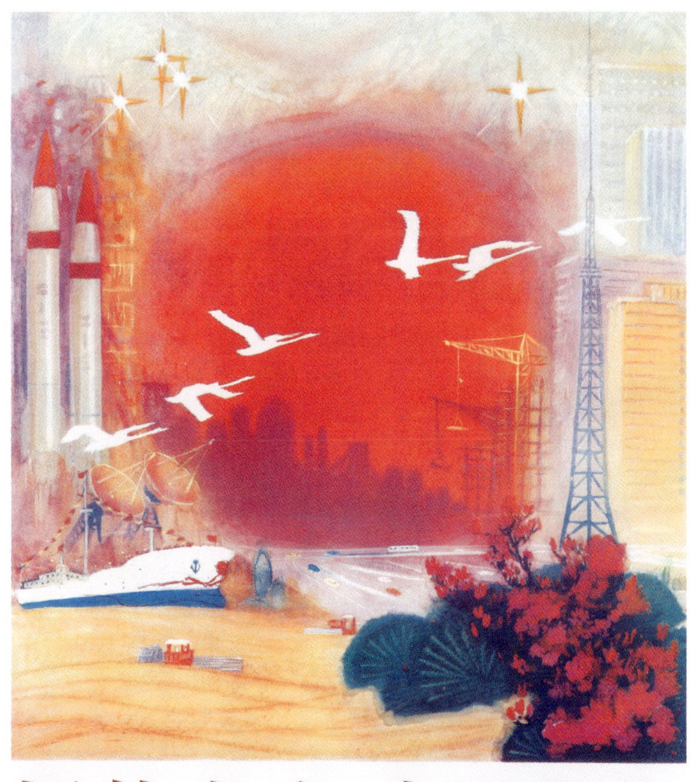

Fight together to build the Four Modernizations* *Artist:* Pan Xiaoqing; Jiangsu People's Publishing House, 1982; 0.18 Yuan
* See page 94.

Gemeinsam kämpfen, um die Vier Modernisierungen* aufzubauen *Gemalt von* Pan Xiaoqing; Volksverlag Jiangsu, 1982; 0,18 Yuan
* Siehe Seite 94.

Luttons côte à côte pour édifier les Quatre Modernisations* *Peintre :* Pan Xiaoqing ; Éditions Populaires du Jiangsu, 1982 ; 0,18 yuan
* Voir page 94.

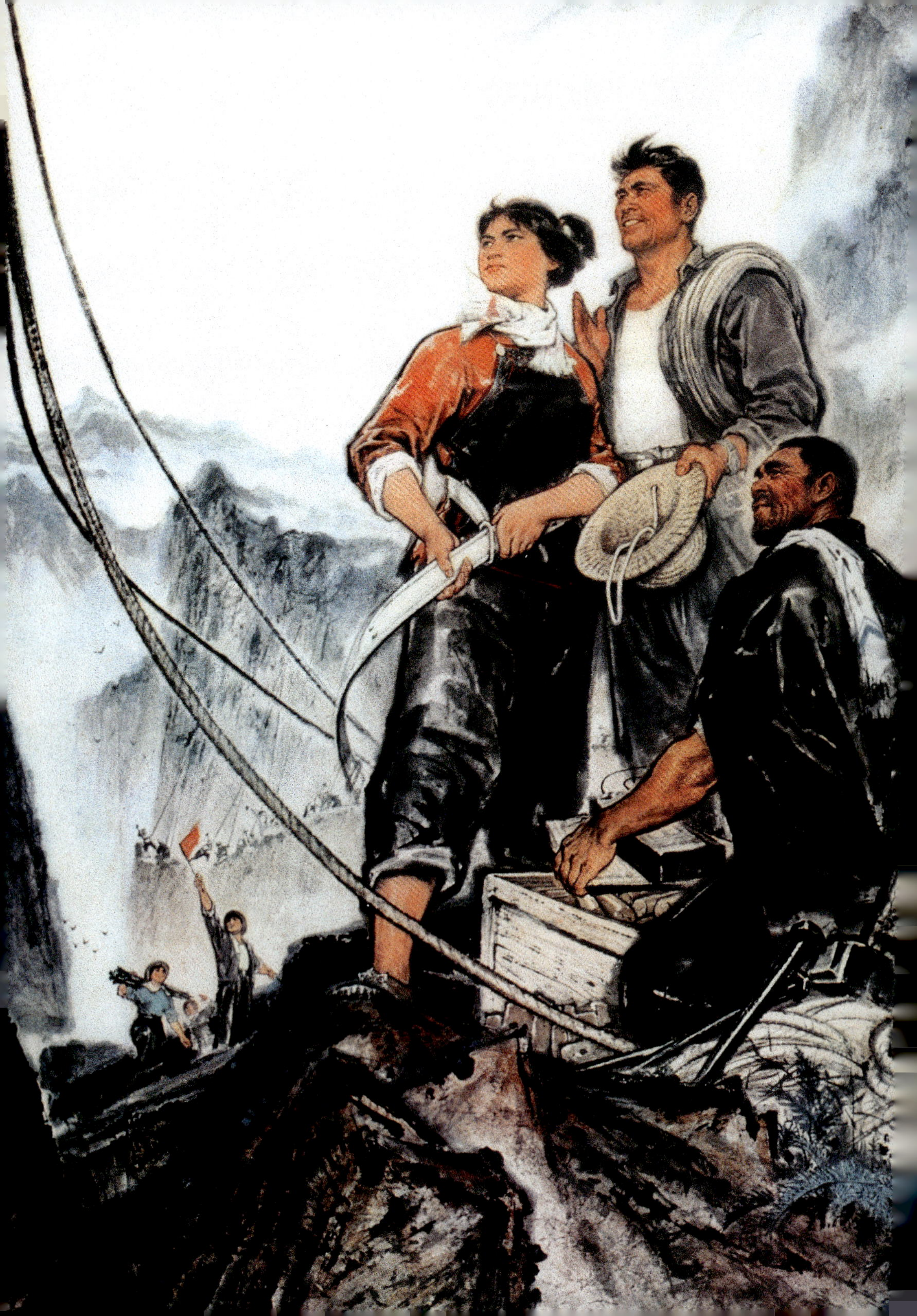

XXI

SELF-RELIANCE AND ARDUOUS STRUGGLE

SELBSTVERTRAUEN UND HARTER KAMPF
CONFIANCE EN SOI ET LUTTE ARDUE

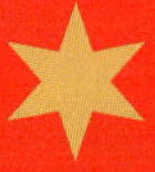

Page 330
There is no difficulty in the world that cannot be overcome *Artist:* Wu Qizhong; Shanghai People's Publishing House, 1977; 0.11 Yuan

Es gibt keine Schwierigkeit auf der Welt, die man nicht überwinden kann *Gemalt von* Wu Qizhong; Volksverlag Shanghai, 1977; 0,11 Yuan

Il n'y a pas au monde de difficulté qui ne puisse être surmontée *Peintre :* Wu Qizhong ; Éditions Populaires de Shanghai, 1977 ; 0,11 yuan

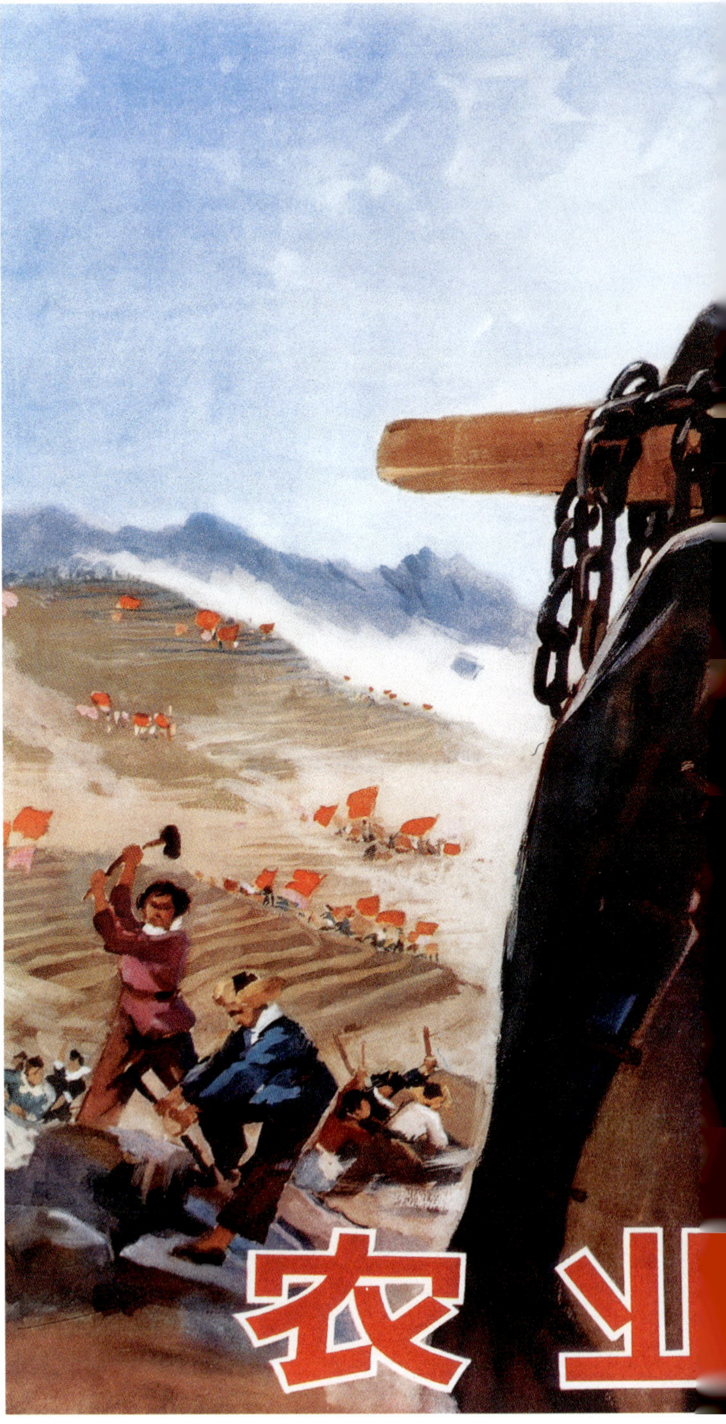

In agriculture, learn from Dazhai! *Book in left hand:* Yu Gung moves mountains. Mao Zedong *Designed by:* Bei An Railway Maintenance Sector, Helongjiang Province; People's Art Publishing House, 1973; 0.11 Yuan

Lernt in der Landwirtschaft von Dazhai! *Buch Mann:* Yü Gung versetzt Berge, Mao Zedong *Entwurf:* Eisenbahn-Wartungsabschnitt Bei An, Provinz Helongjiang; Volkskunstverlag, 1973; 0,11 Yuan

Retenez de l'expérience agricole de Dazhai ! *Sur le livre :* Yü Gung déplace des montagnes. Mao Zedong *Conception :* Équipe d'entretien des chemins de fer de Bei An, province de Helongjiang, Éditions Populaires d'Art, 1973 ; 0,11 yuan

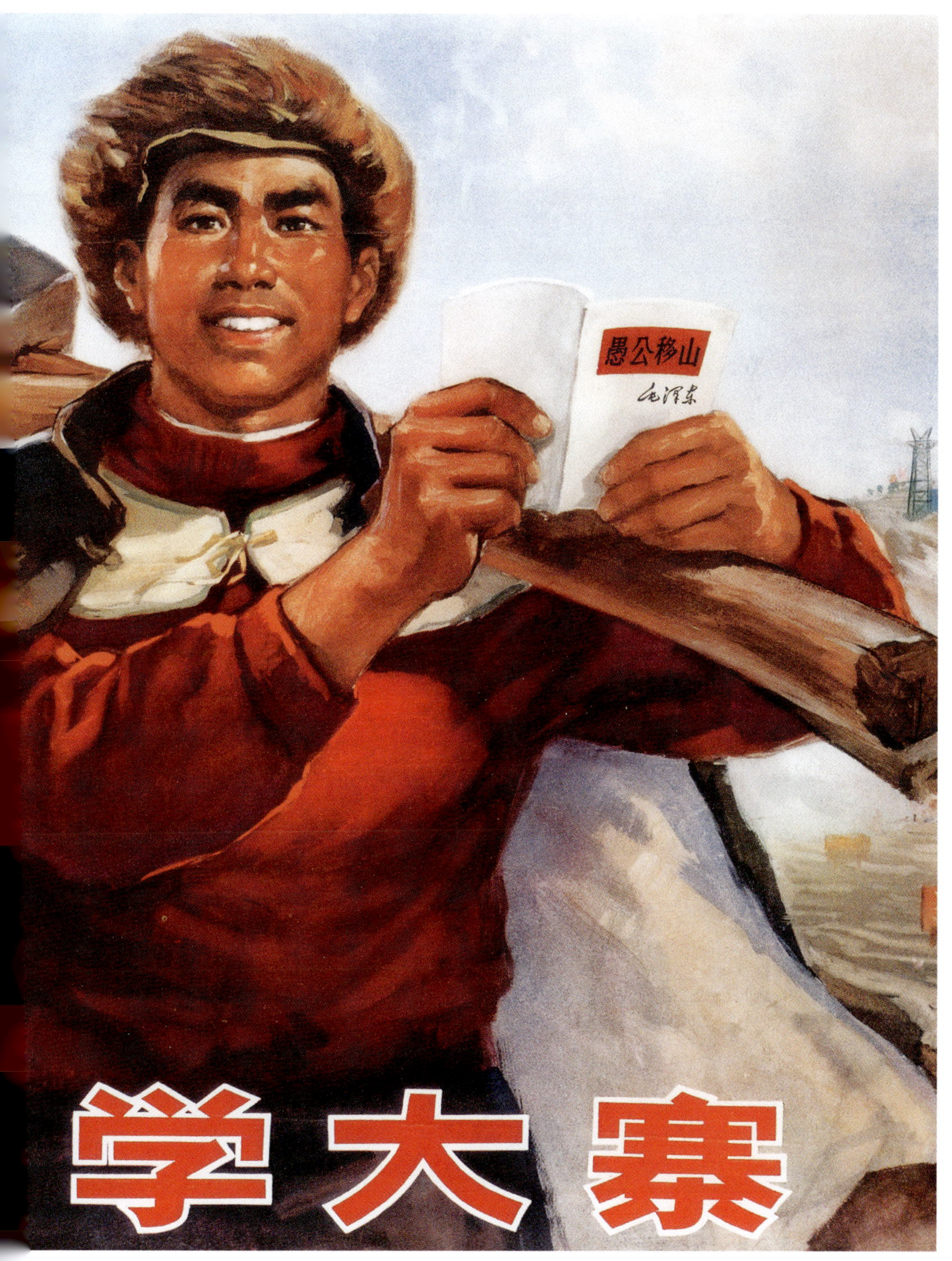
愚公移山
毛泽东
学大寨

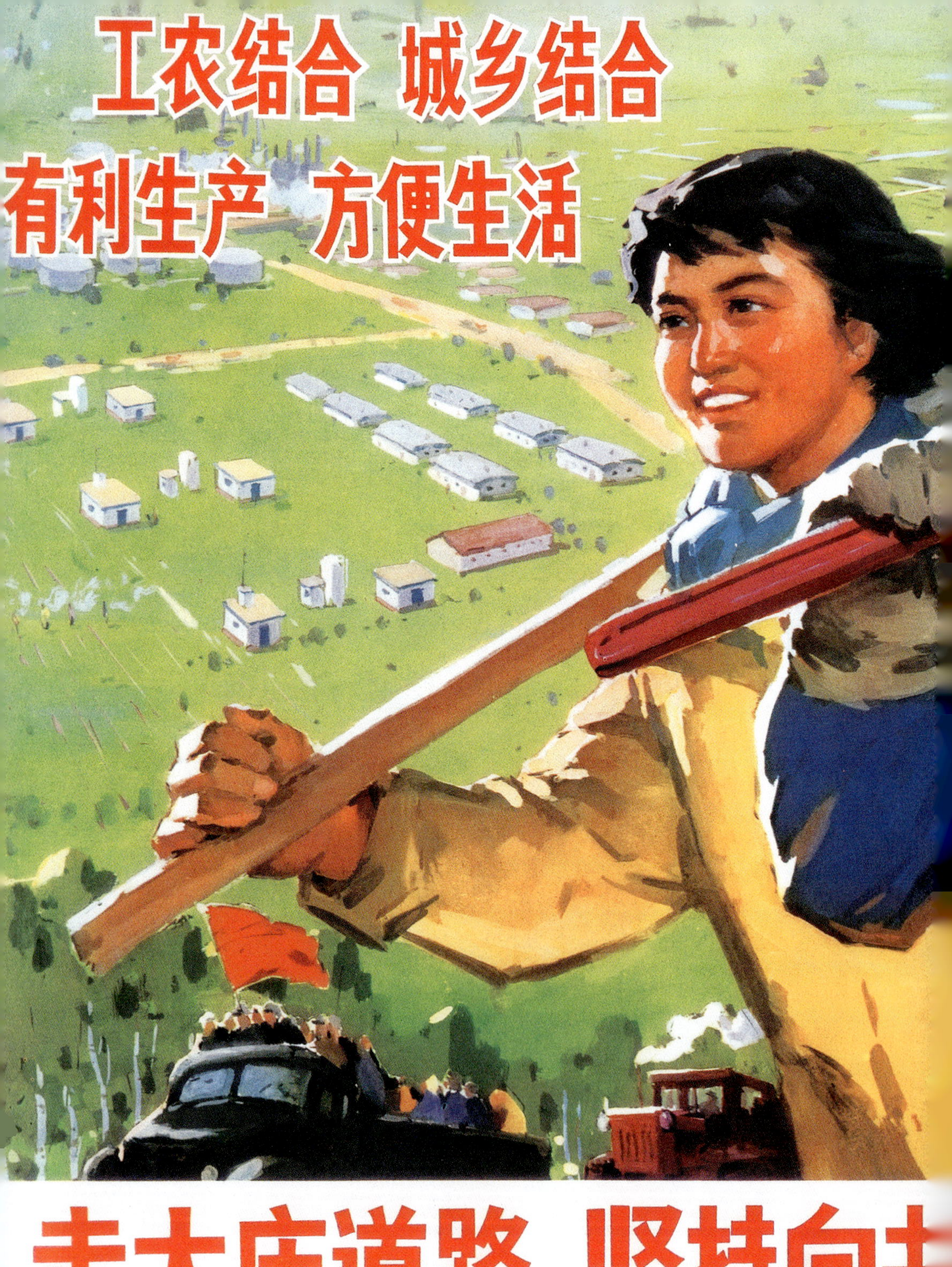
工农结合 城乡结合
有利生产 方便生活
走大庆道路，坚持向

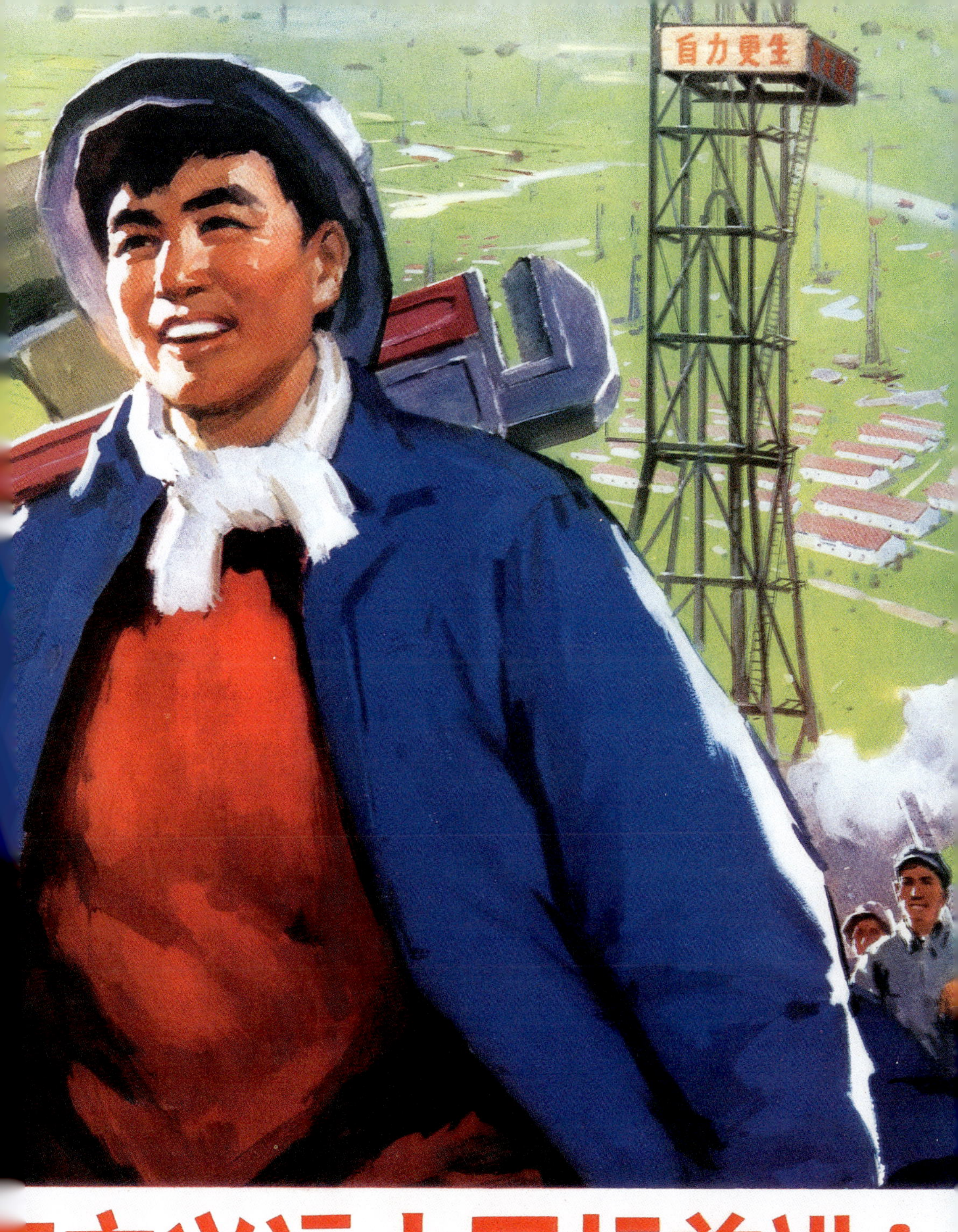

主义远大目标前进！

Pages 334–335
Following Daqing's example we stride forward towards the great goal of Communism *Top left:* Industry shall be connected to agriculture, city to countryside, in order to improve production and make life more comfortable *Top right, on pylon:* Faith in our own strength *Artists:* Ma Changli and Yin Rongsheng; People's Art Publishing House, 1977 *Print run:* 80,000; 0.14 Yuan

Dem Vorbild Daqings folgend voranschreiten, dem großen Ziel des Kommunismus entgegen *Links oben:* Um die Produktion zu begünstigen und das Leben bequemer zu gestalten, soll Industrie mit Landwirtschaft, Stadt mit Land verbunden werden *Rechts oben auf dem Mast:* Vertrauen auf die eigene Kraft *Gemalt von* Ma Changli und Yin Rongsheng, Volkskunstverlag, 1977 *Auflage:* 80 000; 0,14 Yuan

Avançons en suivant l'exemple de Daqing dans la perspective de l'édification du communisme *En haut à gauche :* Pour favoriser la production et rendre la vie plus facile, l'industrie doit être liée à l'agriculture, la ville à la campagne. *En haut à droite sur le pylône :* Ayons confiance en notre propre force *Peintres :* Ma Changli et Yin Rongsheng ; Éditions Populaires d'Art, 1977 *Tirage :* 80 000 ex. ; 0,14 yuan

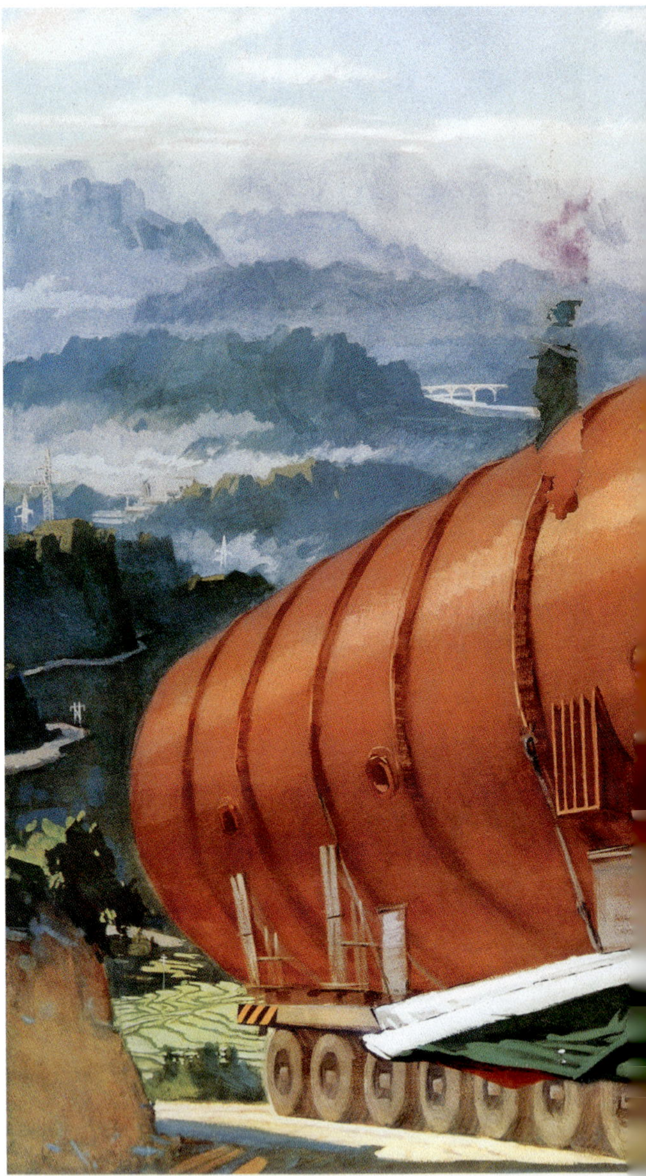

工人阶级有

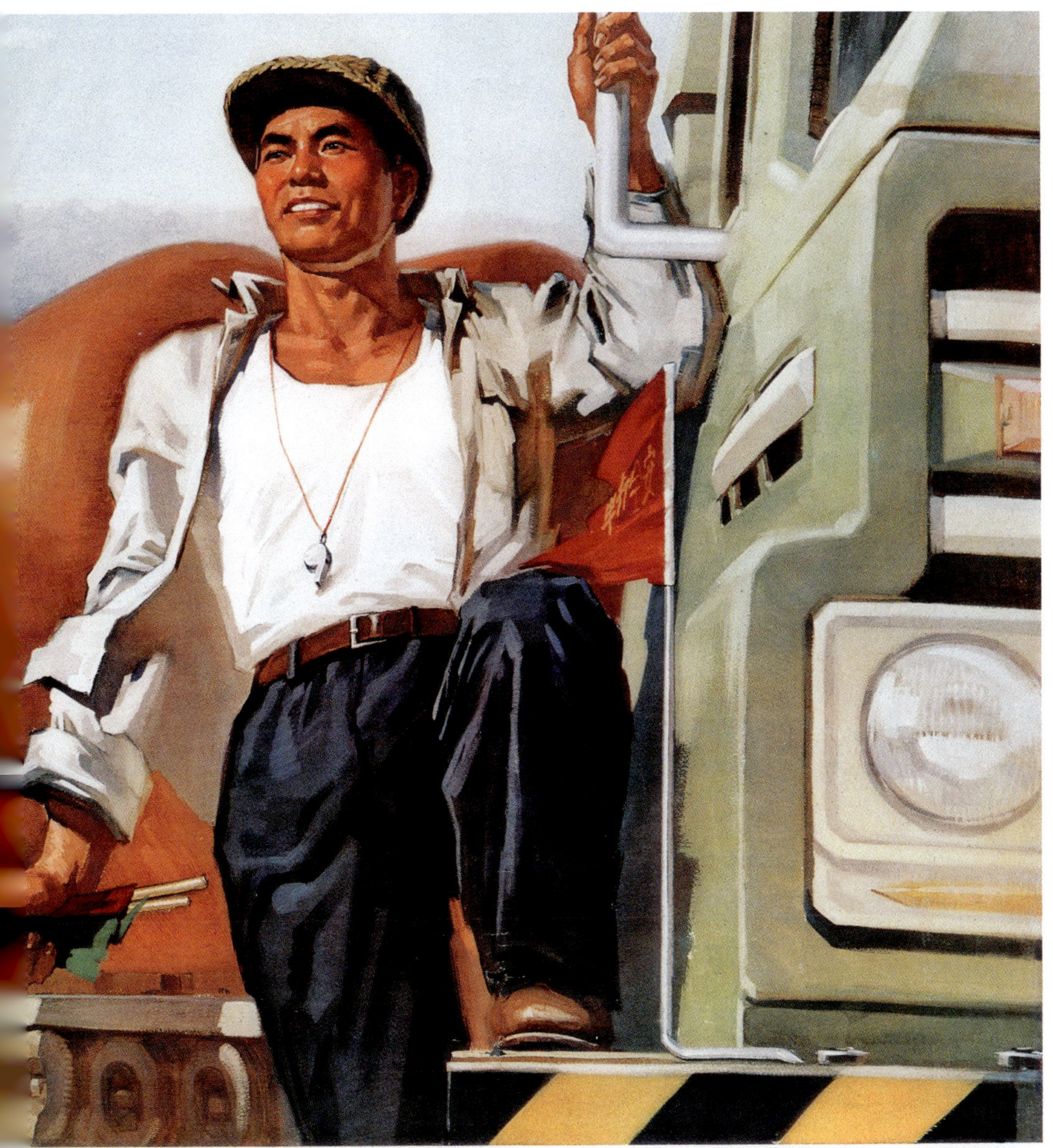

The working class has high ambitions: to be self-reliant and to do pioneering work Shanghai People's Publishing House, 1973 *Print run:* 40,000; 0.12 Yuan

Die Arbeiterklasse hat hohe Ziele vor Augen: Auf die eigene Kraft vertrauen und Pionierarbeit leisten Volksverlag Shanghai, 1973 *Auflage:* 40 000; 0,12 Yuan

La classe ouvrière a de hautes ambitions: ayons confiance en nous et faisons un travail de pionnier Éditions Populaires de Shanghai, 1973 *Tirage :* 40 000 ; 0,12 yuan

Struggle together and rebuild your district following the example of Dazhai *On the sluice gate, left:* Sluice gate of solidarity *Slogan, top:* In agriculture, learn from Dazhai! *Three flags, right:* "The East is Red" People's Commune, "Red Flag" People's Commune, "Victory" People's Commune *Designed by:* Propaganda Poster Painting School for Peasants in the Jin district of Liaoning Province *Artist:* Yan Chengfu; People's Art Publishing House, 1975 *Print run:* 50,000; 0.14 Yuan

Gemeinsam kämpfen und den Kreis nach dem Vorbild Dazhai aufbauen *An der Schleuse links:* Schleuse der Solidarität *Eine Parole oben:* Lernt in der Landwirtschaft von Dazhai! *Drei Fahnen rechts:* Volkskommune „Der Osten ist rot", Volkskommune „Rote Fahne", Volkskommune Sieg" *Entwurf:* Propagandaplakat-Malkurs für Bauern des Kreises Jin, Provinz Liaoning *Gemalt von* Yan Chengfu; Volkskunstverlag, 1975; *Auflage:* 50 000; 0,14 Yuan

Luttons tous ensemble pour édifier le canton d'après l'exemple de Dazhai *Sur la vanne, à gauche :* Vanne de la solidarité *Slogan, en haut :* Retenez de l'expérience agricole de Dazhai ! *Trois drapeaux, à droite :* Commune populaire « L'Est est rouge », Commune populaire « Drapeau rouge », Commune populaire « Victoire » *Conception :* Affiche de propagande du cours de peinture pour les paysans du canton de Jin, province du Liaoning *Peintre :* Yan Chengfu ; Éditions Populaires d'Art, 1975 *Tirage :* 50 000 ; 0,14 yuan

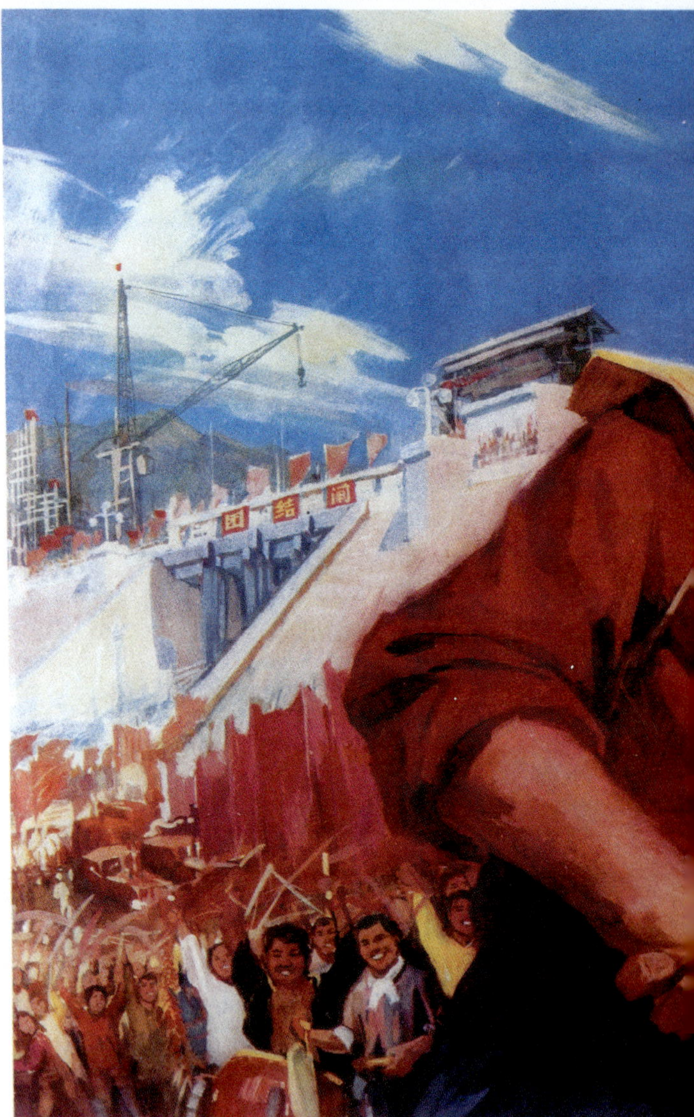

团结战斗

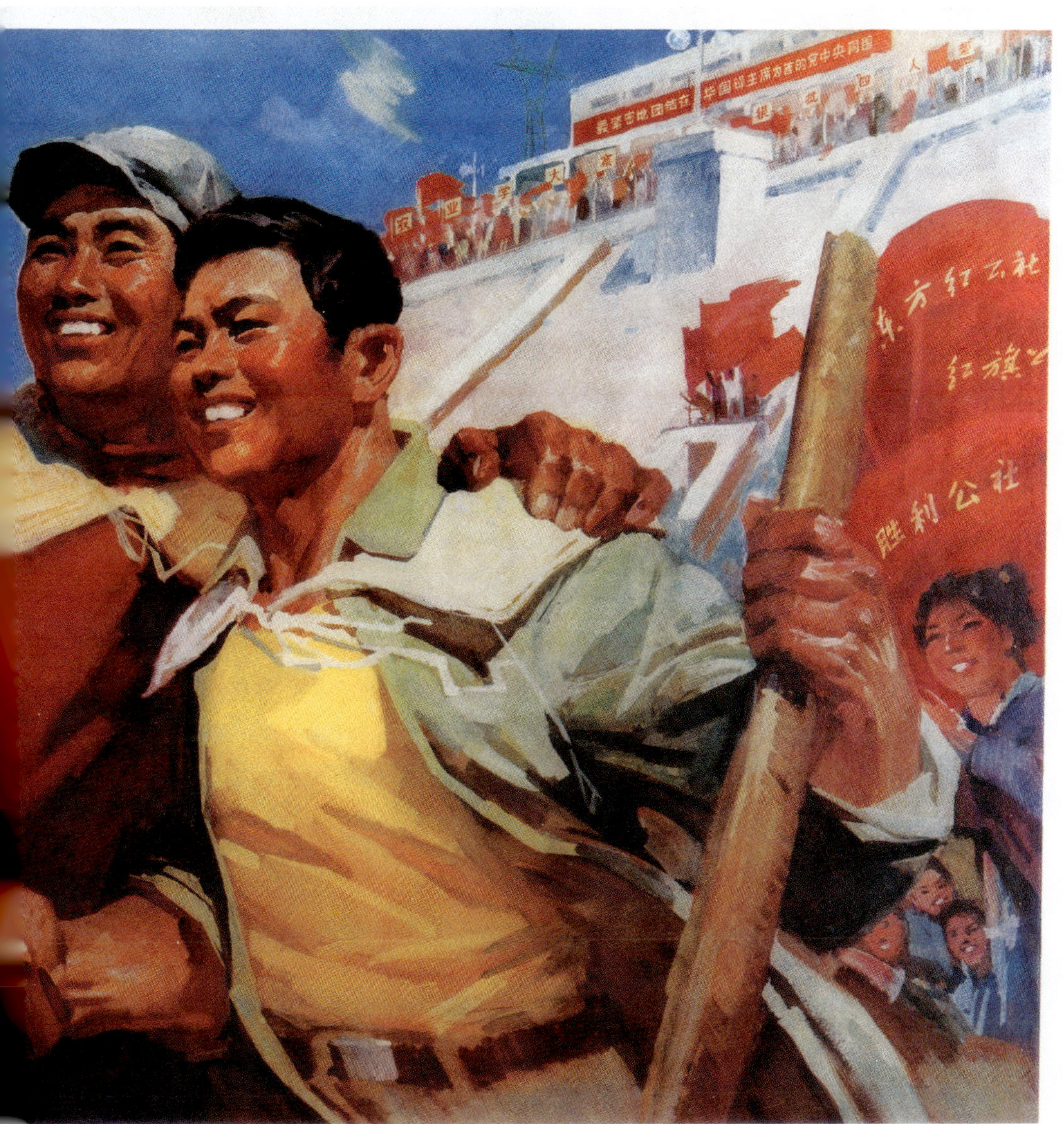

速建成大寨县

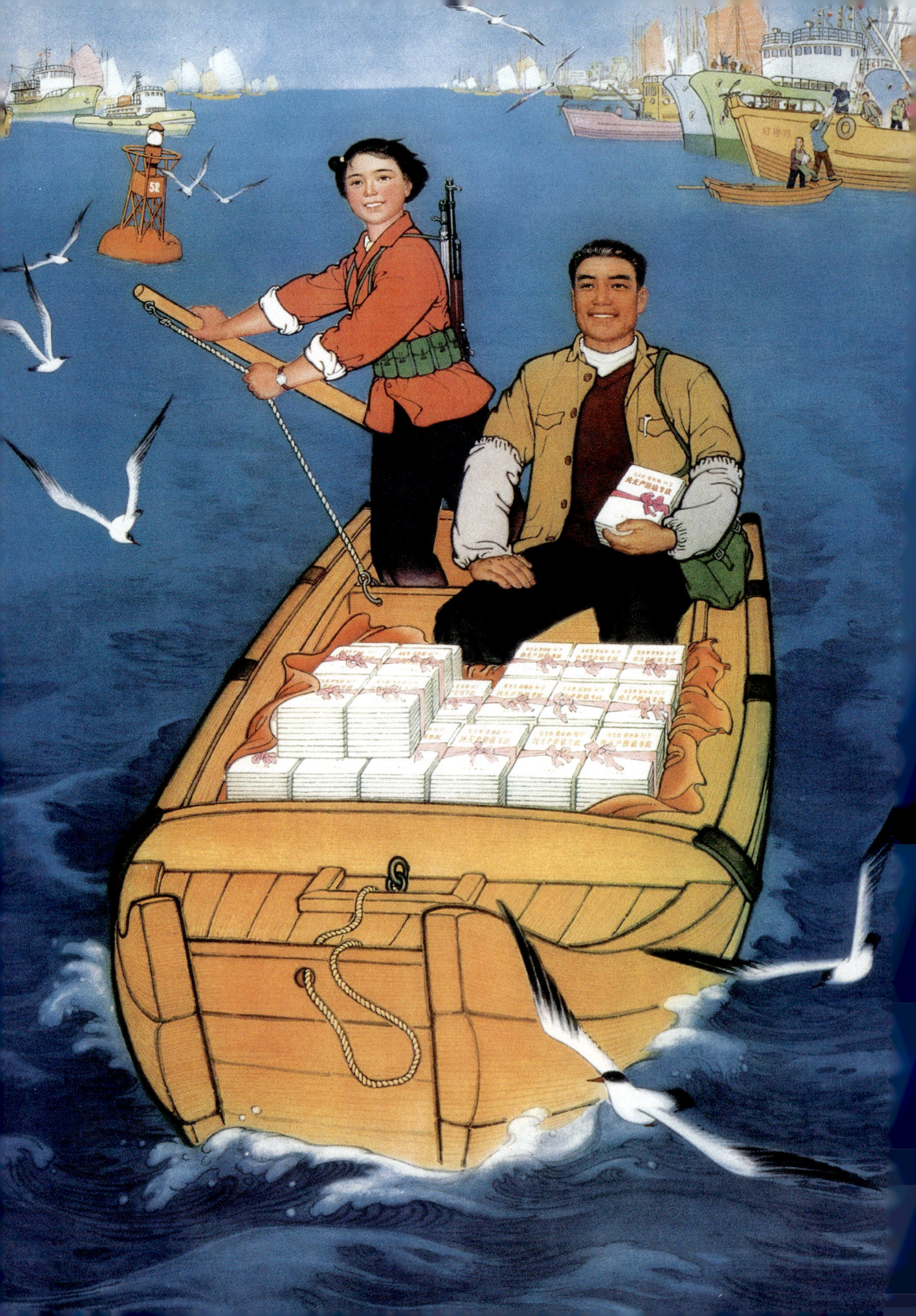

XXII

METHODS OF THINKING AND METHODS OF WORK

DENKWEISE UND ARBEITSMETHODEN
MÉTHODES DE PENSÉE ET DE TRAVAIL

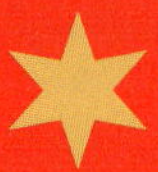

Page 340
The spring brings warmth *Books on the boat:* Marx, Engels, and Lenin on the dictatorship of the proletariat *Artists:* Zhang Jinrong and Yu Huali; Tianjin People's Art Publishing House, 1975; 0.14 Yuan

Der Frühling bringt Wärme *Bücher im Boot*: Marx, Engels und Lenin über die Diktatur des Proletariats *Gemalt von* Zhang Jinrong und Yu Huali; Volkskunstverlag Tianjin, 1975; 0,14 Yuan

Avec le printemps vient la chaleur *Livres sur le bateau :* Marx, Engels et Lénine sur la dictature du prolétariat *Peintres :* Zhang Jinrong et Yu Huali ; Éditions Populaires d'Art de Tianjin, 1975 ; 0,14 yuan

"Listen to both sides and you will be enlightened, heed only one side and you will be benighted."

Hörst du alle an, dann bist du dir im Klaren, schenkst du nur einem Glauben, wirst du im Dunkeln tappen. ★ Qui écoute les deux côtés aura l'esprit éclairé, qui n'écoute qu'un côté restera dans les ténèbres.

The people's desire is a weapon of the revolution *Book:* Selected Works of Mao Zedong, Volume 5 *Designed by:* Guangzhou Province Art Studio; People's Art Publishing House, 1977 *Print run:* 100,000; 0.14 Yuan

Wunsch des Volkes, Waffe der Revolution *Buch:* Ausgewählte Werke Mao Zedongs, Band 5 *Entwurf:* Kunststudio der Provinz Guangzhou; Volkskunstverlag, 1977 *Auflage:* 100 000; 0,14 Yuan

Désir du peuple, arme de la révolution *Livre :* Œuvres choisies de Mao Zedong, volume 5 *Conception :* Studio d'Art de la province du Guangzhou ; Éditions Populaires d'Art, 1977 *Tirage :* 100 000 ; 0,14 yuan

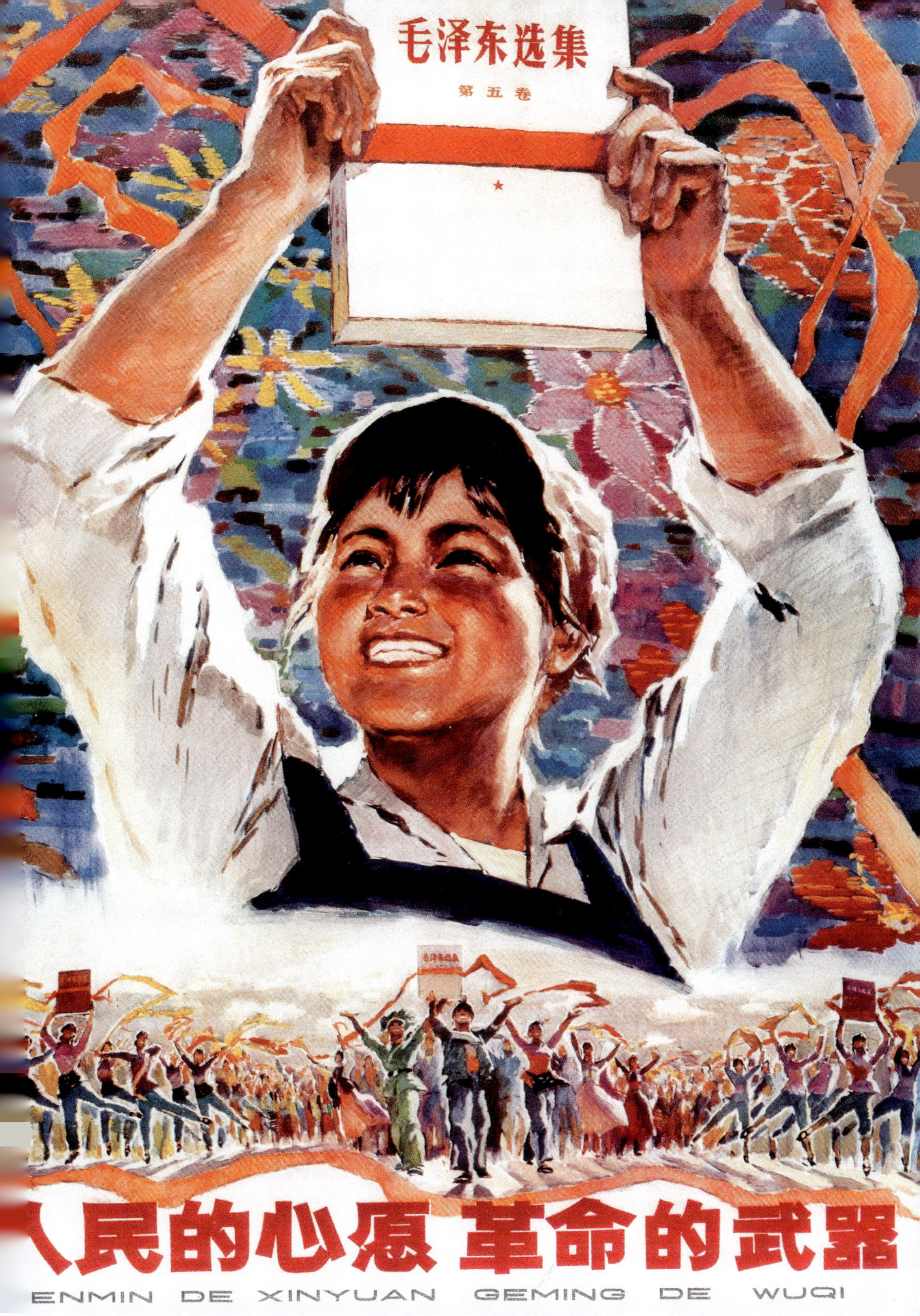
毛泽东选集
第五卷
人民的心愿 革命的武器
ENMIN DE XINYUAN GEMING DE WUQI

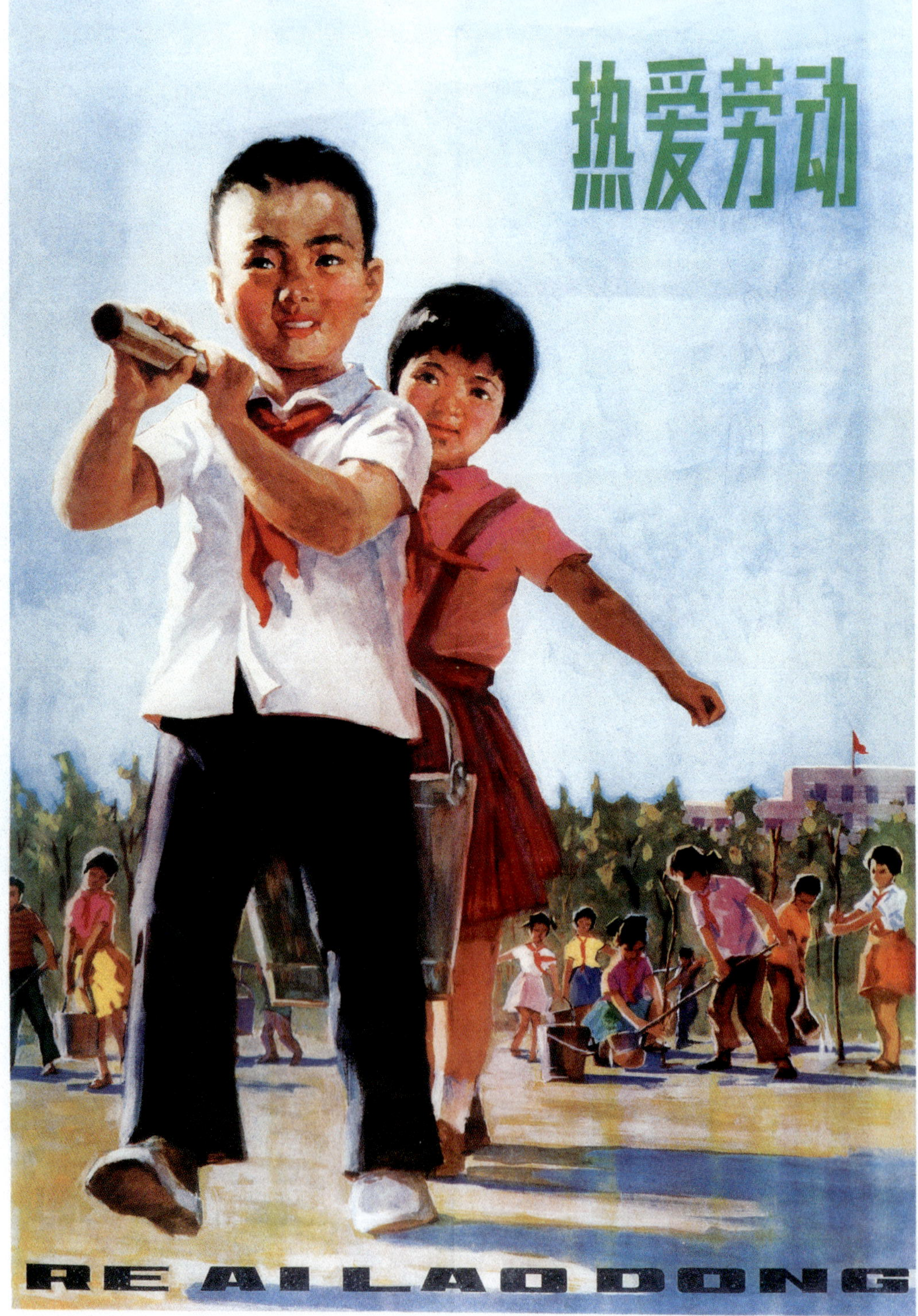
热爱劳动
RE AI LAO DONG

Opposite

Enjoy physical work Poster used as teaching aid; Shanghai Educational Publishing House, 1978; 0.12 Yuan

Die körperliche Arbeit lieben Erziehungsplakat; Erziehungsverlag Shanghai, 1978; 0,12 Yuan

L'amour du travail physique Affiche pédagogique ; Éditions Éducatives de Shanghai, 1978 ; 0,12 yuan

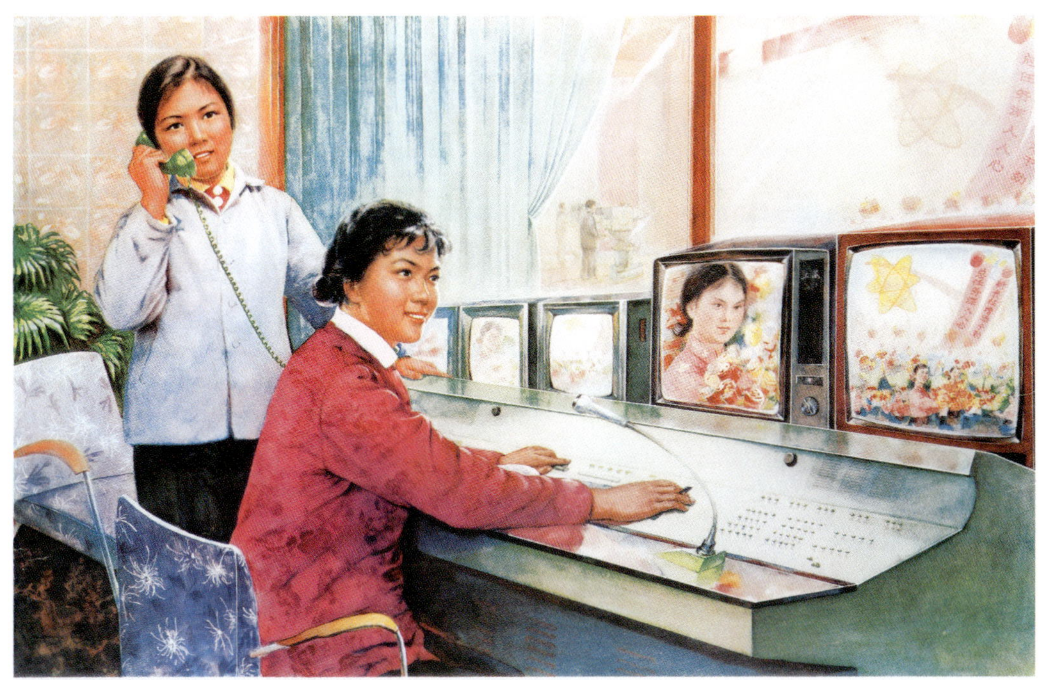

News of victory is spreading to all areas; good news brings joy to every family *Artist:* Zhang Jinbiao; Shanghai People's Publishing House, 1978; 0.11 Yuan

Siegesnachrichten verbreiten sich überall, Freudenbotschaften bringen Wärme in alle Familien *Gemalt von* Zhang Jinbiao; Volksverlag Shanghai, 1978; 0,11 Yuan

Les nouvelles de la victoire se répandent partout, les messages de joie apportent de la chaleur dans toutes les familles *Peintre :* Zhang Jinbiao ; Éditions Populaires de Shanghai, 1978 ; 0,11 yuan

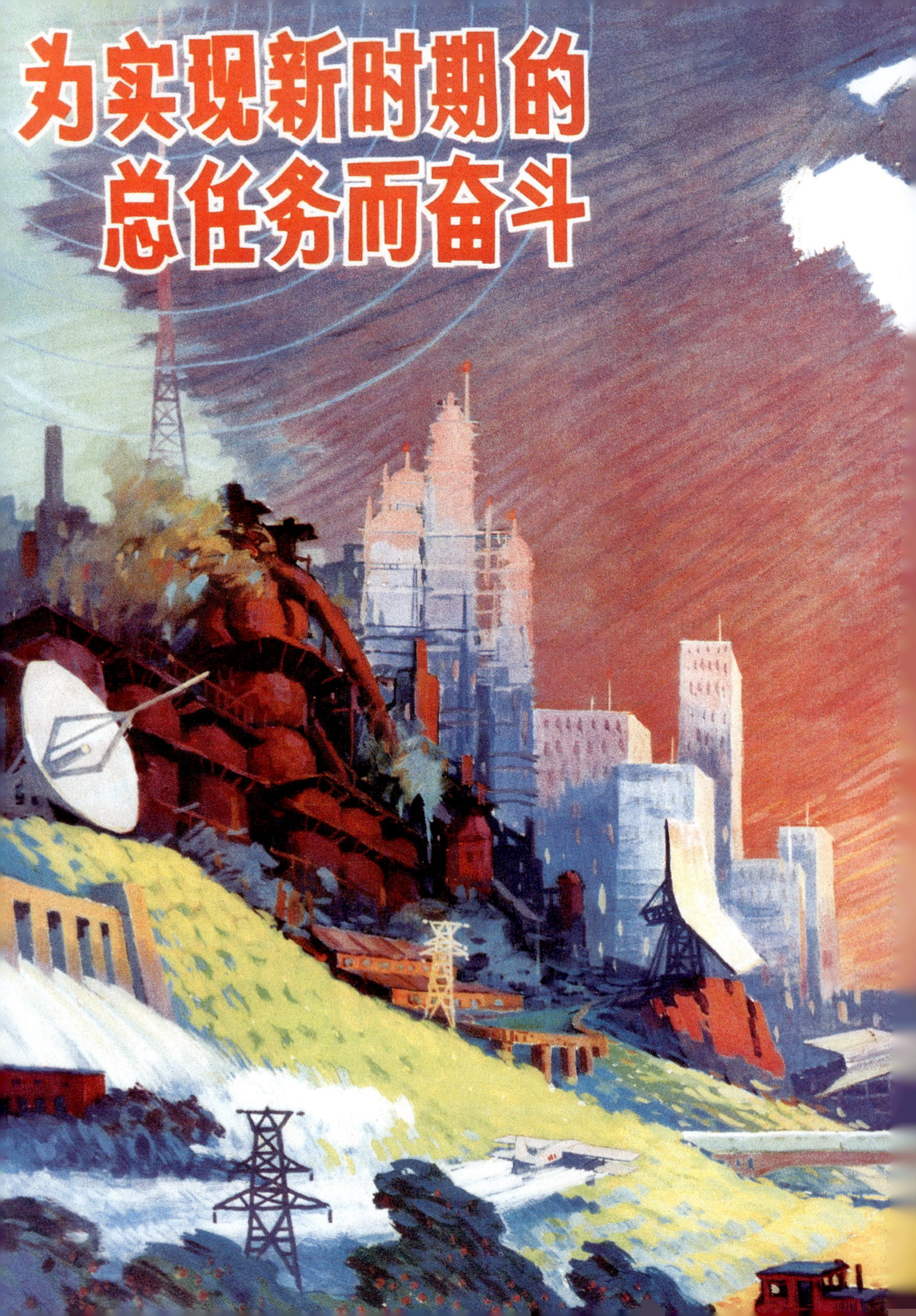
为实现新时期的
总任务而奋斗

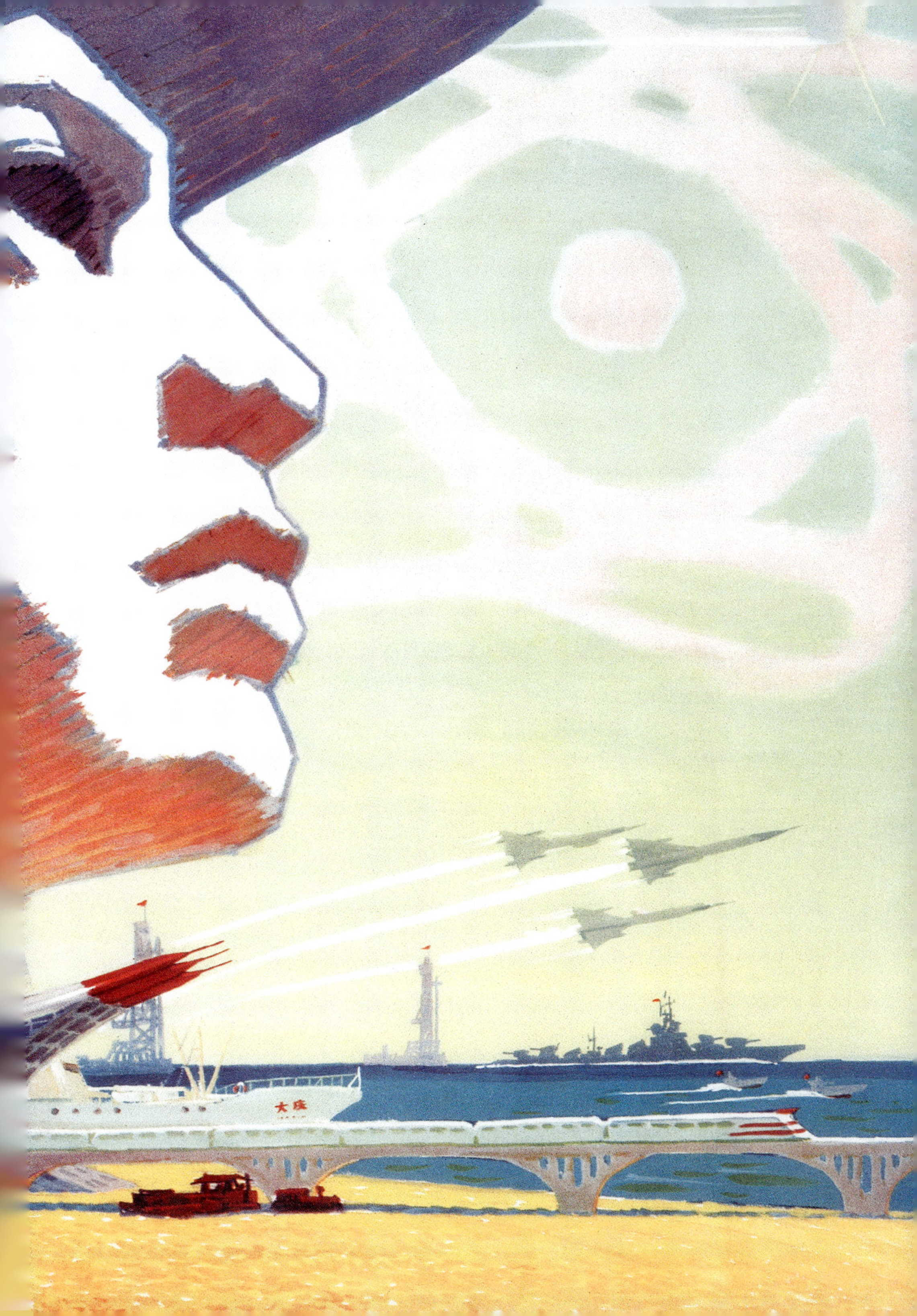
大庆

Pages 346–347
Fight to accomplish all the tasks of the New Era *Published by:* Zhejiang People's Publishing House, 1978; 0.11 Yuan

Für die Verwirklichung der gesamten Aufgaben der Neuen Periode kämpfen *Herausgegeber:* Volksverlag Zhejiang, 1978; 0,11 Yuan

Luttons pour la réalisation de l'ensemble des tâches de l'Ère Nouvelle *Éditeur :* Éditions Populaires du Zhejiang, 1978 ; 0,11 yuan

The rural regions are wide open spaces where our skills can be developed to the full *Book tied to the luggage:* Family records 1959

Die ländlichen Regionen sind eine weite Welt, in der man seine Fähigkeiten unbegrenzt entwickeln kann *Am Gepäck:* Familienbuch 1959

Les régions rurales sont un vaste espace dans lequel on peut développer sans entraves ses facultés *Sur le paquet :* Livret de famille 1959

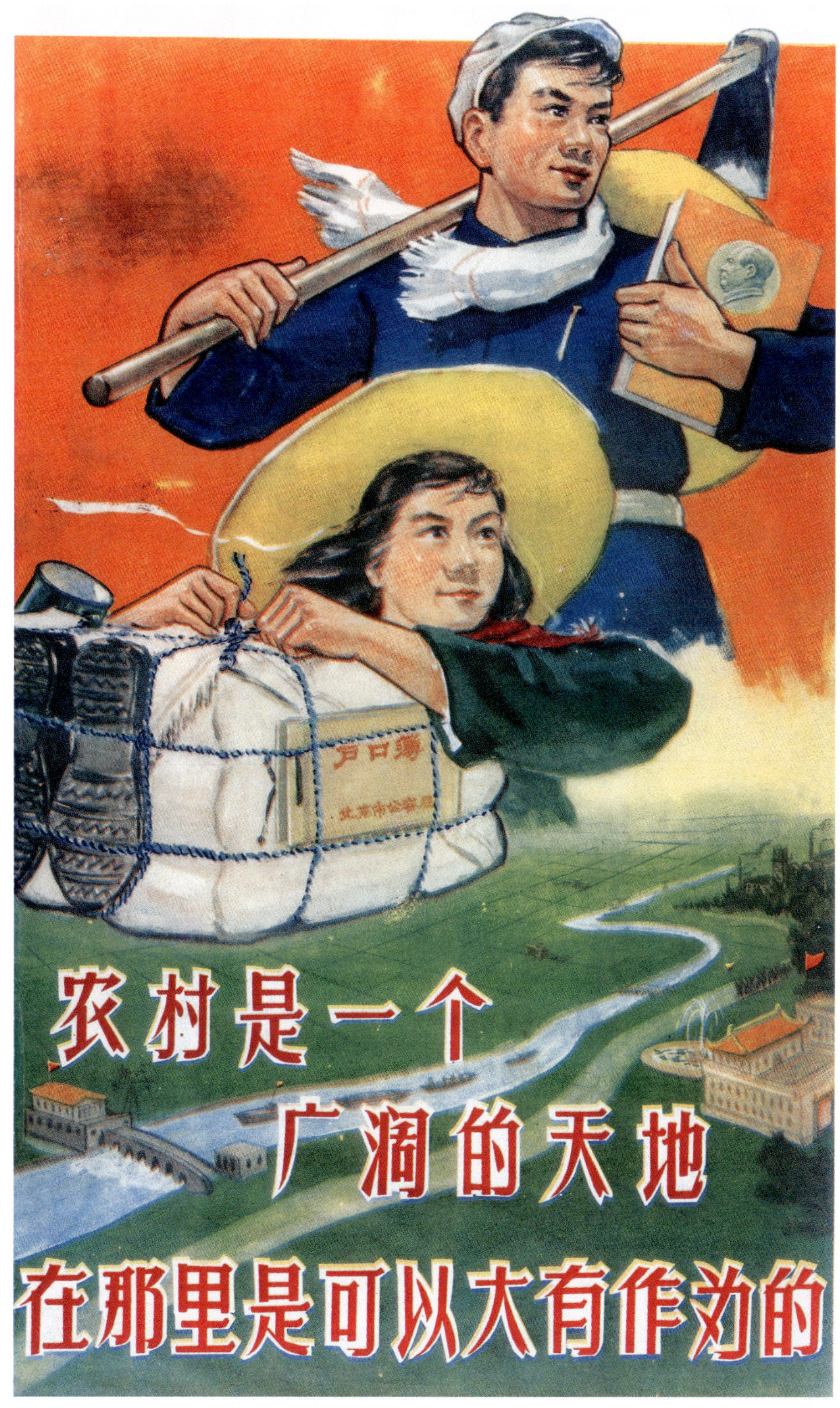
户口簿
农村是一个
广阔的天地
在那里是可以大有作为的

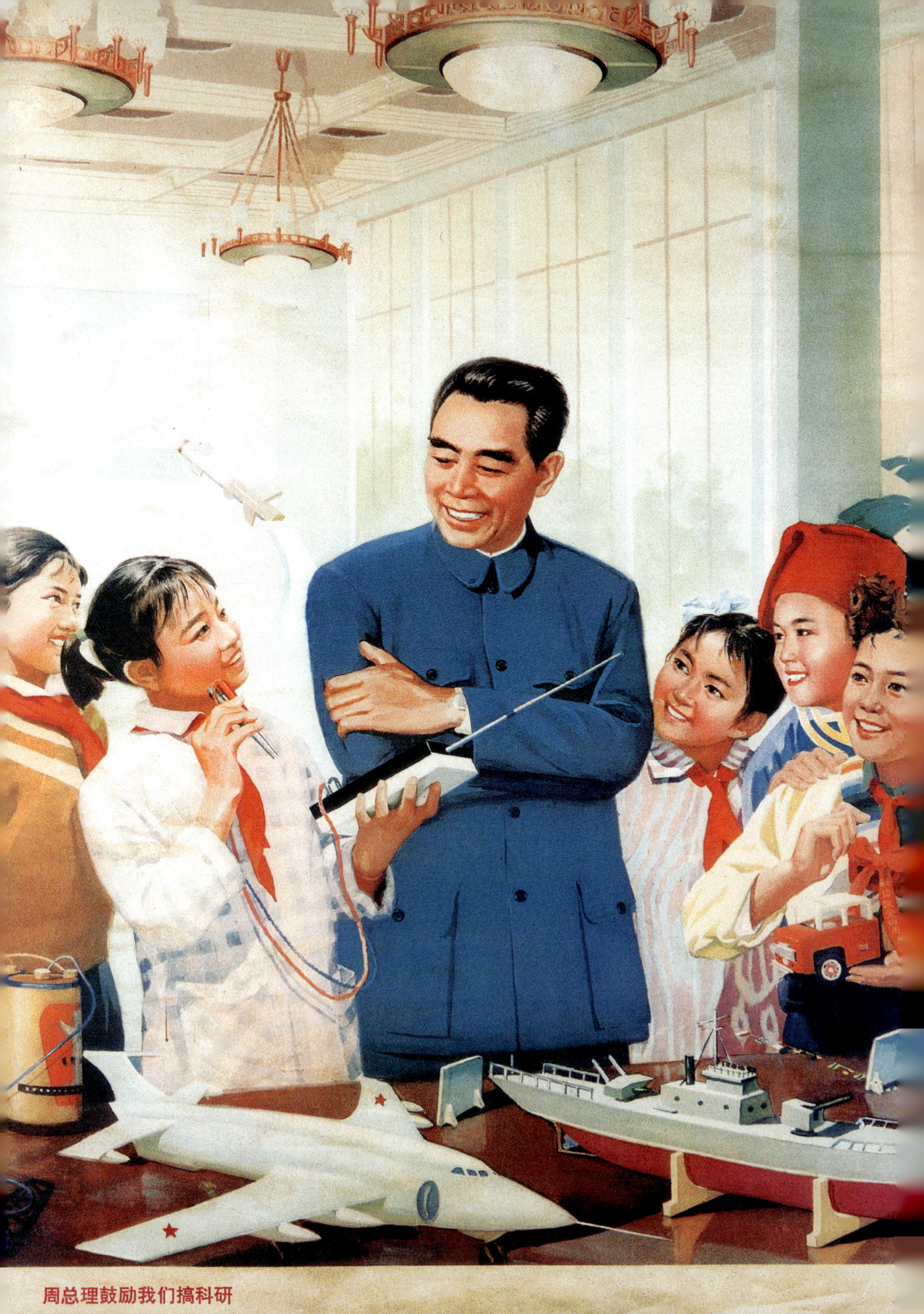
周总理鼓励我们搞科研

XXIII

INVESTIGATION AND STUDY

UNTERSUCHUNG UND FORSCHUNG
ENQUÊTES ET RECHERCHES

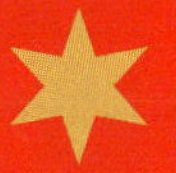

Page 350
Prime Minister Zhou Enlai encourages us to do research *Artist:* Zhou Guo; Shandong People's Publishing House, 1978; 0.14 Yuan

Premierminister Zhou Enlai ermutigt uns, Forschung zu betreiben *Gemalt von* Zhou Guo; Volksverlag Shandong, 1978; 0,14 Yuan

Le premier ministre Chou Enlai nous encourage à faire de la recherche *Peintre :* Zhou Guo ; Éditions Populaires du Shandong, 1978 ; 0,14 yuan

Opposite
Aircraft *Artist:* Hou Xiaoge; Hubei People's Publishing House, 1981; 0.16 Yuan

Flugzeuge *Gemalt von* Hou Xiaoge; Volksverlag Hubei, 1981; 0,16 Yuan

Avions *Peintre :* Hou Xiaoge ; Éditions Populaires du Hubei, 1981 ; 0,16 yuan

Pages 354–355
A great idea *Artists:* Wang Weishu and Yao Zhongyu; Shanghai People's Art Publishing House, 1st edn 1982, 2nd edn 1982 *Print run:* 300,001–960,000; 0.16 Yuan

Ideal *Gemalt von* Wang Weishu und Yao Zhongyu; Volkskunstverlag Shanghai, 1. Aufl. 1982, 2. Aufl. 1982 *Auflage:* 300 001–960 000; 0,16 Yuan

Idéal *Peintres :* Wang Weishu et Yao Zhongyu ; Éditions Populaires d'Art de Shanghai, 1ère éd. 1982, 2e éd. 1982 *Tirage :* 300 001–960 000 ; 0,16 yuan

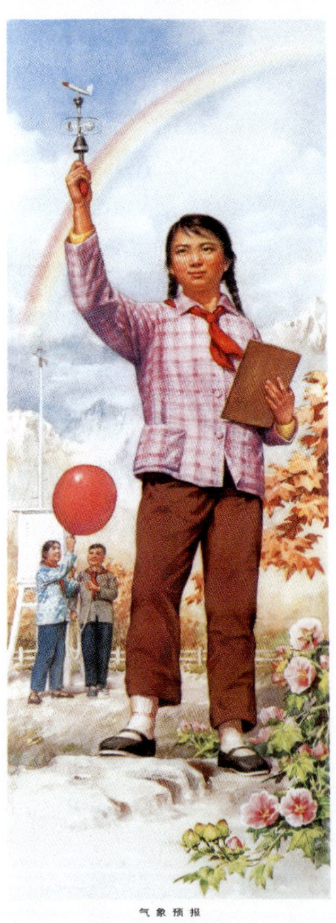

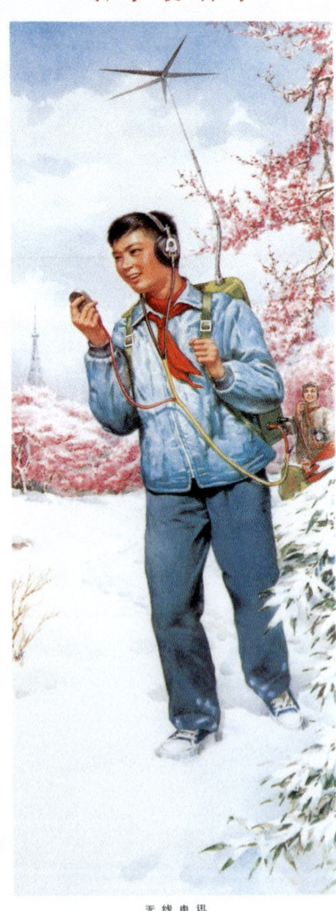

Love science from an early age *Left:* Weather forecast *Right:* Radio contact *Artist:* Pang Ka; Shanghai People's Art Publishing House, 1978; 0.22 Yuan

Von klein auf die Wissenschaft lieben *Links:* Wettervorhersage *Rechts:* Funkverbindung *Gemalt von* Pang Ka; Volkskunstverlag Shanghai, 1978; 0,22 Yuan

Nous aimons la science depuis notre enfance *À gauche :* Prévisions météorologiques *À droite :* Liaison radio *Peintre :* Pang Ka ; Éditions Populaires d'Art de Shanghai, 1978 ; 0,22 yuan

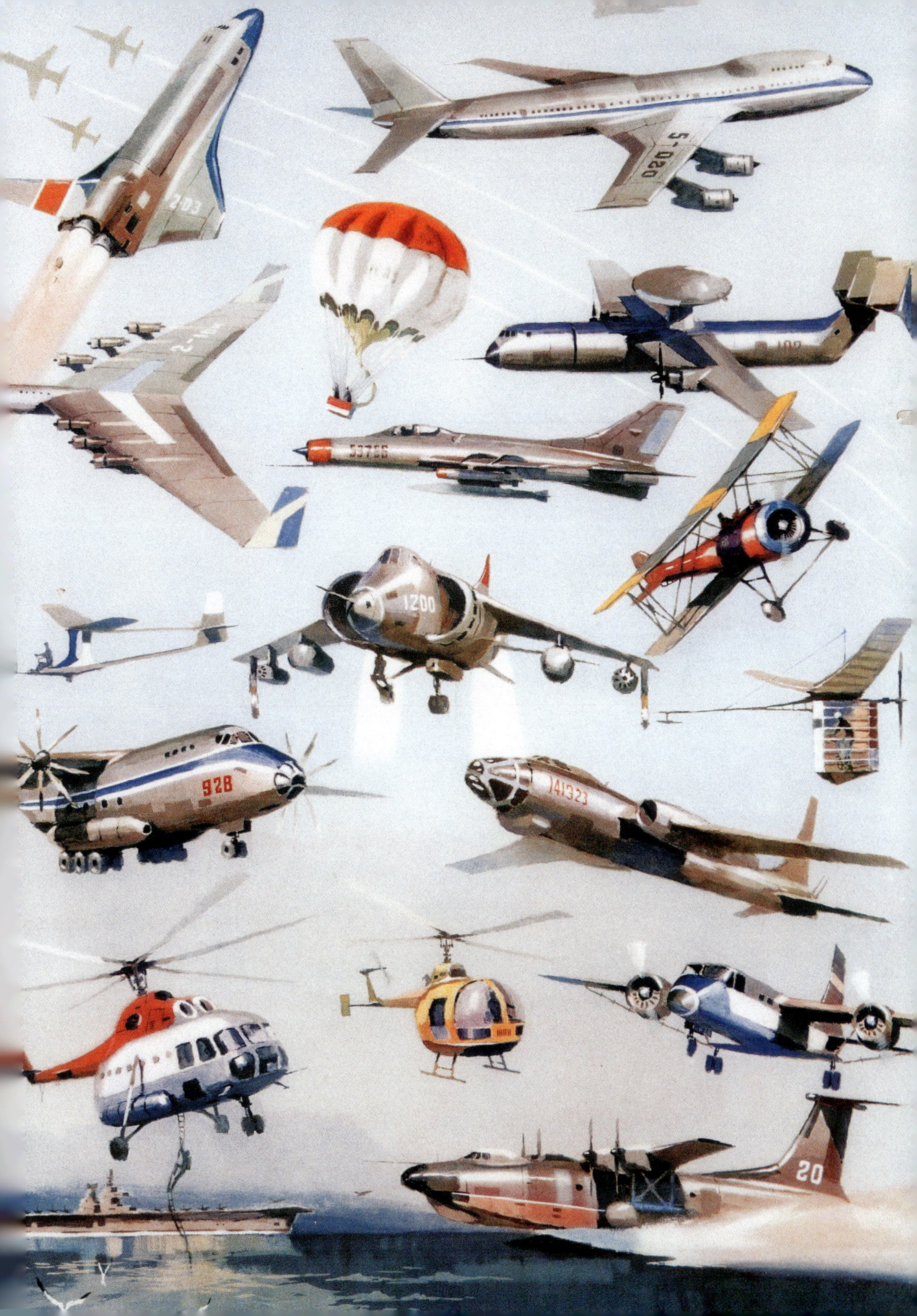
1200
928
20

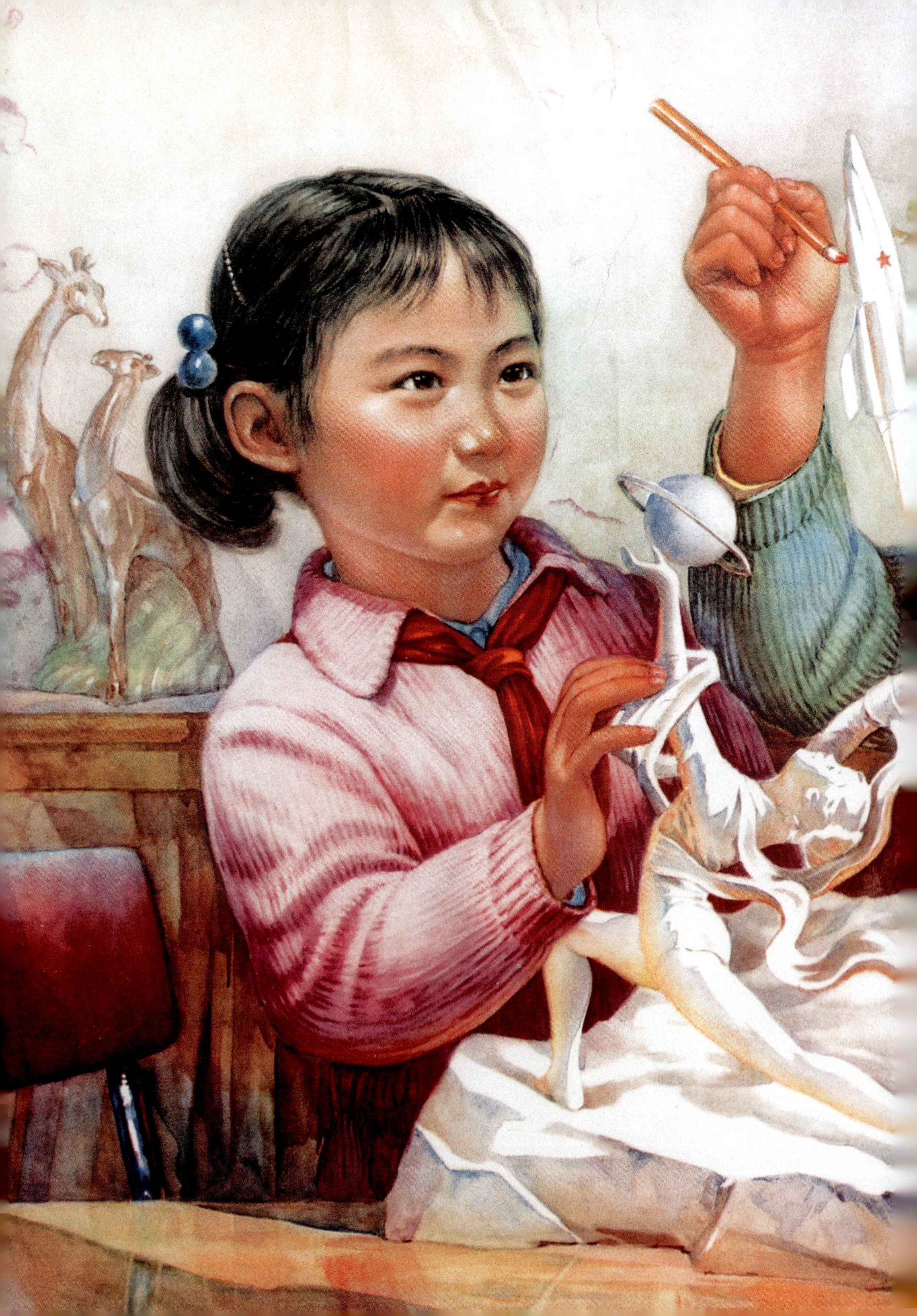

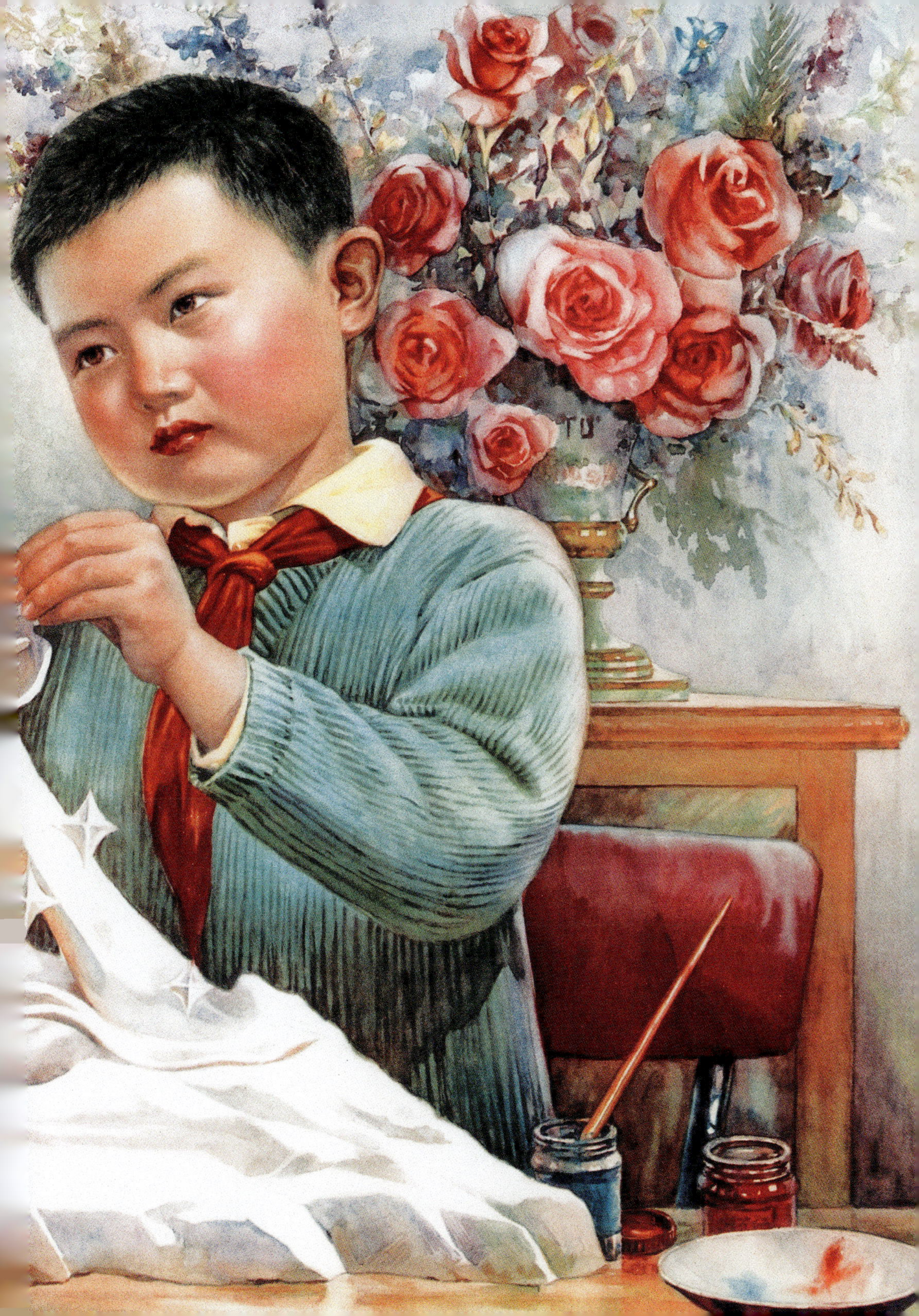

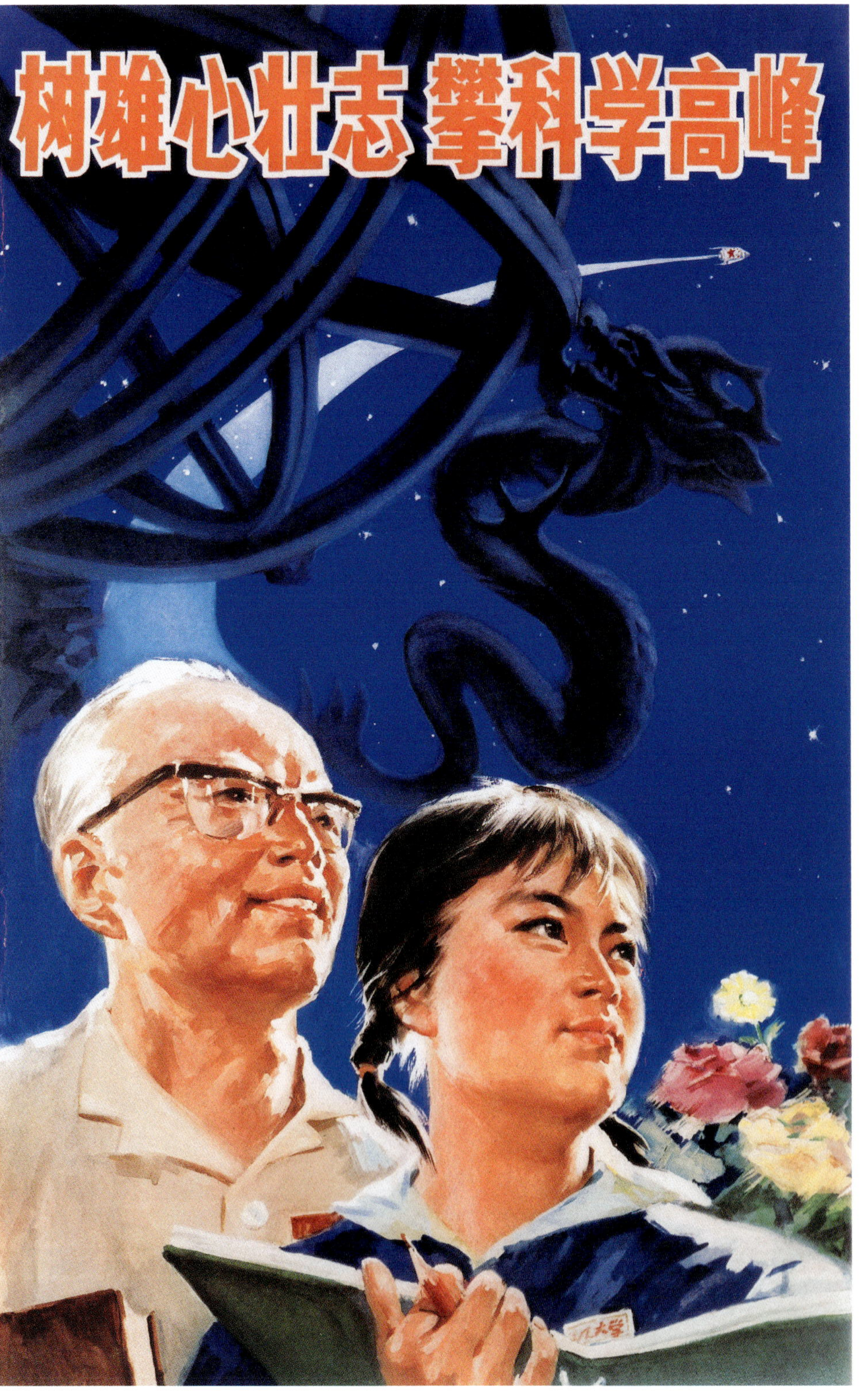
树雄心壮志 攀科学高峰

Opposite
Have a strong will and aim high; conquer the peak of science

Einen starken Willen und hohe Ziele haben, den Gipfel der Wissenschaft bezwingen

Avec de la volonté et de hauts desseins hissons-nous au sommet de la science

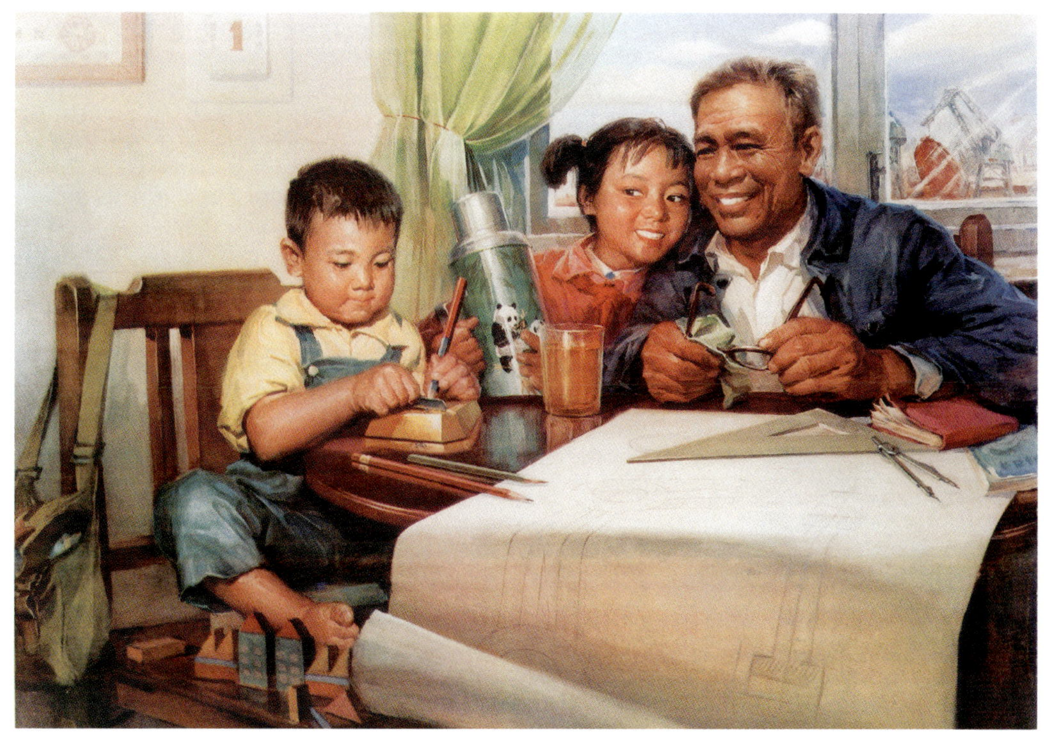

I help grandfather achieve technical innovation *Artists:* Liu Yi, Liu Jinrui, and Chao Deren; Tianjin People's Art Publishing House, 1974; 0.14 Yuan

Ich helfe Großvater bei der technischen Neuerung *Gemalt von* Liu Yi, Liu Jinrui und Chao Deren; Volkskunstverlag Tianjin, 1974; 0,14 Yuan

J'aide grand-père à se familiariser avec les nouveautés techniques *Peintres :* Liu Yi, Liu Jinrui et Chao Deren ; Éditions Populaires d'Art de Tianjin, 1974 ; 0,14 yuan

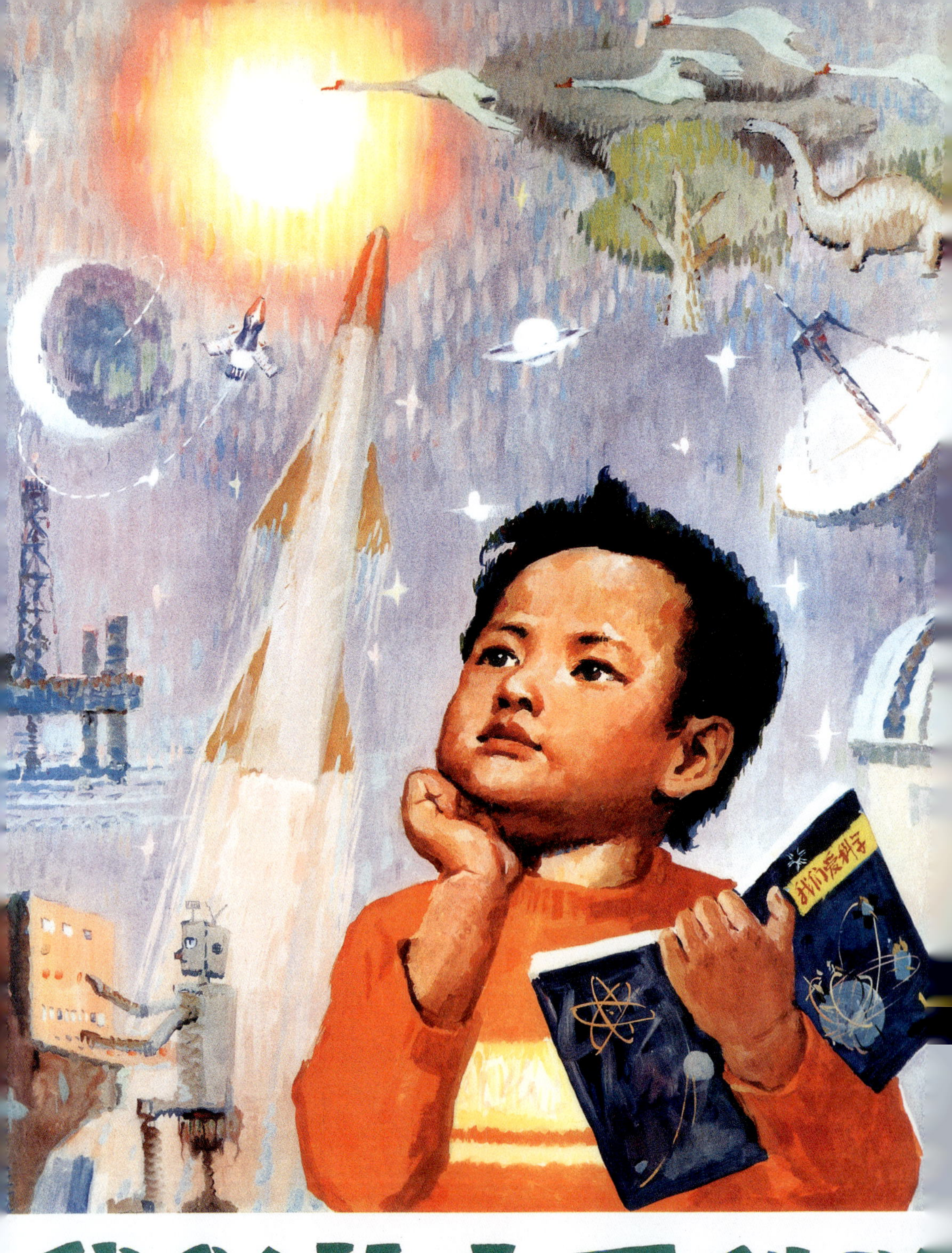

我们从小爱科学

We love science from an early age *Artist:* He Bing, People's Art Publishing House *Published by:* the Association for Popular Scientific Work, 1979 *Print run:* 32,000; 0.14 Yuan

Wir lieben von klein auf die Wissenschaft *Gemalt von* He Bing, Volkskunstverlag *Herausgeber:* Verein des populärwissenschaftlichen Schaffens, 1979 *Auflage:* 32 000; 0,14 Yuan

Nous aimons la science depuis notre enfance *Peintre :* He Bing, Éditions Populaires d'Art *Éditeur :* Association Populaire d'Activités Scientifiques, 1979 *Tirage :* 32 000 ; 0,14 yuan

“Investigation may be likened to the long months of pregnancy, and solving a problem to the day of birth. To investigate a problem is, indeed, to solve it.”

Eine Untersuchung anstellen heißt gleichsam „zehn [Mond-]Monate schwanger gehen“; eine Frage lösen heißt gleichsam „an einem Tag gebären“. In der Untersuchung einer Frage liegt ihre Lösung. ✶ L'enquête est comparable à une longue gestation, et la solution d'un problème au jour de la délivrance. Enquêter sur un problème, c'est le résoudre.

Pages 360–361

Sow new seeds *Magazine (white cover):* Red Flag *Artist:* Qiu Jianpin of the Xiulong brigade of the Zhouxi commune in the Nanhui District; Shanghai People's Publishing House, 1975 *Print run:* 300,000; 0.11 Yuan

Neue Keimlinge züchten *Zeitschrift (weiß):* Rote Fahne *Gemalt von* Qiu Jianpin der Brigade Xiulong der Kommune Zhouxi des Kreises Nanhui; Volksverlag Shanghai, 1975 *Auflage:* 300 000; 0,11 Yuan

Semons de nouvelles graines *Revue (blanche) :* Drapeau rouge *Peintre :* Qiu Jianpin, de la brigade de Xiulong, commune de Zhouxi, canton de Nanhui ; Éditions Populaires de Shanghai, 1975 *Tirage :* 300 000 ; 0,11 yuan

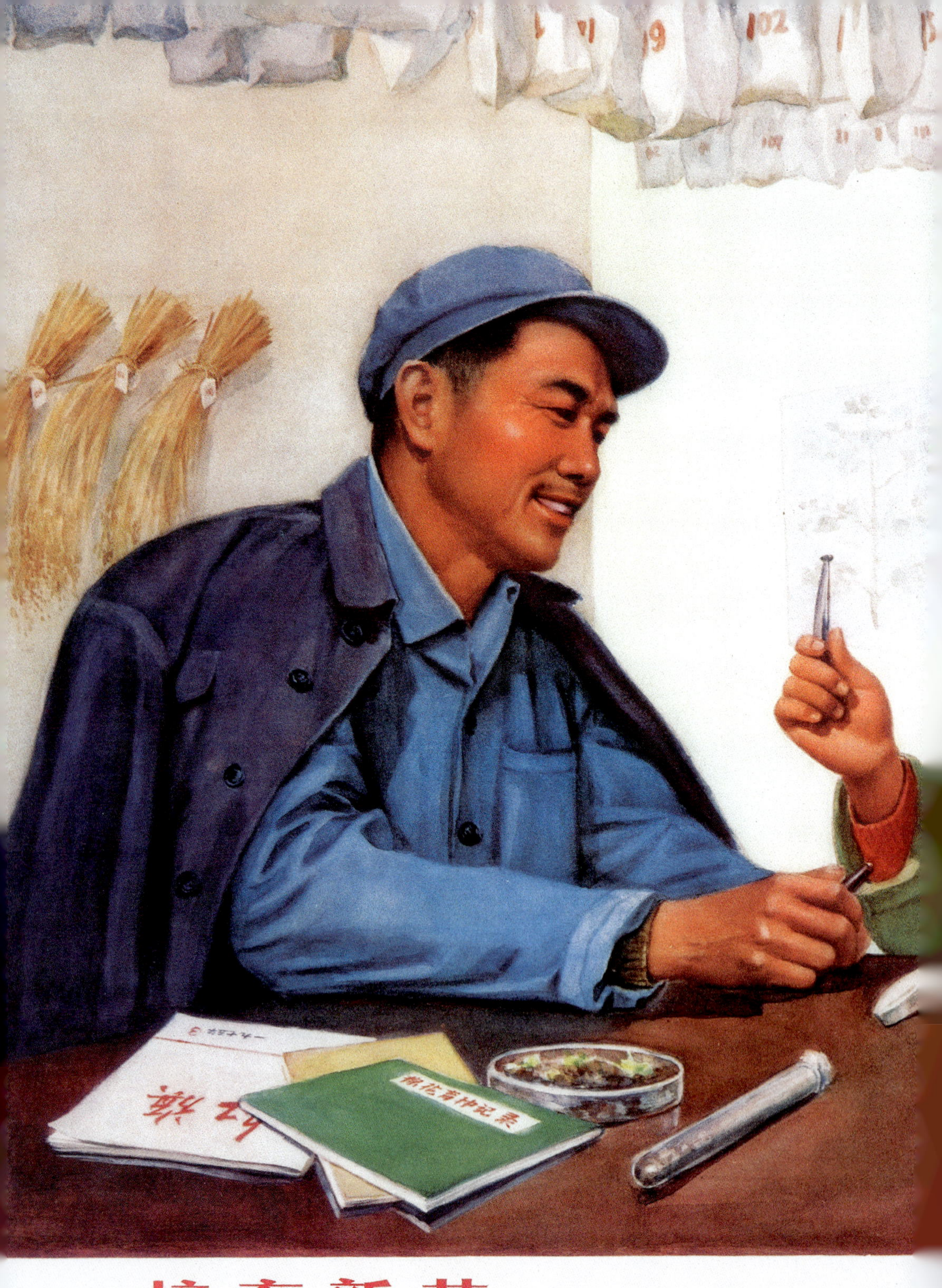

培育新苗

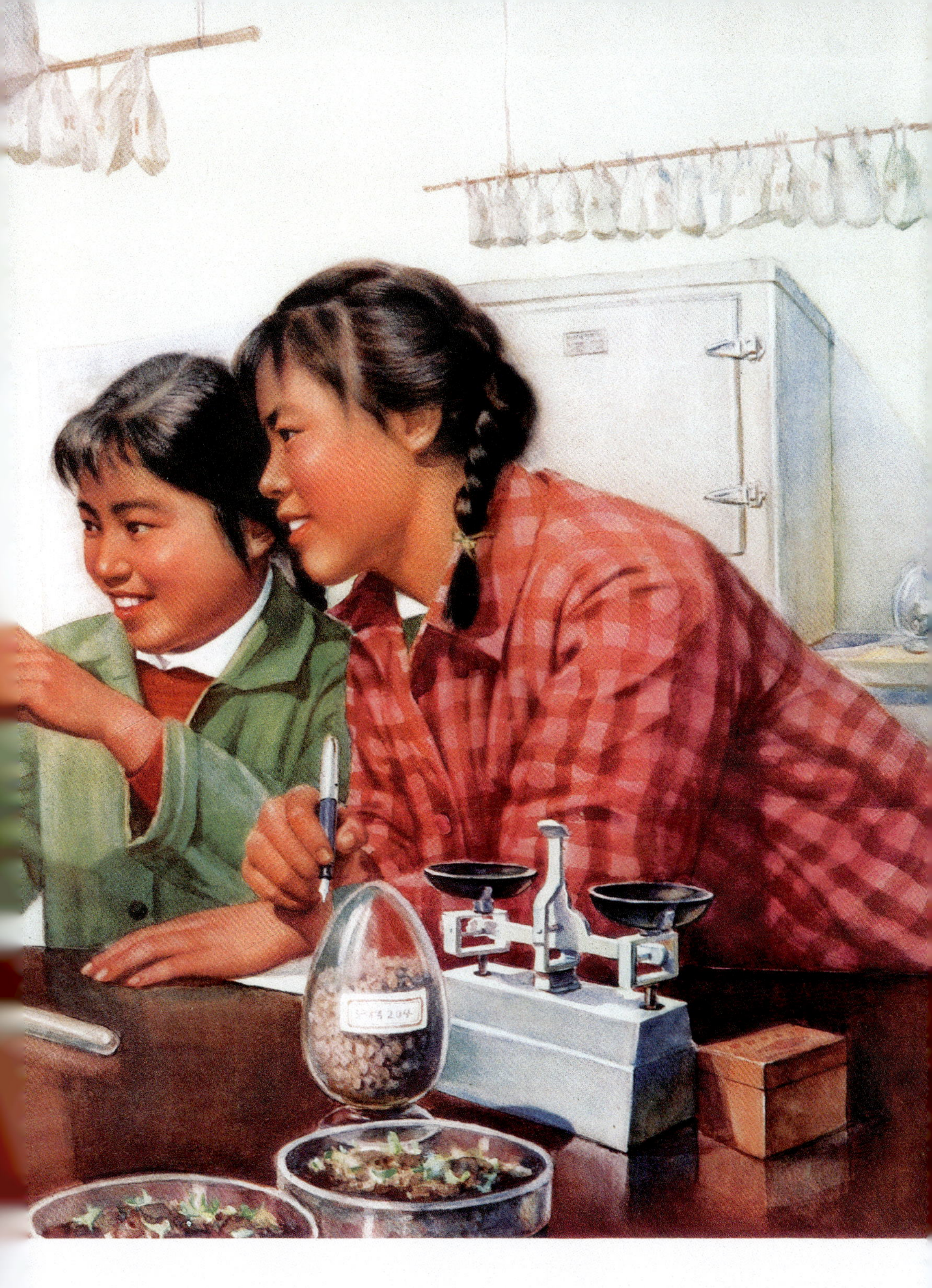

上海人民美术出版社出版 新华书店上海发行所发行 上海中华印刷厂印刷 统一书号 8171·1345
1975年7月第1次印刷 定价 0.11元

First attempt Poster used as teaching aid; Shanghai Educational Publishing House, 1979 *Print run*: 570,000; 0.12 Yuan

Der erste Versuch Erziehungsplakat; Erziehungsverlag Shanghai, 1979 *Auflage:* 570 000; 0,12 Yuan

La première expérience Affiche pédagogique ; Éditions Éducatives de Shanghai, 1979 *Tirage :* 570 000 ; 0,12 yuan

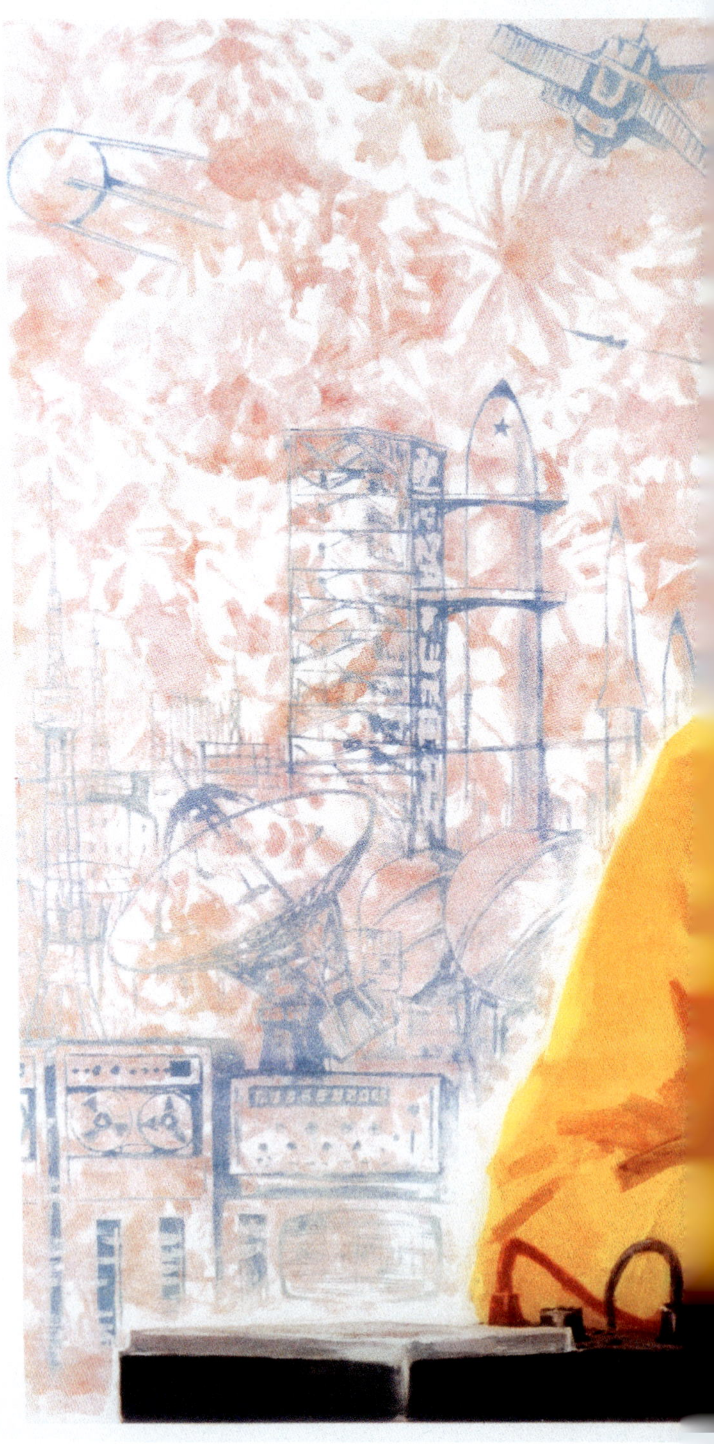

Pages 364–365
Mobilize all Party members to strive towards the goal of modernizing science and technology *Artist:* Chao Deren; Tianjin People's Art Publishing House, 1978; 0.14 Yuan

Mobilisiert alle Parteimitglieder, um dem Ziel der Modernisierung von Wissenschaft und Technik zuzustreben *Gemalt von* Chao Deren; Volkskunstverlag Tianjin, 1978; 0,14 Yuan

Mobilisons tous les membres du Parti en vue d'atteindre l'objectif de modernisation de la science et de la technologie *Peintre :* Chao Deren ; Éditions Populaires d'Art de Tianjin, 1978 ; 0,14 yuan

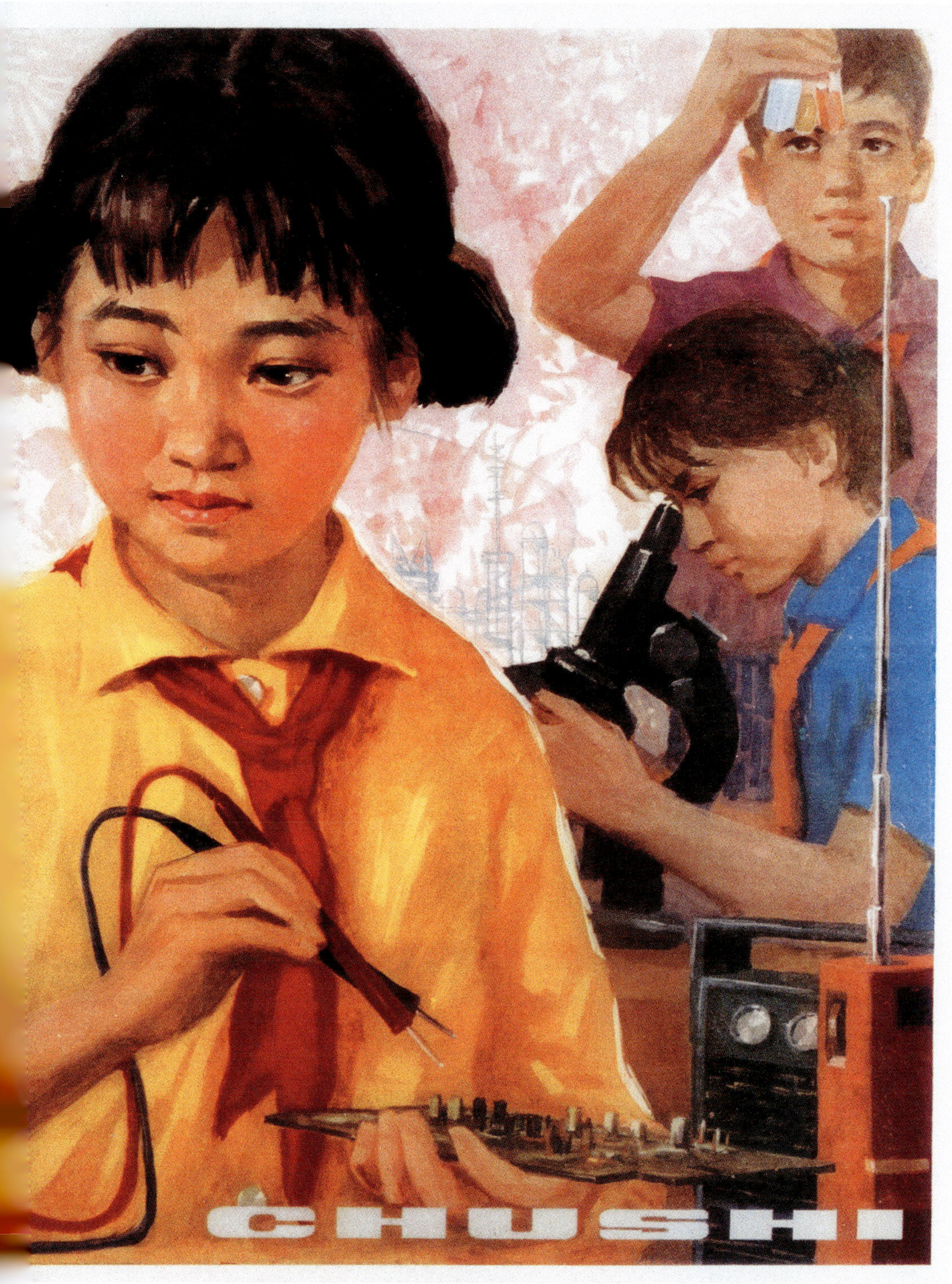
CHUSHI

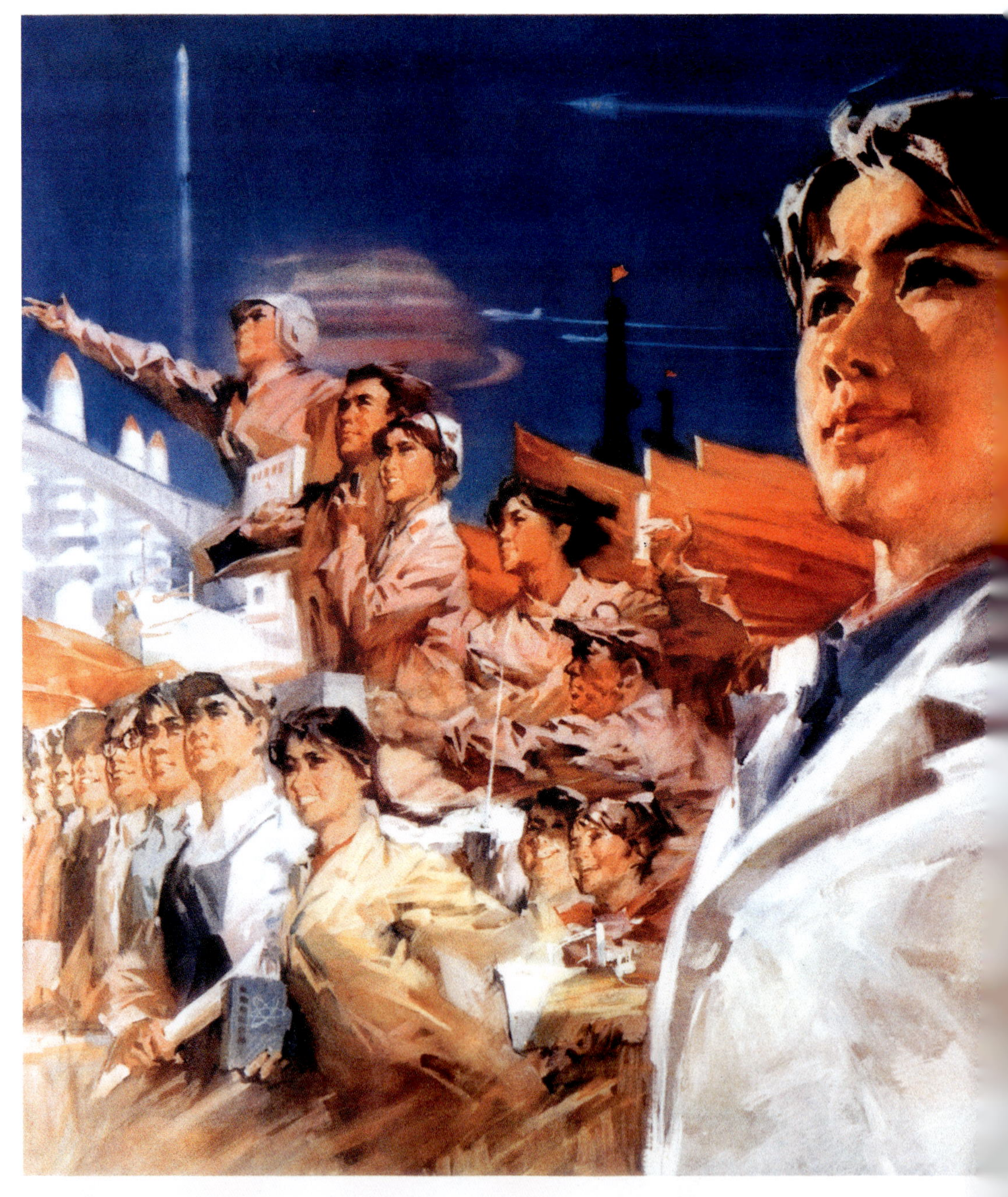

全党动员 向科学

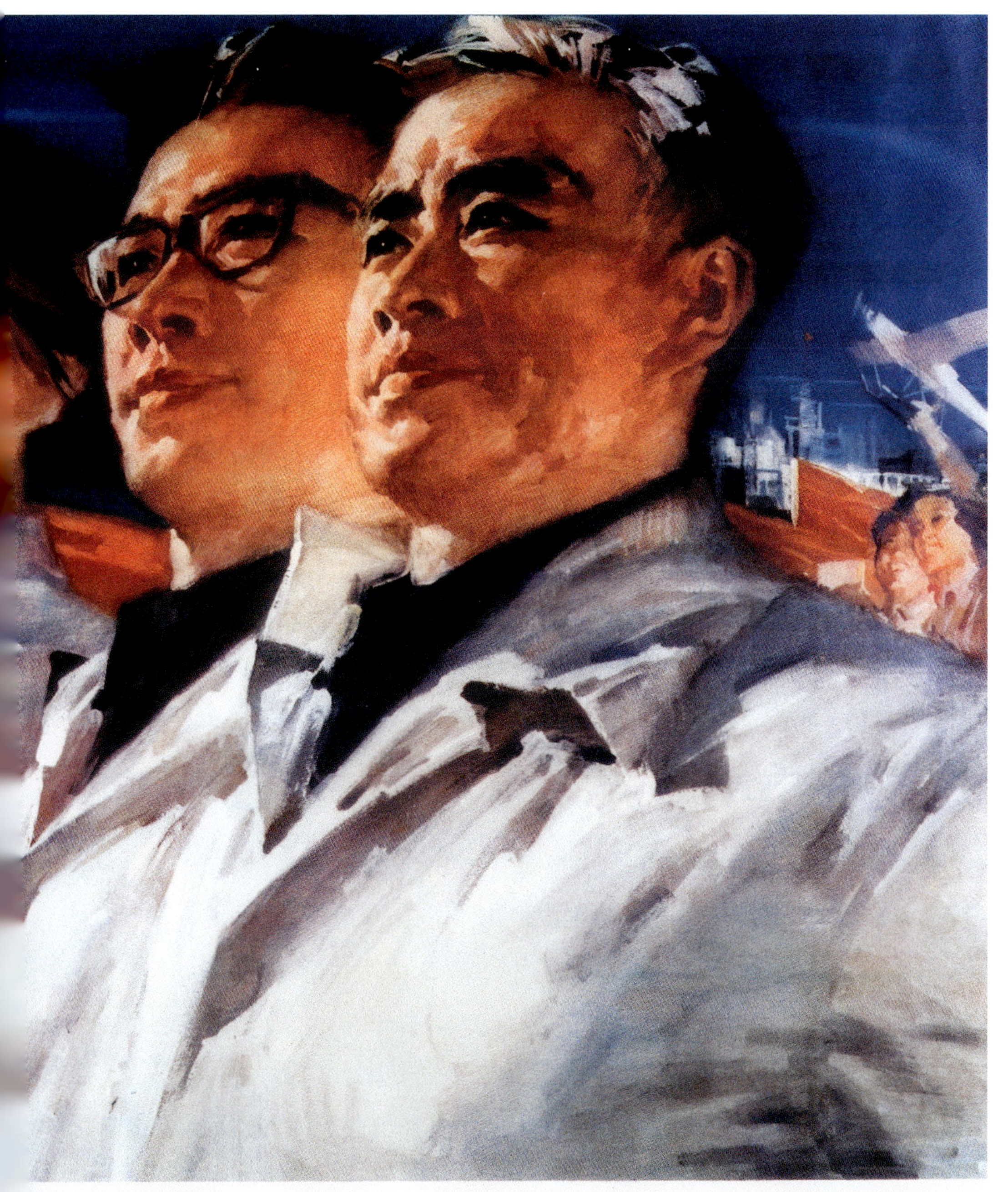

技术現代化进军
晁德仁作

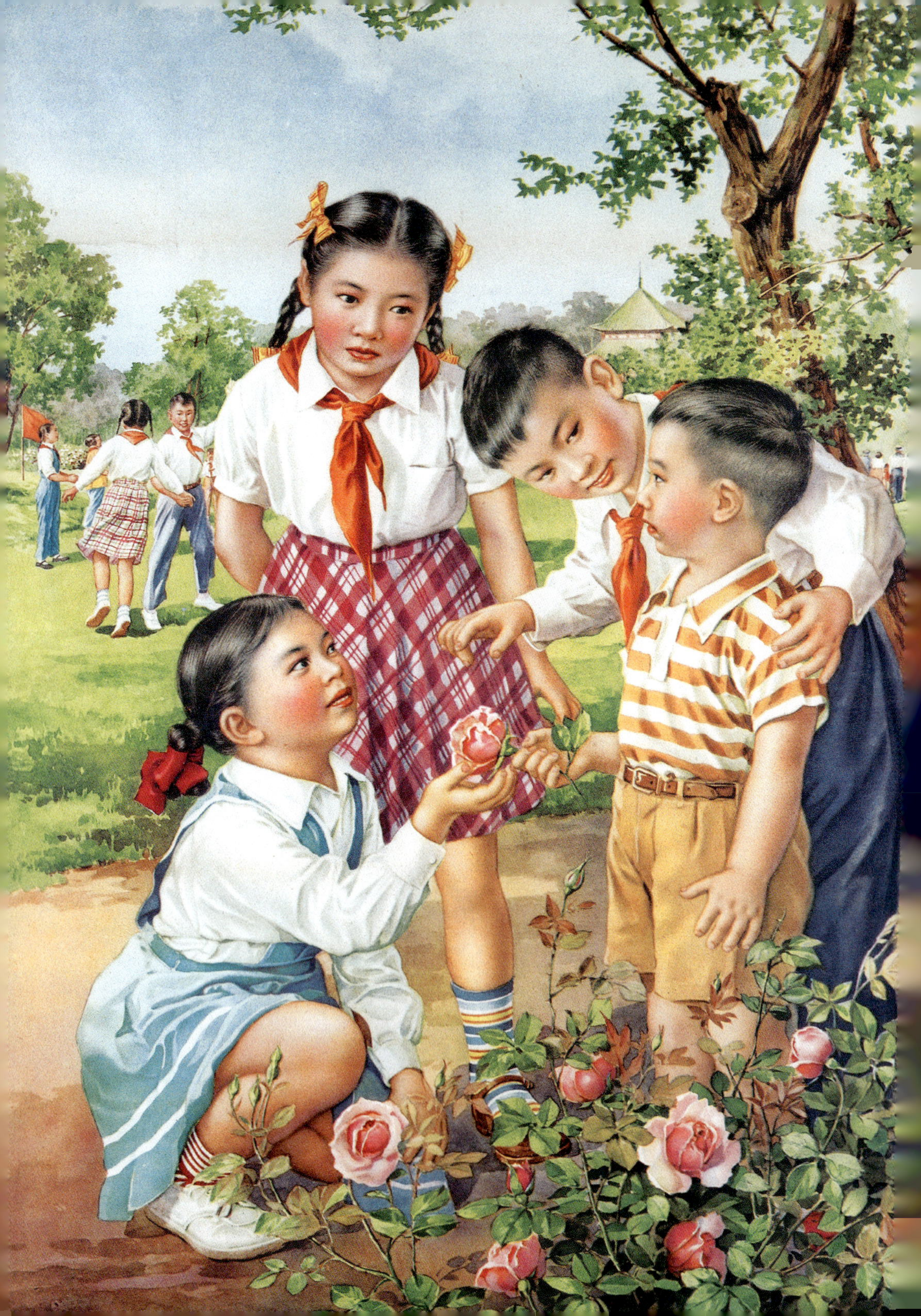

XXIV

IDEOLOGICAL SELF-CULTIVATION

BERICHTIGUNG FALSCHER ANSICHTEN
L'APPRENTISSAGE IDÉOLOGIQUE

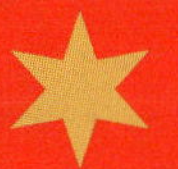

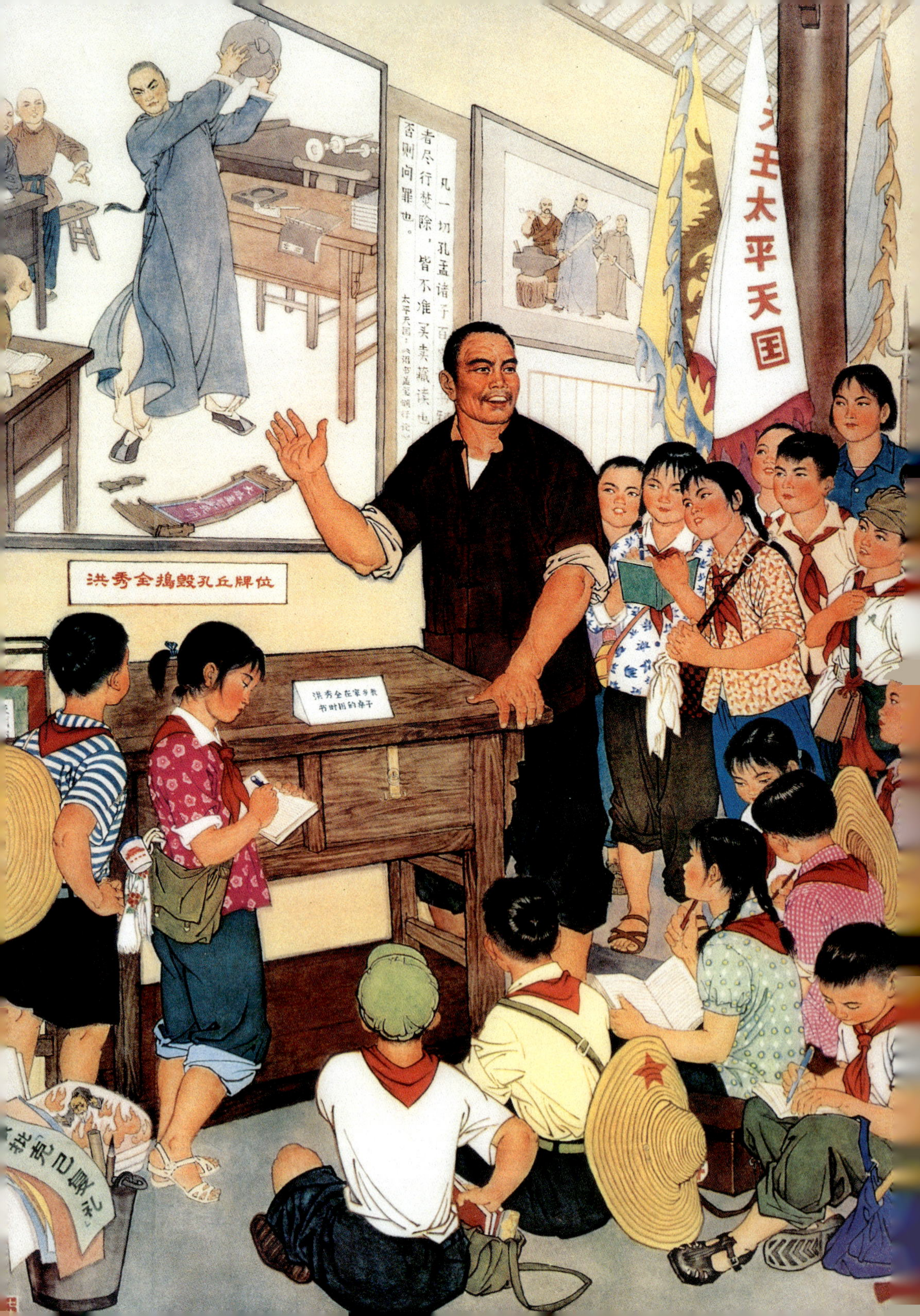

凡一切孔孟诸子百
者尽行焚除，皆不准买卖藏读也
否则问罪也。
太平天国：《诏书盖玺颁行论》
王太平天国
洪秀全捣毁孔丘牌位
洪秀全在家乡教书时用的桌子
批克己复礼

Page 366

We must protect what belongs to us all *Artist:* Li Mubai; Shanghai People's Art Publishing House, 1958; 0.18 Yuan

Wir müssen den Gemeinbesitz schützen *Gemalt von* Li Mubai; Volkskunstverlag Shanghai, 1958; 0,18 Yuan

Nous devons protéger le bien commun *Peintre :* Li Mubai ; Éditions Populaires d'Art de Shanghai, 1958 ; 0,18 yuan

The main subject *Under the picture, left:* Hong Xiuquan* destroys the genealogical table of Confucius *White flag, right:* Heavenly kingdom of eternal peace *Scroll, bottom left:* Be deeply critical of the teachings of Confucius *Artists:* Shan Boxin and Chen Wenguang; Beijing People's Art Publishing House, 1973; 0.11 Yuan

* Hong Xiuquan (1814–1864): Leader of the peasant revolt against the Qing Dynasty (1644–1911) that began in 1851. He called the movement under his control the "Heavenly Kingdom of Eternal Peace" (Tai Ping Tian Guo). In 1864 the revolution was suppressed by the Qing government.

Das Hauptfach *Unter dem Bild links:* Hong Xiuquan* zerstört die Ahnentafel des Konfuzius *Rechts die weiße Fahne:* Himmlisches Reich des ewigen Friedens *Schriftrolle links unten:* Die Lehre von Konfuzius gründlich kritisieren *Gemalt von* Shan Boxin und Chen Wenguang; Volkskunstverlag Peking, 1973; 0,11 Yuan

* Hong Xiuquan (1814–1864): Anführer des 1851 begonnenen Bauernaufstandes gegen die Qing-Dynastie (1644–1911). Er nannte seine Herrschaft „Himmlisches Reich des ewigen Friedens" (Tai Ping Tian Guo). 1864 wurde die Revolution von der Qing-Regierung unterdrückt.

La matière principale *Sous l'image, à gauche :* Hong Xiuquan* détruisant le tableau généalogique de Confucius *Drapeau blanc, à droite :* L'Empire de la Grande Paix *Rouleau en bas à gauche :* Pour une critique radicale de la doctrine de Confucius *Peintres :* Shan Boxin et Chen Wenguang ; Éditions Populaires d'Art de Pékin, 1973 ; 0,11 yuan

* Hong Xiuquan (1814–1864) : Chef de l'insurrection paysanne contre la dynastie des Qing qui commença en 1851 à Guangxi. Il fonda ce qu'il appela « l'Empire de la Grande Paix » (Tai Ping Tian Guo). La rébellion fut étouffée en 1864 par le gouvernement des Qing.

“There may be some communists, who were not conquered by enemies with guns and were worthy of the name of heroes for standing up to these enemies, but who cannot withstand sugar-coated bullets; they will be defeated by sugar-coated bullets. We must guard against such a situation.”

Es mag Kommunisten geben, die sich vom bewaffneten Feind nicht besiegen ließen und wegen ihrer Standhaftigkeit verdienen, Helden genannt zu werden; wenn sie aber mit „Geschossen in Zuckerhülle“ angegriffen werden, halten sie nicht stand, und sie werden von den Zuckergeschossen bezwungen. Wir müssen einer solchen Situation zuvorkommen. ✶ Il peut y avoir de ces communistes que l’ennemi armé n’a pu vaincre, qui se conduisaient devant l’ennemi en héros dignes de ce nom, mais qui, incapables de résister aux balles enrobées de sucre, tomberont sous ces balles. Nous devons prévenir pareil état de choses.

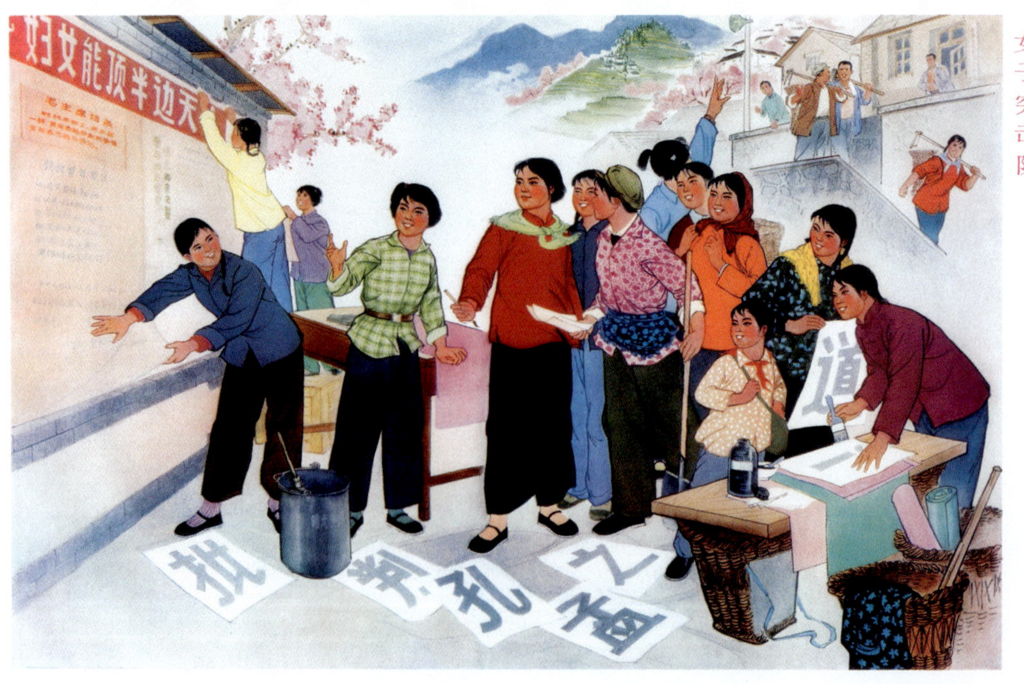

女子突击队

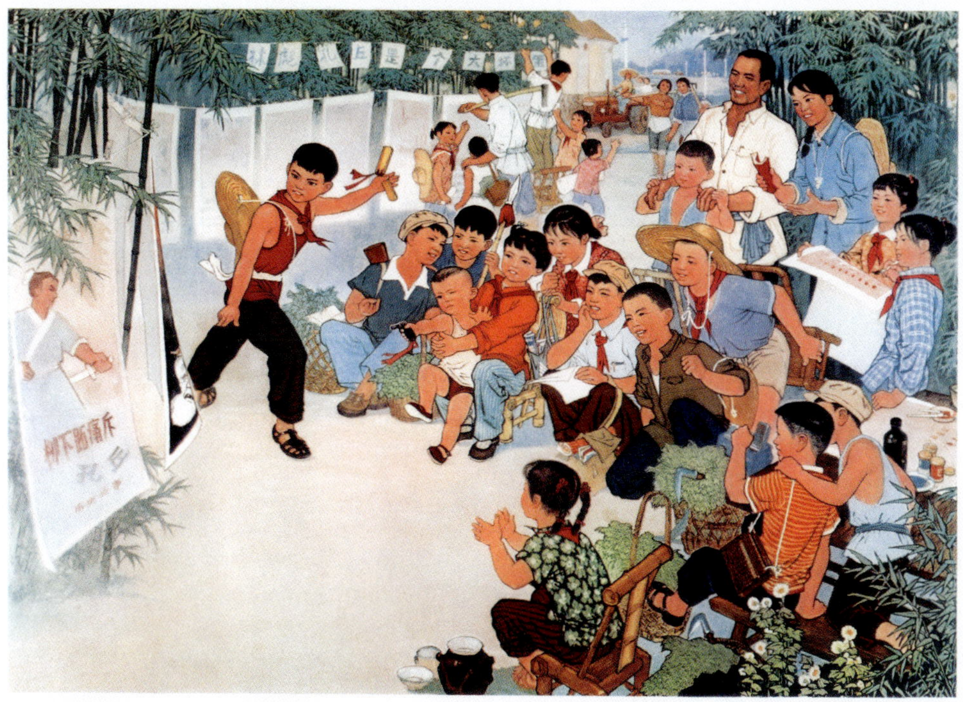

林彪孔丘都是坏东西

Lin Biao* and Confucius are both rogues *On picture, left:* Liu Xiazhi** took decisive action against Confucius *On bamboo, top:* Lin Biao and Confucius are rascals *Artists:* Zhang Chang and Wang Changjin; Shanghai People's Publishing House, 1st edn 1976, 2nd edn 1976; 0.11 Yuan
* See page 132.
** A contemporary of Confucius, leader of a slave rebellion around the end of the Spring and Autumn Period (770–476 BCE).

Lin Biao* und Konfuzius sind beide Schurken *Auf dem Bild links:* Liu Xiazhi** trat Konfuzius entschieden entgegen *Oben am Bambus:* Lin Biao und Konfuzius sind Bösewichte *Gemalt von* Zhang Chang und Wang Changjin; Volksverlag Shanghai, 1. Aufl. 1976, 2. Aufl. 1976; 0,11 Yuan
* Siehe Seite 132.
** Konfuzius' Zeitgenosse, Anführer eines Sklavenaufstandes gegen Ende der Frühlings- und Herbstperiode (770–476 v. Chr.)

Lin Biao* et Confucius sont tous les deux des crapules *Sur l'image de gauche :* Liu Xiazhi** s'est résolument opposé à Confucius *Sur les bambous en haut :* Lin Biao et Confucius sont de méchantes gens *Peintres :* Zhang Chang et Wang Changjin ; Éditions Populaires de Shanghai, 1ère éd. 1976, 2e éd. 1976 ; 0,11 yuan
* Voir page 132.
** Contemporain de Confucius, chef d'une révolte d'esclaves vers la fin de la période de printemps et d'automne (770–476 av. J.-C.).

Opposite
Women's shock brigade
Headline on wall newspaper, left: Women make up half of heaven *Chinese characters on ground:* Condemn the teachings of Confucius and Mencius*; Beijing People's Publishing House, 1972; 0.14 Yuan
*Mencius (c. 372–289 BCE), representative of one of the leading schools in Confucian thought.

Frauen-Stoßbrigade
Titel der Wandzeitung links: Frauen sind die Hälfte des Himmels *Schriftzeichen auf dem Boden:* Lehren von Konfuzius und Menzius* verurteilen; Volksverlag Peking, 1972; 0,14 Yuan
*Menzius (ca. 372–289 v.Chr.), Vertreter einer der wichtigsten konfuzianischen Schulen.

Brigade féminine de choc
Titre du journal mural, à gauche : Les femmes sont la moitié du ciel *Caractères sur le sol :* Mettons Confucius et Mencius* à l'index ; Éditions Populaires de Pékin, 1972 ; 0,14 yuan
* Mencius (vers 372–289 av. J.-C.) : représentant de l'une des plus importantes écoles confucéennes.

This is what the resolute "lefties" are like* *Top left:* Clowns of history** *Book title:* Popular literature on the national revolutionary war by Lu Xun*** *Top right:* Outrageous and extravagant praise**** *On the peach on the table:* Long life *Writing by the trombone:* Chiang Kai-shek leads the struggle against the Japanese aggressors *Bottom left:* In cahoots***** *Lin says:* Jiang Qing is an art expert with a lot of political clout *Jiang Qing says:* Vice-Chairman Lin is always willing to learn *Bottom right:* Dogs barking****** *Sign on door:* Prime Minister Zhou Enlai's sickroom *On Zhang Chingiao's club:* Against empiricism *Jiang Qing says:* Before you haven't[…,] we must get to the root cause of the return of right-wing convictions *Yao Wen-yuan (bottom) says:* The greatest supporter of the school of Confucianism, the greatest ruler on the capitalist path.

* This is a page out of a series of political caricatures about the "Gang of Four."

** The characters are Jiang Qing and Zhang Chingiao.

*** Lu Xun (1881–1936), one of China's major literary figures, thinkers and revolutionaries, best known for his sharp-tongued essays of social criticism, described as "China's Gorky."

**** The picture hanging upside down depicts Chiang Kai-shek. The figures are Jiang Qing and Zhang Chingiao.

***** The man is the one-time successor to Mao, Lin Biao, who died in a plane crash while fleeing the country after a failed putsch in 1971. The woman is Jiang Qing.

****** The figures are the "Gang of Four."

So sind die konsequent entschlossenen „Linken"* *Oben links:* Clowns der Geschichte** *Buchtitel:* Volksliteratur des nationalen revolutionären Kriegs von Lu Xun*** *Oben rechts:* Unverschämte Lobhudelei**** *Auf dem Pfirsich auf dem Tisch:* Langes Leben *Schrift neben der Kontrabasstuba:* Chiang Kai-shek ist der Führer im Widerstandskampf gegen japanische Aggressoren *Unten links:* Unter einer Decke stecken***** *Aus dem Mund von Lin:* Jiang Qing ist politisch stark und eine Kunstexpertin *Aus dem Mund von Jiang Qing:* Der Vize-Vorsitzende Lin ist stets bereit, fleißig zu lernen *Unten rechts:* Hundegebell****** *Das Schild an der Tür:* Das Krankenzimmer des Premierministers Zhou Enlai *Auf der Keule von Zhang Chunqiao:* Gegen den Empirismus *Aus dem Mund von Jiang Qing:* Bevor du noch nicht …, müssen wir der Ursache der Rückkehr der Rechtsgesinnung auf den Grund gehen *Aus dem Mund von Yao Wenyuan ganz unten:* Der größte Anhänger der konfuzianischen Schule, der größte Machthaber auf dem kapitalistischen Weg.

* Hier handelt es sich um eine Seite einer politischen Karikatur-Serie über die sogenannte Viererbande.

** Die Figuren sind Jiang Qing und Zhang Chunqiao.

*** Lu Xun (1881–1936), ein großer Literat, Denker und Revolutionär Chinas, in erster Linie bekannt durch seine scharfzüngigen gesellschaftskritischen Essays, wurde als „Chinas Gorki" bezeichnet.

**** Das auf dem Kopf hängende Bild ist von Chiang Kai-shek. Die Figuren sind Jiang Qing und Zhang Chunqiao.

***** Der Mann im Bild ist der ursprüngliche Mao-Nachfolger Lin Biao, der bei der Flucht nach einem gescheiterten Putsch 1971 mit dem Flugzeug abgestürzt und gestorben war. Die Frau ist Jiang Qing.

****** Die Figuren sind die sogenannte Viererbande.

C'est ainsi que sont les « gauchistes » résolus !* *En haut à gauche :* Les clowns de l'Histoire** *Titre du livre :* Littérature populaire de la guerre nationale révolutionnaire de Lu Xun*** *En haut à droite :* Adulation éhontée**** *Sur la pêche sur la table :* Longue vie *Au-dessus de l'hélicon :* Chiang Kai-shek est le chef de la résistance armée contre l'agresseur japonais *En bas à gauche :* Cachons-nous sous une couverture***** *Lin Biao :* Jiang Qing a une grande force politique, et c'est une experte en matière d'art *Jiang Qing :* Le vice-président est toujours prêt à apprendre de nouvelles choses *En bas à droite :* Aboiements****** *Pancarte près de la porte :* Chambre d'hôpital du Premier ministre Chou En-lai *Sur la massue de Chang Chun-chiao :* Contre l'empirisme *Jiang Qing :* Avant que tu ne …, nous devons savoir le pourquoi du retour de la conscience de droite *Yao Wanyuan, tout en bas :* Le plus grand partisan de l'école confucianiste, le plus grand dirigeant sur la voie du capitalisme.

* Il s'agit ici d'une page extraite d'une série de caricatures politiques sur la Bande des Quatre.

** Les personnages sont Jiang Qing et Chang Chun-chiao.

***Lu Xun (1881–1936) : Grand homme de lettres, penseur et révolutionnaire chinois, connu essentiellement pour la causticité de ses essais de critique sociale, il fut qualifié de « Gorki chinois ».

**** Le portrait accroché est celui de Chiang Kai-shek. Les deux personnages sont Jiang Qing et Chang Chun-chiao.

***** L'homme sur l'image est Lin Biao, le successeur initial de Mao, qui mourut dans un crash d'avion tandis qu'il s'enfuyait après l'échec d'un putsch en 1971. La femme est Jiang Qing.

****** Les personnages sont les membres de la Bande des Quatre.

如此一贯坚定的"左派"

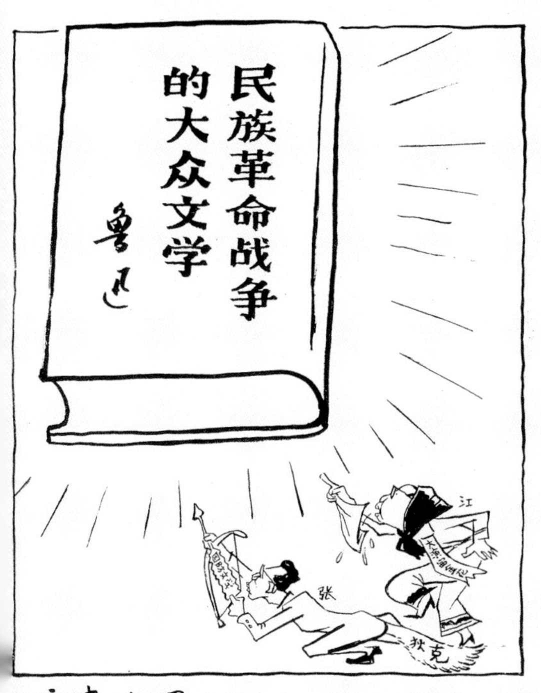

历史小丑

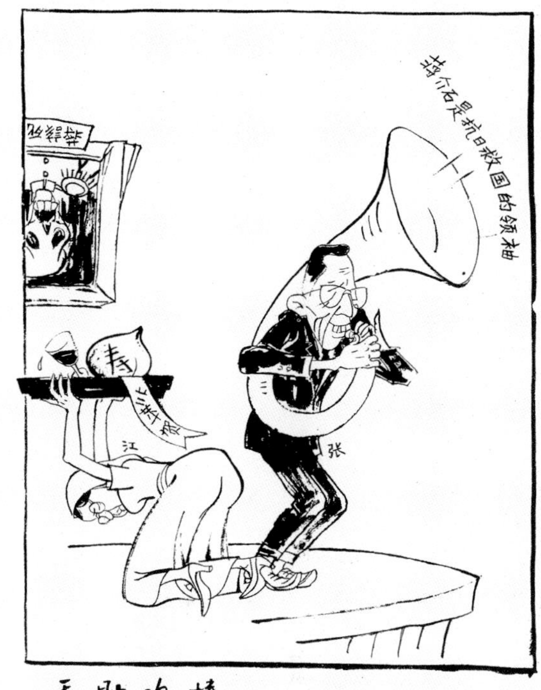

无耻吹捧

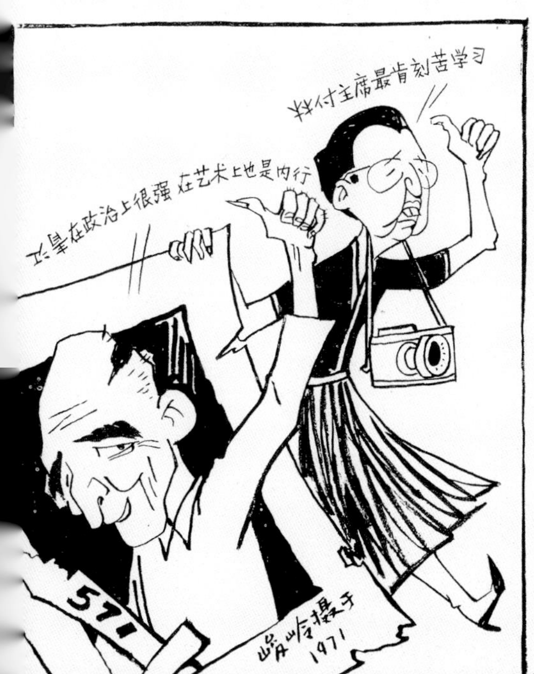

狼狈为奸

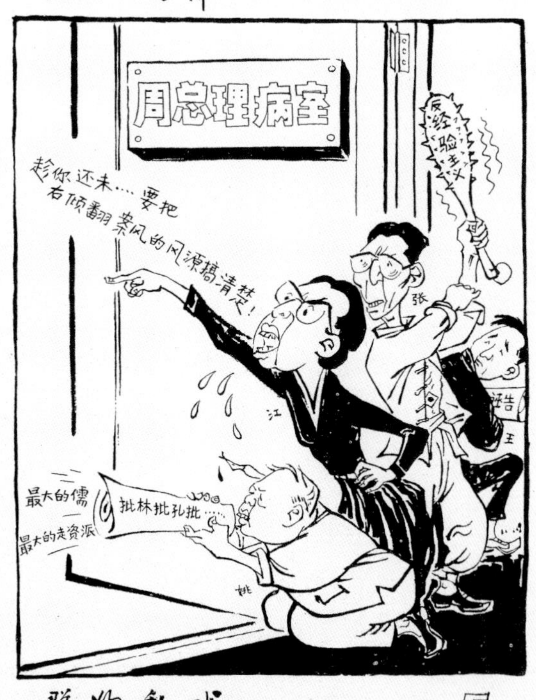

群狗乱吠

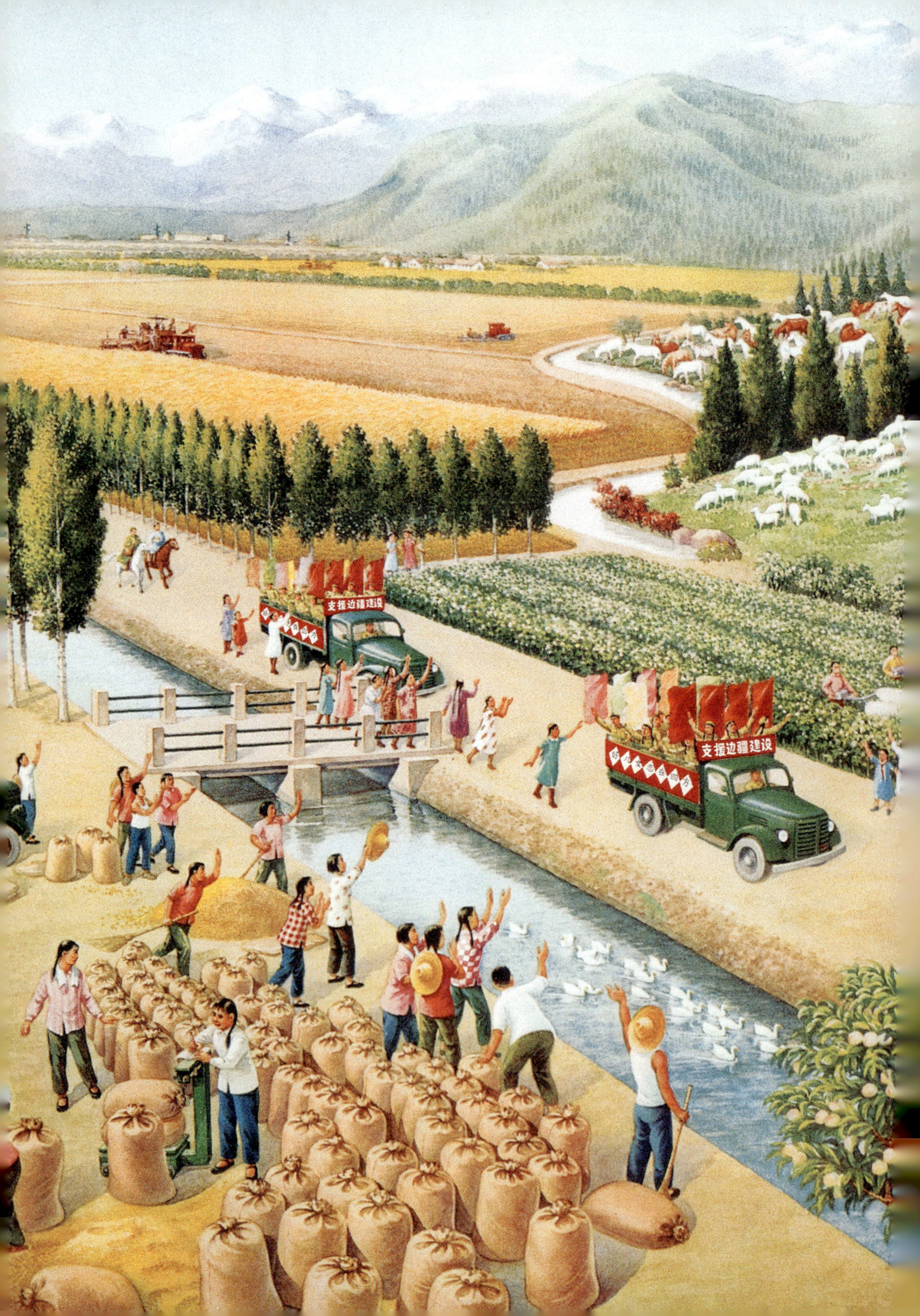
支援边疆建设
支援边疆建设
好儿女志在四方

XXV

UNITY

DIE EINHEIT
L'UNITÉ

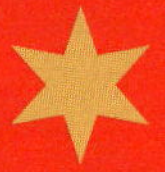

Page 374
A new sight in the frontier zone* *Slogan on the first truck:* Support the development of the frontier zone *Artist:* Zhang Yuqing; Shanghai People's Publishing House, 1st edn 1973, 5th edn 1973 *Print run:* 2,000,001–3,800,000; 0.11 Yuan
* The clothing of the people on the right identifies them as members of the Uigur people, so this is the autonomous region of Xingjiang in western China.

Ein neues Bild im Grenzgebiet* *Parole auf dem ersten Lastwagen:* Den Aufbau des Grenzgebietes unterstützen *Gemalt von* Zhang Yuqing; Volksverlag Shanghai, 1. Aufl. 1973, 5. Aufl. 1973 *Auflage:* 2 000 001–3 800 000; 0,11 Yuan
* An der Kleidung der Leute rechts kann man erkennen, dass es sich um die Völkergruppe Uiguren, also um das autonome Gebiet Xingjiang im Westen Chinas, handelt.

Une nouvelle image de la région frontalière* *Slogan sur le premier camion :* Soutenons l'édification de la région frontalière *Peintre :* Zhang Yuqing ; Éditions Populaires de Shanghai, 1ère éd. 1973, 5e éd. 1973 *Tirage :* 2 000 001–3 800 000 ; 0,11 yuan
* On reconnaît aux vêtements des personnes de droite qu'il s'agit du groupe ethnique des Ouïgours, et donc de la région autonome du Xinjiang (Chine de l'Ouest).

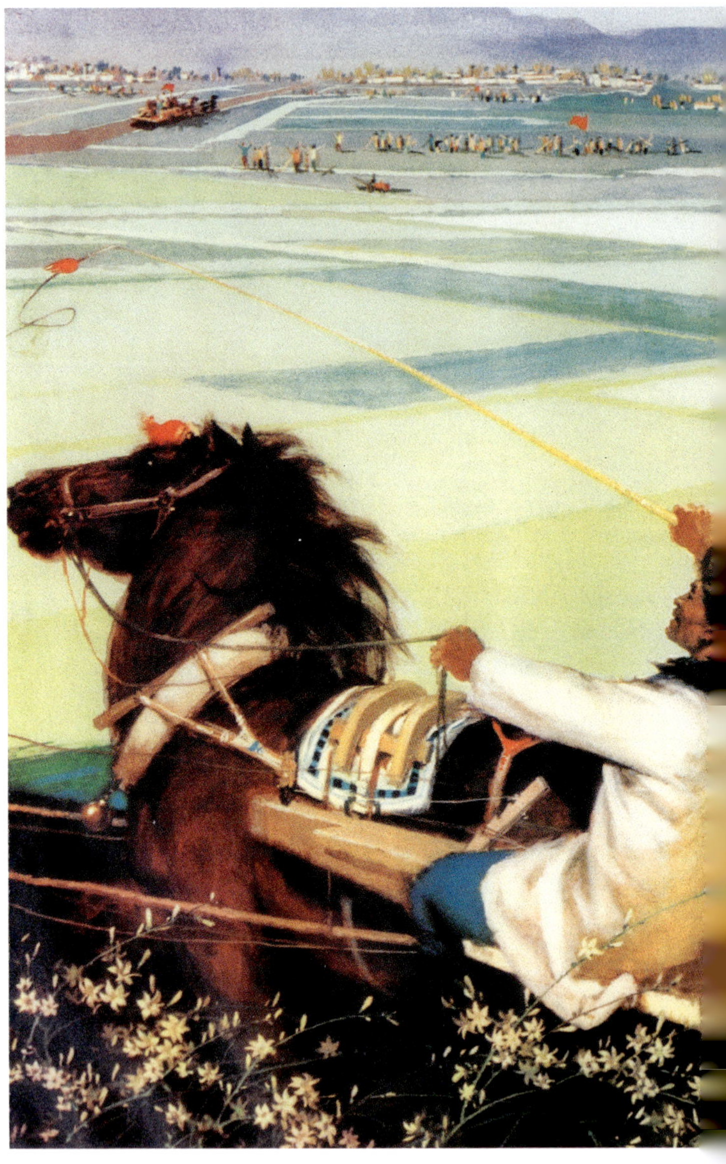

Pages 378–379
On festive holidays we miss our relatives twice as much *Artist:* Ha Qiongwen; Shanghai People's Art Publishing House, 1st edn 1980, 2nd edn 1980 *Print run:* 5,001–23,000; 0.16 Yuan

An frohen Festtagen hat man doppelte Sehnsucht nach seinen Familienangehörigen *Gemalt von* Ha Qiongwen; Volkskunstverlag Shanghai, 1. Aufl. 1980, 2. Aufl. 1980 *Auflage:* 5.001–23 000; 0,16 Yuan

Dans l'allégresse des jours de fête, on a doublement la nostalgie de sa famille *Peintre :* Ha Qiongwen ; Éditions Populaires de Shanghai, 1ère éd. 1980, 2e éd. 1980 *Tirage:* 5 001–23 000 ; 0,16 yuan

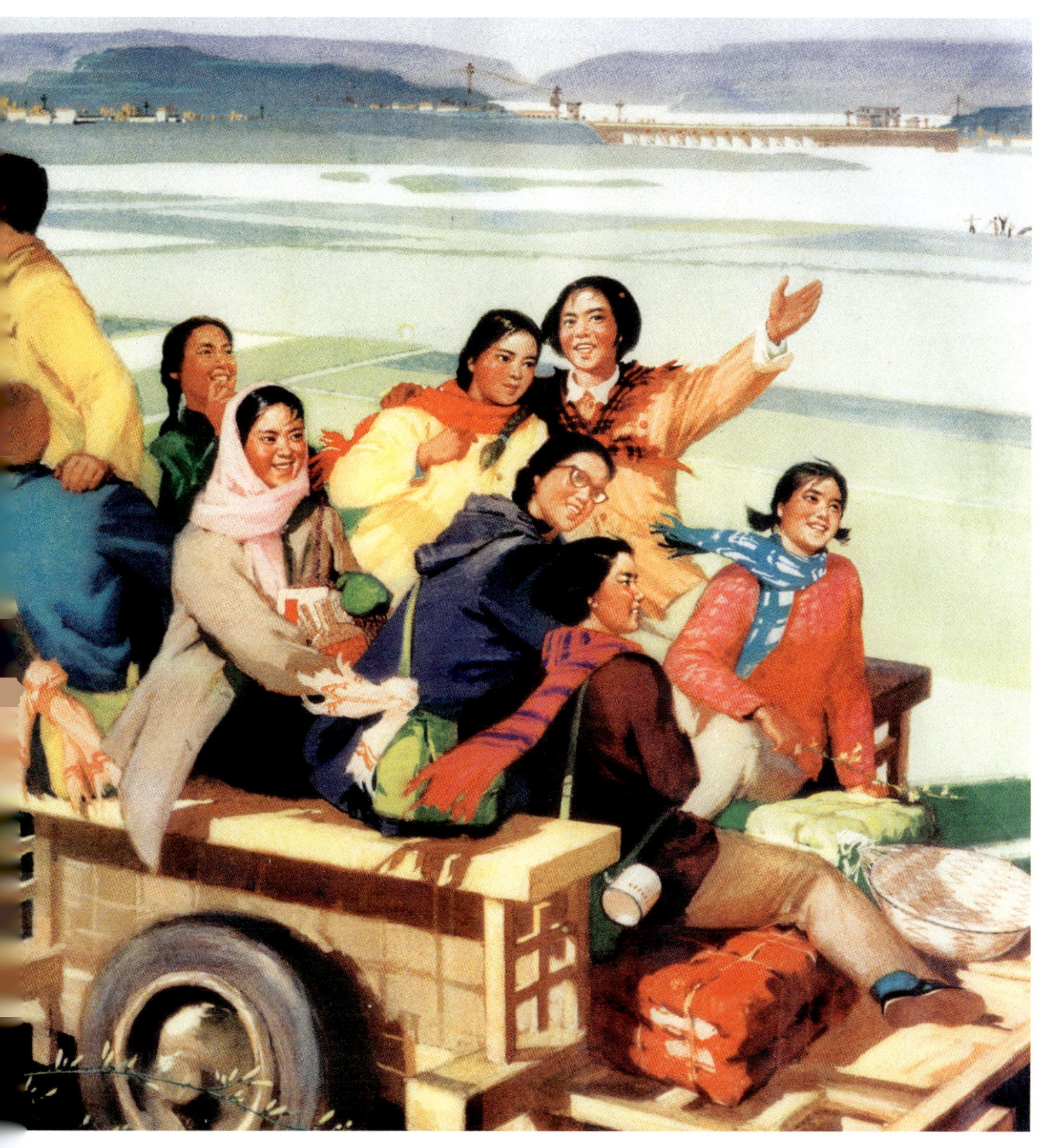

New arrivals, welcome to the wide open spaces of the rural regions! Shandong People's Publishing House, 1974; 0.12 Yuan

Neuankömmlinge, willkommen in der weiten Welt der ländlichen Regionen! Volksverlag Shandong, 1974; 0,12 Yuan

Bienvenue aux nouveaux arrivants dans le vaste espace des régions rurales ! Éditions Populaires du Shandong, 1974 ; 0,12 yuan

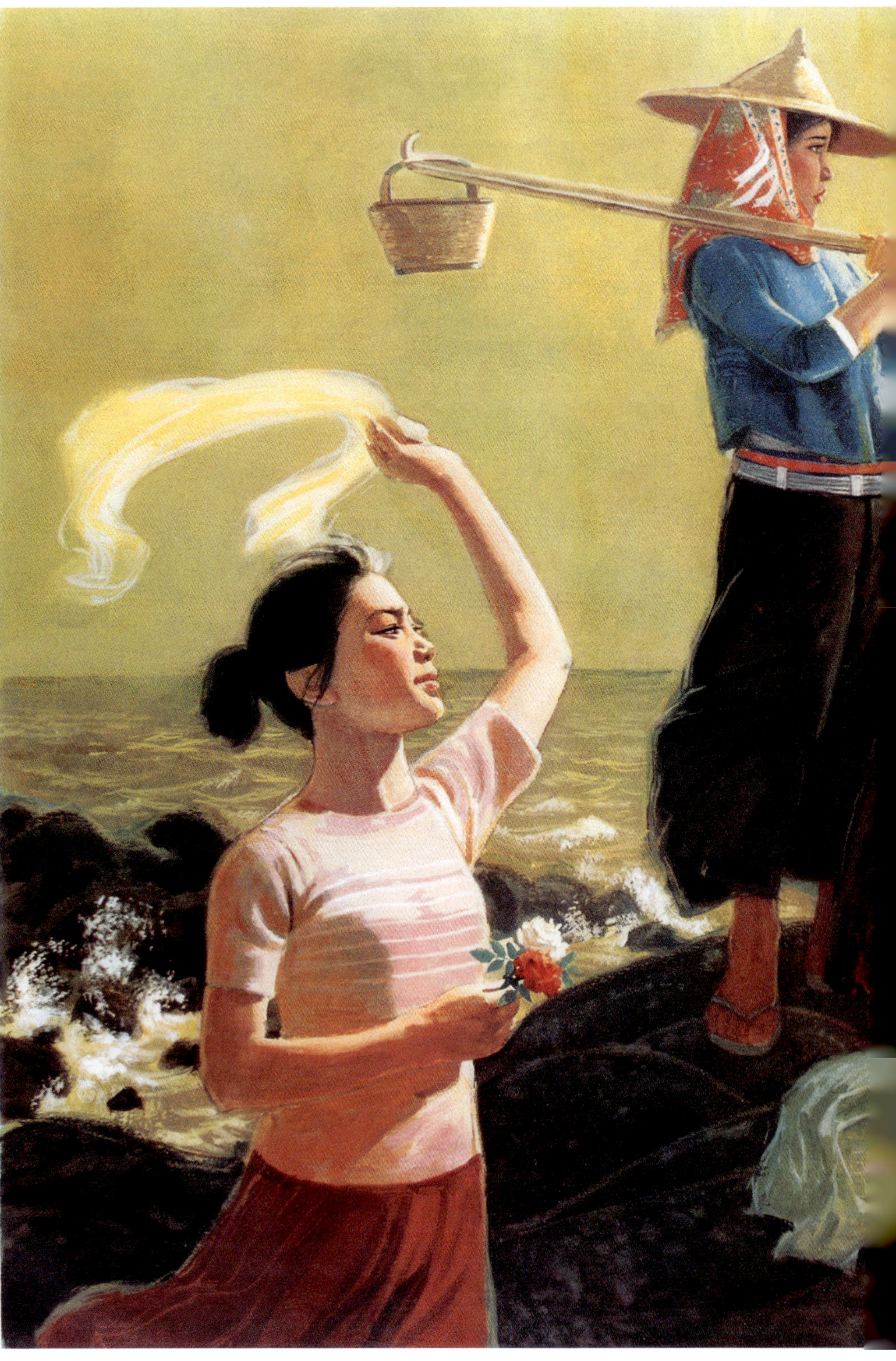

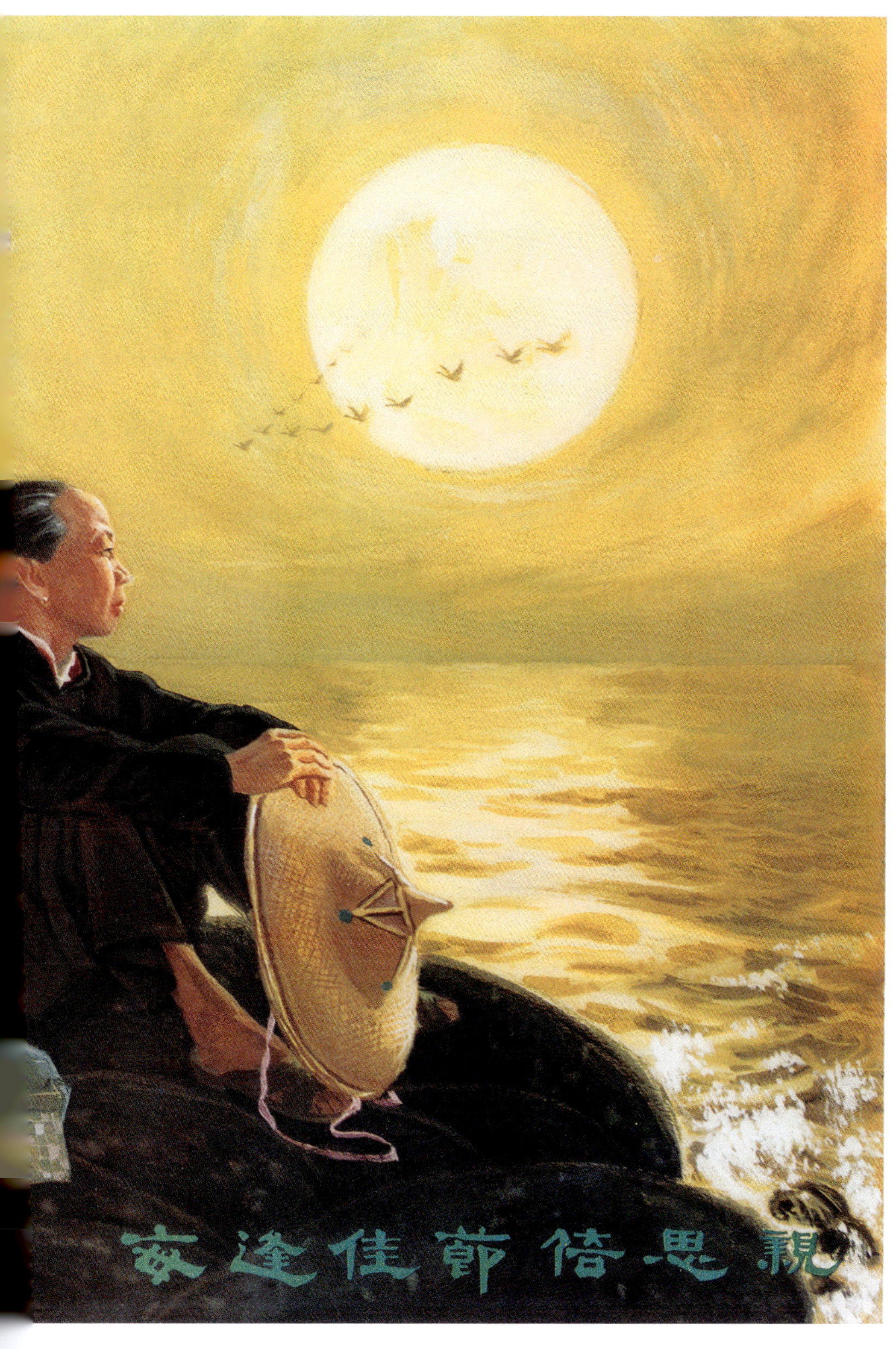
每逢佳節倍思親

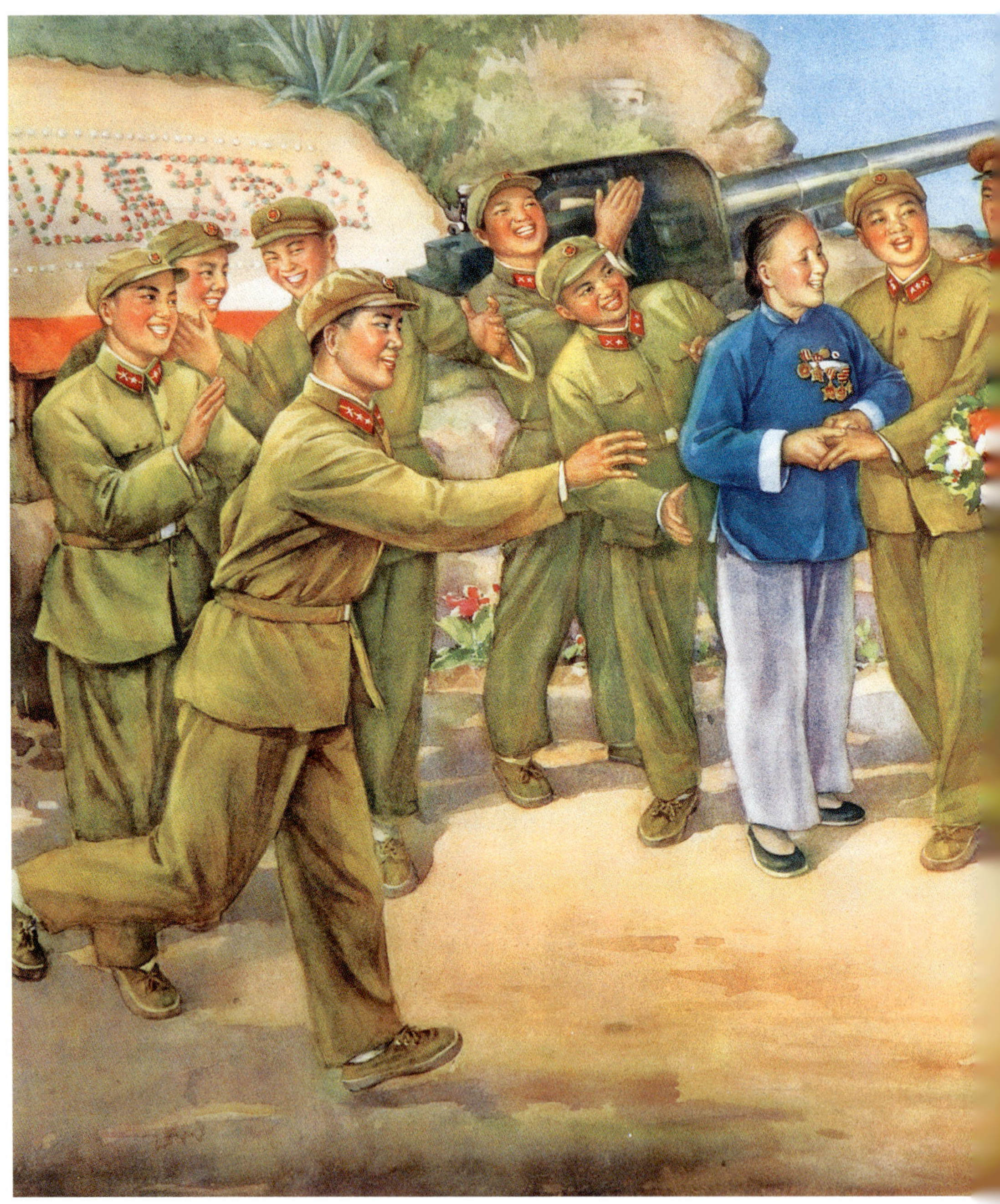

A warm welcome for our favorites* *Top left, on hut:* Gaining a foothold on the island *Artist:* Chen Qiang; Shanghai People's Art Publishing House, 1961 *Print run:* 300,000; 0.13 Yuan

* The five figures on the right are from the Beijing opera *The Pilgrimage to the West*.

Die Lieben herzlich willkommen heißen* *Links oben auf der Hütte:* Auf der Insel Fuß fassen *Gemalt von* Chen Qiang; Volkskunstverlag Shanghai, 1961 *Auflage:* 300 000; 0,13 Yuan

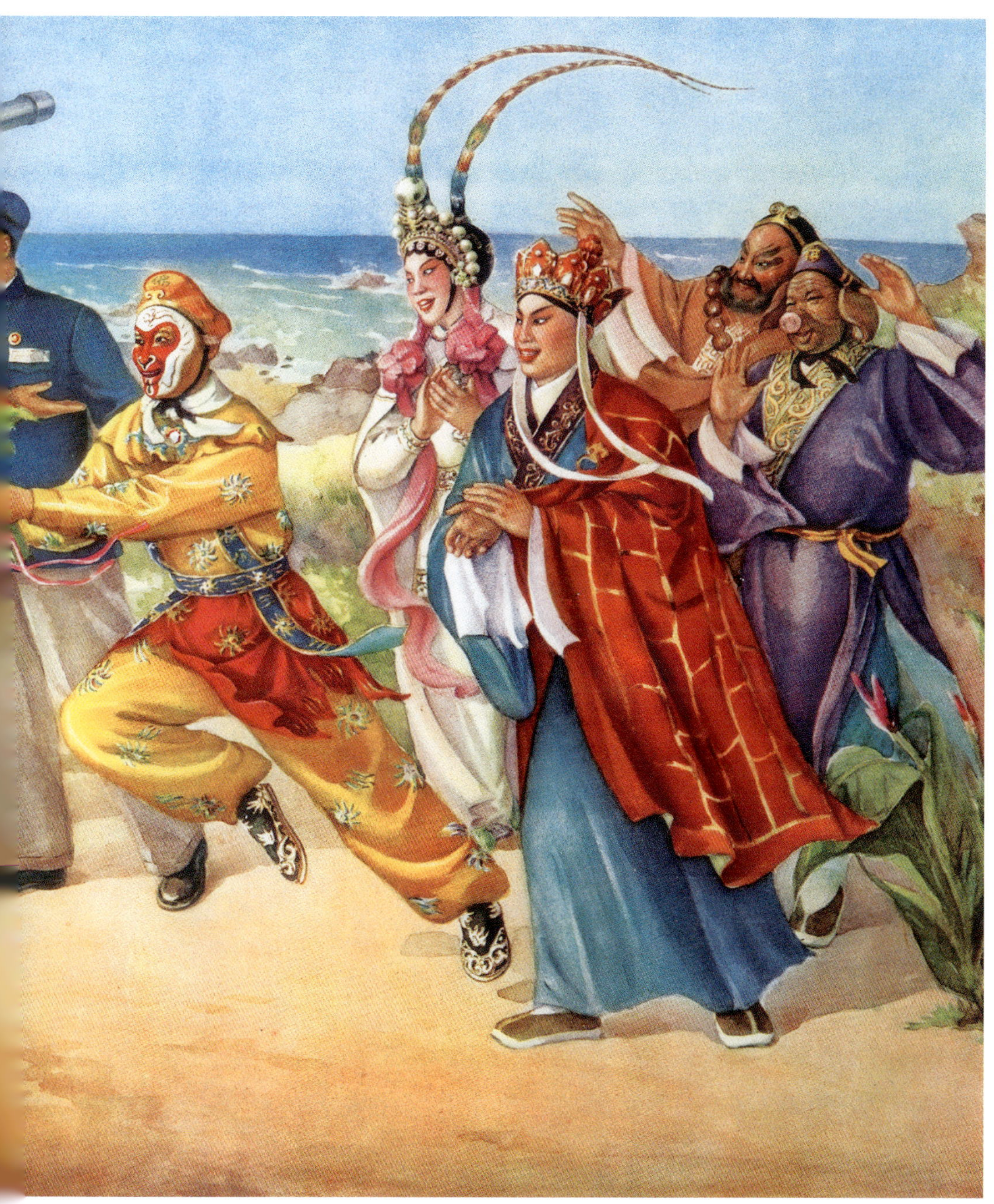

* Die fünf Figuren rechts stammen aus der Pekingoper „Die Pilgerfahrt nach dem Westen".

Souhaitons chaleureusement la bienvenue à nos bien-aimés* *En haut à gauche :* Prenons pied sur l'île *Peintre :* Chen Qiang ; Éd. Populaires d'Art, Shanghai, 1961 *Tirage:* 300 000 ; 0,13 yuan

* Les cinq personnages de droite sont issus du « Pélerinage en Occident », joué à l'Opéra de Pékin.

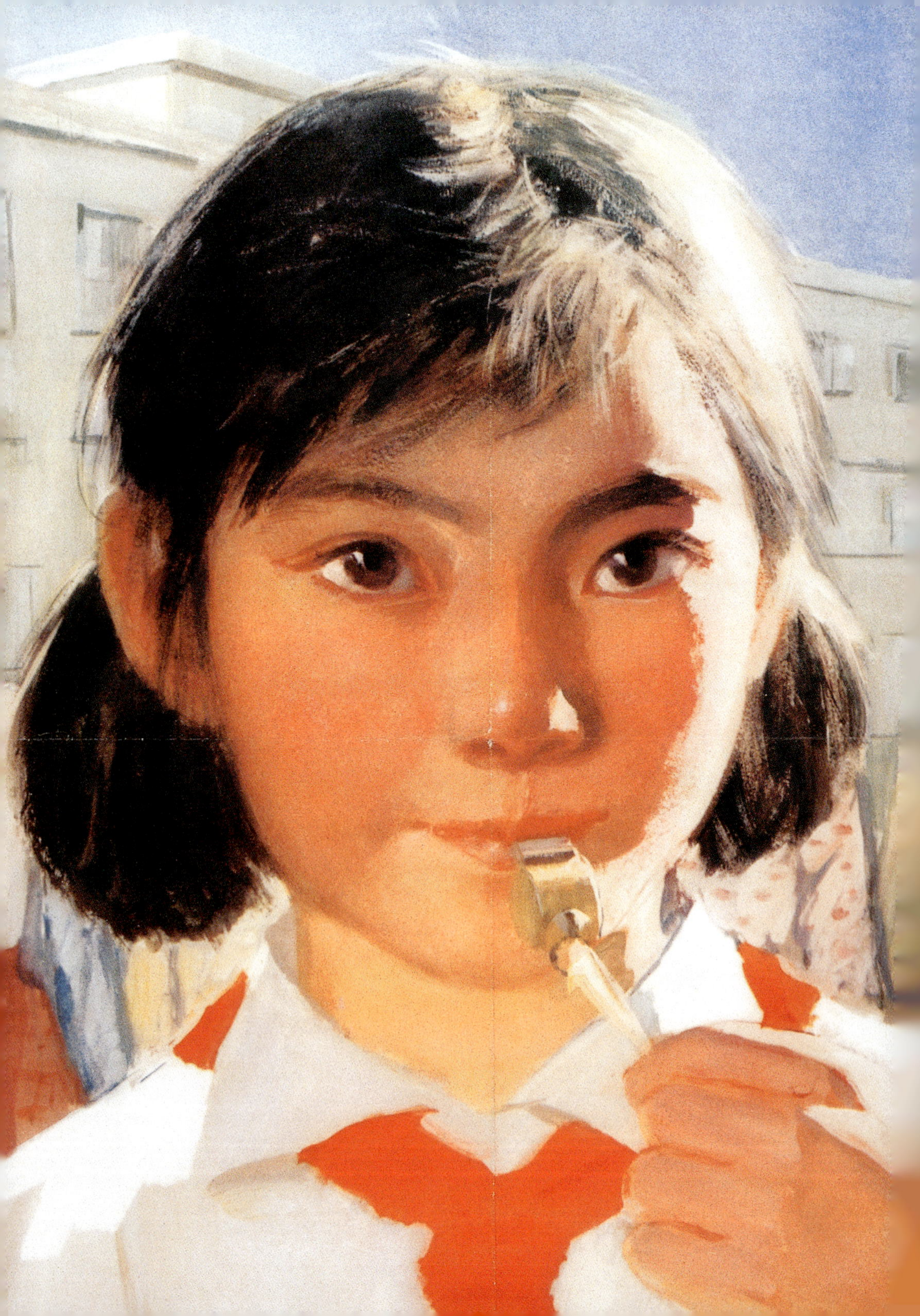

XXVI

DISCIPLINE

DIE DISZIPLIN
LA DISCIPLINE

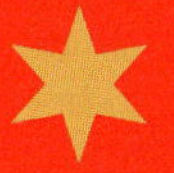

Page 382
Toeing the line of discipline Educational poster *Artist:* Zhao Weiliang; Shanghai Educational Publishing House, 1978; 0.12 Yuan

Sich der Disziplin fügen Erziehungsplakat *Gemalt von* Zhao Weiliang; Erziehungsverlag Shanghai, 1978; 0,12 Yuan

Astreignons-nous à la discipline Affiche pédagogique *Peintre :* Zhao Weiliang ; Éditions Éducatives de Shanghai, 1978 ; 0,12 yuan

Victory will only be achieved when orders are obeyed in all actions and everyone marches in step *On the flag:* The cadres, the masses, the Party members, and the people must be educated in accordance with the Three Main Rules of Discipline and the Eight Points for Attention *On the sheet:* The Three Main Rules of Discipline and the Eight Points for Attention* *Artists:* Liang Zhenxiang, Wang Jiayu and Liu Yuwen; Zhejiang People's Publishing House, 1974 *Print run:* 40,000; 0.11 Yuan
* The Three Main Rules of Discipline: 1. Obey orders in all your actions. 2. Don't take a single needle or piece of thread from the masses. 3. Turn in everything captured.
The Eight Points for Attention: 1. Speak politely. 2. Pay fairly for what you buy. 3. Return everything you borrow. 4. Pay for anything you damage. 5. Do not hit or swear at people. 6. Do not damage crops. 7. Do not take liberties with women. 8. Do not ill-treat captives. Quotations from Chairman Mao Zedong

Der Sieg kann nur erreicht werden, wenn bei allen Aktionen die Befehle befolgt werden und alle im gleichen Schritt marschieren *Auf der Fahne:* Die Kader, die Massen, die Parteimitglieder und das Volk müssen gemäß den Drei Hauptregeln der Disziplin und den Acht Punkten zur Beachtung erzogen werden *Auf dem Blatt:* Die Drei Hauptregeln der Disziplin und die Acht Punkte zur Beachtung* *Gemalt von* Liang Zhenxiang, Wang Jiayu und Liu Yuwen; Volksverlag Zhejiang, 1974 *Auflage:* 40 000; 0,11 Yuan
* Die Drei Hauptregeln der Disziplin: 1. Gehorche dem Kommando in allem, was du tust.
2. Nimm den Massen nicht eine Nadel und nicht einen Faden weg.
3. Liefere alles Beutegut ab.
Die Acht Punkte zur Beachtung: 1. Sprich höflich. 2. Zahle für alles, was du kaufst, den angemessenen Preis. 3. Gib zurück, was du entliehen hast. 4. Bezahle für das, was du beschädigt hast. 5. Schlage und beschimpfe niemanden.
6. Beschädige keine Ackerbaukulturen. 7. Belästige keine Frauen.
8. Misshandle keine Gefangene. Worte des Vorsitzenden Mao Zedong

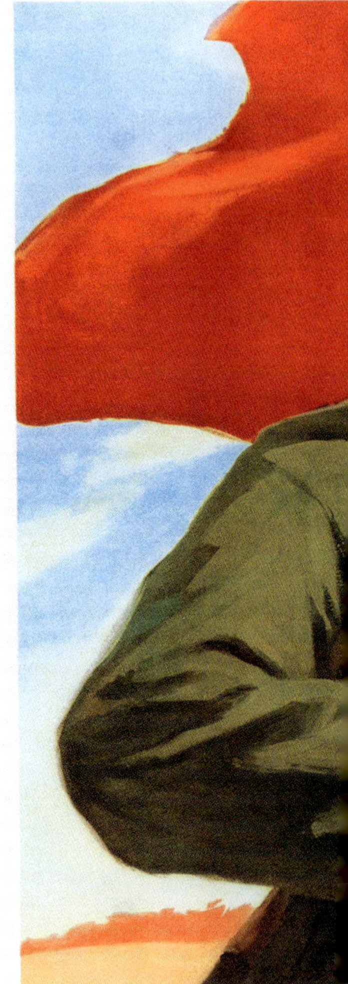

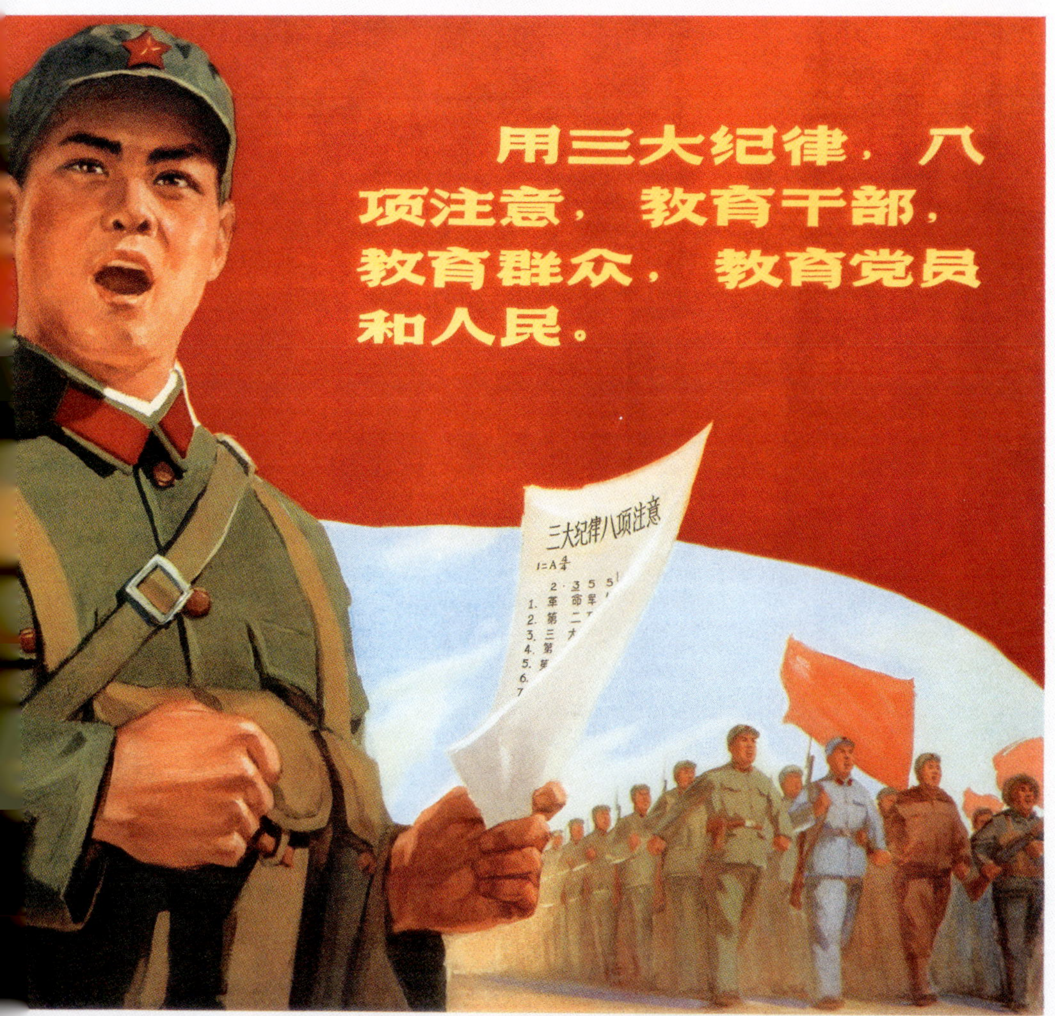

La victoire ne pourra être atteinte que si, dans chacun de vos actes, les ordres sont suivis, et que tous marchent du même pas *Sur le drapeau :* Les cadres, les masses, les membres du Parti et le peuple doivent être éduqués dans le sens des Trois grandes règles de la discipline et des Huit recommandations* *Peintres :* Liang Zhenxiang, Wang Jiayu et Liu Yuwen ; Éditions Populaires du Zhejiang, 1974 *Tirage :* 40 000 ; 0,11 yuan

* Les Trois grandes règles de la discipline : 1. Obéissez aux ordres dans tous vos actes. 2. Ne prenez pas aux masses une seule aiguille, un seul bout de fil. 3. Remettez tout butin aux autorités.
Les Huit recommandations :
1. Parlez poliment. 2. Payez honnêtement ce que vous achetez. 3. Rendez tout ce que vous empruntez. 4. Payez ou remplacez tout ce que vous endommagez. 5. Ne frappez pas et n'injuriez pas les gens. 6. Ne causez pas de dommages aux récoltes. 7. Ne prenez pas de libertés avec les femmes. 8. Ne maltraitez pas les prisonniers. Citations du président Mao Zedong

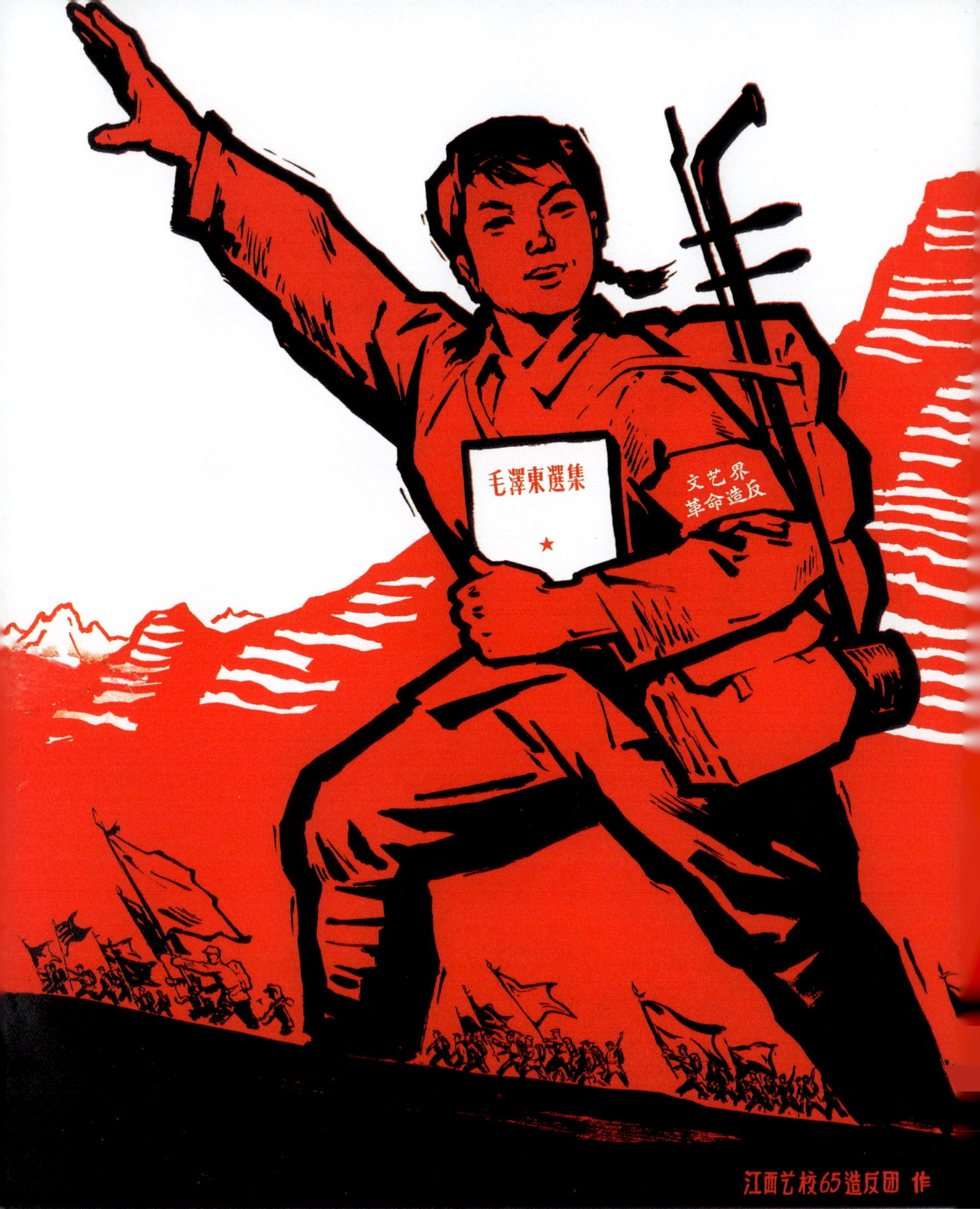

“杀”出文艺界、深入工农兵

XXVII

CRITICISM AND SELF-CRITICISM

KRITIK UND SELBSTKRITIK
LA CRITIQUE ET L'AUTO-CRITIQUE

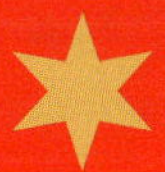

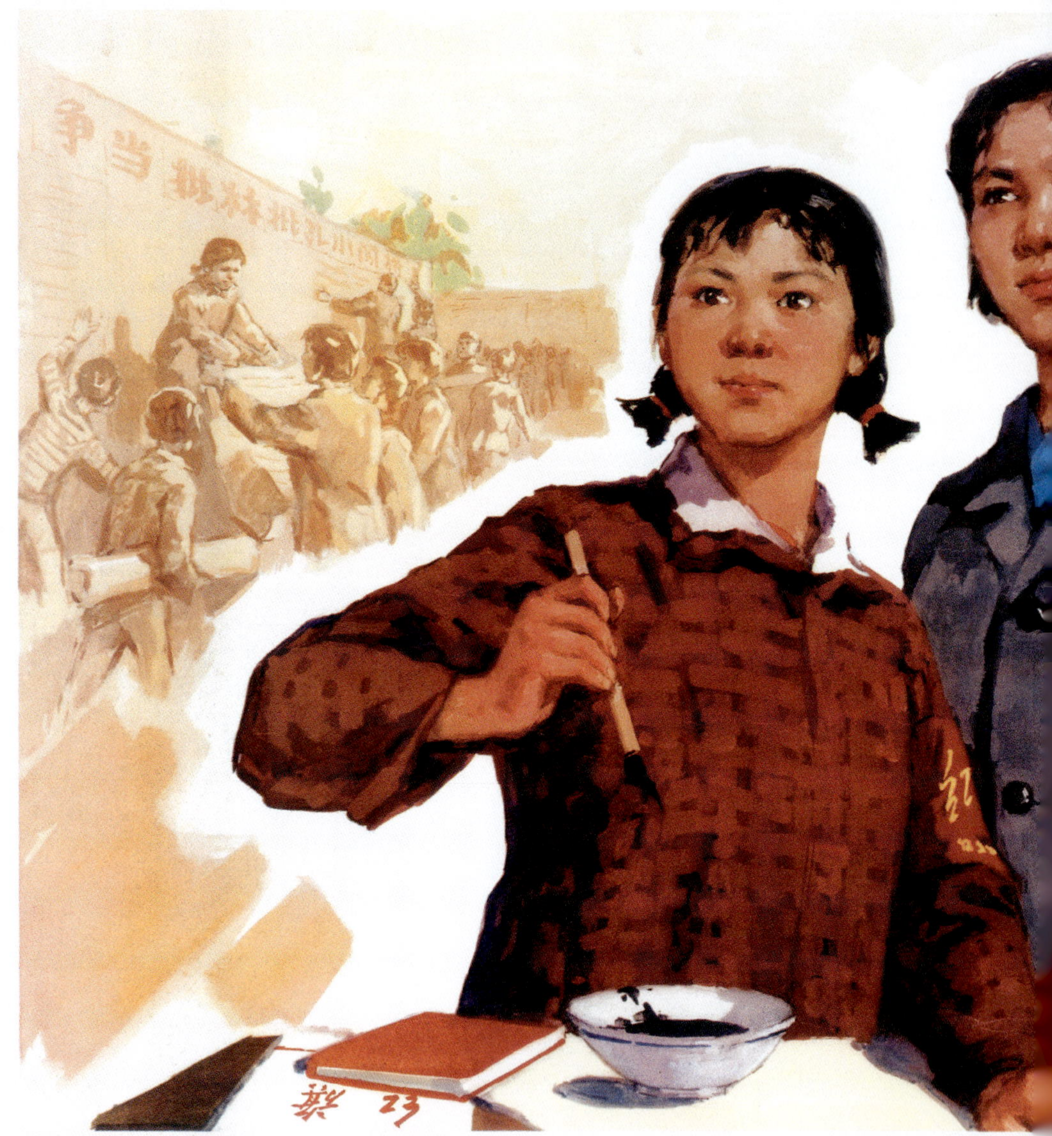

Revolutionary teachers and students are comrades in the same trench *Wall newspaper held by teacher:* Radically condemn the revisionist line in education *Wall newspaper, left:* Become brave activists in the campaign against Lin Biao and Confucius *Banner, right:* Rally to condemn Lin Biao and Confucius *Artist:* Wang Yuanzhen; People's Art Publishing House, 1974 *Print run:* 450,000; 0.14 Yuan

Revolutionäre Lehrer und Studenten sind Kameraden im selben Schützengraben *Wandzeitung Lehrerin:* Die revisionistische Erziehungslinie radikal verurteilen *Wandzeitung links:* Werdet mutige Aktivisten der Kampagne gegen

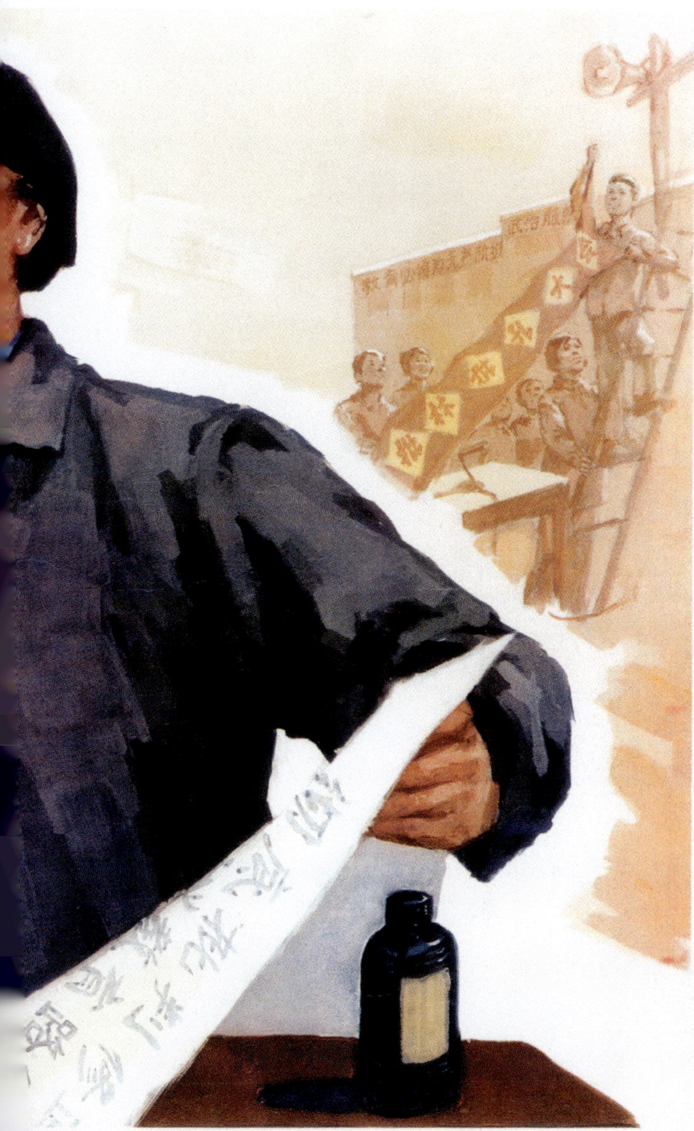

Page 386
Eschew the worlds of literature and art and become familiar with the lives of workers, peasants and soldiers
Commune of the Red Rebels for New Literature and Art, Jiangxi Province *In the bottom right corner of the picture:* Designed by the "65 Rebel Group' at Jiangxi Province Art School *Book:* Selected Works of Mao Zedong *Armband:* Revolutionary Rebels in the field of Literature and Art

Sich aus dem Bereich der Literatur und Kunst befreien und das Leben der Arbeiter, Bauern und Soldaten kennen lernen
Kommune der Roten Rebellen für neue Literatur und Kunst, Provinz Jiangxi *Im Bild rechts unten:* Entworfen von der „Rebellen-Gruppe 65" der Kunstschule, Provinz Jiangxi *Buch:* Ausgewählte Werke Mao Zedongs *Armbinde:* Revolutionäre Rebellen des Bereichs Literatur und Kunst

Libérons-nous des domaines de la littérature et de l'art et familiarisons-nous avec la vie des ouvriers, des paysans et des soldats Commune des rebelles rouges pour une littérature et un art nouveaux, province du Jiangxi *En bas à droite dans l'image :* Conception : « Groupe des rebelles 65 » de l'école des Beaux-Arts, province du Jiangxi *Livre :* Œuvres choisies de Mao Zedong *Brassard :* Rebelles révolutionnaires du secteur littéraire et artistique

Lin Biao und Konfuzius *Transparent rechts:* Versammlung „Verurteilt Lin Baio und Konfuzius" *Gemalt von* Wang Yuanzhen; Volkskunstverlag, 1974 *Auflage:* 450 000; 0,14 Yuan

Les enseignants et les étudiants révolutionnaires sont des camarades de tranchée *Journal mural de l'enseignante :* Condamnons radicalement la ligne d'éducation révisionniste *Journal mural de gauche :* Soyons de courageux activistes de la campagne contre Lin Biao et Confucius *Banderole, à droite :* Rassemblement « Condamnons Lin Biao et Confucius » *Peintre :* Wang Yuanzhen ; Éditions Populaires d'Art, 1974 *Tirage :* 450 000 ; 0,14 yuan

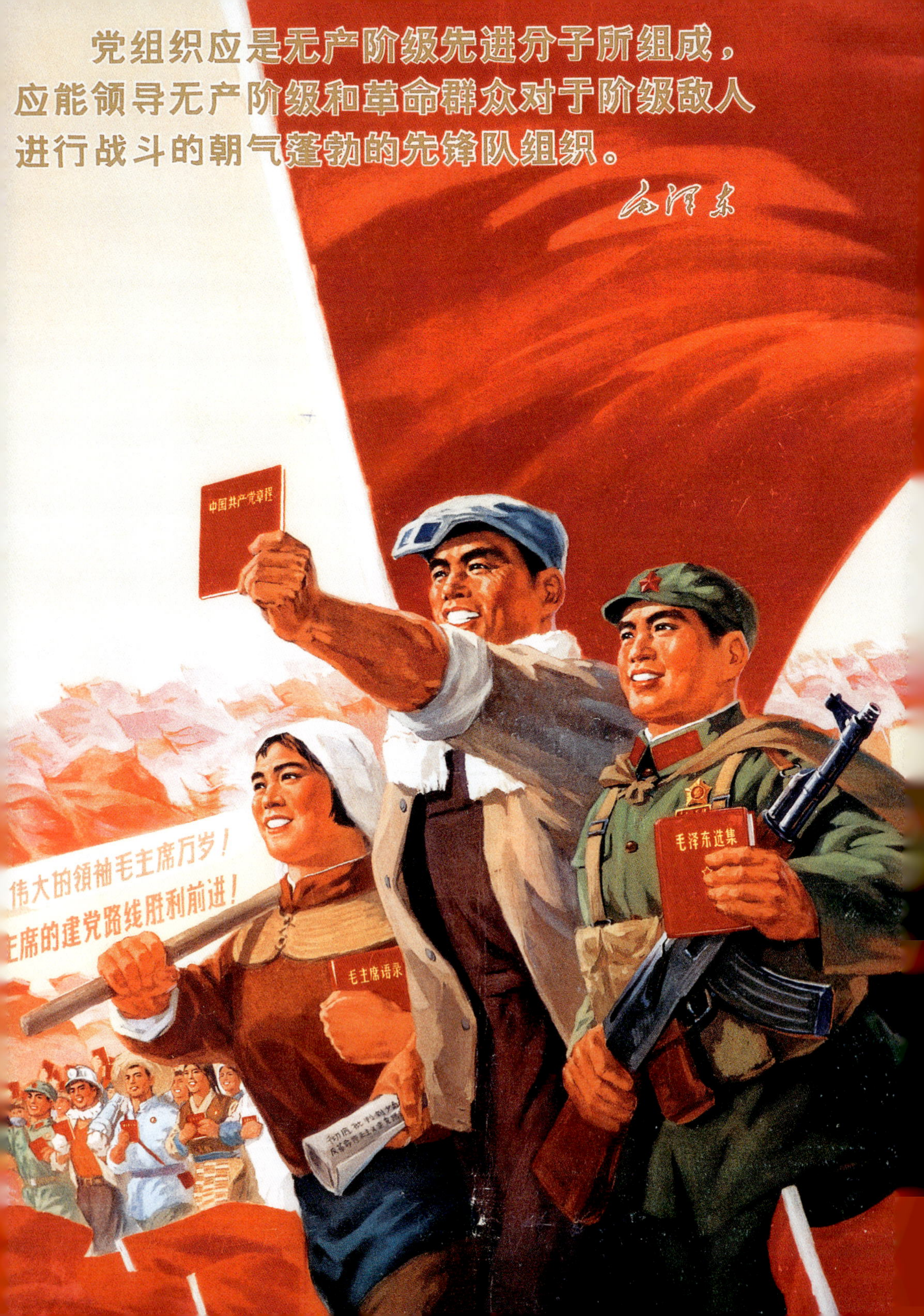
党组织应是无产阶级先进分子所组成，应能领导无产阶级和革命群众对于阶级敌人进行战斗的朝气蓬勃的先锋队组织。
毛泽东
中国共产党章程
伟大的领袖毛主席万岁！
主席的建党路线胜利前进！
毛主席语录
毛泽东选集

XXVIII

COMMUNISTS

DIE KOMMUNISTEN
LES COMMUNISTES

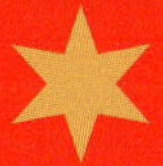

Page 390

Party members must be progressive in their attitude to the proletariat "The Communist Party should be made up of people who are progressive in their attitude to the proletariat. It should be a vanguard organization full of vitality, capable of leading the revolutionary masses in the struggle against class enemies." Mao Zedong *Book title, man, center:* Statute of the Chinese Communist Party *Book title, woman:* Quotations from Chairman Mao Zedong *Book title, soldier:* Selected Works of Mao Zedong *Banners, left:* Long live the great leader Chairman Mao! Striding forwards triumphantly along Chairman Mao's path for building the Party *Banner, right:* Enthusiastically celebrating the 50th anniversary of the founding of China's great, glorious, and correctly acting Communist Party! *Designed by:* Rudong District Art Course for Workers, Peasants, and Soldiers, Jiangsu Province; Jiangsu People's Publishing House, 1971; 0.14 Yuan

Die Parteimitglieder sollen fortschrittlich Gesinnte des Proletariats sein "Die Kommunistische Partei soll aus fortschrittlich Gesinnten des Proletariats bestehen. Sie soll eine Vorhutorganisation voller Lebenskraft sein, die in der Lage ist, das Proletariat und die revolutionären Massen im Kampf gegen Klassenfeinde zu führen." Mao Zedong *Buchtitel Mann Mitte:* Statut der Kommunistischen Partei Chinas *Buchtitel Frau:* Worte des Vorsitzenden Mao Zedong *Buchtitel Soldat:* Ausgewählte Werke Mao Zedongs *Transparente links:* Es lebe der Große Führer, der Vorsitzende Mao! Auf der Linie des Vorsitzenden Mao für den Aufbau der Partei triumphierend vorwärts schreiten *Transparent rechts:* Voller Begeisterung den 50. Gründungstag der großen, ruhmreichen und richtig handelnden Kommunistischen Partei Chinas feiern! *Entwurf:* Malkurs für Arbeiter, Bauern und Soldaten des Kreises Rudong, Provinz Jiangsu; Volksverlag Jiangsu, 1971; 0,14 Yuan

Les membres du Parti doivent être les esprits progressistes du prolétariat « Le parti communiste doit se composer des esprits progressistes du prolétariat. Il doit être une organisation d'avant-garde pleine de force vitale, capable de guider le prolétariat et les masses révolutionnaires dans la lutte contre les ennemis de classe. » Mao Zedong *Titre du livre, homme du milieu :* Statut du Parti Communiste Chinois *Titre du livre, femme :* Citations du président Mao Zedong *Titre du livre, soldat :* Œuvres choisies de Mao Zedong *Banderoles de gauche :* Vive le Grand Timonier, le président Mao ! 2e *banderole de gauche :* Sur la ligne du président Mao, avançons pour l'édification triomphante du Parti *Banderole de droite :* Célébrons dans l'enthousiasme le 50e anniversaire de la création du grand, juste et glorieux Parti Communiste Chinois ! *Conception :* Cours de peinture pour ouvriers, paysans et soldats du canton de Rudong, province du Jiangsu ; Éditions populaires du Jiangsu, 1971 ; 0,14 yuan

I accompany my grandmother to night school *Book:* Communist Party Manifesto *Poem, below:* The night-time rain dampens the spring twigs. The fields become wet and the young seedlings are glad. I light the lantern and accompany my grandmother to night school. Grandmother has a red heart. She is highly aware of the progress of the Revolution and regularly reads the works of Marx and Lenin. In the political storm her position is unshakable. *Artist:* Sun Xuecheng; Tianjin People's Art Publishing House, 1973; 0.11 Yuan

Ich begleite die Großmutter zur Abendschule *Buch:* Manifest der Kommunistischen Partei *Gedicht unten:* Der nächtliche Regen befeuchtet Frühlingszweige. Die Felder werden nass und die jungen Setzlinge freuen sich. Ich zünde die Laterne an und begleite die Großmutter zur Abendschule. Großmutter hat ein rotes Herz. Sie hat ein hohes Bewusstsein in Bezug auf die Fortsetzung der Revolution und liest regelmäßig Werke von Marx und Lenin. Im politischen Sturm ist ihr Standpunkt unerschütterlich.
Gemalt von Sun Xuecheng; Volkskunstverlag Tianjin, 1973; 0,11 Yuan

J'accompagne ma grand-mère aux cours du soir *Livre de la grand-mère :* Manifeste du Parti communiste *Poème en bas :* La pluie de la nuit arrose les rameaux de printemps. Les champs sont mouillés et les jeunes plants se réjouissent. J'allume la lampe-torche et j'accompagne ma grand-mère aux cours du soir. Grand-mère a le cœur rouge. Elle a une connaissance profonde de ce qui touche à la poursuite de la révolution et lit régulièrement les œuvres de Marx et de Lénine. Dans la tourmente politique, son point de vue est inébranlable. *Peintre :* Sun Xuecheng ; Éditions Populaires d'Art de Tianjin, 1973 ; 0,11 yuan

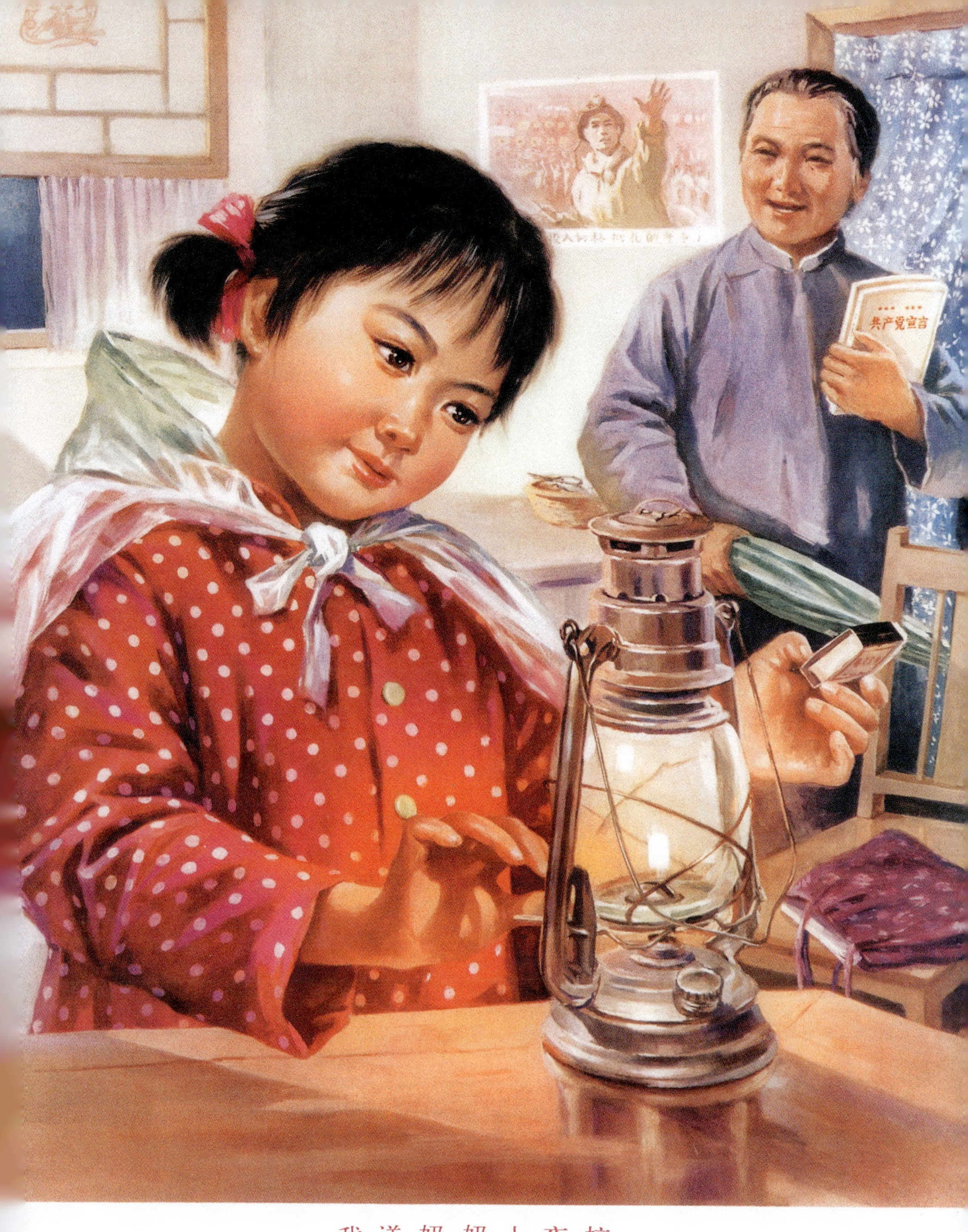

我送奶奶上夜校

春风夜雨洒柳梢
田野滋润新禾苗
划火点亮灯一盏
我送奶奶上夜校

奶奶心红人不老
继续革命觉悟高
长年坚持读马列
几经风浪不动摇

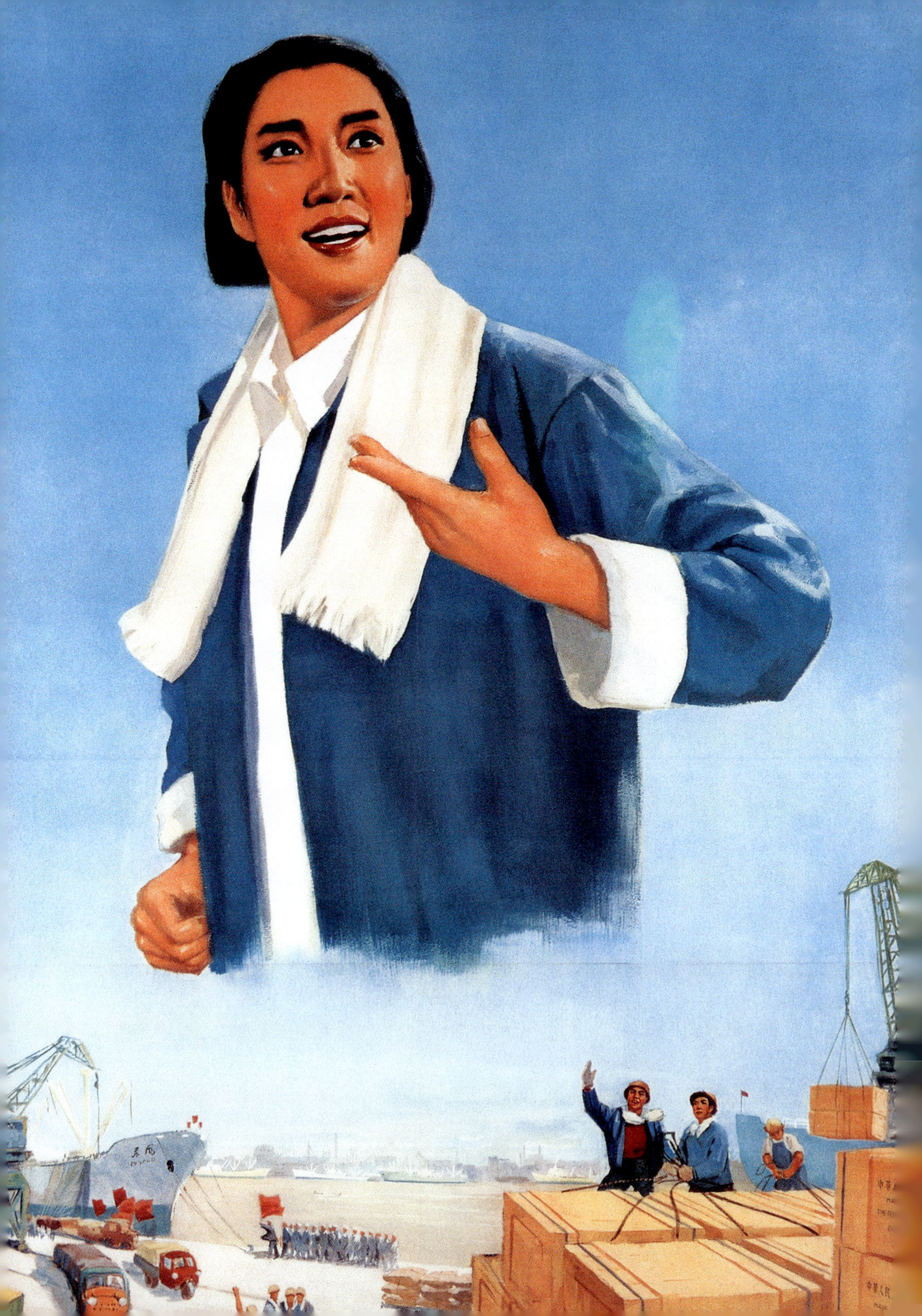

XXIX

CADRES

DIE KADER
LES CADRES

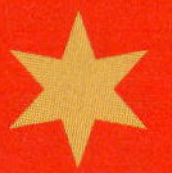

Page 394

Learn from heroes to act immediately Gain a foothold in the harbor, keep an eye on the whole world *Designed by:* Painting Course for Workers, Peasants and Soldiers at Shanghai Art School; Shanghai People's Publishing House, 1st edn 1971, 14th edn 1974 *Print run:* 4,150,001–4,350,000; 0.11 Yuan

Von Helden lernen, sofort handeln Im Hafen Fuß fassen, die ganze Welt im Auge behalten *Entwurf:* Malkurs für Arbeiter, Bauern und Soldaten der Kunstschule Shanghai; Volksverlag Shanghai, 1. Aufl. 1971, 14. Aufl. 1974 *Auflage:* 4 150 001–4 350 000; 0,11 Yuan

Retenons l'expérience des héros, agissons tout de suite Prenons pied dans le port, ne perdons pas de vue le reste du monde *Conception :* Cours de peinture pour ouvriers, paysans et soldats de l'École des Beaux-Arts de Shanghai ; Éditions Populaires de Shanghai, 1ère éd. 1971, 14e éd. 1974 *Tirage :* 4 150 000–4 350 000 ; 0,11 yuan

Supreme Commander Zhu weaving a straw shoe Poster used as a nursery school teaching aid *Artist:* Shi Qiren; Shanghai Educational Publishing House, 1st edn 1978, 2nd edn 1978 *Print run:* 20,001–95,000; 0.16 Yuan

Der Oberbefehlshaber Zhu beim Flechten eines Strohschuhs Unterrichtsplakat für Kindergärten *Gemalt von* Shi Qiren; Erziehungsverlag Shanghai, 1. Aufl. 1978, 2. Aufl. 1978 *Auflage:* 20 001–95 000; 0,16 Yuan

Le commandant en chef Zhu tressant de la paille pour faire une chaussure Affiche pédagogique destinée aux jardins d'enfants *Peintre :* Shi Qiren ; Éditions Éducatives de Shanghai, 1ère éd. 1978, 2e éd. 1978 *Tirage:* 20 001–95 000 ; 0,16 yuan

Pages 398–399

Learn from Zhu Boru* and become models of the development of new human relationships in society *Artists:* Huang Zhenyong and Fei Changqing *Published by:* Political Department (Ministry) of the Airforce

* A former airforce officer, known nationally for his willingness to help others and his selflessness, was considered a model in the "Learning from Lei Feng" movement. In the 1980s he was praised in the media as the "Living Lei Feng of the present."

Lernt von Zhu Boru* und werdet ein Vorbild bei der Entwicklung neuer menschlicher Beziehungen innerhalb der Gesellschaft *Gemalt von* Huang Zhenyong und Fei Changqing *Herausgeber:* Politische Abteilung der Luftwaffe

* Ein ehemaliger Offizier der Luftwaffe, landesweit bekannt durch seine Hilfsbereitschaft und Selbstlosigkeit, galt als Vorbild in der Bewegung „Von Lei Feng lernen". In den 1980er Jahren wurde er in den Medien als „Lebender Lei Feng der Gegenwart" gepriesen.

Retenons l'exemple de Zhu Boru* et devenons un modèle dans le développement de nouveaux rapports humains au sein de la société *Peintres :* Huang Zhenyong et Fei Changqing *Éditeur :* Département politique de l'Armée de l'air

*Ancien officier de l'armée de l'air, connu dans tout le pays pour son dévouement et son altruisme, il fut considéré comme un modèle du mouvement « Retenons l'exemple de Lei Feng ». Dans les années 1980, les médias firent son éloge en le qualifiant de « Lei Feng contemporain ».

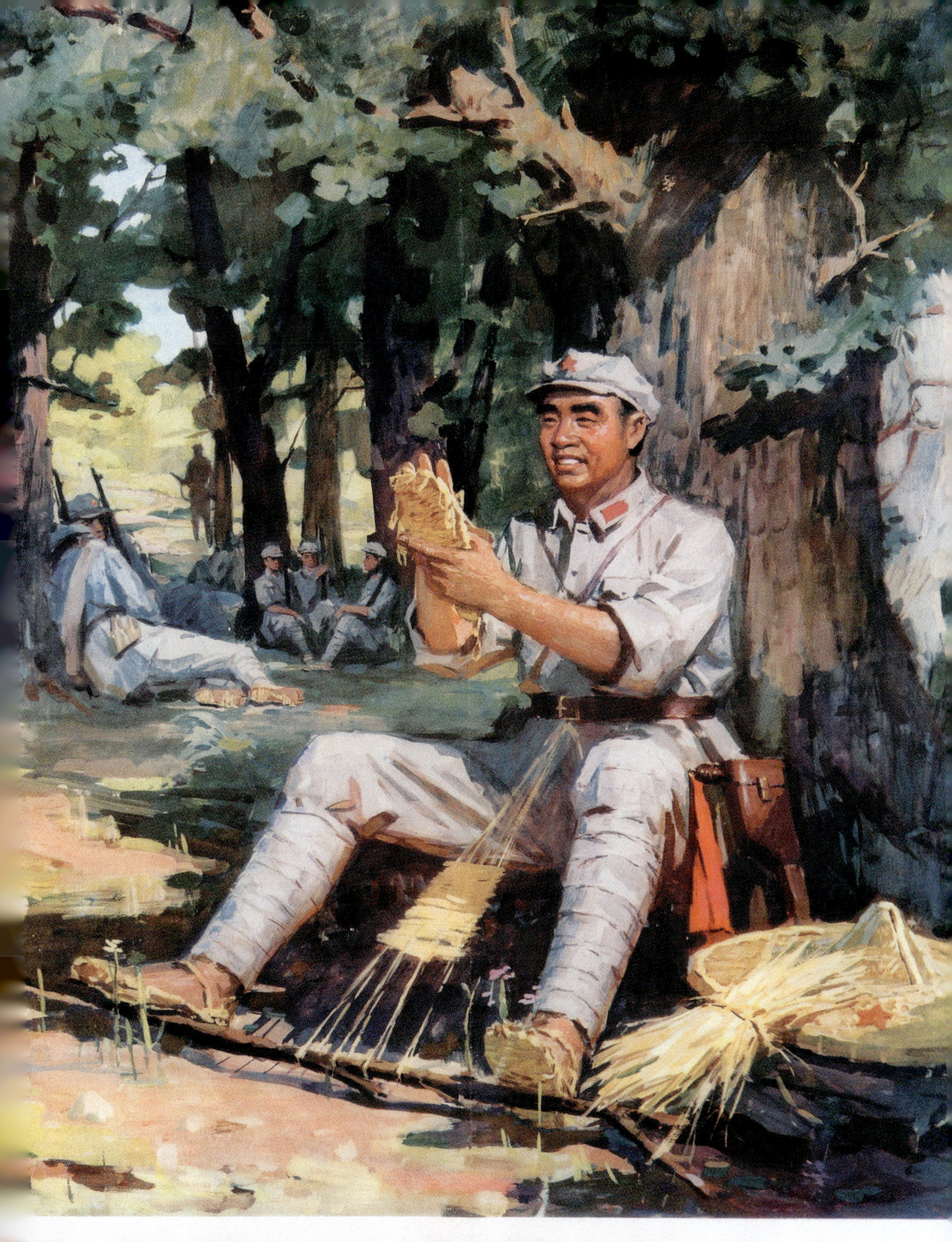

朱总司令编草鞋

ZHU ZONG SI LING BIAN CAO XIE

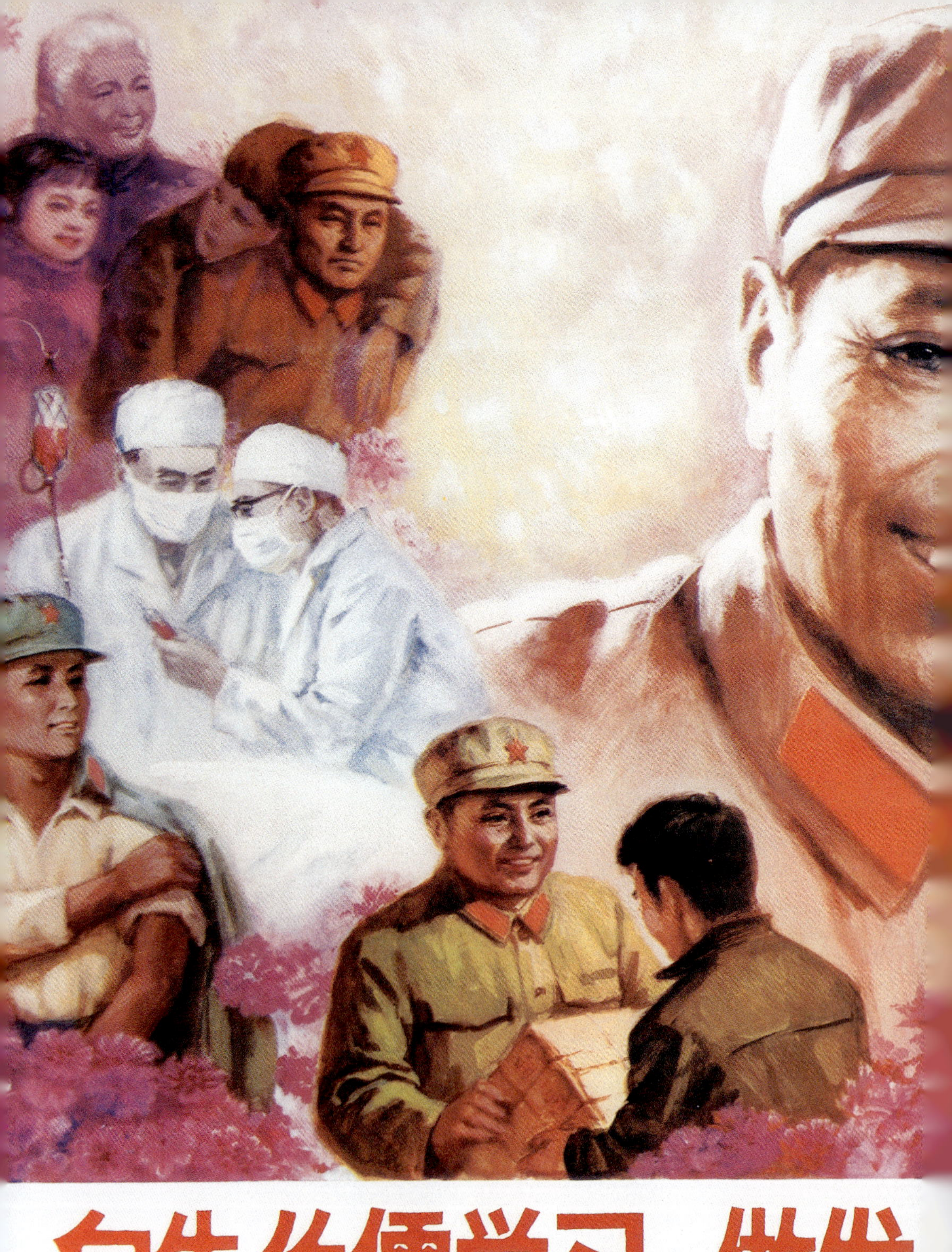
向朱伯儒学习 做发

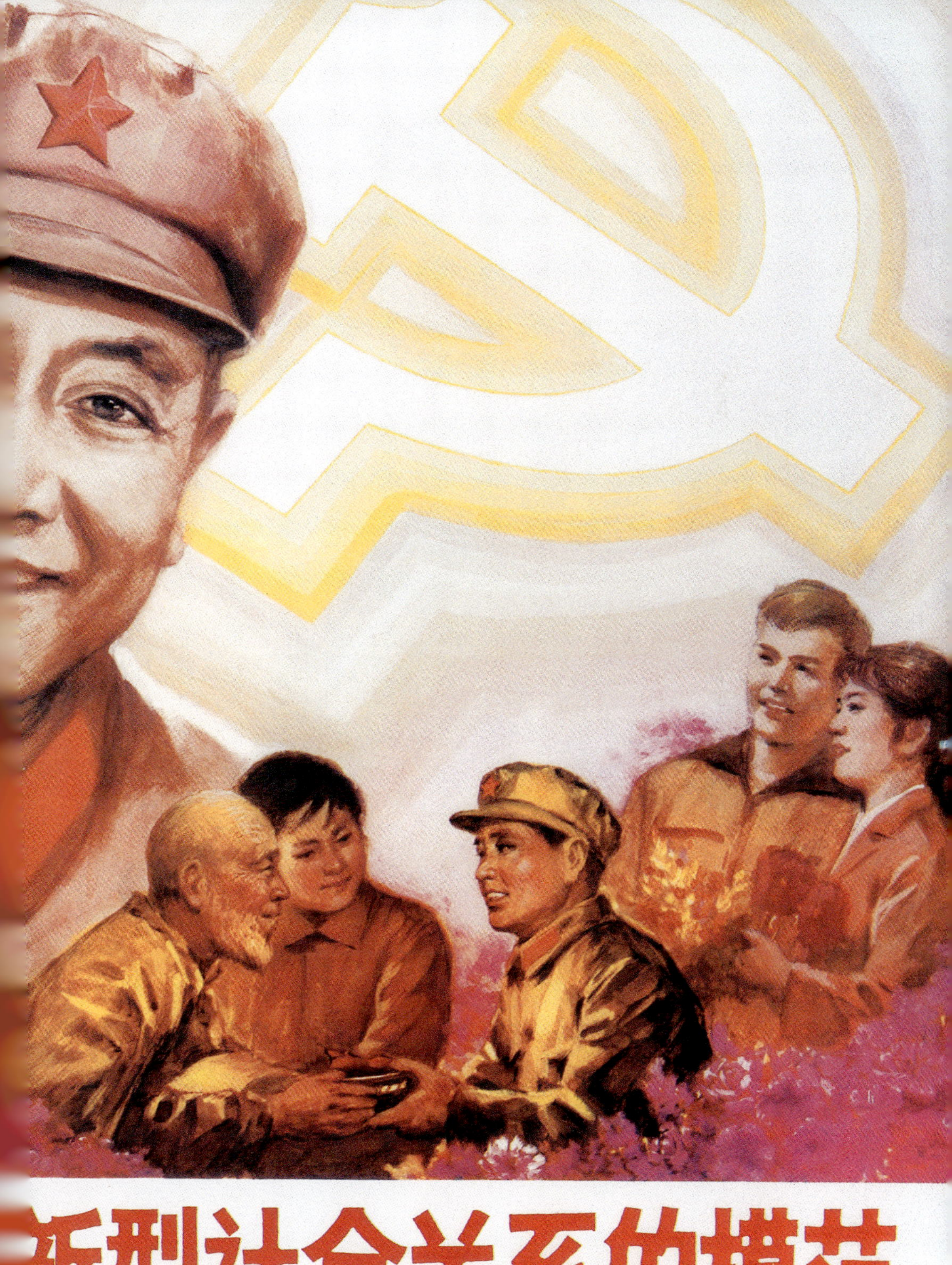

新型社会关系的模范

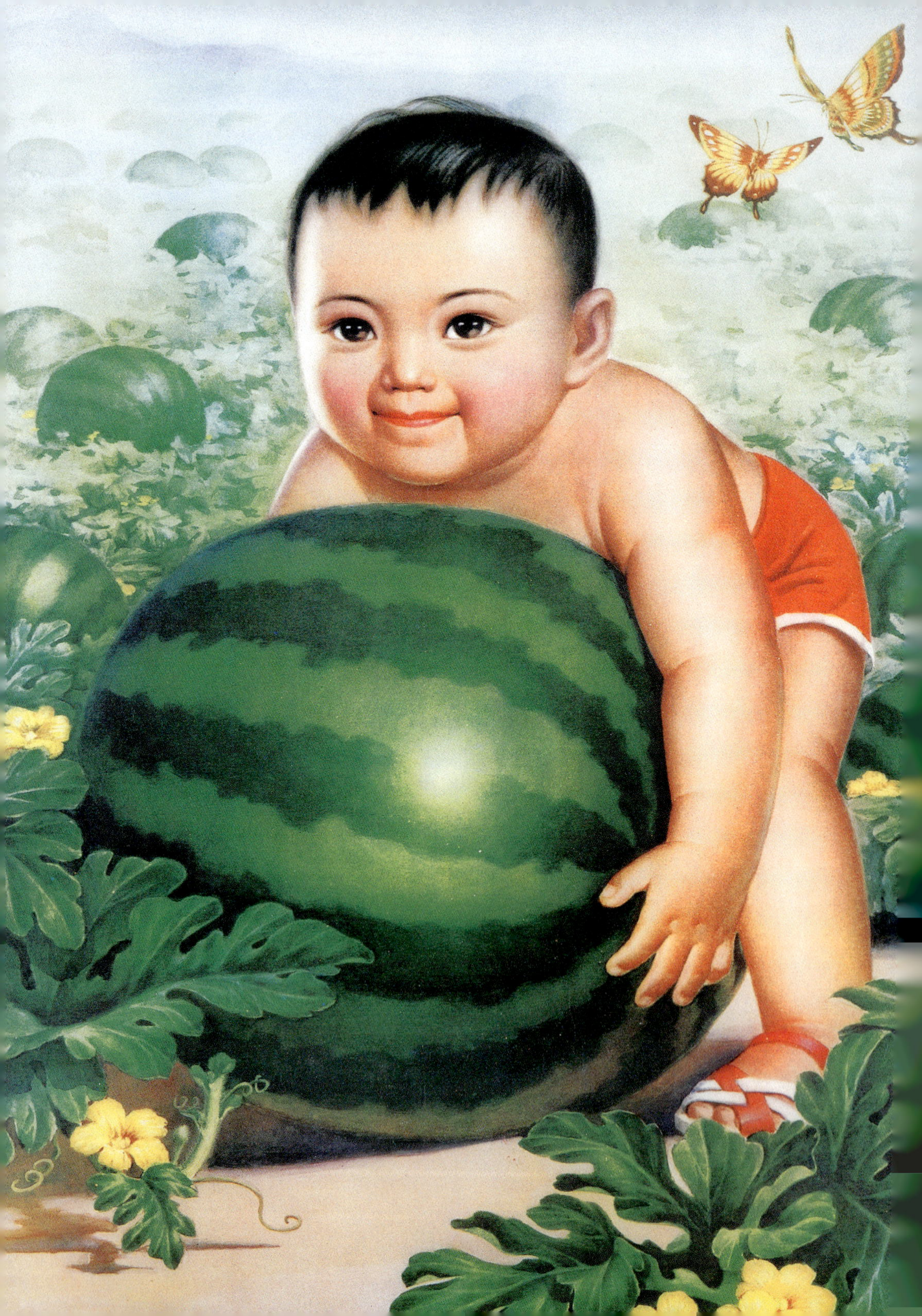

XXIX

YOUTH

DIE JUGEND
LES JEUNES

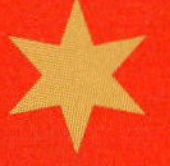

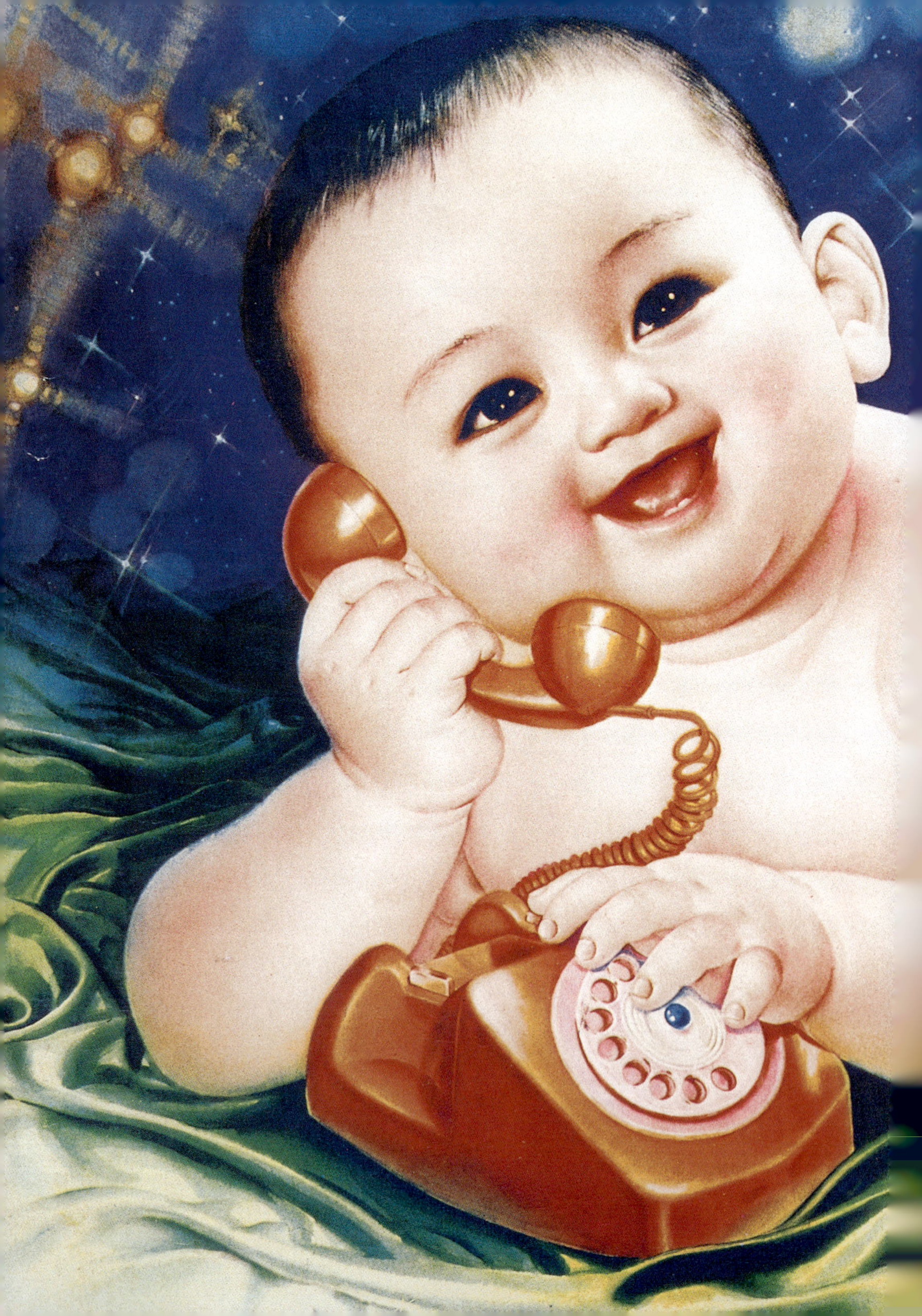

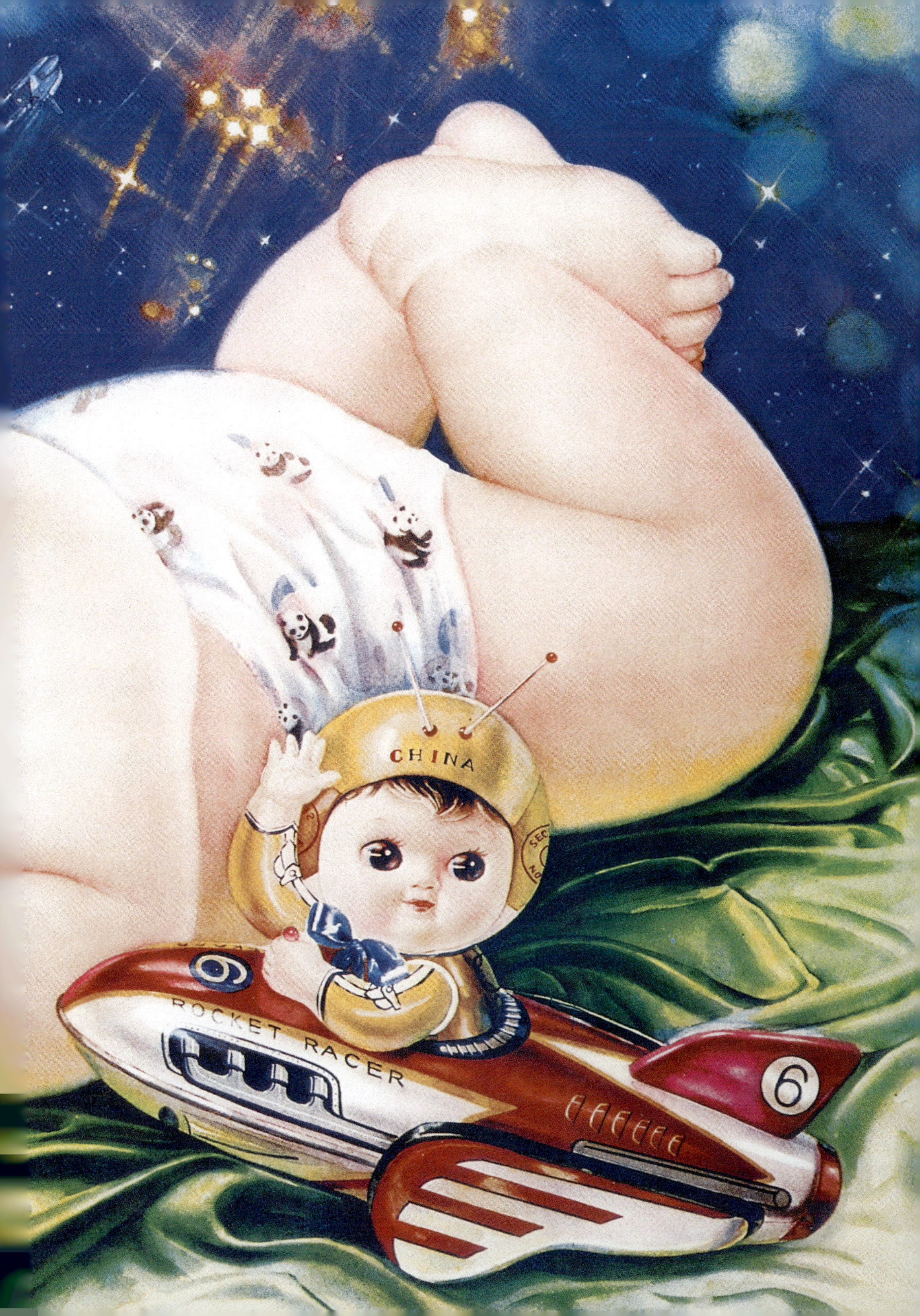
CHINA
ROCKET RACER
6

Page 400

The big watermelon *Artist:* Zheng Xuexin *Published by:* Shandong People's Publishing House, 1983; 0.16 Yuan

Die große Wassermelone *Gemalt von* Zheng Xuexin *Herausgeber:* Volksverlag Shandong, 1983; 0,16 Yuan

La grosse pastèque *Peintre :* Zheng Xuexin *Éditeur :* Éditions Populaires du Shandong, 1983 ; 0,16 yuan

Pages 402–403

I'm calling the stars *Artist:* Cheng Lizhi; Jiangsu Art Publishing House, 1985; 0.21 Yuan

Ich rufe die Sterne an *Gemalt von* Cheng Lizhi; Kunstverlag Jiangsu, 1985; 0,21 Yuan

J'appelle les étoiles *Peintre :* Cheng Lizhi ; Éditions d'Art du Jiangsu, 1985 ; 0,21 yuan

A child's dream The stars light up the sky, I want to observe them closely through my telescope. I shall one day fly into space and turn the most modern scientific ideas into reality. *Artists:* Wang Weishu and Yao Zhongyu *Poem by:* Fan Zhenjia; Shanghai People's Art Publishing House, 1960 *Print run:* 330,000; 0.15 Yuan

Das Ideal der Kinder Die Sterne leuchten am Himmel, mit meinem Fernglas will ich sie genau beobachten. Um die Modernisierung der Wissenschaft zu verwirklichen, fliege ich eines Tages ins All. *Gemalt von* Wang Weishu und Yao Zhongyu *Gedicht:* Fan Zhenjia; Volkskunstverlag Shanghai, 1960 *Auflage:* 330 000; 0,15 Yuan

L'idéal des enfants Les étoiles brillent dans le ciel, je veux les observer de près avec des jumelles. Je volerai un jour dans l'espace pour réaliser la modernisation de la science. *Peintres :* Wang Weishu et Yao Zhingyu *Poème :* Fan Zhenjia ; Éditions Populaires d'Art de Shanghai, 1960 *Tirage :* 330 000 ; 0,15 yuan

Pages 406–407

We are the astronauts of the future Space rocket 086; Popular Science Publishing House, Guangzhou branch, 2nd edn 1986; 0.22 Yuan

Wir sind die zukünftigen Astronauten Raumschiff 086; Verlag der Populärwissenschaft, Niederlassung Guangzhou, 2. Aufl. 1986; 0,22 Yuan

Nous sommes les futurs astronautes Vaisseau spatial 086 ; Éditions des Sciences Populaires, filiale de Guangzhou, 2e éd. 1986 ; 0,22 yuan

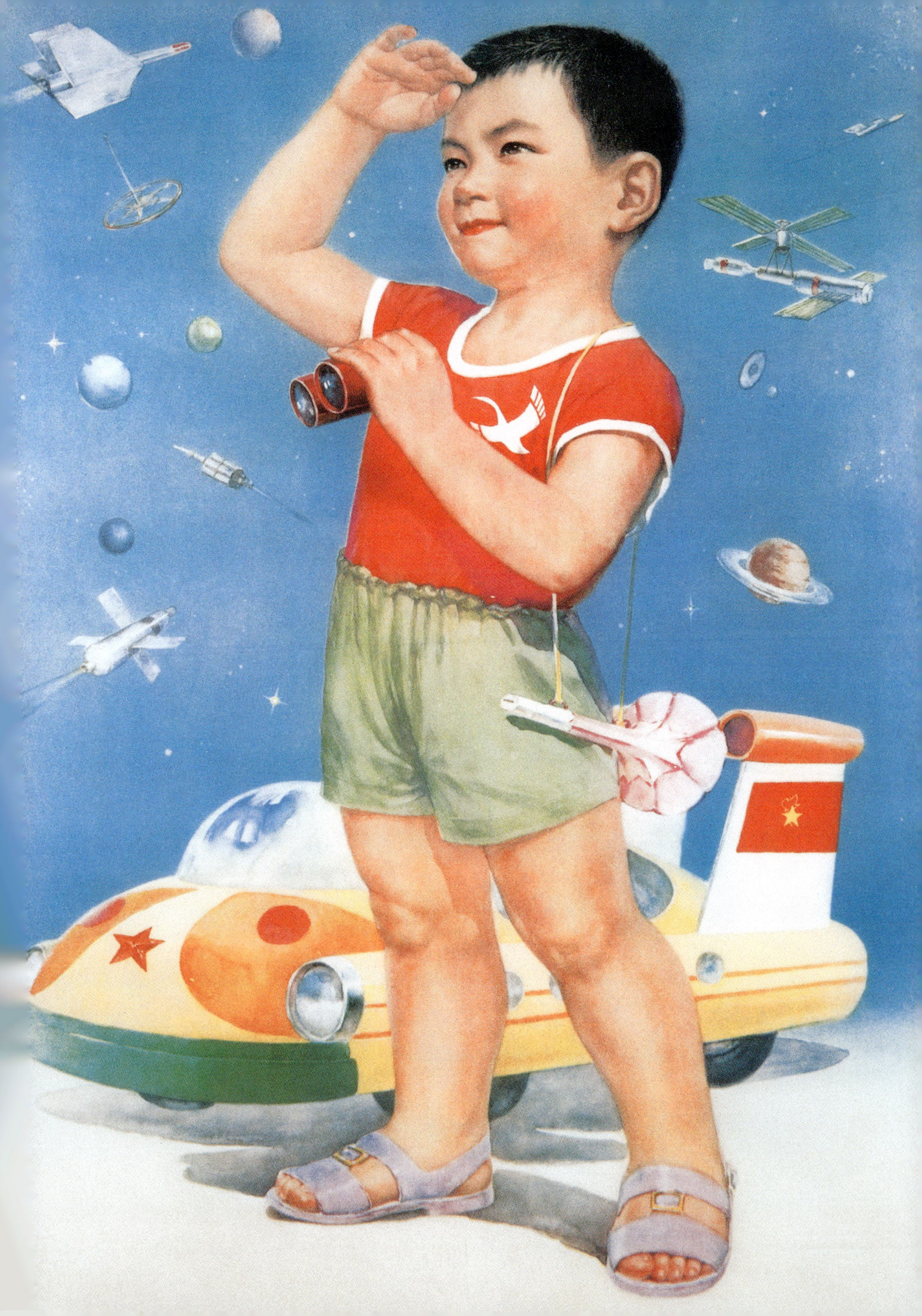

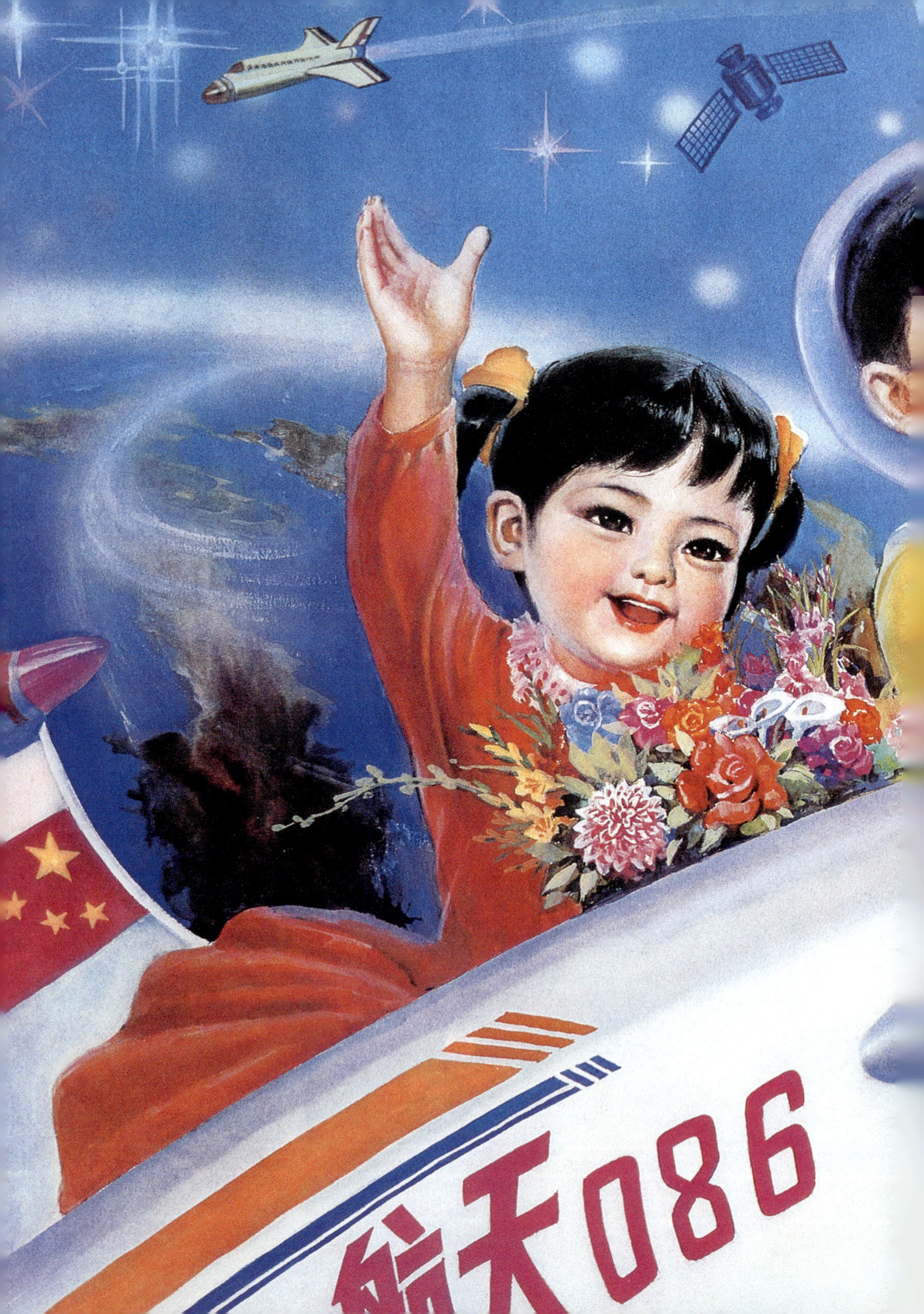
航天086

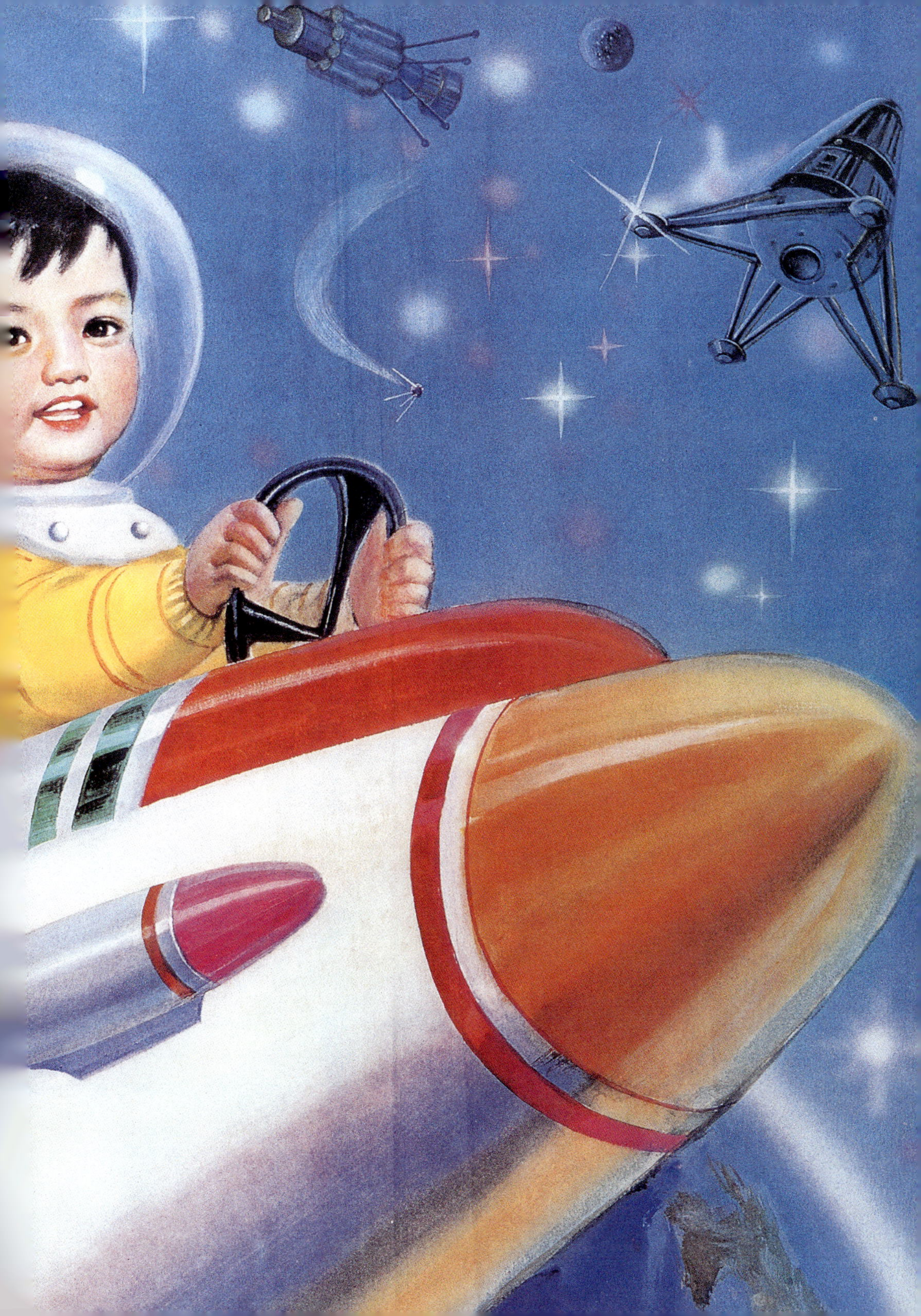

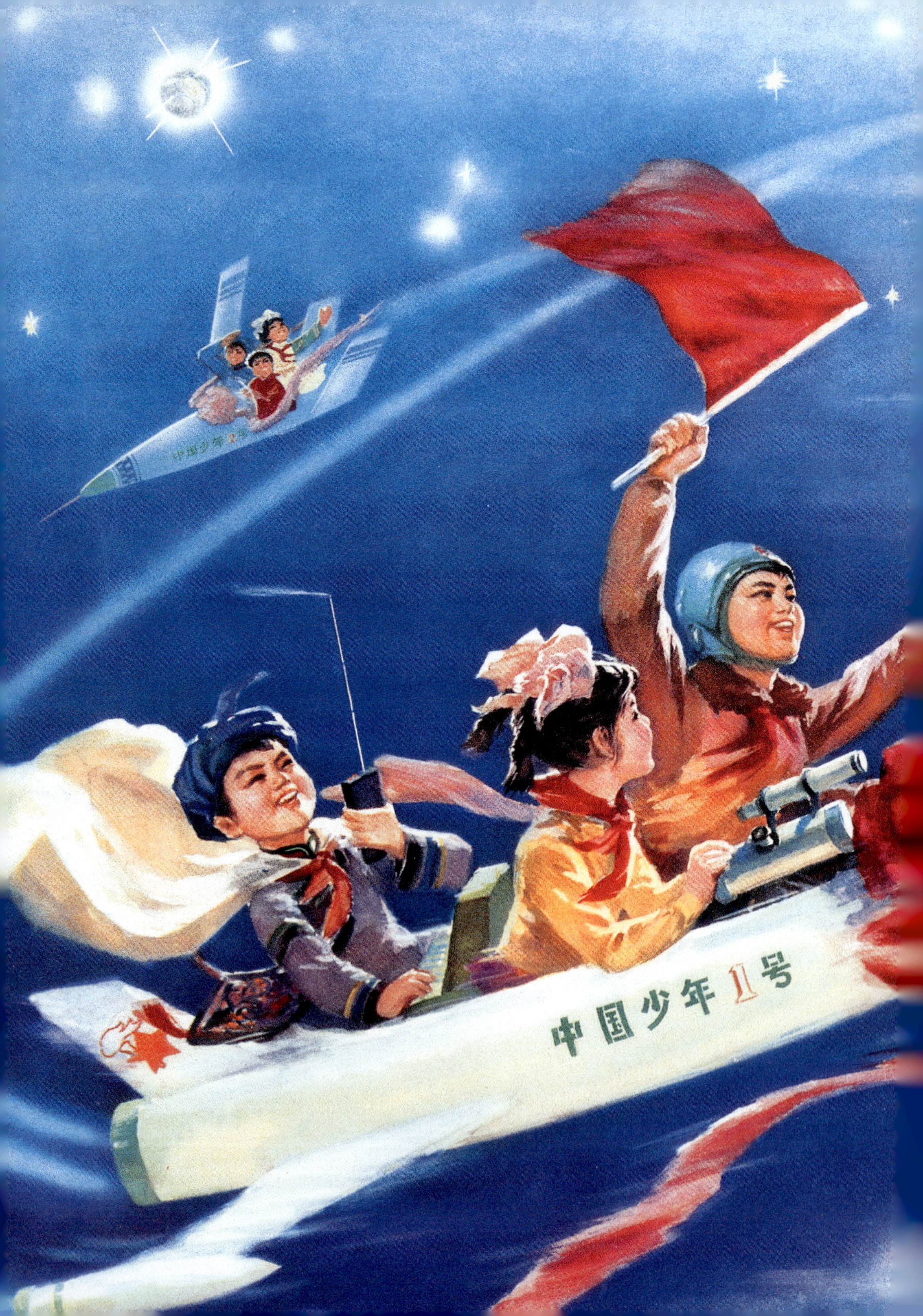
中国少年2号
中国少年1号

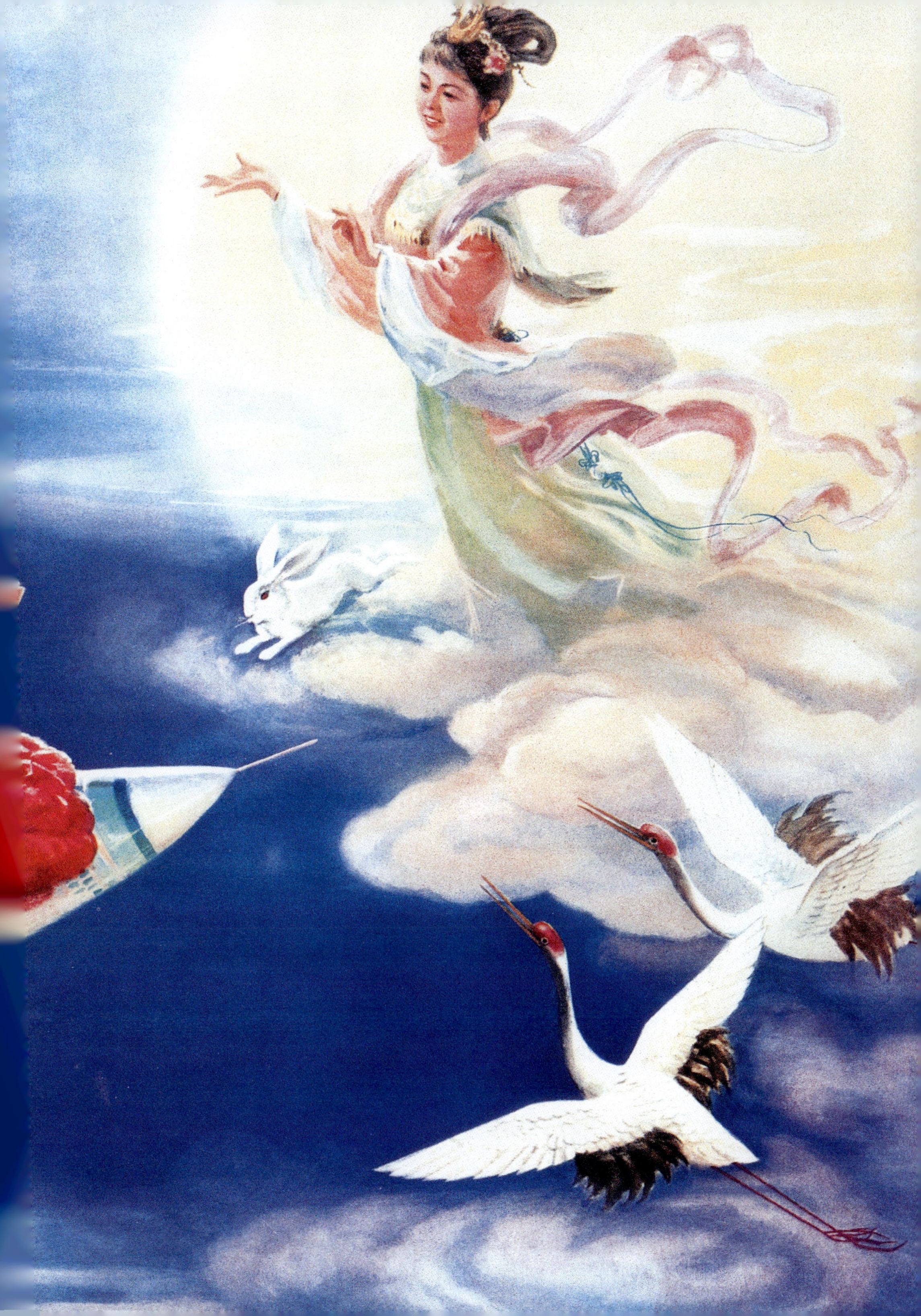

Pages 408–409

Soar, youth of the New China!* *On the rocket:* China's Youth No. 1 *Artist:* Jin Dingsheng, Qingjiang Art and Leisure Centre; Jiangsu People's Publishing House, 1978; 0.11 Yuan
* The woman depicted is the Chinese mythological fairy Chang E who lives on the moon with her rabbit.

Flieg, Jugend des Neuen China!* *Auf der Rakete:* Chinas Jugend Nr. 1 *Gemalt von* Jin Dingsheng, Kulturhaus der Stadt Qingjiang; Volksverlag Jiangsu, 1978; 0,11 Yuan
* Die Frau im Bild ist die auf dem Mond lebende Fee Chang E aus der chinesischen Mythologie mit ihrem Hasen.

Vole, jeunesse de la Chine Nouvelle !* *Sur la fusée :* Jeunesse de Chine n° 1 *Peintre :* Jin Dingsheng, Maison de la Culture de la ville de Qingjiang ; Éditions Populaires du Jiangsu, 1978 ; 0,11 yuan
* La femme sur l'image est Chang E, la fée de la mythologie chinoise qui vit sur la lune, représentée avec son lièvre.

Little darlings reading a picture book *Artist:* Zhang Daxin; Shanghai People's Art Publishing House, 1962 *Print run:* 20,000; 0.15 Yuan

Schätzchen lesen eine Illustrierte *Gemalt von* Zhang Daxin; Volkskunstverlag Shanghai, 1962 *Auflage:* 20 000; 0,15 Yuan

Les petits bouts de chou lisent un illustré *Peintre :* Zhang Daxin ; Éditions Populaires d'Art de Shanghai, 1962 *Tirage :* 20 000 ; 0,15 yuan

Pages 412–413

Looking at a magazine *Artist:* Zhang Daxin; Shanghai People's Art Publishing House 1978; 0.11 Yuan

Eine Illustrierte betrachten *Gemalt von* Zhang Daxin; Volkskunstverlag Shanghai 1978; 0,11 Yuan

La lecture d'un illustré *Peintre :* Zhang Daxin ; Éditions Populaires d'Art de Shanghai, 1978 ; 0,11 yuan

Pages 414–415

Feeding the rabbits *Artist:* Zhang Daxin *Published by:* Shanghai Picture Publishing House, 12th edn 1954 *Print run:* 401,201–440,400

Kaninchen füttern *Gemalt von* Zhang Daxin *Herausgeber:* Bilderverlag Shanghai, 12. Aufl. 1954 *Auflage:* 401 201–440 400

Donnons à manger aux lapins *Peintre :* Zhang Daxin *Éditeur :* Éditions des Images de Shanghai, 12e éd. 1954 *Tirage :* 401 201–440 400

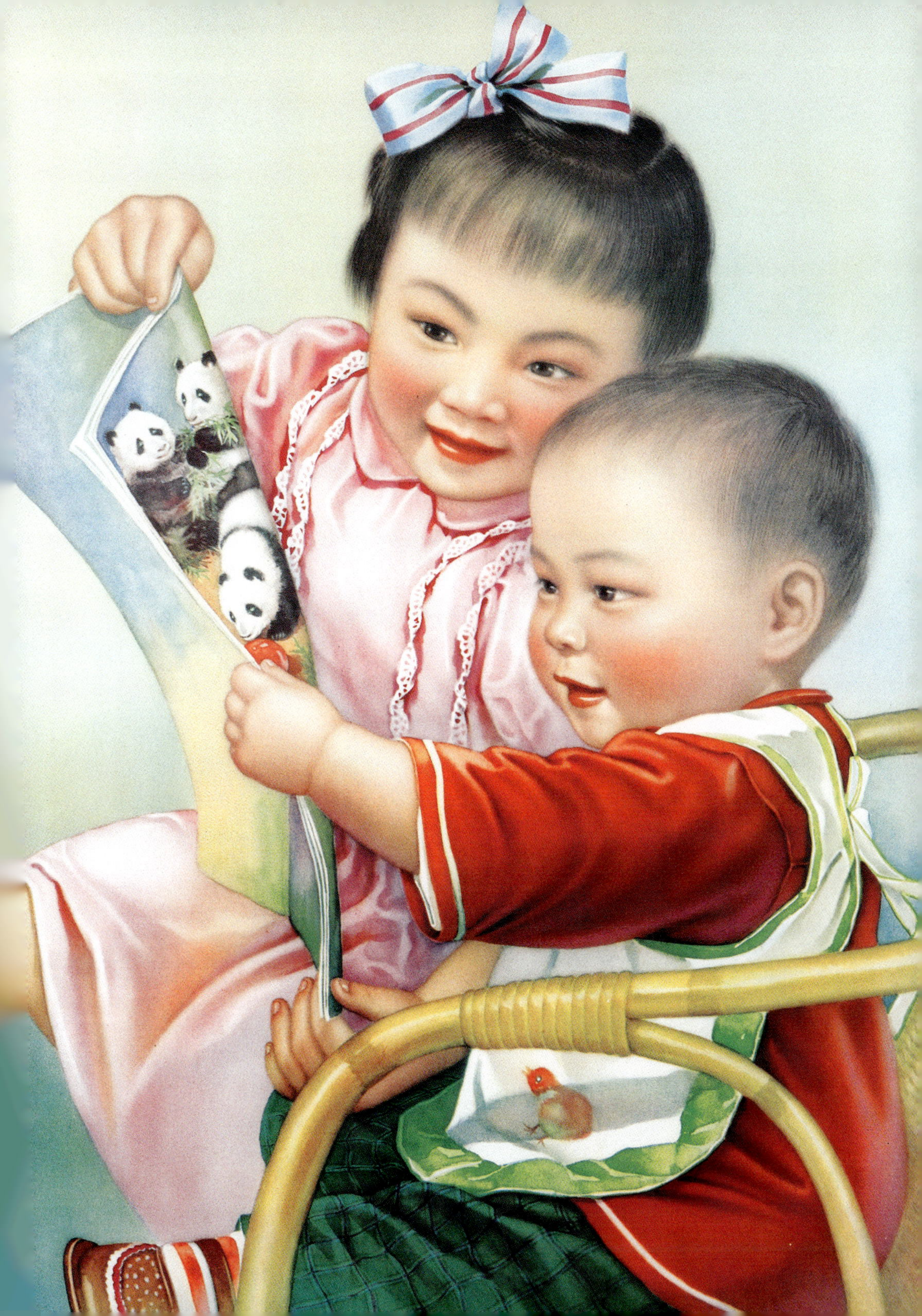

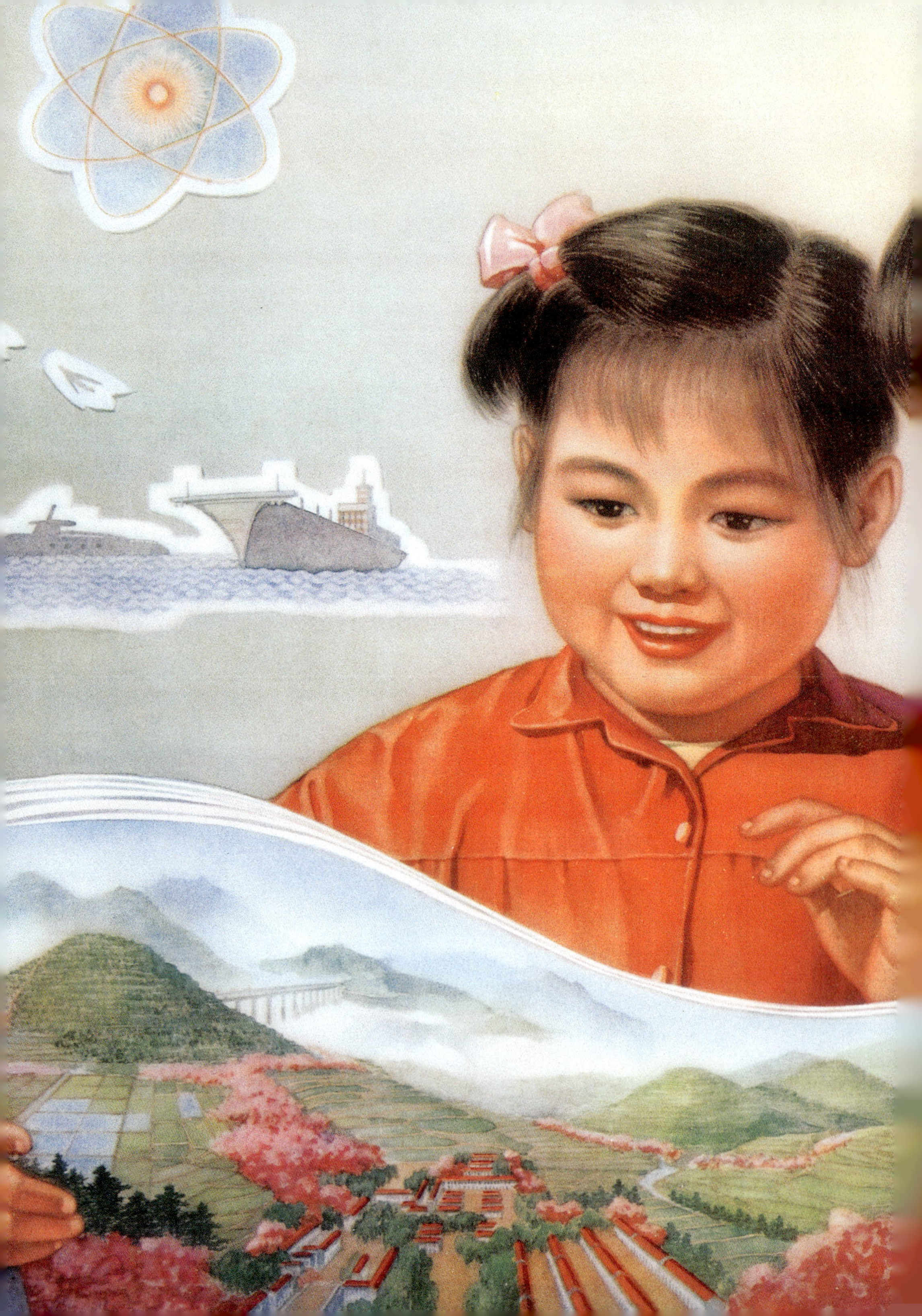

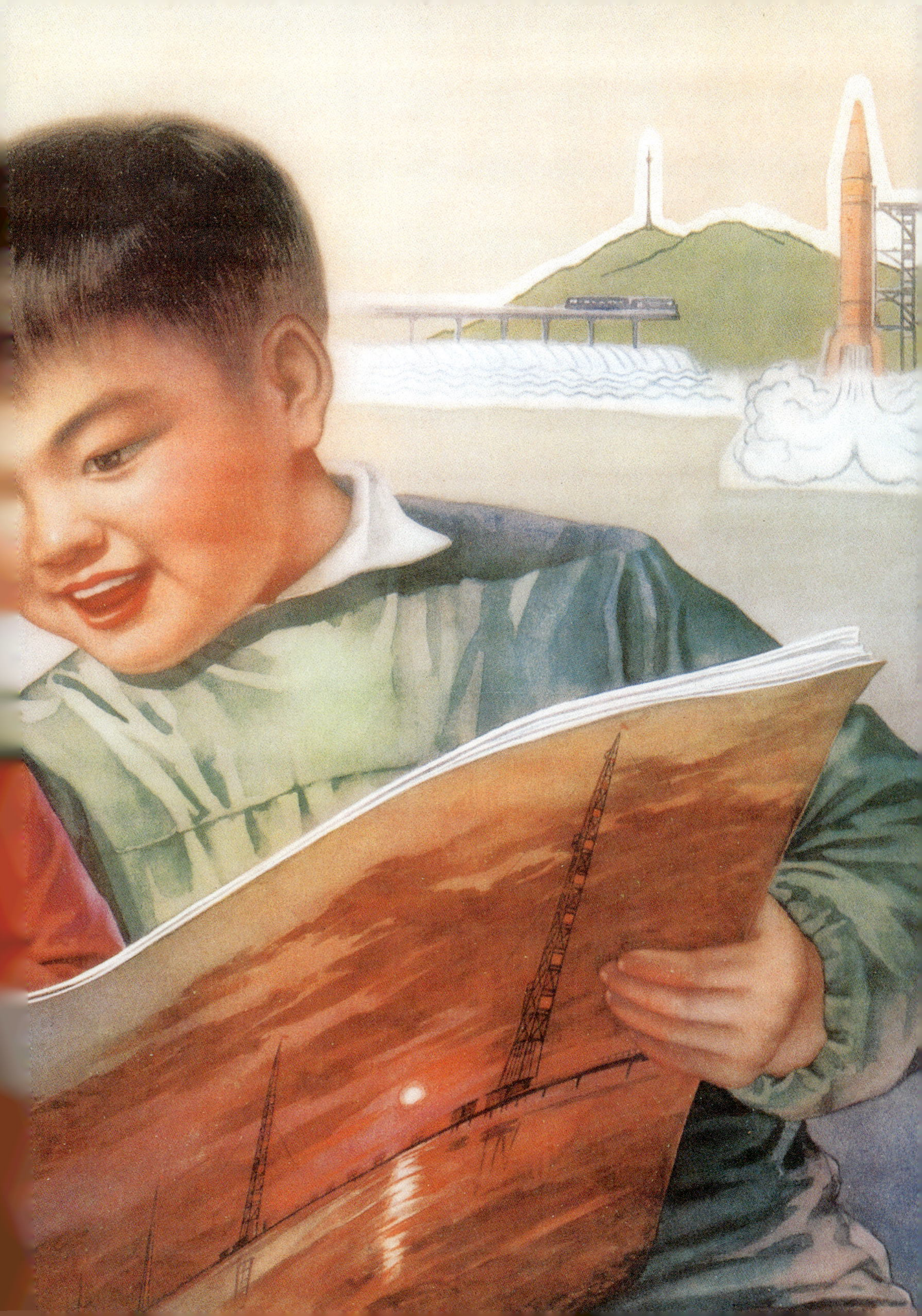

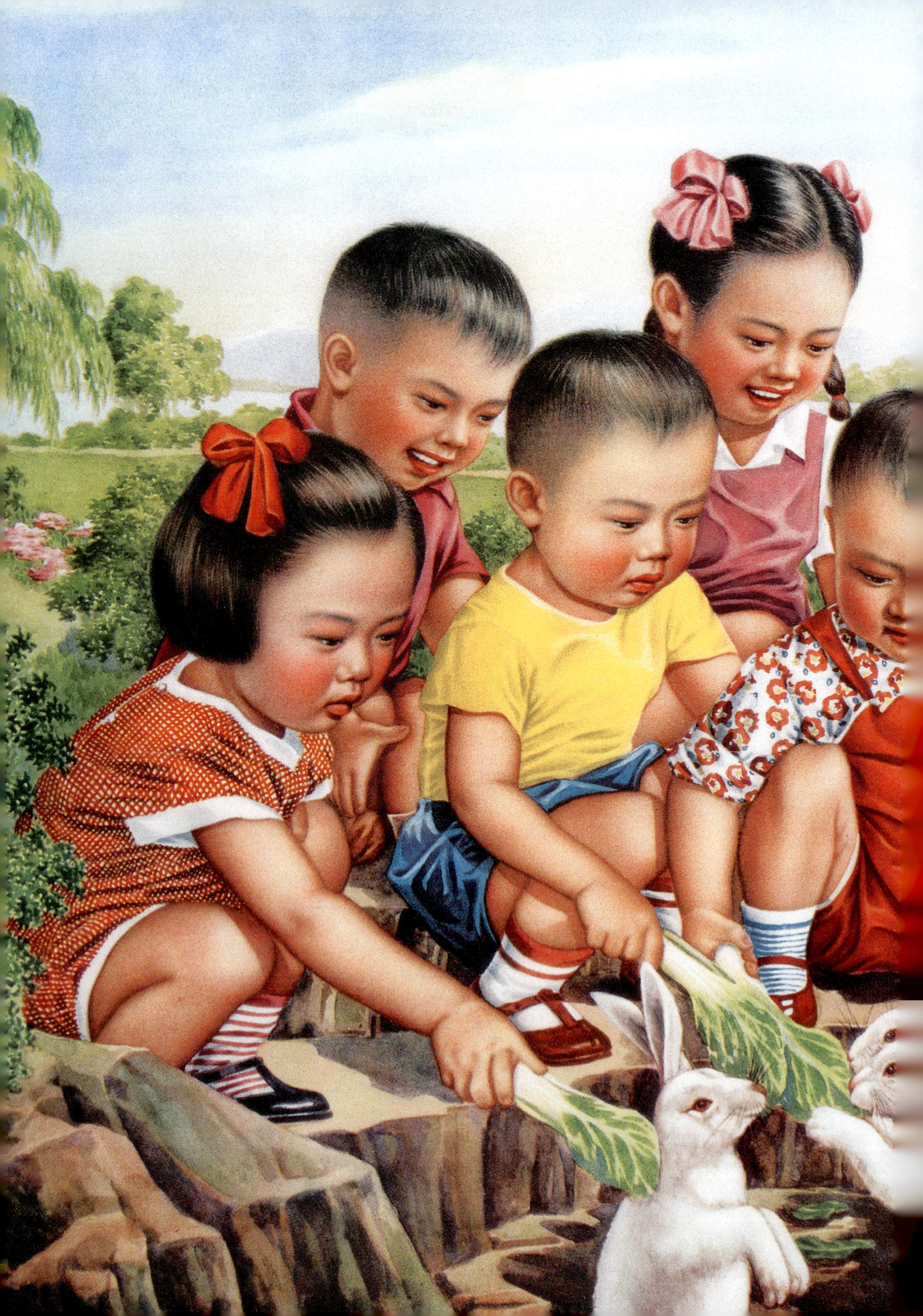

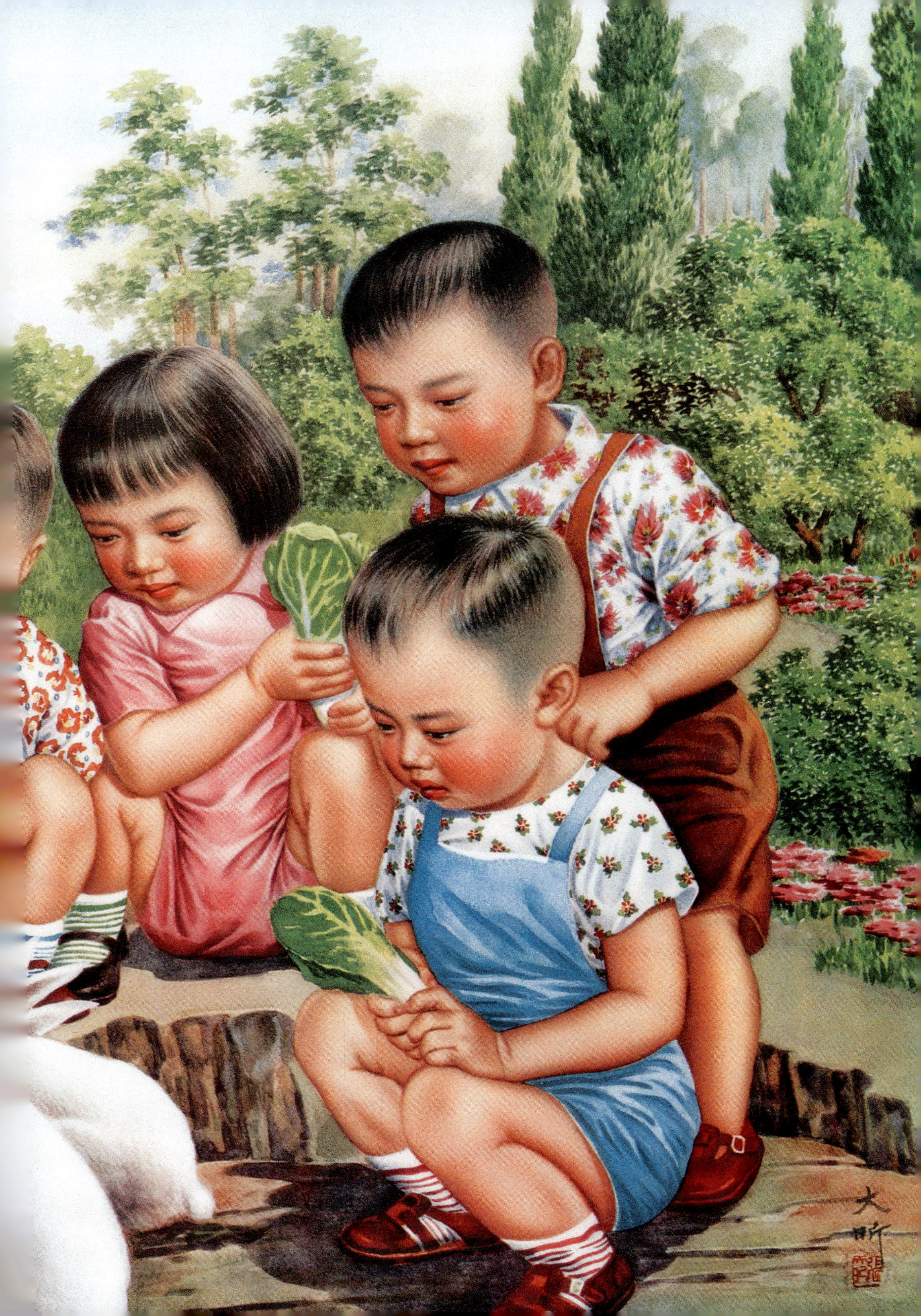
大昕

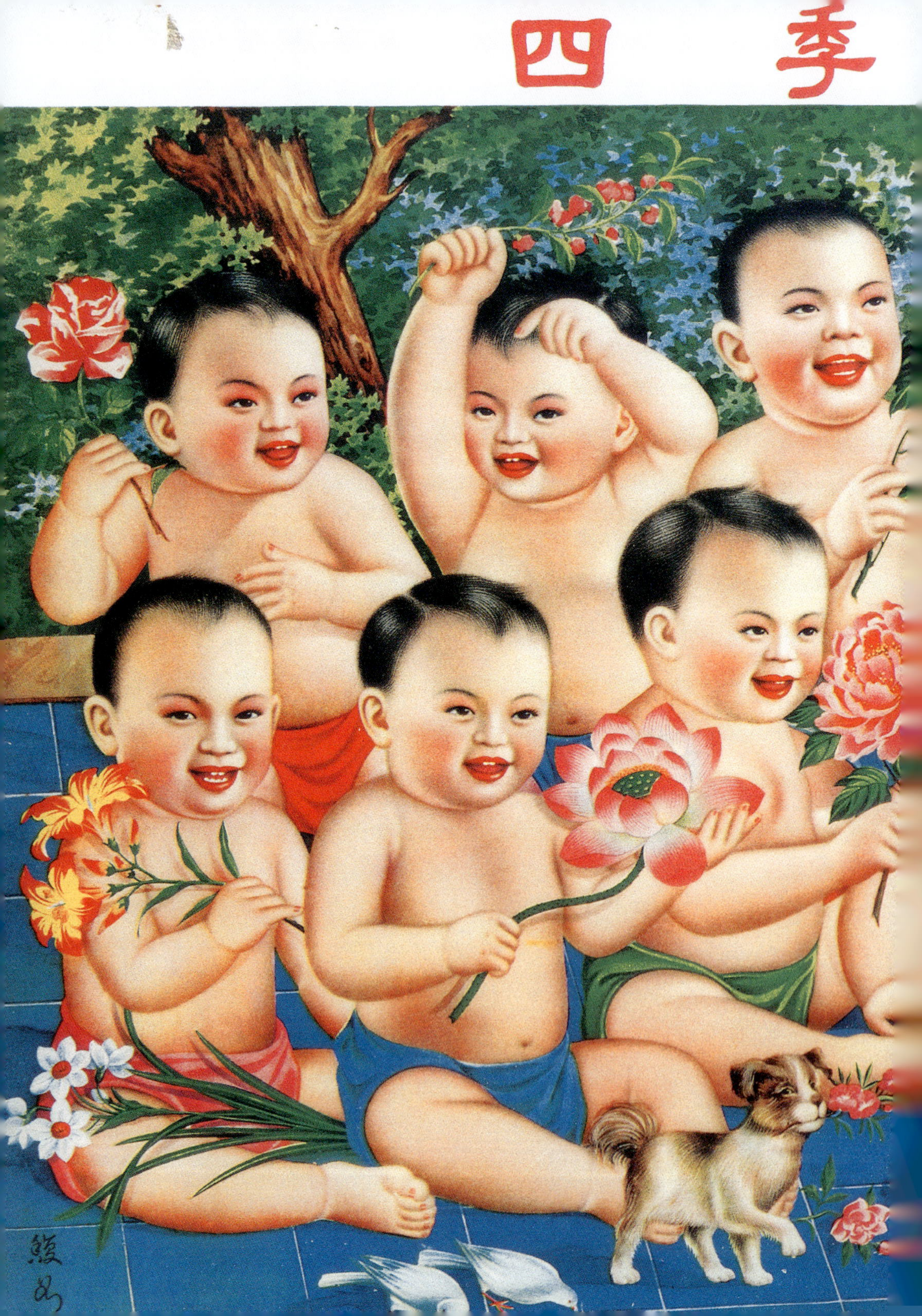

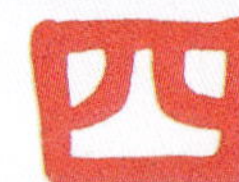
四
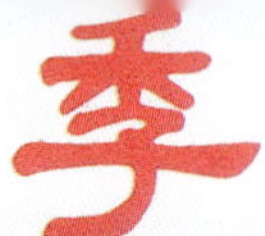
季

花 型

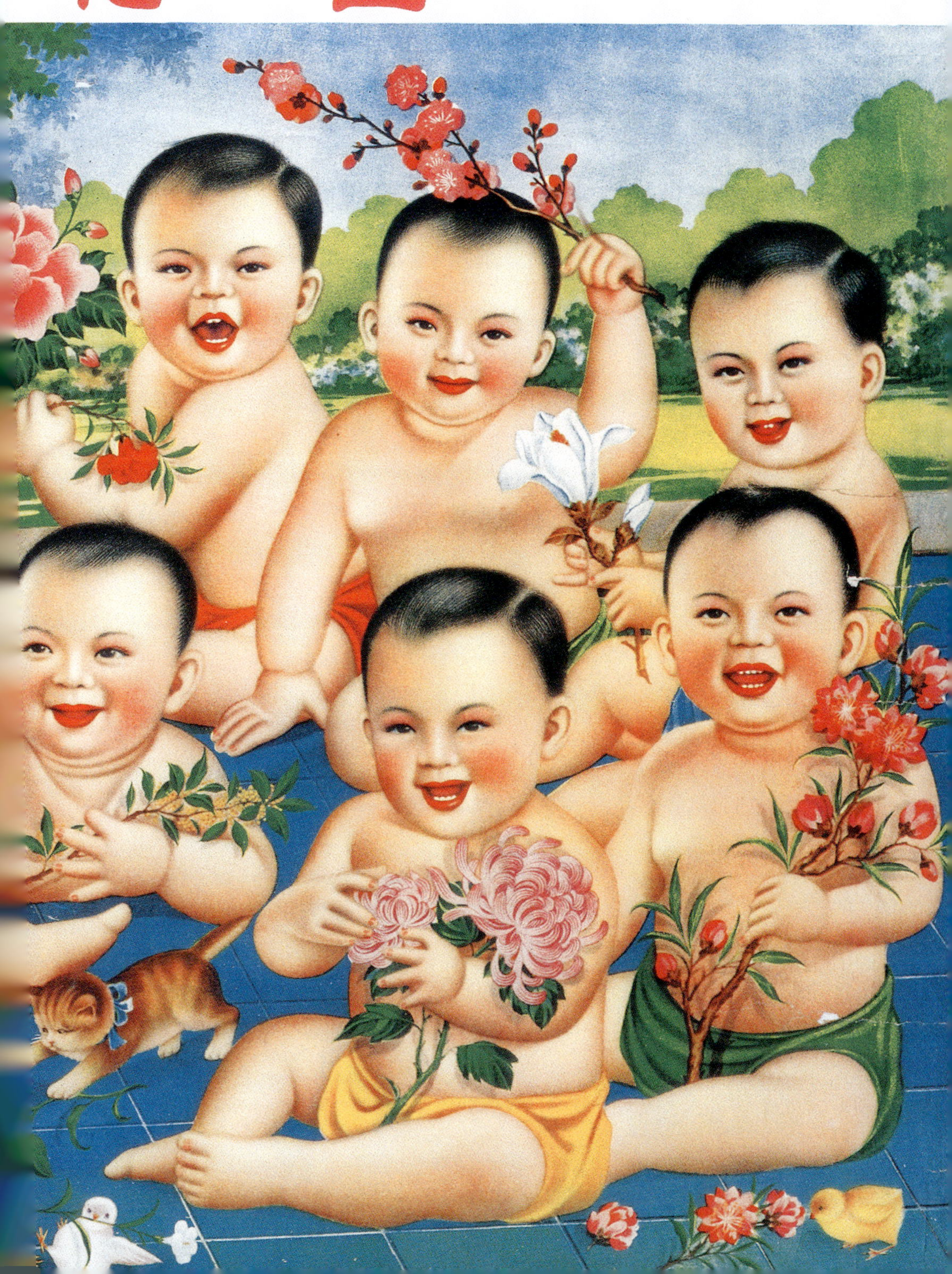

Pages 416–417

The flowers of the four seasons *Artist:* Yang Furu *Published by:* Yihui Poster Shop, Western Beijing Road, No.3 Street 240, Shanghai, 1953 *Print run:* 10,000

Die Blumen der vier Jahreszeiten *Gemalt von* Yang Furu *Herausgeber:* Plakatgeschäft Yihui, Westliche Pekinger Straße, Gasse 240, Nr. 3, Shanghai, 1953 *Auflage:* 10 000

Les fleurs des quatre saisons *Peintre :* Yang Furu *Éditeur :* Magasin d'affiches Yihui, partie ouest de la rue de Pékin, ruelle 240, n° 3, Shanghai, 1953 *Tirage :* 10 000

Wash your hands before eating *On door:* Street Committee's Children's Canteen *On poster:* Observe food-hygiene rules *Artists:* Song Yipin and Zhang Dejun; Shanghai People's Art Publishing House, 1st edn 1980, 3rd edn 1980 *Print run:* 600,001–1,280,000; 0.16 Yuan

Vor dem Essen Hände waschen *An der Tür:* Kinderkantine des Straßenkomitees *Auf dem Plakat:* Auf die Nahrungsmittelhygiene achten *Gemalt von* Song Yipin und Zhang Dejun; Volkskunstverlag Shanghai, 1. Aufl. 1980, 3. Aufl. 1980 *Auflage:* 600 001–1 280 000; 0,16 Yuan

Lavez-vous les mains avant de manger *Sur la porte :* Cantine pour enfants du comité de quartier *Sur l'affiche :* Surveillez votre hygiène alimentaire *Peintres :* Song Yipin et Zhang Dejun ; Éditions Populaires d'art de Shanghai, 1ère éd. 1980, 3ème éd. 1980 *Tirage :* 600 001–1 280 000 ; 0,16 yuan

Pages 420–421

Electric toys are fun *Artist:* Lu Ting; Shanghai People's Art Publishing House, 1983 *Print run:* 105,000; 0.16 Yuan

Lustige elektrische Spielzeuge *Gemalt von* Lu Ting; Volkskunstverlag Shanghai, 1983 *Auflage:* 105 000; 0,16 Yuan

D'amusants jouets électriques *Peintre :* Lu Ting ; Éditions Populaires d'Art de Shanghai, 1983 *Tirage :* 105 000 ; 0,16 yuan

Pages 422–423

Beautiful flowers Qunyitang New Year poster *Artist:* Zhang Yuqing *Published by:* Qunyitang Artists' Requisites Company, 1963 *Print run:* 145,000; 0.18 Yuan

Schöne Blumen Qunyitang-Neujahrsplakat *Gemalt von* Zhang Yuqing *Herausgeber:* Qunyitang-Kunstbedarfsgeschäft, 1963 *Auflage:* 145 000; 0,18 Yuan

De belles fleurs Affiche de Nouvel An Qunyitang *Peintre :* Zhang Yuqing *Éditeur :* Magasin de fournitures pour artistes Qunyitang, 1963 *Tirage :* 145 000 ; 0,18 yuan

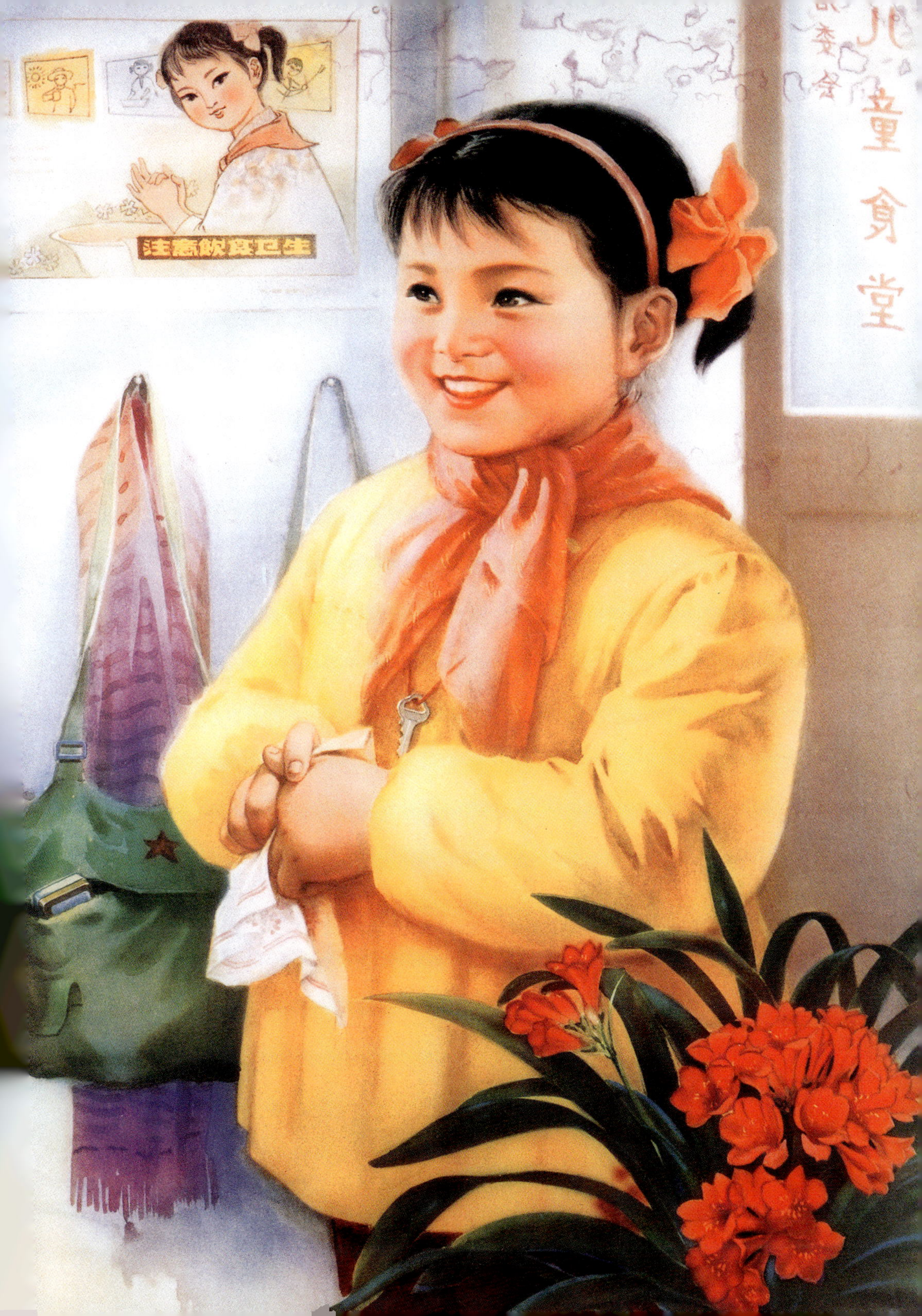
注意飲食卫生
儿童食堂

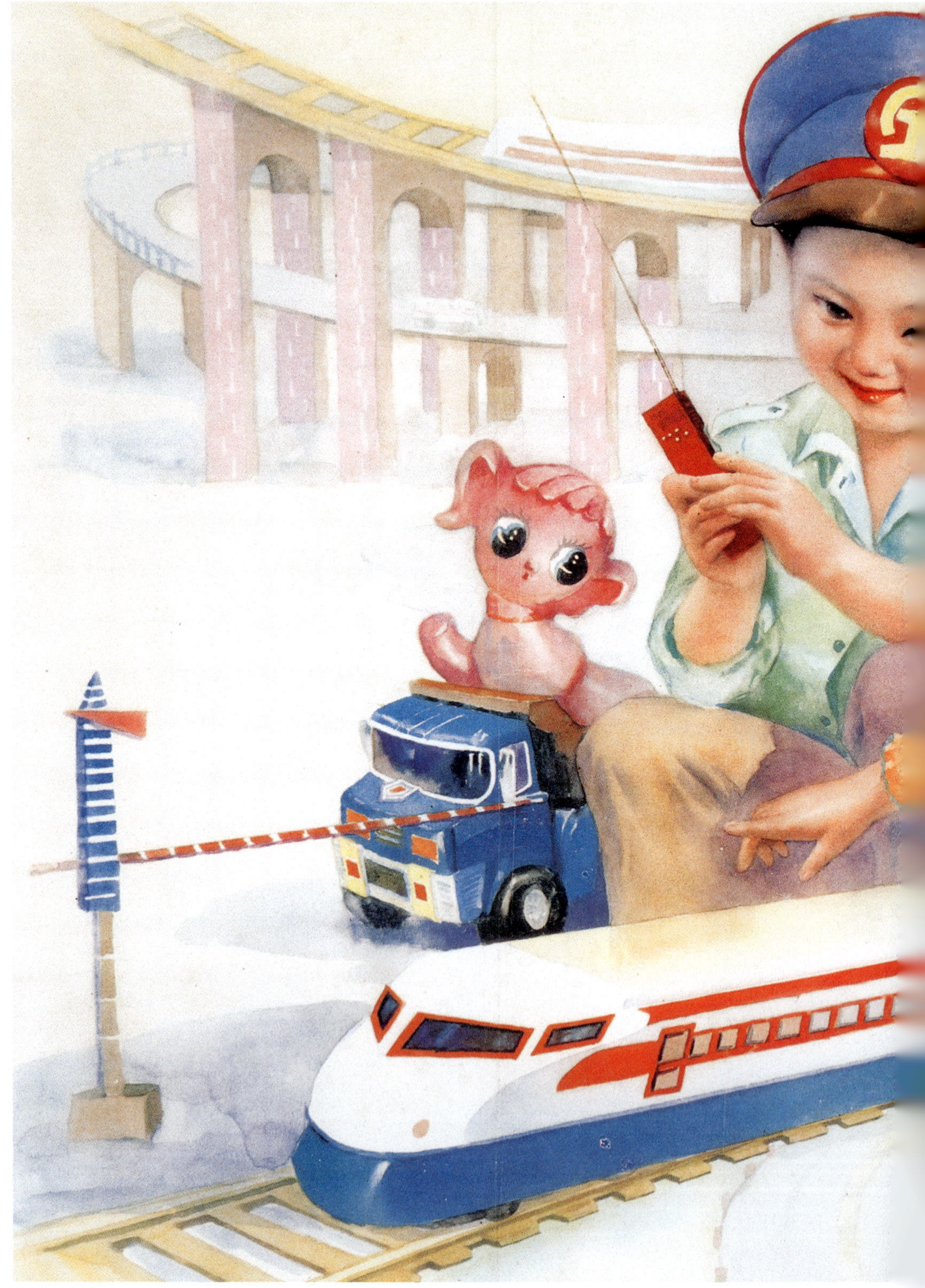

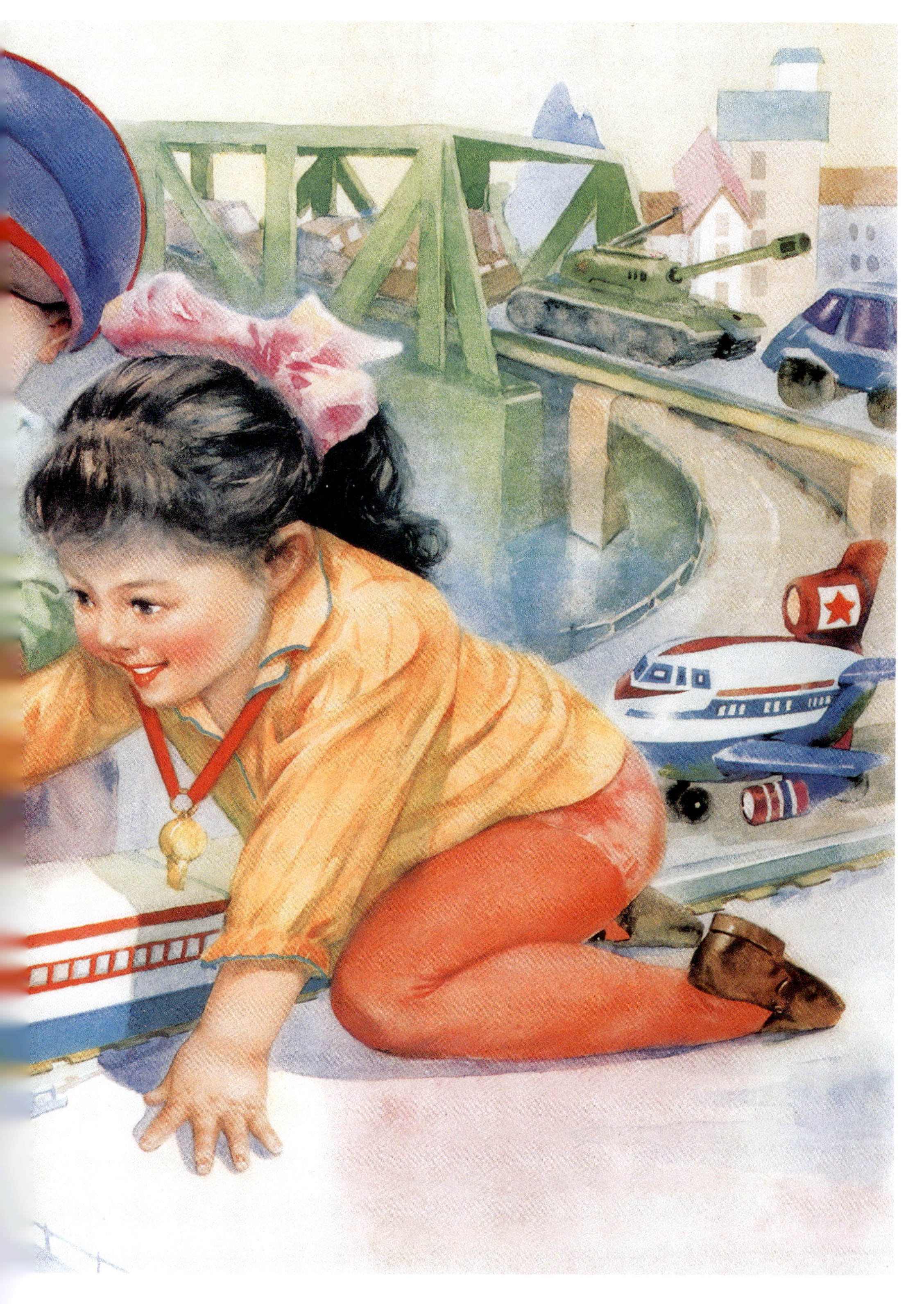

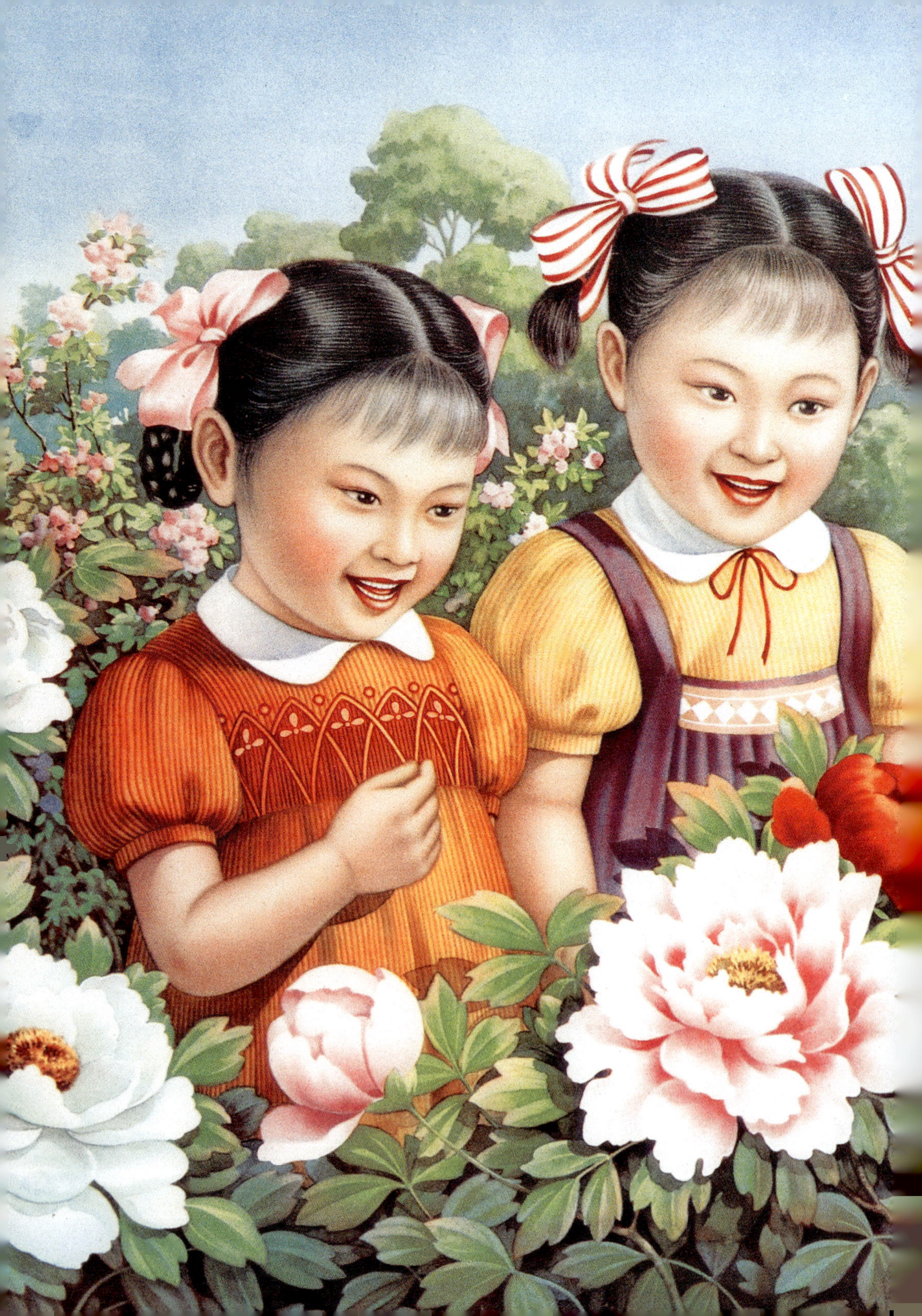

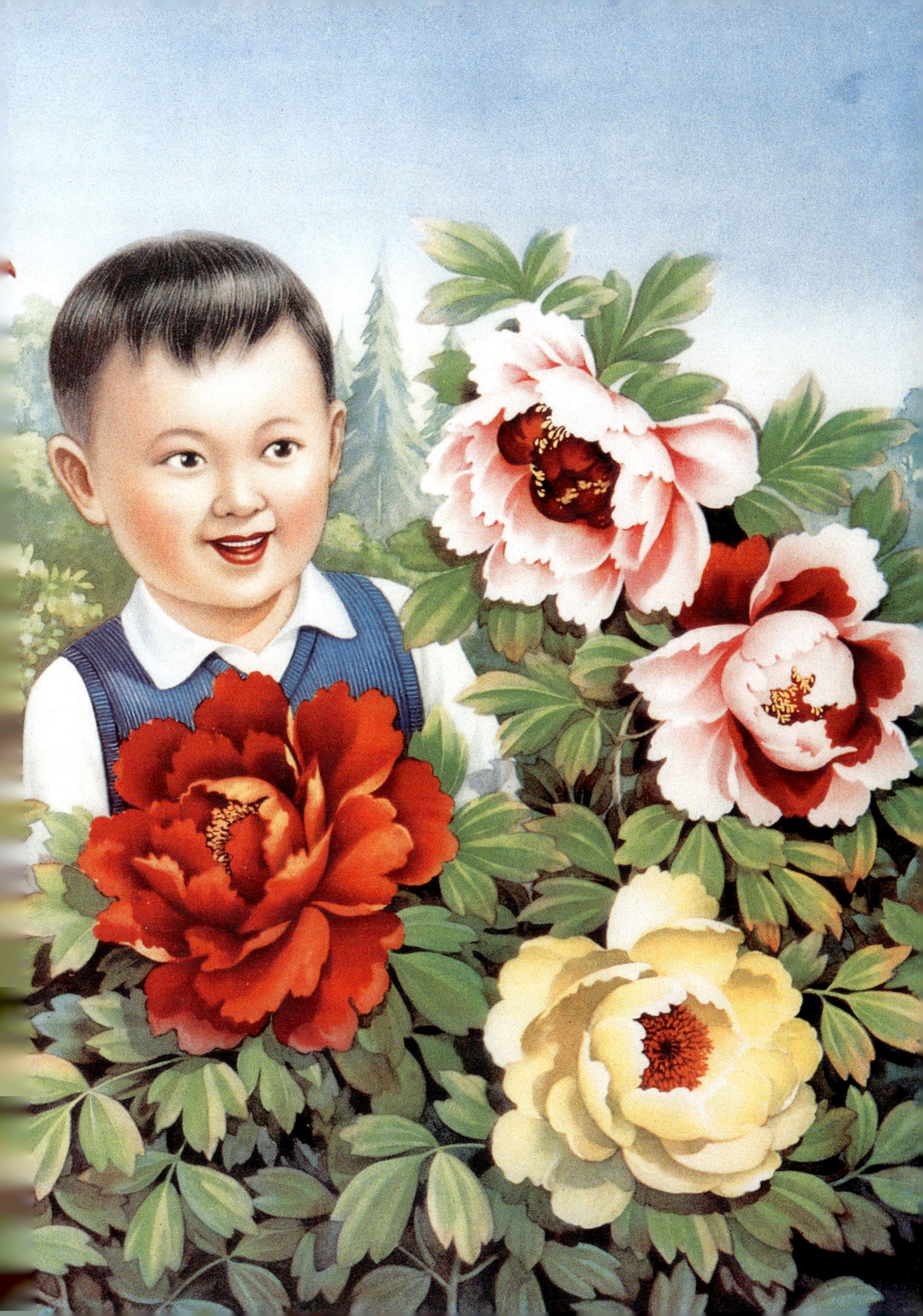

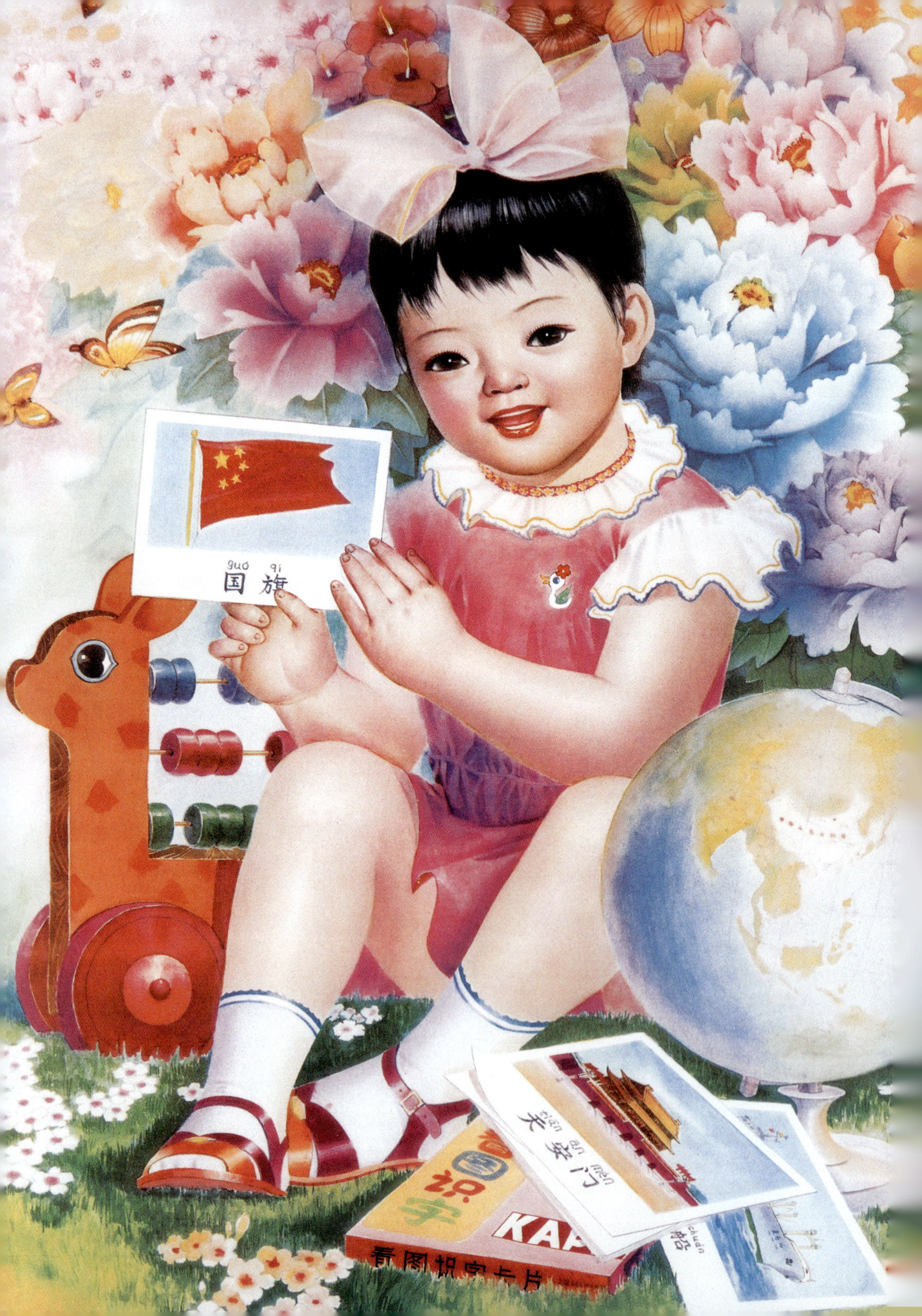
guó qí
国旗
tiān ān mén
天安门
识字
chuán
船
看图识字卡片

Opposite
I love the wonderful fatherland *On postcard held by girl:* The national flag *Postcard below:* The Gate of Heavenly Peace *Artist:* Sima Lianyi; People's Art Publishing House, 1985; 0.21 Yuan

Ich liebe das großartige Vaterland *Auf der Karte in der Hand des Mädchens:* Die Nationalflagge *Karte unten:* Das Tor des Himmlischen Friedens *Gemalt von* Sima Lianyi; Volkskunstverlag, 1985; 0,21 Yuan

J'aime notre magnifique patrie *Sur la carte dans la main de la fillette :* Le drapeau national *Carte en bas :* La Porte de la Paix Céleste *Peintre :* Sima Lianyi ; Éditions Populaires d'Art, 1985 ; 0,21 yuan

Pages 426–427
Wonderful childhood *Artist:* Huang Miaofa; Shanghai People's Art Publishing House, 1960 *Print run:* 100,000; 0.12 Yuan

Die schöne Kindheit *Gemalt von* Huang Miaofa; Volkskunstverlag Shanghai, 1960 *Auflage:* 100 000; 0,12 Yuan

La belle enfance *Peintre :* Huang Miaofa ; Éditions Populaires d'Art de Shanghai, 1960 *Tirage :* 100 000 ; 0,12 yuan

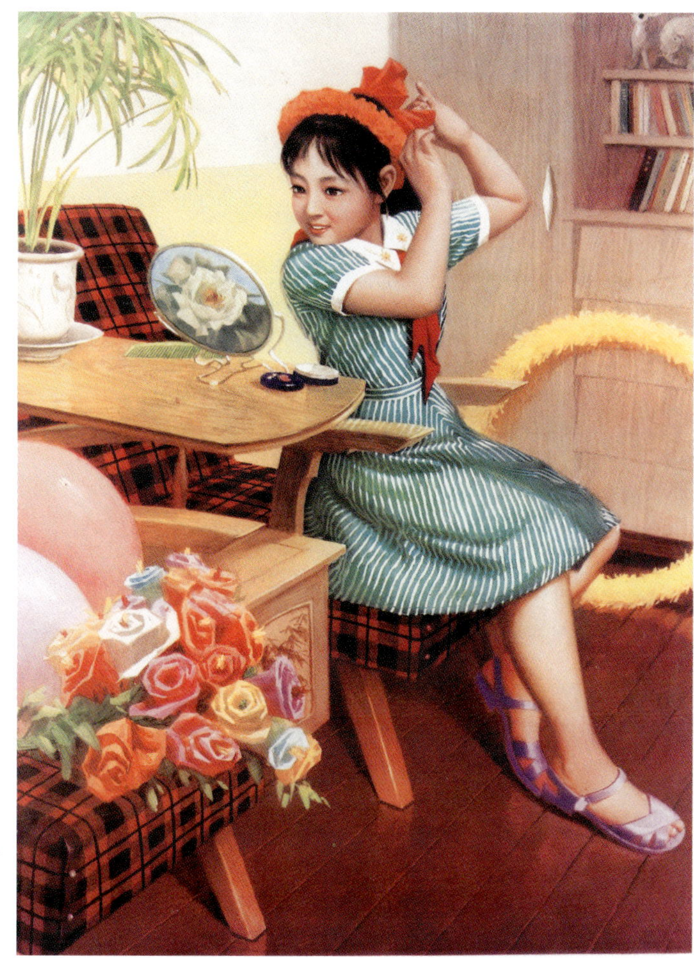

A festive holiday *Artist:* Ji Binggang; People's Art Publishing House, 1951; 0.16 Yuan

Ein Festtag *Gemalt von* Ji Binggang; Volkskunstverlag, 1951; 0,16 Yuan

Jour de fête *Peintre :* Ji Binggang ; Éditions Populaires d'Art, 1951 ; 0,16 yuan

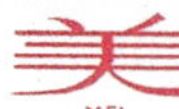
美
MEI
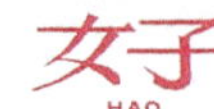
好
HAO

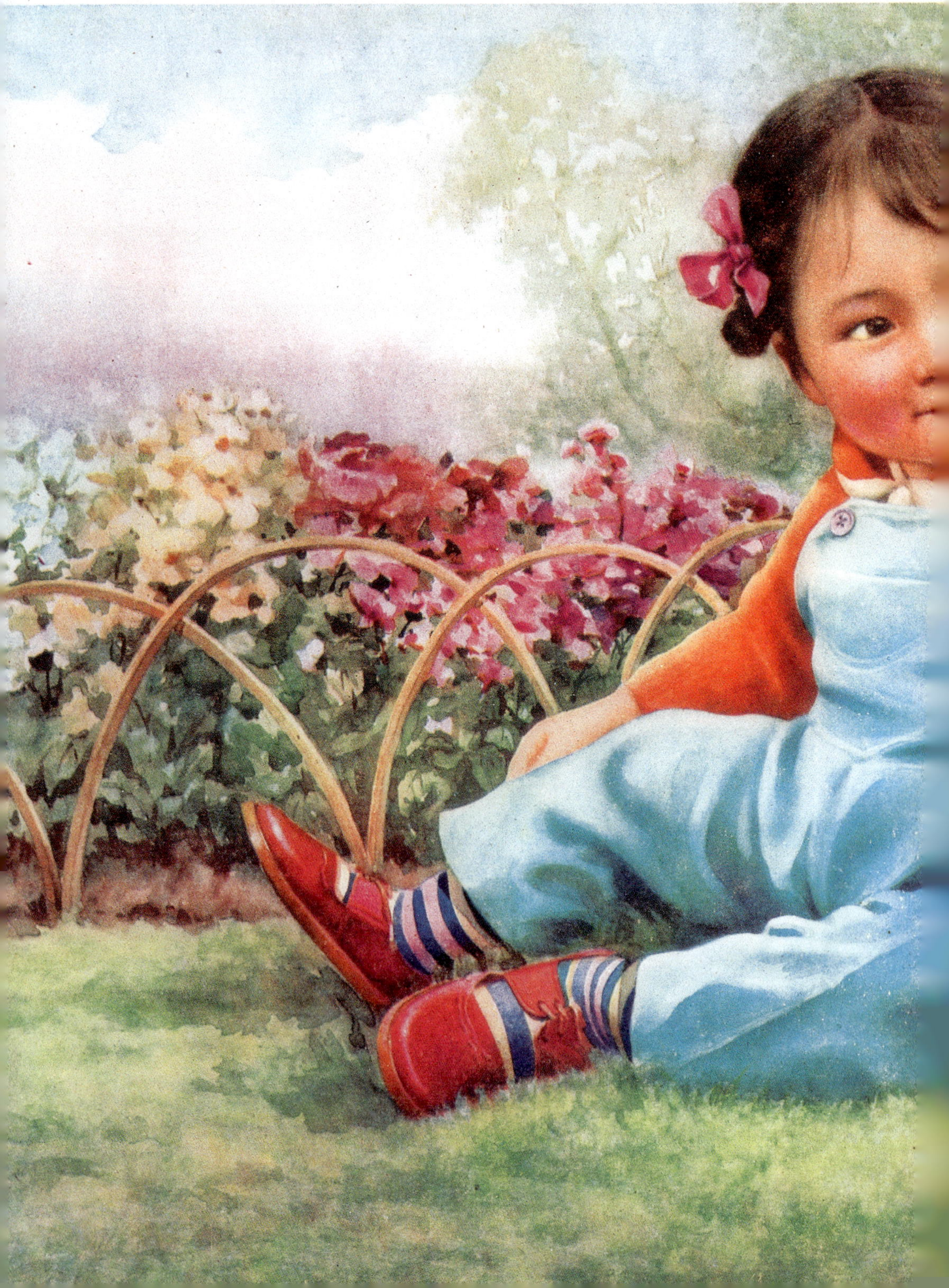

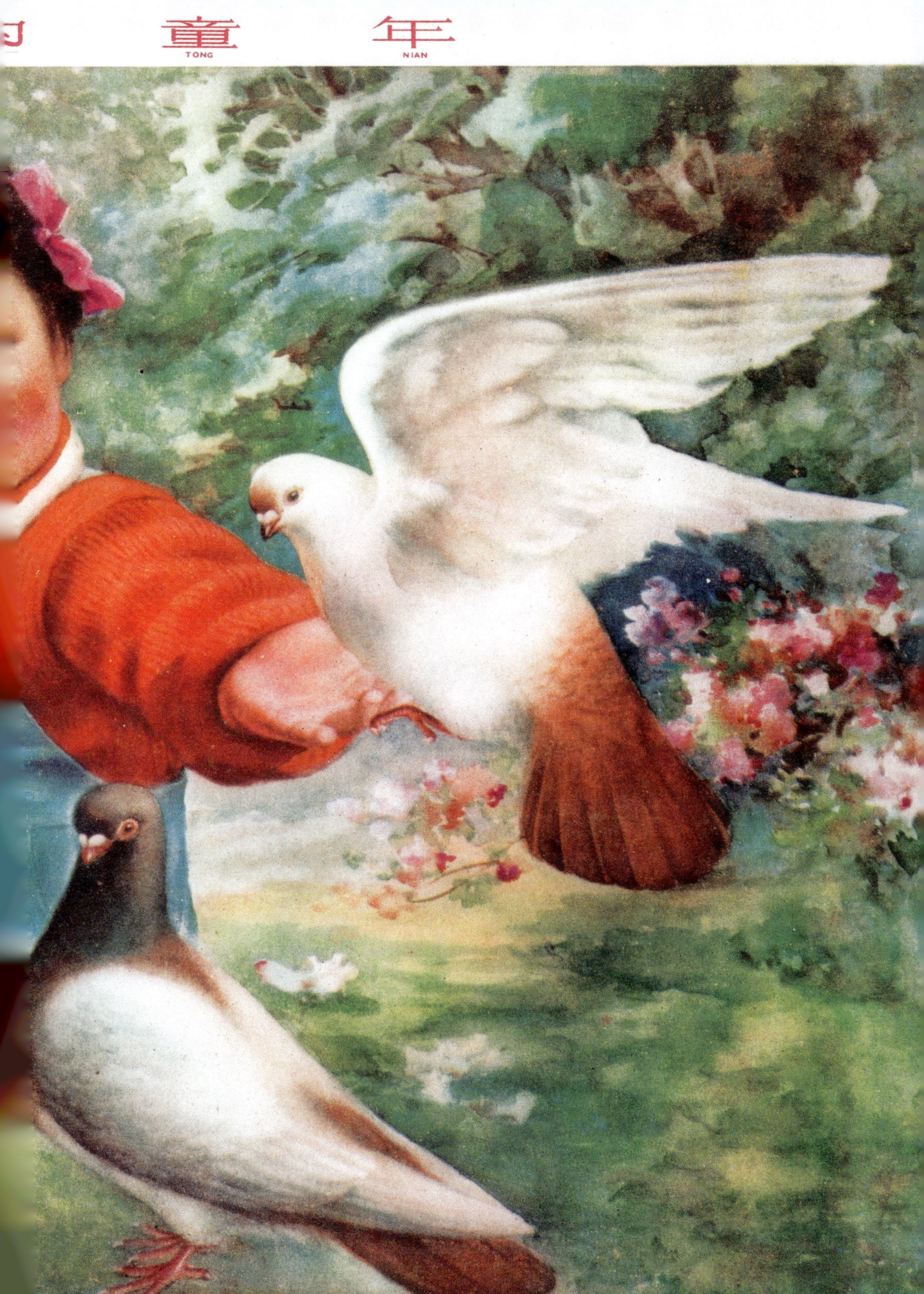

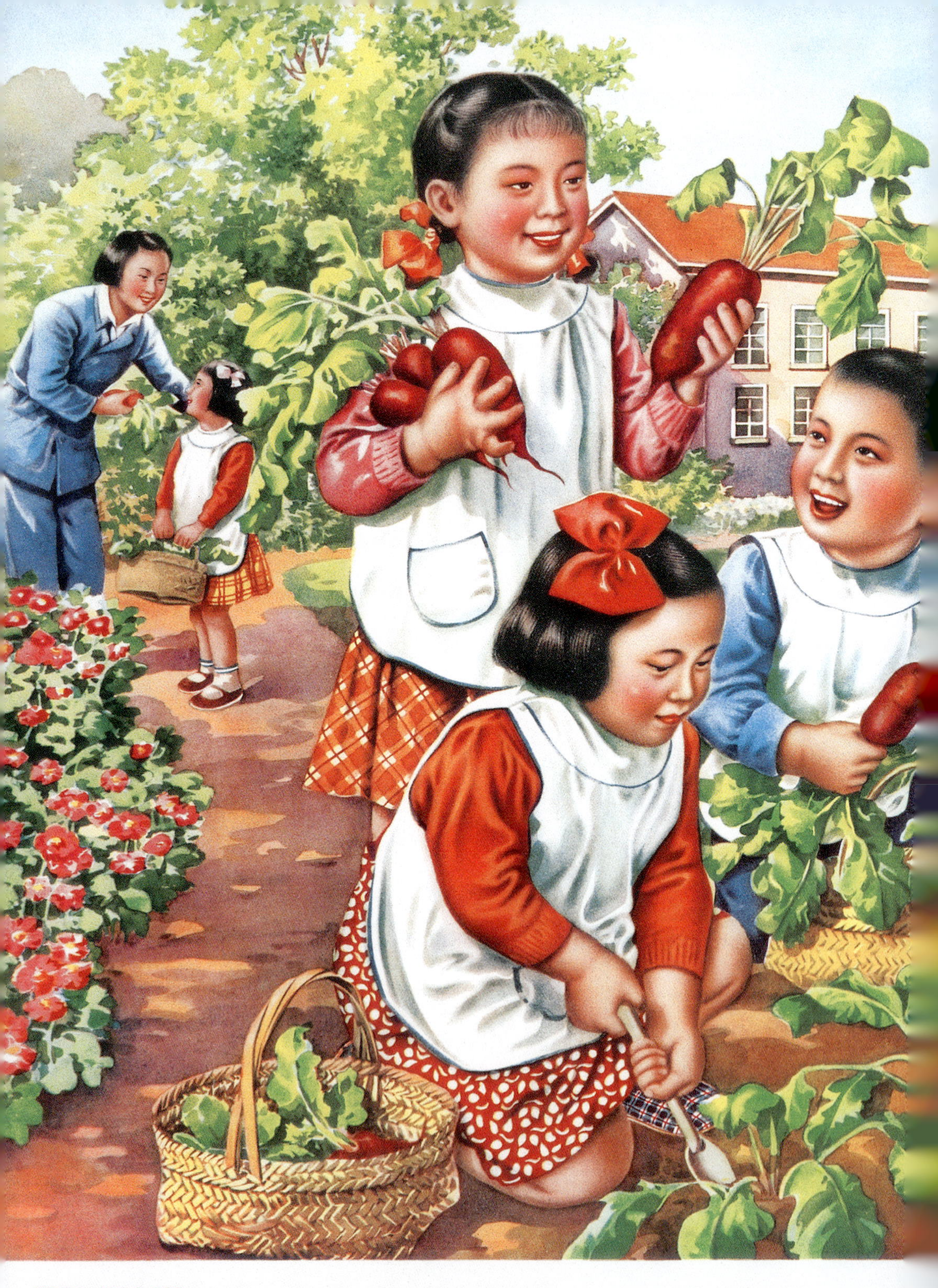

THU HOẠCH

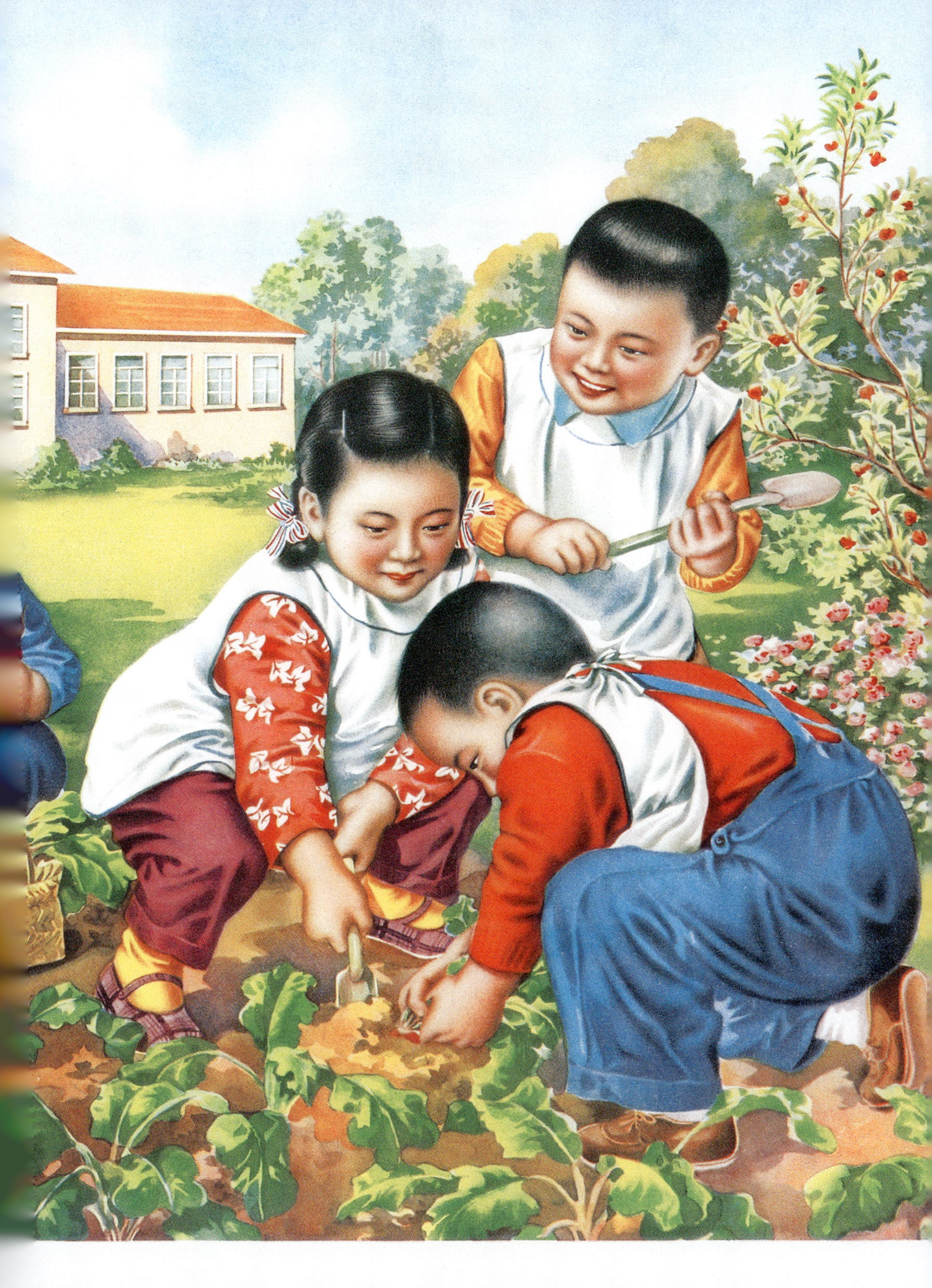

Pages 428–429
Harvest *Artist:* Wu Shaoyun *Published by:* Shanghai Picture Publishing House, 10th edn 1956

Looking at chrysanthemums
Different varieties of chrysanthemums bloom in the garden, brightly colored and beautiful. Let us not forget the gardener, whose diligent and skillful hands planted the flowers. *Artist:* Zhang Yuqing; Shanghai Picture Publishing House, 1st edn 1955, 27th edn 1957 *Print run:* 2,375,001–2,396,000; 0.11 Yuan

Ernte *Gemalt von* Wu Shaoyun *Herausgeber:* Bilderverlag Shanghai, 10. Aufl. 1956

Chrysanthemen betrachten
Verschiedene Sorten von Chrysanthemen blühen im Garten, farbenprächtig und wunderschön. Dabei soll man den Gärtner nicht vergessen, seine fleißigen und geschickten Hände haben die Blumen gepflanzt. *Gemalt von* Zhang Yuqing; Bilderverlag Shanghai, 1. Aufl. 1955, 27. Aufl. 1957 *Auflage:* 2 375 001–2 396 000; 0,11 Yuan

Récolte *Peintre :* Wu Shaoyun *Éditeur :* Éditions des Images de Shanghai, 10e éd. 1956

En regardant des chrysanthèmes
Plusieurs variétés de chrysanthèmes poussent dans le jardin, des fleurs magnifiques aux couleurs merveilleuses. Mais il ne faut pas oublier le jardinier : Ce sont ses mains habiles et courageuses qui les ont plantées. *Peintre :* Zhang Yuqing; Éditions des Images de Shanghai, 1ère éd. 1955, 27e éd. 1957 *Tirage :* 2 375 001–2 396 000 ; 0,11 yuan

Pages 432–433
Ah! Another big apple! *Artist:* Wei Yingzhou, *Published by*: Shanghai Picture Publishing House, 1954 *Print run:* 90,001–120,000; 1.80 Yuan

Ah! Noch ein großer Apfel! *Gemalt von* Wei Yingzhou; *Herausgeber*: Bilderverlag Shanghai, 1954 *Auflage:* 90 001–120 000; 1,80 Yuan

Ah ! Encore une grosse pomme ! *Peintre :* Wei Yingzhou *Éditeur :* Éditions des Images de Shanghai, 1954 *Tirage :* 90 001–120 000 ; 1,80 yuan

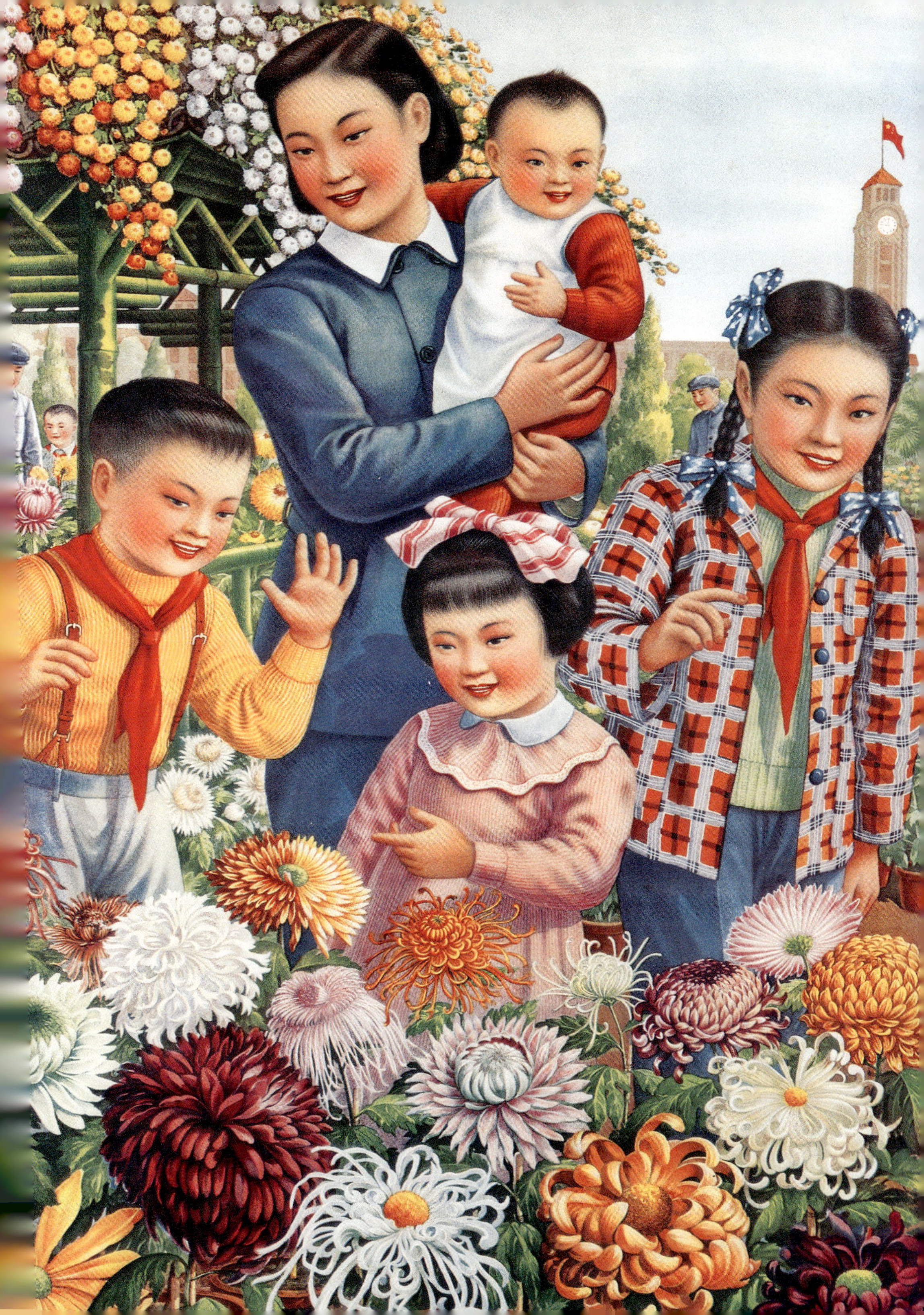

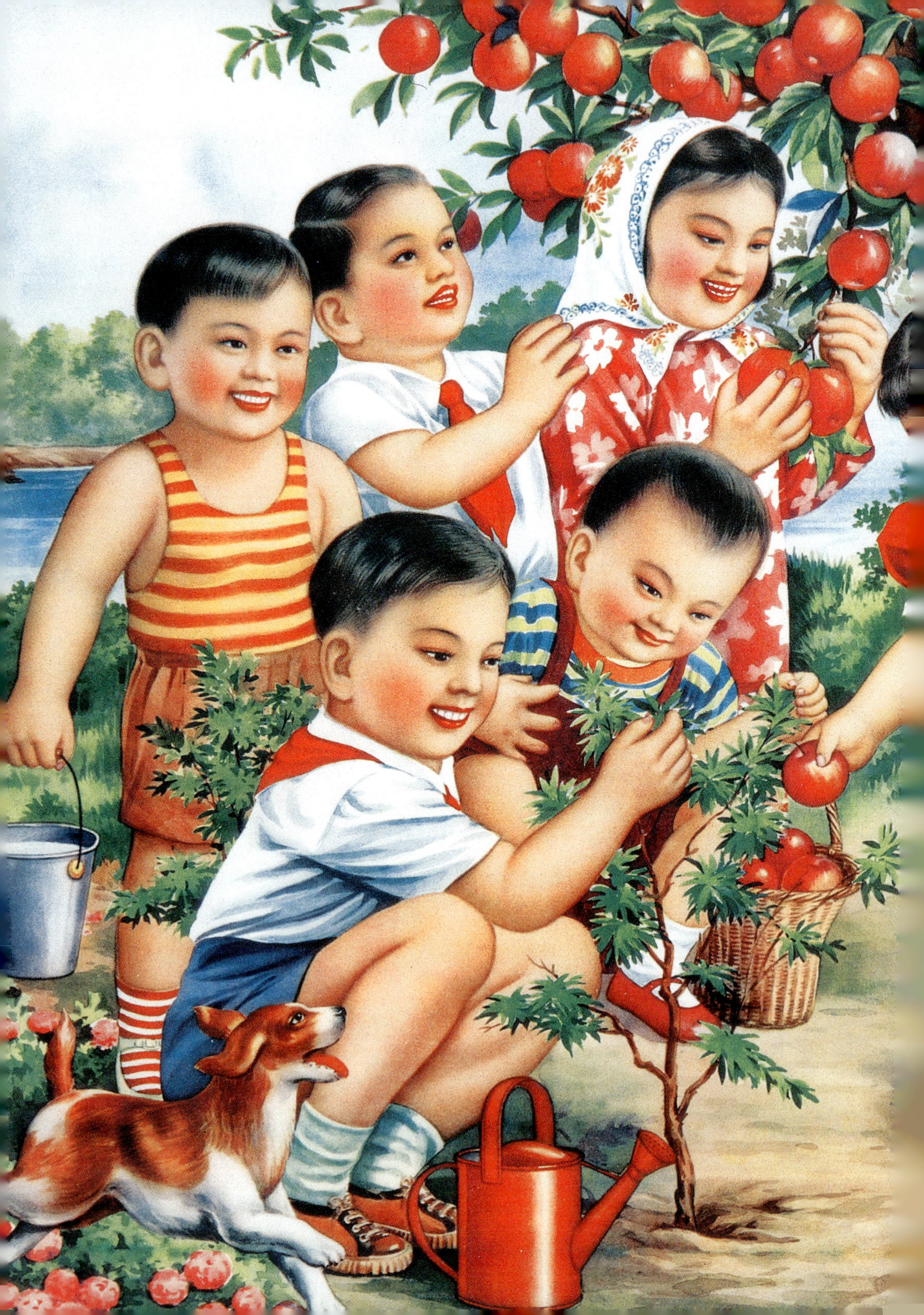

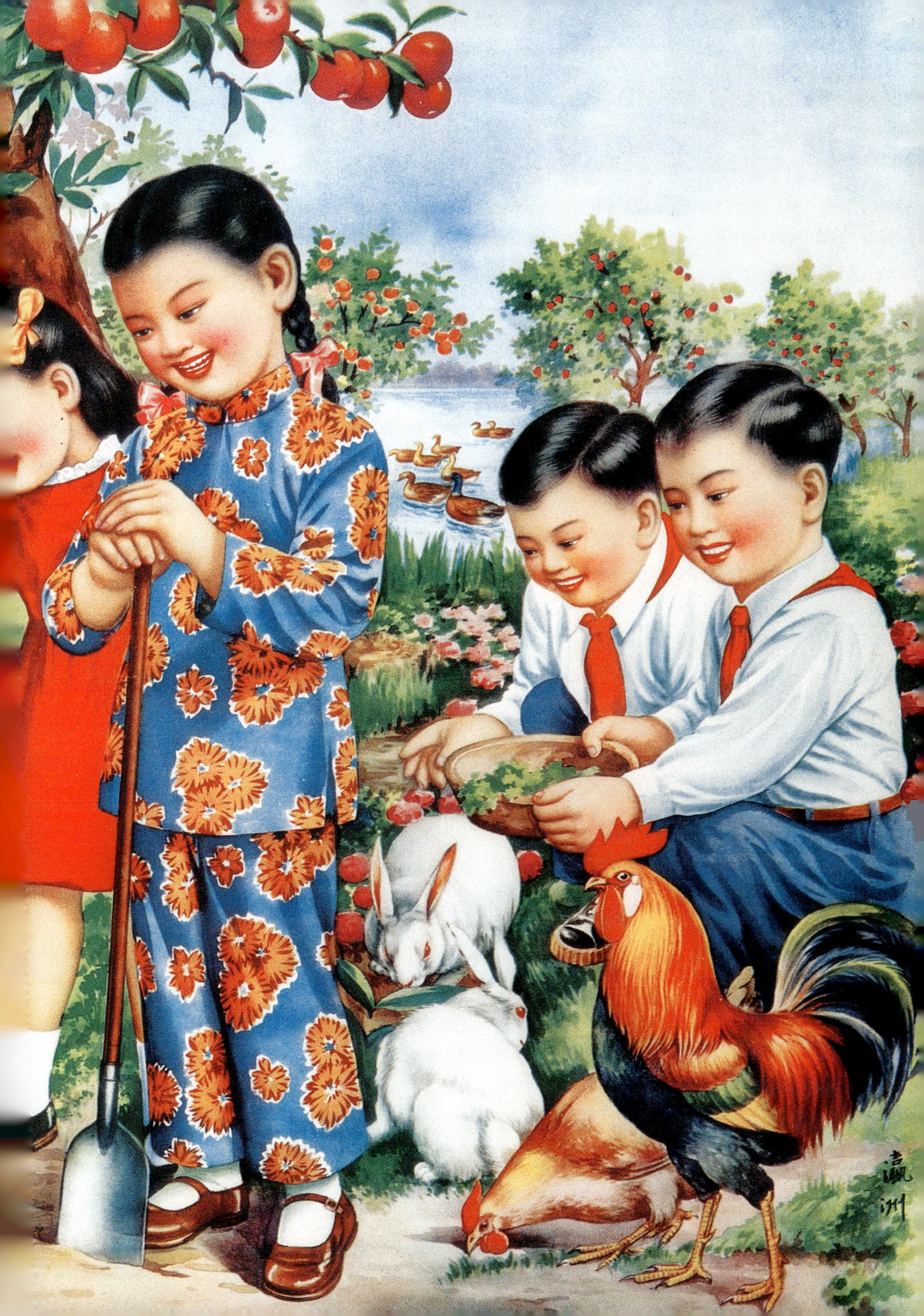
瀛洲

Opposite

Morning gymnastics for good health *Artist:* Wang Ensheng; Tianjin Children's Art Publishing House, 1st edn 1959, 2nd edn 1959; 0.13 Yuan

Morgengymnastik macht gesund *Gemalt von* Wang Ensheng; Kinderkunstverlag Tianjin, 1. Aufl. 1959, 2. Aufl. 1959; 0,13 Yuan

La gymnastique matinale pour rester en bonne santé *Peintre :* Wang Ensheng ; Éditions d'Art pour Enfants de Tianjin, 1ère éd. 1959, 2e éd. 1959 ; 0,13 yuan

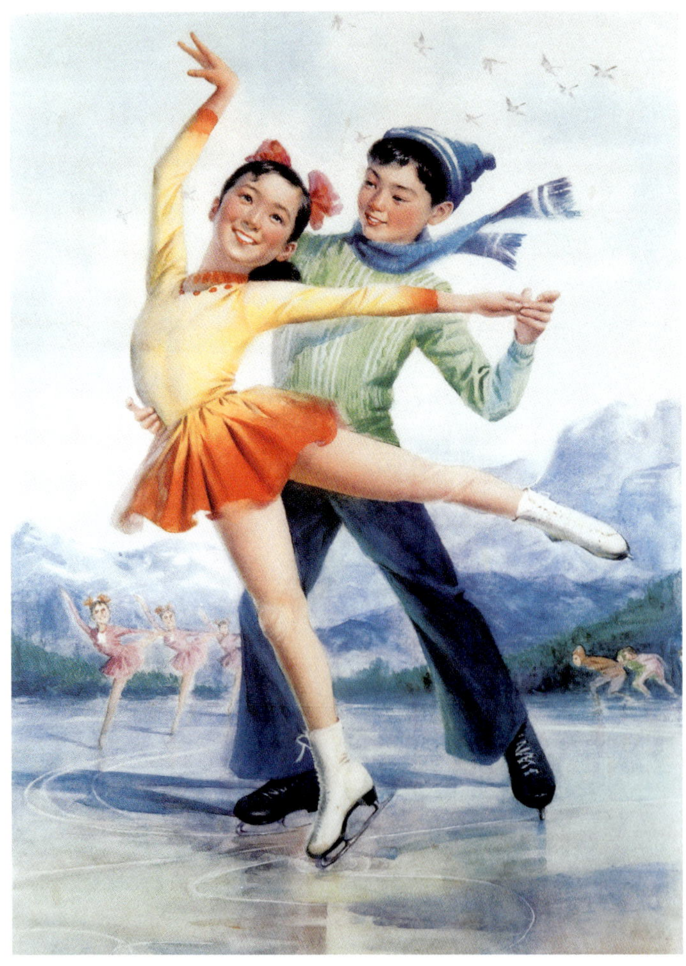

Young swallows learn to fly *Artist:* Zhang Luhong; Shanghai People's Art Publishing House, 1st edn 1981, 2nd edn 1981 *Print run:* 100,001–180,000; 0.13 Yuan

Junge Schwalben lernen fliegen *Gemalt von* Zhang Luhong; Volkskunstverlag Shanghai, 1. Aufl. 1981, 2. Aufl. 1981 *Auflage:* 100 001–180 000; 0,13 Yuan

Les jeunes hirondelles apprennent à voler *Peintre :* Zhang Luhong ; Éditions Populaires d'Art de Shanghai, 1ère éd. 1981, 2e éd. 1981 *Tirage :* 100 001–180 000 ; 0,13 yuan

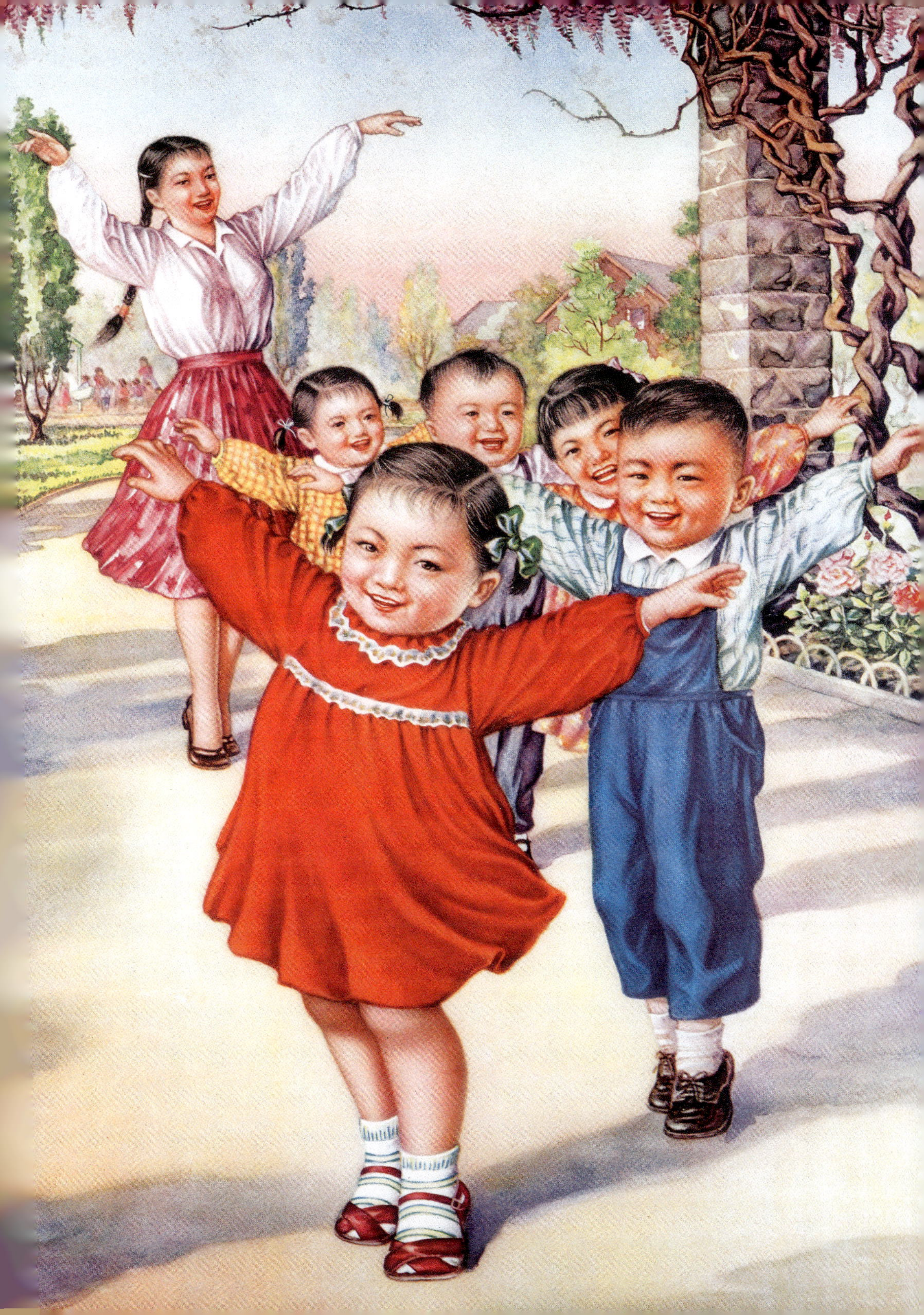

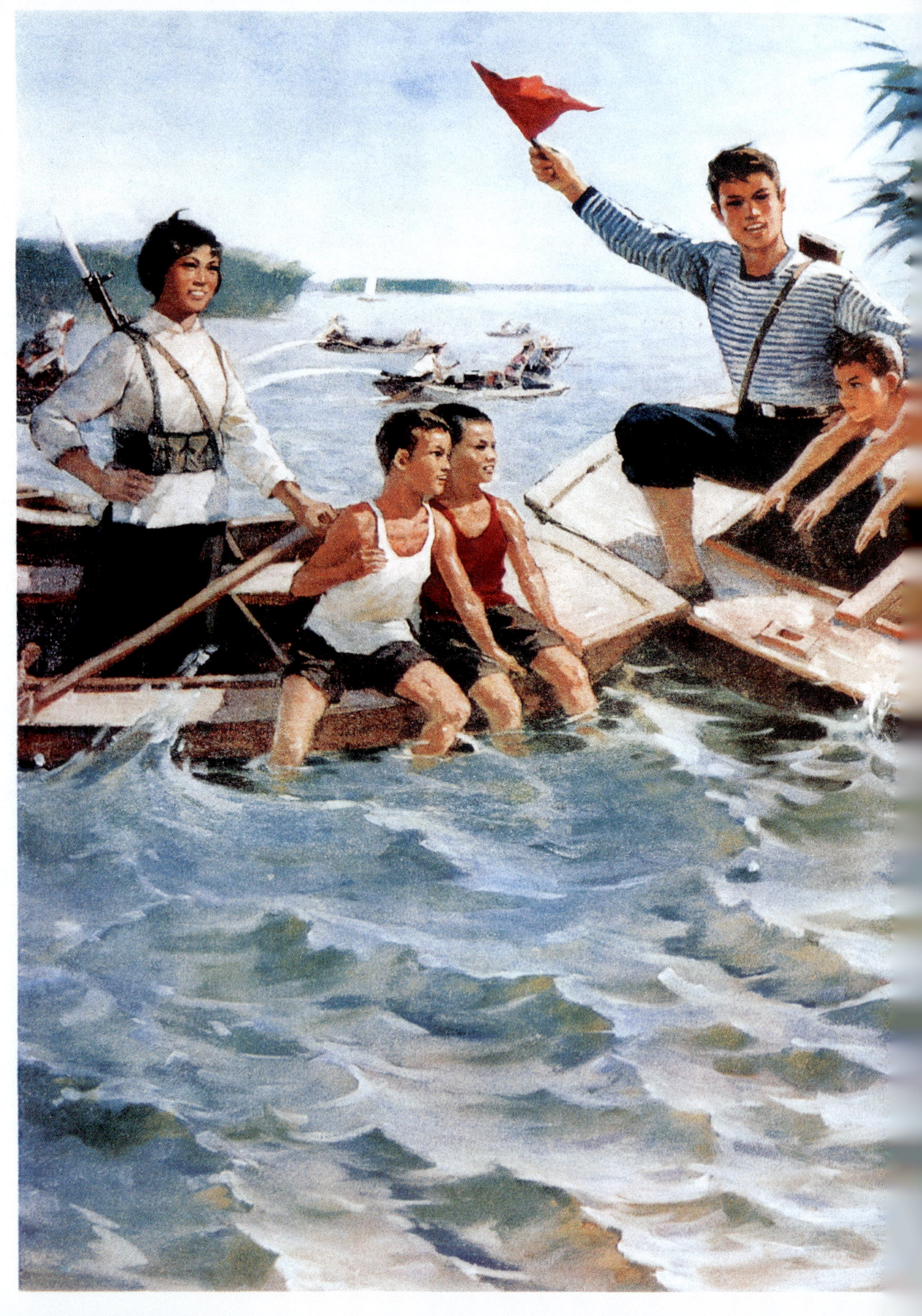

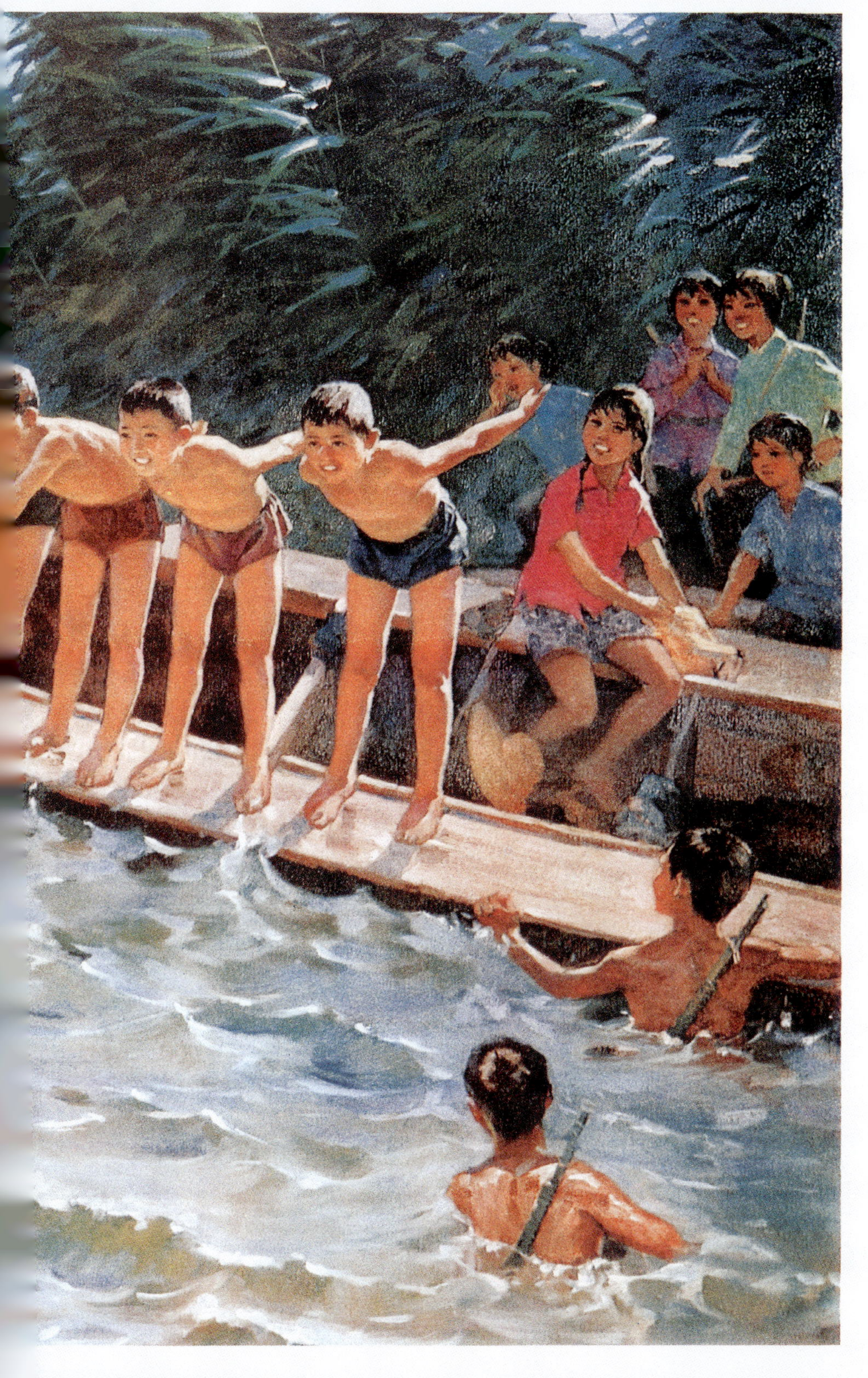

到江河湖海去锻炼

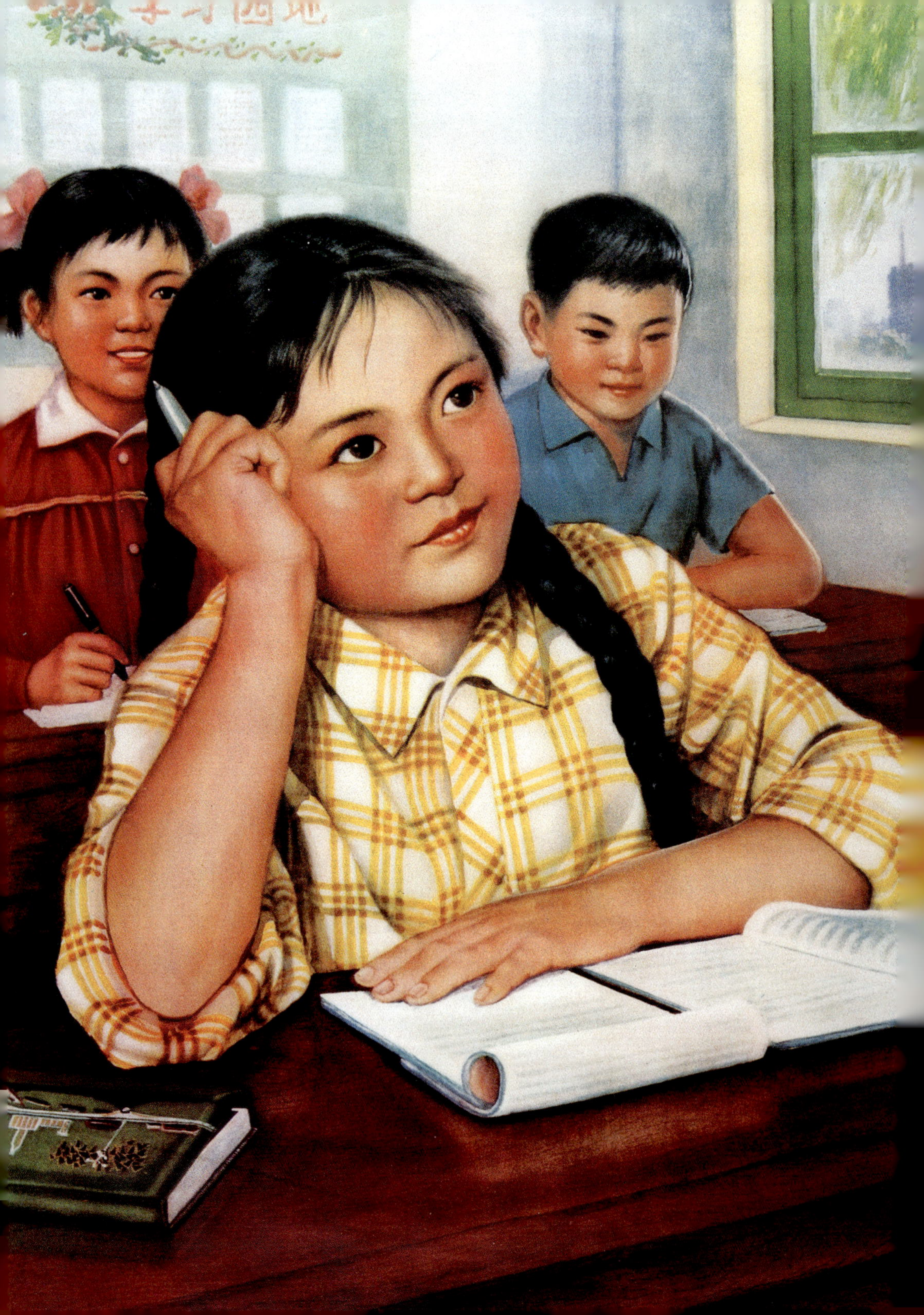

Pages 436–437

Build up strength in lake, river, and sea *Artist:* Wei Kuizhong; Shanghai People's Publishing House, 1st edn 1975; 2nd edn 1975 *Print run:* 30,001–120,000; 0.16 Yuan

Sich im See, Fluss und Meer stählen *Gemalt von* Wei Kuizhong; Volksverlag Shanghai, 1. Aufl. 1975, 2. Aufl. 1975 *Auflage:* 30 001–120 000; 0,16 Yuan

Aguerrissons-nous dans les lacs, les rivières et la mer *Peintre :* Wei Kuizhong ; Éditions Populaires de Shanghai, 1ère éd. 1975, 2e éd. 1975 *Tirage :* 30 001–120 000 ; 0,16 yuan

Deep in thought *Top left:* Wall newspaper with article on learning *Artists:* Ze Yu, Shu Ping, Bao Dong, Xi An, Jun Ting, and Fu Yin; Hebei People's Publishing House, 1980 *Print run:* 294,000; 0.13 Yuan

Konzentriert nachdenken *Links oben*: Wandzeitung zum Thema Lernen *Gemalt von* Ze Yu, Shu Ping, Bao Dong, Xi An, Jun Ting und Fu Yin; Volksverlag Hebei, 1980 *Auflage:* 294 000; 0,13 Yuan

Réflexion et concentration *En haut à gauche :* Journal mural sur le thème de l'étude *Peintres :* Ze Yu, Shu Ping, Bao Dong, Xi An, Jun Ting et Fu Yin ; Éditions Populaires du Hebei, 1980 *Tirage :* 294 000 ; 0,13 yuan

Pages 440–441

China must achieve great things for humanity Study hard for the Revolution *Badges:* Red Guard Youth Section *Designed by:* Lintong and Yuxin Middle School; Shanghai People's Publishing House, 1972; 0.11 Yuan

China muss etwas Großes für die Menschheit leisten Für die Revolution fleißig lernen *Brosche*: Junge Rote Garde *Entwurf:* Mittelschule Lintong und Yuxin; Volksverlag Shanghai, 1972; 0,11 Yuan

La Chine doit faire de grandes choses pour l'humanité Soyons de bons élèves pour la Révolution *Sur l'insigne :* Jeune Garde Rouge *Conception :* Collège de Lintong et Yuxin ; Éditions Populaires de Shanghai, 1972 ; 0,11 yuan

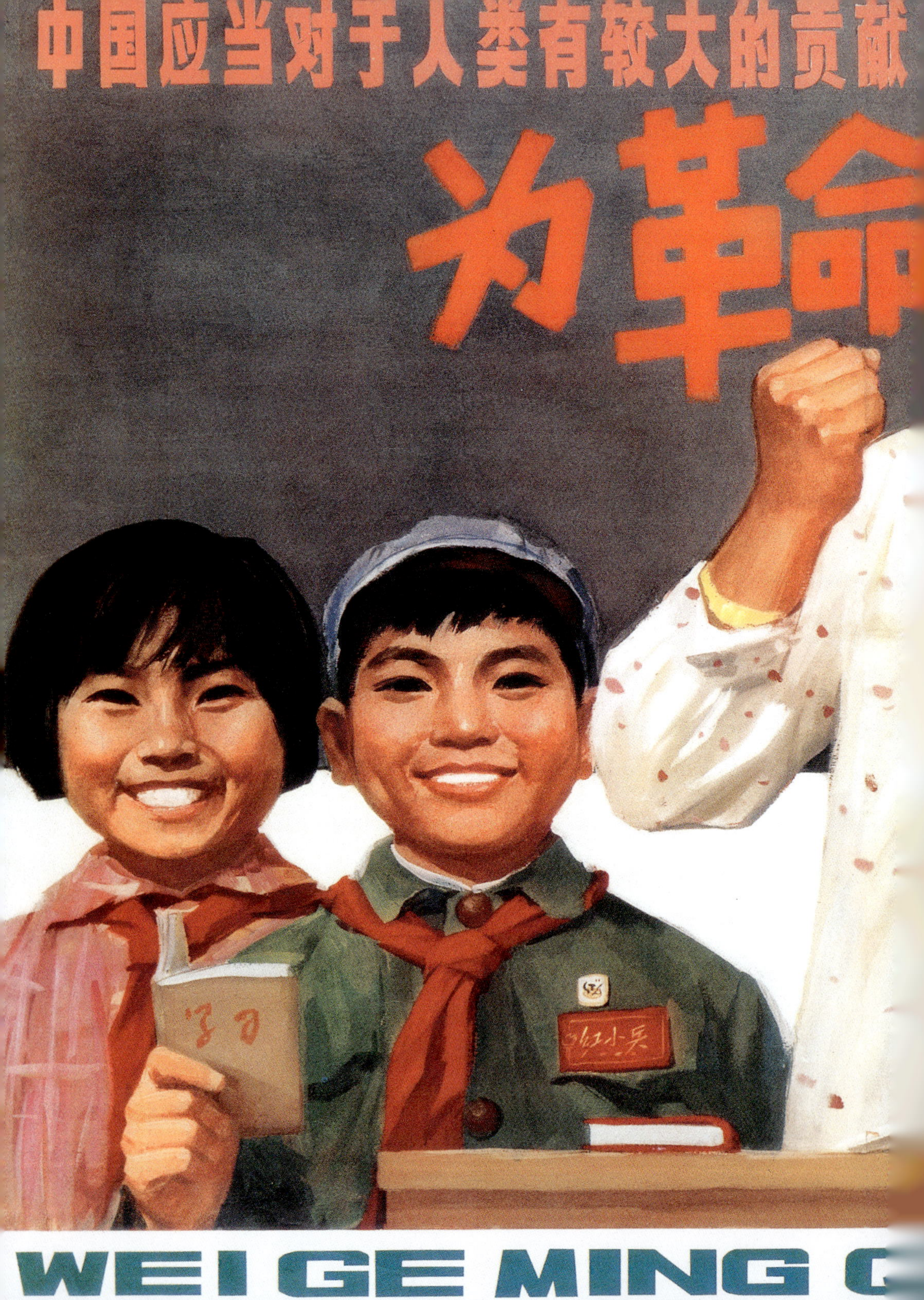
中国应当对于人类有较大的贡献
为革命
学习
红小兵
WEI GE MING

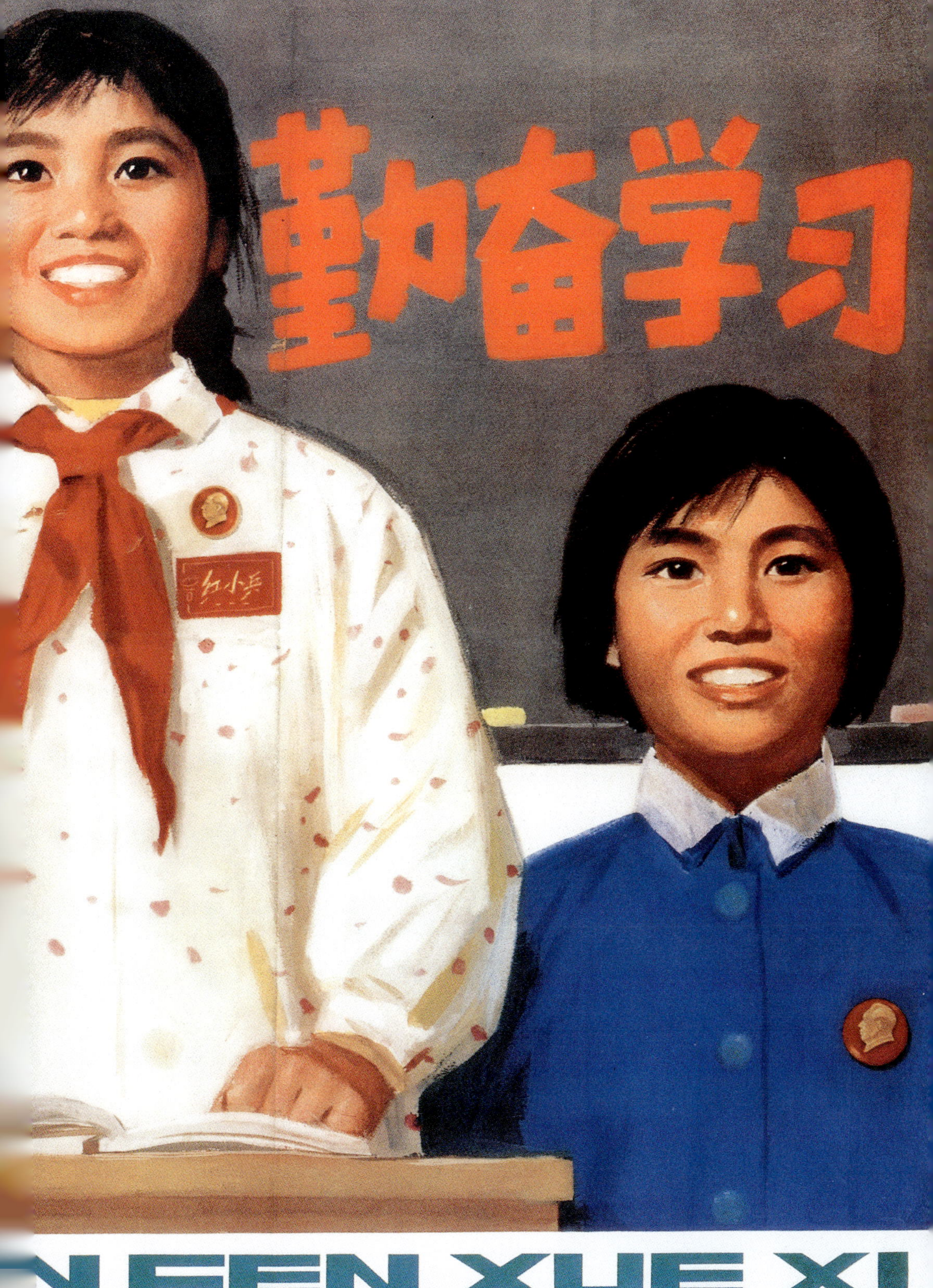
勤奋学习
红小兵
N FEN XUE XI

Opposite
A good pupil *On certificate:* Award. The pupil … is rewarded for her good work in the three points (moral, mental, and physical) and as an incentive is awarded this certificate, Primary school … *Artist:* Shan Xihe; People's Art Publishing House, 1963; 0.15 Yuan

Eine gute Schülerin *Auf der Urkunde*: Auszeichnung. Schülerin … wird für ihre guten Leistungen in den drei Punkten (moralisch, geistig und körperlich) ausgezeichnet und erhält als Ansporn diese Urkunde, Grundschule … *Gemalt von* Shan Xihe; Volkskunstverlag, 1963; 0,15 Yuan

Une bonne élève *Sur le document :* Distinction honorifique. Cette élève … est récompensée pour ses bonnes prestations dans les trois points (moral, intellectuel et physique) et reçoit ce certificat à titre d'encouragement, École primaire … *Peintre :* Shan Xihe ; Éditions Populaires d'Art, 1963 ; 0,15 yuan

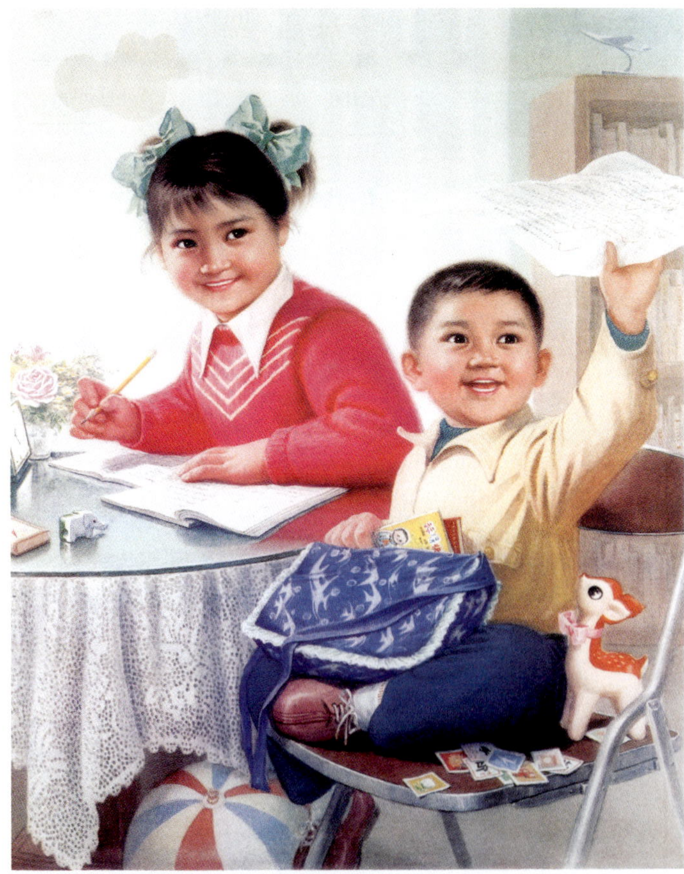

I got 100 per cent again! *Artist:* Chen Hongren; Shanghai People's Art Publishing House, 1st edn 1980, 2nd edn 1980 *Print run:* 200,001–1,300,000; 0.14 Yuan

Ich habe wieder 100 Punkte bekommen! *Gemalt von* Chen Hongren; Volkskunstverlag Shanghai, 1. Aufl. 1980, 2. Aufl. 1980 *Auflage:* 200 001–1 300 000; 0,14 Yuan

J'ai eu de nouveau 100 points ! *Peintre :* Chen Hongren ; Éditions Populaires d'Art de Shanghai, 1ère éd. 1980, 2e éd. 1980 *Tirage :* 200 001–1 300 000 ; 0,14 yuan

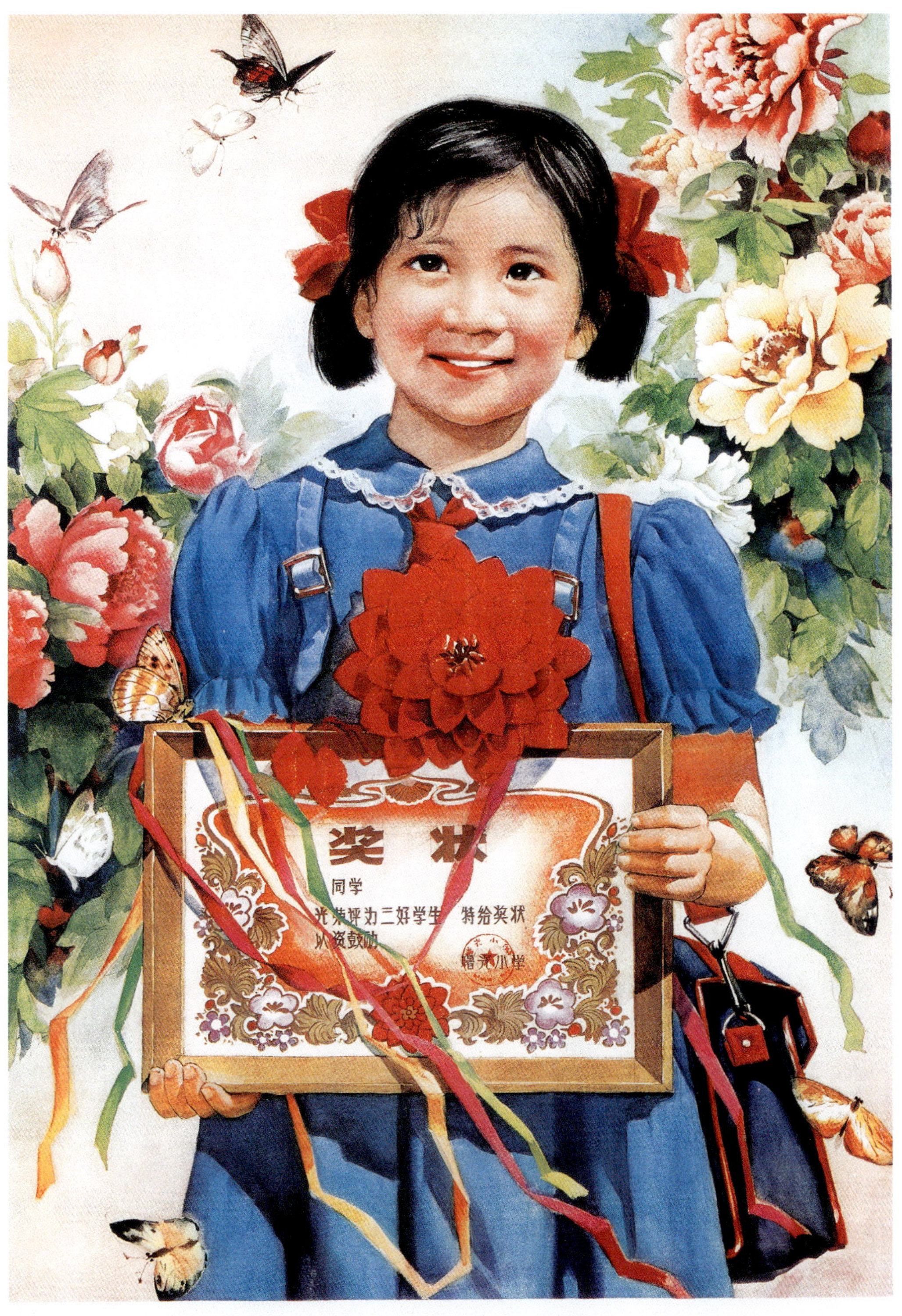

好　学　生

Opposite
We have accomplished it
Artist: Zhang Biwu; Tianjin Art Publishing House, 1953; 0.13 Yuan

Wir haben es geschafft
Gemalt von Zhang Biwu; Kunstverlag Tianjin, 1953; 0,13 Yuan

Nous y sommes arrivés
Peintre : Zhang Biwu ; Éditions d'Art de Tianjin, 1953 ; 0,13 yuan

Pages 446–447
Palace of Youth* *Artist:* Zhang Yuqing; Shanghai People's Art Publishing House, 1960 *Print run:* 200,000; 0.12 Yuan
* The statue in the picture represents Liu Hulan.

Palast der Jugend* *Gemalt von* Zhang Yuqing; Volkskunstverlag Shanghai, 1960 *Auflage:* 200 000; 0,12 Yuan
* Die Statue im Bild stellt Liu Hulan dar.

Palais de la jeunesse* *Peintre :* Zhang Yuqing ; Éditions populaires d'Art de Shanghai, 1960 *Tirage :* 200 000 ; 0,12 yuan
* La statue sur l'image représente Liu Hulan.

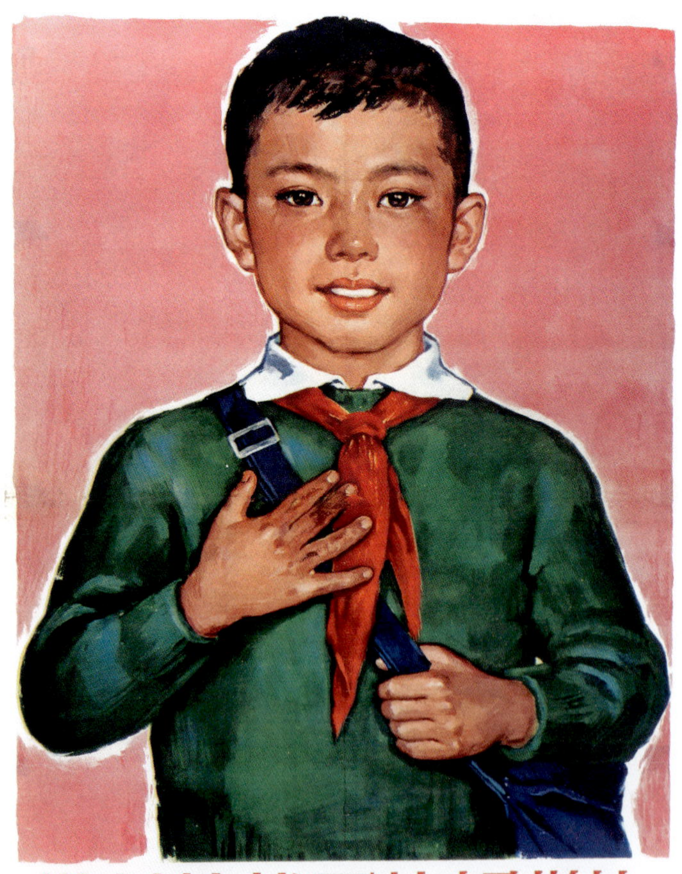

Be a good, virtuous student
Artist: Guo Qian; Shanghai People's Art Publishing House, 1960s; 0.11 Yuan

Ein tugendhafter guter Schüler sein *Gemalt von* Guo Qian; Volkskunstverlag Shanghai, 1960er Jahre; 0,11 Yuan

Je veux être un bon élève vertueux *Peintre :* Guo Qian ; Éditions Populaires d'Art de Shanghai, années 1960 ; 0,11 yuan

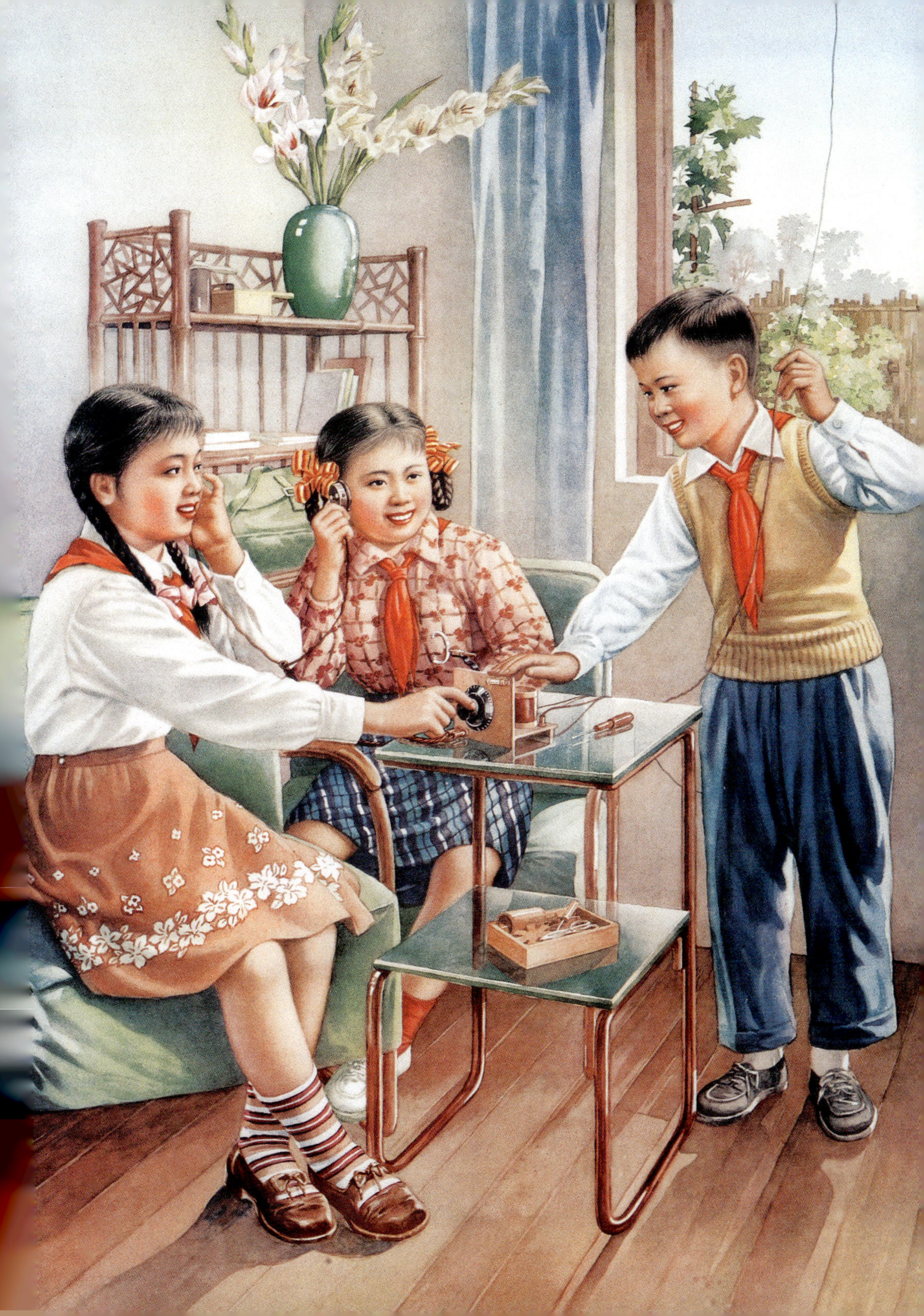

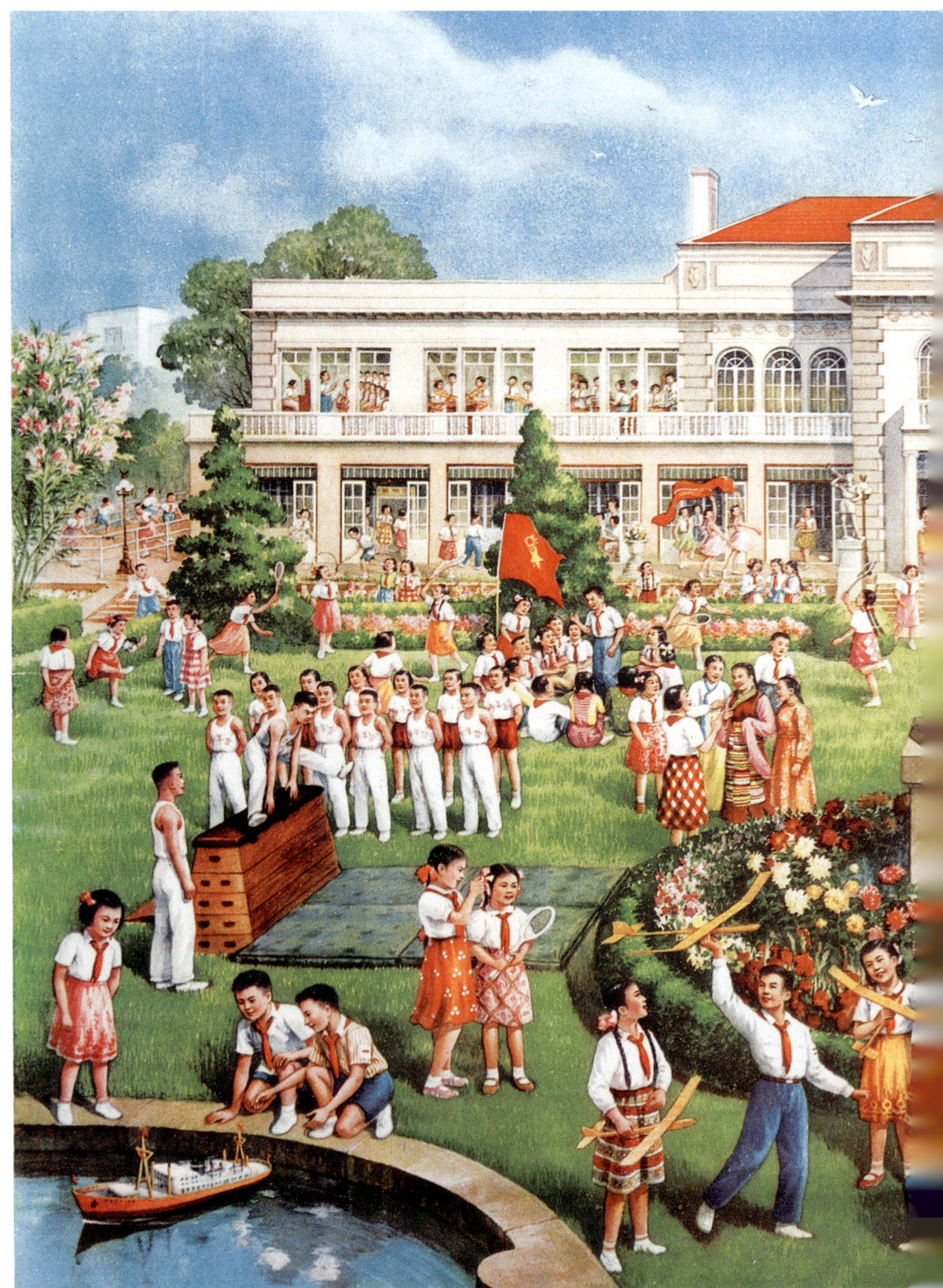

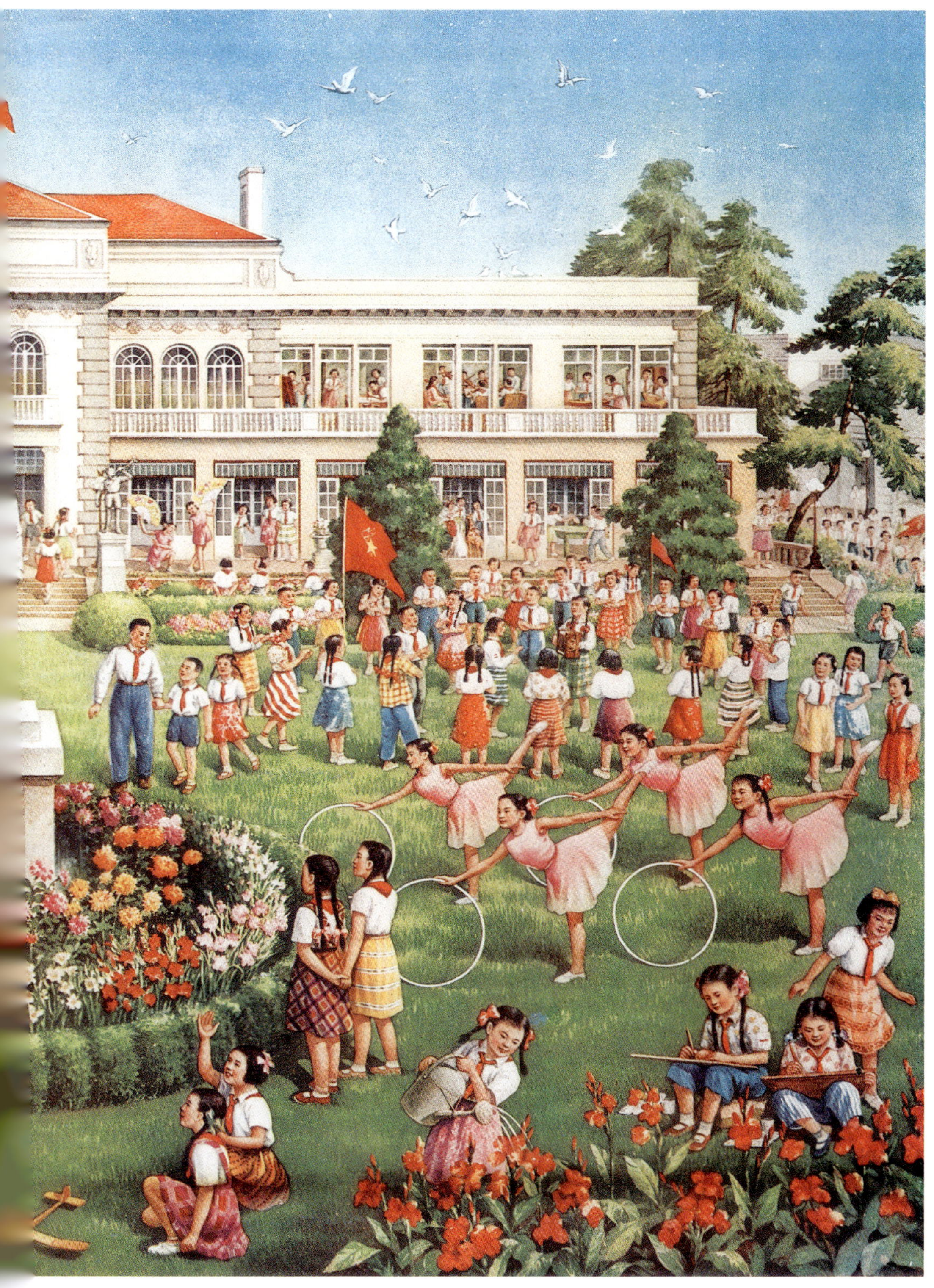

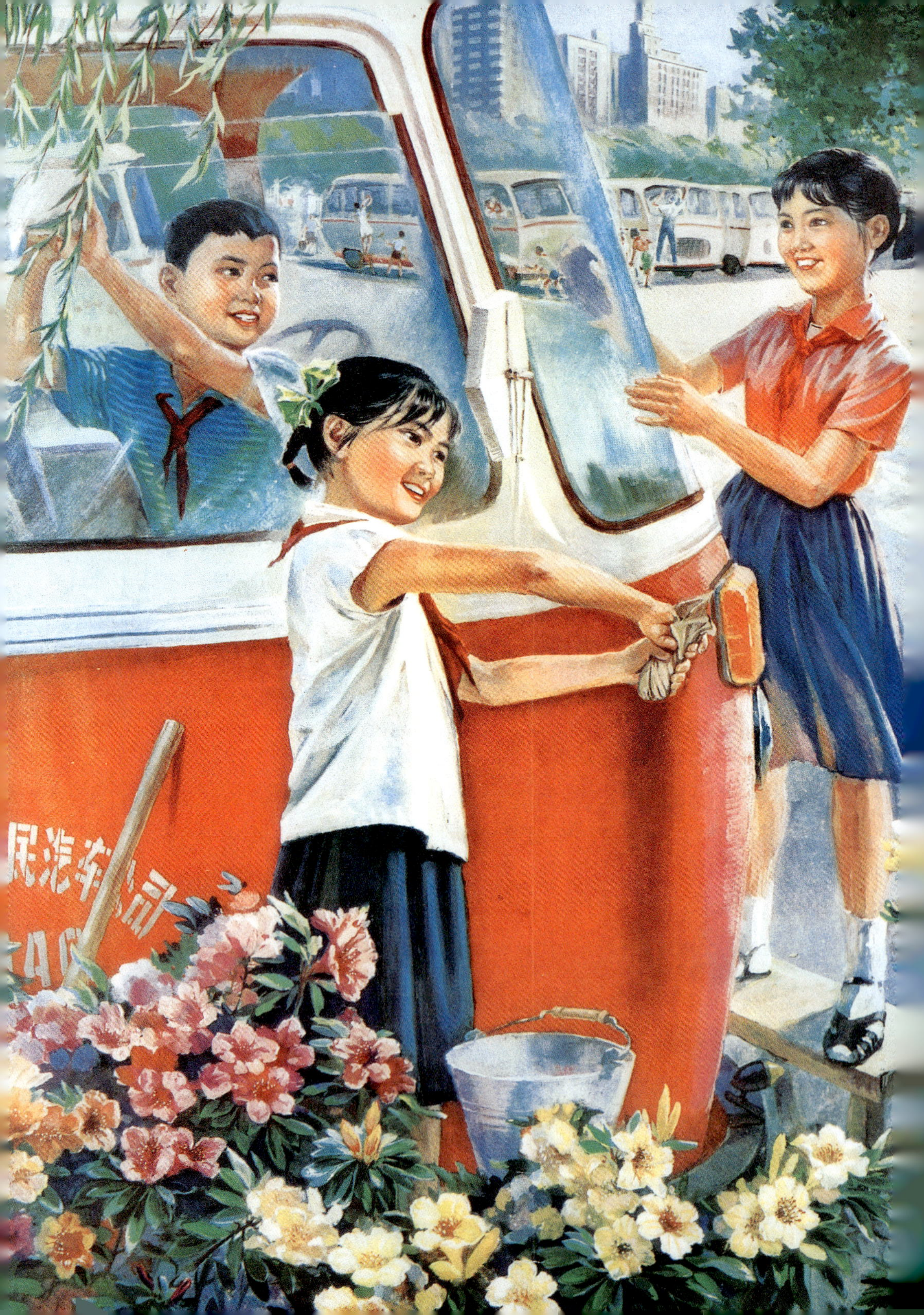

Opposite
The Young Pioneers' Day of Action *Artists:* Zheng Jianshi and Wu Haiying; Hebei People's Publishing House, 1979 *Print run:* 210,000; 0.11 Yuan

Ein Aktionstag der Jungen Pioniere *Gemalt von* Zheng Jianshi und Wu Haiying; Volksverlag Hebei, 1979 *Auflage:* 210 000; 0,11 Yuan

Une journée d'action des Jeunes Pionniers *Peintres :* Zheng Jianshi et Wu Haiying ; Éditions Populaires du Hebei, 1979 *Tirage :* 210 000 ; 0,11 yuan

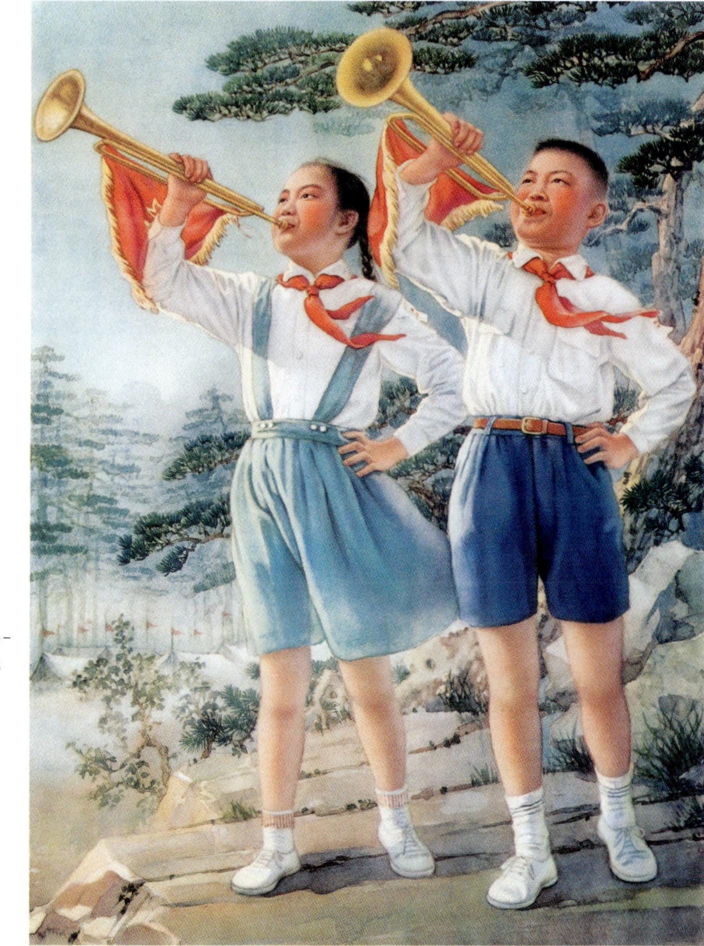

Morning in the summer camp
Artist: Zhang Daxin; Shanghai People's Art Publishing House, 1963 *Print run:* 350,000; 0.15 Yuan

Der Morgen im Sommerlager
Gemalt von Zhang Daxin; Volkskunstverlag Shanghai, 1963 *Auflage:* 350 000; 0,15 Yuan

Le matin au camp d'été
Peintre : Zhang Daxin ; Éditions Populaires d'Art de Shanghai, 1963 *Tirage :* 350 000 ; 0,15 yuan

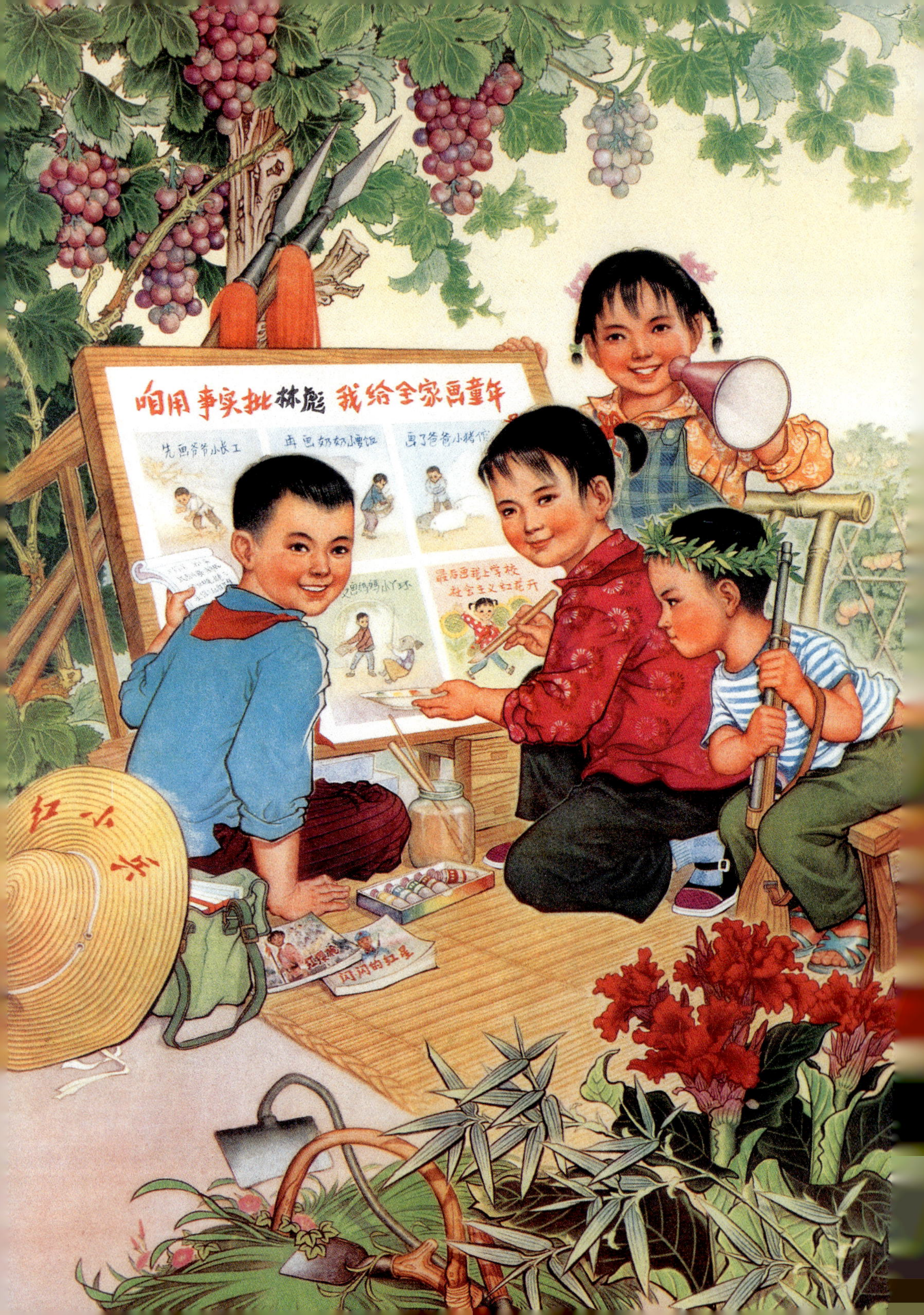
咱用事实批林彪 我给全家画童年
先画爷爷小长工
再画奶奶小要饭
画了爸爸小猪
画妈妈小丫环
最后画我上学校
社会主义红花开
红小兵
闪闪的红星

I paint pictures that represent the childhoods of my parents, my grandparents, and myself *Top of board:* Find Lin Biao guilty on the basis of facts: past and present *On straw hat:* Young Red Guard *Artist:* Wang Fuzeng, Yuncheng District Art and Leisure Centre; Shandong People's Publishing House, 1974; 0.11 Yuan

Ich male Bilder, die die Kindheit meiner Großeltern und Eltern und meine eigene Kindheit darstellen *Über der Tafel*: Mit Tatsachen Lin Biao verurteilen: Vergangenheit und Gegenwart *Auf dem Strohhut*: Junge Rote Garde *Gemalt von* Wang Fuzeng, Kulturhaus des Kreises Yuncheng; Volksverlag Shandong, 1974; 0,11 Yuan

Je peins des images qui représentent l'enfance de mes grands-parents et de mes parents et ma propre enfance *Sur le tableau :* Les faits, passés et présents, condamnent Lin Biao *Sur le chapeau de paille :* Jeune Garde rouge *Peintre :* Wang Fuzeng, Maison de la Culture du canton de Yuncheng ; Éditions Populaires du Shandong, 1974 ; 0,11 yuan

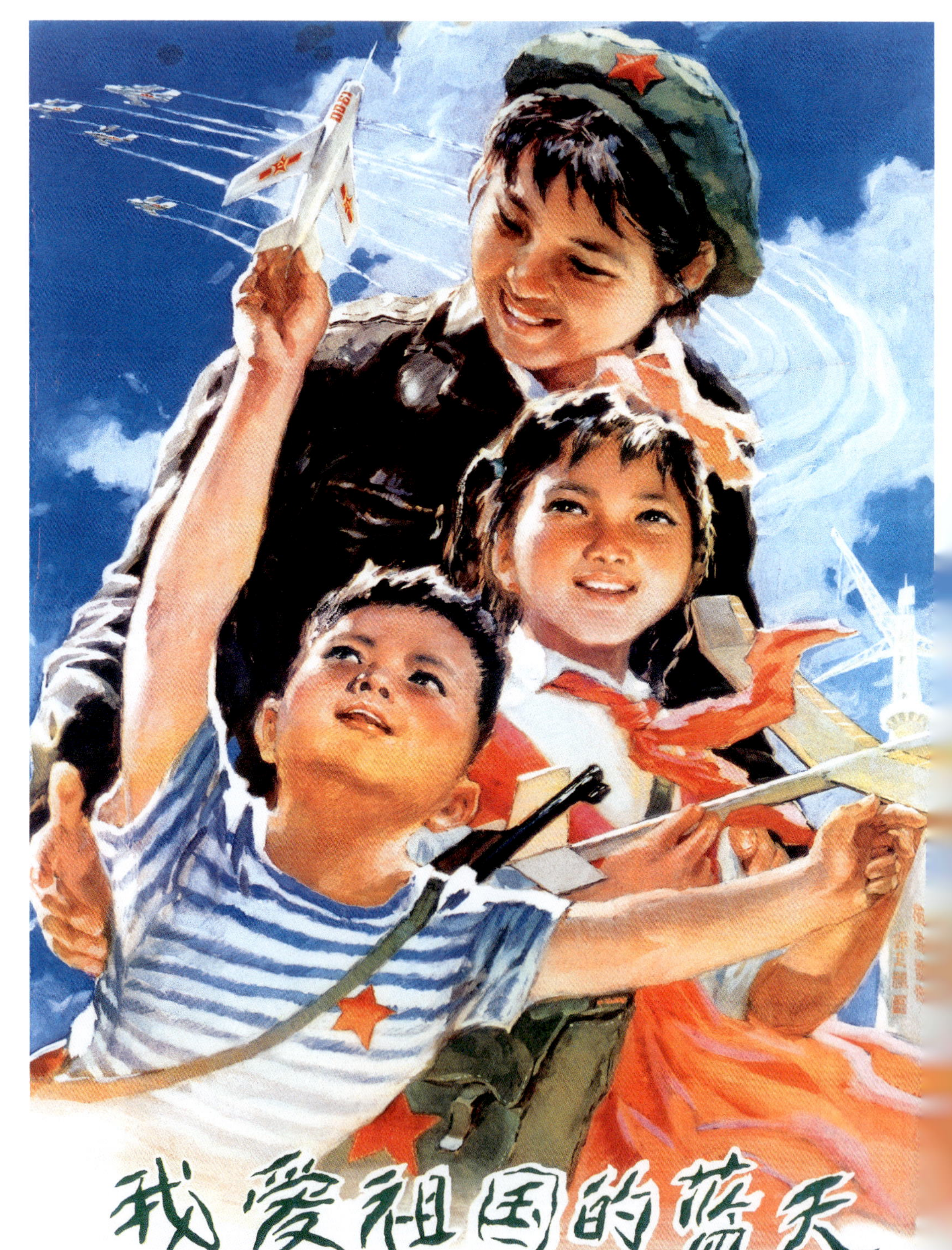
我愛祖国的蓝天
WO AI ZU GUO DE LAN TIAN

Opposite
I love the blue sky of the fatherland The People's Sports Publishing House, 1975 *Print run:* 200,000; 0.11 Yuan

Ich liebe den blauen Himmel des Vaterlandes Volkssportverlag, 1975 *Auflage:* 200 000; 0,11 Yuan

J'aime le ciel bleu de notre patrie Éditions Populaires Sportives, 1975 *Tirage :* 200 000 ; 0,11 yuan

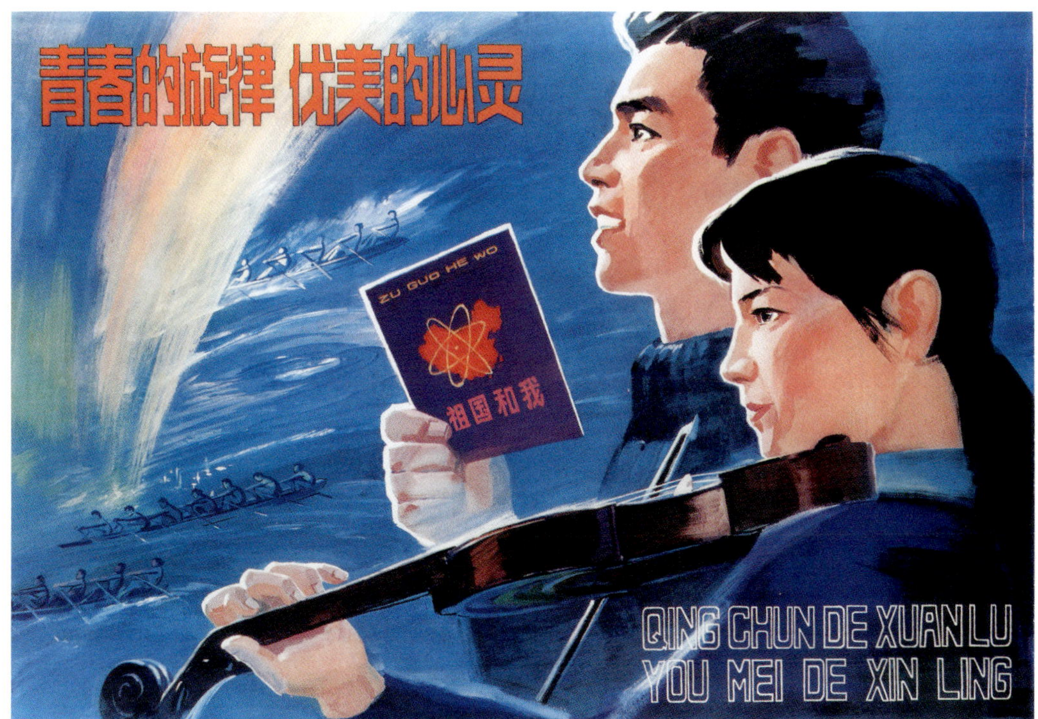

Melody of youth, beautiful soul *On book:* The fatherland and I *Artist:* Shen Shaolun; Shanghai People's Art Publishing House, 1981 *Print run:* 40,000; 0.16 Yuan

Melodie der Jugend, schöne Seele *Auf dem Buch*: Vaterland und ich *Gemalt von* Shen Shaolun; Volkskunstverlag Shanghai, 1981 *Auflage:* 40 000; 0,16 Yuan

Mélodie de la jeunesse, beauté de l'âme *Sur le livre :* La patrie et moi *Peintre :* Shen Shaolun ; Éditions Populaires d'Art de Shanghai, 1981 *Tirage :* 40 000 ; 0,16 yuan

Opposite
The spirit of Lei Feng provides warmth *Over the door:* Family of a member of the armed forces *On the door:* Mao Zedong's ideas are passed on from generation to generation *Artist:* Li Yongshi, a worker at the Fangchang Steel Works, Wuhu District; Anhui People's Publishing House, 1978; 0.11 Yuan

Der Geist von Lei Feng spendet Wärme *Über der Tür*: Familie der Armeeangehörigen *An der Tür*: Mao Zedongs Ideen werden Generation für Generation weitergegeben *Gemalt von* Li Yongshi, einem Arbeiter des Fangchang-Stahlwerks, Bezirk Wuhu; Volksverlag Anhui, 1978; 0,11 Yuan

L'esprit de Lei Feng dispense de la chaleur *Au-dessus de la porte :* Famille des membres de l'armée *Sur la porte :* Les idées de Mao Zedong se transmettent de génération en génération *Peintre :* Li Yongshi, ouvrier de l'aciérie Fangchang, canton de Wuhu ; Éditions Populaires de l'Anhui, 1978 ; 0,11 yuan

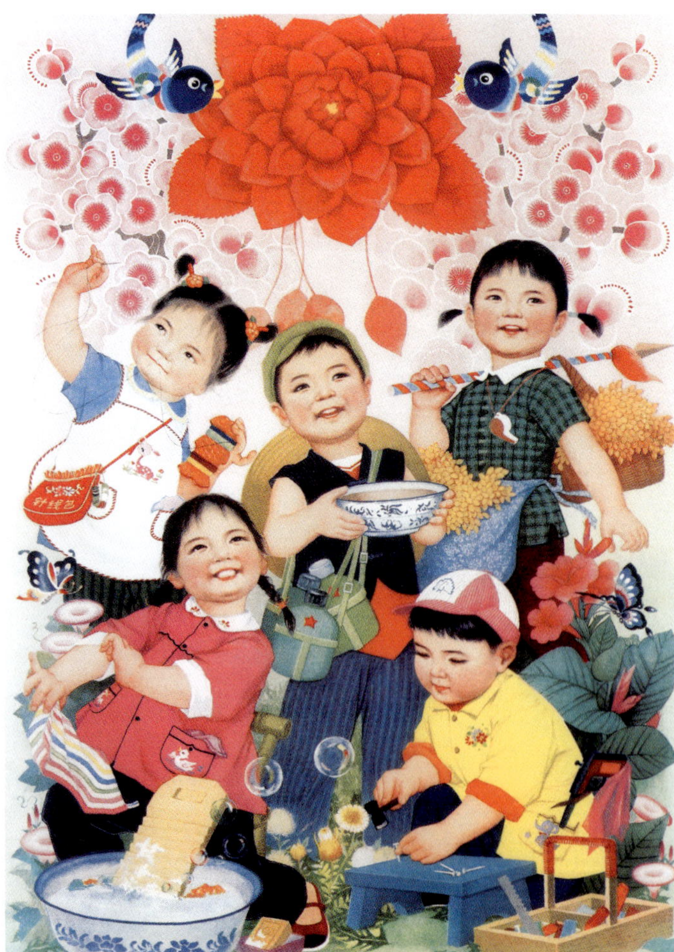

They all aspire to being little Lei Fengs *Left, on the girl's bag:* Sewing bag *Artists:* Wu Xingqing and Chen Juxian; Shanghai People's Art Publishing House, 1st edn 1978, 2nd edn 1978; 0.11 Yuan

Alle wollen ein kleiner Lei Feng sein *Links auf dem roten Täschchen des Mädchens*: Nähtasche *Gemalt von* Wu Xingqing und Chen Juxian; Volkskunstverlag Shanghai, 1. Aufl. 1978, 2. Aufl. 1978; 0,11 Yuan

Tous veulent être un petit Lei Feng *Sur le petit sac rouge de la fillette, à gauche :* Trousse de couture *Peintres :* Wu Xingqing et Chen Juxian ; Éditions Populaires d'Art de Shanghai, 1ère éd. 1978, 2e éd. 1978 ; 0,11 yuan

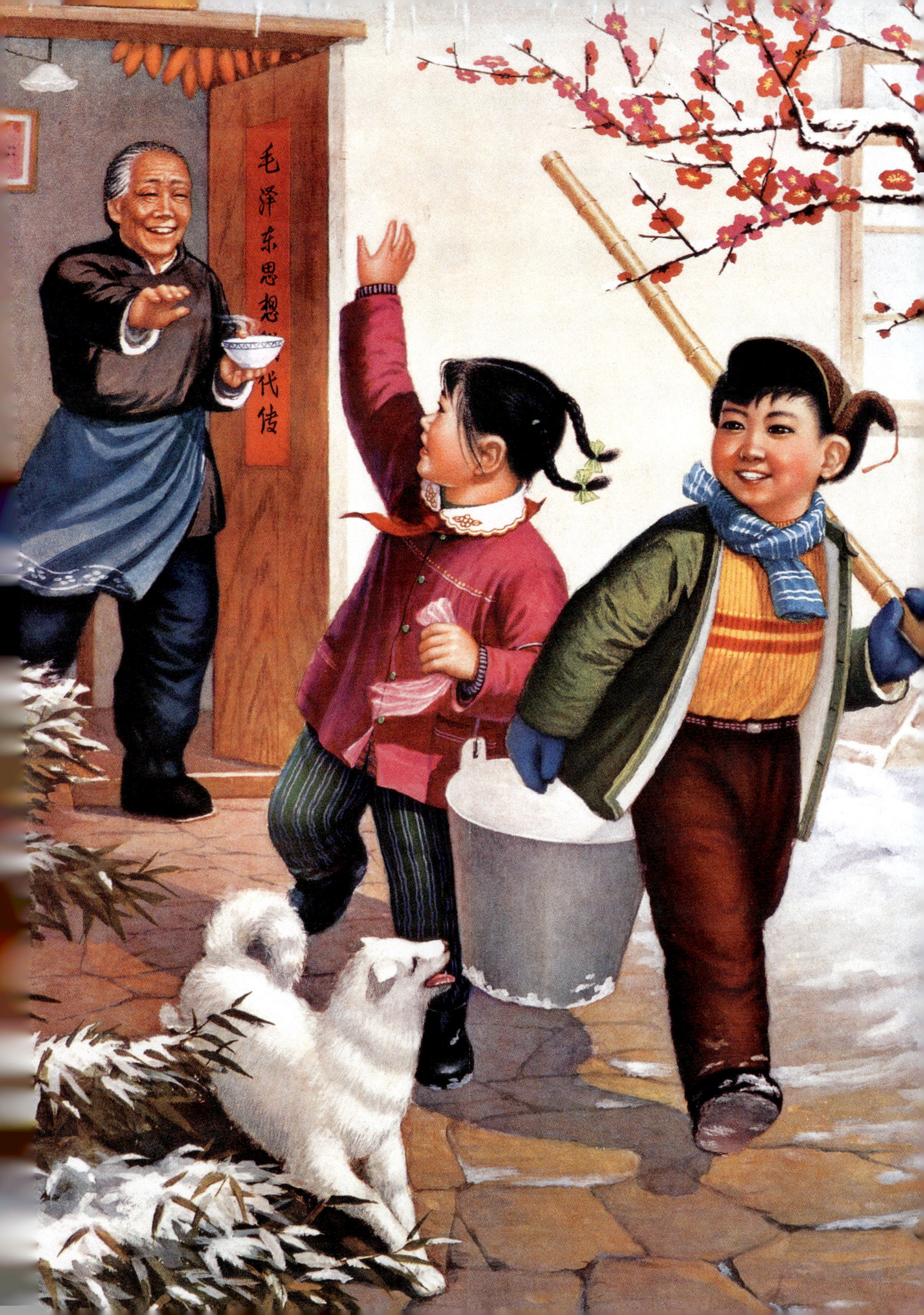
毛泽东思想
代传

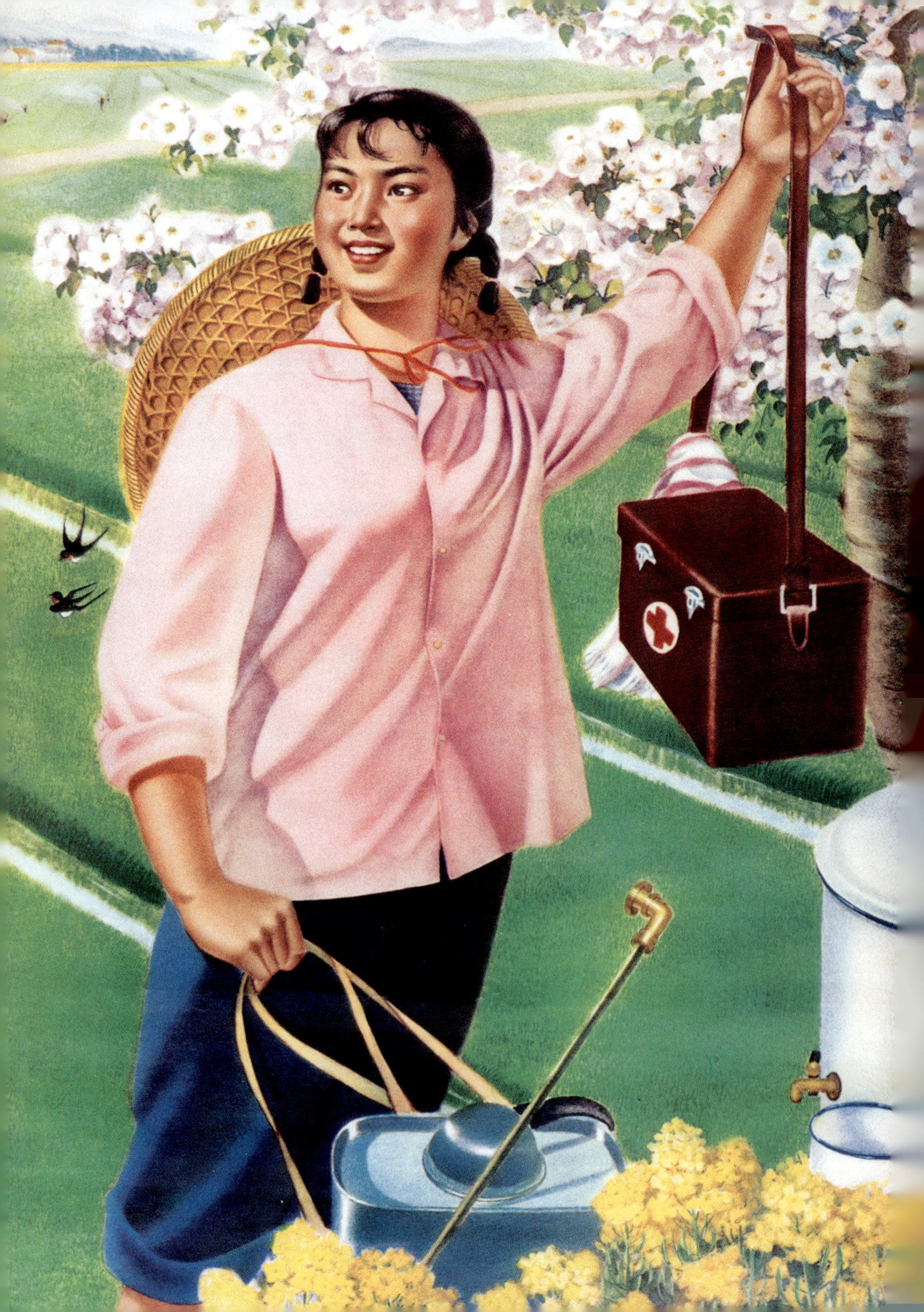

XXXI

WOMEN

DIE FRAUEN
LES FEMMES

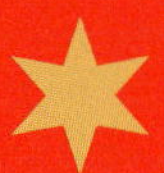

Page 456
For the welfare of the people, combine agricultural work with medical services* Zhejiang People's Publishing House, 1977; 0.14 Yuan
* The woman is a so-called "barefoot doctor"–i.e. she is a self-taught country doctor.

Für das Wohl des Volkes Landarbeit mit dem medizinischen Dienst verbinden* Volksverlag Zhejiang, 1977; 0,14 Yuan
* Diese Frau ist eine so genannte „Barfußärztin" – d. h. eine durch Selbststudium qualifizierte Landärztin.

Pour le bien du peuple, que le travail aux champs et le service médical aillent de pair* Éditions Populaires du Zhejiang, 1977 ; 0,14 yuan
* La femme est ce qu'on appelle un « médecin aux pieds nus », c'est-à-dire un médecin de campagne autodidacte et qualifié.

"In order to build a great socialist society, it is of the utmost importance to arouse the broad masses of women to join in productive activity."

Um eine große sozialistische Gesellschaft zu erbauen, ist es äußerst wichtig, die breiten Massen der Frauen für die Teilnahme an der Produktionstätigkeit zu mobilisieren. ✶ Il est de première importance pour l'édification de la grande société socialiste d'entraîner en masse les femmes à participer aux activités productrices.

Mummy is very famous
Child's T-shirt: Peace

Mama genießt großen Ruhm
T-Shirt des Kindes: Frieden

Maman jouit d'une grande célébrité *T-Shirt de l'enfant :* Paix

Pages 460–461
Mummy and I are going on a holiday *Artist:* Zhao Shaohu; Jiangsu Art Publishing House, 1985; 0.21 Yuan

Ich mache mit Mama eine Urlaubsreise *Gemalt von* Zhao Shaohu; Kunstverlag Jiangsu, 1985; 0,21 Yuan

Je pars en voyage avec maman
Peintre : Zhao Shaohu ; Éditions d'Art du Jiangsu, 1985 ; 0,21 yuan

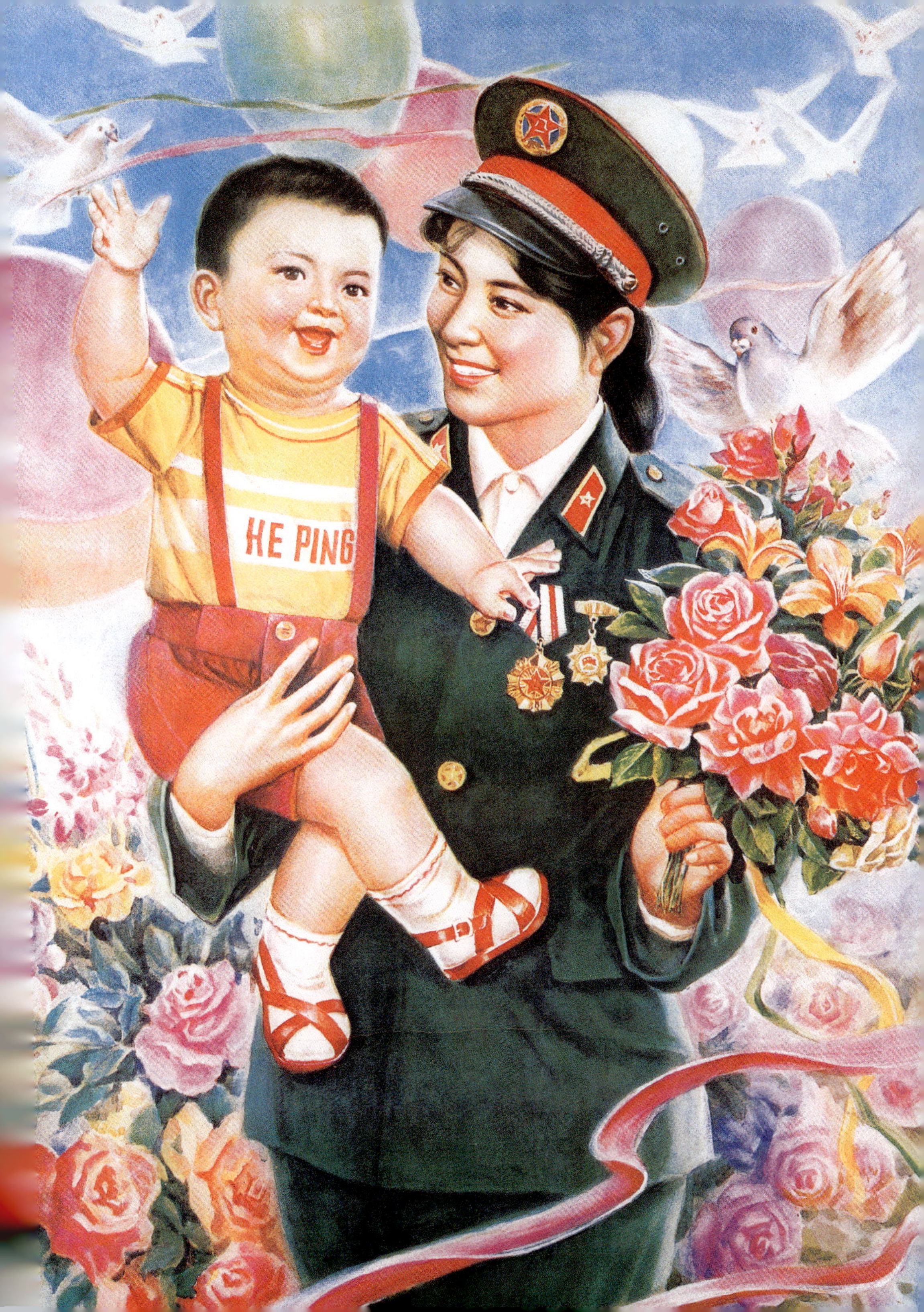
HE PING

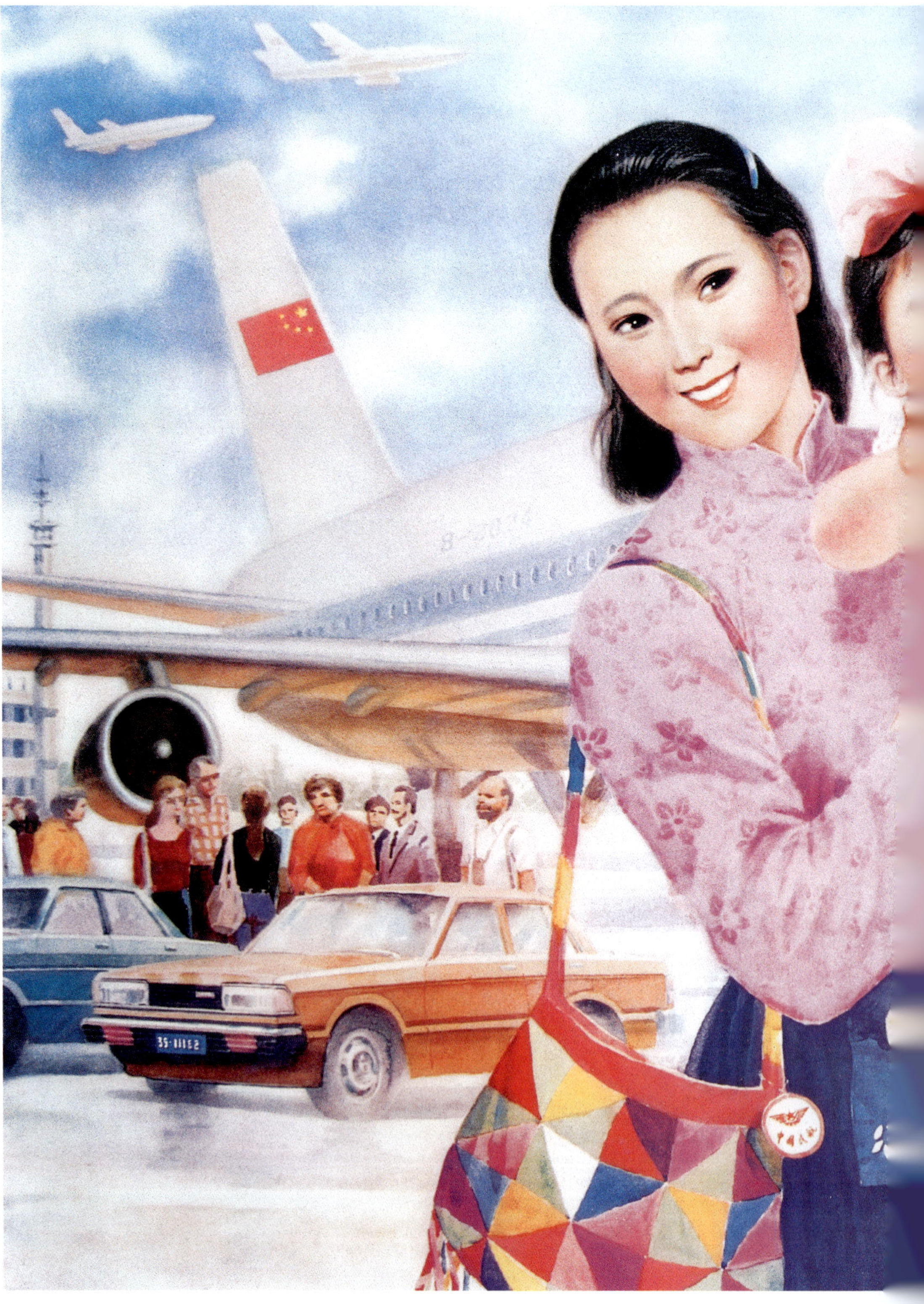

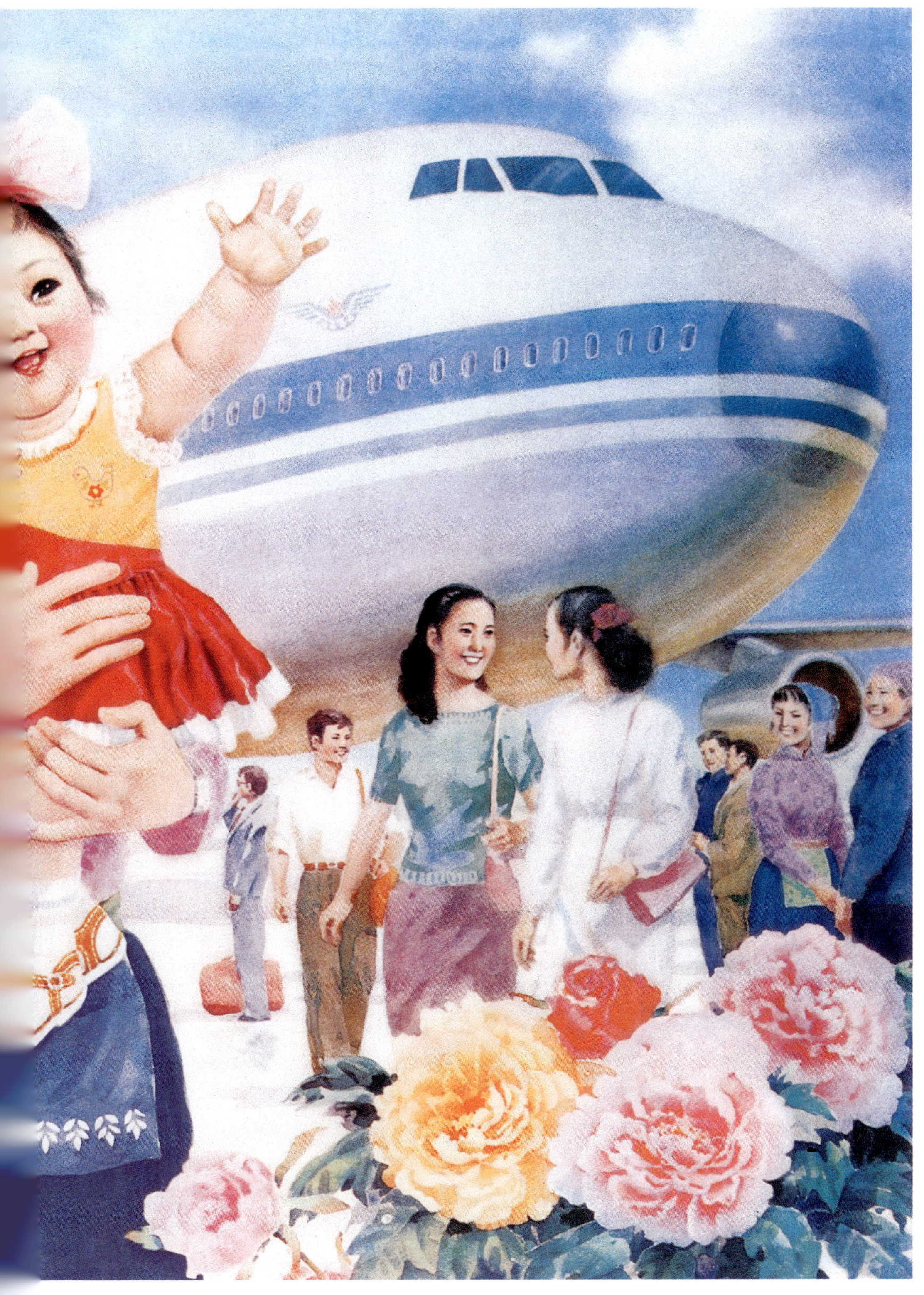

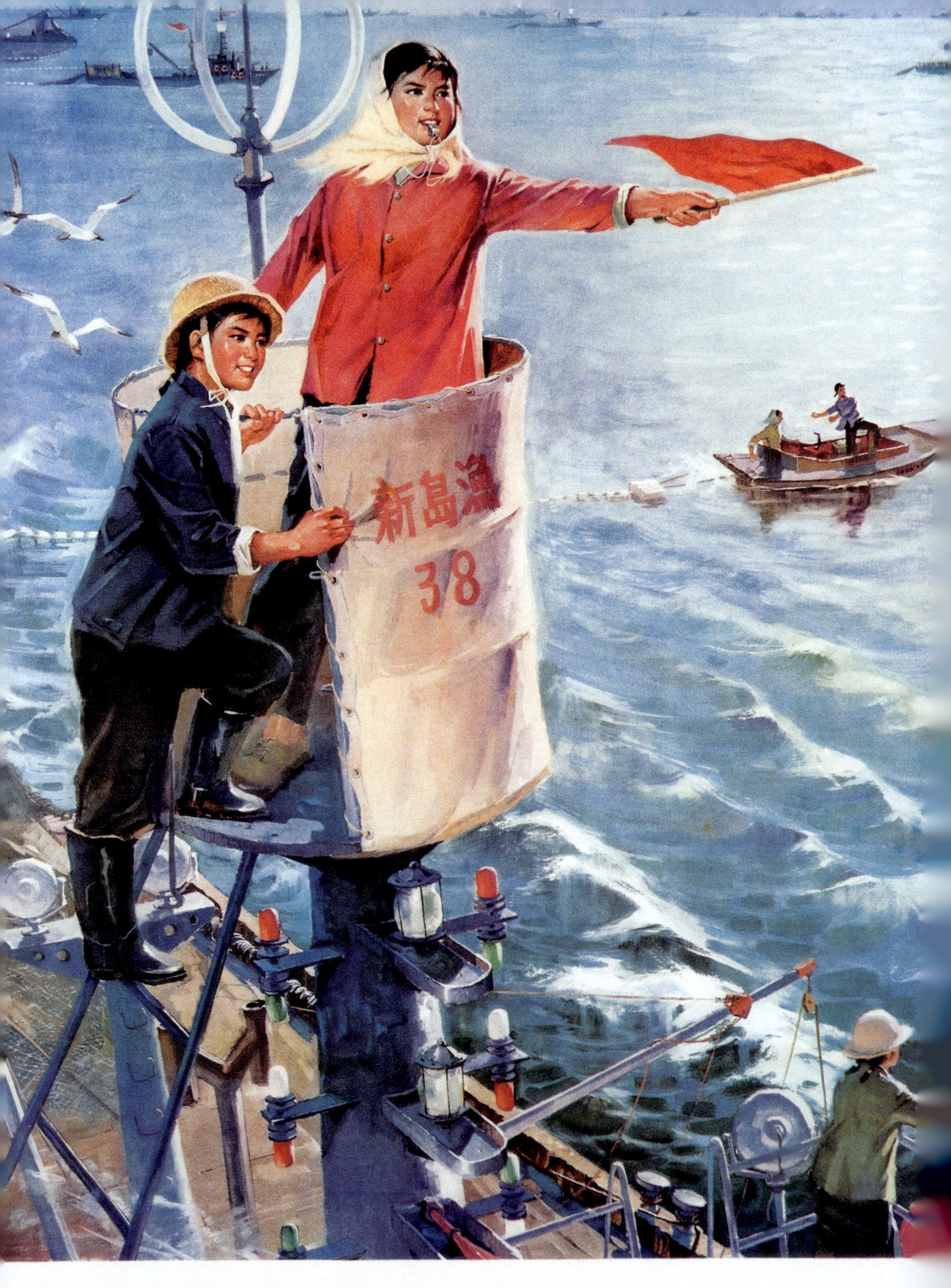

望穿碧海千层浪

“Enable every woman who can work to take her place on the labor front, under the principle of equal pay for equal work. This should be done as quickly as possible.”

Die Forderung, dass sich alle arbeitsfähigen Frauen nach dem Prinzip „Gleicher Lohn für gleiche Arbeit“ in die Arbeitsfront einreihen, muss in möglichst kurzer Frist verwirklicht werden. ✶ Il faut que toute la main-d'œuvre féminine prenne sa place sur le front du travail où sera appliqué le principe « à travail égal, salaire égal », et cela doit être réalisé dans le plus bref délai.

A sharp-eyed observer *On the tarpaulin:* New Island Fishery *Artist:* Liu Zewen of the Xinhua Bookshop of the Yantai District; Shandong People's Publishing House, 1978; 0.11 Yuan

Beobachterin mit scharfen Augen *Auf der Plane*: Fischerei der Neuen Insel *Gemalt von* Liu Zewen aus der Xinhua-Buchhandlung des Bezirks Yantai; Volksverlag Shandong, 1978; 0,11 Yuan

Observatrice à la vue perçante *Sur la bâche :* Pêche de l'Île Nouvelle *Peintre :* Liu Zewen, de la librairie Xinhua du canton de Yantai ; Éditions Populaires du Shandong, 1978 ; 0,11 yuan

Pages 464–465

Women militia members on the Yellow River *Artist:* Cui Zhande; Shandong People's Publishing House, 1976; 0.11 Yuan

Milizsoldatinnen auf dem Gelben Fluss *Gemalt von* Cui Zhande; Volksverlag Shandong, 1976; 0,11 Yuan

Miliciennes sur le Fleuve Jaune *Peintre :* Cui Zhande ; Éditions Populaires du Shandong, 1976 ; 0,11 yuan

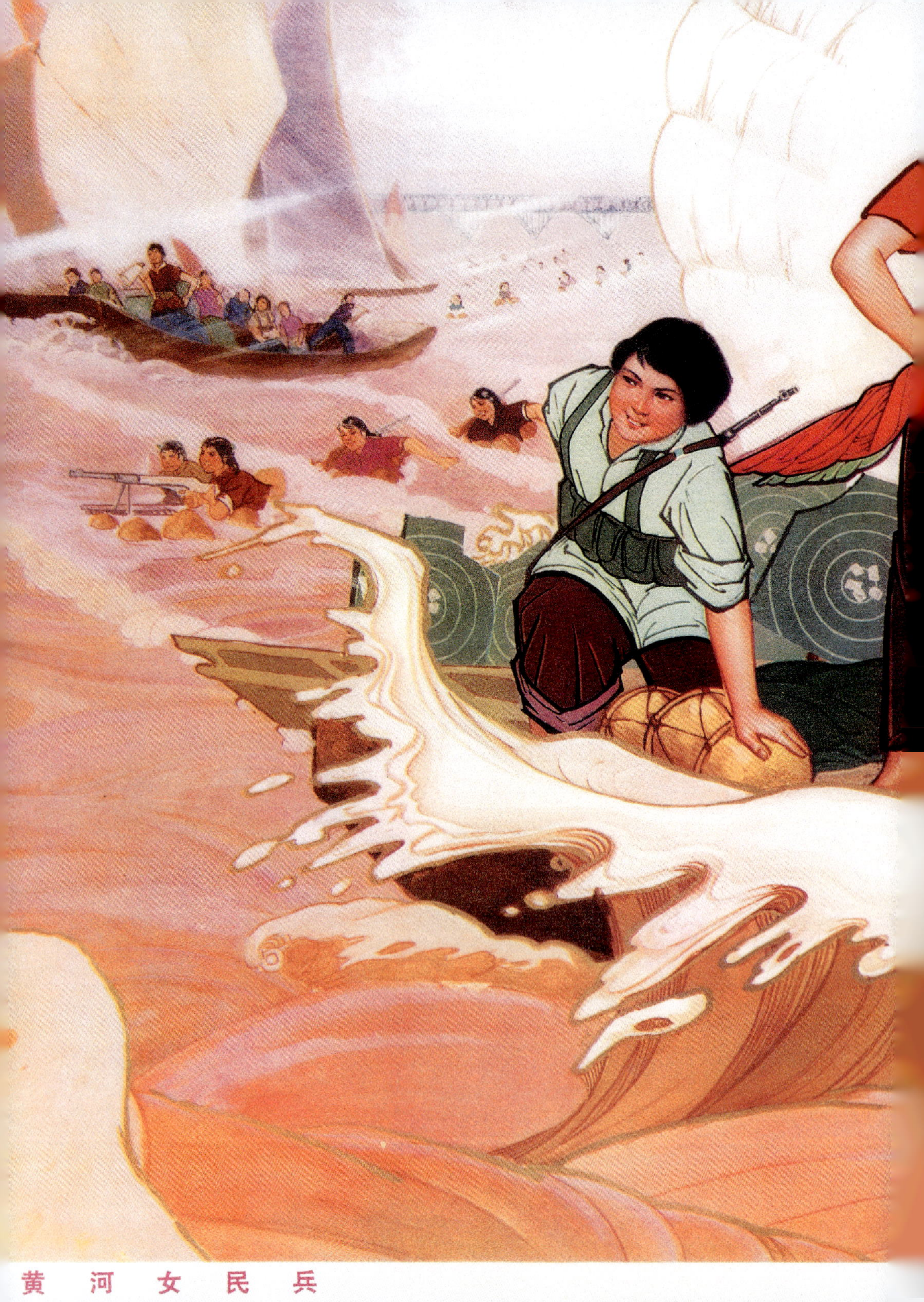

黄河女民兵

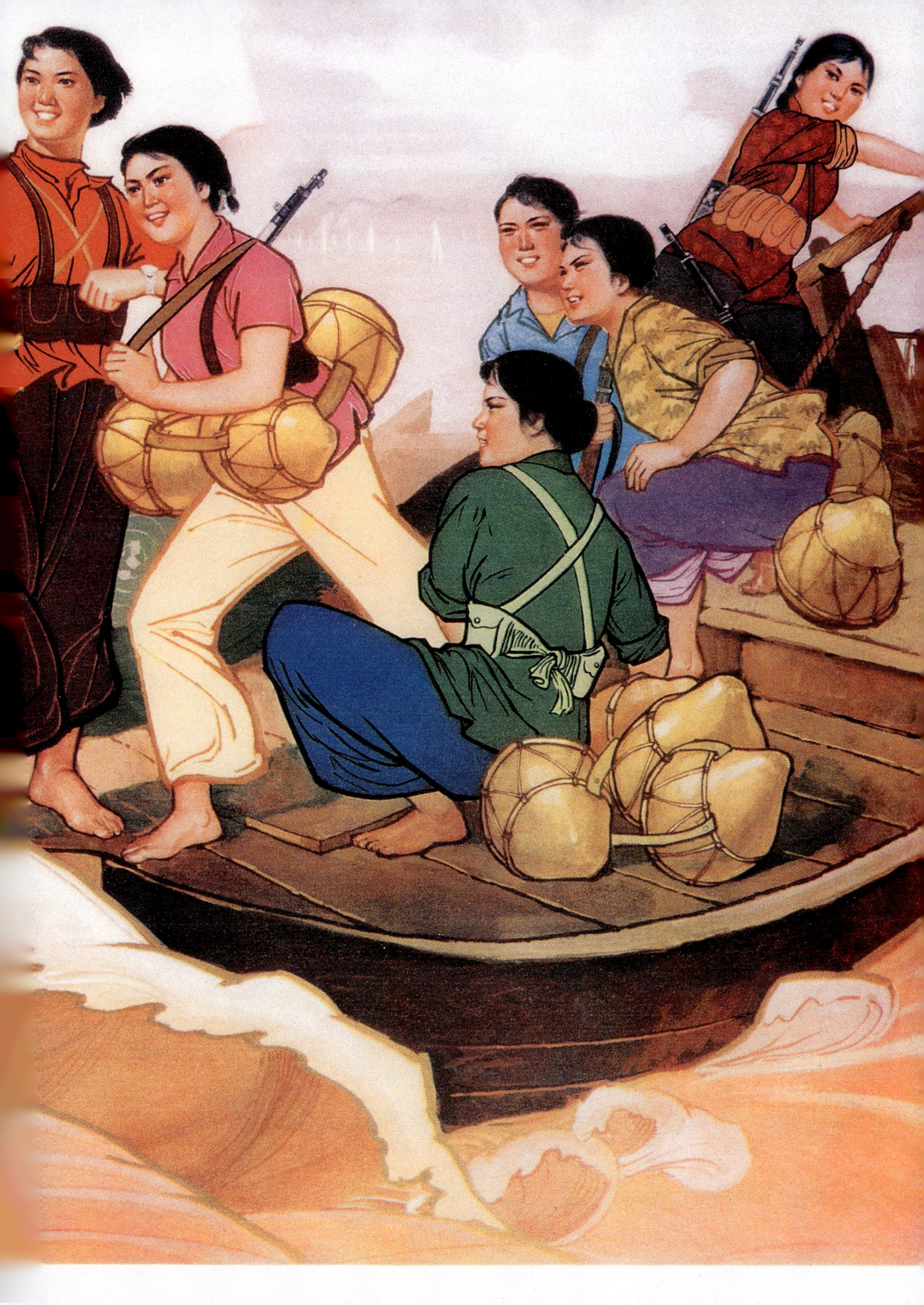

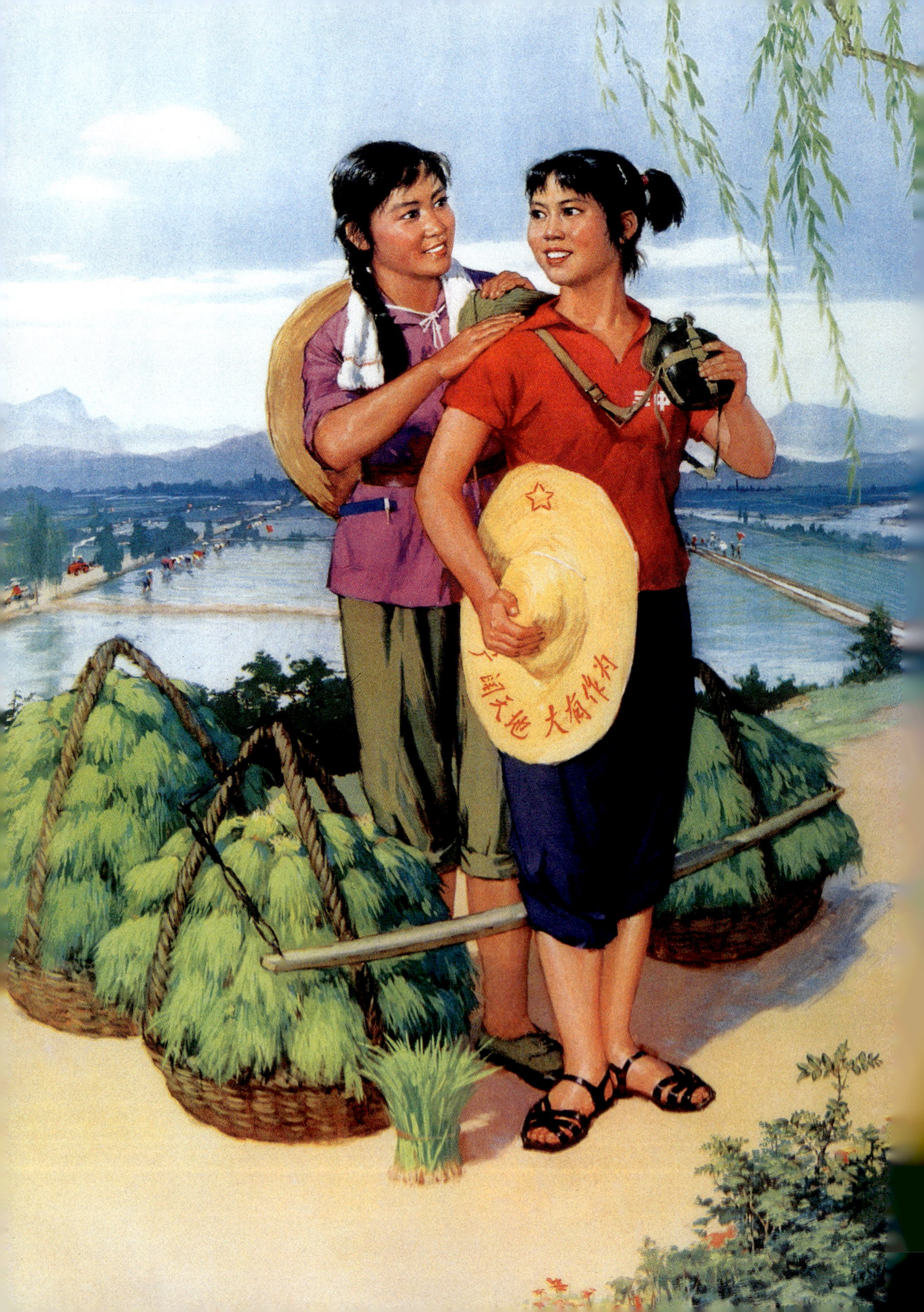
广阔天地 大有作为

Opposite
Two sisters *On straw hat:* On the land there is no limit to the skills we can develop *Artists:* Wang Zunyi and Yin Peihua; Shandong People's Publishing House, 1978; 0.14 Yuan

Zwei Schwestern *Auf dem Strohhut:* Auf dem Land kann man seine Fähigkeiten unbegrenzt entwickeln *Gemalt von* Wang Zunyi und Yin Peihua; Volksverlag Shandong, 1978; 0,14 Yuan

Deux sœurs *Sur le chapeau de paille :* À la campagne, on peut développer sans entraves ses capacités *Peintres :* Wang Zunyi et Yin Pehua ; Éditions Populaires d'Art du Shandong, 1978 ; 0,14 yuan

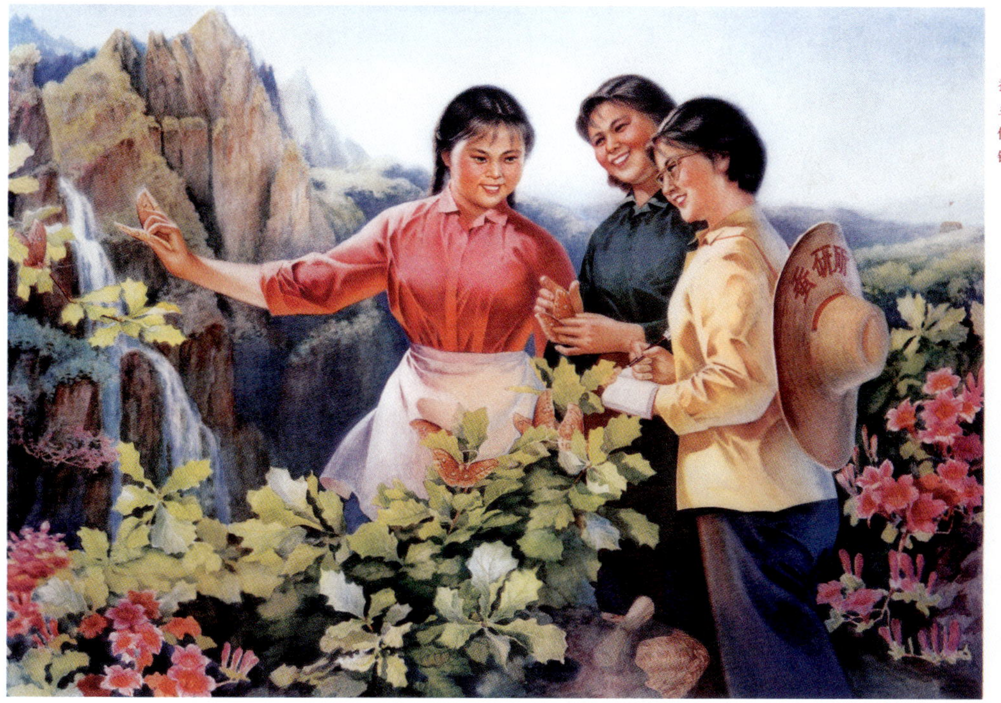

蚕乡似锦

The silkworm's beautiful natural habitat *Artist:* Tong Jingui; Liaoning People's Publishing House, 1978 *Print run:* 500,000; 0.11 Yuan

Die wunderschöne Heimat der Seidenraupe *Gemalt von* Tong Jingui; Volksverlag Liaoning, 1978 *Auflage:* 500 000; 0,11 Yuan

Le merveilleux pays du ver à soie *Peintre :* Tong Jingui ; Éditions Populaires du Liaoning, 1978 *Tirage :* 500 000 ; 0,11 yuan

Up hill and down dale by shank's pony* *Artist:* Jiang Huaqing; Shandong People's Publishing House and People's Art Publishing House, 1977; 0.14 Yuan
* Again, this concerns the work of a barefoot doctor, see page 456.

Zu Fuß über den ganzen Berg* *Gemalt von* Jiang Huaqing; Volksverlag Shandong und Volkskunstverlag, 1977; 0,14 Yuan
* Hier handelt es sich wieder um eine Barfußärztin, vgl. Seite 456.

Traversons toute la montagne à pied* *Peintre :* Jiang Huaqing ; Éditions Populaires du Shandong et Éditions Populaires d'Art, 1977 ; 0,14 yuan
* Il s'agit ici à nouveau d'un médecin aux pieds nus, voir page 456.

"Protect the interests of the youth, women and children (...), help the youth and women to organize in order to participate on an equal footing in all work useful to the war effort ..."

Man muss die Interessen der Jugend, der Frauen und der Kinder schützen (...), den Jugendlichen und Frauen helfen, sich zu organisieren, damit sie gleichberechtigt an allen Tätigkeiten teilnehmen können, die für den antijapanischen Widerstandskrieg (...) von Nutzen sind. ✶ Défendre les intérêts des jeunes, des femmes et des enfants (...), aider les jeunes et les femmes à s'organiser et à participer, de plein droit, à toute activité utile à la Guerre de Résistance contre le Japon ...

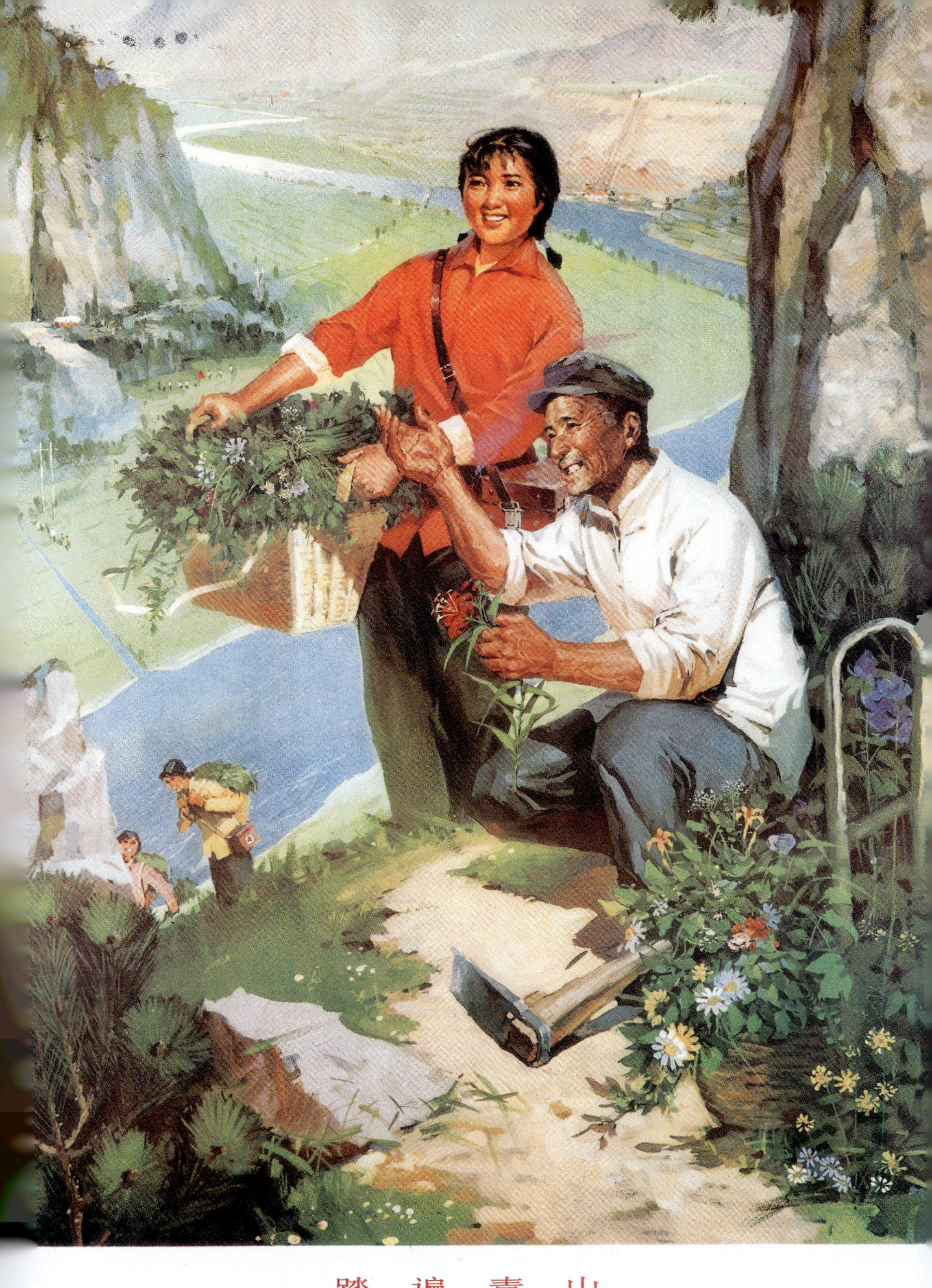

踏 遍 青 山

女工屏

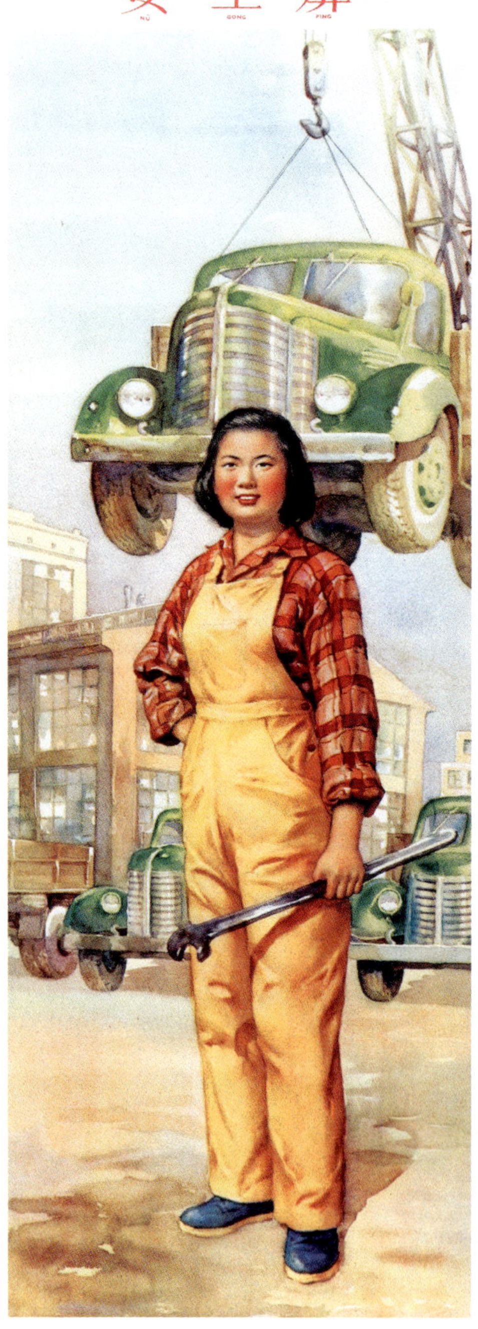

Women workers poster (1)
Arbeiterinnen-Plakate (1)
Affiches d'ouvrières (1)

女工屏

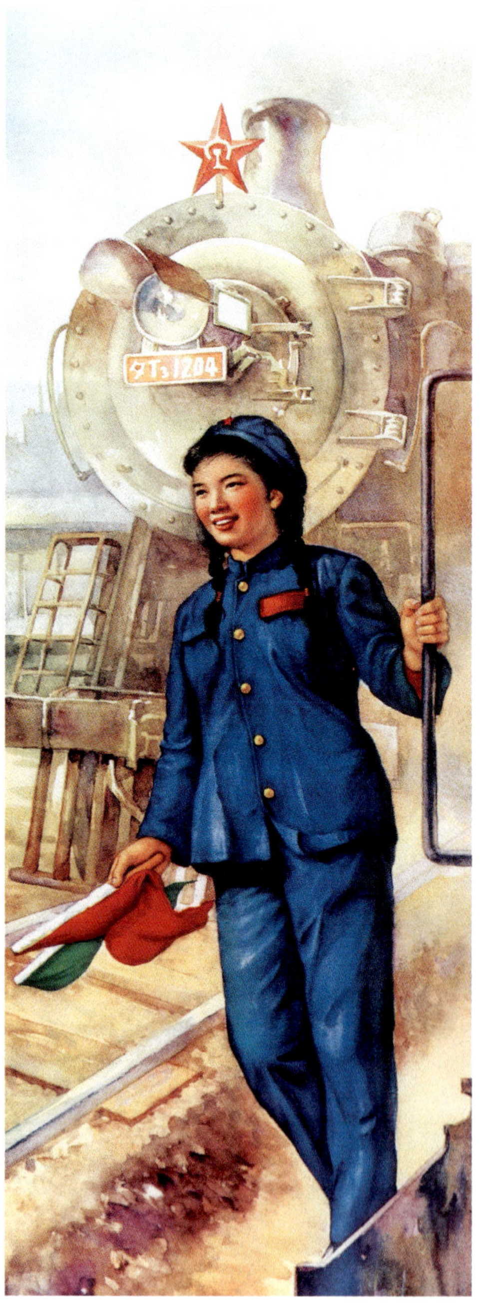

Women workers poster (2)
Arbeiterinnen-Plakate (2)
Affiches d'ouvrières (2)

女工屏
NU GONG PING

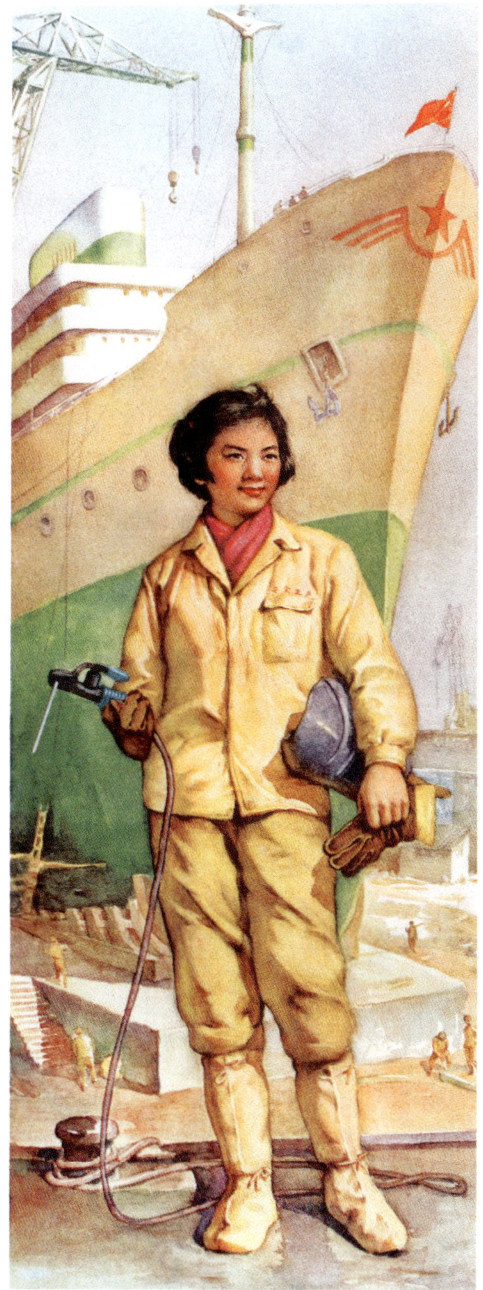

Women workers poster (3)
Arbeiterinnen-Plakate (3)
Affiches d'ouvrières (3)

女工屏
NU GONG PING

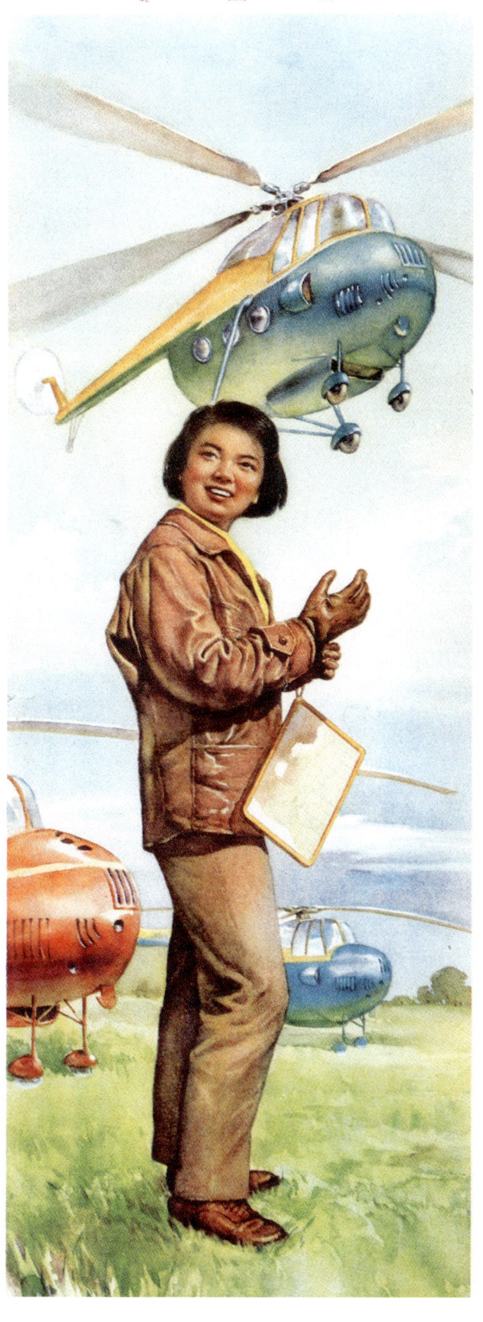

Women workers poster (4)
Arbeiterinnen-Plakate (4)
Affiches d'ouvrières (4)

Attack the "Book of Women"*! *On the board:* Carry out military exercises to consolidate the dictatorship of the proletariat. Attack the "Book of Women"! *Artist:* Feng Youkang of Unit 6386, Shanghai Area Garrison; Shanghai People's Publishing House, 1975; 0.11 Yuan
* An ancient book of feudal and Confucian moral philosophy for women.

Nehmt das „Buch der Frauen"* unter Beschuss! *Auf der Tafel:* Militärische Übungen durchführen, um die Diktatur des Proletariats zu konsolidieren. Nehmt das „Buch der Frauen" unter Beschuss! *Gemalt von* Feng Youkang der Truppe 6386, Garnisonsbereich Shanghai; Volksverlag Shanghai, 1975; 0,11 Yuan
* Ein volkstümlich überliefertes Buch, das die feudale konfuzianische Sittenlehre für Frauen beinhaltet.

Ouvrez le feu sur le « Livre des femmes »* ! *Sur le tableau :* Faites des exercices militaires pour consolider la dictature du prolétariat. Ouvrez le feu sur le « Livre des femmes » ! *Peintre :* Feng Youkang de la compagnie 6386, secteur de garnison de Shanghai ; Éditions Populaires de Shanghai, 1975 ; 0,11 yuan
* Livre populaire traditionnel qui traite de la morale confucéenne réservée aux femmes.

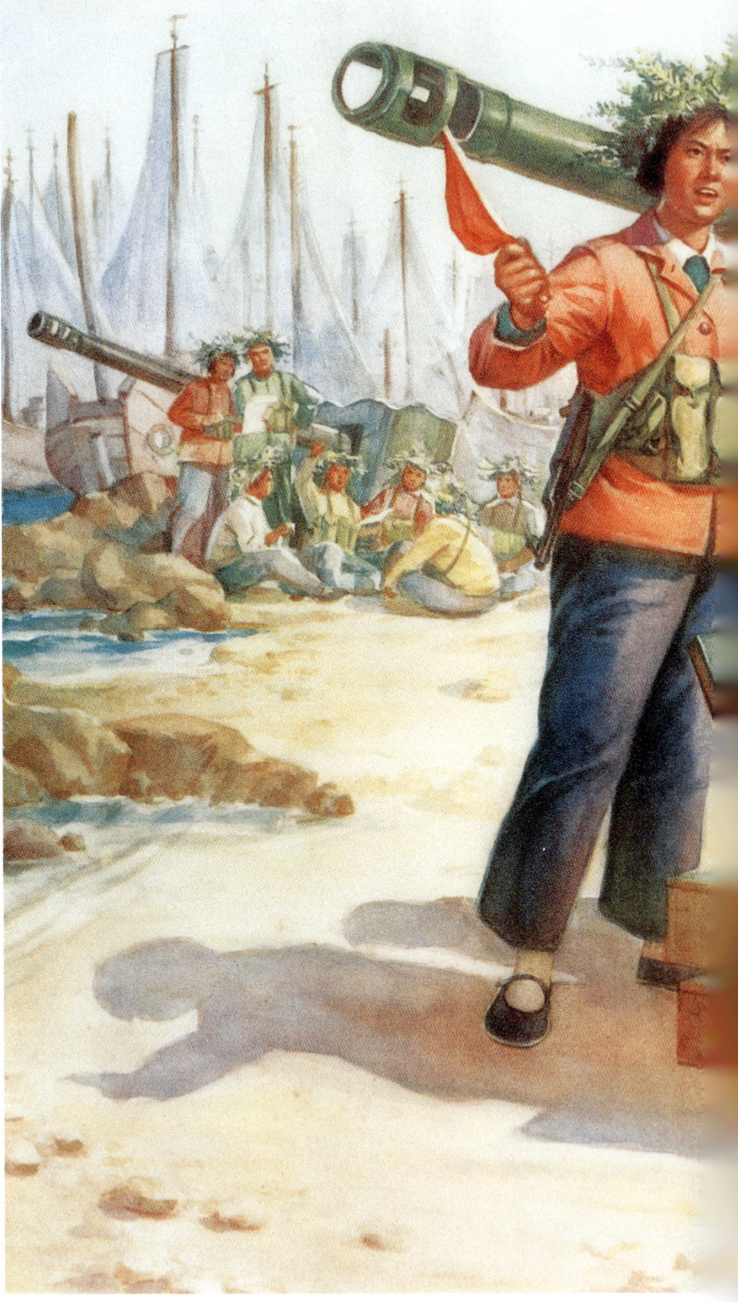

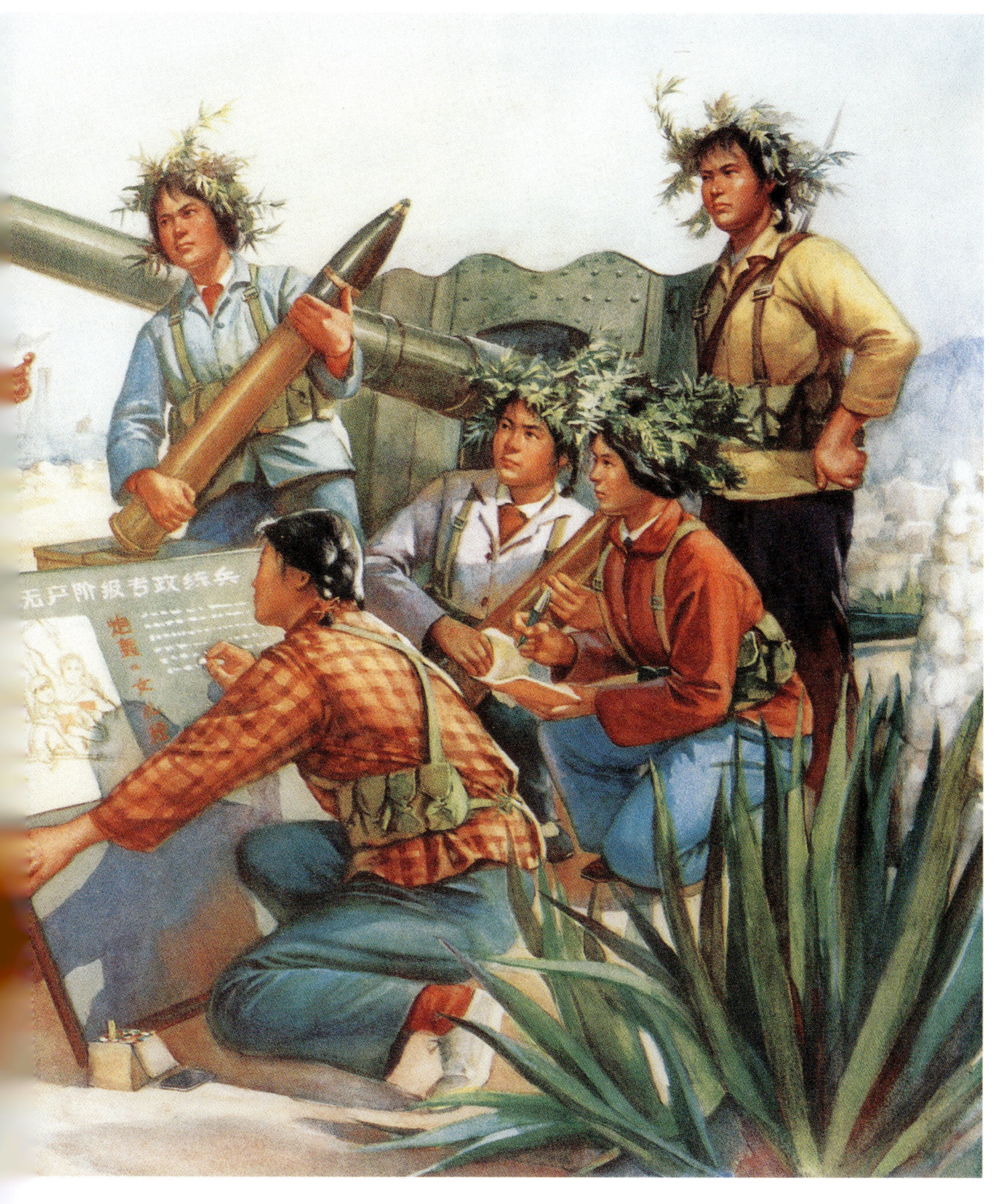
无产阶级专政练兵

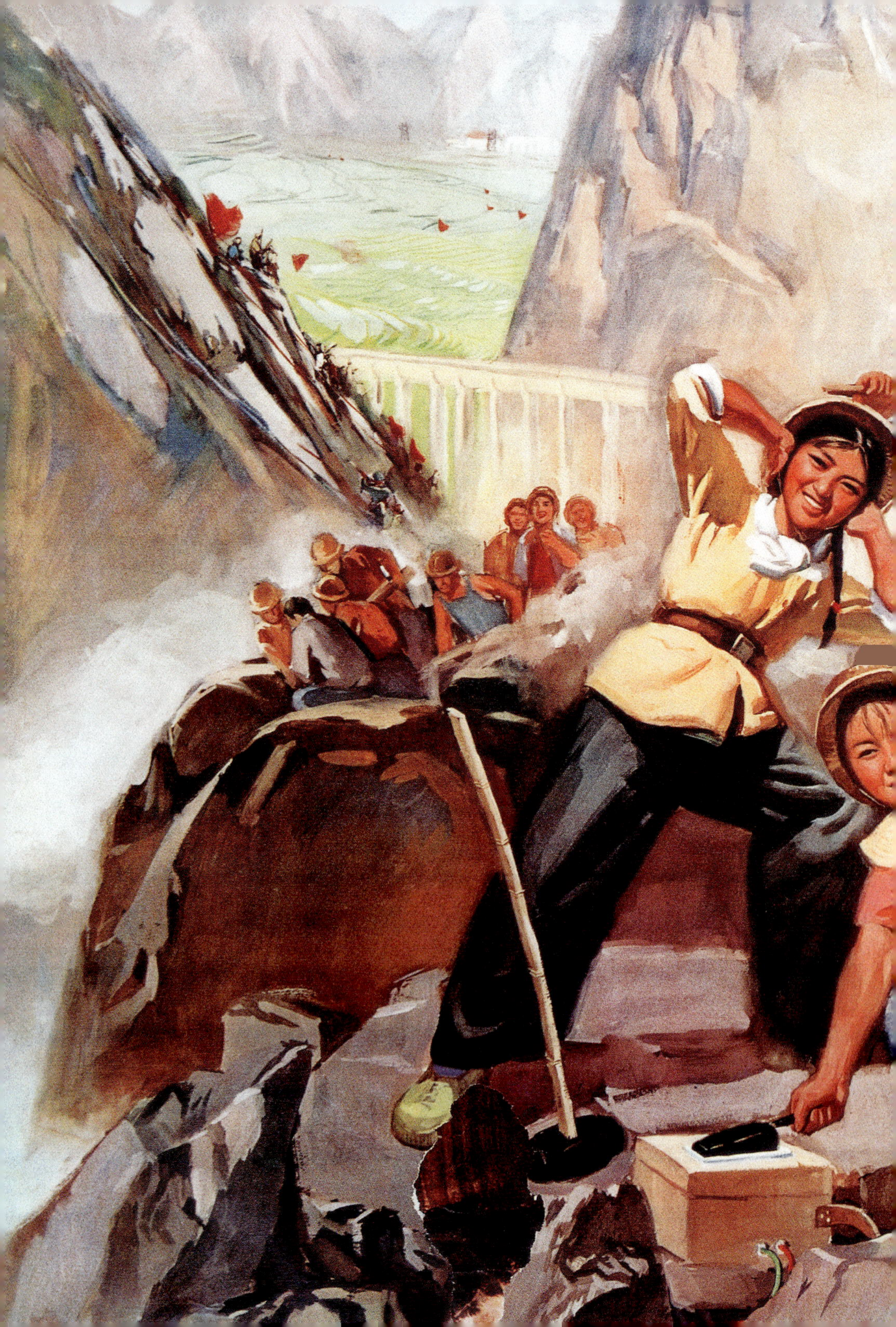

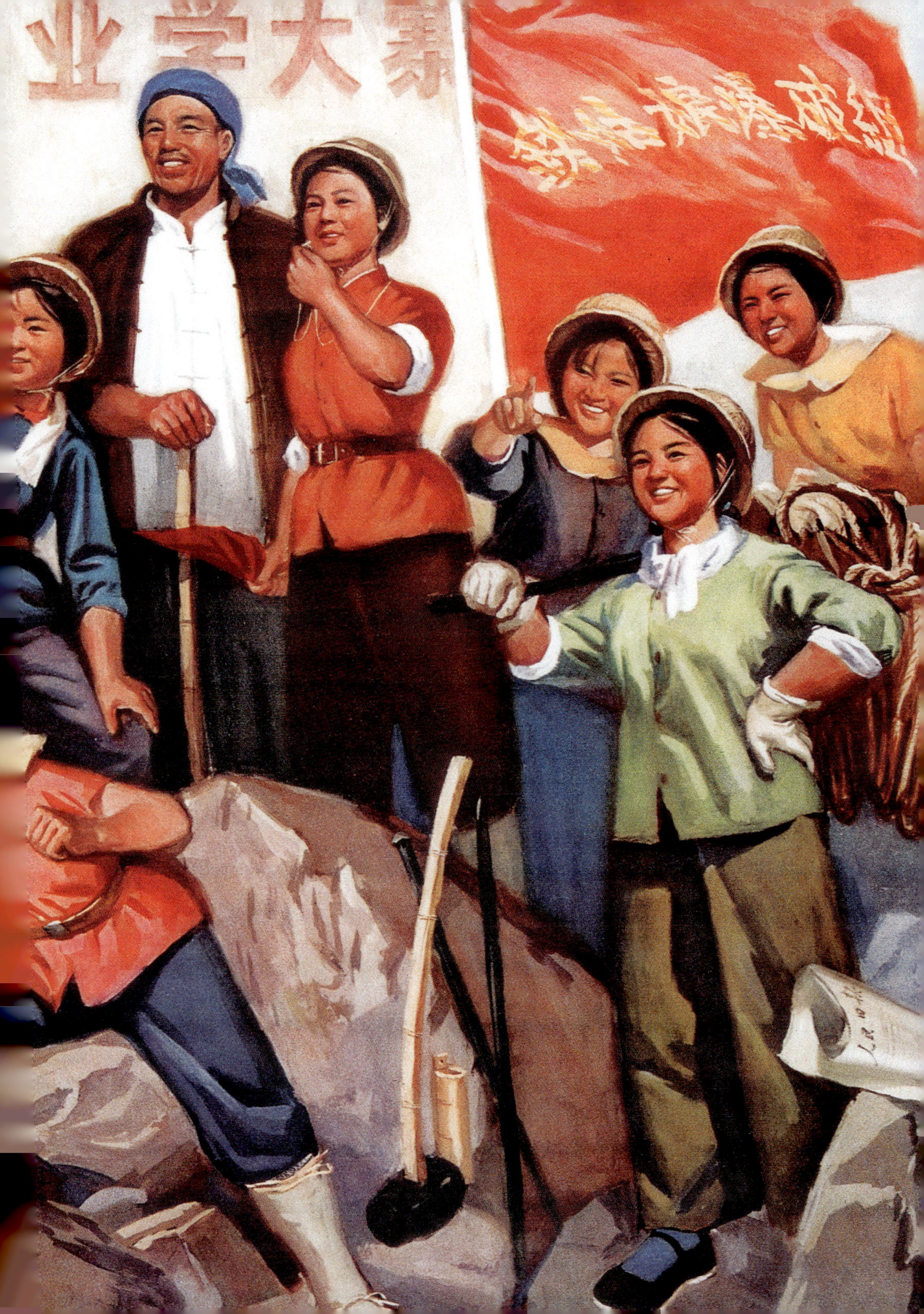
业学大寨

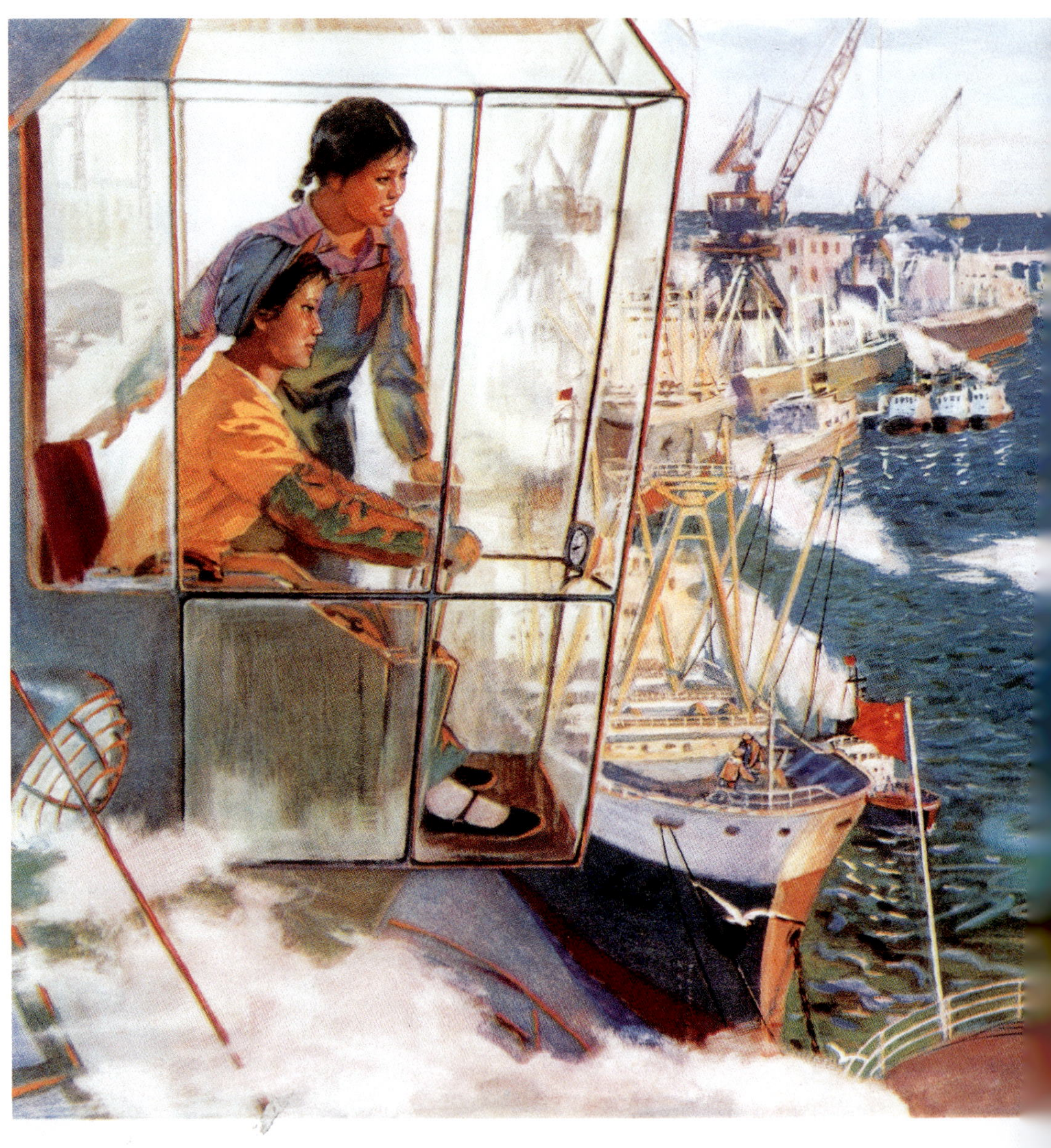

Pages 474–475
The new shot firer *On rock:* Learn from Dazhai's agriculture! *On flag:* The iron women's blasting unit *Artist:* Jin Chen; Jiangxi People's Publishing House, 1974

Die neue Sprengmeisterin *Auf dem Felsen*: Lernt in der Landwirtschaft von Dazhai! *Fahne*: Sprengtrupp der eisernen Frauen *Gemalt von* Jin Chen; Volksverlag Jiangxi, 1974

La nouvelle maîtresse de tir *Sur le rocher :* Inspirez-vous de l'expérience agricole de Dazhai ! *Drapeau:* Équipe de dynamitage des femmes de fer *Peintre :* Jin Chen ; Éditions Populaires du Jiangxi, 1974

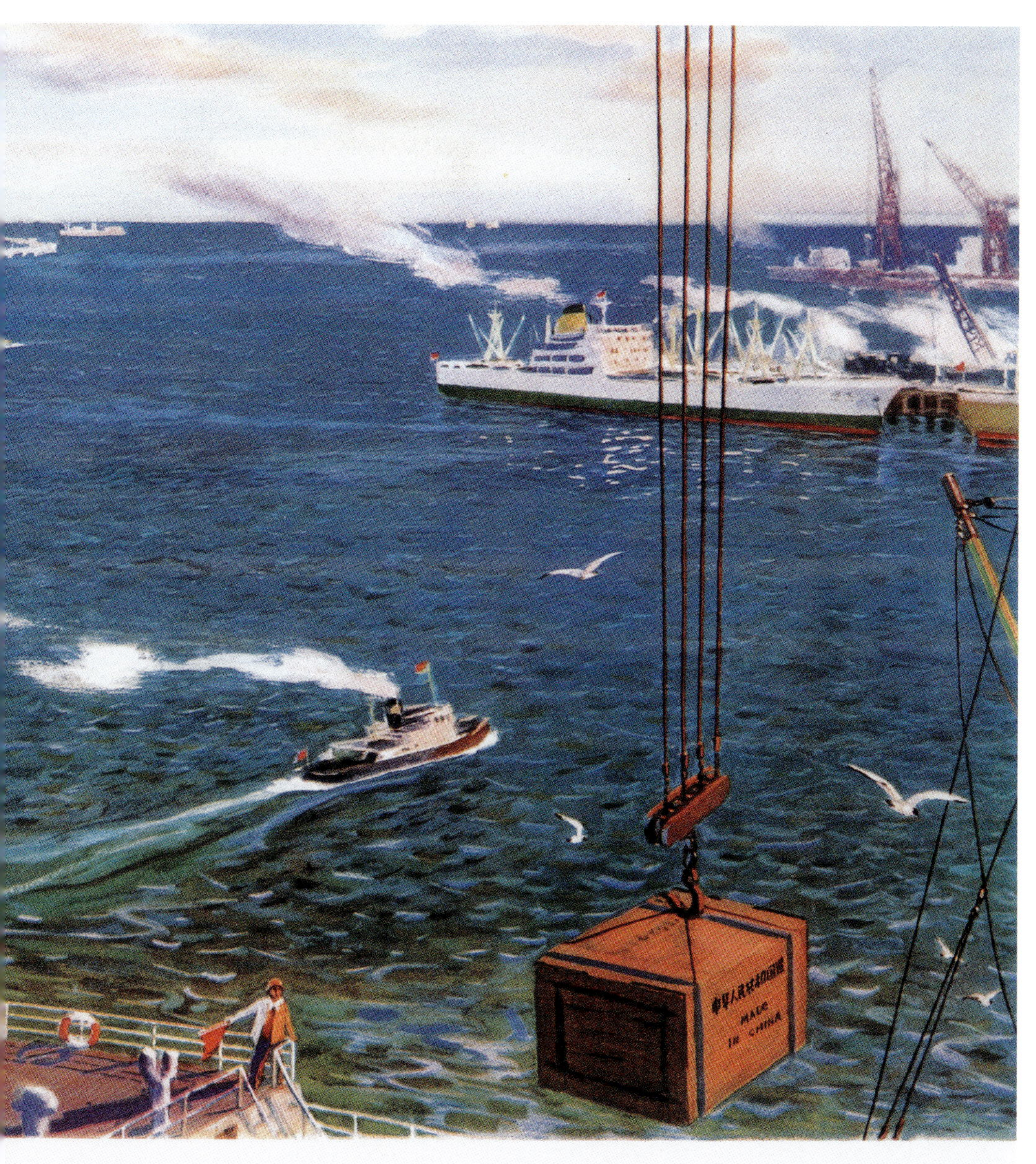

Harbour of the fatherland *Artist:* Fei Zheng; Hebei People's Publishing House, 1974 *Print run:* 830,000; 0.14 Yuan

Hafen des Vaterlandes *Gemalt von* Fei Zheng; Volksverlag Hebei, 1974 *Auflage:* 830 000; 0,14 Yuan

Le port de la patrie *Peintre :* Fei Zheng ; Éditions Populaires du Hebei, 1974 *Tirage :* 830 000 ; 0,14 yuan

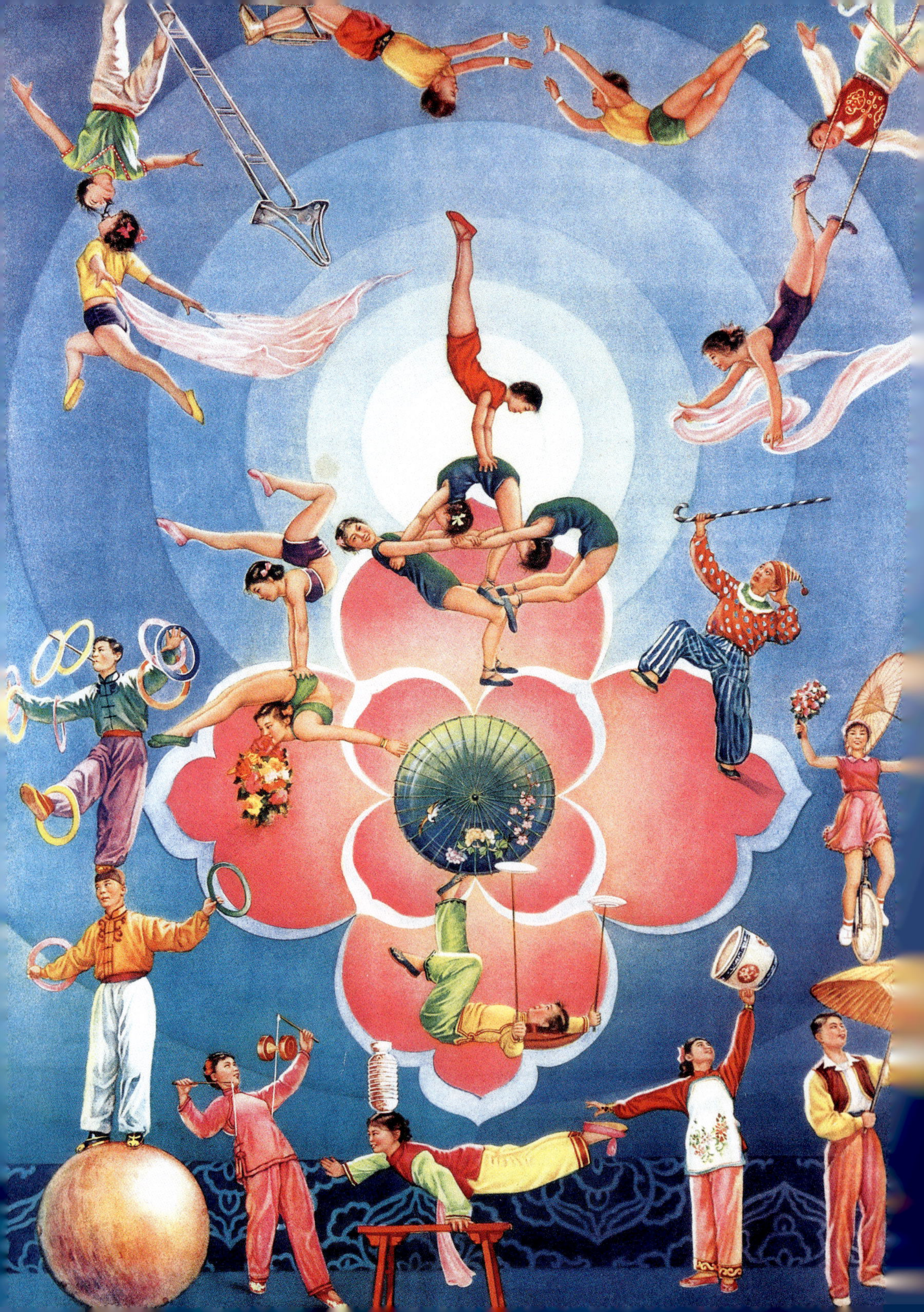

XXXII

CULTURE AND ART

KULTUR UND KUNST
LA CULTURE ET L'ART

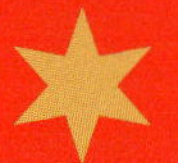

Page 478
Acrobatics *Artist:* Xu Jiping; Shanghai People's Art Publishing House, 1st edn 1962, 2nd edn 1962 *Print run:* 30,001–430,000; 0.18 Yuan

Akrobatik *Gemalt von* Xu Jiping; Volkskunstverlag Shanghai, 1. Aufl. 1962, 2. Aufl. 1962 *Auflage:* 30 001–430 000; 0,18 Yuan

Acrobaties *Peintre :* Xu Jiping ; Éditions Populaires d'Art de Shanghai, 1ère éd. 1962, 2e éd. 1962 *Tirage :* 30 001–430 000 ; 0,18 yuan

"An army without culture is a dull-witted army, and a dull-witted army cannot defeat the enemy."

Eine Armee ohne Kultur ist eine unwissende Armee, und eine unwissende Armee kann den Feind nicht besiegen. ✶ Une armée sans culture est une armée ignorante, et une armée ignorante ne peut vaincre l'ennemi.

Return to Jingzhou* *Artist:* Jin Meisheng; Shanghai People's Art Publishing House, 1st edn 1958, 15th edn 1962 *Print run:* 1,835,001–2,083,000; 0.14 Yuan
* A poster for the Beijing Opera.

Rückkehr nach Jingzhou* *Gemalt von* Jin Meisheng; Volkskunstverlag Shanghai, 1. Aufl. 1958, 15. Aufl. 1962 *Auflage:* 1 835 001–2 083 000; 0,14 Yuan
* Ein Plakat für eine Pekingoper.

Retour à Jingzhou* *Peintre :* Jin Meisheng ; Éditions Populaires d'Art de Shanghai, 1ère éd. 1958, 15e éd. 1962 *Tirage :* 1 835 001–2 083 000 ; 0,14 yuan
* Affiche de l'Opéra de Pékin.

Pages 482–483
Acrobatics (3) *Artist:* Wu Shaoyun *Published by:* Huamei Picture Publishing House, Shanghai, 3rd edn 1954 *Print run:* 135,000; 1.60 Yuan

Akrobatik (3) *Gemalt von* Wu Shaoyun *Herausgeber:* Huamei-Bilderverlag Shanghai, 3. Aufl. 1954 *Auflage:* 135 000; 1,60 Yuan

Acrobaties (3) *Peintre :* Wu Shaoyun *Éditeur :* Éditions d'Images Huamei de Shanghai, 3e édition 1954 *Tirage :* 135 000 ; 1,60 yuan

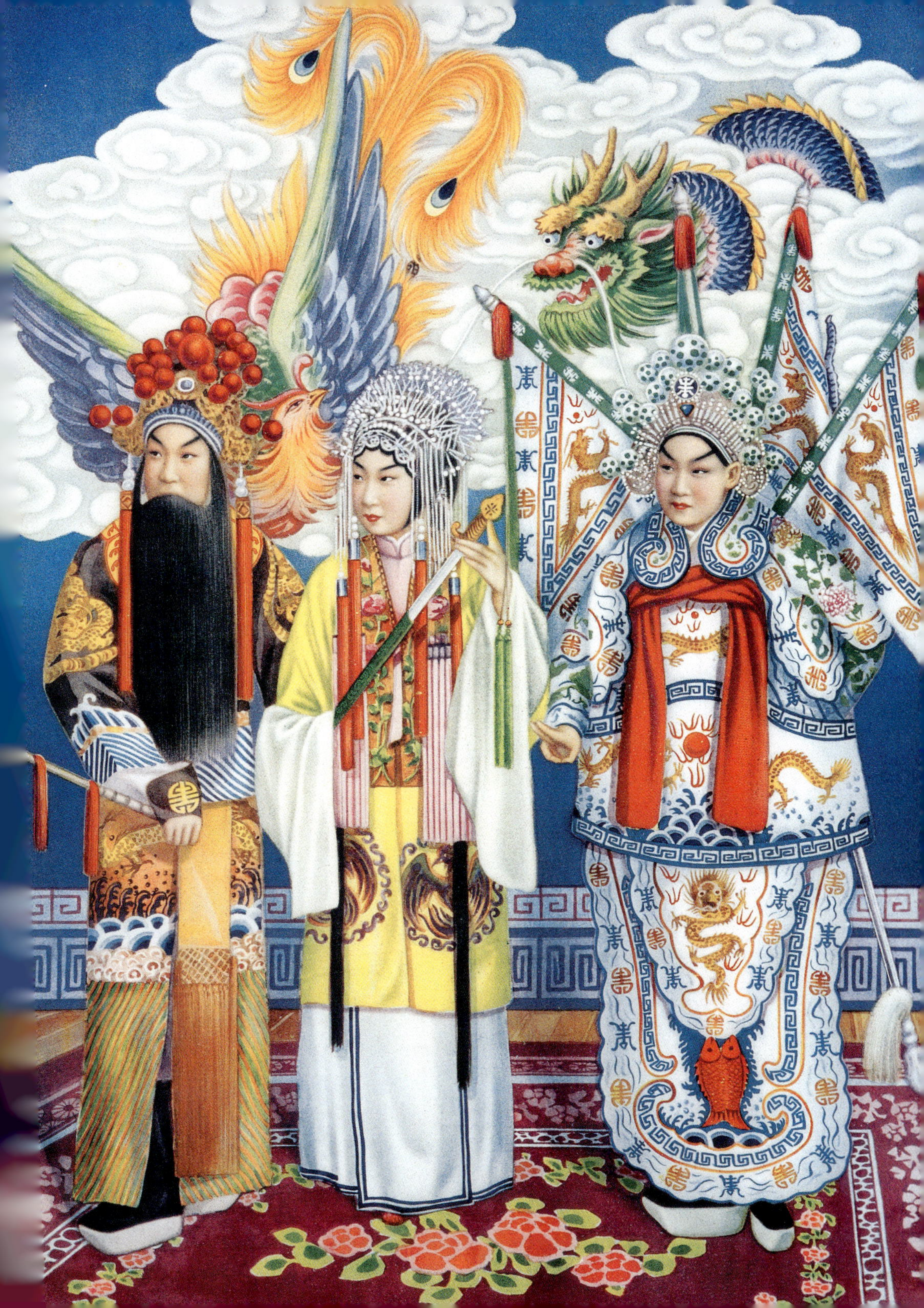

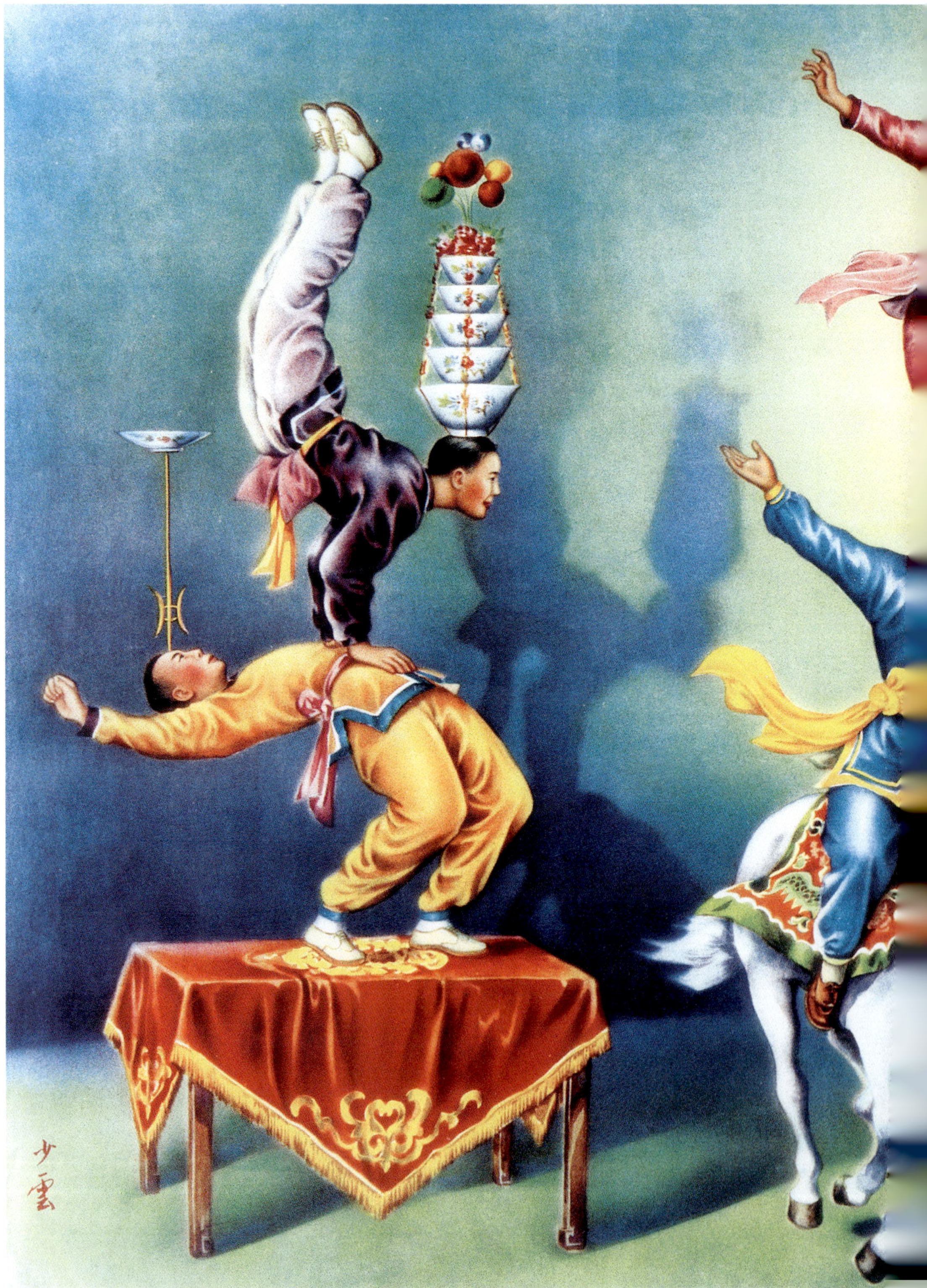
步雲

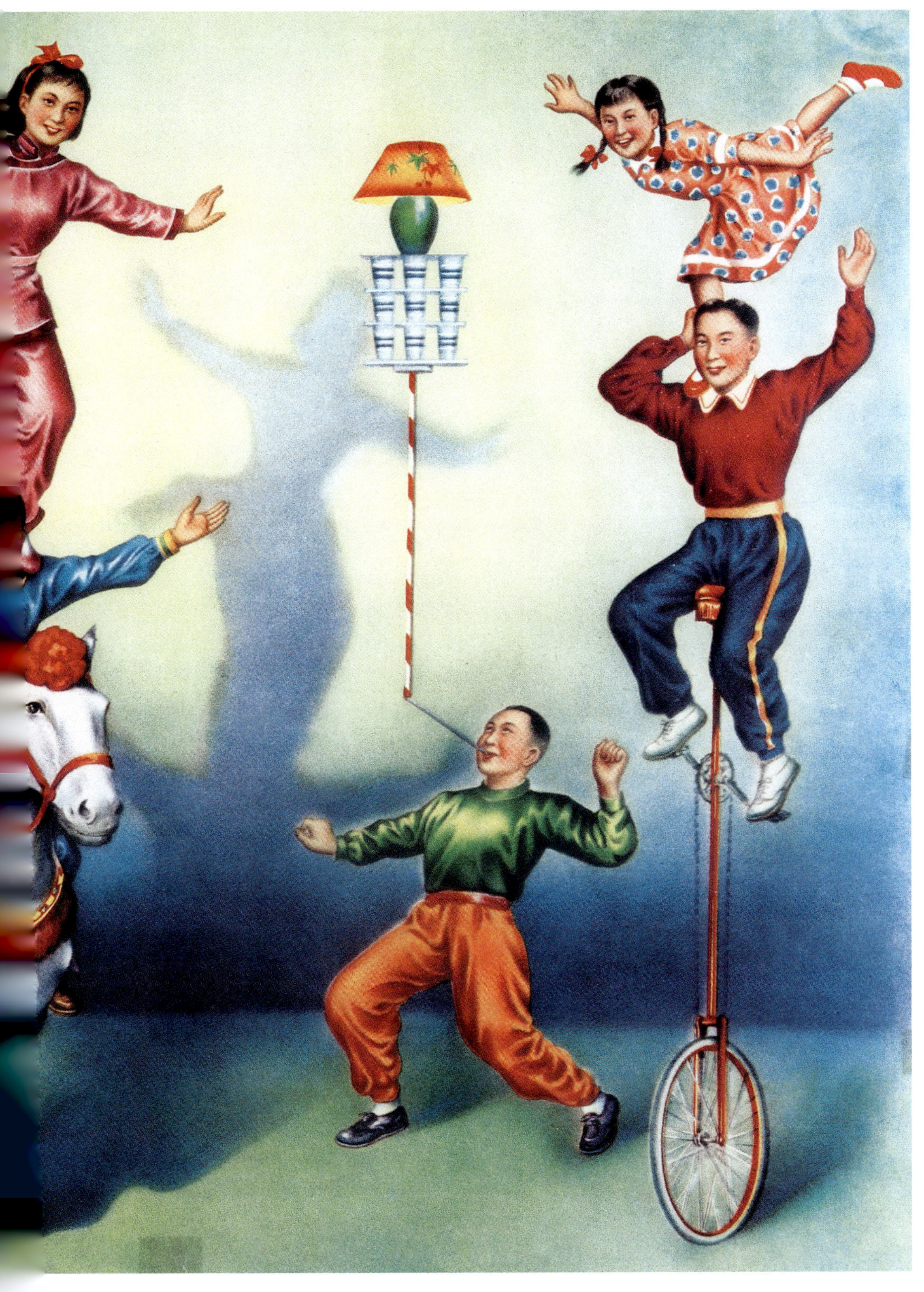

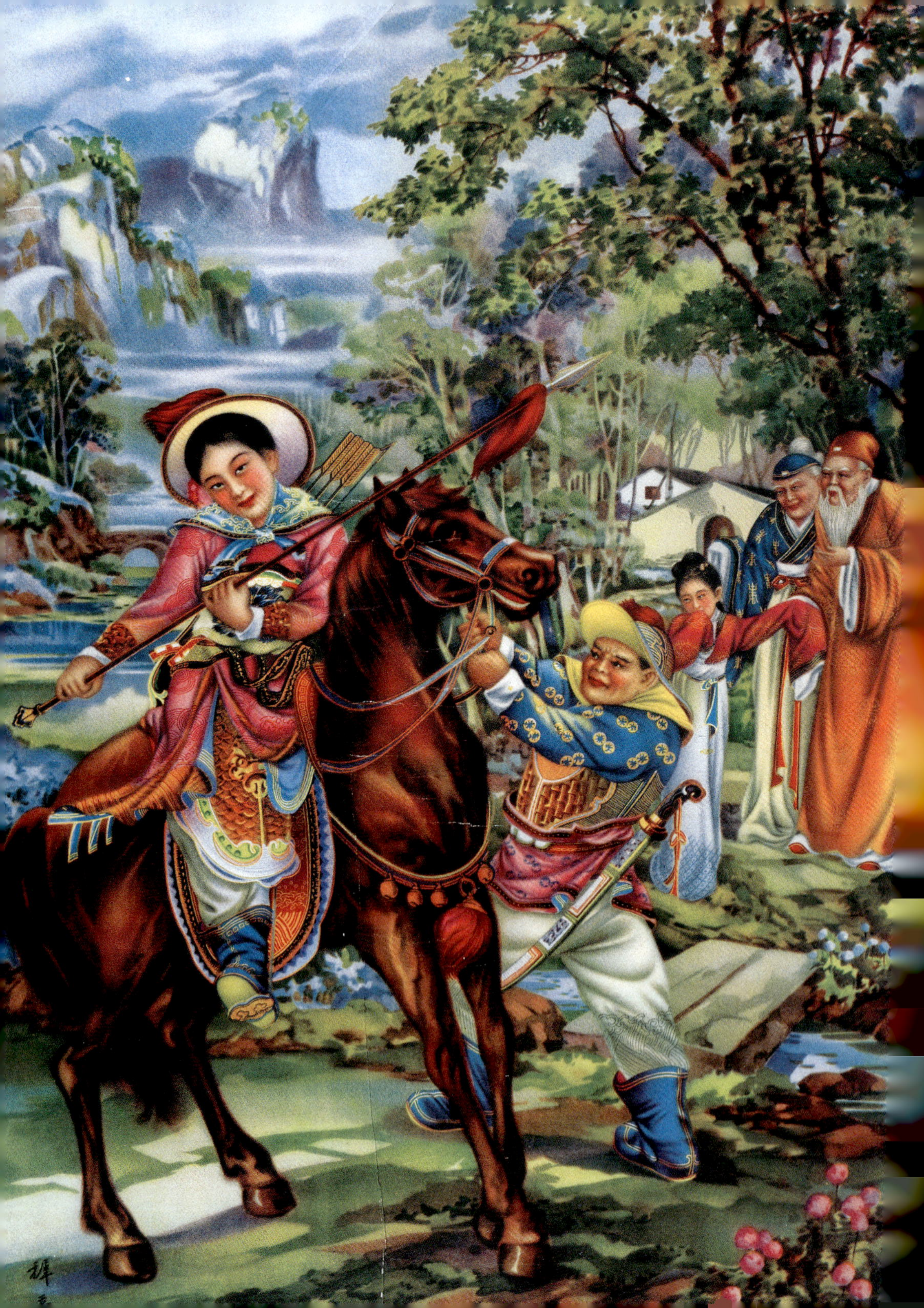

Mu Lan* enlists in the army
Published and distributed by: First Community Picture Publishing House Shanghai, 2nd edn 1954 *Print run:* 20,000, total 260,000; 1.60 Yuan
*A peasant girl who, according to popular legend, dressed as a man and went to war in place of her sick father, and later became a general. The story has been adapted to various forms of art, including an opera by Beijing Opera, literature and film. There is even a feature-length Disney cartoon.

Mu Lan* tritt in die Armee ein
Herausgeber und Vertrieb: Der erste gemeinschaftliche Bilderverlag Shanghai, 2. Aufl. 1954 *Auflage:* 20 000, insgesamt 260 000; 1,60 Yuan
* Laut Volkssage ein Bauernmädchen, das sich als ein Mann verkleidet und für den kranken Vater in den Krieg zieht und später eine Generalin wird. Die Geschichte wird in verschiedenen Kunstgattungen adaptiert, u. a. Pekingoper, Literatur, Film (es gibt sogar einen Zeichentrickfilm von Walt Disney).

Mu Lan* entre dans l'armée
Peintre : Hang Ying *Éditeur et distributeur :* Les premières Éditions d'Images collectives Shanghai, 2e éd. 1954 *Tirage :* 20 000–260 000 ; 1,60 yuan
*Jeune paysanne qui, selon la légende populaire, se travestit en homme pour aller à la guerre à la place de son père malade et devint plus tard général. Cette histoire a donné lieu à plusieurs adaptations artistiques, notamment par l'Opéra de Pékin, la littérature et le cinéma (Walt Disney en a même fait un dessin animé).

Pages 486–487
Lanterns for tea picking
Lanterns for tea picking is a well-known, traditional song and dance. It is very popular with workers because it reflects the working lives of the tea pickers in the west of Fujian Province. Its lively, simple choreography in the local tradition expresses the optimistic spirit of the workers in a region that was once a base for revolutionary activity. The dance is very popular in the west of Fujian Province and is performed everywhere, in the countryside and the cities, and in factories and schools. At the first Chinese Festival of Folk Music and Dance organized by the Ministry of Culture of the Central People's Government in 1953, this outstanding dance was presented by the East China Ensemble. *Artist:* Jin Xuewen *Published, printed and distributed by:* Xusheng Print Works, Shanghai, 8th edn 1954 *Print run:* 20,000–145,000; 1.60 Yuan

Laterne für das Teepflücken
„Laterne für das Teepflücken" ist ein traditionelles, bekanntes Gesang- und Tanzstück. Es ist bei den Werktätigen sehr beliebt, weil es das Arbeitsleben der Teepflücker im Westen der Provinz Fujian widerspiegelt. Seine lebhafte, lokal-volkstümliche, einfache Choreografie bringt den optimistischen Geist der Werktätigen des ehemaligen revolutionären Stützpunktgebietes zum Ausdruck. Dieses Tanzstück ist im Westen der Provinz Fujian sehr populär und wird überall aufgeführt, ob auf dem Land, in der Stadt oder in den Fabriken und Schulen. Auf dem ersten Volksmusik- und Volkstanz-Festival Chinas im April 1953, das vom Kulturministerium der Zentralen Volksregierung veranstaltet wurde, führte das Ostchina-Ensemble diesen hervorragenden Tanz vor. *Gemalt von* Jin Xuewen *Herausgeber, Druck und Vertrieb:* Xusheng-Druckerei Shanghai, 8. Aufl. 1954 *Auflage:* 20 000–145 000; 1,60 Yuan

Lanternes pour la récolte du thé
Le « Lanternes pour la récolte du thé » est un chant traditionnel bien connu et une danse. Ce morceau, qui reflète la vie des cueilleurs de thé de l'Ouest de la province du Fujian, est très aimé des travailleurs. La vivacité et la simplicité de sa chorégraphie, inspirée du folklore local, exprime l'optimisme des travailleurs dans cet ancien bastion révolutionnaire. Très populaire à l'Ouest de la province du Fujian, il est dansé partout, que ce soit à la campagne, en ville, ou dans les usines et les écoles. Cette danse remarquable a été présentée par l'Ensemble de la Chine Orientale lors du premier Festival de danse et de musique populaire chinoises, organisé en 1953 par le Ministère de la Culture du Gouvernement Populaire Central. *Peintre :* Jin Xuewen *Édition, impression et distribution :* Presses Xusheng de Shanghai, 8e éd. 1954 *Tirage :* 20 000–145 000 ; 1,60 yuan

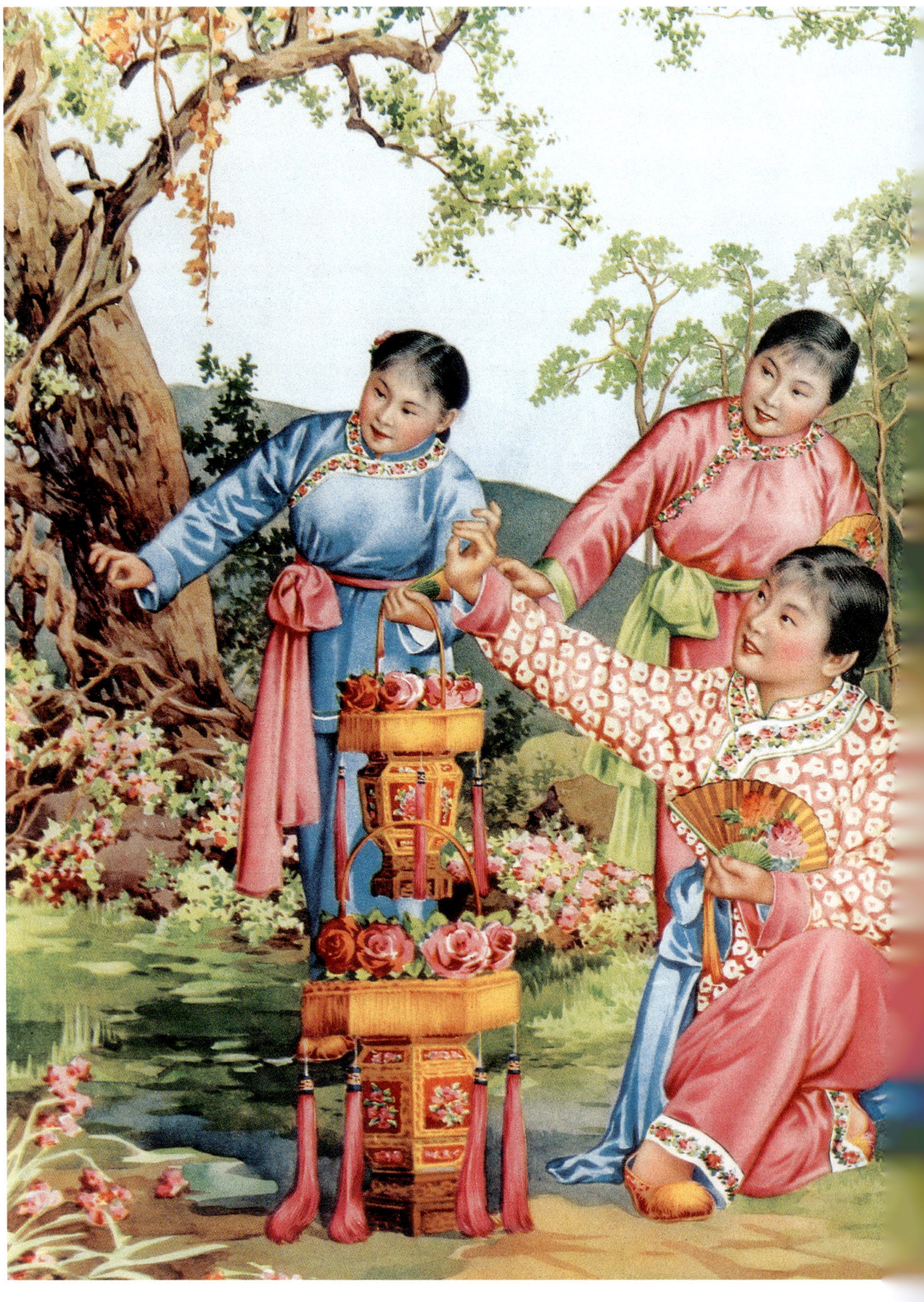

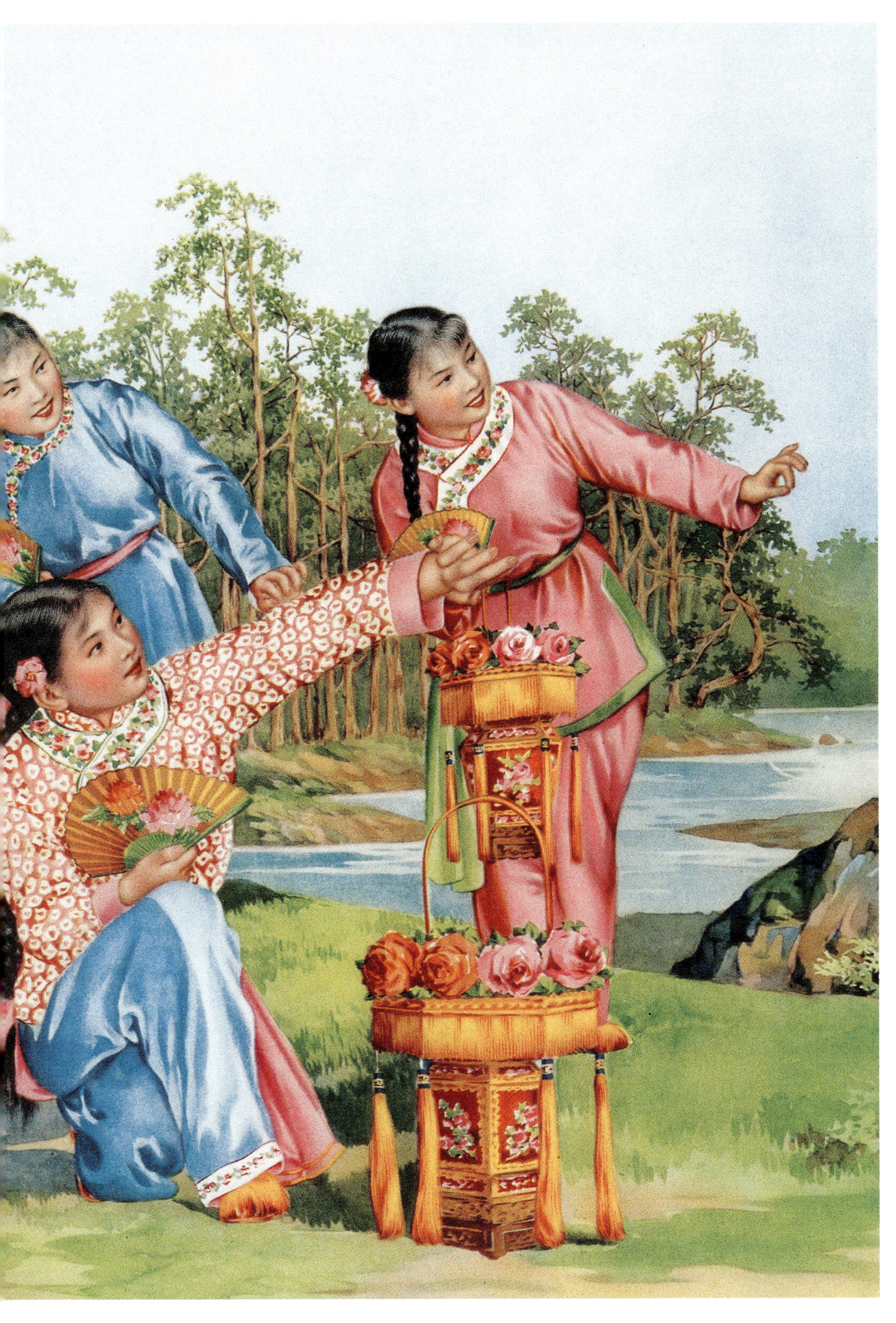

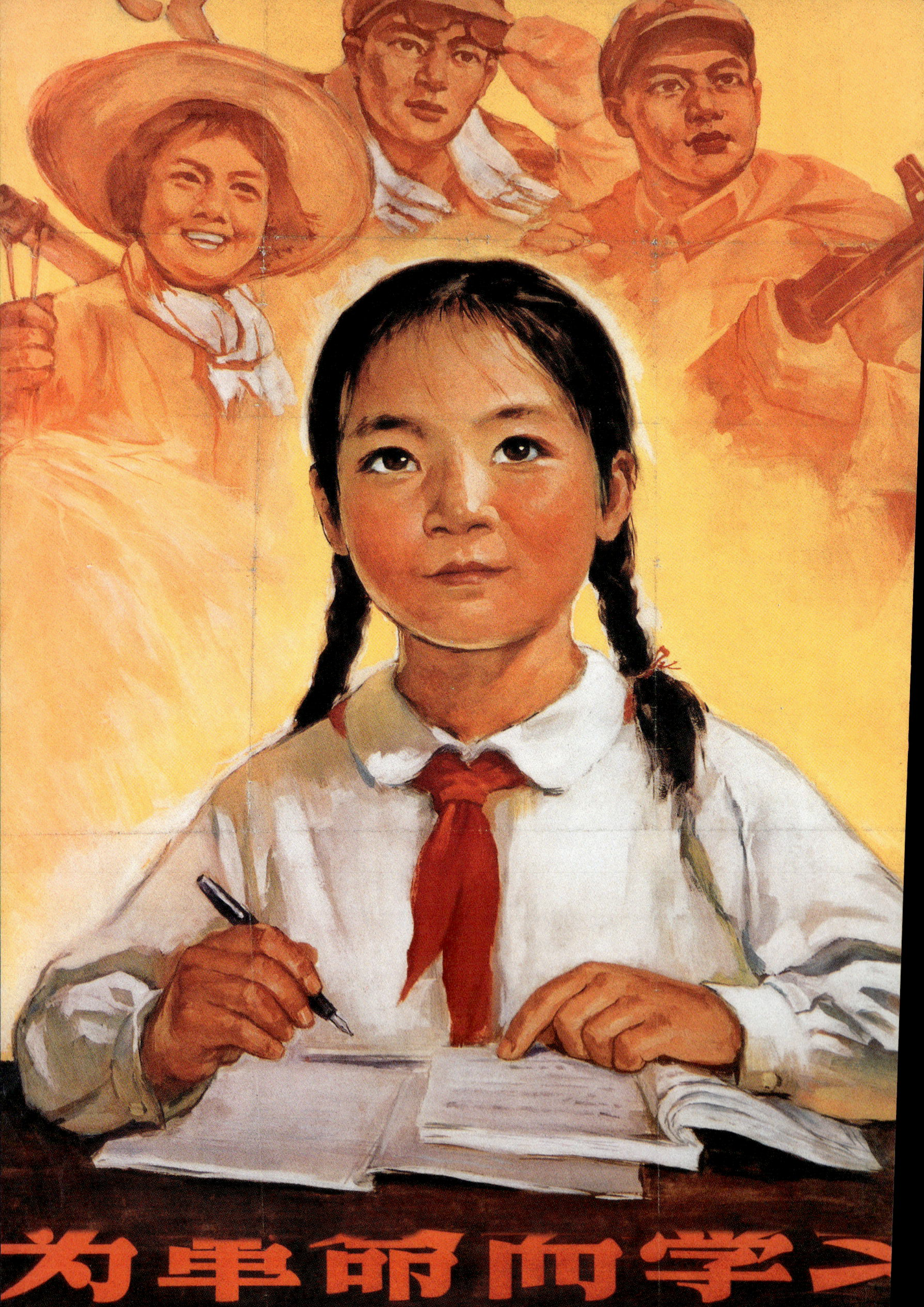
为革命而学

XXXIII

STUDY

DAS STUDIUM
L'ÉTUDE

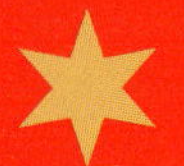

Page 488
Studying for the revolution *Artists:* Ying Fengxian and Zhou Anqi; Shanghai People's Art Publishing House, 1966 *Print run:* 25,000; 0.15 Yuan

Für die Revolution lernen *Gemalt von* Ying Fengxian und Zhou Anqi; Volkskunstverlag Shanghai, 1966 *Auflage:* 25 000; 0,15 Yuan

Faites des études dans l'intérêt de la révolution *Peintres :* Ying Fengxian et Zhou Anqi ; Éditions Populaires d'Art de Shanghai, 1996 *Tirage :* 25 000 ; 0,15 yuan

"We can learn what we did not know. We are not only good at destroying the old world, we are also good at building the new."

Wir sind imstande, das zu erlernen, was wir vorerst nicht wissen. Wir verstehen es nicht nur, die alte Welt zu zerstören, sondern wir werden es auch verstehen, eine neue aufzubauen. ✶ Nous pouvons apprendre tout ce que nous ne savons pas. Nous ne sommes pas seulement bons à détruire le monde ancien, nous sommes également bons à construire un monde nouveau.

Listen to Chairman Mao and be a good student of Chairman Mao *Artist:* Liu Wenxi; Shanghai People's Art Publishing House, 1965; 0.15 Yuan

Auf den Vorsitzenden Mao hören und guter Schüler des Vorsitzenden Mao sein *Gemalt von* Liu Wenxi; Volkskunstverlag Shanghai, 1965; 0,15 Yuan

Écoutons le président Mao et soyons de bons élèves du président Mao *Peintre :* Liu Wenxi ; Éditions Populaires d'Art de Shanghai, 1965 ; 0,15 yuan

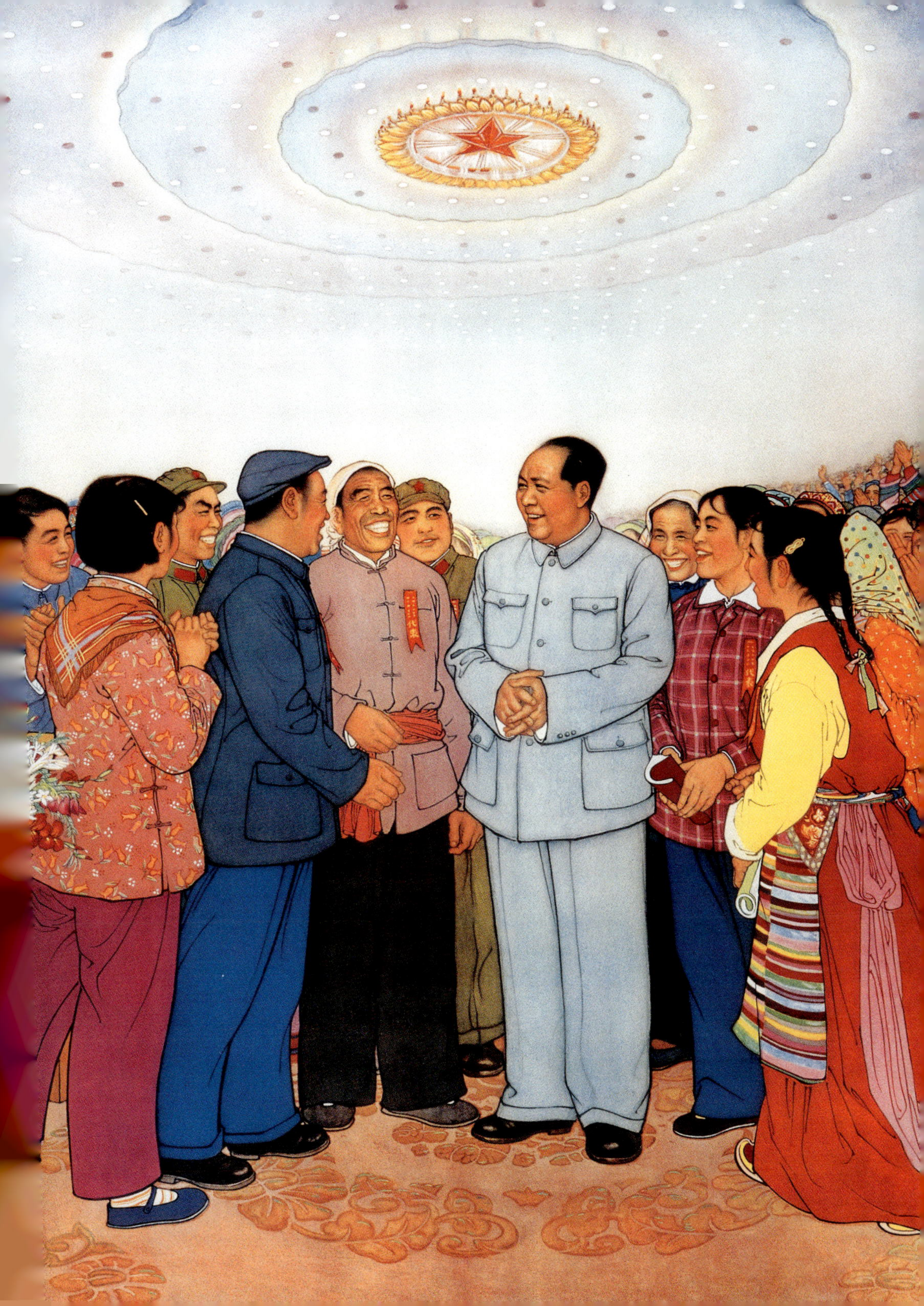
代表

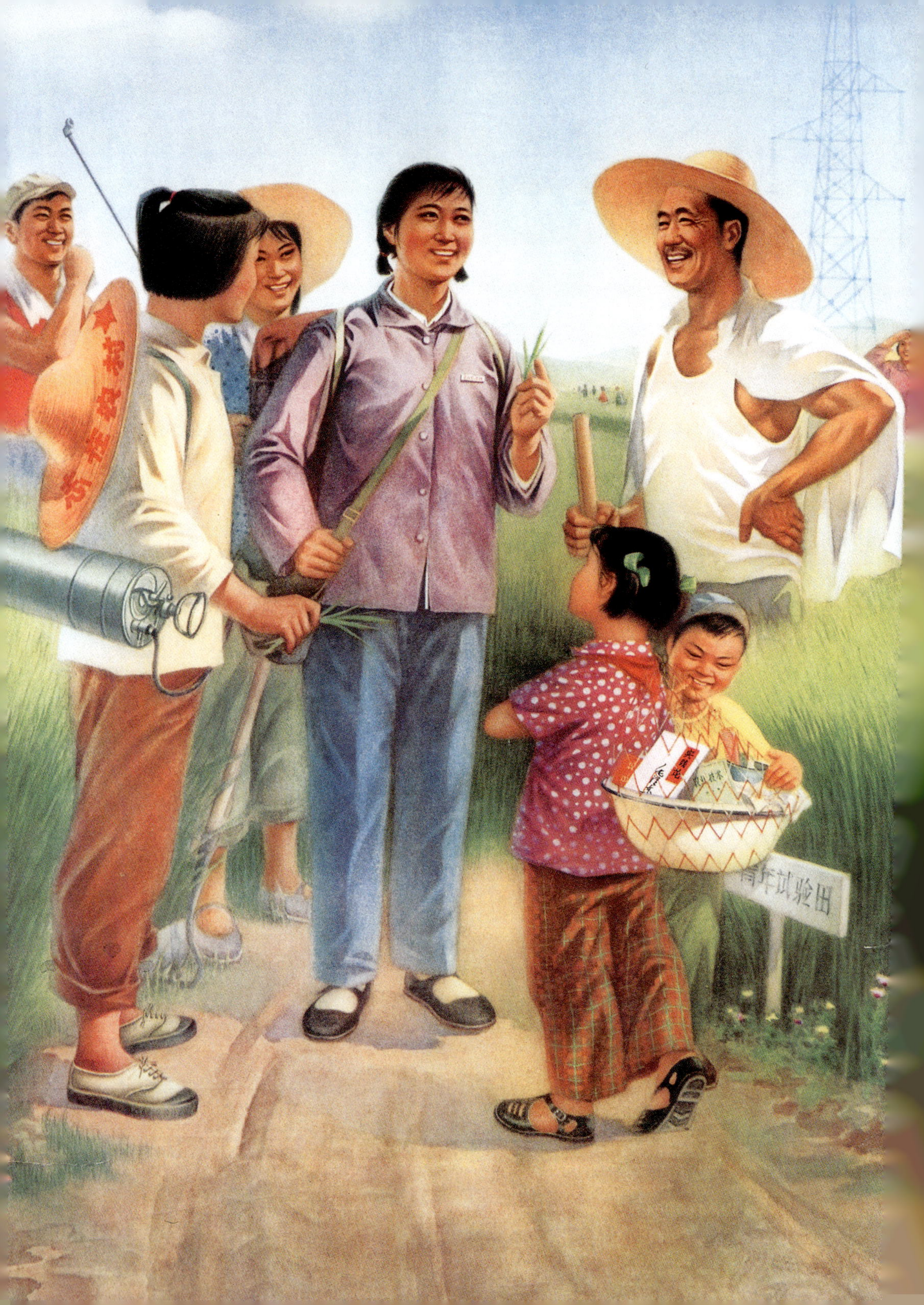
实践论
产试验田

Our student has come home
Straw hat, left: Make the ideal reality by working the land *Sign, bottom right:* Young people's experimental field *Artist:* Zhu Yan; Helongjiang People's Publishing House, 1974 *Print run:* 400,000; 0.14 Yuan

Unsere Studentin ist zurückgekehrt *Strohhut Links:* Das Ideal beim Einsatz auf dem Land verwirklichen *Schildchen Rechts:* Versuchsfeld der Jugend *Gemalt von* Zhu Yan; Volksverlag Helongjiang, 1974 *Auflage:* 400 000; 0,14 Yuan

Notre étudiante est de retour
Chapeau de paille, À gauche : Réalisons notre idéal en travaillant à la campagne *Panonceau, À droite :* Champ expérimental de la jeunesse *Peintre :* Zhu Yan ; Éditions Populaires d'Helongjian, 1974 *Tirage :* 400 000 ; 0,14 yuan

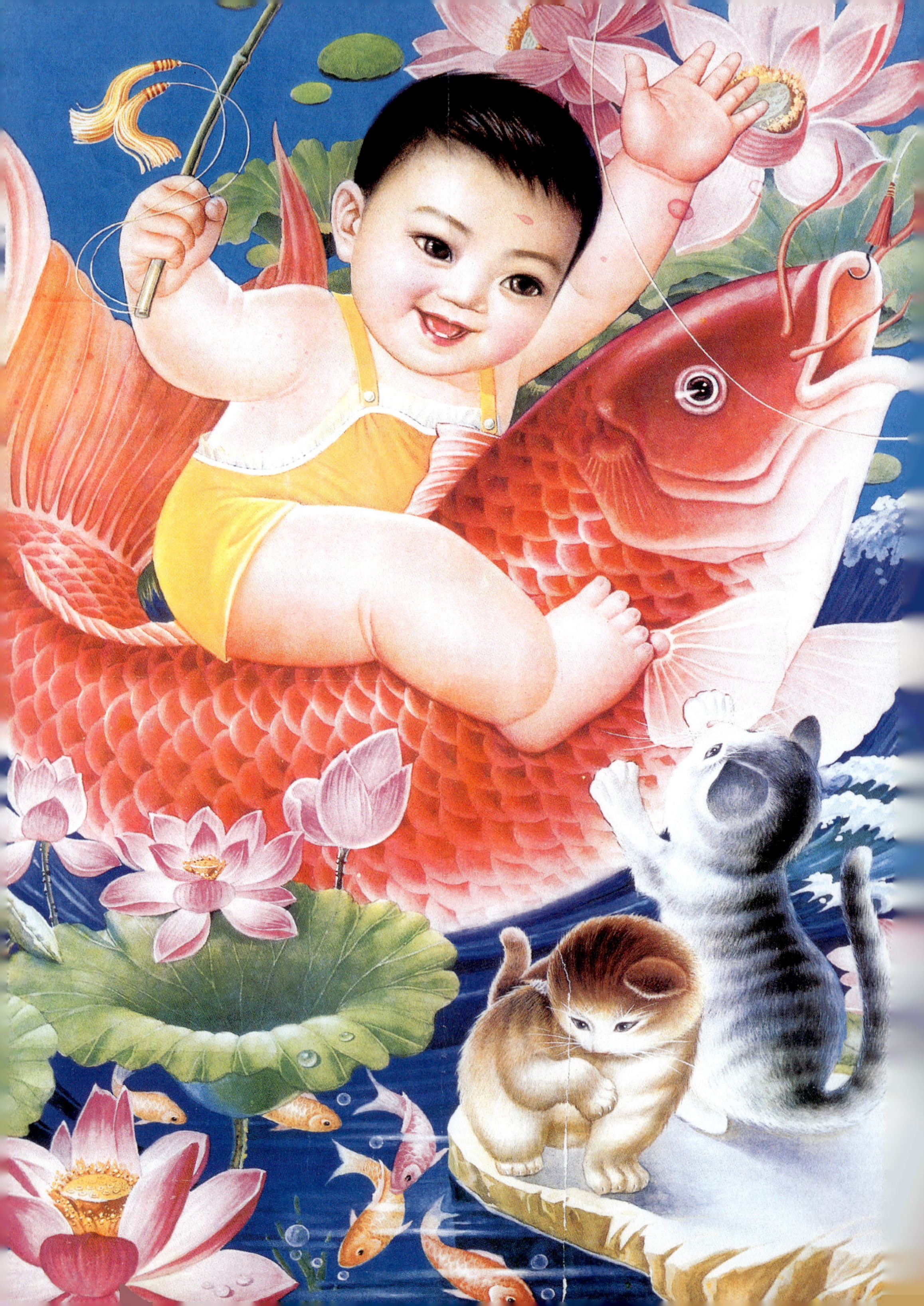

NEW YEAR

NEUJAHR
LE NOUVEL AN

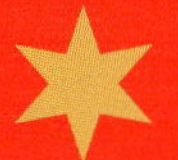

Page 494

All families enjoy sufficient resources* *Artist:* Peng Haiqing; Shanghai People's Art Publishing House, 1987 *Print run:* 235,000; 0.28 Yuan
* The Chinese word for "fish" (yu) is phonetically identical to the word for "abundance." It is therefore an ancient custom to depict images of fish and boys–symbols of an abundance of supplies and/or offspring–on New Year's greetings.

Jede Familie freut sich über ausreichende Versorgung* *Gemalt von* Peng Haiqing; Volkskunstverlag Shanghai, 1987 *Auflage:* 235 000; 0,28 Yuan
* Das chinesische Wort für „Fisch" (yu) ist phonetisch mit dem Wort „überschüssig" identisch. Deshalb ist es ein alter Brauch, Fische und Knaben – als Symbole für Überschuss in der Versorgung, bzw. für den Wunsch von Nachwuchs – auf Neujahrsbildern abzubilden.

Chaque famille se réjouit d'avoir des ressources suffisantes* *Peintre :* Peng Haiqing ; Éditions Populaires d'Art de Shanghai, 1987 *Tirage :* 235 000 ; 0,28 yuan
* Le mot chinois pour « poisson » (yu) est phonétiquement identique à celui qui signifie « surplus ». De là vient la vieille coutume selon laquelle on représente sur les images de Nouvel An des poissons et des petits garçons, symboles de profusion des denrées et de désir de progéniture.

Lotus flowers and mandarin ducks *Artist:* Lu Zezhi; Changchun Art Publishing House, 1958 *Print run:* 285,000; 0.13 Yuan

Lotosblumen und Mandarinenten *Gemalt von* Lu Zezhi; Kunstverlag Changchun, 1958 *Auflage:* 285 000; 0,13 Yuan

Fleurs de lotus et canards mandarins *Peintre :* Lu Zezhi; Éditions d'Art de Changchun, 1958 *Tirage :* 285 000 ; 0,13 yuan

Pages 498–499

The sun rises in the eastern sky and hundreds of birds sing in harmony *Artist:* Jiao Yesong; Shanghai People's Art Publishing House, 1st edn 1960, 2nd edn 1960 *Print run:* 10,001–80,000; 0.12 Yuan

Die Sonne steigt am östlichen Himmel auf und Hunderte von Vögeln singen harmonisch *Gemalt von* Jiao Yesong; Volkskunstverlag Shanghai, 1. Aufl. 1960, 2. Aufl. 1960 *Auflage:* 10 001–80 000; 0,12 Yuan

Le soleil monte dans le ciel de l'Est et des centaines d'oiseaux chantent en harmonie *Peintre :* Jiao Yesong ; Éditions Populaires d'Art de Shanghai, 1ère éd. 1960, 2e éd. 1960 *Tirage :* 10 001–80 000 ; 0,12 yuan

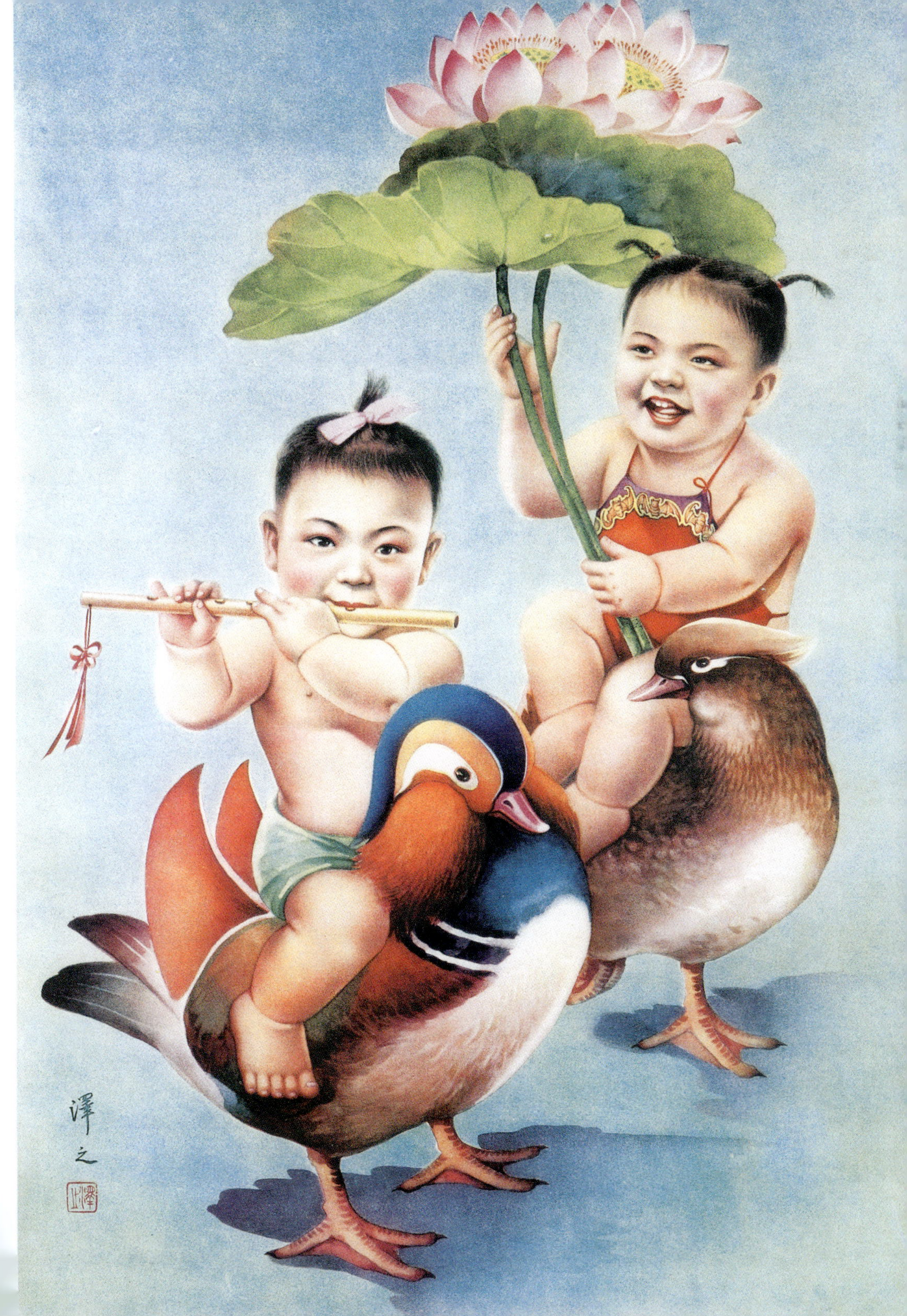
澤之

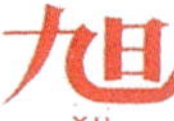
旭
XU
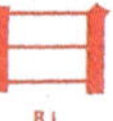
日
RI
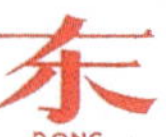
东
DONG
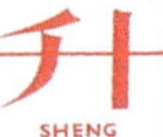
升
SHENG

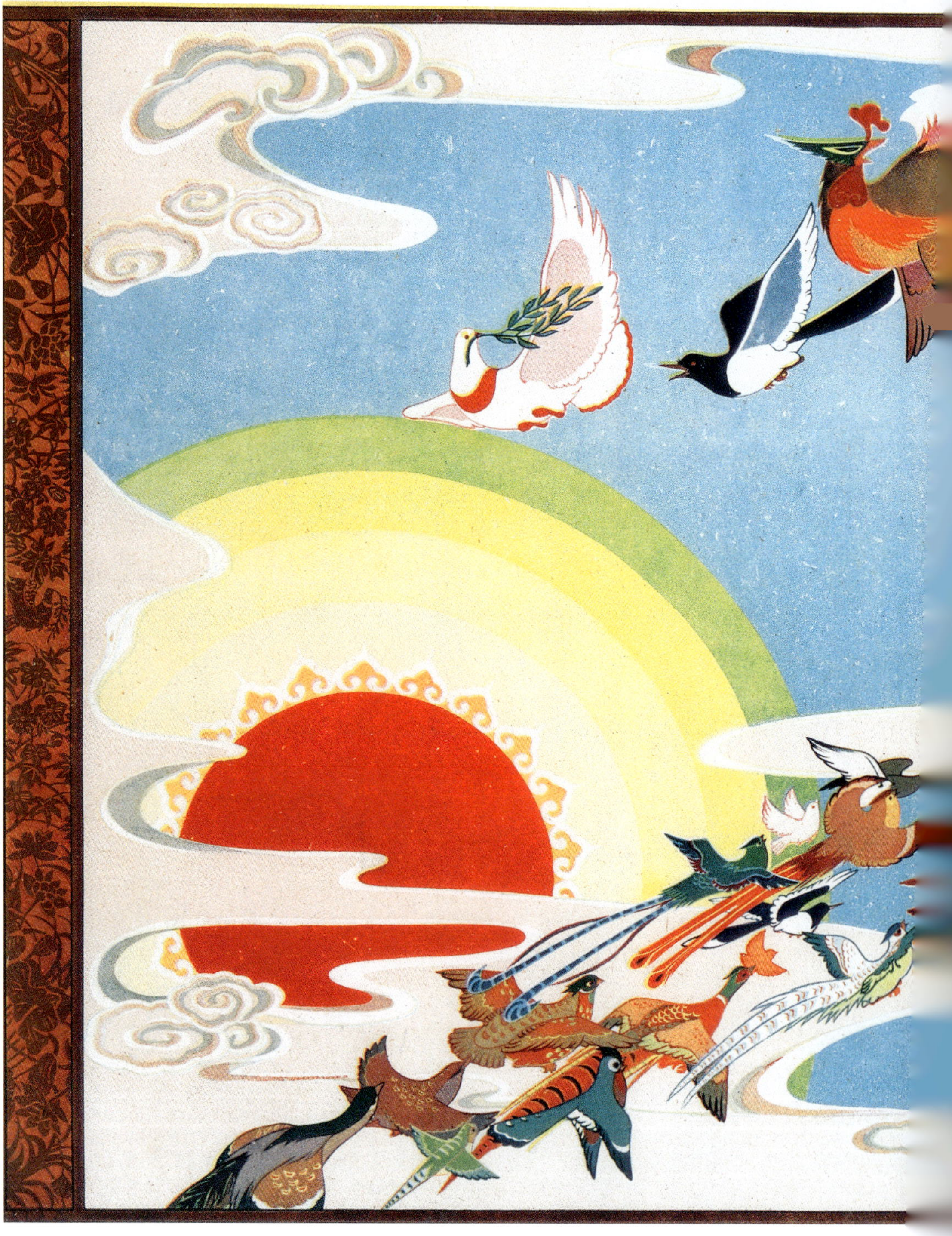

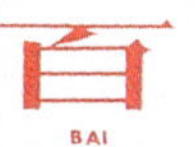

BAI

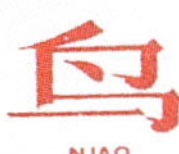

NIAO

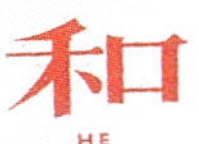

HE

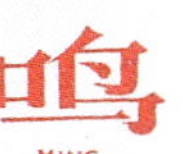

MING

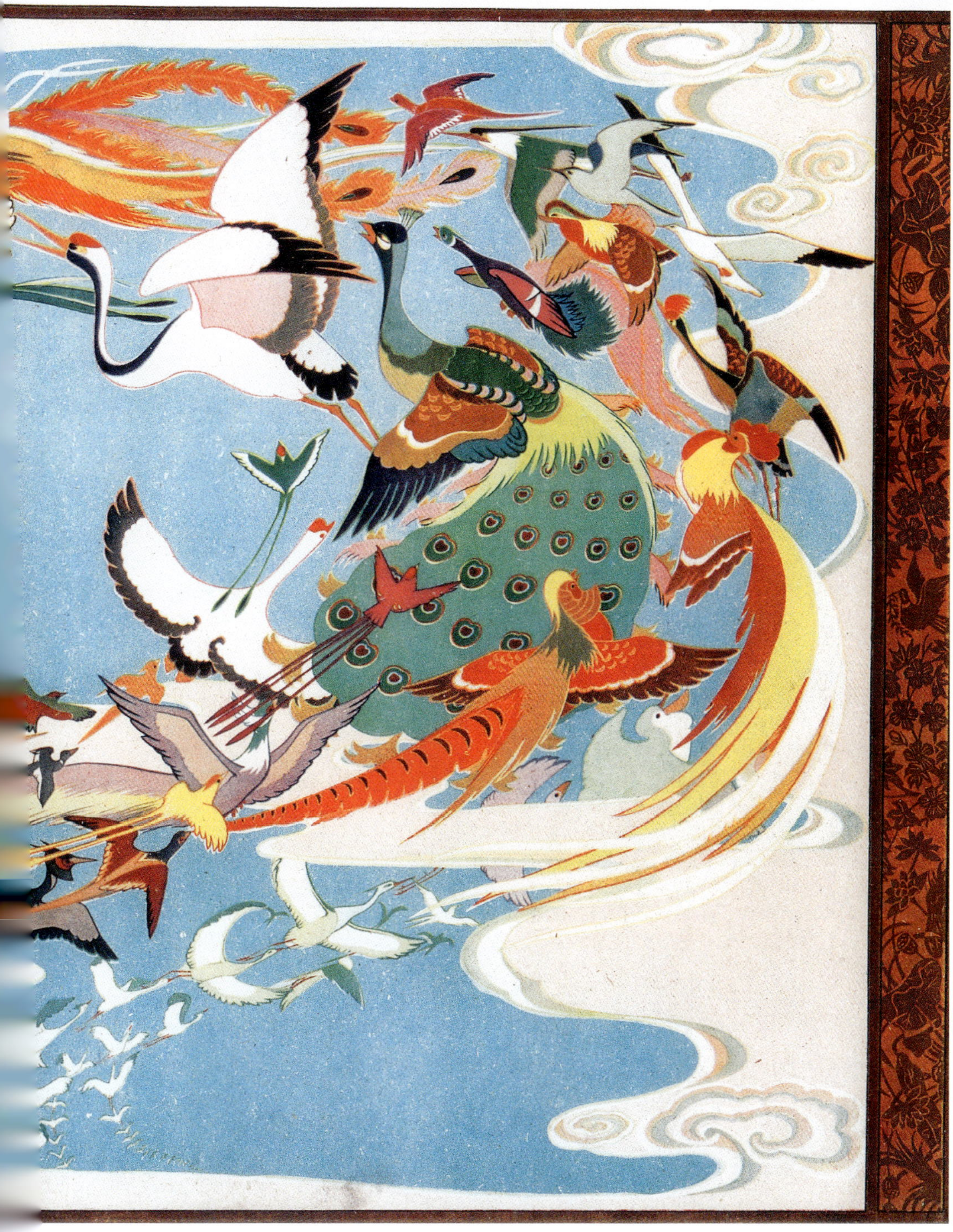

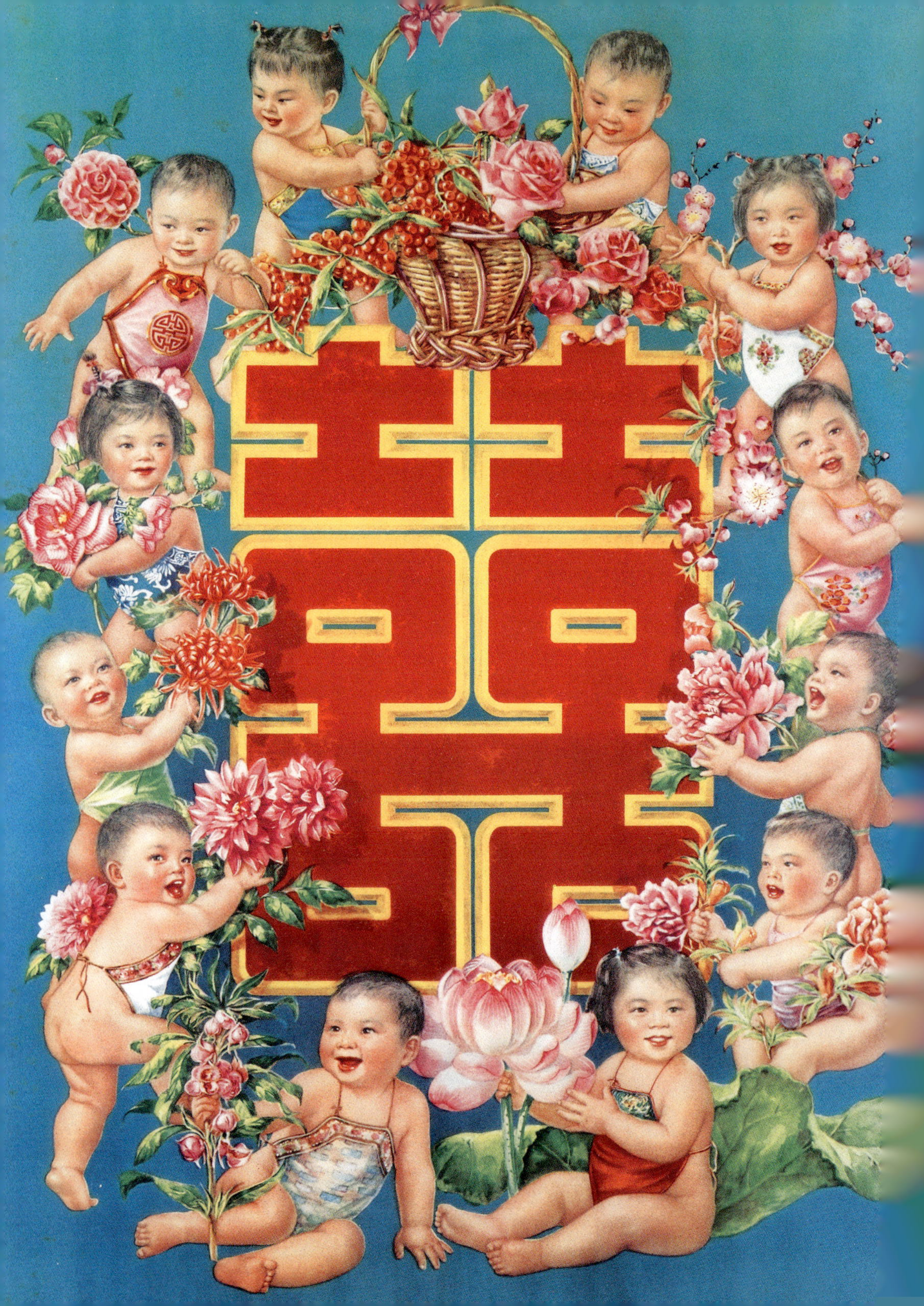
囍

Opposite
Chinese Rose *Large Chinese character:* Happiness *Artist:* Sheng Leitian; *Published by:* Shanghai People's Art Publishing House, 1st edn 1962, 2nd edn 1962 *Print run:* 100,094–200,091; 0.18 Yuan

Chinesische Rose *Das große Zeichen im Bild:* Glück *Gemalt von* Sheng Leitian *Herausgeber:* Volkskunstverlag Shanghai, 1. Aufl. 1962, 2. Aufl. 1962 *Auflage:* 100 094–200 091; 0,18 Yuan

Rose de Chine *Grand signe au milieu de l'image :* Bonheur *Peintre :* Sheng Leitian *Éditeur :* Éditions Populaires d'Art de Shanghai, 1ère éd. 1962, 2e éd. 1962 *Tirage :* 100 094–200 091 ; 0,18 yuan

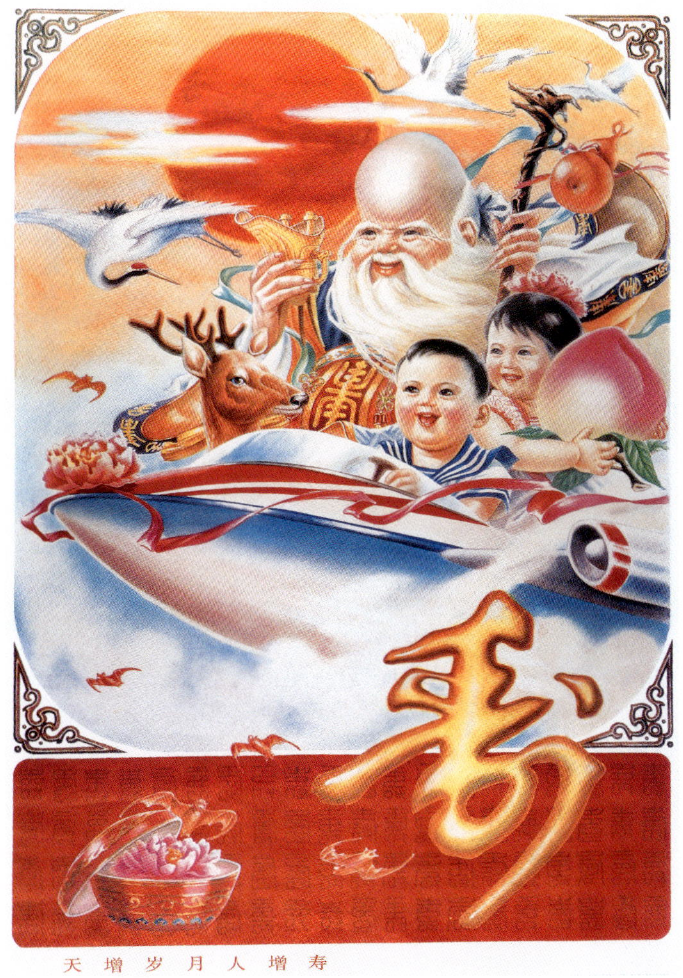

The heavens are enriched by time and man by age *Bottom right:* Long life* *Artist:* Chen Nailiang; Shanghai People's Sports Publishing House, 1989; 0.50 Yuan
* The male figure in the picture is the god of longevity.

Der Himmel wird durch die Zeit und der Mensch durch das Alter bereichert *Rechts unten:* Langes Leben* *Gemalt von* Chen Nailiang; Volkssportverlag Shanghai, 1989; 0,50 Yuan
* Der Mann im Bild ist der Gott der Langlebigkeit.

Le ciel est enrichi par le temps, l'homme par l'âge *En bas à droite :* Longue vie* *Peintre :* Chen Nailiang ; Éditions Populaires Sportives de Shanghai, 1989 ; 0,50 yuan
* Le vieil homme est le dieu de la longévité.

紅花处处开

HONG HUA CHU CHU KAI

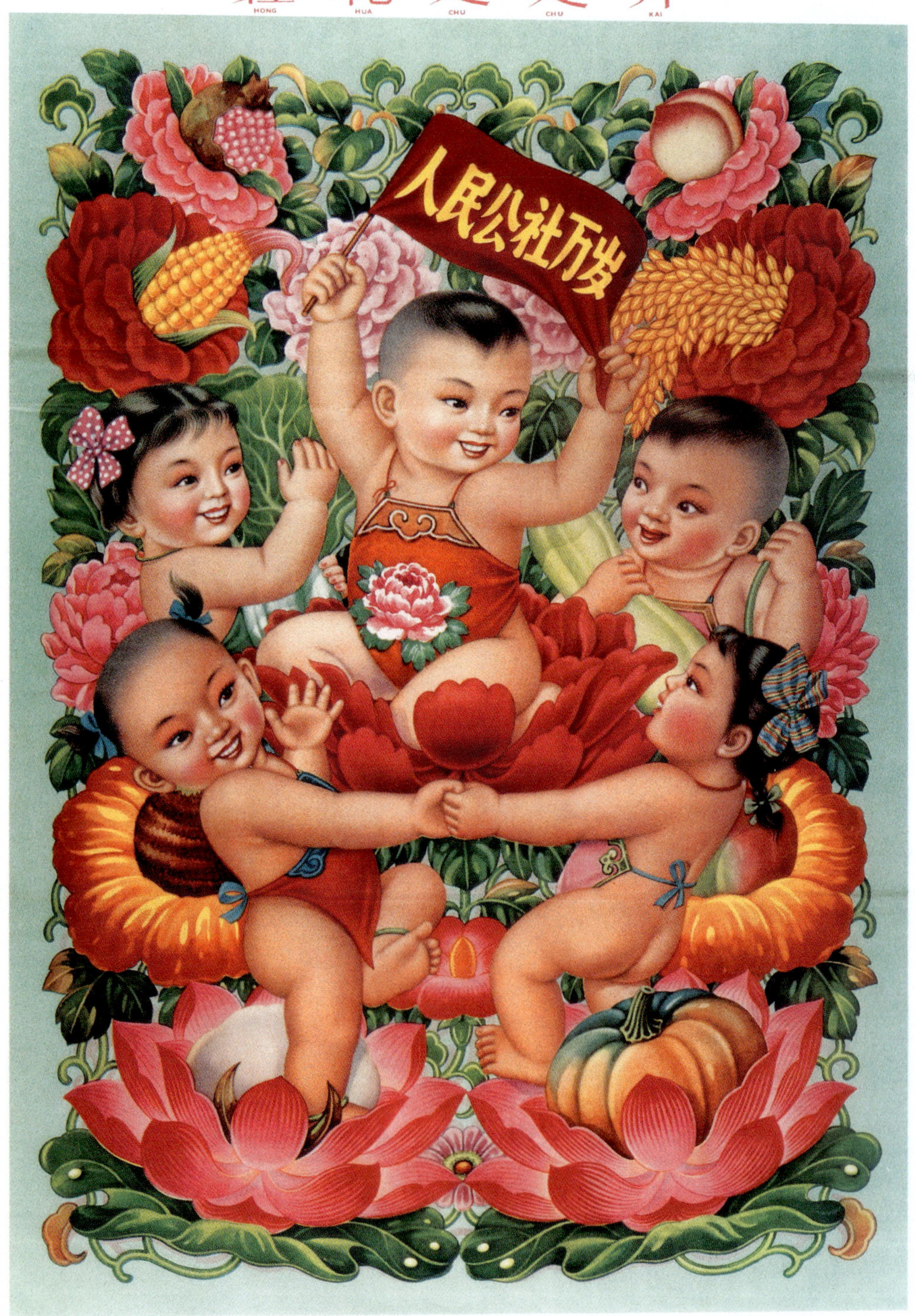

Opposite
Red flowers blossom everywhere *Small flag in the picture:* Long live the People's Commune *Artist:* Yang Furu; Shanghai People's Art Publishing House, 1st edn 1960, 2nd edn 1962; 0.18 Yuan

Rote Blumen blühen überall *Fähnchen im Bild:* Es lebe die Volkskommune *Gemalt von* Yang Furu; Volkskunstverlag Shanghai, 1. Aufl. 1960, 2. Aufl. 1962; 0,18 Yuan

Les fleurs rouges fleurissent partout *Petit drapeau :* Vive la Commune populaire *Peintre :* Yang Furu ; Éditions Populaires d'Art de Shanghai, 1ère éd. 1960, 2e éd. 1962 ; 0,18 yuan

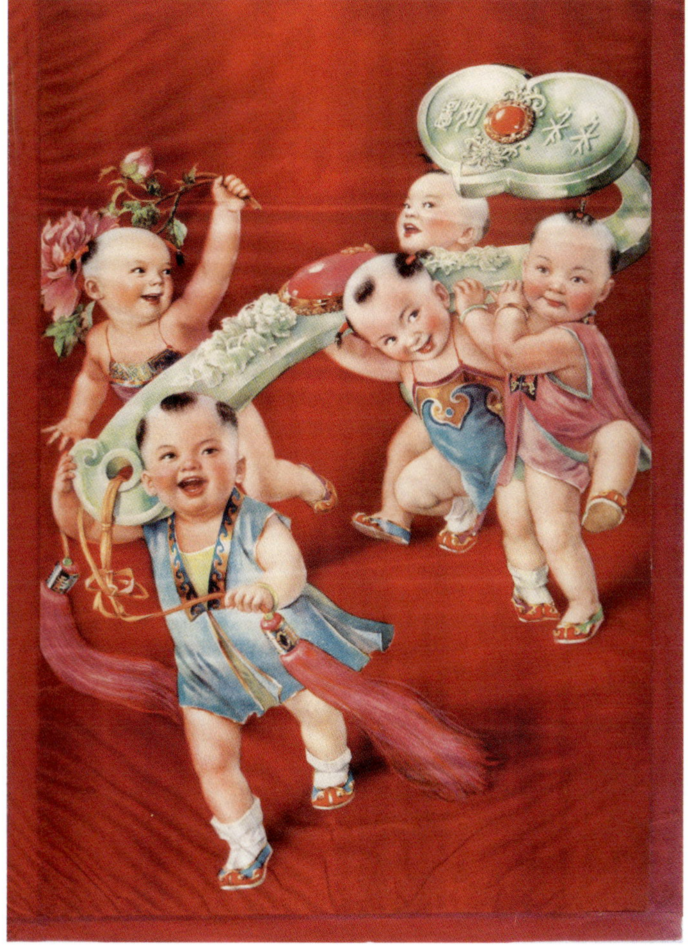

The picture shows a "Ruyi" good luck charm, usually made of jade, ivory or high-grade wood. The Ruyi characters (every wish fulfilled) can be seen on the heart-shaped top piece.

Dargestellt ist der Glücksbringer „Ruyi", meistens aus Jade, Elfenbein oder Edelholz gefertigt. Auf dem herzförmigen Kopf sind die Zeichen Ruyi (Erfüllung aller Wünsche) zu erkennen.

Il s'agit d'une représentation du « Ruyi », porte-bonheur fait le plus souvent de jade, d'ivoire ou de bois précieux. On peut voir sur la tête en forme de cœur les caractères signifiant Ruyi (réalisation de tous les désirs).

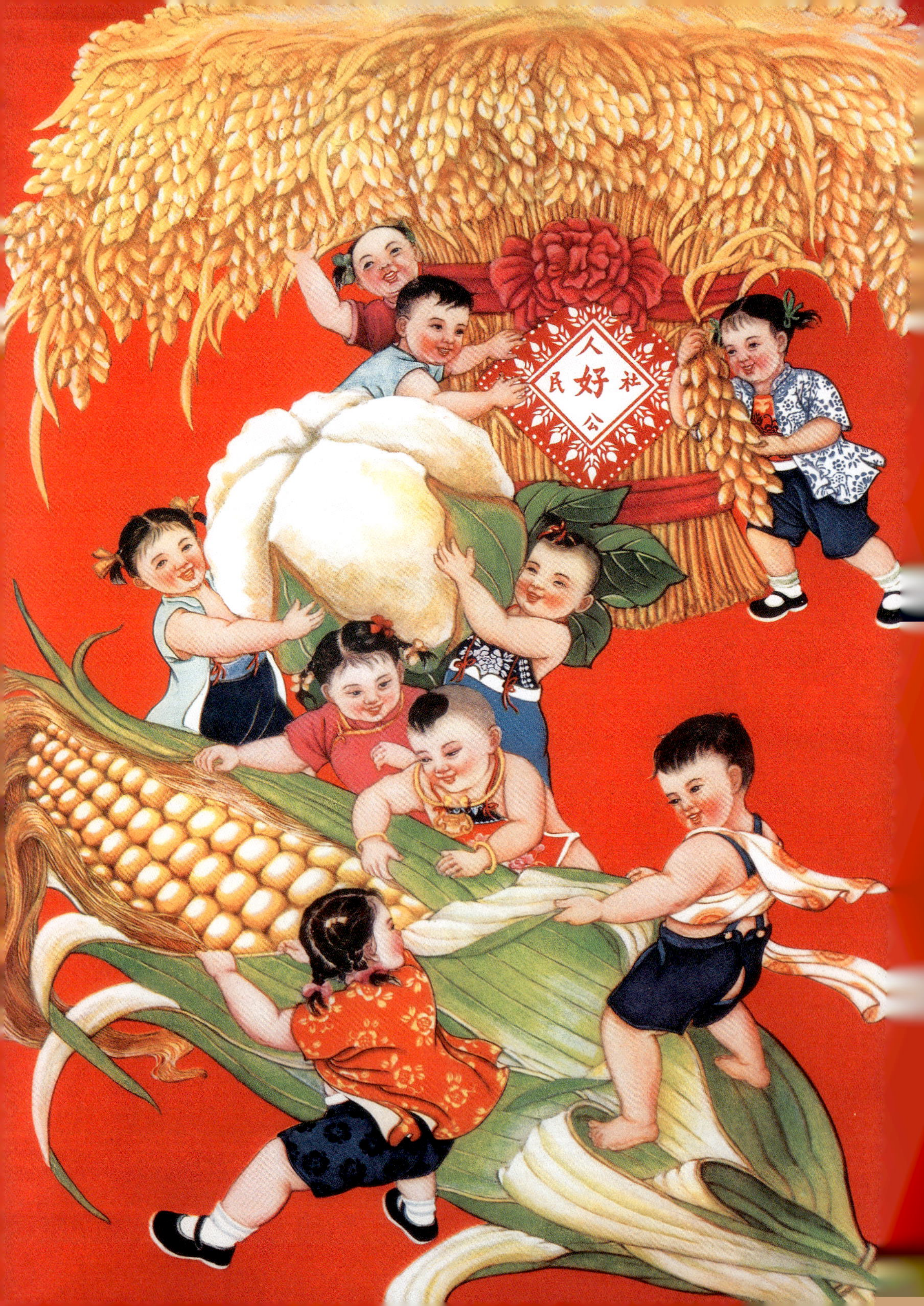
人民公社好

Opposite
Rejoicing at the plentiful harvest *On sheaf of rice:* The People's Commune is good *Artists:* Chen Gupin and Chen Huiguan; Liaoning Art Publishing House, 1st edn 1959, 4th edn 1961 *Print run:* 100,001–550,000; 0.12 Yuan

Freude bei der reichen Ernte *Am Reisbündel*: Die Volkskommune ist gut *Gemalt von* Chen Gupin und Chen Huiguan; Kunstverlag Liaoning, 1. Aufl. 1959, 4. Aufl. 1961 *Auflage:* 100 001–550 000; 0,12 Yuan

Le plaisir d'une récolte abondante *Sur la botte de riz :* La Commune populaire, c'est bien *Peintres :* Chen Gupin et Chen Huiguan ; Éditions d'Art du Liaoning, 1ère éd. 1959, 4e éd. 1961 *Tirage :* 100 001–550 000 ; 0,12 yuan

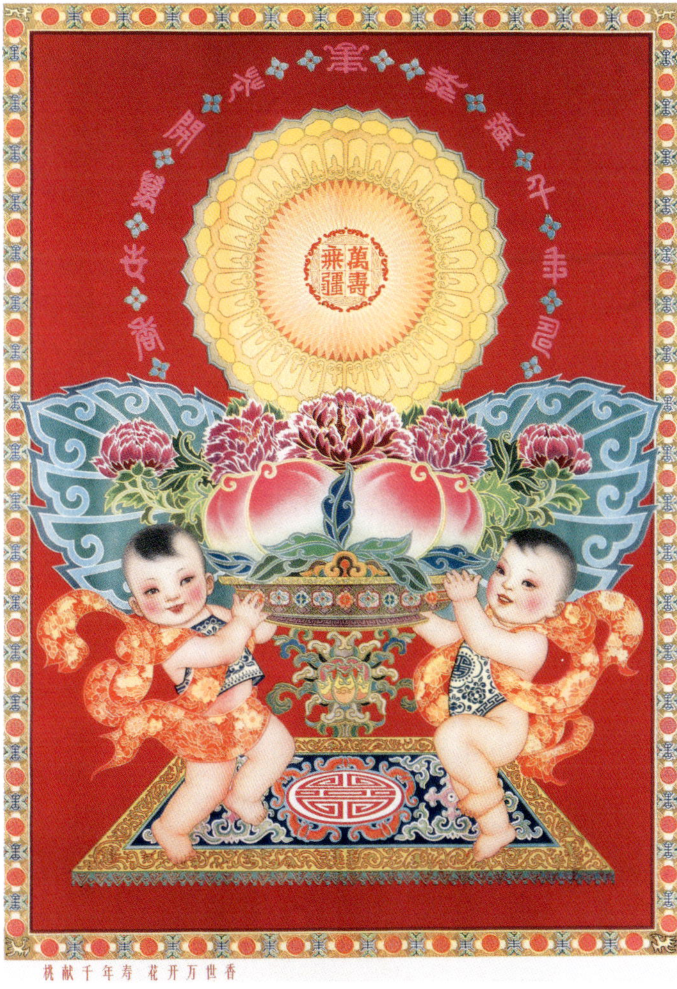

Peaches bring a long life, flowers give out eternal fragrance *In central circle:* Long life *Artist:* Jiang Nanchun; Shanghai People's Art Publishing House, 1962 *Print run:* 100,000; 0.18 Yuan

Pfirsiche bringen ein langes Leben, Blumen spenden ewige Düfte *Im mittigen Kreis*: Langes Leben *Gemalt von* Jiang Nanchun; Volkskunstverlag Shanghai, 1962 *Auflage:* 100 000; 0,18 Yuan

Les pêches prodiguent la longévité, les fleurs des parfums éternels *Cercle du milieu :* Longue vie *Peinture :* Jiang Nanchun ; Éditions Populaires d'Art de Shanghai, 1962 *Tirage :* 100 000 ; 0,18 yuan

CHINA IN THE 20th & 21st CENTURIES

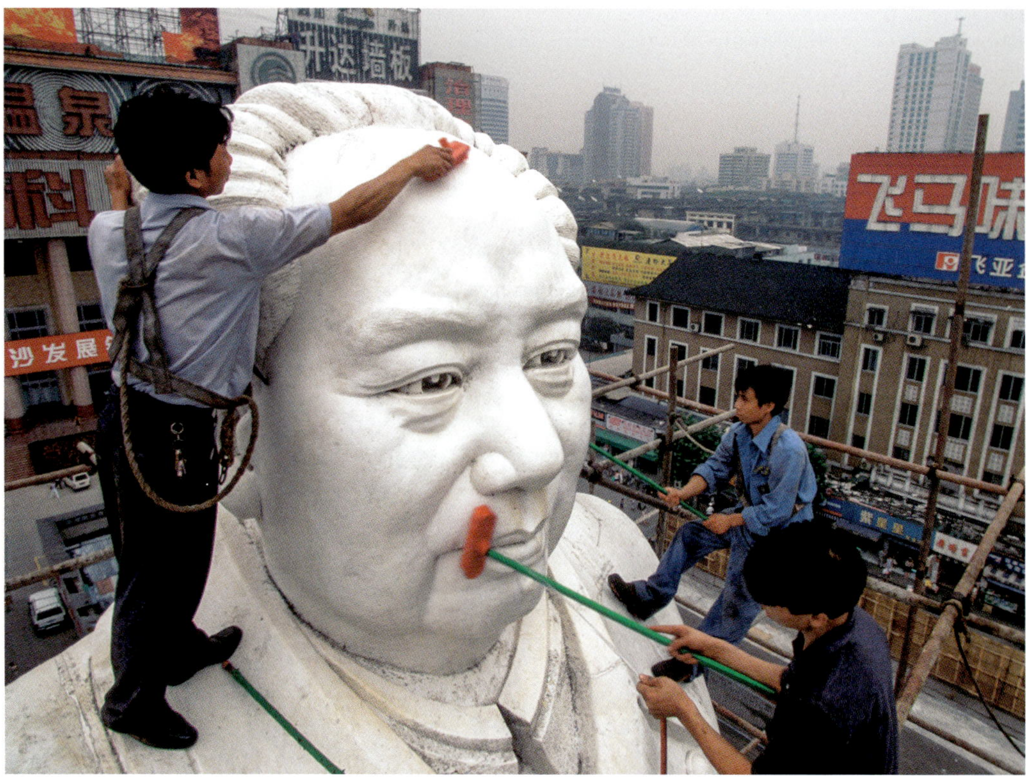

China's largest statue of Mao gets a spring-clean to mark the 50th anniversary of the People's Republic of China. Chengdur, 1999

Für den 50. Jahrestag der Volksrepublik China wird die größte Mao-Statue Chinas gereingt. Chengdur, 1999

Nettoyage de la plus grande statue de Mao à l'occasion du 50e anniversaire de la République Populaire de Chine. Chengdur, 1999

★ **1900** The Boxer Rebellion (the Boxers, a movement bitterly hostile to Westerners, are suppressed by Japanese and allied colonial troops).
★ **1904** The Russian advance into north-eastern China sparks the outbreak of the Russo-Japanese War (1904–05).
In Tokyo Sun Yat-sen founds the Revolutionary Alliance, forerunner of the Nationalist Party (aka Kuomintang or KMT).
★ **1911** Tibet and Mongolia declare independence. In Nanking, Sun Yat-sen proclaims the new republic.
★ **1912** Manchu emperor Yuan Tong abdicates on 12 February.
Yuan Shikai is sworn in as President of the Republic and Beijing becomes the seat of government.
★ **1913** Yuan Shikai outlaws the Kuomintang.
★ **1914** Outbreak of World War I (1914–18). Japan occupies German territory in Shandong. Central and western Tibet remain under British control.
★ **1915** Outer Mongolia becomes a Russian protectorate.
In its "21 Demands" on China, Japan calls for the area under its control to be extended as far as the Yangtze River.
★ **1916** On 1 January Yuan Shikai proclaims a new dynasty with himself as Emperor. In subsequent years there is no de facto central government

control over China as a whole. Instead, hundreds of warlords form constantly shifting alliances.
✱ **1917** October Revolution in Russia.
China enters World War I on the side of the Allies.
✱ **1919** The Treaty of Versailles awards Germany's former Chinese territory to Japan.
✱ **1921** The Chinese Communist Party (CCP) is founded in Shanghai.
In Canton a Nationalist government is formed under Sun Yat-sen's leadership.
✱ **1922** The CCP states its intent to establish a dictatorship of workers and peasants (creating the fundamental difference between the Maoism that would develop later and the Stalinist version of Communism).
Chiang Kai-shek is sent to Russia as a political and military adviser.
✱ **1923** Agreement between the Soviet Union and Sun Yat-sen to form an alliance between the KMT and the CCP.
Zhou Enlai becomes the CCP's first political commissar.
✱ **1925** Sun Yat-sen dies on 12 March.
Chiang Kai-shek takes over the leadership of the KMT. Worker and student unrest in Shanghai and Guangzhou.
✱ **1926** Start of Chiang Kai-shek's northern expedition against the warlords of central and northern China.
✱ **1927** Chiang Kai-shek breaks with the CCP and forms his own government in Nanking.
✱ **1928** Chiang Kai-shek organizes a second military expedition to northern China and takes over Beijing. Red Army founded in Hunan.
✱ **1929** Deng Xiaoping leads a rebellion against Chiang Kai-shek in southern China.
✱ **1930** Mao Zedong and others found the Jiangxi Soviet.
✱ **1931** The Japanese occupy Manchuria.
✱ **1932** The Japanese seize Shanghai and advance into northern China.
✱ **1934** The Japanese control the whole of Manchuria. The puppet state of Manchukuo is established with Pu Yi as the "Last Emperor."
The People's Liberation Army escapes Chiang Kai-shek's campaign to annihilate it. Beginning of Mao Zedong's "Long March" (1934–35).
The official CCP newspaper uses the term "Maoism" for the first time.
✱ **1936** Chiang Kai-shek is captured in Xian. KMT and CCP declare a ceasefire.
✱ **1937** On 7 July the Japanese attack Chinese troops on the Marco Polo Bridge. Outbreak of the Sino-Japanese War (1937–45).
✱ **1939** Beginning of World War II (1939–45). The Japanese occupy the island of Hainan.
✱ **1940** The Japanese occupy Vietnam.
Wang Jingwei forms a puppet administration in Nanking, dependent from Japan.
✱ **1941** The Soviet Union and Japan sign a non-aggression pact.
On 7 December the Japanese attack Pearl Harbor. The USA enters World War II.
✱ **1942** The Japanese occupy the whole of south-east Asia, cutting off the route through Burma into China.
The USA and Great Britain relinquish their territorial rights in China.
✱ **1944** Japanese occupation spreads to Henan and south China.
✱ **1945** Japan surrenders on 14 August. At the Potsdam Conference Japan is compelled to return Taiwan to China. Taiwan is brought under KMT control.
The Soviet Union and Chiang Kai-shek's Nationalist government sign a treaty of friendship and alliance. A face-to-face meeting between Mao and Chiang Kai-shek proves fruitless. Outbreak of civil war (1945–49).
✱ **1946** The French bomb Haiphong, beginning Franco-Vietnamese hostilities.
The CCP and other delegates boycott a constituent national assembly convened by Chiang Kai-shek.
✱ **1947** Military successes for the KMT, whose forces take Yanan and Nanking. The communists advance into Manchuria.
Uprising in Taiwan against the Nationalist government.
✱ **1948** In Nanking Chiang Kai-shek is elected President of the Republic.
North China People's Government is formed.
✱ **1949** Major Communist offensive in south China. Beijing becomes the "northern capital."
On 1 October, Mao Zedong, chairman of the Chinese Communist Party, declares the People's Republic of China.
✱ **1950** Beginning of the Korean War (1950–53).
On 1 March Chiang Kai-shek becomes president of Taiwan. General MacArthur places Taiwan under US protection.
The Soviet Union and the People's Republic of China sign a "Treaty of Friendship, Alliance and Mutual Assistance."
Internal reorganization of the People's Republic of

China, including the introduction of laws giving equal rights to men and women, land reform and improvements in the education system.
✶ **1951** The People's Liberation Army invades Tibet.
✶ **1952** Beginning of the "five-anti" campaign (the first large-scale re-education campaign).
✶ **1953** Stalin dies on 5 March.
The First Five-Year Plan (1953–57) laid down the guidelines for the "transition to socialism" according to the Soviet model.
✶ **1954** France withdraws from Indochina after its defeat in Vietnam.
China and India sign a peaceful coexistence agreement.
Taiwan and the USA sign a mutual defence treaty.
Agriculture is collectivized within the framework of the "transition to socialism."
✶ **1956** De-Stalinization begins in the Soviet Union.
The last part-privatized industrial firm in the People's Republic of China passes to 100 per cent state ownership.
✶ **1957** The "Hundred Flowers Campaign" (so called after a phrase in a speech by Chairman Mao) criticizes the system. The Party reacts with the launch of a campaign against "Right deviationists."
✶ **1958** The 8th Party Congress launches the "Great Leap Forward" (1958–61) as the realization of the radical Maoist model of development.
Collective farms are merged into huge "people's communes," while between 20 and 30 million people starve to death.
✶ **1959** Uprising in Tibet; the Dalai Lama flees to India.
Vice-Chairman of the Communist Party Liu Shaoqui replaces Mao as State President; the Maoist models of the people's communes are virtually withdrawn.
✶ **1960** The Soviet Union cancels its economic aid program and recalls all its technical advisers from China.
✶ **1962** Chinese troops carry out attacks in the Assam and Kashmir regions along the border with India.
The Cuban missile crisis brings about a clear split between the Chinese and Soviet Communist Parties.
✶ **1964** US invasion of North Vietnam begins in April.
In October China explodes its first atomic bomb.
✶ **1965** A play entitled The Dismissal of Hai Rui from Office is seen as veiled criticism of Mao.
Mao removes several important party leaders from power.
✶ **1966** Beginning of the "Great Proletarian Cultural Revolution" (1966–76). The Central Committee resolution launching the revolution calls for "struggle, criticism and change."
In calling the Red Guards into action Mao unleashes an avalanche. In the following months he reviews over 10 million Red Guards on Tiananmen Square.
✶ **1967** The first hydrogen bomb is detonated.
The Red Guards are disbanded. Mao supporters take power in Beijing.
By mid-1968 32 percent of members of the Politburo, 66 per cent of Central Committee members and 80 per cent of provincial Party secretaries have fallen victim to the purge.
✶ **1968** Officials are obliged to do manual work at the so-called "7th May cadre schools."
✶ **1969** Border skirmishes between China and the Soviet Union along the Ussury River.
The 9th Party Congress elects Lin Biao as Mao's successor.
✶ **1970** China joins the UN.
✶ **1971** Beginning of so-called "ping-pong diplomacy" between the USA and the People's Republic of China.
Taiwan's seat at the United Nations is taken over by the People's Republic of China.
An attempted coup against Mao Zedong led by Lin Biao is thwarted. Lin Biao's plane crashes over Mongolia.
✶ **1972** US President Richard Nixon visits China.
Zhou Enlai's more moderate policies gain ground.
✶ **1975** The 4th National People's Congress adopts a new constitution. Zhou Enlai promotes the modernization of agriculture, industry, national defence, and science and technology.
✶ **1976** Zhou Enlai dies on 8 January.
Mao Zedong dies on 9 September at the age of 82.
In October an alliance opposed to the Cultural Revolution takes control and arrests the "Gang of Four."
✶ **1977** Deng Xiaoping is rehabilitated and the Cultural Revolution declared officially at an end.
✶ **1978** The Central Committee endorses the process of reform initiated by Deng Xiaoping.
✶ **1979** Border conflict in Cambodia between invading Vietnamese forces and the People's Republic of China.
Full diplomatic relations established between the USA and China.

CHINA IN THE 20TH & 21ST CENTURIES

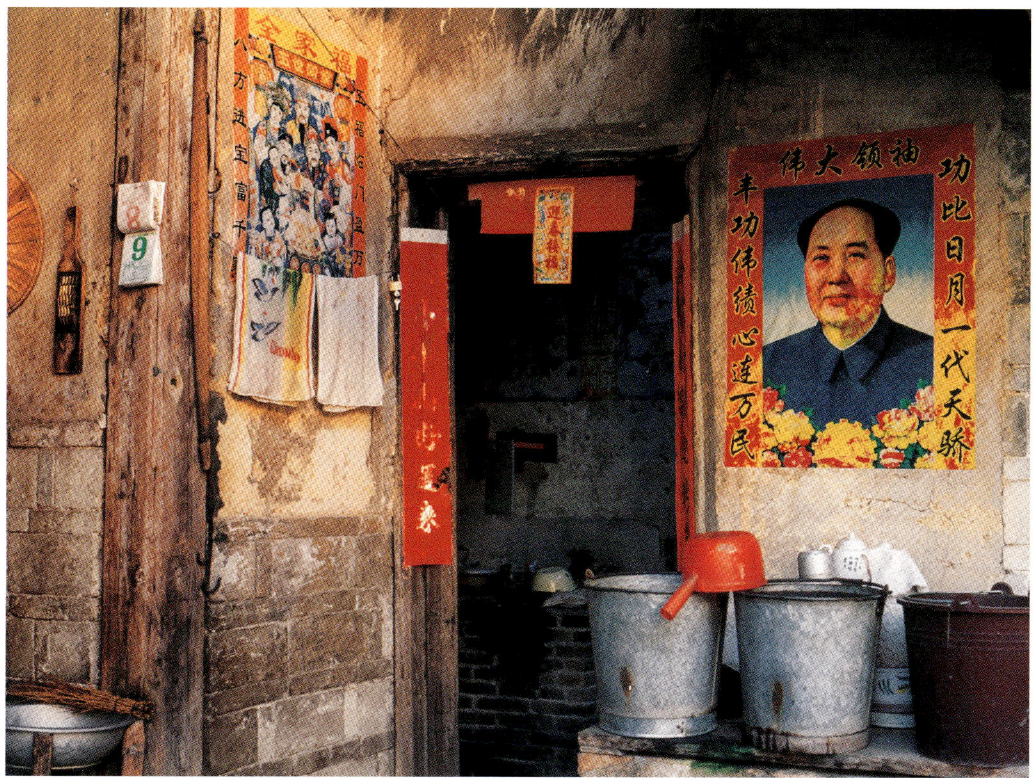

Portrait of Chairman Mao above the sink in a house in Fujian Province, 2000

Maoportrait über der Waschstelle eines Wohnhauses in der Provinz Fujian, 2000

Portrait de Mao au-dessus du lavoir d'une résidence dans la province du Fujian, 2000

★ **1980** Hua Guofeng is replaced as premier by Zhao Ziyang.
★ **1981** The members of the Gang of Four, including Mao's wife Jiang Qing (Chiang Chíing), are condemned to death (the sentences are commuted).
★ **1983** Diplomatic relations with India are resumed.
★ **1988** Yang Shangkun becomes head of state.
★ **1989** Fall of the Berlin Wall.
Unrest in Tibet.
First Sino-Soviet summit for 30 years.
The announcement of the death of Hu Yaobang on 15 April leads to mass demonstrations in Tiananmen Square. On the night of 3–4 June the authorities use extreme violence to clear the square.
Party chief Zhao Ziyang is ousted by Li Peng.
★ **1990** The state of emergency in Tibet is lifted on 1 May.
★ **1992** Chris Patten is appointed Governor of Hong Kong.
Deng Xiaoping introduces a campaign to continue economic reforms.
★ **1994** Underground atomic weapons tests.
★ **1995** In his Eight-Point Plan, Jiang Zemin presents the government with a "one-China policy" under which Taiwan would be regarded as part of China.
★ **1996** The Russian Federation and China agree to a Strategic Partnership for the 21st Century.

Five-nation agreement between Russia, China, Kazakhstan, Kyrgyzstan, and Tajikistan.

✶ **1997** Deng Xiaoping dies on 19 February; Jiang Zemin succeeds him as President.
On 1 July the British Crown Colony of Hong Kong is handed back to the People's Republic of China.
Uyghur separatists are involved in serious disturbances in Beijing and Xinjiang.

✶ **1998** State visit of US President Bill Clinton to the People's Republic of China.
Zhu Rongji is the new Prime Minister.
Government reorganization with the abolition of many commissions and ministries. Followers of the Falungong movement demonstrate in Beijing in support of religious freedom.

✶ **1999** NATO forces bomb the Chinese Embassy in Belgrade.
On 20 December the Portuguese colony of Macao is handed back to China.
The State Council ratifies the "Action Plan for Educational Vitalization Facing the 21st Century."

✶ **2001** A US reconnaissance plane collides with a Chinese fighter aircraft over the South China Sea.
The International Olympic Committee announces Beijing as the venue for the 2008 Olympics.

✶ **2002** 75th anniversary of the foundation of the People's Liberation Army.

✶ **2003** SARS (Severe Acute Respiratory Syndrome) epidemic in China.
Start of work on the bridge between Shanghai and Ningbo, at 36 km the longest in the world.
China's People's Congress elects Wen Jiabao (b. 1942) as the new head of government to succeed Jiang Zemin; the new President is Hu Jintao (b. 1942).

✶ **2004** For the first time since the communist revolution in 1949, the People's Republic guarantees the protection of private property in its constitution: "Legally acquired private property shall not be violated."
Some 800 million people, a good two-thirds of the population, live in the countryside. Their social conditions have deteriorated in spite of the ongoing economic boom.
Hundreds of thousands demonstrate for more democracy on 1 July, the 7th anniversary of the return of Hong Kong to China.

✶ **2005** Hu Jintao formally takes over the function of chairman of the Central State Military Commission from Jiang Zemin and thus unites the most important offices in the state in one person.

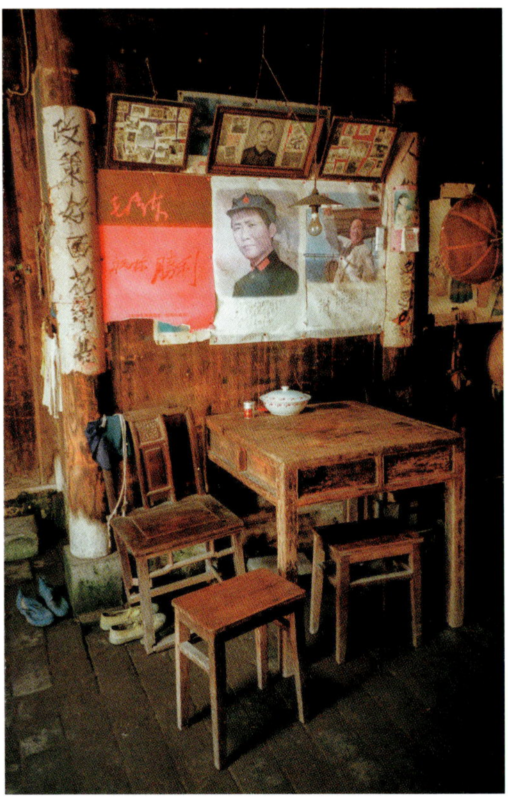

A portrait of Mao as a stern-looking young man hangs over the dining table in a workers' house in the town of Pingyao, 2000

Der strenge junge Mao hängt über einem Esstisch in einem Bauernhaus in der Stadt Pingyao, 2000

Le jeune Mao à l'allure sévère est accroché au-dessus de la table d'une ferme dans la ville de Pingyao, 2000

Data from the Sciamachy atmospheric sensor operated by the German Aerospace Centre (DLR) and from the satellite-based GOME provide evidence of a drastic increase in air pollution over China.

✶ **2006** After a construction period lasting 13 years, the Three Gorges Dam on the Yangzi Jiang begins operation. The controversial largest hydro-electric power-station in the world is intended to generate as much electricity as 15 to 20 nuclear plants.

Hu Jintao opens the 1142 km Tibet railway, a project of superlatives: over long stretches, the trains travel at an altitude of more than 4000 m.
✶ **2007** New labour law introduced after hundreds of men and boys were found working as slaves in brick factories.
China launches its first moon orbiter.
✶ **2008** Staging of the Olympic Games in Beijing. The slogan is "One world, one dream."
During China's third manned space mission, on Shenzhou VII, Zhai Zhigang carries out his country's first ever space walk.
✶ **2009** Mass celebrations are held to mark the sixtieth anniversary of the Communist Party coming to power.
Officials in Shanghai urge couples to have a second child, in order to balance the country's ageing population; it's the first sign of the one-child policy being relaxed.
✶ **2010** China announces a 17.7 per cent rise in exports during December 2009, which may mean that it has overtaken Germany and become the biggest exporter in the world.
There are official protests from the government in Beijing as jailed Chinese dissident Liu Xiaobo is awarded the Nobel Peace Prize.
✶ **2011** China officially becomes the world's second-largest economy, overtaking Japan.
✶ **2012** Chongqing Communist Party chief Bo Xilai is dismissed, in the country's biggest political scandal for years. He is later sentenced to life in prison for bribery, embezzlement and abuse of power.
✶ **2013** Xi Jinping takes over as president, completing the once-in-a-decade transfer of power to a new generation of leaders. He launches an efficiency and anti-corruption drive.
✶ **2014** Attacks in Xinjiang Region and elsewhere in China, attributed to Uighur separatists, leave tens of people dead and more injured.
✶ **2015** China's economic growth falls to its lowest level for more than 20 years - 7.4 percent in 2014.
✶ **2016** The Communist Party announces it has decided to end the decades-old one-child policy.
✶ **2017** The government passes a new cybersecurity law, giving it more control over the data of foreign and domestic firms.
The Communist Party votes at its congress to enshrine Xi Jinping's name and ideology in its constitution, elevating him to the same level as founder Mao Zedong.
✶ **2018** National People's Congress annual legislative meeting votes to remove a two-term limit on the presidency from the constitution, allowing Xi Jinping to remain in office for longer than the conventional decade for recent Chinese leaders.
China announces it will impose 25% trade tariffs on a list of 106 US goods, including soybeans, cars and orange juice, in retaliation for similar US tariffs on about 1,300 Chinese products.
✶ **2019** Hong Kong sees start of months of anti-government and pro-democracy protests, involving violent clashes with police, against a proposal to allow extradition to mainland China.
✶ **2020** Outbreak of Covid-19 in Hubei province spreads worldwide.
China imposes Hong Kong national security law, criminalizing "secession, collusion and terrorism".
✶ **2021** In February, Xi Jinping proclaims "complete victory" over rural poverty.
In July, the CCP celebrates its 100th anniversary.
NATO declares China a "security challenge".
✶ **2022** By March, Hong Kong is suffering the world's highest Covid-19 death rate, after a wave of Omicron-variant coronavirus cases ravages the region.
Xi Jinping is re-elected as General Secretary of the CCP.
✶ **2023** A Chinese spy balloon spent a week in February flying over Canada and the United States. The incident increases tensions between the US and China and leads to the postponement of a US Secretary of State's trip to Beijing.
✶ **2024** The total value of Chinese exports reaches a new record high.
✶ **2025** Trump's newly imposed tariffs intensify the trade war between the US and China.

IMPRINT

This book shows part of Max Gottschalk's propaganda poster collection. The posters have been arranged in an order that corresponds with the chapters in *The Little Red Book* (or *Quotations from Chairman Mao Zedong*). With such a huge variety of posters, this system was necessary to give the book a coherent structure and a logical narrative thread. The posters and quotations from the relevant chapters of *The Little Red Book*, together with the accompanying essays, all serve to illustrate just how much Chinese life was influenced by Mao's ideas and the visualization of those ideas in posters.

Für dieses Buch, das einen Teil von Max Gottschalks Sammlung chinesischer Propagandaposter zeigt, wurde die Einteilung nach den Kapiteln der *Worte des Vorsitzenden Mao Zedong* gewählt, um der Vielfalt der Plakate eine inhaltliche Struktur und einen roten Faden zu geben. Die Plakate und die Zitate aus den entsprechenden Kapiteln der *Maobibel* zeigen ebenso wie die begleitenden Essays, wie stark durchdrungen das chinesische Leben von den Ideen Maos und ihrer Visualisierung in Plakaten war.

Le principe retenu pour la composition de cet ouvrage, qui présente une partie de la collection d'affiches chinoises de propagande de Max Gottschalk, est celui d'un alignement sur les chapitres du *Petit Livre Rouge de Mao*, les Citations du président Mao Zedong. Il s'agissait en effet d'organiser ces nombreuses images en fonction d'une structure interne, et de trouver un fil rouge. Les affiches et les citations empruntées à ces chapitres montrent, tout autant que les textes qui les accompagnent, à quel point la vie en Chine était imprégnée des idées de Mao, dont les affiches donnaient une traduction graphique.

EACH AND EVERY TASCHEN BOOK PLANTS A SEED!
Each year, we offset our annual carbon emissions with carbon credits at the Instituto Terra, a reforestation program in Minas Gerais, Brazil, founded by Lélia and Sebastião Salgado. To find out more about this ecological partnership, please check: *www.taschen.com/institutoterra*.
Inspiration: unlimited.
Carbon footprint: (almost) zero.

Want to see more? Visit *taschen.com* to view our current publications, browse our latest magazine, and subscribe to our newsletter.

Hohenzollernring 53, D–50672 Köln
www.taschen.com

Editorial direction by Benedikt Taschen, Cologne
Photographs by Michael Wolf, Hong Kong
English translation by Isabel Varea and Karen Waloschek for Grapevine Publishing, London

German translation by Jie Zhao, Berlin (captions and essay by Duo Duo), Brigitte Beier, Hamburg (essays by Anchee Min and Stefan R. Landsberger)
French translation by Catherine Henry, Nancy (captions and essay by Duo Duo), Annie Berthold, Angers (essays by Anchee Min and Stefan R. Landsberger)

Printed in Bosnia-Herzegovina
ISBN 978-3-7544-0553-6